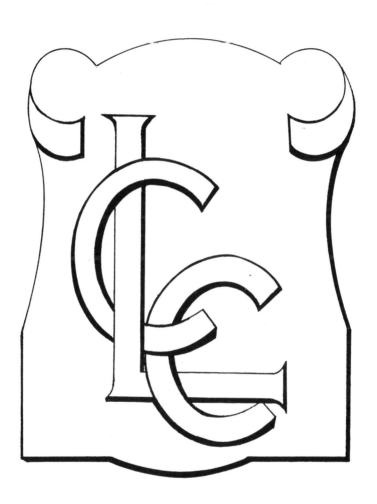

THE
LONDON COUNTY COUNCIL
TRAMWAYS

THE
LONDON COUNTY COUNCIL
TRAMWAYS

VOLUME ONE - SOUTH LONDON

by

E. R. OAKLEY

Published by
The London Tramways History Group
in association with
The Tramway & Light Railway Society
and
The Light Rail Transit Association

The London County Council Tramways, Volume 1
by E. R. Oakley.

First Edition 1989.

ISBN: 0 9513001 0 5

Typesetting by J. Tribe & P. Brill.

Origination by Mosaic, London. E17 6SH.

Printed by W. J. Ray & Co. Ltd., Walsall, West Midlands, WS1 2HQ.

Published by The London Tramways History Group,

Address: 16 Edendale Road, Barnehurst,
           Bexleyheath, Kent. DA7 6RW.
           England.

Printed in Great Britain.

CONTENTS

Frontispiece : One of the several styles of medallion used by the LCC
               on tramway publicity material.

End Papers : Front - The Coat of Arms of the London County Council.
                      The Common Seal of the Council.
                      The embossed shield cast into pole bases and
                      other ironwork.

              Back - An advertisement displayed in the Official
                      Tramways Guide of the LCC, 1908.

Introduction

This work is about the origins, development and consolidation of the tramway systems which eventually became the London County Council Tramways. It describes in some detail the many stages of construction, maintenance and day-to-day working of the several companies which were the forerunners of the LCC Tramways. The history is divided and described in two parts, the south London System being dealt with in this volume, together with some supporting services.

The London County Council Tramways was, by any standard, an enormous undertaking. From its beginning it was an almost-complete public transport industry in its own right; certainly it was much more than a tramway operator, as the authors have attempted to show. The London County Council was also unique, in that it was the only administrative County Authority to own and operate its own tramway network. The subject covers a wide range of topics, from horses and horse cars to track construction, power supplies, electric rolling stock, financial arrangements, routes, services, fares, tickets, politics, staffing and many other facets of this huge undertaking. Each subject is dealt with in a separate chapter or chapters wherever possible, or combined into sub-sections of a chapter where desirable. Some of this material will be presented in Volume 2, including a description of the north London system, and the fares and ticketing arrangements for the whole of the undertaking, together with the modernisation programme that was instituted by the Council in the 1920s.

The period covered is one of about 75 years, from the introduction of the street tramway in London by George Francis Train in 1861, through the times of the companies which worked the tramways in the capital and their acquisition by the London County Council between 1896 and 1909, to the compulsory takeover of the very efficient LCC Tramways by the London Passenger Transport Board in 1933. Much of this story is political in nature, not necessarily of the "party" kind, but often showing the deep differences of opinion in the thoughts and actions of people in public life during those times.

As the period under review was one in which traditional British standards for the spelling of words and for the expression of weights, measures and money were in use, it has been decided that these terms and expressions would continue to be used in this work. Therefore, no reference will be made in the text to any metric or decimal measure or other term which was not in general use in those days. Fractions of a whole number will appear as fractions, except in cases where, for example, parts of the measure of length, known as a chain (22 yards) were often shown in decimal form. All dates are also given in the traditional manner, e.g., 3rd September 1921.

Acknowledgements

In compiling this history, research for which has been undertaken over a period of about twenty-five years, the references, notes and writings of a large number of persons and official bodies have been studied. The intricacies involved in unravelling many of the little-known facets of tramway construction and working, particularly in the early years of this form of public transport, have also entailed undertaking considerable research at many establishments. Two people have actively assisted me during this long and interesting period, and therefore I must firstly very sincerely thank Mr. G. E. Baddeley and Mr. C. S. Smeeton for giving up countless hours of their time to this activity.

The members of the London Tramways History Group have provided the means for enabling us to process the mountain of information collected, and so to Messrs. P. J. Davis, C. E. Holland, D. W. K. Jones, M. B. Leahy, G. W. Morant and C. L. Withey, I express my appreciation of their efforts in this direction. The Tramways & Light Railway Society. together with the Light Rail Transit Association, both as corporate members of the History Group and in their own right, have considerably encouraged me and I offer my thanks to both bodies. In connection with this, I include the members of the Joint Publications Sub-Committee of these two Societies, under the Chairmanship of Mr. G. B. Claydon.

A considerable amount of research has been undertaken at the reference sections of a number of local history and library collections, notably at the London Boroughs of Bexley, Greenwich, Lewisham, Lambeth, Southwark, Wandsworth, the City of London and the City of Westminster, and to all the people in these establishments who have helped, I tender my thanks.

Special mention must be made of the unstinting assistance given in earlier years by Mr. Neate and his staff at the London County Council Library which in more recent years has been transferred to the Greater London Record Office at 40 Northampton Road, Clerkenwell. To all these good people, and to the Keeper of Records and staff at the Public Record Office, Kew, the many staff members of the British Museum Library and Map Room, Bloomsbury, the British Newspaper Library, Colindale, the City of Birmingham Central Library, the Library of the National Tramway Museum, Crich, Derbyshire, the London Transport Museum, the East Anglia Transport Museum and the House of Lords Record Office, I express my thanks.

I particularly wish to thank Messrs. R. Elliott and A. J. Wills for so patiently dealing with my many enquiries regarding rolling stock details and allied subjects, Mr. Baddeley for his work on certain sections and particularly in providing artwork, Mr. Leahy for design work, Mr. Holland for considerable work in compiling text and tables, Mr. T. M. Russell for letting us use his excellent rolling stock drawings, the Light Rail Transit Association for allowing us to use extracts from their printed works "The LCC Trailers" and "The Tramways of Wandsworth and Battersea" and through them, Mr. M. J. D. Willsher and Mr. C. S. Dunbar who were the authors of these papers.

Photographs from many sources have been studied, a large number of which have been used, and I wish to give due acknowledgement to all those who have provided photographic material, in particular to Messrs. G. E. Baddeley, K. C. Blacker (who also helped with the text of the section on Petrol-Electric Cars), C. Carter, R. Elliott, W. J. Haynes, D. W. K. Jones, J. H. Meredith, M. J. O'Connor, A. D. Packer,

J. H. Price, A. H. Spring, W. J. Wyse, the National Tramway Museum Library, the London County Council Library, the Greater London Record Office, the London Transport Museum, the Army Museums Ogilby Trust (courtesy of the London Borough of Lewisham Local History Library), the several London Boroughs as mentioned above, the British Newspaper Libray, Lens of Sutton and Mr. R. J. Durrant of the Omnibus Society. Their assistance has been greatly appreciated.

A great many people have helped in many other ways, particularly with regard to giving information of many kinds, and so to Messrs. H. E. Bellamy, G. E. Budden, E. C. Dawes, F. L. Dix, C. S. Dunbar, H. L. Frost, F. P. Groves, M. L. Harper, A. A. Hunter, R. F. Makewell, J. H. Meredith, J. H. Price, D. A. Thompson and W. J. Wyse, I express my appreciation for their assistance. May I also thank Mrs. J. Tribe, Mrs. C. I. Baker and Mrs. P. Brill for their good work in typing and setting out all the text, to Messrs. Davis, Holland and Smeeton for checking and proof reading, and lastly to Mr. Leahy, the printers and binders for transforming it into this volume. To anyone whose name I have omitted, may I offer my apologies and thanks.

During the long period in which the work has been in progress, several people who had an interest in the project have been taken from us. In this respect I would like to remember the late Frank E. Wilson, whose original idea this history was, F. Merton Atkins, who had collected and collated a considerable portfolio of facts and figures which were made available by the Tramway & Light Railway Society, W. H. Bett, C. E. Lee, S. V. Kempson, A. W. McCall, A. W. Morant, L. A. Thompson and R. E. Tustin, whose notes have been of great help, and lastly, David W. Willoughby, who had worked with me for many years on this history and who had also provided the main system map.

In conclusion, I must sincerely thank my Wife, Irene, for bravely and with good humour putting up with all the intrusions into our family life, that the many years of working on this history have occasioned.

E. R. Oakley,
Hartley, Kent.
Autumn, 1988.

Some Useful Addresses

Museums

East Anglia Transport Museum,
Chapel Road, Carlton Colville, Lowestoft, Suffolk.
London Transport Museum,
Covent Garden, London. WC2E 7BB
National Tramway Museum,
Crich, Matlock, Derbyshire.

Societies

Light Rail Transit Association, Membership Secretary,
6 Hermitage Woods Crescent, St. John's, Woking, Surrey. GU21 1UE
Tramway & Light Railway Society, Hon. Secretary,
216 Brentwood Road, Romford, Essex. RM1 2RP

Drawings

T. M. Russell, "Chaceside", St. Leonard's Park,
Horsham, West Sussex. RH13 6EG

Chapter 1
Origins

London was founded in the pre-Roman era with the establishment of a Celtic settlement known as Llindin or something very similar. It was built on the north bank of the River Thames, about 35 miles up river from the estuary and within the region that was to eventually become Middlesex. The believed interpretation of the name "Llindin" is that "Llin" referred to a pool or lake, and "din" a town or harbour for ships, as it is believed that the Thames at this point spread into a lake on the south or Surrey side. The area was eventually colonised by the Romans, becoming known by them as Londinium.

Llindin, Londinuim and then London became the walled city about which the modern metropolis gradually spread. This city, with an area of about one square mile has, over the centuries, lost most of its protection, as almost all of the wall has disappeared, either being knocked down to make way for new roads and buildings, or falling down through decay. Small settlements grew up around the edge of the city, originally "without" the walls, Shoreditch, Whitechapel and Islington being three of these. The suburbs eventually spread across the Thames to villages almost opposite London, and Southwark and Lambeth, both in the County of Surrey were, by the sixteenth century, considered in some ways to be extensions of the city.

London Bridge was, from the time that the first structure was built, the only crossing over the Thames and, as such, became a focal point point so far as the City was concerned. Several bridges in turn have served to provide this crossing place, some lasting for centuries. What today is generally termed "old London Bridge" was constructed between 1176 and 1209 AD, serving its purpose until 1831 when it was replaced by a new bridge a short distance upstream from the old. This remained until replaced in 1973 by a new structure made of steel and concrete, built on the site of its predecessor.

The gradual increase in population over the centuries ultimately saw an increase in the number of bridges built across the waterway. In what was to become the LCC area, there were to eventually be seven railway bridges and twelve road bridges, together with several railway tunnels built upstream from London Bridge, with only one, Tower Bridge, on the downstream side. This was built during the middle years of the last decade of the nineteenth century at a cost of over £1,000,000, and ceremonially opened on 30th June 1894.

Downstream, things were very different. From time immemorial, the eastern part of the area has been distinctly divided. The River Thames was, and in fact to some degree still is, an effective barrier to the movement of people and traffic from north to south and vice versa. Below Tower Bridge there are to this day only three tunnel crossings for road vehicles, two tunnels for pedestrians, one ferry for road vehicles and foot passengers, one passenger (only) ferry and one railway tunnel. Looking eastwards from Tower Bridge these are:-

1. The Thames Tunnel between Rotherhithe and Wapping, which was constructed by the famous Engineers, the Brunels. Commenced in 1822, it took twenty years to complete. Now used by London Underground trains.
2. Rotherhithe Road Tunnel, built by the London County Council.
3. Greenwich Pedestrian Tunnel, built by the LCC.
4. Blackwall Road Tunnel, built by the LCC.
5. Woolwich Free Ferry for pedestrians and road vehicles, opened by the LCC in 1889.
6. Woolwich Pedestrian Tunnel, built by the LCC.
7. Dartford Road Tunnel, built by Kent and Essex County Councils.
8. Gravesend Passenger Ferry.

The last two however, are just outside the area of influence of Greater London, although Dartford Toll Tunnel takes a lot of the vehicular traffic which would otherwise be funnelled into the road system nearer the capital.

The distance by road between London Bridge and Woolwich is about ten miles and the river crossings are all more or less evenly spaced between these two points, so that it can be seen that communications are still not all that easy from one part of the eastern half of London to the other. This problem, seen from a public transport point of view, has had a profound effect on movement and, due to the natural settlement of the population into two self-contained regions divided by the river, has caused the people to move mainly in easterly or westerly directions. It will therefore be accepted that the main arterial roads are all more or less parallel and follow the course of the river.

Study of the geography of the area as it existed around the year 1860, will show that the only way to cross the Thames from any point below London Bridge was by means of wherries, which were small boats operated by licensed watermen for profit, or by the Thames Tunnel. At that time also, much of the south-eastern part was still open country, or under cultivation as market gardens, while a large part of the area bordering the Thames on the north side was swampy marsh, only then being tamed by large scale construction of railways.

The outposts of the metropolis on the south side were Rotherhithe, Peckham, Camberwell, Kennington, Vauxhall and Walworth, all in Surrey, while Stratford in Essex, and Bow, Stoke Newington and Paddington in Middlesex were their opposite numbers in the north. Streatham and Dulwich were villages in Surrey, with Kensington and Hampstead similarly in Middlesex. Woolwich in the south-east was a country town in Kent, Barnet was a small country town in Hertfordshire, as was Walthamstow in Essex and Croydon in Surrey.

Local Government and the Police

It is necessary to explain the complicated arrangements in force in local government together with the role taken by the police as it applied to the great area surrounding the City of London and since the first tramways were suggested in the area. Geographically and historically the City of London was a self-contained county situated within the County of Middlesex. The remainder of the Metropolis, both north and south of the Thames came within the jurisdiction of the counties of Middlesex, Surrey and Kent.

From the early years of the nineteenth century, great growth was taking place in the area within a ten mile radius of London Bridge. The only form of local government was provided by the "Vestries", which were directly descended from church bodies, together with Local Boards which attempted to undertake public works such as keeping roads in some sort of repair and maintaining the rather primitive drainage systems. Law and order was also under the control of the bodies, who employed "constables" to watch over their areas. This was not very successful.

The first body to be incorporated in a sweeping re-arrangement was the Metropolitan Police, which was brought into existence by an Act of Parliament of 1829 and put under the control of the Home Office, its area of operations stretching from Farnborough (Kent) in the south, to Barnet and beyond in the north; from Seven Kings in the east, to Slough in the west. Its powers were extensive; everything from the detection and prevention of crime, to the licensing of hackney carriages. The only area where it had no authority was, and still is, within the boundaries of the City of London, where a separate force is maintained, administered by the City Corporation.

It was the licensing of cabs and stage carriages with the powers obtained under the 1829 Act, together with a further Act of 1839 and the London Hackney Carriages Act, 1843 which brought the police into contact with omnibuses and later, tramcars. When the early companies were set up to lay and operate tramways, control of their "traffic" was vested in the Commissioner of Police for the Metropolis by virtue of the inclusion in their Acts of Parliament of a statement to that effect. As, of course, the police already had wide powers to control the omnibus and cab traffic which included licensing of vehicles, drivers and conductors, they assumed the same powers with regard to the infant tramways. Every vehicle licensed to operate in public service carried a numbered metal plate fixed in a conspicuous position on it. On tramcars, this plate would be fixed on the end bulkhead at rocker panel level at one end, with the number duplicated in sign-written characters at the other. This item of hardware, known as the Metropolitan Stage Carriage Plate (M.S.C.Plate) would be affixed or removed by a representative of the Metropolitan Police, usually a serving police constable seconded to the special division set up to deal exclusively with vehicle licensing and known as the Public Carriage Office of the Commissioner of Police for the Metropolis. All vehicles of each tramway company had to be inspected annually to see that they were in a roadworthy condition in accordance with police regulations, while all drivers and conductors had to be licensed by the same body before being allowed to carry out the duties for which they were employed. The police could, and did, object to any Bills (either in whole of in part) before Parliament, regarding the construction (or reconstruction) of tramways, and even issued "recommendations" as to how the tramcars should be constructed.

About twenty years after the law and order situation was under control, the government of the day turned its attention to local government. Due to the grossly inefficient arrangements inherent under the parochial system, it resolved to bring into existence a central body to be known as the Metropolitan Board of Works to oversee important projects of several kinds in parts of metropolitan Kent, Surrey and Middlesex. One of these improvements was the construction of a totally new and all-embracing main drainage system for the whole of the Metropolitan area. While very large, this area was not so great as the Police District. The Local Board of Works and Vestries would continue to operate but modified to some extent and guided by the Metropolitan Board. The Metropolis Management Act, 1855, brought the Board into being.

The matter of construction and maintenance of highways, together with all other things referring to them was not straightforward either. In most of the Board's area it was the duty of the Local Boards and Vestries to undertake any work required and to provide the necessary supervision. The local bodies became the 'road authorities' for their areas, while the Metropolitan Board became the 'local authority' for the whole region. There were, however, two departures from this arrangement. In the City of London and its Liberties the authority for both local and road affairs was, and remains the Mayor, Aldermen and Commonalty of the City of London. The second distinction concerned some of the Turnpike Roads north of the Thames under the control of the Commissioners for Turnpike Roads, whose powers were to lapse in 1872, and not having much effect on the developing tramways.

It can be seen that there was split responsibility for many facets of local government, this becoming more obvious as greater areas were given over to housing and industrial development. It showed most of all when tramways first came to the Metropolis and particularly so after the disastrous affairs of George Francis Train. It became woefully obvious that divided responsibility caused many problems as tramway schemes evolved in different parts of the Metropolis.

The Railway Department of the Board of Trade was nominated to deal with all tramway matters and, in its capacity as public works guardian had powers to recommend technically, present Bills to Parliament, authorise and issue Provisional Orders and make inspections of any tramway. The Railway Inspectorate, whose inspectors were all officers of the Royal Engineers, undertook this duty in addition to the inspection and regulation of railways.

The Street Tramway in Britain

In the middle years of the nineteenth century, Britain was in the throes of the vast industrial expansion which was intensified by the coming of the railways, as a result of which people were tending to travel further afield, something that up until then they had not been able to do. Towns and cities were expanding; railways were being built with great speed and enthusiasm to connect them together with ribbons of steel. This expansion affected the metropolitan areas around London, stretching from Hammersmith in the west to Greenwich and Stratford in the east, Highgate in the north to Clapham in the south. Nevertheless, the only way for a large part of the population to travel, apart from "the carriage folk", or those who could afford to use the railways or cramped, expensive omnibuses, was to walk! It was at this time that the street tramway made its appearance.

The tramway operated for the carriage of passengers made its impact on Britain in the mid years of the nineteenth century. Its acknowledged arrival here was quite late, as this method of transport was reputedly first used in the United States of America in Baltimore, in 1828, to be followed by New York and New Orleans in the 1830s and many other American towns and cites soon afterwards. However, it is recorded (as is so often the case) that the American claim may not be so absolutely factual after all, as an article ('The Engineer', 23rd April 1869) states ..'Road and street railways are generally supposed to have originated in so far as this country is concerned, with the notorious George Francis Train. This is not the case. Tramways were projected and in actual use, and successful, in this country long before Train's advent. From 1827 until 1839, when the railway was opened to Preston, a tramway was in constant use in that locality and which, in parts at least, had a grooved rail, that the stage coaches crossed daily at Bamber Bridge without accident or inconvenience'.

The introduction of the tramway into France is said to have come in 1853 when a line was built in Paris by one M. Loubat, while the London General Omnibus Company, which had its beginnings in a French company known as the Compagnie Generale des Omnibuses de Londres and which was later to become (for a time) a French-owned British company, was one of the principal omnibus operators in the capital at that time. On 6th October 1857 the French management suggested that tramways be built in London, issuing a prospectus later that year referring to a British company which was to be known as the London Omnibus Tramways Company Limited. The proposal was to lay a line from Notting Hill to the Bank via Bayswater, the New Road (Euston Road), City Road and Moorgate, with a branch from Kings Cross to Fleet Street via Bagniggewells Road (later known as Kings Cross Road) and Farringdon Street, just over eight miles in all. The recommended capital was quoted as £50,000; the Engineer being named as James Samuel. It was also stated that the 'tramway omnibuses' would be constructed to carry 60 passengers, would weigh two tons and would be hauled by two horses, with a third horse to assist when pulling the cars up the hills on either side of "The Angel", Islington. The track was to be double and of a type which was laid flush with the road, so as not to cause interference with other road users. The gauge would be 4 ft. 6 in. The Bill, when presented to Parliament, met with strong opposition from the local authorities through whose areas the line was proposed, and also from Sir Benjamin Hall, who was M.P. for Mary-le-Bone, as well as being Chief Commissioner for Public Works. The Bill was defeated at its second reading.

No more was heard of this company until, on 6th October 1860 it was re-registered with a recommended capital of £50,000 as before. This was done in an attempt to oppose the activities of the American G. F. Train, who had come to Britain to carry out tramway prospecting. There was also at this time an Englishman by the name of William Joseph Curtis who was trying to raise the enthusiasm of various Boards of Works around the Metropolis with his ideas on tramways. Curtis eventually obtained permission to lay what he called "a line of trams" along Liverpool Road, Islington. He stated .. 'that the rails were on the ground and that the public would soon have the opportunity of trying the value of the system ..', but, in fact, the line was not built by Curtis. Train in the meantime, applied to the Mary-le-Bone Vestry to build a line from Finchley Road, via Baker Street, Wigmore Street and Cavendish Square to Regent Street, then back along Oxford Street, Portman Square and Gloucester Place. This too, was refused.

G. F. Train was born in Boston, Mass. in 1829, eventually becoming involved in the family shipping concern. However, from his other activities it would seem that he was something of an opportunist but, so far as Britain was concerned, he certainly made his mark. His first transport venture in England was in 1859 at Birkenhead where he laid a tramway using the "step" type of rail, which, in fact, was a flat strip of iron with a lip or step on the outside edge, two of these being laid to gauge, thereby forming a "way", which was to prove so very unpopular with other road users, and with those who were antagonistic towards him, accusing him of 'causing all sorts of damage to vehicles and persons'. This line was opened in 1860 and fortunately for him, a man named James McHenry came to his rescue almost immediately by raising the capital necessary to replace the step rails with those of a grooved type which were far superior, being flush with the road.

After much agitation, Train eventually obtained permission from the Commissioners of Turnpike Roads, to lay a line along the Bayswater Road from its junction with the Edgware Road and Porchester Terrace. A company was registered in January 1861 known as "The Marble Arch Street Rail Company Limited". Work proceeded quickly as by 23rd March all was ready, and the line was opened with considerable ceremony. Train had used the notorious step rail and by so doing managed to arouse the wrath of most of the local residents.

An artist's impression of what the Marble Arch Street Rail Co. line may have looked like. The list of places served, as shown on the second car is rather optimistic.

The prospectus of the Marble Arch Street Rail Company Ltd. stated that the company was formed 'for the laying down of street rails or tram plates along any part of Oxford Street and the Uxbridge Road to the west of Marble Arch, Hyde Park. The running of omnibuses or other carriages thereon for the conveyance of passenger traffic by horse power.

And also all such further or more extended objects connected with the laying down and working of street rails or tramways in or near London - within ten miles of the GPO - as the Company in General Meeting may from time to time (agree) in accordance with the Articles of Association.

Capital: £10,000 in 200 shares of £50 each. (Train took 100, twelve others took the rest).

First Directors: Coleridge John Kinnard, William Frederick Splatt and William Evans.

Issued on 22nd January 1861 from 18 Great George Street, S.W.'

Rails for the line were supplied by the Ebbw Vale Company and cars by Prentiss of Birkenhead, with seats for 18 passengers inside and room for as many on top. The cars were about 18 feet long (including platforms), 7 feet wide with the wheels beneath the body, and 9 feet high from the ground, the floor being about 20 inches above the rails. The carriages were drawn by two horses each at an average speed of about 7 m.p.h. and could be stopped within their own length. The fare for the journey was 2d and on Sunday 14th April 1861, it was reported that 3,600 passengers had been carried, with £30 being taken.

As a result of his track laying activities at Bayswater, Train found himself in trouble with the local magistrate when on 5th April 1861 he appeared in Court charged with breaking up the Uxbridge Road. In the report we read '..Mr. G. F. Train has been fined 1/- (one shilling) and costs by the Mary-le-Bone police magistrate for breaking up the Uxbridge Road. The magistrate is of the opinion that the Commissioners for Turnpike Roads* exceeded their powers in granting a license to Mr. Train'. Commenting further, the report stated 'as only a single line of rails is laid down, the car on its return journey is necessarily

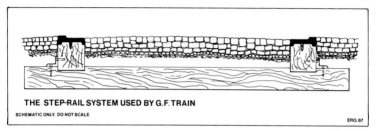

THE STEP-RAIL SYSTEM USED BY G.F. TRAIN

SCHEMATIC ONLY. DO NOT SCALE

ERO. 87

on the wrong side of the road, an infringement of the rules by which street traffic is regulated, which obliged Mr. Yardley (the magistrate) to inflict a nominal fine of 1/-'. At the same time, Mr. Yardley pointed out that a tramway was not an obstruction and that this assent of the Commissioners of Roads to lay it down was sufficient licence. The bad feeling that had been caused by Train over the use of his step rail, fuelled by the vehement opposition of the people who lived in this area, gave rise to much wrangling and argument which resulted in the local Vestry insisting that it be removed, giving the company until 4th October to do this and make good the road. It had all gone by mid-September.

His second London venture was the well-known Victoria Street line. This was opened in a flamboyant manner with a "Yankee Breakfast", whatever that may have meant, on 15th April 1861, ten days after his appearance before the magistrate over the Uxbridge Road affair. The line commenced in Victoria Street close to the north entrance to Westminster Abbey, then traversed Victoria Street for abour half a mile, to end at the parish boundary. Although the line had been opened, the company was not registered until 20th April, when it became known as the Westminster Street Rail Company Limited. The Directors were G. F. Train, James B. Kitcat, George Starbuck Jnr., Thomas Corner, Charles Burn. The Secretary was James S. Oliver (pro-tem). Horses were supplied by William Sheldon.

In a return dated 15th October 1861, the names of four directors, totally different from the originals were Elijah Freeman Prentiss, Hiram Saunders, George Barclay Bruce and Richard Michael Mugeridge. The only original director remaining was George Starbuck, and these five were to run the company during its short but stormy existence. The usual complaints were levelled at this undertaking and, after

---

* Turnpike, or main roads in the Metropolitan area north of the Thames were, until 1872 under the control of the Commissioners for Turnpike Roads. After this date, responsibility passed to the Local Boards of Works or Vestries.

The single deck car that worked on the Victoria Street line appears to be of early Starbuck design, similar to those used at Marble Arch.

about eight months, the Westminster Board of Works served a Notice of Removal, effective as from 10th December 1861, in which the rails should be removed and the roads reinstated. Service continued until about four days before the Notice expired, the line finally closing on 6th March 1862. During the early months of operation, the normal fare was 2d, but this was reduced in later months to 1d in an effort to gain additional passengers. Only one single deck car, 'The People', was in use, this being a nine-a-side window version of a simple four-wheeled car of the Starbuck type. Brightly painted in a selection of gaudy colours, with a complicated design over each window, the car also sported a large bogus coat of arms. Two horses hauled the vehicle.

The third and last tramway built by Train extended from the south side of Westminster Bridge to Kennington Gate. As with his other lines, a separate company was formed. This one was "The Surrey Side Street Rail Company Limited", incorporated on 9th May 1861, with a nominal capital of £100,000 in 10,000 shares of £10 each. In this case, the Articles of Association are reproduced in full, as this line, even though it was short-lived, was to be the fore-runner of something much more important.

The Surrey Side Street Railway Co. Ltd.

"Prospectus for ... the laying down of Street Rails or Tramplates (in) Westminster Bridge Road, Borough Road and other streets and roads south of the Thames.
The running of omnibuses or other carriages thereon for the conveyance of passenger traffic by Horse Power.
(The use of) ... Patent Rights and Licenses to use Patents ...
Capital: £100,000 into 10,000 of £10 shares. Half to be deferred, the other half to be preferred.
Subscribers: Deferred Stock, all 5,000 shares, G. F. Train.
Preferred Stock; 100 shares, G. F. Train.

50	"	Geo. Starbuck, Jnr.
20	"	James B. Kitcat.
10	"	Joseph Griffiths Oliver.
10	"	William Davies.
50	"	Chas. Hathaway.
100	"	Chas. Rowe.
20	"	Hiram Saunders.
50	"	Henry Potter Burte.
20	"	Joseph Rodney Croskey.

Dated: 16th May 1861

Articles of Association of the Company

1. ... power to alter name ...
2. ... power to extend objects ... as follows:-
   Laying down Street Rails or Tramplates within ten miles of GPO.
   The running of omnibuses or carriages thereon for conveyance of
   passenger traffic by horse power.
   The running of carts or waggons uopn the original or any other
   street rails for ... conveyance of goods traffic of all descriptions
   by horse power.
3. ... power to increase or decrease capital ...
4. ... power to purchase ... other businesses ...
5. ... power ... subject to (conditions) to ... sell the business ...
Quorum for General Meetings ... five shareholders, holding not less than
£2,000 in shares.
Quorum for Directors ... not less than three or more than six.
Qualifications ... to ... hold shares to nominal amount of £200.
G. F. Train,   H. P. Burte,   Jas. Rodney Croskey,
Geo. Starbuck Jr,   Jas. B. Kitcat.

Full List of Shareholders

G. F. Train, Geo. Starbuck Jr., J. B. Kitcat, J. S. Oliver, C. Hathaway,
H. Saunders, W. Davies, C. Rowe, H. P. Burte, J. R. Croskey, R. Maitland,
David Kitcat, W. H. Turley, A. H. Knight, W. H. Fairfax, H. Clowick,
James McHenry, B. Mozley, G. Rae, C. Burn, I. Hutchinson, T. S. Cutbill,
James Samuel C.E., Wm. F. Splatt, J. W. Kennard, Henry Hewitt Kincaid,
Col. J. Kennard.

Date of Incorporation, 16th May 1861."

Train and his enterprise was keenly opposed by omnibus proprietors
(but the LGOC is not specifically mentioned) and, as before, they
went to great lengths to embarrass him. However, acting upon the
terms of a formal contract concluded with the Lambeth Vestry on
13th March 1861, Train arranged to construct the line. His contract,
among other things, obliged him to complete the work within three
months, but it was to be 15th August before the line was ready for
traffic, and the 'sidings' were not ready for use until September. The
step rail was again used, with the road between and for two feet on
either side of the rails being paved at the expense of the company.
Horses were supplied by Sheldon. Notices announced that 'the cars
of this company leave Kennington Park for Westminster Bridge and
vice-versa, every eight minutes. Fare 2d, 8 tickets for 1/-'. (The
reduced rate tickets were in the form of metal tokens). It seemed
that the cheaper tickets proved popular with workmen, but even so,
1½d was a lot to pay in those days for a ride of just over a mile.

In October 1861, just over two months after the opening of the line,
Train, with others, was indicted for making the roads dangerous to
the public. The matter was taken to Kingston (Surrey) Assizes, where
on 7th April 1862 a verdict of 'guilty' was recorded against Train,
but not against the Vestrymen of Lambeth who had appeared with
him. Train was ordered to remove the line, but he carried on working
until the last possible moment. On the morning of 20th June, a party
of 20 men began to pull up the rails by order of the Sheriff of Surrey,
forcing Train to close the line and sell off the stud of 50 horses.

With closure the company faded out. After years of unsuccessful
attempts to secure statutory returns, or even a reply to enquiries,
the company was dissolved by Order of the Registrar, being removed
from the Register on 7th March 1882. Even though Train's efforts

were largely wasted, he did leave his mark as the following extract from "The Engineer" of 26th April 1861 shows:- 'Mr. Train .. has actually got two such railways at work in London and who, if he does nothing else, deserves the gratitude of the English Lady for shaming the proprietors of the dirty, inconvenient nuisance called the "British Omnibus", by producing a vehicle into which a woman can step decently and sit in cleanliness and comfort. Also for substituting neatly uniformed and civil men for the "coarse cads" who at present "bawl behind the 'bus"'!

It is important to note that in 1868, Parliament gave authority for the construction of a large network of tramways in Liverpool and there is no doubt that this influenced attitudes to this mode of transport. In December 1868, John Bright, a warm supporter of tramways, became President of the Board of Trade (Works), which was the department concerned with the authorisation of tramways. Therefore, the future looked better for the people who were attempting to obtain powers to lay tramways in and around London.

Following the success of the Liverpool Bills, proposals were once again put forward on a more definite and substantial basis involving two groups of promoters, whose companies were described as "The Metropolitan Tramways" and "The Metropolitan Street Tramways". Meanwhile, the promoters of a third company, with the title of "The Pimlico, Peckham & Greenwich Street Tramways Company", made proposals overlapping to some extent those of the Metropolitan Street Tramways Company. The first of the three was mainly concerned with lines north of the Thames, the other two mainly on the south side.

In statements concerned with the construction of street tramways, the Metropolitan Board of Works made it known in 1869 that:- 'with regard to the Tramway Bills now before Parliament, the Board are ready to concur with any plan which would have the effect of facilitating the traffic of the Metropolis, but that, as the laying of tramways in public streets involves such great changes, the Board are of the opinion that there should be an experiment of the system before any extensive scheme is sanctioned by Parliament, and that the Solicitor be instructed to confer with the Agents for the Bills now before Parliament, and endeavour to arrange with them for an experiment of the system to be carried out between Westminster Bridge and Kennington Park'.

In effect, what Train did in 1861/2, re-appeared in 1869 ... "an experimental tramway", but only as a small part of what was to be eventually constructed. After this came the long legal arguments regarding the "experiment" and, during this process, it was gradually widened in scope, as later events will show.

After the Acts obtained by the Metropolitan Street Tramways Company, the North Metropolitan Tramways Company and the Pimlico, Peckham & Greenwich Street Tramways Company in 1869, and before anything was done to implement the terms of these, the Metropolitan Board of Works let it be known that it would oppose all further Bills until it was certain that tramways were a satisfactory means of conveyance. This did not apply, however, to the three original companies, for in 1870 they again presented proposals which were accepted. These were all again seeking to obtain extensions to their lines together with certain amendments to the content of their 1869 Acts.

Meanwhile, John Bright, President of the Board of Trade, with his Board behind him, proposed, in 1870, to introduce a method whereby tramways would be built under the authority of Board of Trade Cert-

This pen-and-ink drawing of the Houses of Parliament, also shows a tramcar, working on the Victoria Street line of G. F. Train, near the doors of Westminster Abbey.

ificates and without the need for formal parliamentary approval. There was considerable opposition to this idea and, due to Bright falling ill at this critical time, his opponents won the day and the proposal was withdrawn. This situation led to the presentation of a comprehensive Bill to Parliament. In this, every possible contingency was catered for and was the cause of much argument and debate. It passed through the various parliamentary stages to emerge as "The Tramways Act, 1870, (33-34 Vic. cap. 78)", receiving the Royal Assent on 9th August 1870. This Act, with a few minor amendments, is still extant to the present time. In the Act, the 21-year purchase clause was clearly stated. It had been proposed by Lord Redesdale that an initial 50-year term would be the accepted period of tenure, but this was overturned in favour of the lesser term.

The 1870 Act also set out a clearly defined procedure which all promoters of tramways would be expected to follow. It authorised the Board of Trade, subject to subsequent approval of Parliament, to grant Provisional Orders authorising the construction of tramways, provided that the Metropolitan Board of Works (so far as London was concerned) gave its consent together with those of the District Boards of Works and Vestries. Should there be more than one "road authority" involved, and one dissented, the Provisional Order would still be granted if assents had been given to more than two-thirds of the tramways proposed.

On 10th August 1870, the Royal Assent was given to the three Private Acts promoted by the existing companies, all numbered 33-34 Vic. cap. 167 and 171 to 174. In the main these were amending Acts with additions put in, but the important provision was that, in exchange for the 21-year term of tenure granted by the 1869 Acts, a 28-year term was granted, coupled with probable compulsory purchase arrangements by the local authority which, in the case of the Metropolis was the Metropolitan Board of Works. Such purchases were to be approved by the Board of Trade.

By the mid-1870s, a number of companies had become involved in operation in and around the Metropolitan area. Details of each are set down in separate chapters. Ultimately there were seven undertakings working south of the Thames, all of which are described in this Volume. The other three, all north of the river, will be dealt with in Volume 2.

The Formation of the London County Council

Before the passage of the Local Government Act, 1888, the only "real" London was the County and City of London situated within the boundaries of the County of Middlesex. The Metropolitan Board of Works was set up by Act of Parliament in 1855 in an attempt to remedy the rather chaotic state of affairs obtaining in local government in the region surrounding the City of London, but not including it. This new board was, however, defective in that it was not elected by the ratepayers. The Corporation of the City of London, together with the Vestries and Local Boards, each sent representatives to sit on the Metropolitan Board and to act in the best interests of the Metropolis so far as they were able. During the course of their years in office much good work was done, including the provision of a completely new main drainage system, the construction of the Victoria and Albert Embankments and the construction of the Woolwich Free Ferry. The Board was also given powers under the Tramways Act, 1870 to purchase any tramway, normally after a 21-year period from the date of the passage of the relative Act authorising such a tramway within the Metropolitan area.

In the mid-1880s, Parliament decided that a re-arrangement of the responsibilities of the Shire Counties should extend to the areas surrounding the City of London. An administrative County was set up under the terms of the 1888 Act, and a body to be known as the London County Council (LCC) would replace the Metropolitan Board of Works, its members to be elected by the County ratepayers. The City of London Corporation, while being brought into the area and becoming part of it, would still be considered to be a County in its own right, autonomous to a considerable degree, as by ancient charters and rights, many privileges were bestowed upon the Lord Mayor and Commonalty which did not exist elsewhere. Vesting day for the new Council had been settled as 1st April 1889.

The two main parties in the first election on 17th January 1889 were the Moderates and Progressives, the first reflecting a traditional conservative approach. On the other hand, the Progressives had their roots in the Fabian Society, founded in 1883. This Society had brought together Liberal politicians, Socialist intellectuals and trades unionists to fight the election. Their avowed aim was to make the "new" London a better place in which to live and work and in their opinion one way to achieve this aim would be to bring the various services, including the tramways, into municipal ownership. The Progressives won the election with a large majority, taking two seats for every one that went to the Moderates. To prepare for the takeover, a number of meetings of the Provisional Council was held. Nineteen committees were formed, with one, the Highways Committee, given responsibility for matters concerning tramways.

Due to alleged problems associated with the proposed construction of Blackwall Tunnel, which was being dealt with by the Metropolitan Board of Works, the Council decided to appeal to the Local Government Board, seeking a date earlier than 1st April on which to take office. This resulted in the Council taking over on 21st March, ten days earlier than planned, in order to forestall any repercussions that might occur in connection with tunnel contracts. The first meeting of the LCC took place on that day. Because of this change, the Board was denied the pleasant duty of inaugurating the new service provided by the Woolwich Free Ferry as from Saturday 23rd March. Thus, the LCC immediately became a public transport operator.

The new Council inherited all the powers with regard to tramways which had been invested in the Metropolitan Board of Works and lost no time in obtaining detailed information of every company operating or constructing tramways within the county, also taking note of those on its borders. It also made it known that a policy of municipalisation of all the London tramways would be pursued as soon as it was in a position to do so, and by the end of the first year in office had commissioned an investigation to be made by A. Bassett Hopkins, Vice-Chairman of the Highways Committee. This document, "Tramway Legislation in London", outlined parliamentary involvement in tramways in the Metropolis since 1869, together with details of all the companies and their day-to-day working throughout this period.

After the formation of the County Council, plans were quickly made by that body to take advantage of the conditions of purchase allowed by the Tramways Act of 1870. A study was undertaken by the Chairman of the Highways Committee early in 1891 regarding tramways in Britain already belonging to local authorities. His findings were published in the form of a memorandum in which he pointed out that, of 29 tramways owned by local authorities at that time, only

Huddersfield operated its lines. The rest contracted with public or statutory companies to work them, normally under the terms of leases for clearly defined periods, usually 21 years, due to the fact that even though municipal bodies could own lines, that state of the law at the time forbade them to work them, except by special dispensation (as at Huddersfield). It was therefore necessary for the County Council to consider ways in which it could free itself from these restrictions, which resulted in a further long report being published. In this, the County Council showed the results of a study of all tramway Bills submitted to Parliament, to enable them to give a measure of control at various stages of the parliamentary process. However, municipal ownership and operational control was the real aim of the Council.

It was fortuitous that, in 1891, the first 4 miles 1 furlong of the tramways belonging to the London Street Tramways Company would come up for consideration for purchase by the Council under the 21-year term granted to the company by its Act of 1870. This short and rather insignificant piece of tramway was to eventually be the cause of considerable and costly litigation, bitterness and bad blood between the Council and the company. Eventually, five years later, as is described elsewhere, the Council got its way and the lines were purchased, to be leased back to the company until the whole of its assets could be taken into municipal ownership. (See the London Street Tramways Company and the North Metropolitan Tramways Company chapters in Volume 2).

As previously mentioned, the Tramways Act of 1870 appeared to prevent the Council from becoming a tramway operator in its own right, although this was disputed by the LCC, so it was decided to submit a Bill to Parliament in 1895 with a view to regularising the position, with the expectation of a straightforward and speedy response. This hope was dashed, however, by the sudden dissolution of Parliament and a subsequent change of government, together with considerable opposition from representatives of the tramway companies. The Bill had to lie over until the 1896 Session, when the powers were eventually granted under the London County Tramways Act, 1896.

The LCC, now being the owner of a fairly large and important network of horse tramways, even though leased back to a company to operate, entered into the year 1898 with some enthusiasm. In March that year, the "pro-tramway" party, the Progressives, won a decisive victory in the Council elections, ensuring that plans made to purchase the tramways within the County as they fell due would be likely to be fruitful. They then set about acquiring the various companies as and when the 21-year rule allowed, beginning with the London Street Tramways Company as mentioned above and ending with the Highgate Hill Tramways Company on 24th August 1909.

A description of the following companies is given in this Volume:-
The London Tramways Company Limited.
  (The Metropolitan Street Tramways Company)
  (The Pimlico, Peckham & Greenwich Street Tramways Company)
The South Eastern Metropolitan Tramways Company.
The London, Deptford & Greenwich Tramways Company.
  (The Southwark & Deptford Tramways Company)
The London, Camberwell & Dulwich Tramways Company.
  (The Peckham & East Dulwich Tramways Company)
The Woolwich & South East London Tramways Company Limited.
  (The Woolwich & Plumstead Tramways Company)
The South London Tramways Company.
The London Southern Tramways Company.

The following companies will be described in Volume 2:-
The North Metropolitan Tramways Company.
The London Street Tramways Company.
The Highgate Hill Tramways Company and its predecessors.

The other companies, operating short sections of line in the LCC area, will be mentioned in outline form only.
The Harrow Road & Paddington Tramways Company.
The West Metropolitan Tramways Company, its predecessors and
  successor.
The Lea Bridge, Leyton & Walthamstow Tramways Company.

Chapter 2
The London Tramways Company Limited
The Metropolitan Street Tramways Company

Original Intentions and Historical Notes

On the south side of the River Thames, the two undertakings known as the Metropolitan Street Tramways Company and the Pimlico, Peckham & Greenwich Street Tramways Company came into existence on the same day by virtue of two Acts of Parliament, both of which received the Royal Assent on 12th July 1869.

Dealing with the Metropolitan Street Tramways Company first, the intended area of operations covered the main roads running out of London in a southerly direction. From a terminus on the Surrey side of Westminster Bridge, its lines were to serve Newington ("The Elephant & Castle" and St. George's Circus), part of Lambeth, Kennington, Brixton, Streatham, Clapham and later, Tooting (Totterdown), while it was also intended to lay lines along the New and Old Kent Roads and through Hill Street Peckham to Rye Lane.

The second undertaking, the Pimlico, Peckham & Greenwich Street Tramways Company intended to work lines from Victoria Railway Station, along Vauxhall Bridge Road to the west side of the bridge, over the bridge and then from the east side along Harleyford Road to Kennington, Camberwell, Peckham, New Cross and Deptford Bridge to the foot of Blackheath Hill, and from Deptford Bridge to East Greenwich; from the Surrey side of Blackfriars Bridge to St. George's Circus, Southwark ("The Obelisk"), where the proposed Metropolitan Street Tramways line was to converge, then along London Road to the "Elephant & Castle"; from St. George's Church, along Newington Causeway to the "Elephant"; through the Walworth Road to connect up with the line from Vauxhall; and finally, from St. George's Circus, along Westminster Bridge Road to Hercules Buildings.

The inner urban areas on the Surrey side of the Thames were well established and heavily populated by the time the tramways were being developed. Southwark, once a village almost opposite the City of London was drawn into the influence of London around the sixteenth century and served as a residential suburb of the city from that time on. Newington, the area around and to the north of the great road junction made famous by the "Elephant & Castle" public house, became a mixed industrial and housing community, mainly for the many artisans who lived near to their workplaces in the many factories and workshops established there by the middle years of the nineteenth century.

Lambeth, like Southwark, became a suburb of the metropolis in the early nineteenth century. In the County of Surrey, it is the Metropolitan Seat of the Archbishop of Canterbury who resides in Lambeth Palace when in town. As for Kennington, Brixton, Steatham, Clapham and Balham, these were all residential small towns and villages which became dormitory appendages to the Metropolis.

On the west bank of the Thames opposite Vauxhall lies Pimlico and the long, straight road which leads to Victoria, the name given to a railway station, later extending to the district around it in honour of the late Queen.

Camberwell, Peckham, Hatcham and New Cross were all orginally hamlets grouped around tollgates, while the Old Kent Road (or "Kent Road" until about 1860) leading in to Southwark and outwards to Rochester and Maidstone, is of great antiquity. The old town of Deptford, about a mile to the east of New Cross, lies alongside the River Ravensbourne, with part of the town extending north to front the Thames.

Lastly to Greenwich, a place steeped in history with Royalty playing a large part in its activities. The Royal Observatory, the Queen's House, the Dreadnought Seamens' Hospital and later, the Royal Naval College all lie within a few hundred yards of each other.

The Metropolitan Street Tramways Company;
Original Bills and Acts, 1869-1870

A number of proposals had been made by several promoters from 1865, beginning with the "Metropolitan Tramways Company" and, from 1867 by the Metropolitan Street Tramways Company and the Pimlico, Peckham & Greenwich Street Tramways Company for authority to construct tramways in the districts previously mentioned, but it was not until 1869 that their Parliamentary Bills succeeded. The Metropolitan company was applying for powers to build tramways in areas where, in fact, it never did operate, either because it was unsuccessful in its application or because the Pimlico company took over the responsibility for building part of the network. The original promoters were William Evans, John Humphrey, Charles Oppenheim and William White.

As the first of the authorised tramways in the Metropolitan area were to have such a great effect on the future of public transport, the Bills and subsequent Acts for the first two years are described. The proposed lines in the 1869 Bill were:-

Nos. 1 & 1A. A double line, from South Lambeth Road, along Clapham Road to Kennington Park.

Nos. 2 & 2A. A double line, from Tramway No. 1 at Kennington Park, along Brixton Road to Stockwell Road.

Nos. 3, 3A & 3B. A single line, along Stockwell Road linking Tramway No. 1 with No. 2.

Nos. 4 & 4A. A double line, from the end of Tramways Nos. 1 and 2 at Kennington, along Kennington Road to Westminster Bridge Road.

Nos. 5 & 6. A single line, from the end of Tramway No. 4A, along Westminster Bridge Road, Stangate, Palace Road, Crosier Street, Royal Street, Allen Street and Hercules Buildings, back to Kennington Road (end of Tramway No. 4).

Nos. 7 & 7A. A double line, from Kennington Road, along Westminster Bridge Road and Borough Road to Southwark Bridge Road.

Nos. 7B & 7C. Two short junction lines at Christchurch, Westminster Bridge Road and Kennington Road.

Nos. 8 & 8A. A double line, from the end of Tramways Nos. 7 & 7A, along Southwark Bridge Road, Newington Causeway, "Elephant & Castle", New Kent Road, Old Kent Road, then by **Nos. 9 & 9A** to Park Street.

Nos. 10 & 10A. A double and single line from Tramways Nos. 9 & 9A, along Park Street and Hill Street to High Street, Peckham.

Nos. 11 & 11A. A single line, from the end of Tramways Nos. 7 & 7A, along Borough Road, Great Suffolk Street, Gravel Lane, Southwark

Street, Bridge Street and Southwark Bridge Road, back to Borough Road (end of Tramways Nos. 7 & 7A).

No. 12. From Westminster Bridge Road, along York Road, Stamford Street and Southwark Street to Tramway No. 11 at Gravel Lane.

No. 13. From Kennington Cross, along Upper Kennington Lane to Wandsworth Road. The lines to continue by **No. 14** along Nine Elms Lane and Lower Wandsworth Road to Battersea Park. Then along Queens Road and Prince of Wales Road to Lower Wandsworth Road.

The tramways to be laid down were to be "5 ft. 3 in. wide", the uppermost surface of the rail being on a level with the surface of the street.

The resulting Act, one of a trio passed on the same day, authorising the laying and working of tramways in the Metropolitan area, heralded a new era for public transport, even though it only allowed the use of horse power and did not authorise all lines proposed. It contained 82 clauses of which the most important are stated below.

The Metropolitan Street Tramways Act, 1869, (32-33 Vic. cap. xciv)   12th July 1869

An Act to authorise the construction of Street Tramways in certain parts of the Metropolis south of the River Thames and for other purposes. **Whereas** the laying down in certain streets in the Metropolis south of the River Thames in this Act mentioned of Tramways to be worked by animal power only, and constructed so as not to impede or injure the ordinary traffic of the streets would be of great local and public advantage.

And whereas it is expedient that the persons hereinafter named, with others, should be incorporated into a Company and should be empowered to lay down and maintain the several street tramways in this Act particularly described.

And whereas plans and sections showing the lines and levels of the tramways and works by this Act authorised to be made and the lands to be taken for the purposes thereof and books of reference to those plans containing the names of the owners or reputed owners, lessees or reputed lessees and occupiers of those lands, have been deposited with the Clerk of the Peace for the County of Surrey and those plans, sections and books of reference are in this Act referred to as the deposited plans, sections and books of references.

And whereas the objects of this Act cannot be attained without the Authority of Parliament, **May it please Your Majesty** that it may be enacted by the Queen's Most Excellent Majesty by and with the advice of the Lords Spiritual and Temporal and Commons in this present Parliament assembled and by the authority of the same as follows:

Short Title

1. This Act may be cited for all purposes as The Metropolitan Street Tramways Act, 1869.

Company Incorporated

4. William Evans, John Humphrey, Chas. Oppenheim, Wm. White the Younger and all other persons and corporations who have already subscribed or shall hereafter subscribe to the undertaking, their executors, administrators, successors and assigns respectively shall be united into a Company for the purpose of making and maintaining the tramways and for other than the purposes of this Act, and for those purposes shall be incorporated by the name of "The Metropolitan Street Tramways Company" and by that name shall be a body corporate with perpetual succession and a common seal and with power to purchase, take, hold and dispose of lands and other property for the purposes of this Act.

Power To Make Tramways

5. Subject to the provisions of this Act, the Company may make, form, lay down and maintain in the lines and according to the levels shown on the deposited plans and section, the street tramways hereinafter described ... and use such of the lands ... as may be required for the purpose.

The Tramways referred to and authorised by this Act are:-

Nos. 1 & 1A. A line 7 f. 0.25 ch. long, commencing in Clapham Road near South Lambeth Road, along Clapham Road and Kennington Park Road, terminating opposite William Street.

Nos. 2 & 2A. A line 1 ml. 2 f. 4 ch. long, commencing in Brixton Road by Gresham Road, along Brixton Road to Tramway No. 1 at Kennington.

No. 3. A line 5 f. 4.25 ch. long, along Stockwell Road from Clapham Road into Brixton Road.

No. 3A. A line 6.75 ch. long, a passing place at Stockwell Green.

No. 3B. A line 2 ch. long, a passing place at Stockwell Park Walk.

Nos. 4 & 4A. A line 1 ml. 6 ch. long, from Tramways Nos. 1 & 1A at Kennington, along Kennington Road to a point just south of Westminster Bridge Road.

No. 13. A line 4 f. 6.50 ch. long, from a junction with Tramway No. 4A near Kennington Cross, along Upper Kennington Lane to Wandsworth Road and High Street.

6   Mode of Formation.
    Two rails, 5 ft. 3 in. apart, to be maintained that the upper surface of the rails shall be on a level with the surface of the road.

9   The Company shall not ... open up a greater length than 100 yards of street ... and ... shall leave 440 yards between openings.

10 The time taken to work on any section is not to exceed six weeks, including making good.

11 The Company shall ... keep in repair ... the road between the tracks.

21 The Company ... cars to use flanged wheels and animal power.

22 The Company ... to have exclusive use of flanged wheels.

29 Only Tramway Cars to use rails ...

33 Powers for Police ... to regulate traffic on tramways ...

36 Tramways ... if discontinued ... to be removed ...

39 Capital: £120,000 ... in shares of £10 each ...

51 Borrowing powers ... to a maximum of £30,000 ...

55 Money raised ... only to apply to this Act ...

58 Directors ... (to be) six, but not less than three ...

61 First Directors ...Wm. Evans, John Humphrey, Chas. Oppenheim, Wm. White the Younger, and two others ...

62 Completion (of works) in two years ...

64 Tolls ... 1d per mile, but minimum of 3d ... may be charged ...

65 Luggage ... of passengers ... maximum of 28 lbs weight ...

66 Cars for workmen ... two each way each weekday ... not later than 7 a.m. or earlier than 6 p.m. ... minimum of 1d may be charged.

67 Cars ... not to carry goods ...

68 (List of) tolls to be exhibited in cars ...

77 Company ... to have power to recover tolls in Court ...

78 "Twenty-one year purchase clause for full value and goodwill" ...

81 Tramways ... not exempt from provisions in any General Act ...

82 All costs of the Act to be paid for by the Company.

The Parliamentary Agents to the Company were J. Dorington & Company: Solicitors were Ashurst, Morris & Company.

The reference to the track gauge being 5 ft. 3 in. was evidently the cause of considerable confusion. Although it appeared in this form in the 1869 Bill and Act, this was not the intention. In evidence given to the House of Commons in a report dated 8th April 1869, George Hopkins, Engineer to the Company (and also the North Metropolitan Tramways and Liverpool Tramways Companies) stated "... that the gauge is 4 ft. 8½ in. as in a railway, that is, to the outside of the flanges. It would be 4 ft. 9 in. to the extreme edge of the groove to allow of a little play. From the outside of the rail to the outside of the other is 5 ft. 1 in. It stands at 5 ft. 3 in. in the Bill and is explained by adding 3 inches to either side, but the intention was to keep the gauge at 4 ft. 8½ in. It is a little overstated in the Bill as the extreme measurement is 5 ft. 1 in. In other words, the gauge is the same as at Liverpool".

The same inaccuracy occurred in the 1869 Act of the Pimlico, Peckham & Greenwich Street Tramways Company, in both cases being rectified in the Acts of 1870, together with other far-reaching powers, including one which authorised the company to give up some of its selling power in exchange for an extra seven years' tenure, and another to enable the company to be sold, if desired, to a new Limited Company.

The Metropolitan Street Tramways Act, 1870 (33-34 Vic. cap. clxxiii) authorised the following tramways:-

Nos. 1 & 2. A double line, 2 f. 8 ch. long, from Kennington Road (at end of Tramways Nos. 4 & 4A, 1869 Act), along Westminster Bridge Road to Stangate.

Nos 5 & 6. A double line, 1 ml. 3.50 ch. long, from Clapham Road (at end of Tramways Nos. 1 & 1A, 1869 Act), along Clapham Road, Clapham Rise and High Street, Clapham to Park Road.

No. 7. A connecting curve 2 ch. long, between Stockwell Road and Clapham Road.

Nos. 8 & 9. A double line, 2 f. 6 ch. long, from Brixton Road (at end of Tramways Nos. 2 & 2A, 1869 Act), along Brixton Road to Brixton Rise at Acre Lane.

No. 9A. A passing place in Stockwell Road at Brixton Road.

Nos. 10 & 11. A double line, 2 f. 8 ch. and 3 f. long respectively, along Brixton Rise from end of Tramways Nos. 8 & 9 to Water Lane.

No. 12. A line 2 f. 5.50 ch. long, from end of Tramways Nos. 10 & 11, along Water Lane to Lower Tulse Hill.

An early Stephenson car, No. 212, is seen approaching St. George's Church, on a journey to Old Kent Road "Lord Wellington" via Brixton.

No. 13. A line 1 f. 7.50 ch. long, along Water Lane.
No. 14. A line 3 f. 4 ch. long, from Brixton Rise at Acre Lane, along Effra Road and Water Lane to Tramway No. 12.
No. 15. A line 3 f. 3.75 ch. long, from Brixton Road at Cold Harbour Lane, along Cold Harbour Lane to Barrington Road.

A number of the clauses written into the Act were of considerable importance, some extracts of which are reproduced here:-
10. .. existing funds may be made available for use ...
11. .. additional capital not to exceed £30,000 ...
12. .. additional mortgage sum of £17,500 authorised ...
14. .. 1869 mortgages have priority ...
37. (This also applied to the Pimlico, Peckham & Greenwich Co.)
The Metropolitan Board of Works may, if by resolution passed at a Special Meeting ... decide ... within six months **after the expiry of 28 years from the passing of this Act and within six months after the expiry of every subsequent period of seven years ...** require the Company to sell ... to them their undertaking upon the terms of paying **the then value** (exclusive of any allowance for past or future profits of the undertaking, or any compensation for compulsory sale, or other consideration whatsoever) of the Tramway ... and all powers ... **may be exercised by the Metropolitan Board of Works in like manner as if that Board had been authorised by the Acts of 1869 and 1870 ... and had been named in the 1869 Act instead of the Company.** One month notice to be given ... two-thirds of the members of the Board to be present ... and the Metropolitan Board may, in order to raise money for the purpose of carrying this section into effect, create additional stock not exceeding £300,000 under the "Metropolitan Board of Works (Loans) Act, 1869".
59. The Company and the Pimlico Company are empowered to enter into agreements, with respect to:-
   1. The user working, maintenance and management of their respective undertakings, etc.
   2. Provision of rolling and working stock.
   3. The appointment, removal and payment of officers and servants.
   4. The fixing, collection, division, appointment and appropriation by and between the companies of the rates, tolls and charges upon their respective undertakings.
   5. All incidental things, etc. ...

Track construction commenced in Brixton Road early in 1870, with about 120 men working on the first 400 yard section of road to be broken open, commencing at "The Russell" public house, approximately midway along the projected route. The type of rail devised by the Engineer to the company, George Hopkins, was corrugated on its inside face to enable the horses using the road to obtain a more positive foothold on all parts of the surface, and was similar to that used at Liverpool. This version of the "bar" rail was four inches wide and 1⅜ inches thick with an extension piece or lip on the inner edge, extending another half-inch downwards, and each bar was generally either 20 feet or 24 feet long.

The surface of the street was first removed to a depth of about nine inches and of sufficient width to enable a double or single line to be laid and including a space of two feet on either side. Longitudinal trenches about nine inches deep and sixteen inches wide were then dug, corresponding to the positions that the sleepers supporting the rails would take. The four-inch wide by six-inch deep sleepers were then laid in cast-iron "clip" chairs, spaced at about five feet intervals, with bar-iron cross ties maintaining the track to gauge. The rails were then spiked to the sleepers with nails passing vertically through holes in the grooves. The whole excavation was then packed with concrete and rammed.

The dovetailed tie-bars proved to be of very little use. They were not very precise, as due to vibration caused by the passage of cars over the track, they tended to work loose and rise up to the surface, causing damage to the paving. In addition, they tended to rust, and this, together with the ingress of surface water on to the fixings, made the whole assembly unstable after several years use.

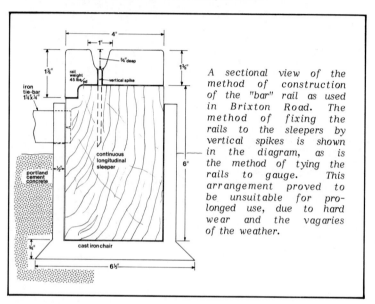

A sectional view of the method of construction of the "bar" rail as used in Brixton Road. The method of fixing the rails to the sleepers by vertical spikes is shown in the diagram, as is the method of tying the rails to gauge. This arrangement proved to be unsuitable for prolonged use, due to hard wear and the vagaries of the weather.

The First Section Opens

The line between Gresham Road Brixton and "The Horns" Kennington opened on 2nd May 1870. It was an occasion tinged with an air of festivity, which had been preceded by a number of trial runs at which many members of local bodies, Parliament and the press were present. A report of the opening states that "commodious cars, some seating 46 (22 inside, 24 out), others carrying 42 graced the line, decked out in a blue livery. The inside seats were fitted with red velvet cushions and backs; sun blinds were provided, as were 'winding ladders' to enable passengers to gain access to the outside seats". No inspection of the line is recorded.

Starbuck of Birkenhead supplied the 46-seat cars, while those seating 42 and probably 44 were by Stephenson of New York and Rowan of Randers, Denmark. Each vehicle was hauled by two horses, which had their bridles fitted with small bells with which to warn other road users of their presence.

The first depot and stables were situated "somewhere near Brixton". From such information as is available, it is most likely that a line

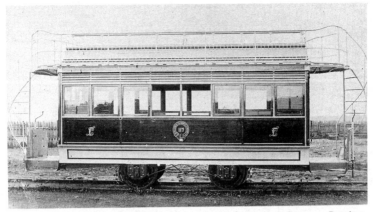

One of the original 8-window cars ordered from F. J. Rowan, Randers, Denmark, by the Metropolitan Street Tramways Company in 1871.
(Courtesy: P. S. Eilertsen)

was laid along Canterbury Road (as a branch of or as an extension to the main line) to a depot which had been installed in several of the railway arches which had recently been built in the area. This is borne out by the fact that in 1884 (some 14 years later) the London Tramways Company made proposals for a line which would meet "the Company's line at the entrance to the (Company's) tram depot at Canterbury Road".

On 5th October 1870 an extension along Kennington Road from "The Horns" to Westminster Bridge Road was opened for traffic, while a short extension at the other end of the line, from Gresham Road to Brixton Church (Acre Lane) opened at the same time. Finally, the line along Westminster Bridge Road from Kennington Road to the foot of Westminster Bridge opened on 22nd October. No inspections are recorded. The through fare was set at 3d and a five-minute service was provided. In the following year the line was extended south from Brixton Church to Water Lane, at the foot of Brixton Hill, and was opened to traffic on 21st August 1871. It has been said that a property standing at the foot of Brixton Hill, known as "Bethel House" was purchased by the company for use as a depot and stables, but this cannot be confirmed.

Meantime, track construction was proceeding on the Clapham Road line, a junction being formed with the Brixton Road line at St. Mark's Church, Kennington. This was opened as far as "The Swan" Stockwell on 7th December 1870, and was followed by an extension from "The Swan" to "The Plough" Clapham being completed at the beginning of April 1871. When the company informed the Board of Trade that it intended to commence services, Capt. H. W. Tyler, one of the Railway Department Inspectors, insisted that the line be properly authorised by inspection, a duty that he carried out on 5th April. After some small repairs to the road had been carried out, the line opened on 1st May 1871. For some years Clapham remained as the outpost of the operations of the company.

A further length of line opened on 11th September 1871 along Lambeth Road between Kennington Road and St. George's Circus, a distance of 19.45 chains. This had been constructed to allow cars from Kennington to obtain access to Blackfriars Bridge terminus. Due to the narrow width of Newington Butts, just to the south of the "Elephant & Castle", it was not possible at that time to build a direct line from Kennington to "Elephant", so this route was devised instead. It remained in use until 1874, when the Newington Butts route became available, after which it fell into disuse for a time, only to be revived by the South London Tramways Company in later years.

Cars for Artisans and Daily Labourers

The Acts obtained by the company made it obligatory for them to work two special journeys each weekday morning between Brixton and Westminster for artisans and daily labourers, with corresponding evening journeys from Westminster. It was not long after the introduction of this service however, before some of the regular passengers asked that the times of the evening cars be varied, in response to which the company suggested that workmen could use any car leaving Westminster between 6 and 8 p.m. provided that they rode on the top decks. This was agreed to, after which the company took off one of the special evening cars. Before long, possibly with the onset of bad weather, complaints were made that these passengers were not being allowed to ride inside the cars. The matter was taken up by the Board of Trade, who insisted that the company must not discriminate and, by law, should run a full quota of special evening cars. The company gave way, allowed workmen to ride inside if there was room, and again put on one additional special car.

The Newington Butts Extension

Newington Butts, connecting the northern end of Kennington Park Road with the "Elephant & Castle" junction, about a quarter of a mile in length, was very narrow in places. Late in 1871, the local Vestries and the Metropolitan Board of Works, together with the Ecclesiastical

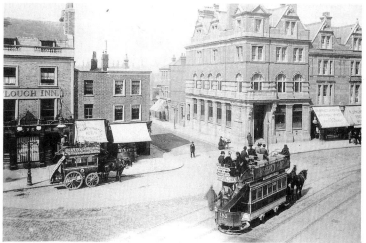

An 1890s view of car No. 151, standing at "The Plough", Clapham. By this time, the "knifeboard" top deck seats had been replaced with transverse "garden" seats.

Commissioners and the Bishop of London decided that the Parish Church of St. Mary could be demolished to make way for the new widened road if a new church would be provided elsewhere. It would also be necessary for the Board and Church to arrange for part of the church-yard to be cleared, which would require an Act of Parliament. The **Metropolitan Street Improvements Act, 1872 (35-36 Vic. cap. cliii)** gave the necessary authority. Work was sufficiently advanced in 1874 to allow the company to lay a double track tramway along the route.

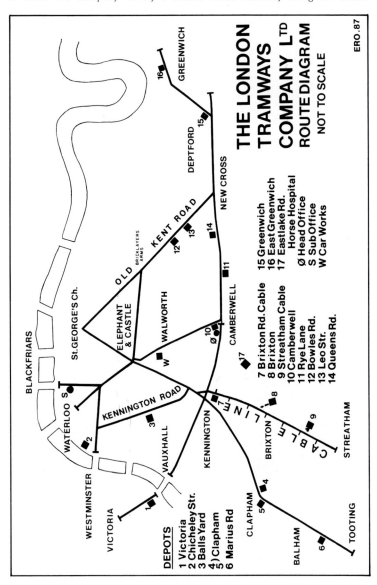

THE LONDON TRAMWAYS COMPANY LTD ROUTE DIAGRAM

NOT TO SCALE

ERO.87

7 Brixton Rd. Cable
8 Brixton
9 Streatham Cable
10 Camberwell
11 Rye Lane
12 Bowles Rd.
13 Leo Str.
14 Queens Rd.

15 Greenwich
16 East Greenwich
17 Eastlake Rd.
   Horse Hospital
Ø Head Office
S Sub Office
W Car Works

DEPOTS
1 Victoria
2 Chicheley Str.
3 Balls Yard
4) Clapham
5) Marius Rd

Chapter 3
The London Tramways Company Limited

The Pimlico, Peckham & Greenwich Street Tramways Company

Original Bills and Acts, 1869-1870

The original promoters of this company were William Morris, William Sheldon and John William Thomas, who became the first directors. Their 1869 proposals were presented early in the year, being formulated into a Bill to Parliament, seeking to authorise the construction of the following lines:-

"The proposed tramway will commence in the Vauxhall Bridge Road, then along Harleyford Road and both sides of Kennington Oval to Harleyford Street, thence along Camberwell New Road to Camberwell Green, and along Church and High Streets to Peckham, thence along Queen's Road and New Cross Road to Deptford and along the Blackheath Road opposite Lewisham Road, being about seven miles in length. It will be a single line of tramway throughout having at certain intervals a duplicate line to allow the passing and re-passing of the traffic on the tramway which, like those of the other two schemes, will be 5 ft. 3 in. in width."

The many secondary clauses in the Bill were similar in most respects to those in the 1869 Metropolitan Street Tramways Bill, providing for the protection of the authorities having responsibility for the streets, drains and sewers; the responsibility of the company in maintaining the rails and surrounding areas in good condition; the rights of the company to the sole use of the lines; together with other general clauses designed to give the police the power to regulate traffic, etc.

On 12th July 1869, the Royal Assent was given to **The Pimlico, Peckham & Greenwich Street Tramways Company Act, 1869 (32-33 Vic. cap. xcv),** which authorised the following tramways:-
No. 2. A line 1 ml. 4 f. 1.50 ch. long, from Upper Kennington Lane, along Harleyford Road, Kennington Oval (south side), Harleyford Street, and Camberwell New Road to Camberwell Green.
No. 2A. A line 2 f. 3.50 ch. long, round Kennington Oval (north side).
No. 2B. A passing place, 3 ch. long, in Camberwell New Road.
No. 3. A line 1 ml. 9 ch. long, from end of Tramway No. 2 at Camberwell Green, along Church Street to High Street, Peckham at Hill Street.
No. 3A. A passing place, 3 ch. long, by the Vestry Hall.
No. 4. A line 7 f. 8.50 ch. long, from end of Tramway No. 3 at Peckham, to Queens Road, Peckham.
No. 4A. A passing place 3 ch. long, near Carlton Grove.
No. 5. A line 7 f. 7 ch. long, from end of Tramway No. 4 at Queens Road, along New Cross Road to Broadway, Deptford.
No. 5A. A passing place 3 ch. long, in New Cross Road at North Road.
No. 6. A line 3 f. 5.25 ch. long, from end of Tramway No. 5 at Deptford Broadway, along Deptford Bridge, Greenwich Road and Blackheath Road to South Street.

A Stephenson 7-window car in original condition, standing with its crew in Rye Lane, Peckham depot yard. (Courtesy: G. E. Baddeley)

No. 6A. A line 1 ch. long, in Blackheath Road at South Street (making a double track terminal stub).

Other conditions were similar to those applying to the Metropolitan Street Tramways Company except for clause 42, which authorised the company to raise capital to the sum of £45,000 in £10 shares. The Secretary to the company was J. Foulston Hunt.

On 17th December 1869, the Engineer to the Metropolitan Board of Works, J.W. Bazalgette, was notified of the intention of the company to commence roadworks at the beginning of January 1870. At the same time, proposals were being made for the company to present an amending Bill, similar in many respects to that presented by the Metropolitan Street Tramways Company, in which it asked for authority to extend the system, as yet unbuilt, and which was to include lines north of the Thames; to redefine the gauge of the lines, and for other purposes. A second Bill was also being written to enable the company to build additional passing places and to double some single line sections on the route.

The first of these Bills passed through Parliament, received the Royal Assent on 10th August 1870 and was:-
**The Pimlico, Peckham & Greenwich Street Tramways Act, 1870
(33-34 Vic. cap. clxvii).**
The Act authorised three additional passing places:-
No.1. 3 ch. long in Harleyford Road.
No.2. 3 ch. long at Kennington Church.
No.3. 3 ch. long in Camberwell New Road at Wyndham Road.

Another provision of the Act allowed for doubling parts of Tramways Nos. 3, 4, 5 and 6 of the 1869 Act. A number of regulating clauses were contained in the Act, and those of particular importance were:-
5. .. abandon ... construction of several authorised tramways or passing

Westminster Bridge Road in the 1870s. A Greenwich-bound car is seen leaving the terminus, followed by one for Brixton.

(*Courtesy: Aberdeen University Library*)

places, viz: Nos. 2B, 3A, 4A and 5A now unnecessary.
6. Gauge to be 4 ft. 8½ in.
13. Completion ... within 18 months.
14. Monies from the 1869 Act may be applied ...
15. Further additional capital to the maximum of £56,000 authorised ...
17. An additional £14,000 authorised ... to be raised on mortgage ...
22. The **whole** of the tramways to be **simultaneously** opened at one time for traffic (including parts authorised under the 1869 Act).
23. The Company and the Metropolitan Street Tramways Company may from time to time enter into ... contracts or arrangements ... regarding rolling stock, staff, etc.
24. During ... any such agreement the companies shall, for the purpose of tolls and charges be considered as one tramway ...

Under the terms of the Extensions Act, the lines authorised were divided into Groups to give priority in building the first "experimental" lines, this being required as Parliament and other bodies were very wary of giving too much headway to speculative companies. These were, in the eyes of Parliament, in a position to "monopolise" the centre section of some of the most important thoroughfares in the metropolis.

The second Bill to receive Royal Assent on 10th August 1870 was:-
The Pimlico, Peckham & Greenwich Street Tramways (Extensions) Act, 1870 (33-34 Vic. cap. clxxxiv).
The lines authorised were:-
Group A. "Elephant & Castle" to Vauxhall and Victoria Station.
Nos. 1 & 2. A double line, 2 mls. 7 f. long, in St. George's Road, Lambeth Road, Church Street, Lambeth Bridge, Horseferry Road, Greycoat Road, Old Rochester Row, Artillery Row and Victoria Street.
Nos. 1A & 2A. A double line junction between Kennington Road and Lambeth Road.

37

No. 3. A single line, 2.10 ch. long, from Tramway No. 1 in Victoria Street, into Vauxhall Bridge Road.

Nos. 5 & 6. A double line, 1 f. 1.28 ch. long, in St. George's Road between Lambeth Road and Westminster Bridge Road.

Nos. 7 & 8. A double line, 1 ml. 1 f. 2.77 ch. long, from Upper Kennington Lane at Goding Street, over Vauxhall Bridge, along Vauxhall Bridge Road to the end of Tramway No. 3 at Victoria.

Group B. "Elephant & Castle" to Westminster and Blackfriars Bridges.

Nos. 9 & 10. A double line, 7 f. 3.05 ch. long, from "Elephant & Castle" along London Road and Blackfriars Road to Holland Street.

Nos. 11 & 12. A double line, 5 f. 2.25 ch. long, from St. George's Circus (junction with Tramways Nos. 9 & 10), along Westminster Bridge Road to Belvedere Road.

Group C. Miscellaneous junctions.

Nos. 13 & 14. A double line, 3.20 ch. long, from Tramways Nos. 1 & 2 from St. George's Road into New Kent Road.

Nos. 15 & 16. A double line, 3 ch. long, from Tramways Nos. 9 & 10 from London Road into New Kent Road.

Nos. 17 & 18. A double line, 1 f. 4.47 ch. long, along Lambeth Road from St. George's Road to St. George's Circus.

Group D. "Elephant & Castle" to Camberwell.

Nos. 19 & 21. A double line, 1 ml. 4 f. long, from "Elephant & Castle" along Walworth Road to Camberwell Green.

No. 20. A line 1 ch. long, at "Elephant & Castle" into Walworth Road.

No. 22. A line 1 ch. long, at Camberwell Green.

Group E. "Elephant & Castle" to New Cross.

Nos. 23 & 24. A double line, 5 f. 0.32 ch. long, from end of Tramways Nos. 15 & 16, along New Kent Road to Old Kent Road.

Nos. 25 & 26. A double line, 2 mls. 1 f. 8 ch. long, from end of Tramways Nos. 23 & 24, along Old Kent Road and New Cross Road to Queens Road.

A rare view of the opening ceremony of the Pimlico company's line between Deptford and Greenwich on 4th March 1871. (G. E. Baddeley)

Group F. Extensions to Greenwich and Woolwich.

Nos. 27 & 28. A double line, 1 ml. 4 f. 6.30 ch. long, from Deptford Bridge Along Greenwich Road, London Street, Church Street, Nelson Street, Trafalgar Road, Greenwich and Woolwich Lower Roads to Hatcliffe Street, Woolwich.

No. 29. A single line, 1 ml. 5 f. 9.45 ch. long, from end of Tramway No. 27, along Woolwich Lower Road to Albion Road.

Nos. 30 & 31. A double line, 3 f. 3.26 ch. long, from Blackheath Road, along South Street to London Street (Tramways Nos. 27 & 28).

No. 32. A passing place, 3.10 ch. long, in Woolwich Lower Road at Lombard Road.

No. 33. A single line, 5 f. 4.34 ch. long, from end of Tramway No. 29, along Woolwich High Street, Edward Street, Powis Street and Beresford Street (Tramway No. 35).

No. 35. A single line, 2 f. 5.30 ch. long, from Powis Street to Beresford Square (Tramway No. 33).

There were several important clauses contained in the Act:-

21. ... 1869 funds may be applied ...
22. Additional capital not to exceed £160,000.
24. Mortgage ... maximum of £40,000 ...
28. ... agreement between Pimlico Company and Lambeth Bridge Co. ... 2d toll on each car crossing the Bridge.

First Construction

A considerable amount of preparatory work, such as the diversion of pipes was undertaken prior to laying the first section of the line at Blackheath Road Greenwich in March 1870. By the end of October, work was complete as far as New Cross, and a junction line had been installed into Greenwich Road. Land near the "Red Lion" public house in Greenwich Road had been purchased upon which a depot and stables were to be built.

Following completion, a series of trial runs took place early in December, with employees of the company acting as passengers. The line opened to traffic on 13th December, but had only been open for a few days when a great snowstorm swept across the area and stopped all activity. It was not until 7th January 1871 that services were resumed.

Early in 1871, the company stated its intention to commence the construction of the line between Blackheath Road and Christchurch, Greenwich, working from both ends simultaneously. Just over a mile long, the line was opened with all due ceremony on 4th March when, at 2 p.m., five cars, decorated with flags, started out from the depot and made for Greenwich, after which all the invited guests made for the "Ship Hotel" at Greenwich, where a reception was held, presided over by one of the Directors, Mr. J. Morris.

Public service commenced the following day which, according to Capt. H. W. Tyler of the Board of Trade, was irregular. He pointed out that under the Act obtained by the company in 1870, lines were to be properly inspected before being opened to public traffic. As this line was constructed by powers obtained in 1869, it is doubtful whether any inspection was required, nevertheless Capt. Tyler carried out an inspection on 17th March and authorised its use. One piece of track specially mentioned was that at Deptford Bridge, where it was stated that "... these is a curious piece of engineering at Deptford Bridge upon this line. For a considerable length the line is double, but the trams (sic) are laid so close together that the cars cannot pass each other. One of them has to wait for the other, or go back

Another of the original Stephenson cars, now No. 338 of the London Tramways Company fleet, stands for a few moments at Greenwich terminus, prior to making the return journey to Westminster.

if it meets another within this space". For this reason, a timekeeper was stationed at the interlaced track, acting also as a "policeman" for the cars, ensuring that only one was on this section at any one time. The first holder of this position was a gentleman named Mott.

Original Track Construction

The original track employed timber tie-bars in its construction, transversely laid at between five and six feet intervals at the bottom of the excavation, which provided the main bearing surfaces to the concrete. Longitudinal sleepers were then placed on top of the tie-bars and secured by means of angle brackets spiked to the sleepers, one outside each longitudinal. The bar rails, with extended fillets on either side were fitted to the tops of the pre-formed sleepers and held fast by vertical spikes driven through holes in the grooves. The bar rail was four inches wide, and weighed 48 lbs/yard.

When the rails had been laid, the whole assembly was levelled and then packed with concrete to the height necessary for receiving the stone pavement or asphalte as required. It had been thought that the use of asphalte would provide a quieter road surface, but it was structurally weak and broke away from the sides of the rails and was not successful. The other problem of instability of the rail, caused by the use of vertical spikes was to remain.

Further Construction

The company was originally authorised to construct a line from Pimlico to Greenwich by way of Kennington, Peckham and New Cross. The Act gained in 1870 transferred some of the authorised lines of the Metropolitan Street Tramways Company to the Pimlico Company and it was these that were dealt with next. Tracklaying commenced at New Cross Gate and proceeded along New Cross Road and Old Kent Road as far as the "Shard Arms" public house, a distance of about one mile, which was opened to traffic on 1st May 1871. This was followed on 2nd July by an extension to the Bricklayers Arms Railway Station, and in neither case does it appear that the lines were inspected prior to opening.

Continuing onwards from Bricklayers Arms Station, the lines along Old Kent Road, then New Kent Road, London Road, St. George's Circus and Blackfriars Road, Stamford Street were completed in two parts. The section between St. George's Circus and Stamford Street opened on 1st September 1871, to be followed on 6th by the line between Bricklayers Arms Station and St. George's Circus. A connecting line between Hercules Buildings (Oakley Street) and St. George's Circus completed the main line of the company from Westminster to Greenwich when it opened on 25th September. It also formed a junction with the Kennington line of the Metropolitan Street Tramways Company. There are no reports of any inspections having taken place.

Meanwhile, the line along Walworth Road from the "Elephant" to Camberwell Green and from there to Peckham and New Cross was nearing completion. Part of this had been authorised by the original Act obtained by the company. The Walworth Road line opened on 25th September, with the remainder to New Cross following on 29th January 1872. Lastly, the Vauxhall to Camberwell line, although it was completed and, apparently, inspected on 30th December 1871, did not open to traffic until 15th April 1872, and when it did, it worked as an isolated line for a number of years.

In conjunction with the construction of its network, the company obtained several sites for depots and stables, among them a large area in Penrose Street, Walworth where the main workshops were to be situated, together with a depot for 40 cars. Stabling for 100 horses was also provided for in several railway arches nearby.

The section of line from the north side of Vauxhall Bridge to the "Windsor Castle" public house near Victoria Street was completed in October 1872, but due to difficulties experienced by the company

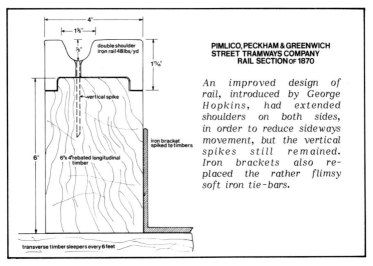

PIMLICO, PECKHAM & GREENWICH STREET TRAMWAYS COMPANY RAIL SECTION OF 1870

An improved design of rail, introduced by George Hopkins, had extended shoulders on both sides, in order to reduce sideways movement, but the vertical spikes still remained. Iron brackets also replaced the rather flimsy soft iron tie-bars.

double shoulder iron rail 48 lbs/yd

vertical spike

iron bracket spiked to timbers

6"x 4"rebated longitudinal timber

transverse timber sleepers every 6 feet

The isolated line between Vauxhall and Victoria Street was worked in later years by several standard 7-window cars, which were rebuilt from the original Stephenson vehicles. These lasted until August 1906.

in negotiations over a site for a depot near Bessborough Gardens, the line did not open to traffic until 20th October 1873. It had also been intended that the lines on both sides of Vauxhall Bridge would be connected by a line over the bridge, but authority could not be obtained from either the bridge owners nor the Metropolitan Board of Works, mainly because of the narrowness of the steeply humped bridge. It was left to the company to operate an omnibus service over the bridge at ½d fare.

In all Acts of Parliament gained by tramway companies, the Metropolitan Police were given considerable powers for regulating traffic, and this they used to the full. A difficulty soon to be seen was that, as the cars operated on fixed tracks, they were considered by the police to be "obstructive", particularly at terminal points where they stood in the centres of the roads. As early as March 1872, a conductor was summoned for leaving his tramcar and allowing it to stand in the roadway "for longer than was considered necessary". Even though the conductor said that he was allowed an eight-minute break at the terminus, the police would not agree, resulting in his being fined 5/- for his "misdemeanour". Eventually, by tacit agreement, this problem receded, but tramcar crews were never entirely freed from the threat of prosecution for "obstruction".

Another difficulty, which eventually became a financial burden on tramway companies in the Metropolitan area, concerned the payment of a rate to every local authority through whose districts the tramways were laid. Although a large part of the roadways had to be kept in repair by the tramway company and these sections of road could be used by all and sundry, the principle was always upheld, right through the period of tramways operation, before and after acqusition by the London County Council.

Chapter 4
The London Tramways Company Limited
Amalgamation of the Companies

Almost from the beginning of operations it was seen that the two companies had much in common, both in the choice of termini that they were using in central London and also in parts of the routes that they were taking to the suburbs. Amalgamation was proposed, which was to be arranged by the purchase of both by another limited company which had been formed and registered on 12th December 1870 under the regulations of the Companies' Acts, 1862 and 1867. The new company, The London Tramways Company Limited, had two of the directors of the Metropolitan Street Tramways Company and one from the Pimlico Peckham & Greenwich Street Tramways Company as founder shareholders.

Nevertheless, both existing companies submitted their separate proposals to Parliament in 1871 for extensions which in the main were for lines in areas where they were never to be allowed. Apart from several short lengths in the suburbs, the rest concerned lines over London, Waterloo, Southwark, Blackfriars and Westminster Bridges and into the central parts of the City and West End. Nothing came of these; no routes were ever laid over London Bridge or Waterloo Bridge, while it was left to the London County Council to obtain powers to lay tramways over the others many years later.

The Memorandum and Articles of Association of the London Tramways Company Limited were:-

1. Title: The London Tramways Company Limited.
2. Registered Offices of the Company will be in England.
   Certificate No.5198 NL - 4979/2.   12th December 1870.
3. Objects:
   a. To purchase the undertakings of the Metropolitan Street Tramways Company and the Pimlico, Peckham & Greenwich Street Tramways Company respectively under the powers in the Acts of Parliament relating to those companies, and in the meantime to acquire and hold the shares in those companies respectively.
   b. To equip the lines and to work the tramways of those companies.
   c. To acquire, to make, and to equip and work any extensions of such tramways which have been or which may hereafter be authorised by Parliament or by the Board of Trade.
   d. To acquire any land, buildings, plant, machinery, carriages, horses, chattels or other property (whether real or personal and of whatever nature) the possession of which may be useful for or conducive to the attainment of any of the objects of this company.
   e. To take and hold shares in any other tramway companies under any General Act, or any right or interest in any tramway for the furtherance of the objects of this company.
   f. To do all such other things as are incidental or conducive to the attainment of the above objects.

4. The liability of the Members is Limited.
5. The Capital of the company is £250,000, divided into 25,000 shares of the nominal amount of £10 each.

The original shareholders in the new company were Anthony John Mundella, M. P.; Wm. Evans, Director, Metropolitan Street Tramways; James Reynolds; Wm. Morris, Director, Pimlico, etc. Tramways; John Foulson Hunt, Secretary; John Humphrey, Director, Metropolitan Street Tramways; James Ridley, Solicitor.   A scheduled list of conditions was included in the content of the Articles of Association, giving the new company certain rights over the other two undertakings.

Sale of the Metropolitan Street Tramways Company;
The London Tramways Company to allot to shareholders 9,750 paid-up shares representing £97,500 of capital, plus 5,500 "scrip certificates" representing the right of the holder to one part in twelve thousand five hundred of half the surplus profits at a maximum dividend of 6% in both cases.

Sale of the Pimlico, Peckham & Greenwich Street Tramways Company:
When the lines are built, the allocation of shares to be agreed, plus 7,000 transferable scrip certificates.   The contractors are to complete the work and the London Company (is) to pay the Pimlico Company at the rate of £5,650 per mile of single track.   £1,000 to be paid to the Directors of the Pimlico Company ... The London Company is to provide rolling stock.

The method of sale was to be that the shareholders were to transfer their holdings from the old companies to the London Tramways Company Limited and, in foregoing any payment for goodwill, would each receive an allotment of scrip certificates, to hold for as long as the shares were retained. The two companies were subject to the sale and purchase conditions as laid down in the Tramways Act, 1870, Section 44, which said " ... and where any tramway in any district has been open for traffic for a period of six months, the promoters may, with the consent of the Board of Trade, sell their undertaking to any person, persons, corporation or company".

Messrs. Ashurst, Morris & Co., the Solicitors to all the companies, decided to attempt to go ahead with the sale of the Metropolitan Street Tramways Company, advising the Board of Trade of this on 21st July 1871.   The decision had been taken not to proceed with the sale of the Pimlico Company until sufficient of the line had been built in order to make the transaction possible.   The Board of Trade, in turn, referred the matter to a Parliamentary Committee, who said that " ... if the sale can be legally made then it will be. If not, the Company shall, if they see fit, apply for and obtain an Act of Parliament, provided that the selling parties and the Board of Trade agreed to this course of action".   The Committee also advised the Board of Trade that, until such sale was arranged, the London Company would be able to work both undertakings on their behalf, but the separate administration and organisation of both must be maintained.   The Board also advised the Limited Company on 13th December, to proceed with caution, as the Metropolitan Company "were not yet in a position to transfer the whole of their undertaking".

In November 1872, the Board of Trade asked whether the companies were in a position to sell, but the Solicitor intimated that it would be two more years before this could take place. The line from Vauxhall to Victoria, although built, was not open; the line from Greenwich to Woolwich was not built; neither was the one from the "Elephant & Castle" along Lambeth Road and Bridge to Victoria.   In view of this, they had all decided to apply to Parliament in the 1873 Session to effect the change.

The London Tramways Company Limited Purchase Act, 1873 (36-37 Vic. cap. cciv) received Royal Assent on 28th July, allowing the sale and purchase of the two earlier companies to take place. Although the London Tramways Company was given powers to become the legal owner, the two operating companies had each obtained a Provisional Order from the Board of Trade, allowing them to construct further extensions to their lines.

The Metropolitan Tramways Orders Confirmation Act, 1873 (36-37 Vic. cap. ccxv) received Royal Assent on 5th August, confirming the Provisional Order granted by the Board of Trade. The new extensions were authorised under the following sub-headings:-

Metropolitan Street Tramways:-
Nos. 1 & 1A. A double line, 1 ml. 3 f. long, from "The Horns", along Kennington Park Road, Newington Butts, Newington Causeway, Stones End and Blackman Street to St. George's Church. The lines were not to be opened north of the "Elephant & Castle" until a connection had been made with the lines of the Pimlico Company ...
The company may make arrangements with the Pimlico, North Metropolitan and London Street Companies ...

The Pimlico, Peckham & Greenwich Street Tramways:-
Nos. 2 & 3. A double line, 5 f. long, from St. George's Church, along Great Dover Street to Bricklayers Arms Station.
No. 9. A line in Short Street linking Walworth Road with Newington Butts and St. George's Road.
No. 10. A line 4 ch. long connecting London Road with Newington Butts. Nos. 2 & 3 are not to be opened until Nos. 1 & 1A and short junctions are completed.

Notice was given to the Board of Trade and local Vestries on 13th May 1874 of its intention to commence construction of the authorised lines at the north-west end of Old Kent Road and Great Dover Street, and on 21st July 1874 for those in Kennington Park Road, Newington Butts, Newington Causeway and Blackman Street. By Christmas, all

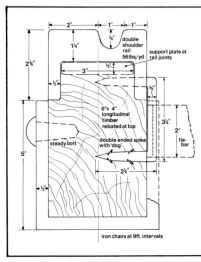

By 1873, it had become clear that the rail fixings were of little use, and resulted in yet another type of rail and fastenings being introduced. This time, the double-shouldered rails were dog-spiked to the sleepers with double-ended staples, which also assisted in holding the tie-bars in position. The sleepers were also locked into the chairs by the use of "steady-bolts" which were driven through holes in the sides of the chairs.

Stephenson cars were well-known in many parts of the world. Large numbers were purchased by the London Tramways Company and its two predecessors. No. 284 of the LTC is seen here, prior to shipment from the John Stephenson Company of New York, USA.

(Courtesy: John Stephenson Album)

was complete. Services commenced on 28th December 1874 without consent of the Board of Trade. However, this state of affairs did not last long, as on 4th January 1875, Maj. Gen. Hutchinson visited the lines and was very critical of the work. He ordered the company to cease operations "at once" and not resume until remedial work had been carried out on the tracks. A further inspection was made by the General on 11th January, after which he agreed to its re-opening. Services commenced the same day.

In 1874, the company obtained premises at "Balls Yard", situated at the junction of Kennington Road and Kennington Lane, for use as a depot and stables to house the growing fleet. Until this time, the horses had been hired from the LGOC, but with the expansion of the tramway company, the decision was taken to purchase a stud of horses for its own use.

The Act which authorised the company to purchase its predecessors also contained a clause making it conditional upon the Limited Company that all Acts and Orders obtained by the two earlier companies were to remain in force after the transfer. The rights of the Metropolitan Board of Works were also protected.

By 1875, almost almost all the works authorised by the various Acts and Orders had been completed. The London Tramways Company Limited became the largest operator in the Metropolitan area south of the Thames. It had offices at 80 Blackfriars Road, which were later removed to 303 Camberwell New Road, where they remained for the rest of the time that the company was in business and which, after the LCC Tramways came into being, continued to serve as Head Office for several years. The first Managing Director of the Limited Company was Thomas Kenworthy Robotham, who was previously General Manager of the North British Railway Company.

Management in Crisis

The year 1877 was a difficult one for the company, with much criticism being directed at the management over the alleged very bad condition of much of the track. While this company was not the only one to be involved in accusations of this type, it received its share of bad press. Several reports were compiled by individuals commissioned by various bodies, one John S. Pierce, C.E. among them, who published his findings on 2nd March 1877 in the form of a letter to Col. Marcus Beresford, M. P. It was highly critical of the general state of the rails and roads, laying most of the blame on the heads of the tramway companies. Resulting from the bad publicity, some remedial work was carried out and the worst parts of the tracks were attended to, but it seems that they were hard put to cope with the scale of repair required.

It was also becoming apparent that a deep division was forming between factions within the governing body of the company. The problem was its financial condition and criticism of the way in which affairs were being handled. It was also alleged that capital had been "lost" and that sums set aside for depreciation and reserve were not sufficient, the result being that assets had been over-estimated by an alleged £114,000. Certain individuals meantime, had banded together and registered a new company in an effort to provide a "cushion" should disaster befall the London Tramways Company. The South Metropolitan Tramways Company Limited was registered on 26th August 1878.

Despite the warning signs, the management of the London Company were still pursuing their own policy aims. The Chairman had reported to the shareholders on 9th February 1878 that the company was dealing with the track repairs in a positive way and that, generally, the undertaking was in a stable condition. Nevertheless, at the next meeting of shareholders in July, the bad condition of much of the track was still the main talking point and, after acrimonious discussion the report was rejected. At yet another meeting on 28th August, the report finally got a hearing and was accepted.

On 20th November another extraordinary meeting was called for the purpose of considering terms for leasing the company to the South Metropolitan Tramways Company. At this gathering, which was chaired by Capt. Gillies, one of the shareholders, Mr. Harrison, who expressed displeasure at the performance of the company, together with a friend, proposed and seconded the motion but, after a poll had been taken, the resolution was lost. The London Tramways Company was not to be leased away. The problems, however, were to remain as, on 18th February 1879, one of the scripholders applied for and obtained an injunction restraining the directors from declaring and paying a dividend on the ordinary shares for the second half of 1878, due to their being no net profits available for such a payment. It was not long afterwards that some members of the Board, including the Chairman and Secretary were unseated. David Plenderleath Sellar, who had been a leading figure in the launching of the South Metropolitan Tramways Company, took Capt. Gillies' place as Chairman, while James Connell took over for a one-year period as Secretary, after which W. H. Andrews filled the position. Following this, the South Metropolitan Company was wound up on 19th February 1879.

A Bill was prepared for the 1880 Parliamentary Session in which it was proposed that the company be recapitalised, and that several more extensions to the system be authorised. The Metropolitan Board of Works refused to allow the extension clauses to be included, unless

The London Tramways Company also operated omnibuses in conjunction with the tramway services, connecting their termini with destinations in the City of London and "West End". Omnibus No. 101 stands outside Chicheley Street depot, together with its confident driver, reliable conductor and patient horses. (Courtesy: London Transport)

the company agreed to maintain all new and existing tramways up to a standard specified by the Board, which the company declined to do. Resulting from the terms of **The London Tramways Company Limited (Capital) Act, 1880 (43-44 Vic. cap. clv)**, which received Royal Assent on 12th August, the company was given the opportunity to rearrange its affairs and by the end of 1880 there was promise of more normal working again. A lawsuit, entered into late in 1880, completed the story, with authority to recover the deficit of £98,240 from the Sinking Fund in the first instance and, if the shareholders desired, to take further action through the Courts to recover it from "those upon whom the responsibility rested in allowing the capital of the company to be lost to this extent".

Resulting from the earlier litigation, track renewals played a large part in the activities of the company during the next few years. In 1881, the Kennington Park Road line was completely reconstructed, using the "Spielmann" type of rail, consisting of two half-rail sections mounted back to back. Details of this unusual type of construction were:-

> Length of rail, 24 feet (reversible).
> Weight, two sections, each of 32½ lbs/yard.
> Wooden sleepers, 6 in. x 4 in. x 6 ft. (the old ones were retained).
> Rail groove, 1 in. deep x 1 in. wide.

No fishplates were used. Each half-rail section was "staggered" so that the joints were 6 ft. apart.

"Derby Day" loomed large in the calendar of the period and although the event was staged on Epsom Downs, about ten miles south of Kennington, great concern was felt that the tramway rail renewal programme would be liable to upset the passage of the large numbers of vehicles of all kinds which would be used to convey the "punters" to the shrine! The Chairman of the Poplar Board of Works, Henry Fainfield pointed this out quite forcibly to the Board of Trade as well to the Tramway Company and the Lambeth Vestry. However, it was promised that the work would be completed by then, or if not, operations would be suspended so that the faithful could all safely negotiate Kennington Park Road. It was also said that the company had money on the event too. It stood to gain some extra patronage from people who would be only too pleased to ride to Clapham - and walk the rest of the way to Epsom!

A proposal had been made in 1882 on behalf of the "Clapham, Balham & Tooting Tramways" for a line to be built from the terminus of the London Tramways at Clapham Common to Church Street Balham. This was unsuccessful but was raised again by the London Tramways Company, which resulted in **The London Tramways Company (Various Powers) Act, 1888 (51-52 Vic. cap. cxliv).**
The extension was divided into three Tramways, namely:-
No. 1. A double line, 6 f. 2 ch. long, from High Street Clapham, along the east side of Clapham Common to Cavendish Road.
No. 1A. A double line, 5 f. 9 ch. long, from the end of Tramway No. 1, along Balham Hill and Balham Road to Balham Station. This included two single track sections totalling 8 ch. in length.
No. 1B. A double line, 4 f. 7 ch. long, from the end of Tramway No. 1A, along Balham Road to Tooting Bec (sic) Road. This included 1.50 ch. of single line (terminal stub).

"Derby Day" in the 80s. This animated scene in Clapham Road, with St. Mark's Church in the background, shows the fervour displayed by some race-goers to get to the races. The reaction of the tram driver can only be imagined! (Courtesy: Aberdeen University Library)

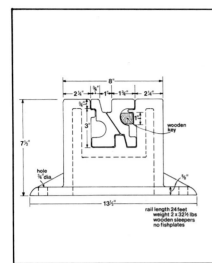

The Spielmann System of track construction, using reversible rails was little used on the LTC system. The only known example was installed in a part of Kennington Park Road.

The original Bill had included a proposal for the extension of the Brixton line to Streatham, with operation by mechanical traction (other than steam), but this was deleted. In addition, plans were deposited, together with a Bill for a tramway across Westminster Bridge, but the Metropolitan Board of Works opposed this and it failed.

The Act also specified that roads should be of a minimum width of 47 feet and stated that, if any part was less than this, it was to be widened at the expense of the company. A "new standard rail" was to be used, made of steel in 24 ft. lengths and weighing either 58 or 61 lbs/yard and supported in cast-iron chairs weighing 39 lbs each. Fishplates 14 inches long were to be used at rail joints.

Construction of the section between "The Plough", Clapham and Nightingale Lane was completed and inspected by Maj. Gen. Hutchinson on 2nd July, and services commenced on 28th. The extension to Tooting Bec Road was inspected by the General on 30th November and was opened to traffic on 15th December.

The final extension to Tooting (Totterdown) was authorised by **The London Tramways Company (Extensions) Act, 1889 (52-53 Vic. cap. cxxiv)**, which received Royal Assent on 12th August. This was:- **No. 1C**. A double line, 4 f. 3.50 ch. long, from the end of Tramway No. 1B to Totterdown Street.

Approval was given to use the "new standard rails" on the extension. The completed line was inspected on 1st December 1890 by Maj. Gen. Hutchinson and public traffic commenced on 16th December. The same Act also authorised the extension of the line from Brixton, Water Lane to Streatham, Telford Avenue, details of which are contained in the next chapter.

Car No. 163 at "The Plough" Clapham. The two tracks into the small depot at the side of the public house are also visible.

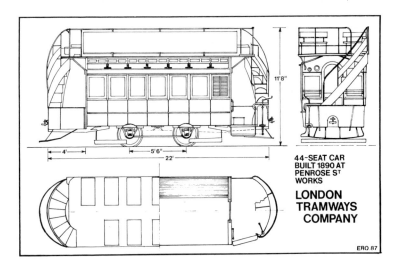

11'8"

4' — 5'6" — 22'

44-SEAT CAR
BUILT 1890 AT
PENROSE S^T
WORKS

**LONDON
TRAMWAYS
COMPANY**

ERO 87

Chapter 5
The Kennington and Streatham Cable Line

The horse-drawn line of the company terminated at the foot of Brixton Hill at Water Lane. The directors decided to submit a Bill to Parliament for an extension up the hill as far as Telford Park, with eventual ideas on a further extension to Streatham Village. The **London Tramways Company (Extensions) Act, 1889 (52-53 Vic. cap. cxxiv)** authorised the following Tramways:-

No. 2. A double line, 2 f. 4 ch. long, from Water Lane to Endymion Road.

No. 2A. A double line, 3 f. 3.50 ch. long, from the end of Tramway No. 2 to Mill Lane.

No. 2B. A double line, 2 f. 2 ch. long, from the end of Tramway No. 2A to Telford Avenue, where a depot will also be sited.

On this extended section, the Wandsworth Board of Works was authorised to widen the roads where necessary to allow for a double line with a 9 ft. 6 in. clearance on either side of the outer rails, charges for this work to be settled by the tramway company.

It was realised that if services were not to be maintained at snail's pace up Brixton Hill, something other than horsepower would be needed. After much deliberation, the directors decided that cable traction would probably provide the best means of giving a good and reliable service. The company obtained an Act in 1890, authorising the use of cable traction on the new line, together with the conversion to cable working of the line between Water Lane and Kennington. **The London Tramways Company Act, 1890 (53 vic. cap. xxiv)** gave this authority for an initial maximum term of seven years, renewable for a further maximum term of seven years, subject to the approval of the Board of Trade, the London County Council and the local Boards and Vestries.

This system was reputed to have been patented as long ago as 1838 by a man named Curtis. A similar idea was taken up by Andrew Smith Hallidie of San Francisco, who was a successful businessman engaged in the manufacture of wire rope. The method involved the use of an endless stranded steel cable, supported by pulley wheels, running at a depth of between eight and nine inches in a conduit or open tube placed centrally between the tramway running rails. The cable was driven from an engine house, where a huge steam-driven winch ran continuously, hauling the cable through the conduit at a speed of about 8 m.p.h.

Track Construction

The Engineer responsible for the construction of the cable line, power house and depot, together with all ancillary equipment was Mr. W. N. Colam, M. Inst. C. E., who worked in conjuction with the main contractor, Messrs. Dick, Kerr & Co. Ltd., and their Engineer, James More, A. M. Inst. C. E.

The running rails were laid on cast-iron yokes shaped like a letter -u-, the centres of which formed the line of a concrete conduit, through which the cable was to run. When the road was built up to rail level, all that could be seen was the centre slot between the rails, formed by two steel "z" rails. These were supported by cast-iron yokes, each weighing about 150 lbs., standing two feet high from the concrete base and 1 ft. 6 in. wide, and laid at intervals of 3 ft. 7 in. throughout the length of the line. The permanent way was a variation of, but broadly similar to the Hallidie system, adopted in San Francisco, but of lighter construction. Girder rails weighing 95 lbs/yd with shouldered fishplates were used, laid into portland cement concrete six inches thick, being kept to gauge by short, adjustable tie-bars bolted into the rails and slotted into the yokes. The conduit tube was 19 inches deep and 9 inches wide, formed with concrete. A drainpipe was laid beneath each set of rails, with gulleys leading in from the conduits at regular intervals.

On the straight sections of track, vertical pulleys 14 inches in diameter, were spaced about 50 feet apart, while on curved sections, horizontal pulleys 14 inches in diameter and set at suitable intervals, each provided a broad flat face vertically and wide flanges at the bottom, upon which the cable could run easily. Hatches were set into the surface of the road above each pulley, in order that the wheels could be attended to when necessary without disturbing the roadway. The surface was paved with granite setts between the tracks and for eighteen inches on either side of the outer rails.

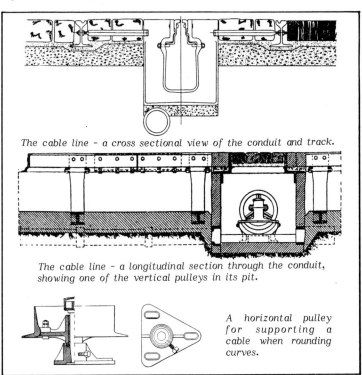

The cable line - a cross sectional view of the conduit and track.

The cable line - a longitudinal section through the conduit, showing one of the vertical pulleys in its pit.

A horizontal pulley for supporting a cable when rounding curves.

The Engine House, Depot and Cable

The power station was built on a one-acre site at Telford Park, at the top of Streatham Hill, almost opposite Telford Avenue. The building, constructed by Messrs. Lucas & Aird, also housed the depot for tractor cars ("dummies") and passenger cars (double deck horse cars, suitably modified), as well as office accommodation.

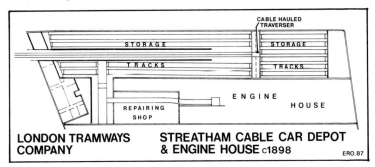

LONDON TRAMWAYS COMPANY — STREATHAM CABLE CAR DEPOT & ENGINE HOUSE c1898   ERO.87

Sufficient engine power was provided at the outset to allow for an extension of the line to Streatham Village, with the possibility of another northwards from Kennington. Four Babcock & Wilcox coke-burning double furnace water-tube boilers, each working to a pressure of 140 lbs/sq. in. and equipped with Benniss mechanical stokers were provided, of which three were generally in use at any one time. These supplied steam at a maximum pressure of 100 lbs/sq. in. to the two compound horizontal engines, each with a 20-inch diameter high pressure cylinder with Proell valve gear, and a 32-inch diameter low pressure cylinder with Corliss gear. Each engine developed 700 horsepower, which was estimated to be sufficient to drive 12 miles of cable. In the event, it was only necessary to use the low pressure cylinders to drive the initial cable.

A common shaft connecting the two pairs of engines in parallel could, if required, be driven by either set and, at its centre point, had a heavy carrier wheel 10 feet in diameter and grooved for 24 woven hemp ropes, each two inches in diameter. These in turn drove a grooved wheel 30 feet in diameter on a countershaft, at the outer ends of which were clutch-actuated cable driving wheels. Only one cable driving mechanism was required for the original section of the line; the second was brought into use when the extension to Streatham Village was commissioned.

The distance between Telford Avenue and Kennington was about 2 miles 6 furlongs, requiring a cable of about 30,000 feet in length, weighing 30 tons and costing £1,200, to provide the means of propulsion for a double track line. The first cable was supplied by Messrs. George Craddock & Co. of Wakefield, on the "Lang Lay" system to the following specification:-

Formation: The cable to be laid up with the lay in the rope in the same direction as the lay in the strands. Six strands are to be laid round a manilla heart. Each strand to consist of seven wires of 0.115 in. laid round five wires of 0.061 in. and round one wire of 0.049 in.

Wire: The wire used shall be of the very Best Selected Patent Improved Crucible Steel evenly drawn throughout.

Size: To be 3⅝ inches in circumference.

Spinning:	Each strand to be spun in one length long enough to lay up the full length of the cable and evenly wound direct from the spinning machine on to the reel. Where it is necessary to join the outside or inside wires they shall be properly braized. (sic)
Closing:	The six reels containing the above named lengths of strands shall be mounted in the closing machine and laid round the heart.
Heart:	To be made of the Best White Manilla Hemp Rope, three strands, hard laid, and well soaked in oil.
Lays:	The lay of the strands to be two inches and the lay of the wires in the strands to be $3\frac{7}{8}$ inches.
Length:	The cable to be 30,000 feet long in a single length.
Tests:	Each of the outer wires to stand an average breaking strain of 2,000 lbs. and a torsion of 33 twists in eight inches. Each of the inner wires to stand an average breaking strain of 560 lbs., and the centre wire 350 lbs. and a torsion of 40 twists in eight inches.
	The cable shall stand a test of 40 tons without fracture.

Subsequent cables were manufactured by Messrs. Craddock; Messrs. Wilkins of Wapping, London and Messrs. Newall & Sons, Washington, Co. Durham.

Purchase on the cable as it passed through the engine house on its endless journey was attained by a "grip pulley", 11 feet in diameter, which had a deep groove lined with renewable white metal sections into which the cable was laid. Movement of the wheel tended to pull the cable into the "jaws", thus drawing it along. After this, the cable was fed round the two pulleys of the tension carriage, which had the

A general view of the winding house at the Telford Avenue cable depot.
(Courtesy: Greater London Photograph Library)

capability of varying in length up to a maximum of 100 feet. In this way the cable could be tensioned for all variations in the load and also to counteract the natural stretching and wear suffered by it on its journey through the conduits. The carriage was maintained in tension by a counter-weight suspended in a special shaft beneath the building. Guide wheels carried the cable through the subway on its journey to and from the street. An engine governor was fitted and placed in a special secure cage (to prevent it being tampered with) and was set to ensure that the cable did not run at more than the permitted speed of 4 to 5 m.p.h. in the first few months of operation, after which the speed was increased to an absolute maximum of 8 m.p.h.

The Tractor Cars or "Dummies"

Upon the introduction of cable cars on the line, it was decided to use separate tractor cars (or "dummies") to haul the standard horse cars used. In this way a service could be provided between the London termini, Brixton and later Streatham, without the need for passengers to change cars. The earliest of these vehicles were 9 ft. 2 in. long, 6 ft. 2 in. wide and quite lightly constructed. Each consisted of a platform mounted on a fixed four-wheel truck, which was where the driver stood to his task, manipulating the levers and screw-wheel handle, a cover on four tubular corner posts protecting him from the worst of the weather. Those of the second series had the covers supported by a series of tubular arches, twelve in all.

Two couplings were used to connect the tractor to the trailer. The main one was - to quote the words of the company manager - "a kind of Norwegian coupling", consisting of a male and female plug and socket, with a locking pin mechanism, while the secondary one was a stout length of wire rope (probably made up from abandoned cable lengths).

A gripper car, otherwise known as a "tractor" or "dummy", standing with its horse-car trailer, crew and interested bystanders, outside the cable depot at Telford Avenue. (Courtesy: W. J. Wyse)

Two braking systems were used; on the dummy, all four wheels were braked; those on the car could be applied from the tractor by the driver, by the operation of an additional lever.

The car shed was large enough to hold an estimated maximum number of 75 passenger cars, plus an adequate number of "dummies" to supply the service. There were initially 30 tractors, eventually being increased to 42, at least one of which was always kept at a small depot at Kennington. Tractors were moved around the depot by means of supplementary cables driven from the mainshaft in conjunction with the use of a traverser. Access between road level and depot area was by means of a 1 in 20 ramp, downwards to the road.

The Gripper Mechanism

The gripper gear fitted to each tractor was quite complex, both in its design and application. As the vehicle was reversible and as the cable ran about an inch to the left of the centre of the slot-rail aperture, to protect it from dirt and moisture which entered the slot, the mechanism was designed to allow the cable to be picked up on either side of the centre line. It was therefore necessary to have gripper jaws on both sides of the central vertical rod. When the gear was locked into place on the tractor, it was capable of a small amount of sideways movement, necessary when rounding curves. A roller-wheel bearing was incorporated into the shaft at slot rail level to prevent the sides of the shaft rubbing along the sides of the slot rail at any point, more particularly when rounding curves.

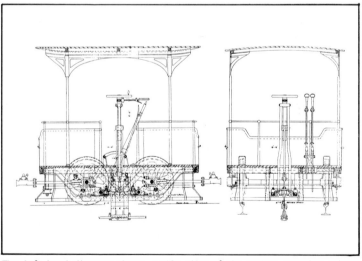

The left hand diagram shows a side view of the rather complex gripper operating mechanism used on the cable "dummies". Two couplers were fitted, effectively making the tractor car easily reversible. In the right hand diagram, the position of the control wheel and mechanism levers can be clearly seen, together with the double sided gripper jaws. The flimsy top cover was all the protection that the driver had against the elements.

The mechanism was controlled by the use of a handwheel mounted horizontally on top of the mechanism shaft. The gripper jaws, twelve inches long, were lined with soft cast-iron "dies" which were renewable and which, when closed around the greased cable, allowed for a smooth take-off from rest. The upper section of the jaws was fixed, the lower part having a downward movement of about six inches, to allow for picking-up, dropping and gripping the moving cable. To over-ride the cable when picking-up, the base of the lower jaw was rounded, allowing the cable to be pushed gently to one side as the jaw was lowered. Once it had been picked-up, there was no need to drop it again until the car reached the engine house or the terminus, except when, through accident or when the car was in the depot, it was necessary to remove the gear completely from the cable conduit. By unlocking a set of wedges which released the locked, lower section, the whole mechanism could be raised above road level.

Conversion of the Line

Reconstruction of the horse tramway construction of the extension from Water Lane to Telford Avenue were carried out as two distinct operations. The new section up Brixton Hill was dealt with first but, as the line was not likely to be used for cable working for some time, the cable was omitted. Maj. Gen. Hutchinson inspected the completed line on 11th August 1891, but authorised its use "for horse traction only, for the present, until the completion of the remainder of the line". Service is said to have commenced the next day by extending cars through from Water Lane, but if so, the horses had a mammoth task in pulling these heavy cars up Brixton Hill. Due to this long climb, more than one chain horse would have been required.

Meantime, the line between Water Lane and Kennington was being relaid and when completed, the cable, about 5½ miles long was hauled into place by heavy steam traction engines. After all the tests had been carried out, several tractor and trailer sets were run for driver training purposes. During this period the cable speed was restricted to 5 m.p.h. On 7th December 1892, Maj. Gen. Hutchinson inspected the work and authorised its use.

Licensing

Board of Trade Regulations concerning mechanical operation of tramways required that special permits were necessary in addition to the normal inspection certificates, before lines could be used for public services. In order to gain this, the company had to obtain the permission of the local authorities through whose areas the cars were to work, in this case, the London County Council, Lambeth Vestry and Wandsworth Board of Works. The first such permit was for 12 months as from 21st December 1892 and included stringent operating conditions. It stated (among other things) that:-
1. Each wheel of each carriage shall be fitted with a break (sic) block which can be applied by a screw or treadle or by any other means.
2. A governor which cannot be tampered with ... shall be attached to each stationary engine and be so arranged that when the engine exceeds the number of revolutions sufficient to move the cable at a speed of 8 m.p.h., it shall cause the steam to be cut off.
3. Each "dummy" and carriage shall be numbered.
4. Each "dummy" and carriage shall be fitted with a suitable wheel-guard to push aside obstructions ... and each shall be fitted with a special bell, whistle or other apparatus ...

5. ... the driver ... shall have the fullest possible view forward.
6. Every carriage ... is to be constructed for the safety of passengers' entry, exit and accommodation.
7. Carriages are always to be attached to the cable except when stopping. No gravity descents are to be made.

Terminal Arrangements

The premises at No. 20 Brixton Road, Kennington consisted of an entrance for a tractor car and trailer in the centre part of the facade, an entrance for horses to one side of the centre and a staff entrance on the other. At least one car set was kept there overnight, in order to provide the early morning service. The premises also housed one of the cable tensioning devices. It was here, too, that trailers were uncoupled for forward working by horses. At this point, the road was on a down gradient towards London and, after the dummies had been disengaged from the cars, they were run across to the "down" line by horsepower. On this track, a tractor would wait for the next car to come in, and after the horses had been removed, the tractor was coupled to the trailer, the cable picked up and the unit taken away to Streatham.

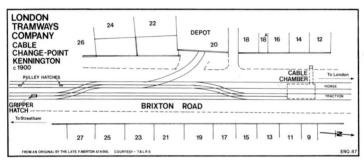

On arrival at Telford Avenue, the tractor was connected up by the front coupler to the trailer car left behind by the previous car, and the trailer brought up was disconnected. The new formation was then drawn on to the single track section, the outgoing cable being dropped before the car crossed the junction line leading into the depot. Once clear of the outgoing cable, the driver of the tractor was able to pick up the ingoing cable and return to Kennington.

Shortly after the commencement of cable services, the system failed. On 13th December at about midnight a mechanical fault occurred, when a gripper on a dummy fouled the cable and "stranded" it, i.e., broke one of the strands of the cable, causing it to bend outwards and, in turn, damage or foul one or more pulley wheels. Due to inexperience, the management brought the line to a halt and decided to change the cable, with the consequent disruption to all services. Horse traction was resumed, originally for one day only, but due to Board of Trade insistence it was continued until, on 21st December after the cable had been replaced, a further inspection of the line by Maj. Gen. Hutchinson showed that all was well once again and services resumed.

By the spring of 1893, protests were coming in from residents who lived and did business on the line of route, with a fair number coming also from people living well away from it, complaining of noise, disturbance and distress, directly resulting from the introduction of cable operation.

One of the main complaints was that the noise made by the cable passing over the pulley guide wheels was intolerable. The company managed to satisfy the large majority of the complainants that it was doing all it could to alleviate the problem during the spring and summer months of that year, but in October a great blast of outrage came in the form of a request for a deputation of "memorialists" to be seen by none other than the President of the Board of Trade at that time, The Right Hon. Anthony John Mundella, M. P. It was getting near to the time when the company would be seeking a renewal of its license, this being conveniently seen by the hundred or so signatories to the plea as being the lever with which to force some suitable action from the company. The petitioners pointed out that they did not want the company to go off the road, but only to come to terms with the frontagers.

The company was given a temporary extension of its license while an enquiry was arranged. This took place at the Brixton Hall on 8th December 1893. The company, meantime, had arranged a counter-petition, collecting over 700 signatures of persons who claimed that there was nothing amiss with the operations of the cable line. After a study of all the conflicting evidence, the result of the enquiry was, to say the least, inconclusive. Nothing was gained, but neither was anything really lost by either party. The main problem, and that outside the control of the company was that of alleged congestion at the change-point at Kennington, where the road was exceptionally narrow. Even that was suspect, as was pointed out by Maj. Gen. Hutchinson, when he made an inspection of the line on 12th December 1893. He said that, if there was any congestion occurring at Kennington, it was the concern of the police, who should deal with it. He then granted a license to operate for another year, which was again renewed in 1897, this time for three months, as the extension southward to Streatham was about to be built. One small side issue which had emerged was that the Wandsworth Board of Works had alleged that the line was being flooded with water to quieten down the sounds made by the cars, which the company denied. However, the "dummies" were all fitted with water tanks, so that the drivers could use water sparingly when it was thought prudent to so do.

The Streatham Extension

The London Tramways Company Act, 1894 (57-58 Vic. cap. cxxxii) was obtained to allow the extension southwards to Streatham Village to be built. It received Royal Assent on 31st July and authorised the following Tramways:-

No. 1. A double line, 2 f. 6 ch. long, from the existing line at Telford Avenue, along Streatham Hill to Leigham Court Road.
No. 2. A double line, 2 f. 1 ch. long, from the end of Tramway No. 1 to Leigham Avenue.
No. 3. A double line, 1 f. 4.75 ch. long, from the end of Tramway No. 2 to the Tate Library.

During the summer of 1895, Messrs. Dick, Kerr & Co. were busy extending the tracks and attending to ancillary works at the depot. Maj. Marindin inspected the completed line on 23rd November, while the LCC and Lambeth Vestry also agreed to its use. Wandsworth, however, would not at first agree to more that a "conditional" consent, but as the original part of the line was licensed only until 2nd May 1896, agreement was reached that a further permit for the whole line would then be sought. In May 1896, after much discussion, a three-year permit was obtained, at last allowing the company to settle

Telford Avenue cable car depot, with a tractor and trailer on the exit ramp. Two other tractors can be seen at the back of the depot.

down to a relatively calm existence that was to remain until it was taken over by the London County Council in 1899.

The extension from Telford Avenue to Streatham Village was on a gently sloping gradient downwards to the new terminus, for which a cable of some 10,000 feet in length, weighing about 10 tons was required to provide the necessary motive power. The original engines had sufficient spare capacity to deal with this load, the only extra equipment required being the drive and tension pulleys to carry the second cable. A large pit, 81 ft. long, 12 ft. wide and 8 ft. deep was constructed beneath the road outside the depot, where all the guide and tension pulleys for both cables were installed. At this point, the driver of each car, in whichever direction he was travelling would need to release one cable completely before gaining the other. At a specified place which was marked on the roadway, the driver opened the jaws of the gripper as wide as possible, thereby allowing the car to coast along, free of the cable. The outgoing cable was deflected round a pulley and away from the line of route, to be followed almost immediately by the incoming cable, which was lined up by a pulley, allowing the driver to pick up the second cable without delay.

Take-off pulleys for the "London" end were at the Streatham end of the pit, with the "Streatham" cable at the London end. From the main pit, subways were provided beneath the building, to and from the engine house. Electricity was used to illuminate the subways and depot, generated by a dynamo driven by shafting connected to a "take-off" from an auxiliary 60 h.p. engine. The dynamo also provided current to recharge the "Froggatt" secondary batteries used on the cars to provide illumination at night.

All the main guide pulleys were 9 ft. 3 in. in diameter and all were constructed in two parts bolted together, the running grooves having loose segments and beech wood linings to deaden the sound made by the cable passing around them. The large pulleys were all fitted with Stauffer's automatic lubricators which, by the use of a lever and balance weights, put constant pressure on the greasing mechanism to ensure that the cables were continually lubricated. Auxiliary cables were used to provide the motive power on the depot roads and traverser, and were driven from the main countershaft during normal hours, or from bevelled gearing connected to the auxiliary engine during silent hours. Speed of all interior cables did not exceed 2½ m.p.h.

Streatham Terminus

When the extension line to Streatham Village was built, double track was laid throughout, including at the terminal stub so that the line could be extended further south should the opportunity occur. A crossover was installed about 20 yards from the end of the line, with points spring-biassed in order to give an "up" car the correct routing to get it on to the "up" track from the stub-end. The procedure adopted was that on arrival at the terminus the tractor and car would be stopped before the crossover. The trailer from the previous car, standing just before the crossover, would be coupled to the front end of the next tractor to arrive. The whole lot would be moved forward a few yards

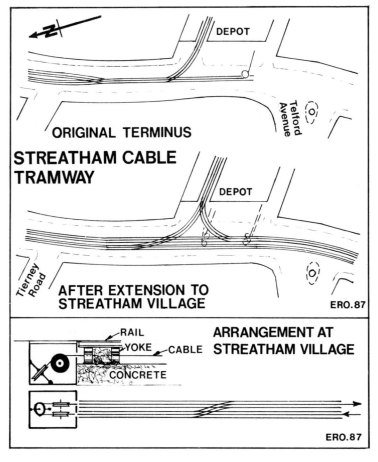

to allow the towed car to take the place of its predecessor and to be uncoupled from the tractor, which would then be moved slowly - still using the cable - until the car being pushed and the dummy were at the end of the line and clear of the points. The gripper would then be opened wide and, as the last few yards of the line in the "down" direction were on an upward gradient, the tractor now leading, could coast forward once the brakes were released, together with its new trailer, over the crossover on to the "up" line, where the cable having been turned through a set of pulleys beneath the road at the end of the line, would once again be available to be gripped and so take the unit towards London.

The Passenger Cars

From the inception of cable haulage, standard 44-seat horse cars were used, being run as through cars, with the cable-horse traction change point situated at Kennington Church. An innovation - for those days - was the installation of electric lighting inside the saloon and with one bulkhead lens in the bulkhead nearside panel beneath the canopy showing the route colour and also with two bulkhead roof lights, each of which had a lens showing the route colour of red, yellow or blue for Westminster, St. George's Church or Blackfriars respectively. The power supply was from "Froggatt" secondary batteries carried on each car. When the accumulator lights were eventually abandoned in favour of the earlier-used oil and then acetylene lighting and the roof lights removed, an additional signal lens was installed in the bulkhead to show the route colour.

On the extension of the line to Streatham, the Board of Trade recommended that the leading end platform steps on the "nearsides" of cars used on mechanically propelled tramways be blocked up. This resulted in the company introducing an improved type of car designed by the manager, Mr. McGill, which involved an almost complete re-building of some of the standard cars in the company workshops.

A number of horse cars were converted by the LTC and LCC into self-contained cable cars, and No. 923 is seen in this condition.

(LCC Tramways)

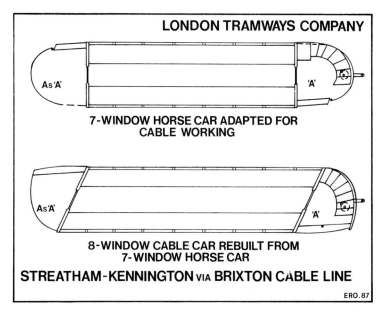

LONDON TRAMWAYS COMPANY

As 'A'   'A'

**7-WINDOW HORSE CAR ADAPTED FOR
CABLE WORKING**

As 'A'   'A'

**8-WINDOW CABLE CAR REBUILT FROM
7-WINDOW HORSE CAR**

STREATHAM-KENNINGTON VIA BRIXTON CABLE LINE

ERO.87

One of the main features of the reconstruction was that a double-width platform was provided at either end, which enabled passengers to board or alight from both decks of the car at the same time. In conjunction with this, the saloon was slightly lengthened by replacing the squared bulkheads with diagonally placed ones, which allowed an extra side panel to be inserted, so making an eight-window body, which could accommodate an extra passenger on each of the benches inside the car, but at the same time, the overall length of the car remained at 22 feet.

During 1898 some of the passenger cars were adapted to enable them to accept cable gripper equipment, doing away with the need to use "dummies". A mechanism had been designed and patented by Mr. Geo. Woolley, the Superintendent of Works to the company, which could be run beneath the "country" end of an outbound car, or removed from an inbound one by a member of a two-man change-pit crew. This mechanism consisted of a metal-framed carriage with an arm extending down into the conduit, on the bottom end of which was the usual set of screw operated jaws, through which the cable passed. Long rods extended forwards and backwards from the carriage, to connect with the wheel-operated gear at either end of the car. After bolting the mechanism into place on a cradle mounted upon two angle irons, which were fitted between the horn blocks on either side of the truck, the control rods from the carriage were then connected to the bottom ends of vertical shafts, the tops of which were just beneath the third stair tread at either end of the car.

The gripper equipment was operated by a handwheel which had an extended spindle with a socket end, which fitted on to the top of the vertical shaft, a hole about 2 inches in diameter being bored through the stair tread to give access for placing the wheel. By turning the wheel at the forward end of the car, the driver could rotate the rod leading to the carriage gearing, which in turn rotated the screw-

No. 928 in its rebuilt condition, and seen with the double width steps and angled bulkheads. A towing bolt was also provided at each end to enable the car to be taken on to London by horses. (London Transport)

gear to close or open the grip jaws as required. Cars rebuilt in 1896/97, together with some of the unrebuilt cars were modified and, by 1899 there were 39 fitted out of a total of 76 cars suitable to receive the equipment, the remainder being attended to during that year.

The license to operate the line was due to expire on 17th May 1900, but this time it was the LCC who had to ask for renewal, with a permit for twelve months being given. However, when it came to the next renewal, Lambeth, by now a Borough Council, would only offer six months, due in part to the continuing argument with the LCC over who should pay for the road widening at Kennington. After more discussion, all parties agreed to a longer period.

In 1903, just after the opening of the electrified line to Tooting, an attempt was made to run 4-wheeled class B electric cars on the cable line, via a complicated change-over point at Kennington, which was reached by a short extension of the conduit track from Kennington Park Road. A service to Westminster opened on 2nd August and to Blackfriars on 11th September. Due, however, to the weight of the cars, compounded by an accident involving one of the class B cars, the experiment was deemed to be a failure and was discontinued on 14th October. The cable section reverted to working with the old cars, passengers changing at Kennington. During this period, the cars were reversed with the aid of a horse whose sole occupation, together with its handler, was to walk back and forth across the road as required. The horse handler would connect the car to the horse harness, then lead the animal over the crossover while the car driver controlled the speed of the car by means of the handbrake.

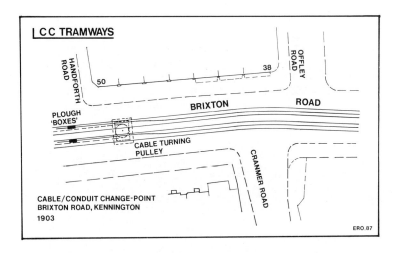

LCC TRAMWAYS

HANDFORTH ROAD

OFFLEY ROAD

50

38

BRIXTON   ROAD

PLOUGH 'BOXES'

CABLE TURNING PULLEY

CRANMER ROAD

CABLE/CONDUIT CHANGE-POINT
BRIXTON ROAD, KENNINGTON
1903

ERO.87

On 7th December 1903 Mr. A. L. C. Fell took up his duties as Chief Officer of the LCC Tramways. Early in 1904, he arranged for one of the old unrebuilt horsecars to be mounted on to a motorised Brill 21E four-wheeled truck, in order to evaluate the possibility of using this hybrid unit on the cable line. As no more was heard of the experiment, it must be assumed that it was not taken any further. In any case, the cable line was closed down on 5th April 1904 to enable the line to be rebuilt for conduit electric working. The steam-driven winding engine was adapted to drive an electric generator, which was used to supply power to the cars for the period prior to the provision of supplies from Greenwich.

Chapter 6
The London Tramways Company Limited
Purchase by the LCC

Staff Problems

In the spring of 1889 the company found itself up against a problem involving staff relations. At midnight on Monday 19th May, the first protest meeting was held at Lamb Lane School, Greenwich, by some conductors and drivers who were complaining about their working conditions and were attempting to form a trade union. There was some opposition to this however, from other members of the staff who held a meeting at the company's yard at Greenwich Road at 1 a.m. on 22nd May "to air their grievances to the company in a more orderly way".

During the following weeks, a number of other such meetings took place at various venues in south London, at some of which at least one member of the LCC, together with a member of Parliament took part in the proceedings.

At an Extraordinary General Meeting which took place at the offices of the company at noon on 14th July 1889, Mr. T. G. Gillespie, the Chairman announced that the total number of passengers carried during the previous half-year was 27,778,531; that the number of car miles run was 3,139,965 and that the dividend on £10 shares was to be 7/3d for the half year. After this statement, he said that "he felt it his duty to refer to the 'agitation' which had taken place of late among the men". He went on to talk of the "liberal wages" paid for a twelve-hour day and compared it with the pay of men of other companies. He mentioned the custom of the company to give all employees who had been in its employ for two years or more a bonus of £1 at Christmas. He also attempted to justify "in the interests of the shareholders" the policy of the company whereby the men were expected to work seven days a week, saying that the travelling public required a seven days' service and the men knew this when they joined the company.

Col. C. M. Davidson, a member of the Board made the comment that "fully seven years ago, the working hours of the conductors and drivers of this company were reduced to an average of less than twelve hours a day, at the following wages:-

On entering the service	4/6d a day
After about six months	5/- a day
After a further twelve months	5/6d a day
Teachers of new hands rise to	6/- a day

All promotions and positions of Inspectors and Foremen of Stables "are made from the ranks of the Service".

The Waterloo Road Line

Proposals were made on behalf of the City of London & Metropolitan Tramways Company to enable it to obtain a Provisional Order for the construction of the following lines:-

No. 1. From Lambeth Bridge, along Lambeth Road and Southwark Bridge Road to the south side of Southwark Bridge.

No. 2. From the south end of Waterloo Bridge, along Waterloo Road to St. George's Circus.

No. 3. From Lambeth Road, along St. George's Road to Temple Street.

An Order was granted and confirmed by the **Tramways Orders Confirmation (No. 3) Act, 1881 (44-45 Vic. cap. clxii).** The lines were never built by the company and, almost as soon as authority was obtained, the City Company was looking for a prospective purchaser. This came in 1882, when the South London Tramways Company took over the rights and built and worked the lines. On 24th July 1891, the Waterloo Road line was leased to the London Tramways Company at an annual rental of £150. The access tracks near St. George's Circus were re-arranged at no cost to the South London Company.

Unfulfilled Proposals

The London Tramways Company (Limited) Extensions Bill, 1891 included a renewal of the request to extend the tramway across Westminster Bridge and along Victoria Embankment as far as Charing Cross Railway Bridge. Even though a massive effort was made to enlist support from the population of south London, and the LCC involvement in a subsequent application to Parliament in the following year, it got no further than that. The Bill was thrown out. Powers were also being asked for in 1892 to enable the company to lay new tramways in Peckham and Camberwell, but due this time to the company disagreeing over certain conditions imposed by the LCC regarding the hours to be worked by the conductors and drivers, the proposals were withdrawn.

In the middle years of the 1890s, the company was expressing an interest in the operation of the Thames steamboats and in October 1895 the Directors decided to ask the sanction of the shareholders to embark upon a scheme empowering them to undertake "the passenger traffic of the Thames" and to alter the name of the company to "The London Tramways & Steamboats Company Limited". It was proposed to develop the river traffic "upon the most enterprising lines" (according to the "Kentish Mercury"). The steamboats were to be 32 in number, each designed to carry 500 passengers. Although this proposal was agreed to by the shareholders, it never got any further than that as in 1896 the LCC armed itself with an Act of Parliament giving it authority to own and operate tramways and, with the possibility of dispossession looming large, it was likely that many of the shareholders were having second thoughts, particularly as the Council was still attempting to negotiate with the company.

The Company Purchased by the LCC

The London County Council made its first attempt to negotiate with the company in 1892 when, under the terms of the Tramways Act, 1870, small parts of the system, authorised in 1871 would become available for purchase. After months of discussion and delay, the LCC Highways Committee Chairman, Mr. A. Bassett Hopkins complained that the company "would not come to terms". Two years later, on 26th July 1894, with the argument still raging, the LCC indicated that, subject to the approval of the Board of Trade, it intended to exercise its right to purchase short lengths of line along Kennington Park Road, Newington Butts and Causeway, Great Dover Street and part of Old Kent Road, amounting to about two miles in all, which had been authorised by Acts of 1873, together with one depot at Lawson Street, but excluding any cars or horses.

On receipt of this information, the company immediately objected, stating that these were only small sections, of no use to the LCC and, if they (the Council) cared to wait until 1898, virtually the whole of the system could be negotiated upon. The discussions dragged on through 1894 with no sign of a settlement and in January 1895 the Council again insisted that it had every right to purchase the sections already mentioned and that it intended to do so.

Eventually, on 21st February 1896, after much hard talking, the Board of Trade decided to appoint an arbitrator to settle the issue. Sir. Frederick W. Bramwell, Bt. accepted the appointment and began his enquiry. Negotiations continued into 1897 when, on 6th January, Sir Frederick announced that his valuation on the lines in dispute was £22,872. This did not satisfy the company management or the share-holders and, at an extraordinary general meeting held on 12th July, the Chairman, David P. Sellar, after castigating the arbitrator, intimated that "the company was going to law on the whole question". In the meantime, the LCC getting to hear of what was about to happen, retaliated by also going to law as, in its opinion the company would owe rent for the lines still being used and would be making a profit in which the Council felt that it had a right to share in. It was not until Mr. Justice North, on 6th May 1898 found for the LCC that a true basis for agreement was reached, both parties stating that the whole of the undertaking would now be under negotiation for sale and purchase. The prospective date for the change to be made was announced as being 31st December 1898/1st January 1899.

On 30th June 1898 the Council paid a deposit of £12,000 to the company, with conditions attaching to cross payments being made by the company to the Council for the use of lines "now belonging to the Council", and by the Council as interest on the unpaid portion of the purchase money for those lines. The whole of the remainder of the assets were to pass to the LCC on the agreed date for the sum of £850,000, this being over and above the £22,872 previously agreed to for the first sections of line. To this was added the cost of all unexpired licenses.

As each car entered its depot at the end of its schedule on the evening of 31st December, the name of the company was obliterated, being replaced by "London County Council Tramways, Charles John Stewart, Chief Clerk to the Council". It was also announced that all lines south of the Thames were to be known as "The Council's (Southern) Tramways", while those north of the river would be referred to as "The Council's (Northern) Tramways", a distinction that was to remain until 1906. The LCC Tramways were at last a reality.

Rolling Stock
Early Vehicles of the Metropolitan Street Tramways Company.

The type of car put into service on 2nd May 1870 on the first sections of line was the cause of much complimentary comment, mostly because of its "light and airy" design. Orders had been placed with various firms for varying numbers of vehicles, these being:-

a). Messrs. Stephenson of New York
b). Messrs. F. J. Rowan, Jernbanevøgn Fabrik, Randers, Denmark
c). Messrs. Starbuck
d). The Metropolitan Railway Carriage & Waggon Co.

The Starbuck/Stephenson/Rowan cars were of the 8-window, 46-seat (22 inside, 24 out) type, while the Metropolitan Carriage Company cars were for 42 passengers (20 inside, 22 out).

Double-deck cars were used exclusively, with the inside seats of longitudinal pattern, fitted with red velvet cushions and seat backs. Sunblinds were also installed as was floor matting. Access to the "outside" seats of "knifeboard" formation was by means of a fixed "winding ladder", one of which was fitted at each end of the car.

On the open top deck, or "outside", seating consisted of two long wooden benches, fixed back to back in "knifeboard" formation, so that passengers were seated facing outwards. Access to the seats from the tops of the iron ladders was by means of duckboards, which gave only the minimum of foothold. The "outside" at that time, was only accessible to agile people, usually men, either young and healthy or young-in-heart! It was not considered (nor was it easy) that ladies should attempt to climb the narrow winding ladders. To prevent passengers from falling over the sides of the cars, iron railings were fitted along the whole length of each side of the upper deck. First livery was blue.

By 5th October 1870 when the line was extended from Kennington to Lambeth (Hercules Buildings) a number of Rowan/Randers cars were in use and to quote from notes of the day "... the cars are of elegant construction; the floor is about 18 inches above the road surface and an entrance at each end is approached by two convenient 'lifts' or steps". This description is borne out by a photograph of Car No.117 which clearly shows the trunnion plates fitted insert into the underside of the bodywork. Cost of cars was between £192.10s and £200.

Early Vehicles of the Pimlico, Peckham & Greenwich Street Tramways Co.

Some of the first cars to be used on the Blackheath Road to New Cross line, opened on 13th December 1870, were said to have been supplied by Messrs. Drew & Burnett of Fountainbridge. Weight of the cars was stated as being between 2 tons 5 cwts and 2 tons 7 cwts. It is not known how many were supplied, but it is known that there were at least nine, as Nos. 7, 8 and 9 are mentioned in connection with other matters.

These were of the double-deck type, in a style developed from the original Starbuck cars of 1861-2. Inside the cars, two benches each seating 10 passengers were fixed along either side of the bodywork. The seats were covered with velvet cushions; fancy velvet curtains were hung in the windows; a carpet was provided to enhance the appearance of the interior and provide additional comfort for the "inside" passengers. Oil burning lamps were fitted in the bulkheads at both ends of the car, which served to illuminate the interior during the hours of darkness and to provide an indication to intending passengers of the route being run on by displaying coloured glass aspects to the outside.

The London Tramways Company and the Cars

Due to the prospect of amalgamation of the two companies, it was agreed that the nominal ownership of the cars should be vested in the London Tramways Company Limited and before long this title appeared on the vehicles. The device used was a circular "strap and buckle" with the company name inscribed in the "strap" and the stock number of the car in the centre of the device. The name of the company was also shown in the form of the initials "LTC" in upper case interwoven script in gold.

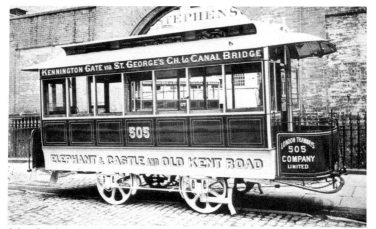

*John Stephenson also supplied several one-man single deck cars to the
London Tramways Company, principally for use on lightly-loaded routes.
No. 505 was delivered as a single-ended vehicle, but probably did not
stay in this condition for very long. No. 507, as yet incomplete, can
be seen in the background of the picture.* (John Stephenson Album)

Soon after the introduction of the "knifeboard" design, the iron
ladders were dispensed with, replaced by curved staircases leading
from the platform deck to the floor of the upper deck. In conjunction
with this innovation, iron safety rails were provided on the outside
of the stairs and the exposed knifeboard passengers, although safely
ensconced on the top deck, were gradually given extra privacy by "decency
boards" being fixed to the railings, along the whole length of the car.
The time had come when ladies could, and did, make the hazardous
climb to the "outside". It was a man's world no longer! It was not
long before the managers of the undertakings realised that the decency
boards could be used to serve another purpose and advertising matter
began to appear, to the advantage of both the advertisers and the
treasurers of the tramway companies.

The next advance was the introduction in about 1880 of a type of
car fitted with "garden seats" on the top deck. These, in two rows
of double seats, were made reversible, to enable passengers to face
the direction of travel. Many of the "knifeboards" were converted
to this new arrangement, by removing the knifeboard seats and fitting
a new, wide floor over the top of the clerestory roof, upon which to
fix the new seating. Capacity was also increased by six, eight or
ten passengers, depending on the length of the car and by 1890 had
become standard practice.

One curious mention of the need to increase horsepower in the renewals
account of the London Tramways Company for 1891 states that " ... more
power had to be used by the horses to pull the cars as, with passengers
seated across the top deck in rows of four, more resistance was offered
to the wind"!

The company became large enough to support its own comprehensive
workshops and staff, who were able to build as well as repair its own
vehicles. The main works were at Penrose Street, Walworth where
all stores and supplies were held, being distributed to depots as required.
Timbers used in car construction were:-

Underframe:	Best Oak
Pillars and Framing:	Ash
Panelling:	Mahogany
Roof Boards:	Inside - alternate Walnut and White Pine
Roof Seats:	Longitudinal slabs of walnut and American Ash
Platforms and outside Roof Boards:	Dry Pitch Pine
Inside Floor:	Best Yellow Deal topped with moveable gratings of Pitch Pine
Inside Seats & Backs	Perforated Birch
Fittings Inside and End Linings	Lime Framing and Walnut Panels
"Landscape" space	Maple

All woods were thoroughly seasoned before use. All ironwork was of best S.C. Crown Iron, except side-steps and hand-grips, which were made from Lowmoor Iron.

Advertisements

Most of the cars displayed advertisements on their sides, on both the decency panels and the lower side panels (rocker panels), as well as in other suitable places. One of the prominent advertisers was the old-established firm of Tarn & Company. This emporium was situated on the corner of the New Kent Road and Newington Causeway, more or less opposite the "Elephant & Castle" public house. Another well-known name in business was the hatter, Isaac Walton & Co., whose premises were situated at the corner of Acre Lane and Brixton Road and, like Tarn, the name was displayed on many of the cars. There was also, of course, "Oakey's Wellington Knife Polish", one of the products of John Oakey & Sons, Wellington Mills, Westminster Bridge Road, where a thriving business was carried on for many years. Almost every tramcar in London carried an advertisement paid for by this company, this extending into the electric tramcar era as well. There were many others, too numerous to mention, some of a local character, but all giving a "personality" to the cars and the areas in and through which they worked.

Depots

A number of depots, stables, workshops and stores were situated at various points on the system at:-
Balham, Marius Road.
Brixton, Railway Arches.
Brixton Road, near St. Marks Church, Kennington.
Camberwell, two depots, Camberwell Green and Camberwell New Road.
Clapham, two depots, (1) near "The Plough" (2) in High Street.
Greenwich Road, (first depot and works of P.P.&G.Co.)
Greenwich, Park Road.
Kennington, near Church, small workshop.
Kennington, Balls Yard, Upper Kennington Lane.
Lawson Street, Great Dover Street.
Leo Street, Old Kent Road.
Old Kent Road, Bowles Road (near "Lord Wellington").
Queens Road, Peckham, in railway arches beneath Queens Road Station.
Basing Road, High Street, Peckham.
Streatham, Telford Avenue (cable car depot).
Vauxhall Bridge Road.

Walworth, Penrose Street, depot and main works.
Chicheley Street, York Road, Lambeth, omnibus depot.

Omnibuses

The company ran omnibuses in conjunction with, and as feeder services to the tramways, the most notable of these being the service across Vauxhall Bridge to connect the two tramway termini. Buses for this service were housed at the tram depot in Vauxhall Bridge Road, as were those used on a service between Victoria, Vauxhall and Upper and Lower Kennington Lanes to the Elephant & Castle. Finally, there were three omnibus services worked as extensions to tramway routes:-

      a). Westminster Bridge to Charing Cross via Whitehall.
      b). Waterloo Bridge to the Strand.
      c). Blackfriars Bridge to Ludgate Circus.

for which the vehicles and horses were accommodated at Chicheley Street depot.

These useful connections were operated for some years with up to 39 omnibuses, mostly two-horse and, apart from the journey between Elephant and Victoria, all other journeys attracted a ½d fare.

Human Sideshow

Timekeeper Mott, the Deptford Bridge Regulator, was assaulted whilst on duty one day in August 1871 by George Overton, aged 42, a cab driver (badge 588), of No.1, Victory Place, Locksfield, Walworth. It appeared that Overton and several other men drove a horse and cart on to the bridge and stopped, thus causing an obstruction to the tramcars. When asked to move by the conductor of the car which was being held up, they refused, and when Mott intervened and sent the conductor for a constable, the gang set about him and beat him up. Overton appeared in Court, was found guilty and fined £5. He said he had not got £5 and was sent to prison for one month instead.

Headlines in a local newspaper (The "Kentish Mercury") told of "Another Fatal Tramway Accident". On Saturday 10th August 1872 in the afternoon between three and four o'clock, a lad named John James Jenkins was fatally injured when he was struck by a tramcar when standing in the road outside the South Eastern Railway Station, New Cross, watching the departure of some soldiers. The inquest was adjourned until 2 o'clock on the following Tuesday afternoon. The company consented to pay the father of the boy the sum of £25 plus £7 for funeral expenses and £5 for the cost of the father's attorney.

"Resulting from the inquest, an important decision as to an 'unlicensed driver' was given". The report continues:- "On Tuesday, Mr. Hunt, the Secretary of the Pimlico, Peckham & Greenwich Street Tramways Company and William Bennett of Arthur Street, Peckham were summoned at the Greenwich Police Court at the instance of the Police Authorities. The former was charged with allowing two horses and a car belonging to the company to be driven by an unlicensed person, and the latter acting as driver without being licensed. Mr. Charles, from the office of Messrs. Morris & Co., attended for the defence.

"P.C. Barnes, 288R, was called to prove the case, and from his evidence it appeared that on the afternoon of Saturday 10th August, a lad was run over in the New Cross Road by a car, the reins of the horses drawing which the defendant Bennett had hold of at the time. On demanding his - Bennett's - number of license, he said he had none, as he had

73

received orders to drive, there being a fresh horse put to work. In answer to a question, the constable said that a man named Cox, who was the licensed driver of the car was standing at the side of Bennett at the time. Mr. Charles said that he admitted all that had been stated by the constable, but the reason why Bennett had been put to drive the horses of the car in question was because one of the horses was fresh to the work on that journey, and Bennett was engaged as a breaker of horses by the company. In fact, he was employed as an extra precaution for the safety of the public and not for the purpose of saving the time or wages of the licensed driver. In answer to the charge, he had to direct his Worship's attention to the 10th Section of the Act, 6 & 7 Vic. cap. 86, (Public Carriage Act, 1844), which allows proprietors of public carriages to employ unlicensed persons as drivers for any time not exceeding 24 hours, or on occasions of necessity. He held that it was necessary so to employ the horse-breaker and that the case came within the section of the Act quoted.

"Mr. G. Metcalf, manager of the horse department of the company, having given evidence that Bennett had driven the horses on the particular occasion by his directions and under the circumstances stated, Mr. Maud (the magistrate) said he considered that the law had not been infringed; that what had been done was as a precaution, and both summonses would therefore be dismissed".

Tickets and Fares

Ticket Styles and Colours

The original tickets issued by the Metropolitan Street Tramways Company, and probably the Pimlico, Peckham & Greenwich Street Tramways Company as well, were of a style which can only be described as "cloakroom" type. An example, at the fare of 2d shows a ticket 3½ inches long by 1½ inches deep which had been torn from a pack.

From records researched, it is understood that the serial numbers also appeared on the stubs of the tickets, which were retained by the conductor and accounted for on his waybill. As there was only one fare of 2d on the various sections of line then open between 1871 and 1873 (before the isolated sections were joined up), it was a fairly simple matter for the conductor to account for tickets sold. There is no evidence that the tickets sold were torn or cancelled in any way upon issue. The tickets were deep orange in colour.

After the London Tramways Company Limited took over operation of the two earlier companies in 1873, a distinctive set of tickets was devised, developed and printed. Being very early in the field of tramway operation, the company was in some measure a pioneer in the matter of ticket issue and control, the more so as many omnibus operators were still using the waybill method of control, which entailed the "booking" of each passenger on a waybill form.

Several styles of ticket were produced. On some, the company title was printed along the left-hand edge with the fare value and other information shown beneath it; fare stages were displayed in geographical form in "ladder" fashion from top to bottom, while the ticket serial numbers were overprinted in black ink, in line with the title of the company. Other tickets were printed with the whole of the information shown "landscape" along them. All tickets were supplied by a predecessor of the Bell Punch Company (and later by Bell Punch) in the years prior to 1879, after which other arrangements were made, leading up to the tramways company deciding to produce its own sets of tickets.

From the earliest days of the London Tramways Company, it became the practice to use white card for tickets of the one penny value, pink or magenta coloured card for 2d and pale blue for 3d values. The first tickets of this type were supplied by Messrs. T. J. Whiting of London and were almost all of a nominal 2½-inch by 1⅜-inch format. Farestage information consisted of a "geographical" layout, showing the limits between which a passenger could travel for the fare tendered, e.g., "Vassall Road & Brixton Station" for a penny, the same sections on the ticket being used for either "up" or "down" journeys. These were issued to passengers after being passed through a registering punch, which made a circular hole in the ticket, almost ¼-inch in diameter.

After several years, the contract for the supply of tickets went to the Bell Punch Company who, while retaining the general style of the previous printer, clarified the text somewhat and, at the same time placed the serial numbers at the head instead of "landscape" on the body of the printed matter. The serial letters, used in conjunction with the numbers however, still appeared as overprints in different colours on the body of the tickets. A 1½d value also appeared, printed on light green card. A standard ticket width of 1¼ inches was used, the length of various issues usually between 2 and 2½ inches, depending upon the amount of information required.

With the introduction of ½d fares in 1891, the salmon-coloured ticket made its appearance, shown in full geographical form, with both "up" and "down" sections being displayed, "up" on the right and "down" on the left. Tickets were also getting longer, some ½d and 1d issues by now 3 inches long. The 2d value had also changed colour slightly, being more "purple-pink" than hitherto, while a single issue of 4d value appeared in the magenta colour. Serial letters as well as the numbers began to appear at the head of the printed matter, while the words "UP" and "DOWN" appeared as overprints. The production of all tickets used had also passed to the company itself, who set up a comprehensive ticket printing section in its works at Penrose Street, Walworth. It was this works together with its distinctive ticket set which passed to the London County Council when it took over the company in 1899.

Fares

Services provided and fares charged were comprehensive and in line with declared practice authorised by the Acts of Parliament which brought the company into being. The usual standard of one penny for about one mile of travel was adopted, but allowing the minimum of 3d to be charged. However, right from the beginning, 2d as well as 3d fares were charged, and on the inauguration of the through services from Greenwich to Westminster and Blackfriars via Old Kent Road and "Elephant", a number of fares at the rate of 1d a mile were charged as 1d stages with overlapping stage points, thus giving a continuity of fares that was to eventually spread to all the other services on all routes, but it was to be some years before this arrangement was fully implemented.

The fares for workmen were somewhat different. Legislation had provided for this section of the community in a special way by making it a requirement that special cars be run for them at fixed times each weekday morning and evening at reduced fares. The rate decided upon was ½d a mile with a minimum of 1d being payable, so that from Clapham, one penny would be charged as far as Kennington with a second penny fare from there to Westminster. On the Clapham route, early cars were from 5.30 a.m., then at half-hourly intervals until 7.30 a.m. Corresponding evening return cars ran from Westminster as from 6 p.m. Only daily labourers and artisans were carried, but just how it was proved that the people concerned were of these categories must have been an interesting exercise.

From 1881, the fares policy was drastically altered when, due to a change in management it was decided that the best way of ensuring that people rode on the cars was to arrange fare scales in such a way that all passengers paid for the length of ride taken and not a minimum fare of 1d or 2d, however long or short the journey taken would be. The general rule of 1d a mile was used and on all routes new fare stages came into being, each named stage being a nominal half-mile from the next in either direction, although some stages were longer, while a few were less than half a mile in length.

The Greenwich to London services via Old Kent Road were already working with penny fares and these did not change in any way, neither did the 2d stages or 3d through fares. However, the New Cross Gate to Westminster or Blackfriars Bridges and "Lord Wellington" services were re-arranged, as were those from Clapham and Brixton.

In all cases, workman fares were still charged at ½d a mile, with a maximum fare of 1½d on the Clapham and Brixton services, and 2d on the Greenwich services. In April 1884, the company decided to make some changes on the Greenwich via Old Kent Road services by slightly extending the distances given for the fare paid.

The line from Kennington to Brixton was converted to cable working in 1891 and extended to Telford Avenue, Streatham. The management decided to mount an experiment on this line by introducing ½d fares throughout its length. This proved to be so successful that the arrangement was extended to cover the whole of the company's services after just a few months of the experiment commencing. The standard then became ½d for about half a mile, with 1d, 1½d, 2d and 3d tickets to cover the full range of fares.

Sunday Fares

The arguments that broke out from time to time surfaced in the Company's area in 1893 when complaints were levelled about the fares charged on Sundays and Bank Holidays. The normal weekday charges were by now, ½d, 1d, 1½d, 2d and 3d on the Greenwich (6¼ miles), Streatham (4¾ miles) and Tooting (6½ miles) routes, but on Sundays and Bank Holidays a throughout fare of 2d any distance was charged and all the lower fares suspended. The Board of Trade and Parliament were both brought into the discussion but, as the level of fares charged had been fixed by Act of Parliament, the only way that these could be altered or amended was by the passing of an amending Act to allow the use of a fare scale similar to that applied on weekdays, or for the company to do this voluntarily, which it was not prepared to do. The only concession made was the reduction from 3d to 2d of the weekday throughout fare from London to Streatham.

Chapter 7
The South Eastern Metropolitan
Tramways Company

The main roads of south-east London radiate from the centre to the suburbs and beyond rather like the spokes of a wheel. Lewisham is situated close to the junction of two of these and, as a Village has existed for over 1,000 years, being known as "Lieuesham" in past ages, the name pronounced almost as it is today. Rushey Green (Catford) was the most southerly outpost of Lewisham, beyond which the whole area was quite rural. Regarding Greenwich, a few notes on the history of this important and ancient town appear in the section dealing with the London Tramways Company.

When tramways were being laid in many districts of the Metropolis during the last three decades of the nineteenth century, it became of some importance to the population of Lewisham to have a connection into the network. An application to secure a Provisional Order was made as early as 1873 by the South London Tramways (Company) for authority to construct lines connecting Catford, Lewisham, Blackheath Hill, Lee and Eltham together. This application was rejected by the Parliament of the day, and it was to be another nine years before further proposals were made. In 1882, the announcement was made that the Lewisham & District Tramways would promote a line which would commence by a junction with the London Tramways at New Cross Road, run along Lewisham High Road and Lewisham Road, to terminate at Rushey Green (Broadway). Due to many objections from several quarters, the matter was dropped.

In 1884, however, further proposals were made by two opposing groups, The South-East Metropolitan Tramways Company and The South-Eastern Metropolitan (Lewisham, Greenwich & District) Tramways Company. The first-named proposed to lay lines from New Cross, along Lewisham High Road and Loampit Vale to Lewisham, then on to Rushey Green, with a branch line from Lewisham to Greenwich. The intention of the second-named group was for much the same, except that it was proposed that the line to Rushey Green should be continued along Southend Road (now part of Bromley Road) as far as Beckenham Hill, and that the projection of a line towards New Cross should only go as far as Loampit Vale. It also proposed a short junction line from Blackheath Hill, along Blackheath Road, to meet the tracks of the London Tramways Company. Of the two sets of proposals, the "South-East" Company was the one to succeed, but with only the line between Rushey Green and Greenwich authorised.

The South-East Metropolitan Tramways Act, 1884 (Vic. cap. cxlvii) gave powers to the company to construct and maintain the following lines:-
1. Along South Street Greenwich, Lewisham Road and High Street, 1 ml. 3.80 ch. long, with passing places.
2. A short double line 2.40 ch. long, in High Street Lewisham and Loampit Vale.

3. A continuation of No. 1 along through High Street and Broadway, Rushey Green, Rushey Green, 1 ml. 3.40 ch. long, with passing places. After this flurry of activity, the matter rested. Nothing was built and no further request was made to obtain an extension of time to allow work to commence. The powers lapsed.

At the end of November 1896, proposals were again published on behalf of the South-Eastern Metropolitan (Lewisham, Greenwich & District) Tramways, for the construction of lines between Greenwich, Lewisham, New Cross and Catford. Nothing came of this either.

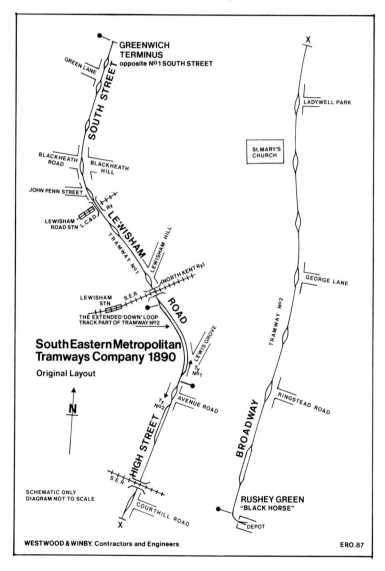

Finally, a Bill was presented to Parliament in 1888, almost echoing the main points of the Act of 1884, but with minor modifications. The **South-Eastern Metropolitan Tramways Act, 1888 (51-52 Vic. cap. clxxxvi)** authorised the construction of:-

No. 1. A line from South Street Greenwich to High Street Lewisham.

No. 2. A continuation line to Rushey Green near the "Black Horse" public house, a total length of 2 mls. 3 f. 7.50 ch. long, with passing places.

Fares to be at the rate of 1d per mile, but certain cars to be run for the "labouring classes" at the rate of ½d per mile.

Directors included J. Atherton, J. B. Atherton and K. H. Behrend, the manager was Chas. Hart, while the contractors and engineers were Messrs. Westwood & Winby.

Authorised capital was £50,000, with borrowing powers for up to a further £12,500.

The Tramways to be completed within two years.

Thus it was, fifteen years after the first proposals were made and four years after the first Act was passed, the prospect of there being a tramway in Lewisham finally became a reality. However, no construction was undertaken in 1888 or 1889. Finally, track laying began in 1890 and continued, slowly, all through the spring and summer, with no sign of completion. However, early in August came the news " .. that the completion of the tramway is at hand .. " The powers given to the company were due to expire on 7th August and, although the tracks had been laid, there were no cars. In order to be able to comply with the terms of the Act, a car and horses was borrowed from the North Metropolitan Tramways Company so that the line could be inspected by Maj. Gen. Hutchinson on 5th August.

The Line Opens

Although the line had passed inspection, there was still no sign of the cars which had been ordered to work upon it. The situation

High Street, Lewisham

High Street Lewisham, at its junction with Loampit Vale, with a car bound for Greenwich in the foreground. The water course on the left is a very dried-up River Quaggy. (Commercial view)

79

prevailed throughout August, September and into October, much to the annoyance of the local population. At last, after delivery of the cars, it was announced that the opening ceremony would take place on Saturday, 11th October 1890, at about 1 p.m., when the first car in the procession would leave the depot. On this day, all those invited to attend, travelled to Greenwich terminus, from whence they made their way to the "Ship Hotel", where a reception was held.

After the official celebrations were over, the public were allowed to ride on the new cars, a ten-minute service, working to a journey time of 28 minutes was provided at a through fare of 2d. Intermediate 1d stages were also advertised. On the opening day and the Sunday, the weather was fine, but on Monday a thick blanket of fog descended, reducing visibility to just a few yards. The drivers of the cars had great difficulty in completing their journeys.

Thomas Tilling Ltd. was operating many omnibus services in south-east London, and it seemed that this would be likely to provide serious competition with the new trams. However, an arrangement was made for Tilling to provide the horses necessary to run the service at a cost to the company of 5½d per car mile, in return for which Tilling agreed not to compete with the tram service.

Beanfeasts and Bunfights

A social activity indulged in by many groups of working men during this period was the annual "beanfeast" which, in reality was one of the few occasions during the year when they could forget their daily cares and take a day out during the summer to a chosen resort. On Thursday 20th June 1893, one half of the men went to Margate for their day out, the rest doing the same thing, one week later. A similar event took place during 1894, but additionally, on 10th October 1894, the company celebrated its "4th birthday" by giving a tea party to the wives and children of their employees, at which function nearly 100 attended and, apparently, a good time was had by all. Two days later, on 12th October, it was the turn of the employees themselves to enjoy the largesse offered by the company, when 70 guests sat down to a midnight supper, under the chairmanship of Mr. C. Hart, the Manager. The proceedings concluded at about 4.30 a.m.

Electrification Proposal

In 1899, the company considered the possibility of obtaining an Act of Parliament, authorising it to electrify its line on the conduit system and a Bill was submitted in 1900. The outcome was **The South Eastern Metropolitan Tramways Act, 1900 (63 - 64 Vic. cap. cxlvii)** which received the Royal Assent on 30th July. In the Act, authority was given to enable the company to reconstruct the tracks in order to introduce electrical working of the line. Electric power was to be supplied by the Blackheath & Greenwich District Electric Lighting Company Limited, "... or any other ... source ... as agreed", subject to the Electric Lighting Acts of 1882 and 1888.

The Act had been obtained in order to strengthen the hand of the company in its negotiations with the London County Council regarding the purchase of the line by the Council. The company could not be purchased under compulsory powers until 1909 and, as it was quite small by comparison to the London Tramways Company, which had been recently purchased, it was felt that by proceeding in this way it would be more likely to obtain a reasonable price from the LCC

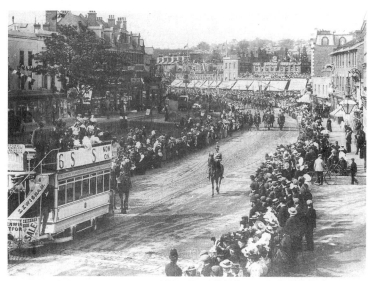

On the occasion of the Diamond Jubilee of Queen Victoria in 1897, a Royal Visit to Lewisham provided a colourful display in the locality. SEMT car No. 3 acted as a grandstand for a number of loyal subjects.
(Courtesy: The Ogilby Trust)

An LCC (ex-London Tramways Co.) car awaits passengers at Lewisham.
(Lewisham Borough Libraries)

if powers to electrify were included. The management, armed with their Act, confidently suggested to the LCC that it should enter into a voluntary agreement with the company on sale and purchase.

According to a reference from the company's Minute Book for Tuesday, 25th February 1902, an Extraordinary General Meeting was held at the offices of the company, to approve the sale of the undertaking to the London County Council for £50,000, to which agreement was unanimous. All employees, with the exception of the Manager and the Secretary were to be taken into the employ of the Council. Mr. Downs, the Manager, was to receive £75 as an ex-gratia payment for loss of employment. Other safeguards written into the agreement included the continuation of advertising contracts; the agreement made with the Ticket Punch & Register Company for the supply of ticket punches; all unexpired contracts with season ticket holders, together with other sundry agreements. Mr. A. Baker, the Chief Officer of the LCC Tramways, assisted by Inspector R. E. Grant were to receive the company on behalf of the Council at midnight, 31st March/1st April 1902.

The Council forecast that when the line came into its control, fares would be brought into line with the standard it had set. The maximum fare would be reduced to 1½ d, while the 1d fare would cover two halfpenny stages. The line would be divided into four sections:- Greenwich Terminus to Albion Hill; Albion Hill to Lewisham Obelisk; Obelisk to Ladywell Road; Ladywell Road to Rushey Green. The custom of charging full fare for any journey made on Sundays and Bank Holidays would be abolished.

The South Eastern Metropolitan Tramways Company was the last to commence operations in the London area, and had an independent life of only about eleven years, albeit quite eventful for the size of the undertaking.

Immediately after takeover, an application was made on behalf of the company for it to be issued with a Certificate of Incorporation as a Limited Liability Company, to enable it to be voluntarily wound up and the purchase money distributed to the shareholders. This task took another six months to complete, after which the company closed down on 15th October 1902.

LCC Operation

After acquisition, things settled down under the management of the new owner; the staff were eventually paid the standard LCC rate for the job, while their working hours were reduced to an average of 60 a week for a six day week, with no penalty for taking a Sunday off if the roster allowed it. A few cars were repainted in the LCC colours, while those which were not considered fit for service were replaced by others from elsewhere and, as there was no connection at that time with other lines, had to be brought in via Greenwich Road and dragged across the road the few yards between the two sets of tracks.

The company had been using hired horses for most of the time that it had been in existence. These had been supplied by Thomas Tilling Ltd. on an annual contract basis. A new agreement was reached with the company, by which the Council were to pay 5¾ d per car mile, with a maximum of 100 miles a day per car. In return for this contract, Tilling agreed not to run competing omnibuses along the line of route.

The Rushey Green terminus of the line was almost outside the depot and next door to the "Black Horse" public house. Car No. 878, one of those transferred from other depots by the LCC, is being prepared for its return to Greenwich.   *(Commercial view)*

When the time came to consider the electrification of the section between Lewisham and Greenwich late in 1905, work was already in progress between New Cross and Lewisham on the construction of a new electric line, with the reconstruction of the Lewisham - Catford section also in hand. This resulted in the horse cars working only between Lewisham and Greenwich which, after some disagreement, Tilling agreed to horse at the original rate per car mile.

On 10th June 1906, electric cars began running between London and Rushey Green via New Cross and Lewisham. For a time, horse and electric cars worked together over the section between Lewisham and Catford, but due to the delays caused to the electric cars, this only lasted for a short time. In any case, the line to Greenwich was due to close for reconstruction, resulting in the Council arranging for Tilling to operate a horse 'bus service while this work was being carried out. On Saturday, 4th April 1908, the new electric cars began working between Greenwich and Catford.

The Cars

A car had been borrowed from the North Metropolitan Tramways Company, had been used for trial runs over the line on Monday and Tuesday 4th and 5th August 1890, and then used for the Board of Trade inspection. Following this, however, no date was announced for the opening of the line to traffic and the borrowed car was returned. Meantime, a fleet of seven cars, soon increased to ten were on order from the North Metropolitan Tramways Company and under construction at their Union Road Works, Leytonstone. Each cost about £245 and was of the standard 46-seat double deck type, the lower saloon having seven windows on each side of the body, suitably curtained as was

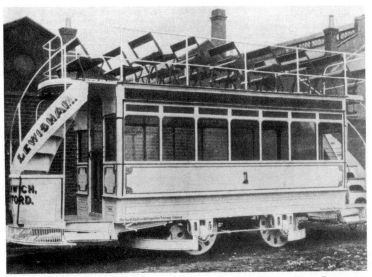

The company purchased ten cars from the North Metropolitan Tramways Company and, apart from several minor detail differences were of standard 7-window pattern. No. 1 is seen at the Union Road Works of the North Metropolitan Company.   (Tramway & Railway World)

the custom at the time.   A clerestory ceiling with ventilator lights was specified. The seats in the saloon were of the longitudinal pattern and fitted with cushions, each bench seating 11 passengers.   On the upper deck or "outside", there were rows of "garden seats" which had reversible backs to enable passengers to face the direction of travel. Each seat, in two rows of six placed on either side of the central gangway, accommodated two passengers.

Livery was white, lined out in gilt and brown, but no monogram or other device was displayed, except for the fleet number of the car midway along each waist panel.   The name of the company and that of the manager was written at the bottom of the rocker panels on either side of the car. Unladen weight of each vehicle was about two tons. As was the custom of the period, the destinations and places served were displayed on boards fixed over the saloon windows, with additional displays over the end panels of the top decks and on the stair stringers.

The Depot

Situated at the extreme southern end of the line, the depot was next to the "Black Horse" public house. After the buildings were constructed and tracks laid, no other alterations were ever made.   The premises were approached through a narrow arch, over which was the office of the company, together with living accommodation for the company manager.

Many years after the demise of the company, part of the premises was acquired by Messrs. Timpson for a coach station, and had been redeveloped for this purpose. All traces of the horse car depot were eradicated by this reconstruction.

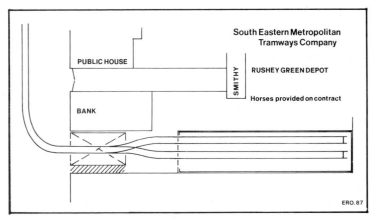

South Eastern Metropolitan Tramways Company

PUBLIC HOUSE

SMITHY

RUSHEY GREEN DEPOT

Horses provided on contract

BANK

ERO. 87

Fares and Tickets

The fare system was very simple and straightforward, only 1d and 2d tickets being on issue. As was usual, a passenger was able to travel up to two miles for 1d, with the exception that workmen had a cheaper fare of 1d single or 2d return throughout, provided that they travelled very early in the mornings. In common with most other undertakings at that time, a premium fare of 2d was charged on Sundays and Bank Holidays for any journey. No concession was given to children and, so far as is known, there was no staged fare for the passage of luggage.

Ticket colours were white for 1d and magenta or pink for 2d. A "Free Pass" was also on issue, which was a brown coloured ticket, with numbered "Up" and "Down" stages, the text stating "Entitling the Bearer to travel a Single Journey on the South Eastern Metropolitan Tramways, (Thomas Prior) Manager", which would have been on issue after a change of Manager, about 1899. Most unusually, annual season tickets, available for unlimited travel, were on offer during the last few years of company operation. As from 1st January 1896, these tickets could be purchased at the following rates:-

To and from Catford and Greenwich	4 gns.
To and from Catford and Obelisk	2 gns.
To and from Greenwich and Obelisk	2 gns.

It is not known how many of these tickets were sold, but it is known that they were in use until after the LCC took over, as that body allowed them to be used for the remainder of the year following the transfer of the company to the Council.

Chapter 8
The London, Deptford & Greenwich
Tramways Company

Southwark is probably one of the best known districts (outside the old City of London) which has a history that can be traced back for almost two thousand years. Situated on the south bank of the Thames almost opposite the City of London, Southwark was originally of much the same size as the City although today, its changed character as a London Borough makes its officials responsible for a large wedge-shaped area stretching from the Thames to Sydenham Heights.

About two miles to the east of Southwark, but still within the sphere of influence of London, lie Bermondsey and Rotherhithe. Further east is Deptford, the modern name of which is a corruption of the older "Deep Ford" or "Fiord". The ford in question however, is not of that of a crossing over the Thames, but of the river now known as the Ravensbourne, which runs into Deptford Creek, which in turn empties into the Thames. A naval dockyard was founded there by King Henry VIII in 1513, upon a prime site at Deptford Strand. This site was maintained for naval purposes until the mid-1950s.

It was into this area that the operations of the Southwark and Deptford Tramways Company took place. The main line was to be from Deptford, "Noahs Ark" at the junction of Evelyn Street with High Street, westwards through Rotherhithe and Bermondsey to Tooley Street near London Bridge, about four miles from Deptford. A second main line was to run from Rotherhithe, "Red Lion", via Raymouth Road and Southwark Park Road, to terminate at the "Bricklayers Arms" at the corner of Old Kent Road at its junction with New Kent Road. A short branch line was to run from Raymouth Road to terminate at Canal Bridge, with another along Spa Road, Bermondsey to join the two main lines together.

The company deposited a Parliamentary Bill in the 1879 Session, which subsequently became an Act, after receiving the Royal Assent on 3rd July 1879. **The Southwark & Deptford Tramways Act, 1879, (42-43 Vic. cap. lxxii)** authorised the "laying down and working of tramways in the counties of Surrey and Kent in certain places, and to be worked by animal power only".

The first directors were Christopher James, Henry Carver Briggs, William James Lethbridge, Henry Lee Corlett and William Frederick Wigg. The engineer was Wm. Shelford C.E., the contractors were Messrs. Westwood & Winby, and the secretary was A. J. Davis.

Gauge of the line was to be 4 ft. 8½ in. An inspection of the lines was to be carried out by an Officer of the Railways Inspectorate of the Board of Trade, before any sections were opened for public service. Fares were to be levied at the rate of 1d per mile, but a minimum sum of 2d could be charged. The company would be permitted to carry parcels at the rate of 7 lbs for 3d; 14 lbs for 5d; 28 lbs for 7d and

56 lbs for 9d. Special cheap fares for workmen were to be instituted. The company was authorised to construct the following tramways:-

No. 1. 3 f. 7.70 ch. long, from near "Bricklayers Arms", along Bermondsey New Road and Grange Road to the junction with Spa Road.
Nos. 1a, 1b, 1c, passing places.
No. 2. 3 f. 8.40 ch. long, from end of Tramway No. 1, along Spa Road to Jamaica Road. **Nos. 2a, 2b, 2c,** passing places.
No. 3. 1 ml. 2 f. long, from end of Tramway No. 2, along Jamaica Road, Union Road and Lower Road to "Red Lion", Rotherhithe.
Nos. 3a to 3g, passing places.
No. 4. 1 ml. 4.45 ch. long, from end of Tramway No. 3, along Lower Road and Evelyn Street to "Noahs Ark", Deptford.
Nos. 4a to 4f, passing places.
No. 8. 1 ml. 4 f. 2.45 ch. long, from end of Tramway No. 1 (Spa Road), along Grange Road, Blue Anchor Road, Raymouth Road and Rotherhithe New Road to "Red Lion". **Nos. 8b to 8h,** passing places.
No. 9. 1.20 ch. long, connecting curve at "Bricklayers Arms" between Bermondsey New Road and Old Kent Road.
No. 10. 1.30 ch. long, a junction line at "Bricklayers Arms".
No. 11. 1.65 ch. long, a connecting line at "Bricklayers Arms", between Bermondsey New Road and New Kent Road "down" line.
No. 12. 1.65 ch. long, a junction line at "Bricklayers Arms".
No. 13. 1.55 ch. long, connecting curve at "Red Lion", Rotherhithe.

A plan was sent to the Board of Trade showing the methods of construction that the engineer proposed to use for the permanent way about to be laid in Bermondsey, in accordance with the 1879 Act, in which a specific type of rail was mentioned and which had been agreed with the Bermondsey Vestry, sealed by a Deed of Covenant signed by both company and vestry representatives. It called for the use of the "Barker" system. The company, however, attempted to lay something different; a rail which was an adaption of the Vignoles method. It was not approved by the Bermondsey Vestry, who insisted on "Barker" rail.

Two cars on the main line pass outside Southwark Park main entrance in Lower Road, Rotherhithe. (*Commercial view*)

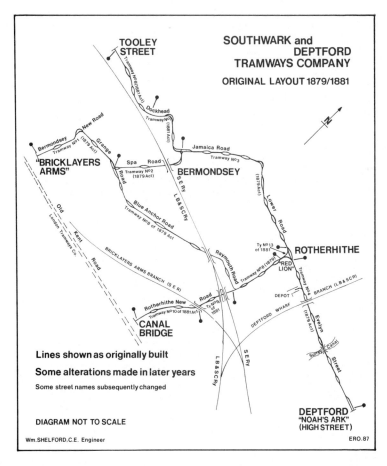

TOOLEY
STREET

SOUTHWARK and
DEPTFORD
TRAMWAYS COMPANY

ORIGINAL LAYOUT 1879/1881

Dockhead

Tramway N°1 (1881 Act)

Jamaica Road

New Road

Bermondsey

Tramway N°1 (1879 Act)

Grange

Road

Spa Road

Tramway N°2 (1879 Act)

"BRICKLAYERS
ARMS"

BERMONDSEY

Tramway N°3

LB&SCRY

SER

Blue Anchor Road

Tramway N°6 of 1879 Act

Lower Road

Old Kent Road

London Tramways Co.

BRICKLAYERS ARMS BRANCH (SER)

Raymouth Road

Tramway N°8 (1879)

Ty N°13 of 1881

ROTHERHITHE

"RED LION"

Tramway N°4

BRANCH (LB&SCR)

DEPOT

Road

Ty N°9 of 1881

Rotherhithe New

Tramway N°10 of 1881 Act

DEPTFORD WHARF

(1879 Act)

Evelyn Street

Surrey Canal

CANAL
BRIDGE

Lines shown as originally built

Some alterations made in later years

Some street names subsequently changed

LB&SCRy

SERy

DIAGRAM NOT TO SCALE

DEPTFORD
"NOAH'S ARK"
(HIGH STREET)

Wm.SHELFORD,C.E. Engineer

ERO.87

A specification was next presented to Bermondsey proposing the use of a rail system described as the "Rotherhithe" section, as it had been agreed that this could be used in that district. But still the Vestry wanted the Barker system. Shelford next suggested that the "Nicholls" section be used, as it was much more likely to withstand heavy use, but to no avail. In the end the Vestry got its way, after insisting on an enquiry by the Board of Trade, which took place on 28th June 1880. The result was the use of an "improved" version of the Barker system, which was, in fact a mixture of the Barker and Rotherhithe rail.

It was later revealed that the Metropolitan Board of Works had opposed the Southwark & Deptford Bill of 1879; it was only because of the support given by the Vestry of Bermondsey that it got a hearing and succeeded. Once settlement had been reached, work commenced on laying the rails. Maj. Gen. Hutchinson inspected the lines in Spa Road, Jamaica Road, Union Road and Lower Road (Deptford Wharf Railway Bridge) on 16th Oct 1880, declaring the line fit for traffic. It is believed that services commenced on 28th October.

Construction then commenced on the Spa Road and Grange Road sections as far as the "Bricklayers Arms". At the same time, the line was being constructed along Evelyn Street to the "Noahs Ark". Together with this, work was proceeding along Rotherhithe New Road as far as Raymouth Road. All three sections of line were inspected by Maj. Gen. Hutchinson on 31st May. The Deptford line opened on 5th June, but the rest had to wait until the completion of drainage works in Raymouth Road. Meanwhile, track was being laid along Blue Anchor Road towards Raymouth Road which, after completion, was inspected on 12th September 1881. Both sections opened to traffic on 12th October, being finally connected on 15th December. The whole of the system so far built, was laid with the approved "modified Barker" rail.

By this time, the company had submitted a set of proposals to Parliament in the 1881 Session, applying for powers to make further extensions to the system, as well as increasing the number of passing places on the lines already open.

The Southwark & Deptford Tramways Act, 1881, (44 & 45 Vic. cap. clxxiii), authorised the construction of new lines which were virtually a continuation of those approved by the preceding Act, the "Tramways" being numbered in ascending sequence:-

No. 7. 2 f. 7.80 ch. long, from Jamaica Road, along Parker's Row to Dockhead, with three passing places.
No. 8. 4 f. 8.10 ch. long, from end of Tramway No. 7, along Dockhead to Tooley Street, with three passing places.
No. 9. 1 f. 3.10 ch. long, in Rotherhithe New Road.
No. 10. 4 f. 1.45 ch. long, from end of Tramway No. 9, to St. James' Road, with three passing places.
No. 11. Five short lengths of line totalling 1 f. 1.40 ch. in length.

Work on the Tooley Street extension commenced in the summer of 1882. The line was inspected on 14th December and opened on

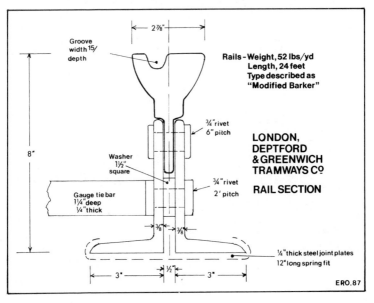

17th. At the same time, the line along Rotherhithe New Road to Canal Bridge was inspected and opened. This marked the end of new construction by the company.

In its continuing efforts to get an extension built from Deptford to Greenwich, the company was prepared to meet some of the costs for a new length of road between these two places, which would be wide enough to allow a tramway to be included, but this idea was thwarted by the London County Council upon its constitution in 1889. Nevertheless, the company pursued its policy of expansion. The present-ation of a Bill to Parliament during 1889 was quite comprehensive, including (again) the proposal to extend to Greenwich; to extend along Tooley Street (again); to make a short extension in Jamaica Road, together with a line to be laid along the whole length of St. James' Road. It was due to the opposition of the LCC, however, that the Bill was badly mauled in Parliament, with the result that the Act gained was very much less in content than had been hoped for. The **Southwark & Deptford Tramways Act, 1889 (52-53 Vic. cap. cxlvii)** authorised the construction of:-

(a) A line from Jamaica Road, along St. James' Road to the end of Rotherhithe New Road by Canal Bridge, 7 f. 1.70 ch. long, of which 4 f. 3.85 ch. is double.
(b) Fourteen short junction lines or passing places at different points on the old lines.

The Act made it quite plain to the company that there was no escape from the purchase clause in the 1870 Tramways Act, and that if the LCC took over the company, this newly authorised line was to be included. In fact, mainly because of this restriction, line (a) was never built, although much of the small work in (b) was carried out.

The company persevered in its attempts to build further sections of line, notably the desired extension from Deptford to Greenwich. A Bill was presented to Parliament in 1891, with a copy sent to the London County Council for its consideration. During the first week of February 1891, the LCC agreed to the proposals, which were that the company be authorised to construct six new tramways; to extend the time for the completion of the lines sanctioned in 1889; to authorise the use of mechanical power; and to change the name of the company to "The London, Deptford & Greenwich Tramways Company".

It seemed that success was just around the corner, but it was not to be. On March 19th 1891, the Bill came before Mr. Thomas, one of the examiners on Standing Orders of the House of Commons who reported against it as, in his opinion, compliance was not proved and the Bill failed. It was presented again for the 1893 Session, but with all provisions removed, except for the change of name of the company, it left nothing to look forward to in the way of expansion. There was no alternative but to just soldier on, until such time as the LCC decided to exercise its compulsory purchase option. **The London, Dept-ford & Greenwich Tramways Act, 1893 (56-57 Vic. cap. ccxii)** could do nothing for the company.

Staff Problems

During 1889, the tramwaymen of south London were attempting to gain some recognition of their right to form themselves into an organised body, to assist them in putting their grievances to their employers without the constant fear of dismissal. A description of their activities is given in the London Tramways Company section. The result was that some concessions were gained by the men, including one day off in twelve with full pay, but with no reduction in daily hours; a bonus at Christmas dependent upon the success of the company; and consideration by the company to setting up a pension fund. Apparently, this met with the approval of the men, for "three cheers" were given for the Chairman at the meeting at which the concessions were announced, with three more for the Manager. In 1892 and 1893, however, the problem occurred again, eventually being resolved by giving an increase in pay in exchange for the one day off in twelve, which meant a monetary increase of up to 4/11d a week for each man.

The LCC Interest

On 3rd July 1900, the London County Council under the powers of Section 43 of the Tramways Act, 1870 resolved to purchase the first sections of the lines of the company which had been built under the authority of the Southwark & Deptford Tramways Act, 1879.

The company responded by objecting in strong terms, saying that the sections involved would be useless to the Council but would upset the company's own arrangements. It was suggested that the Council wait another two years when the whole of the undertaking could be negotiated upon. Nevertheless, after some delay, the Council served the Notice of Intent upon the company on 20th August 1900, stating that it intended to purchase about five route miles of line. Reaction of the company was predictable by complaining to the President of the Board of Trade that the Council was acting in a precipitate manner. In reality, the LCC had no option, as the terms and conditions of the 1870 Tramways Act dictated that this could only be done "after twenty-one years ... after the passing of the relevant Act ... or every seven years thereafter ..."

Having served the Notice, the Council applied to Parliament in the Session of 1901 for powers to authorise extensions to the lines (among other things), including a new double line to be built to an approach road (not yet constructed) from the end of Bermondsey New Road to Tooley Street, which would eventually become a direct route from Lambeth and Southwark to the new Tower Bridge. The Act which was obtained authorised the LCC to undertake the work. So far as the London, Deptford & Greenwich Tramways Company was concerned, the following "Tramways" were authorised:-

No. 23. 4 f. 0.45 ch. long, a double line along Bermondsey New Road, between Grange Road and Tooley Street, with provision for extension to Tower Bridge southern approach.
No. 24. 1.90 ch. long, a double line connection between New Kent Road and Bermondsey New Road.
No. 24A. 1.25 ch. long, a double line at the end of Tramway No. 24 in Bermondsey New Road.
No. 25. 1.17 ch. long, a single line connection between St. James' Road and Old Kent Road.
No. 25A. 1.08 ch. long, a single line connection between St. James' Road and Old Kent Road.

It was to be February 1902 before the section between Grange Road and the "Bricklayers Arms" was doubled (for horse traction only). It was inspected by Col. Yorke on 12th March and opened immediately.

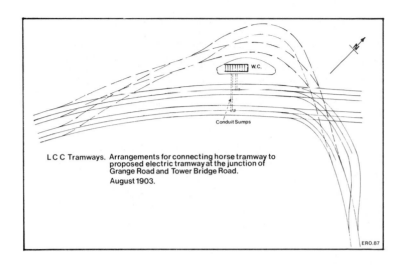

L C C Tramways. Arrangements for connecting horse tramway to proposed electric tramway at the junction of Grange Road and Tower Bridge Road. August 1903.

ERO.87

On 1st October 1902, notice was again given by the LCC that it intended to purchase the remainder of the undertaking, including the sections which fell due in 1900. The Board of Trade appointed Sir. F. Bramwell, Bt. to act as arbitrator between the two parties, but during the proceedings he died. His partner, H. G. Harris took his place on 17th December 1903, being appointed as arbitrator on 2nd March 1904.

One of the points at issue was that the company had made a claim for the Council to bear the cost of "hypothetical widenings". This was based upon the assumption that as the company was freed from liability to contribute to widenings which had never been made, then the value of the tramways was enhanced. After considerable argument which ended in a legal decision, the demand was overruled, at a cost to the company of £165. 6. 5.

The arbitrator made his award on 2nd May 1904. The LCC should pay £91,363. 7. 6d for the undertaking, plus the costs of the reference and award. This sum included payment for leasehold land and buildings, stables, works and depots, but excluded rolling stock, horses, harness, tools, furniture, stores and all other moveable plant or equipment in use at the time. All staff, with the exception of the directors and the manager were to be taken into the employ of the Council. The undertaking became Council property on 7th July 1904. In order that the affairs of the company could be terminated after takeover, a separate Limited Company was set up under the Companies' Acts of 1862-1900. The Certificate of Incorporation was issued on 11th March 1905, which then allowed the shareholders to be paid off and the company to be wound up on 9th April 1906.

Under The LCC

On takeover, there were 42 cars on the books of the company, of both single and double deck types, together with 300 horses. A total of 7 miles 1 furlong 160 yards of track were handed over, of which only 2 miles 3 furlongs 114 yards were double. 1d, 1½d, and 2d fares were in operation, although a cheaper fare (1d single any

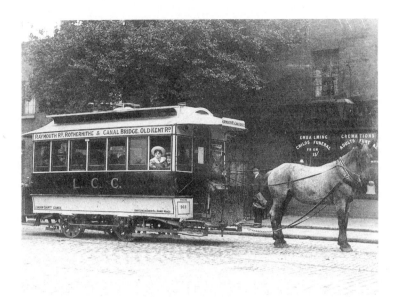

"The ha'penny bumper". In the last days of horse car operation, this single deck car, No. 36, was worked along the Rotherhithe New Road line, which closed in July 1913. (London Transport)

distance) was available for workmen early in the morning and between 6 p.m. and 7 p.m. on weekdays. It was the aim of the LCC to carry out fares revisions (mainly reductions) and service improvements.

Almost as soon as the purchase had been completed, the LCC talked about electrification. In the meantime, the two main lines continued to be worked as in company days with, generally, a 5 to 7 minutes combined service. The frequency of cars on the branch lines was also improved. Other changes occurred from time to time; the cars were completely overhauled, with some being replaced by others painted in the LCC livery, while the fare structure was occasionally amended. In February 1909, the Spa Road to Tower Bridge Road via Grange Road service was interrupted through damage caused to the line and road by a gas explosion in Spa Road. The area was totally closed for some time, and traffic of all kinds was suspended for upward of six months. Tram service resumed on 9th September.

During the latter half of 1909, reconstruction for electric traction commenced. The tracks on Blackhorse Bridge were dealt with first, in conjunction with the complete rebuilding of the bridge. On 5th December, single line working was instituted to enable work to proceed. This was followed up on 20th January 1910 with the closure of the road bridge over the railway line at Deptford Road Station (later to be changed to and at present still known as Surrey Docks). Horse cars worked to either side of the bridge.

It had been intended that the line via Southwark Park Road would be electrified, and during the reconstruction of the tracks in Lower Road, provision was made for the connection by the insertion of a conduit junction at the "Red Lion". Meantime, on 10th August the horsecar service was suspended between "Noahs Ark" and Dockhead on the main line in order to facilitate the work. The depots and stables remained open to service the other lines.

The line over Deptford Road Bridge was re-opened to traffic on 3rd September, service being re-introduced between "Noahs Ark" and Jamaica Road, only to be suspended again on 19th between St. James' Road and the railway bridge. This was followed by closure between "Noahs Ark" and "Red Lion" on 29th November, which isolated the car depot from the sections of track still open. A piece of waste ground at Tower Bridge Road was used as a car stand, while the horses were still stabled at Evelyn Street. On completion of track reconstruction, all cars were returned to Evelyn Street on 9th February 1911, but only for a few more weeks. Electric car working commenced between "Red Lion" and Tooley Street (Bermondsey Street) on 25th February and, at the same time, the horse car service along Spa Road was abandoned. This was followed on 22nd June 1911 by electric cars taking over on the section between "Red Lion" and "Noahs Ark".

Abandonment of the short line along Rotherhithe New Road between Raymouth Road and Canal Bridge came in July 1913, but the line from "Red Lion" via Southwark Bridge Road to Tower Bridge Road lingered on for almost another two years, before it too, passed into oblivion. The line was never electrified.

The Cars

The provision of cars was undertaken by an Agent, Mr. J. Dixon, who placed an order with the Metropolitan Carriage & Wagon Company Limited of Saltley, Birmingham in 1880 for a total of 32 vehicles, of which five or six were to be small single deck cars for working on the two short branch lines, then awaiting Parliamentary approval. A total of £7,191 was allocated for the purchase of this rolling stock, which gave a probable first cost of about £240 for the double deck cars and £140 for the others.

All the double deck cars were of the 7-window pattern, designed to carry 22 passengers in the saloon and 24 on the knifeboard seating on the open top deck. The single deck vehicles, also of the 7-window type, carried 22 passengers. During the late 1880s and early 1890s, several of the cars were rebuilt with new top decks, upon which were placed the later pattern "garden seats". From 1896, a fleet of five omnibuses was added, in order to enable the company to work through to Greenwich Church from the tram terminus at Deptford. It is not known what these vehicles cost.

The number of cars shown in Board of Trade returns showed losses and gains from time to time, but in the early years of the twentieth century, a continual increase in the number of passengers carried, saw the undertaking with 42 cars at the time of the LCC takeover in 1904.

Colours Of Cars

The cars were painted in distinctive colours, usually using a different colour for each service on each route. The main lines were:-

Tooley Street	and Deptford "Noahs Ark", Blue	
"Bricklayers Arms"	and Rotherhithe "Red Lion", Green	
"	and "Noahs Ark", Green	
"	and St. James' Church, White	
Canal Bridge	and Raymouth Road, White	

The two "white" services were on the short branch lines, and were provided by single deck cars, usually with only one car on each line. In each case, this gave a long headway, the time taken to do a journey on the Spa Road line, together with the turn-round time at each end giving a 28-minute service, while on the Canal Bridge route a 20-minute service was provided.

The Connelly Motor

On 25th May 1892, the Chairman of the tramways company asked the Board of Trade for permission to operate an oil-driven engine, known as a Connelly Motor, on an experimental basis. He suggested that the Motor could, subject to agreement, commence working on 28th or 29th June. Although the LCC gave its permission, in the first place for a two-month period, other problems delayed the introduction of the experiment.

The Connelly Oil-Gas Tramway Locomotive was described as being a four-wheeled carriage of American design (with a horsecar-type body without platforms). Length, 11 feet; weight 4½ tons, wheelbase, 5 ft. 6 in.; two-cylinder internal combustion type engine, with electric ignition from a dynamo (magneto); friction wheel transmission having "infinitely variable gear ratio" (also said to be a "flat disc" connection between engine and wheels by means of gearing). The machine was built by Weymann & Co., Guildford, Surrey.

Maj. Gen. Hutchinson carried out his first inspection of the Motor on 29th June 1892, but refused to sanction its use until the following requirements were met.-

Drivers to be as close as possible to the front of the Motor in whichever direction it is running, and regulator and brake handles arranged to meet this object.

The Connelly Motor, as used at Deptford and Croydon.

(Courtesy: G. E. Baddeley)

Brake blocks to be fitted to all four wheels and not only two "as at present".

He also said that pointwork incorporating movable tongues be installed in place of the fixed castings in use.

On his second inspection on 5th August, he still refused to allow the Motor to be used, as the trackwork had not been attended to. He also let it be known that "as he was off to Russia (St. Petersburg) shortly, he suggested that he might have a further look at the car and track about the third week in September". In the event, his next visit was not to be until 12th December 1892, when he finally gave his permission to use the Motor for an initial period of six months. The certificate was issued subject to the Motor being worked only on specified routes; to a regular check and repairs being made to rail joints; to suitable fenders being fitted to the Motor, together with a special bell, whistle or other warning device; and no "clatter" from the machinery, which was to be concealed at all points above four inches from the ground.

The Motor was restricted to working only on the Rotherhithe New Road line, which it did regularly for the next six months. The company then requested renewal of the license for another six months, and then subsequently at regular intervals, which were granted without further inspection. On 17th October 1895, Maj. Marindin carried out an inspection at the request of the Board of Trade and renewed the license for twelve months. This was subject to the flywheel being covered with a wire guard to protect the driver, and subject also to certain sections of the track being properly repaired. He also made the recommendation that the Board of Trade enquire into the object of the experiment being continued beyond the twelve month period just authorised. No more applications were made for the Motor to be "experimentally worked". During the period of operation, it is recorded that the Motor ran 5,348 miles in service with the company, carrying 40,897 passengers in the cars used in conjunction with it.

The Depot

The only depot used by the company was situated at the London end of Evelyn Street, Deptford, alongside the L.B.&S.C. Railway branch line into Deptford Wharf. It was built on leasehold land taken on an 81 year term at £100 per year for the eastern part of the premises, and an 80 year term at £80 per year for the smaller, isolated, south-western part. Originally, the whole of the plot was a single unit, but at about the time the line was built a new road was constructed, forming an extension of Crooke Road and running south-east under the railway embankment, to connect with other new roads, Alloa and Scawen, then being laid out. Consequently, the main part consisted of the car shed, offices, granary and some stabling, while the detached part contained additional stables, the smithy, and some smaller buildings used as stores. The manure store was also at the rear of this section. The car shed was built with six roads, four of which were connected into a depot fan to form a single line with a passing loop about half way between the depot entrance and the main road. The other two roads were connected by crossovers inside the depot. Connection with the main line was by means of an east-to-south curve into the single track which, almost immediately opened out into a passing loop just north of the railway bridge, under which the line passed.

Fares and Tickets

The earliest tickets of this company were simple geographicals with the stages set diagonally around the ticket. As in the case of most companies, the rate was ½d a mile with the minimum fare of 1d usually being charged. On issuing the ticket, the conductor of the car would tear off one corner of it corresponding with the journey the passenger was to make. This method of fare collection was open to abuse and very soon conductors were issued with hand-held punches which, when operated caused a hole to be cut in the ticket; a bell to ring inside the punch and a small register to move one digit forward.

Very soon after the use of the punch began, the style of the tickets was altered, geographical information being printed either across or along the length of the tickets in the "To and From" format. In common with many other undertakings the Southwark & Deptford Company began to use plain white tickets for the 1d value, pink or magenta for the 2d (and sometimes the 1½d as well), and blue for the ½d. The through fare on each main line was 2d and there were ½d through fares on each of the branch lines.

Upon the change of name of the company in 1893, new tickets were introduced, partly geographical but retaining fare stage numbers on some printings, in conjunction with red stripes on the left hand sides of them. The ½d fare on Rotherhithe New Road between the "Red Lion" and Raymouth Road Junction, about ½-mile in length, sported its own ticket, while the short shuttle service between Raymouth Road and Canal Bridge shared a ½d ticket with the Spa Road service.

On the main line, the 1d stages overlapped quite considerably, with a passenger able to travel from Deptford to St. James' Church, Rotherhithe or from "Red Lion", Rotherhithe to Tooley Street, while the full journey could be taken for 1½d. In 1902 however, ½d fares were introduced between Deptford and Tooley Street. Sunday fares on the main lines were fixed at 1½d for any distance on any one car, but this was not always adhered to as, from time to time the company reverted to charging "ordinary" fares on those days.

With the cessation of a through service between Deptford and the "Bricklayers Arms", a transfer system was introduced, with passengers changing cars at "Red Lion". The exchange tickets issued were green with a large red "E" overprint, stocks of which were carried by conductors on both services. These were dealt with by being issued on the second car in exchange for the through ticket presented by the passenger.

When the company introduced an omnibus service between "Noahs Ark" and St. Alphege Church, Greenwich a fare of ½d was charged, for which a blue ticket striped red and marked "Omnibus Ticket" was issued. There was also a special 1d ticket for the journey of about ¾-mile between "Noahs Ark" and the Tramway Depot, Evelyn Street, which seems to have been a "one way only" issue. It can only be surmised that this would be issued on cars "running in" and after all other tickets and cash had been accounted for.

Special cars were run for "artisans and daily labourers" before 7.30 a.m. and after 5.30 p.m. on weekdays, upon which fares at about half the normal rate were charged, with a minimum fare of 1d. This however, did not apply on the short branch lines where ½d fares were charged. Luggage was carried at 2d per package per journey, except for journeymens' tools, which were carried free.

Human Sideshow

Pathos, tragedy and comedy are all parts of human existence. They were all very much in evidence in many ways, as seen in the snippets of information given from week to week in the columns of local newspapers of the period. After all, tramways were built and operated by people for people, so it is inevitable that people will intrude into the daily lives of the undertakings.

Firstly, stark tragedy. On Monday, 5th September 1892, at one o'clock in the afternoon, a tiny girl of just two years old followed her mother out from their shop in Evelyn Street Deptford when mother, one Marian Meager, wife of Robert Meager carpenter and joiner, went across the road to attend to her son, aged 6, who had cut his hand on a broken bottle. The child, Anne Webb Burgess Meager wandered into the road and was knocked down by a tram horse as the car passed at some speed. She was killed outright. It was said at the inquest that the driver of the tramcar did all he could to pull up the horses to try to save the child, and in no way was he to blame.

Wm. Archmead, a labourer, at 11 p.m. on 12th May 1884, threw Samuel Trevallyan, the conductor of a Deptford car, off the car in Bermondsey New Road, fracturing his skull and breaking two ribs. His brother, James Archmead, also assaulted a tramways inspector, John Morgan, then ran after the car, abusing the conductor. Both were remanded in custody. (If the conductor died, so did Archmead - he would have been hanged for murder).

Pathos next. A retired Police Inspector, R. W. Ahern, was summoned to Southwark Police Court on 18th June 1893, accused with infringing the Bye-laws of the tramway company for refusing to show his ticket when requested to do so at the instance of an official of the company. Mr. Ahern complained of the arbitrary way in which he was dealt with, saying that he had paid his fare but could not find his ticket when asked to produce it, and was then asked to pay a second time, which he refused to do. He was then given into custody. Afterwards he wrote to the company threatening legal action and this was why he was summoned by the company. He was fined 1/- with 13/- costs for his misdeed, the magistrate saying "that he had behaved foolishly".

Lastly, a sort of comedy. Henry Sherer was delivering ice to the shop of Mr. King when a tram appeared. On reaching Mansion House loop, the tram driver, John Cross said that he could not pass the cart of the defendant, and Sherer said "that he was not going to move" until he had finished weighing the ice. The company had summoned Sherer, and the magistrate who heard the case found him "guilty" and fined him 5/- with 2/- costs. It seemed that the traders on one side of the road at this point had been trying to get the loop removed to the other side of the road. It was implied that Sherer had been "instigated to cause a fuss". Cars were delayed for five minutes.

A number of reports like this bring to life the goings-on in every street in every town, day in, day out. Probably much more note was taken of some of these incidents in the days when tramways were a novelty, as many people resented their intrusion into their set ways, particularly those in the ranks of the "carmen", who were delivering goods to business premises. The tram had become in their eyes the "King of the Road" to be challenged at every opportunity.

Chapter 9
The London, Camberwell & Dulwich
Tramways Company

Before the spate of house building in the districts around Peckham, the area was mainly open land where market gardens flourished. With the coming of suburbia, came also industry, with factories and works making furniture from the wood brought along the Surrey Canal; others concocting vinegars, sauces and the like; while at least one other was in the paper processing business.

To the south of Peckham lies Peckham Rye, a large open space which, at one time was part of the "waste of the Manor", eventually becoming common land and saved from extinction by the London County Council purchasing what was left of it in the early years of the last decade of the nineteenth century.

So far as the Dulwich part of the original title of the company is concerned, the southern end of a tramway was eventually built in East Dulwich which, like parts of Peckham, mainly consisted of small to medium sized houses built in continuous rows, in streets laid out in the years between 1875 and 1890.

It was into this busy area that the promoters of an undertaking to be known as the "Peckham, East Dulwich & Crystal Palace Tramway" decided to attempt to provide a connection between the line of the London Tramways Company at Peckham and the shopping area of Rye Lane, with the residential districts to the south. A Bill was submitted to Parliament in 1882, seeking authority to construct a line between High Street, Peckham and Bews Corner, Lordship Lane (now the junction with the South Circular Road). The Act which was gained, incorporated the company under a revised name and a truncated route. **The Peckham & East Dulwich Tramways Act, 1882 (45-46 Vic. cap. ccxiii)** of 10th August, authorised the making of Tramways in the Parish of Camberwell in the County of Surrey, and for other purposes. The company was empowered to lay lines to the standard gauge of 4 ft. 8½ in. in the following streets:-

No. 1. 2 f. 1 ch. long, along Rye Lane, Peckham from High Street to the railway bridge over Rye Lane.
No. 2. 4 f. 4.40 ch. long, from Tramway No. 1, along Rye Lane and Peckham Rye to East Dulwich Road, "Kings Arms".
No. 3. 1 ml. 9.60 ch. long, from Tramway No. 2, along East Dulwich Road, Crystal Palace Road and Lordship Lane to the "Plough Inn".

Paul Wallace Sharp and William Fairmainer Rowell were named as two of the directors (the others not being named). Authorised capital was to be £30,000, with borrowing powers on mortgage to a maximum of £7,500.

In the following year, the company obtained powers by the **Peckham & East Dulwich Tramways (Extensions) Act, 1883 (46-47 Vic. cap. ccxxvii)** for the following new lines:-

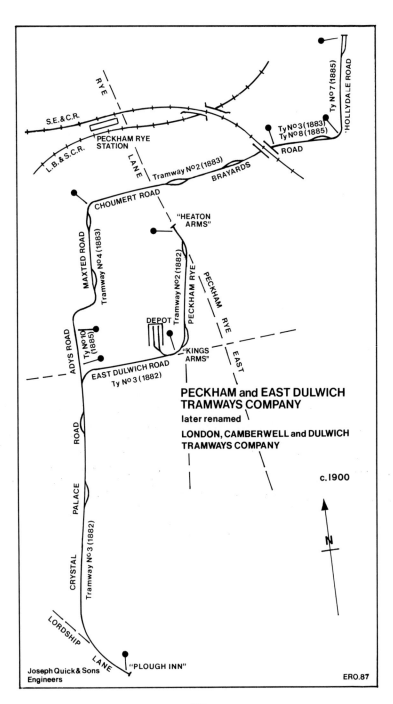

RYE

S.E. & C.R.

L.B. & S.C.R.

PECKHAM RYE STATION

LANE

Tramway No 2 (1883)

BRAYARDS

Ty No 3 (1883)
Ty No 8 (1885)

ROAD

'HOLLYDALE ROAD

Ty No 7 (1885)

CHOUMERT ROAD

"HEATON ARMS"

MAXTED ROAD

Tramway No 4 (1883)

Tramway No 2 (1882)

PECKHAM RYE

PECKHAM RYE EAST

ADYS ROAD

Ty No 10 (1885)

DEPOT

"KINGS ARMS"

EAST DULWICH ROAD

Ty No 3 (1882)

ROAD

CRYSTAL PALACE

Tramway No 3 (1882)

LORDSHIP LANE

"PLOUGH INN"

PECKHAM and EAST DULWICH TRAMWAYS COMPANY

later renamed

LONDON, CAMBERWELL and DULWICH TRAMWAYS COMPANY

c.1900

N

Joseph Quick & Sons
Engineers

ERO.87

No. 2. 4 f. 9.90 ch. long, from Bellenden Road Peckham, along Choumert Road, Atwell Road, Crowley Road and Brayards Road to the corner of Kirkwood Road.

No. 3. 3 f. 9.95 ch. long, from Tramway No. 2, along Kirkwood Road, Kimberley Road, Evelina Road and Hollydale Road to the corner of Cemetery Road.

No. 4. 4 f. 7.0 ch. long, from Choumert Road, along Bellenden Road, Maxted Road, Nutbrook Street, Adys Road, Ondine Road and Champion Hill Road.

No. 5. 6 f. 7.40 ch. long, from Tramway No. 4, along Champion Hill Road and Lordship Lane to Crystal Palace Road, terminating by a junction with Tramway No. 3 authorised by the Peckham & East Dulwich Tramways Act, 1882.

Meanwhile, construction of the line between "Heaton Arms" and Crystal Palace Road had begun, but appeared to be quite a leisurely affair. When completed, no attempt was made to gain authority to work the line. In any event, there were no cars, no depot, nor any staff to work on the line.

Two years later, the **Peckham & East Dulwich Tramways Act, 1885, (48-49 Vic. cap. cxcix)** was obtained, to enable the company to build several more new lengths of line, together with several which had already been mentioned in previous Acts. These were:-

No. 1. 4 f. long, along Rye Lane from High Street to the existing tramway at the southern end of Rye Lane.

No. 7. 3 f. 4.60 ch. long, from the authorised tramway at Evelina Road, along Hollydale Road, to a point adjacent to the lines of the London Tramways Company in Queens Road.

No. 8. 1 f. 3.30 ch. long, along Brayards Road from Kirkwood Road.

No. 9. 4 f. 6.8 ch. long, from the "Kings Arms", along Peckham Rye Common, Nunhead Lane and Evelina Road, to a junction with Tramway No. 3 authorised by the 1883 Act at Kimberley Road.

No. 10. 1 f. 0.40 ch. long, from Crystal Palace Road, into and along Adys Road to Ondine Road.

No. 11. 3 f. long, from the authorised tramway in Maxted Road, along land lying between Oglander Road and Wild Ash Road, then along Wild Ash Road to Grove Vale at a junction with Tramway No. 12.

No. 11A. 0.60 ch. long, a junction line at Grove Vale.

No. 12. 1 f. 3.20 ch. long, from the junction of Ondine Road with Grove Vale to East Dulwich Railway Station.

Authorisation was also given to raise the share capital by £5,000 to £35,000. Regarding the progress of construction work, the company was given until 21st December 1885 to complete the tramways which had been authorised in 1883. Lastly, a site for a depot and stables had been secured in premises next door to the "Kings Arms". In July 1885, another effort was made to get construction work restarted, this time through Hollydale Road, Choumert Road and Maxted Road to Adys Road at East Dulwich Road. This was inspected by Maj. Gen. Hutchinson on 5th January 1886 and certificate was issued. Apart from one car which was borrowed for the inspection, the company had nothing to work on the line.

During the next two years, several more sections of track were laid, but no inspections were requested, and there were still no cars. However, the company went to Parliament with another Bill, by which means it obtained the **Peckham & East Dulwich Tramways Act, 1887, (50-51 Vic. cap. clxxxiii),** authorising the company to:-

(a) Change the name of the undertaking to the London, Camberwell & Dulwich Tramways Company.

One of the several single deck one-man "toastrack" cars waits for passengers at the Peckham Rye terminus of the line. (Commercial view)

(b) Enable them to abandon certain lines authorised by previous Acts.
(c) Authority to increase capital to £40,000 and borrowing powers to a maximum of £10,000.
(d) Obtain a further extension of time in which to construct "certain" of the lines authorised.

So far as abandonment was concerned, the following authorised lines were to be given up:-

1. From Rye Lane (High Street) to "Heaton Arms".
2. The sections in Kirkwood, Kimberley, Ondine, Champion Hill Roads and Lordship Lane (western part).
3. Practically the whole of the content of the 1885 Act, except for one short length across the end of Goose Green into Adys Road.

Even after all this activity, the company did not manage to get any part of the lines open for traffic for several more years. Much pressure was put upon them by the local Vestry and other interested bodies, but to no avail. The Board of Trade even sent an Inspector along to attempt to induce the management to start a service, but this did no good either.

Meantime a sub-contractor, Messrs. Sharp & Son began laying rails along the south side of Peckham Rye, along East Dulwich Road to a junction with the line in Adys Road, and along Crystal Palace Road and Lordship Lane to "The Plough". This was inspected by Maj. Gen. Hutchinson on 11th August 1888, who also took another look at the original lines, commenting that when they were properly repaired, he would issue a certificate. The repairs were executed, the certificate was issued, but there were still no cars. There were still no cars in 1889 or 1890.

For another five years things just coasted along. In 1895, the local authority sent a deputation to the Board of Trade, in an attempt to get the lines removed as, in their opinion they constituted a danger to other road users. Once more an Inspector, this time Maj. Marindin was sent to report on the condition of the tramways. His findings were not good. However, the company set to and made good where necessary, with the avowed intention of opening the undertaking to traffic.

In 1896 it happened! A total length of 2⅞ miles of line opened, upon which small, single deck, open sided "toastrack" cars, hauled by hired horses began their journeys. The cars had been constructed by the Midland Wagon Company of Birmingham and Shrewsbury, and each carried 40 passengers on cross bench seats and with only curtains as a protection against the vagaries of the British climate. Weight of a car was shown to be 2 tons 3 cwts, while it believed that four were delivered, although car No. 5 is shown in an advertisement.

In March 1896, considerable discussion took place between the company and the Board of Trade regarding the collection of fares. The company wanted to install fareboxes, but the Board was not sure whether this could be done within the bye-laws. In the end, the rules were revised to allow a passenger to pay a fare without receiving a ticket in exchange.

An elaborate service was advertised, while a time and faretable worthy of the best was issued in November 1896. Such niceties as special cars to meet "church trains" to and from the City from Queens Road Station is shown in the Sunday section. Although services of sorts were worked, it seems that the company never made a profit. Neither did the proposed junction with the London Tramways Company materialise. The company never published proper accounts, or sent to the Board of Trade any annual return as required by law. In 1900, the operations of the undertaking finally ended, after fitful running at weekends and, occasionally, on Bank Holidays.

After several more attempts in 1901 by the local authority, the County Council and the Board of Trade to induce the company to re-open the lines, a move was made to have the tracks removed, as they were considered by some to be a danger to other road users. In the end the LCC made an offer to purchase the undertaking outright, as it was in the process of negotiating the laying of new conduit tracks over two short sections of road in Lordship Lane and East Dulwich Road where company tracks were laid. Ownership of these would prove to be useful in these negotiations. However, it was still to take some time before the purchase could take place.

By the time the "system" was purchased by the Council for the sum of £6,500, it was in the hands of the Official Receiver. After purchase, it was all promptly abandoned, except for the two sections which were to be incorporated into the new electrified routes.

It had apparently been the intention of the company to lay tracks in practically every back street in the locality. Comment in "The Engineer" as early as 1883 will show what they thought of the idea then:- "The reflection most likely to arise in the mind of a person acquainted with the above district on reading this notice (the proposals for the Bill of 1883) is that it must emanate from a working mans' association of some sort, for if ever a tramway could be devised for the express purpose of setting a tolerable percentage of that exemplary class down at their own front doors, some of these extensions must come pretty near to it".

In later years, with the change of name of the company to The London, Camberwell & Dulwich Tramways Company, there can only be the supposition that the reference to Camberwell may have been due to the fact that the area of "operations" was within the Parish

Weekdays, *except Sat's. & Mon's.*			Saturday and Monday Service.		

RYE LANE CHOUMERT RD. TO PLOUGH INN	RYE LANE HEATON ARMS TO PLOUGH INN	PLOUGH INN TO RYE LANE HEATON ARMS.	HEATON ARMS TO PLOUGH INN	PLOUGH INN TO HEATON ARMS.	QUEEN'S RD. ST'N TO PLOUGH INN.
8 5 3 22	9 15 5 4	9 35 4 56	9 40 6 15	10 1 6 37	7.57, 8.57 a.m.,
8 35 10 23	10 1 5 19	10 0 5 11	10 2½ 6 30	10 23 6 52	3.0, 4.10, 5.20,
9 35 10 46	10 23 5 34	10 22 5 26	10 23 6 45	10 45 7 7	6.30, 7.40, 8.50,
	10 45 5 49	10 41 5 41	10 46 7 0	11 7 7 22	and 10 p.m.
	11 7 6 4	11 6 5 56	11 8 7 15	11 29 7 37	
PLOUGH INN	11 29 6 19	11 28 6 11	11 30 7 30	11 52 7 52	PLOUGH INN, LORD- SHIP LANE TO
TO RYE LANE CHOUMERT RD.	11 51 6 34	11 50 6 26	11 52 7 45	12 13 8 7	QUEEN'S RD. ST'N
	12 13 6 49	12 12 6 41	12 14 8 0	12 35 8 22	7.30, 8.0, 8.30,
	12 35 7 4	12 34 6 56	12 36 8 15	12 57 8 37	9.26, 10.35
7 30 2 46	12 57 7 19	12 56 7 11	12 58 8 30	1 22 8 52	a.m., 3.32, 4.44,
8 0 10 6	1 19 7 34	1 18 7 26	1 20 8 45	1 38 9 7	5.56, 7.4, 8 10,
8 30 10 33	1 41 7 49	1 40 7 41	2 0 9 15	2 0 9 22	9.26, and 10 35
9 0	2 3 8 4	2 2 7 56	2 15 9 30	2 22 9 37	p.m.
	2 25 8 19	2 24 8 11	2 30 9 45	2 37 9 52	
QUEEN'S RD. TO PLOUGH INN	2 47 8 34	3 11 8 26	2 45 10 5	2 52 10 7	**SUNDAY SERVICE.**
	3 4 8 49	3 26 8 41	3 0 10 25	3 7 10 24	
7 57 3 14	3 34 9 4	3 41 8 56	3 15 10 45	3 37 11 4	BETWEEN HEATON ARMS AND
8 27 10 15	3 49 9 19	3 56 9 11	3 30 11 5	3 52 11 29	PLOUGH INN
9 27 10 38	4 4 9 33	4 11 9 26	3 45 11 25	4 7 11 44	*Every 20 min.*
	4 19 9 45	4 26 9 52	4 0	4 22	*through the day*
Pass	4 34 10 13	4 41	4 15	4 37	Leave Rye Lane
Kirkwood	4 49		4 30	4 52	First Car 10 a.m
Choumert	Pass	Pass	4 45	5 7	Last ,, 11 p.m,
Oglander	K'g's Arms	Silvester 4	5 0	5 22	Leave Plough
Goose G'n 1	Goose Gr'n 7	N'th Cross 6	5 15	5 37	First 10.20 a.m.
min. later	N'rth Cross	Goose Gr'n 8	5 30,	5 52	Last 11.20 p.m.
	Silvester 11	K'g'sArms 11	5 45	6 7	A Car leaves
PLOUGH INN TO QUEEN'S RD.	min. later,	min. later.	6 0	6 22	Plough Inn Sun day morning at
7 30 2 46			Saturdays only.	Saturdays only.	9.30 for Queen's Road Station, to
8 0 10 6					meet church tr'ns
8 30 10 33					to City & Victoria
9 0	FARES:— ½D.				A Car leaves
Pass	Heaton Arms and King's Arms—King's Arms				Queen's Road Station Sundays
Silvester	and Goose Green—Goose Green and Northcross'				at 1.47 p.m, meet-
N'rth Cross	Rd.—Northcross Rd. and Goodrich Rd.—Good-				ing church tr'ns
Goose Gr'n	rich Rd. and Plough Inn—Queen's Rd. and Kirk-				from City and
Oglander 12	wood Rd.—Kirkwood Rd. and Rye Lane—Rye				Victoria.
Choumert 17	Lane and Oglander Rd.—Oglander Rd. and				
Kirkwood 20	Goose Green.				
min. later.					

1D.

Rye Lane (Heaton Arms or Choumert Rd.) and Northcross Rd.—King's Arms and Silvester Rd.— Goose Green and Goodrich Rd.—Northcross Rd. and Plough Inn—Queen's Rd. and Rye Lane— Kirkwood Rd. and Oglander Rd.—Oglander Rd. and Silvester Rd.

1½D.

Heaton Arms and Goodrich Rd.—King's Arms and Plough Inn—Queen's Rd. and Goose Green—Kirkwood Rd. and Northcross Rd.—Oglander Rd. and Plough Inn.

Beyond the above distances - **2D.**

The above Time Table will be carefully adhered to, but the Co. cannot hold itself liable for any deviation from same through unforseen causes.

of Camberwell. It is probable that the London part of the title was wishful thinking! This little back street system had an impressive title but precious little else. The late Frank Merton Atkins described it in his notes as "the premier tin-pot tramway of London". This just about sums it up.

It had cost over £30,150 to set up, construct and fitfully operate two and seven eighths miles of back street tramways. It surely must have been the classic "white elephant" tramway ever to have been constructed anywhere in the metropolitan area - or anywhere else for that matter!

Chapter 10
The Woolwich & South East London
Tramways Company Limited

The ancient town of Woolwich, about ten miles to the east of the City of London nestles alongside the south shore of the River Thames and had, until a reorganisation of local government boundaries in 1965, a couple of small tracts of land on the north side of the river within its area of authority.   Until the coming of the railways, the towns-people relied almost entirely on the river as their means of getting about, often in preference to traversing the few roads in the area, which were noted for being particularly susceptible to the dark deeds of highwaymen and other unsavoury characters.   There were stage coach and omnibus services to and from Greenwich and London, one of the first being established in 1831, but these were spasmodic and diminished in importance once the railways became reality.   Such an ancient area must have had as its name something similar to the present-day one and in fact it is named in Domesday as "Hulviz".

The same air of antiquity can be seen in what was once the village of Plumstead, about one mile to the east of Woolwich, and mentioned in Domesday by the name of Plumstede.   At one time it was a well-known fruit growing area.   About a mile to the east of Plumstead is Abbey Wood, which almost certainly got its name from the woodland surrounding the ancient Abbey of Less-Ness, founded in 1178.

Moving westwards from Woolwich, the next district is Charlton. As with the greater part of this area, it is a district of great interest, and at one time, of great importance.   And so to Greenwich.   This ancient town of Royal Patronage owes its name in all probability to a mixture of the Danish and Saxon languages, as at one time, the area was regularly overrun by invaders.

During the early years of the 1870s, the Pimlico, Peckham and Greenwich Tramways Company had connected Greenwich to London by one of the first tramways to be laid in the Capital.   It had originally been the intention of the Pimlico Company to extend to Woolwich and, in fact it obtained a Provisional Order in 1869-70 for this purpose. The powers lapsed, however, and the company made no attempt to renew the application.   It was left to the Woolwich and Plumstead Tramways Company, which had been formed by a group of local people led by Robert Alexander Mayer, to make an application to the Board of Trade for authority to construct lines in its area.

Thomas Floyd, the engineer to the company, obtained the agreement of the Plumstead Board of Works to the proposal on 13th December 1879, following this up on 17th January 1880 by signing a document in company with the members of the Board.   Because of the many narrow roads with severe curvature and tortuous bends, the proposals would only be accepted if the company agreed to adopt the narrow gauge of 3 ft. 6 in. for the track, making this tramway unsual in that it was the only horse tramway to be constructed to this gauge

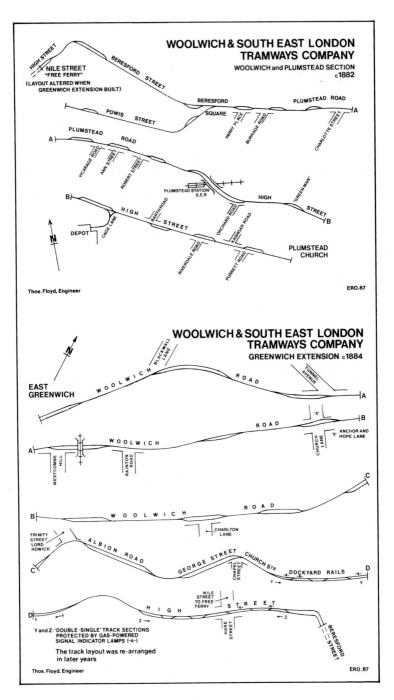

WOOLWICH & SOUTH EAST LONDON
TRAMWAYS COMPANY
WOOLWICH and PLUMSTEAD SECTION
c1882

HIGH STREET
NILE STREET
"FREE FERRY"
(LAYOUT ALTERED WHEN
GREENWICH EXTENSION BUILT)

BERESFORD STREET

BERESFORD SQUARE
PLUMSTEAD ROAD
PARRY PLACE
BURRAGE ROAD
CHARLOTTE STREET
POWIS STREET
A

PLUMSTEAD ROAD
A
VICARAGE ROAD
ANN STREET
ROBERT STREET
PLUMSTEAD STATION S.E.R
"GREEN MAN"
HIGH STREET
B
B
N
DEPOT
CAGE LANE
HIGH STREET
MARTIN ROAD
ORCHARD ROAD
KASHGAR ROAD
RIVERDALE ROAD
PURRETT ROAD
PLUMSTEAD CHURCH

Thos. Floyd, Engineer

ERO.87

WOOLWICH & SOUTH EAST LONDON
TRAMWAYS COMPANY
GREENWICH EXTENSION c1884

N

EAST GREENWICH
BLACKWALL LANE
WOOLWICH ROAD
TUNNEL AVENUE
A

ROAD
'X'
B
'X' ANCHOR AND HOPE LANE
CHURCH LANE
A
WESTCOMBE HILL
WOOLWICH
RAINTON ROAD

C
B
WOOLWICH ROAD
CHARLTON LANE

TRINITY STREET 'LORD HOWICK'
ALBION ROAD
GEORGE STREET
CHURCH STR
CHAPEL STREET
DOCKYARD RAILS
D
C
Y →
Y

D
Y → Y
HIGH STREET
NILE STREET TO FREE FERRY
HARE STREET
Z
BERESFORD STREET

Y and Z: 'DOUBLE-SINGLE' TRACK SECTIONS
PROTECTED BY GAS-POWERED
SIGNAL INDICATOR LAMPS (-s-)

The track layout was re-arranged
in later years

Thos. Floyd, Engineer

ERO.87

106

in what was to become the London area.

Authority to construct the lines was secured by means of the **Woolwich & Plumstead Tramways (Provisional Order), 1880,** which was confirmed in the **Tramways Orders Confirmation (No. 2) Act, 1880 (43-44 Vic. cap. clxxiii),** with Robert Alexander Mayer receiving powers to make and maintain the following tramways:-
(a) A line 1 ml. 3 f. 1.20 ch. long, along Plumstead Road from High Street, Woolwich to Plumstead Church.
(b) A line, 1 f. 4.90 ch. long, from the corner of Hare Street, Woolwich, to Beresford Square, passing along Powis Street.

The western terminus of the proposed line at the end of High Street by Nile Street was near the landing stage of a steam ferry which plied between north and south Woolwich, and it was hoped that some traffic would generated by having this connection. At the other end of the line, the terminus was quite close to Plumstead Church, at the eastern end of the village; it was also almost outside the doors of the "Plume of Feathers" public house!

Almost as soon as the company had received its powers, it was put up for sale. **The Woolwich & South-East London Tramways Company Limited** had been formed during the autumn of 1880 by a group of seven men, some of whom already had tramway interests elsewhere. It had been agreed that the old company should be purchased from Mayer for £19,750, which was to be paid to him in instalments. The Board of Trade was notified of this change and, by the end of the year, the terms of sale and purchase had been completed.

The objects and aims of the new company, which were written into the Memorandum of Association were:-
1. To make, equip and work tramways from Woolwich to Plumstead in the County of Kent and in the District of South East of London within 20 miles of the Plumstead Station of the North Kent Railway.
2. To acquire .. the rights and interests of Robert Alexander Mayer under the Woolwich & Plumstead Tramways Order 1880 as confirmed by the Tramways Orders Confirmation (No. 2) Act, 1880 (V.c.clxxiii).
3. To run omnibuses and vans in connection with ... and generally to carry on the business of an omnibus proprietor and common carrier of passengers, goods and merchandise.
4. To obtain any Provisional Order of the Board of Trade and any Act of Parliament for enabling the company ...
5. To manufacture ... any article ... in connection with tramways.
6. To enter into contracts, etc ...
the tramways are to be built with heavy steel girder rails, suitable for the use of mechanical power if hereafter adopted.
Capital authorised up to £60,000 in £5 shares.
The Directors: H. L. Corlett, J. Hardcastle, J. R. Jolly, L. S. Northcote.
The Engineer: Thomas Floyd, C.E., F.G.S.
Secretary: A. J. Davis.
Line contractor: Chas. Lovedale.

Once construction work commenced, it proceeded at the rate of about 500 yards a week, and was completed early in April 1881. Cost of the line, including granite sett paving was £4,282.14. 2d per mile. On 2nd April, as a "thank you" to those employed on laying the track, Lord Teynham invited 50 men to a "tea" provided by him.

In May 1881, the engineer asked the Board of Trade to arrange for the line to be inspected, suggesting that "it would be convenient at the end of the month". He must have said that with some conviction as there were no cars available to run upon the line. However, at

Car No. 10, bound for Greenwich, standing outside the main gate of Woolwich Arsenal. The reference to "Bostal Heath" was optimistic, as the tram terminus was a mile from the heath. (Courtesy: D. W. K. Jones)

3 a.m. on Saturday 28th May, the first of the six cars ordered, arrived at Cage Lane depot. This was a double deck vehicle having seats for 16 passengers inside and 16 ouside. It was well appointed, being provided with crimson cushions on the inside seats. At noon, it was out on the road, making a special journey for test purposes, the driver and horses being loaned from the London Tramways Company.

Inspection and Opening

Maj. Gen. Hutchinson inspected the line on Monday, 30th May, when he walked the whole length of the route from Woolwich to Plumstead Church behind the special car. At Plumstead, he commented that, at one time, he had been a churchwarden at St. Nicholas' Church and was pleased to renew his acquaintance with the place, "even if the churchyard did seem more crowded". After this interlude, he boarded the special car to return to Woolwich. He authorised the use of the line, subject to an alteration being made to the canopies of the car he was on, and to the rest of them when they arrived.

Public service was promised as from Whit Saturday, 4th June, by which time three cars were available, together with 20 horses out of a stud of 41 ordered from a farm in Wales. The first depot and stables, a temporary affair, was sited on the south side of High Street, Plumstead a few yards into Cage Lane on the east side.

On the opening day, after the ceremonial runs in the morning, the fare paying passengers took to the cars. With only three at work, a ten to fifteen minute service was the best that could be hoped for. Even so, 11,776 passengers were carried in the first ten days. The fares charged were:-

Powis Street or Beresford Street	&	Middle Gates	1d
Arsenal Main Gates	&	Plumstead Railway Station	1d
Middle Gates	&	Plumstead Church	1d
Beyond these distances			2d

It was not long before the first accident involving a tramcar was reported in the local press and was the cause of considerable alarm. On Sunday, 26th June 1881 at about 5 p.m. a car overturned opposite Inverness Place caused, it was said, by the horses becoming restive. The car was heavily loaded and several of the passengers were injured. There was an enquiry which, while inconclusive, gave indications of more than a suspicion of deliberate action, by stones being placed in the lines to upset the car. The sixth new car was put into service to make up the shortage, while the damaged vehicle was stored at the back of the depot, with the intention that eventually, it would be repaired.

By early July, with few passengers using the line from Beresford Square to Nile Street, it was decided "for the time being, until the Greenwich extension is built", to withdraw service along Beresford Street. However, by the end of October, so few people were travelling along Powis Street that it was decided to close this section as well, leaving only the section between Beresford Square and Plumstead in operation. Next, it was announced that due to poor patronage generally, the car service would be reduced for the winter, which would result in the discharge of several drivers and conductors, together with the manager! However, by mid-November, there appeared to have been a change in the fortunes of the company, as it was announced that improvements could be expected. It seems that the company was in crisis. Frederick W. Huddleston took on the task, as the new manager of getting them out of it, in company with J. R. Jolly, J. P. one of the directors, who had energetically pursued the aims of the company since its inception.

The Greenwich Extension

The new company made application to the Board of Trade at the end of 1880 for authority to construct an extension to the line from High Street, Woolwich, onwards to Greenwich. The **Woolwich & South-East London Tramways Order, 1881** as confirmed by the **Tramways Orders Confirmation (No. 1) Act, 1881 (Vic. cap. cv),** which amended the Woolwich & Plumstead Tramways Order, 1880 authorised the construction of a tramway 2 mls. 6 f. 5.2 ch. long, of which about half was single track, from the north end of Beresford Street, through High Street, Church Street, Woolwich Lower Road and Trafalgar Road, to terminate near Old Woolwich Road, end-on with the line of the London Tramways Company. There was, however, considerable misgiving by the Board of Trade and other authorities over the narrowness of parts of High Street, Woolwich which, in some places was less than 16 feet wide. After considerable discussion, headed in the main by Mr. Jolly, all parties including the Board of Trade agreed to the line being laid. As a result, the company in turn agreed to assist in the work of widening the narrowest sections of road wherever possible, so that a minimum of 16 feet should be obtained.

A condition imposed upon tramway operators was that a minimum distance of 15 inches should always be maintained between the widest parts of any two cars passing one another. In the case of the narrow gauge cars used in Woolwich, these had a maximum width of 6 ft. 4 in., which meant that the track centres should have been 7 ft. 10 in. apart. At some passing places however, this distance was 7 ft. 6 in. which was the cause of some concern to the Board of Trade. Further, it had been agreed that double track could only be employed where the width of the road was more than 30 ft., but could be used at the discretion of the Board in places where more than 22 ft. could be obtained. In the case of parts of both High Street and Church Street, Woolwich, it was not possible to obtain more than 22 ft., and an agreement was reached whereby the "double-single" arrangement could be employed. This, in reality was double line laid with track centres at less than the statutory width, which opened out in places to normal width where cars could pass. Special gas-powered lamps were to be installed at the expense of the company at each passing place, in order that drivers would be able to drive safely between the points.

The method of construction of the tracks in Plumstead and Woolwich was quite unusual, consisting of a continuous inverted steel channel upon which each rail was bolted, two channel sections being used for each pair of rails. Gauge was maintained by the rigidity of the all-metal structure with, in this case, the channels being buried in mass concrete. It had been the intention to use the same method for the extension, but the Greenwich Board of Works refused to allow this. Instead, the company had to use the more traditional method, with the rails being supported in cast-iron chairs, each laid on a baseplate 3 feet long, the whole lot standing on a concrete bed.

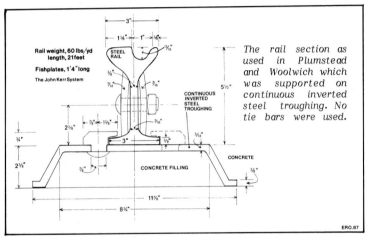

The rail section as used in Plumstead and Woolwich which was supported on continuous inverted steel troughing. No tie bars were used.

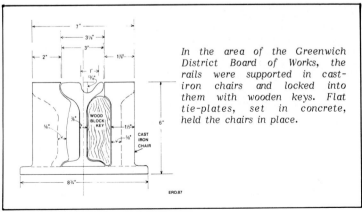

In the area of the Greenwich District Board of Works, the rails were supported in cast-iron chairs and locked into them with wooden keys. Flat tie-plates, set in concrete, held the chairs in place.

Construction commenced during the spring of 1882, being completed at the end of August. A test car was run over the whole route on 7th September. The company, meantime, had concluded an agreement with the freeholders of a piece of land on the west side of Cage Lane, upon which to build a depot and stables at an estimated cost of £4,000. Six more cars were also on order, together with the horses needed to haul them.

Maj. Gen. Hutchinson, at his inspection on 18th September was confronted with an irate representative from Charlton Vestry, who protested that single lines had been laid in some places where double should have been. Hutchinson agreed, refusing to sanction the line for use until the alterations were made. On 20th November, he finally authorised its use and services commenced on the following day.

And so the line was opened, the company advertising that "now that the line is open 'through to Westminster', the people of Plumstead and Woolwich may now have a two-hour drive with coachman, footman and pair for sixpence". This really meant that passengers used the narrow gauge cars as far as Greenwich and then changed to those operated by the London Tramways Company. Through fare was set at 3d, with 1d and 2d intermediate stages, and cars ran every eight minutes.

In January 1883, an attempt was made to extend the branch line westwards from the end of Powis Street, to connect up with the main line, but permission was not forthcoming. This left the branch as a rather useless appendage, which was closed to regular traffic shortly afterwards. The company contented itself with providing more passing places on various parts of the line.

Staff Problems

At this time, some agitation was apparent in the ranks of the drivers and conductors, as they, in company with the men from other London companies were attempting to form a trade union in order to improve their pay and working conditions. To some extent they were successful, probably more so than with some of the larger companies. In general, the management were mindful of their obligations to the staff, and this is evident from the following:-
"In order to give the drivers and conductors on the Woolwich line the opportunity of eating their dinners in warmth and comfort and of otherwise sheltering while waiting to go on duty, suitable accommodation has been provided on ground in High Street Plumstead. A large tramcar has been converted into a shelter with a fireplace and convenience for keeping the dinners warm for the men, who appreciate the extra comfort afforded to them". It is quite possible that this was the body of the car damaged in the accident soon after the line opened.

The Woolwich Free Ferry

There had been ferry services of sorts plying between the banks of the Thames for centuries. With the coming of the railway to North Woowich, a steam ferry service was started between North Woolwich and the Town, for which a fare of 1d was charged. During the 1880s, the Metropolitan Board of Works agreed to provide a free steam ferry between the same two points. Construction of piers was put in hand and boats purchased, while the official opening was set for 23rd March 1889, with considerable ceremony.

111

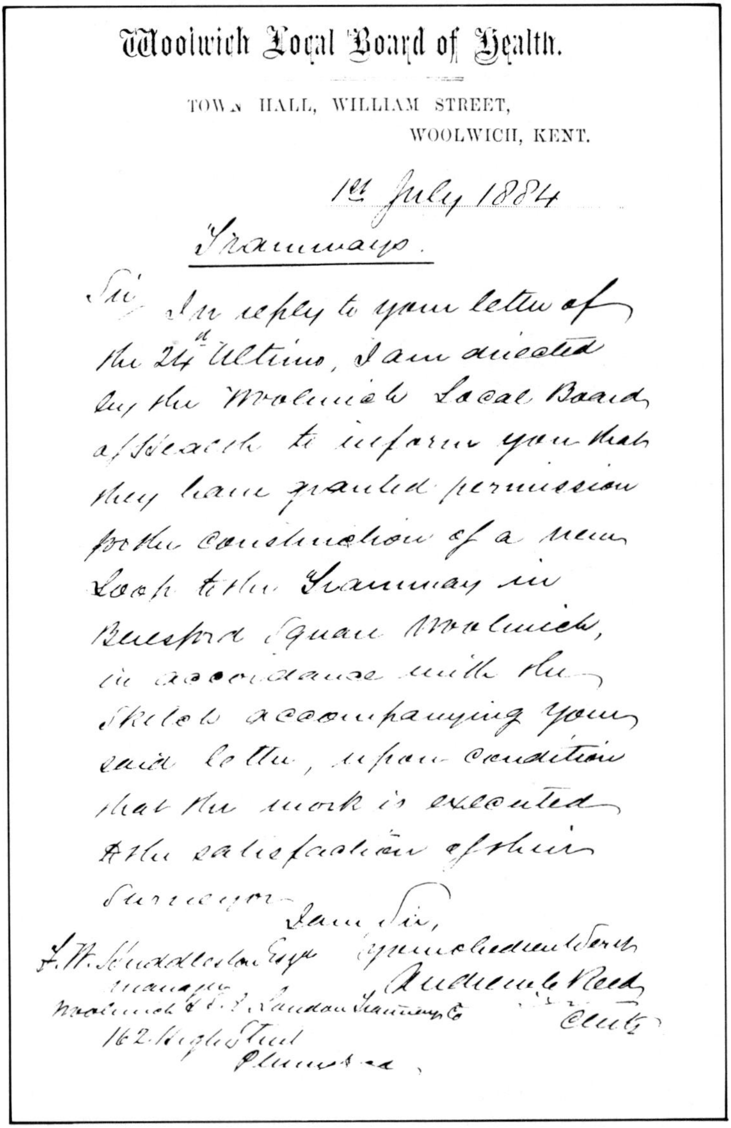

Woolwich Local Board of Health.

TOWN HALL, WILLIAM STREET,
WOOLWICH, KENT.

1st July 1884

Tramways.

Sir, In reply to your letter of
the 24th Ultimo, I am directed
by the Woolwich Local Board
of Health to inform you that
they have granted permission
for the construction of a new
Loop to the Tramway in
Beresford Square Woolwich,
in accordance with the
Sketch accompanying your
said letter, upon condition
that the work is executed
to the satisfaction of their
Surveyor.

I am Sir,

F. W. Huddleston Esq.
manager,
Woolwich & S.E. London Tramway Co.
162 High Street
Plumstead.

Superintendent Works

Andrew L. Reed
Clerk

A letter from the clerk of the Woolwich Board of Health, authorising the company to lay in a passing loop at Beresford Square, Woolwich.

Under the terms of the Local Government Act, 1888, a new body, the London County Council was to take office on 1st April 1889 to replace the Metropolitan Board of Works. It happened that the new County Council took over on 21st March, which meant that it was the Council and not the Board of Works who had the pleasant duty

112

The original boats on the Woolwich Free Ferry service were later joined by two other, the "Gordon", seen here, and the "Squires".

(Courtesy: J. H. Price)

of inaugurating the new ferry service. The two new boats, "Duncan" and "London" conveyed the party over the river at 3 p.m. and back again later in the afternoon. These boats were unusual and novel. They could turn round in their own length; go forwards, backwards and even sideways with the aplomb of a water ballerina. They proved to be of great value to the people of the district.

It was also convenient that, not more than two or three minutes' walk from the southern pier of the ferry, the trams of the Woolwich Company plied on their journeys to and from Plumstead and Greenwich. They took advantage of this fact by boldly advertising that the cars ran "TO & FROM THE FREE FERRY", which legend appeared on the rocker panels of some of the cars.

Express Cars

An unusual service provided by the company was the running of "dinner cars" between Woolwich and Plumstead for the benefit of Royal Arsenal employees. In September 1893, a local newspaper reporter induced an acquaintance to travel on one of the cars and give his impressions of the journey.

"Hearing that Ladies and all well-dressed men are rigorously excluded from the cars running without stopping between Beresford Square and Plumstead Church, a 'gentleman' dressed up as an 'Arsenal Workman' with a view to observing 'the carrying-on in the express cars'. He was challenged with the query 'are you a working man?' and managed to satisfy the conductor. He found the car laden with Arsenal mechanics all eager to get to dinner, their wives knowing 'to a tick' the exact moment they will arrive. On the out and return journeys, a lot of wit, well worth listening to, is flying about on the cars and the men are a jovial crew. The reason that Ladies and Strangers are not carried is that no-one is allowed to get up who cannot jump up and get down whilst the cars are running at a fast rate. All who travel by them are trained to this and never meet with an accident. For the cars to stop whilst the Workmen are hurrying to and from dinner would be treason and upset the whole arrangement; the line being cleared of all other cars to make way for the express to pass".

The Later Years

The company continued to re-arrange, increase and extend the number of passing places on the line, in order to provide as efficient a service as narrow streets and horse traction would allow. During 1891, Frederick Huddleston retired, T. J. W. Dudding taking his place, while towards the end of 1892, the secretary, A. J. Davis was replaced by A. W. Good.

The signal lamps earlier referred to had apparently been used only fitfully. On 21st February 1893, the company asked permission to dispense with them altogether, as road widening and track doubling would make them obsolete. While Maj. Gen. Hutchinson agreed in principle, he insisted that they be put in order and used until the work had been completed. He inspected the new work on 25th September, at the same time authorising the removal of the lamps.

In 1901, Bexley Urban District Council obtained powers to enable it to construct an electric tramway from Bexleyheath and Welling in Kent, then through East Wickham to the boundary with London and the Metropolitan Borough of Woolwich, and continue the line down Wickham Lane to Plumstead Church. When this line opened in 1903, the Woolwich Company extended its line by a few yards to meet the Bexley cars end-on.

Under LCC Control

The shadow of municipalisation materialised early in 1901 when the LCC began exploratory talks regarding takeover. The first possible date for the purchase of the Plumstead to Woolwich section was 4th June 1902, with 21st November 1903 for the Woolwich to Greenwich section. During the course of the discussions, the LCC referred to it as "a good purchase", but admitted that the narrow gauge line would have to be completely rebuilt. Fares charged by the company were higher than the Council would like them to be, while staff wages were lower and working hours longer. It was expected that the extra costs which would be incurred would be about £5,000 per annum, plus the cost of eventually renewing the whole line.

A figure of £85,813. 2. 8d had been mentioned by the company as its valuation of the undertaking, which was totally rejected by the LCC. Due to the disagreement, arbitration was resorted to in order to resolve the dispute. Maj. Philip Cardew, R.E. inspected the undertaking on 21st October 1904, following this up during December 1904 and January 1905 with his enquiry. On 16th February, he announced that the sum to be paid by the LCC should be £46,152. 3. 1d, plus an agreed sum of £515 for consumable stores, such as food and bedding for the horses. Vesting day was to be 1st June 1905.

With the transfer of the tramway to the LCC, all staff with the exception of the management were taken into Council employment. Rolling stock consisted of 32 cars, for which there was a stud of 200 horses. Ordinary services were worked with 17 cars, with another seven being used during the busy hours, while on Sundays, up to 22 were in use depending upon the time of year.

Three cars stand outside the main gate of the Royal Arsenal at 1 p.m. on a summer day in 1904, awaiting passengers for the "dinner" run.
(Commercial view)

The Cars

The Metropolitan Railway Carriage & Wagon Company Ltd. received the first order from the company for six double deck five-window narrow gauge cars with "knifeboard" top deck seating. It was specified "that the seats and railings on the roof and the spiral staircases be made so that they can be easily removed". This instruction was in accordance with the original idea of the company management, that the cars could be used as either double deck or single deck as required, depending upon the amount of traffic offered. Cost of these was £165 each.

Six more were ordered from Metropolitan in the summer of 1882, to be delivered to Plumstead prior to the opening of the Greenwich extension. These were of heavier construction, being two-horse six-window double deck cars, the cost of which was £209 each. In 1884, ten more were purchased for £221 each, but in the following years, five of these were taken out of service, possibly for rebuilding. Things then remained static until 1892, when the five delicensed cars were brought back into service. Five more were purchased in 1895-96, at a book value of £100 each, which probably means that they were secondhand, to be followed in 1900-01 by another six at £115 each and finally, two more in 1902 at £60 each. During the life of the company, several of the cars were damaged, two so seriously that they were written off the company books.

There is some uncertainty about the colour scheme used on the cars, if indeed any definite livery was maintained. Various colours have been recorded, including light blue and pale yellow, with deep maroon in later years. Reference to photographs shows that the earlier cars at least, had a light-coloured livery, with panels lined out in brown or black and the fleet number of each vehicle shown within a "garter" device in the centre of the waist panels. As was usual, names of places served were signwritten on boards fitted to the end panels over the platforms, as well as on boards mounted above the saloon windows and on the stair stringers.

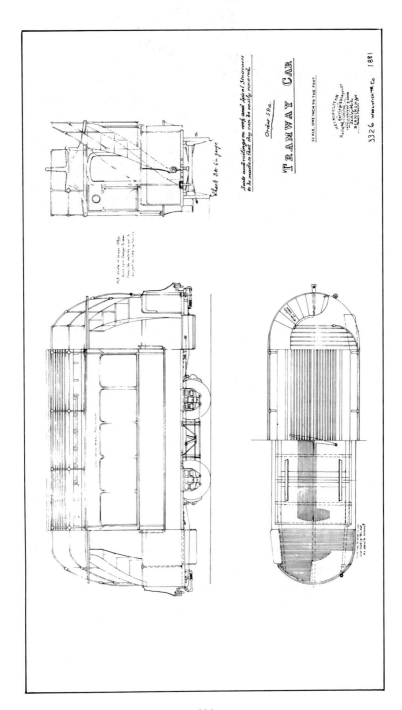

TRAMWAY CAR

Order 59a.

SCALE, ONE INCH TO THE FOOT

Seats and railings on roof and paint. Staircovers
to be made so that they can be easily removed.

METROPOLITAN
Railway Carriage
WAGON COMPANY LIMITED
Saltley Works
BIRMINGHAM

3326 Woolwich R.Co. 1881

Wheels 3ft. 6in gauge

At the workshop at Lakedale Road depot, all car repairs and renovations were carried out. No. 25, in LCC livery, has just had its annual repaint.
(O. W. Thynne)

The Depot

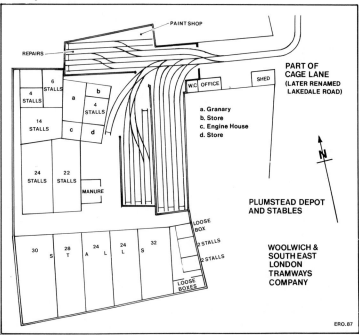

PAINT SHOP

REPAIRS

6 STALLS

4 STALLS

a

b

4 STALLS

14 STALLS

c

d

24 STALLS

22 STALLS

MANURE

W.C OFFICE

SHED

a. Granary
b. Store
c. Engine House
d. Store

30 S

28 T

24 A

24 L

32 S

LOOSE BOX

2 STALLS

2 STALLS

LOOSE BOXES

N

PART OF
CAGE LANE
(LATER RENAMED
LAKEDALE ROAD)

PLUMSTEAD DEPOT
AND STABLES

WOOLWICH &
SOUTH EAST
LONDON
TRAMWAYS
COMPANY

ERO.87

117

Fares and Tickets

In common with most other undertakings, the fare structure of the company was quite simple, passengers being able to travel for about two miles for one penny. From the beginning, an overlapping fare stage system was in use, with 1d white, 2d pink or magenta and 3d blue tickets on issue. All passengers, whether adult or child, were charged the same fares. Luggage carried on the cars was charged for at the rate of 2d per package, a special printed section on the tickets catering for this.

As was also customary, the stages were progressively laid out, being in "ladder" fashion on the 1d and 2d tickets and "landscape" on the 3d through fare ticket, the "up" journeys from Plumstead to Greenwich on the left and "down" on the right in each case.

Workmen were catered for by being able to travel the whole length of the line for 1½d single or 3d return, with 1d sections between, but passengers requiring this facility were only carried early in the mornings before 7.30 a.m. One unusual feature was that "dinner hour" return tickets were available to workmen travelling between Plumstead and Woolwich. These had to be purchased at the same time as the normal morning journey ticket was obtained, and handed to the conductor of the "dinner" car for the midday journey.

Fare stages shown on the 1d tickets were:-

Plumstead Church	and	Beresford Square (and vice versa)
Plumstead Station	and	Free Ferry
Middle Gates	and	Dockyard Main Entrance
Beresford Square	and	"Lord Howick"
Free Ferry	and	"Horse & Groom"
Dockyard Main Entrance	and	Church Lane, Charlton
"Lord Howick"	and	Angerstein Railway Bridge
Church Lane, Charlton	and	Greenwich

while those on the 2d tickets were:-

Plumstead Church	and	"Lord Howick"
Middle Gates	and	Church Lane, Charlton
Beresford Square	and	Greenwich

After the acquisition of the company, the fares structure remained intact until the line was cut back at the Greenwich end, to allow for the electrification of the line as far east as Blackwall Lane. The through ordinary single fare was then reduced to 2½d, and the workman return fare reduced to 2d. Fare stages remained as before.

Chapter 11
The South London Tramways Company

The area of operations of this company consisted of a long strip of suburbia on the south side of the River Thames, stretching from Wandsworth in the south-west, through Battersea, "Clapham Junction", Nine Elms, Vauxhall, part of Lambeth and part of Southwark to the north of the "Elephant & Castle" public house, Newington, and to a point near London Bridge. The districts of Southwark and Lambeth have been mentioned in connection with the operations of the London Tramways Company.

Vauxhall was originally the site of a manor owned by a Norman knight, Fulke de Breaute, in the thirteenth century at the time of King John. He named his house "Fulke's Hall" or, as it came to be known in later years, "Fauke's Hall", subsequently being declined to Vauxhall. The famous gardens were in use for about 200 years, closing on 25th May 1859. Dealing next with Battersea, which was virtually in the centre of the operational area of the company, this town has a long history, as being a residential district within easy reach of the metropolis, it became the home ground for many historically well-known personalities.

"Clapham Junction" is just a name. Until the coming of the railways, the area was an outpost of Battersea, with lavender fields through which Lavender Hill now runs. It is some two miles from Clapham, but the railway companies made this the junction point of a number of lines which they called Clapham Junction. Just over a mile to the west lies Wandsworth, whose name derives from the River Wandle which empties into the Thames just north of the town.

Proposals had been put forward in 1878 for a tramway to be built by the Wandsworth Road Tramways; in 1879 for the South-west Metropolitan Tramways (who had obtained a Provisional Order) and the South London Tramways who eventually obtained an Act in that year. All these proposals covered virtually the same roads. The **South London Tramways Company Act, 1879 (42-43 Vic. cap. cxcvii)** authorised the following tramways:-
No. 15. 6 f. 9.58 ch. long, from Plough Road, along York Road and Battersea Park Road to the junction with Albert Road.
Nos. 15A & 15B. Passing places.
Nos. 16 & 16A. Two lines, each 5 f. 2.71 ch. long, from end of Tramway No. 15, along Battersea Park Road to Queens Road.
No. 17. 9.20 ch. long, from Tramway No. 16 and crossing Queens Road.
Nos. 18 & 18A. Two lines, each 3 f. 7.74 ch. long, from Tramway No.17, along Battersea Park Road to junction of Moat Street.
No. 19. 2 f. 7.86 ch. long, from Tramway No. 18, along Battersea Park Road and Nine Elms Lane to railway crossings near Wandsworth Road.
No. 19A. Passing place.

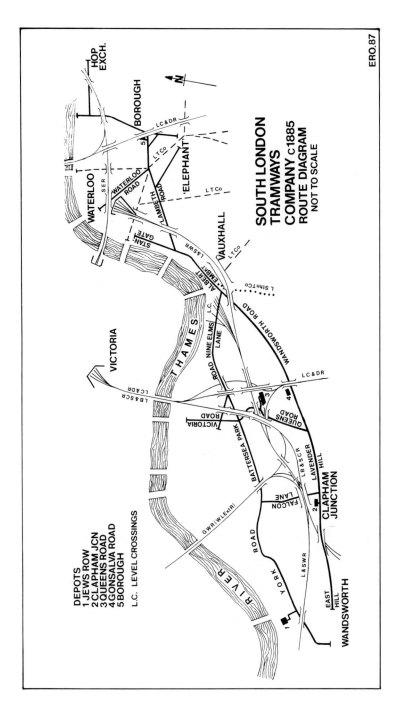

SOUTH LONDON
TRAMWAYS
COMPANY c1885
ROUTE DIAGRAM
NOT TO SCALE

ERO.87

DEPOTS
1 JEWS ROW
2 CLAPHAM JCN
3 QUEENS ROAD
4 GONSALVA ROAD
5 BOROUGH

L.C. LEVEL CROSSINGS

HOP EXCH.

BOROUGH

WATERLOO

ELEPHANT

VAUXHALL

VICTORIA

WANDSWORTH

CLAPHAM JUNCTION

THAMES

RIVER

WATERLOO ROAD

LAMBETH ROAD

STAN. GATE

ALBERT EMBKT.

NINE ELMS LANE

WANDSWORTH ROAD

QUEENS ROAD

LAVENDER HILL

FALCON LANE

BATTERSEA PARK ROAD

VICTORIA ROAD

YORK ROAD

EAST HILL

LC & DR

LT Co

SER

L & SWR

LTCo

L Sthn Tco

L.C.

LB & SCR

LC & DR

GWR (W L Ex IR)

L & SWR

LB & SCR

The promotors were W. G. Beattie, A. Chadbourne, H. L. Corlett and C. J. Lethbridge. The engineer was A. J. D. Cameron, M. Inst. C. E.

Authorised capital was to be £70,000, issued as £10 shares. Any borrowing on mortgage was not to exceed £17,000. Fares were to be charged at the rate of 1d per mile, but a minimum sum of 2d could be charged. Special cheap fares for workmen were to be instituted. A restriction placed upon the company was that no bells were to be used, either attached to cars or to horses, without the written consent of the road authority.

Wandsworth Board of Works agreed to the use of the Barker system of track construction. The rail weighed 52 lbs/yard with the continuous angle iron of 30 lbs/yard securely rivetted to the rail head section. The space between the rails was to be paved with materials as required by the Wandsworth Board. The completed lines were inspected by Maj. Gen. Hutchinson on 21st December 1880. Opening day was to be 1st January 1881, but there is doubt whether any service was worked until 5th when the line was stated as "being open". The depot was at Queens Road, Battersea where 28 cars and 108 horses were housed.

The company next obtained the **South London Tramways (Extensions) Act, 1880 (43-44 Vic. cap. xvi)** authorising the following lines:-
No. 1. 3 f. 7.31 ch. long, from the south side of Chelsea Bridge to Battersea Park Road by Queens Road.
Nos. 1A & 1B. Passing places.
No. 2. 5 f. 6.18 ch. long, from Tramway No. 1, across Battersea Park Road and along Queens Road to Wandsworth Road.
Nos. 2A, 2B & 2C. Passing places.
No. 3. 5.22 ch. long, from Tramway No. 2 to a junction with Wandsworth Road.
No. 4. 1 ch. long, junction line from Queens Road to Wandsworth Road.
No. 5. 4 f. 4.45 ch. long, from Tramway No. 4, along Wandsworth Road to Westbury Street.
Nos. 5A & 5B. Passing places.
No. 6. A connecting line at Wandsworth Road into Lavender Hill.
No. 7. 0.95 ch. long, connecting Queens Road with Lavender Hill.
No. 8. 2.20 ch. long, from Tramways Nos. 6 & 7, along Lavender Hill to Wycliffe Grove.
No. 9. 5 f. 6.10 ch. long, from Tramway No. 8, along Lavender Hill to St. John's Road.
Nos. 9A, 9B & 9C. Passing places.
No. 10. 3.55 ch. long, from Tramway No. 9 into St. John's Hill.
No. 11. 6 f. 6.45 ch. long, from Tramway No. 10, along St. John's Hill and East Hill to Alma Road.
Nos. 11A, 11B & 11C. Passing places.
No. 11D. 5.6 ch. long, a connecting line between St. John's Hill and Lavender Hill.
No. 12. 3.25 ch. long, a connecting line from Tramways Nos. 10 & 11 into Falcon Lane.
No. 13. 3.45 ch. long, a junction line connecting Lavender Hill and Falcon Lane.
No. 14. 3 f. 6.75 ch. long, in Falcon Lane to Battersea Park Road.
No. 14A. Passing place.
No. 15. 4 f. 8.31 ch. long, from Battersea Park Road, along Bridge Road to Battersea Bridge.
Nos. 15A & 15B. Passing places.
No. 16. 3 f. 8.24 ch. long, from Plough Road, along York Road to Jews Row, Wandsworth.
No. 16A & 16B. Passing places.

Clapham Junction, Lavender Hill in the 1890s, with a well-loaded car, No. 92, seen working on the Westminster service. (Commercial view)

No. 17. 2 f. 1.21 ch. long, from Tramway No. 16 to near North Street.
No. 17A. Passing place.
No. 18. 3.63 ch. long, from Tramway No. 17, along North Street.
No. 19. 1 f. 0.10 ch. long, from Tramway No. 18, along North Street to High Street, Wandsworth.
Additional capital was authorised up to £75,000, together with further borrowing on mortgage up to £18,500.
Completion of the works to be made within two years.

The next line to be completed was the section between Chelsea Bridge and Wandsworth Road along Queens Road, and this was successfully inspected by Maj. Gen. Hutchinson on 23rd April 1881.

Early in 1881, the Engineer, A. J. D. Cameron, submitted the design for a "modified" rail for consideration by the Wandsworth Board, with the idea of using it in future construction. Although the weight of the 24 ft. lengths of rail, at 52 lbs/yard was similar to the approved type already in use, it was the method of assembly that was different. The sections on the original type were bolted together and the angle irons were continuous, but those on the "modified" type were held together with keys and pins, while the angle irons were in 15-inch lengths and were only laid at 3-feet intervals.

The Board of Trade demurred over its use, while the Wandsworth Board appeared to object, but later events proved otherwise. In any case, the Board of Trade relented about 18 months later, authorising its use elsewhere.

Resulting from this rebuff, Cameron found himself in some difficulty as he had intended to use the method on the York Road line, stating that he had received permission from Wandsworth to so do. Due to the road widenings not having been completed at York Road, he had set his contractor to work on the Falcon Lane (later Road) line, using the "modified" rails which should have been put in at York Road.

Having laid the line, he asked the Board of Trade to arrange for an inspection to be made and, at the same time, for the Nine Elms Lane line, which had been laid with an approved type of rail, to be inspected also. It was therefore left to Maj. Gen. Hutchinson to make a decision regarding the suitability of the rails that had been laid in Falcon Lane. On 19th March, the Inspector approved the use of both sections, but demanded an explanation from the company as to why the "modified" rails had been laid. Cameron still insisted that Wandsworth had agreed to its use at York Road, and thought that it could be used elsewhere. Eventually, Wandsworth Board admitted that it had agreed to its use in York Road and the matter was dropped.

The company next obtained the **South London Tramways Act, 1881 (44-45 Vic. cap. clxxxiv)** which authorised the construction of tramways:-
No. 45. A single line, 7.40 ch. long, from Vauxhall Cross, along Albert Embankment to High Street, Lambeth.
No. 46. A double line, 3 f. 8.85 ch. long, along Albert Embankment.
No. 47. A single line, 2.40 ch. long, along Albert Embankment.
No. 48. A double line, 3 f. 2 ch. long, from Tramway No. 47 to Stangate.
No. 49. A single line, 1 ch. long, in Stangate.
No. 50. A single line, 1 f. 0.42 ch. long, from Albert Embankment into Church Street (Lambeth Road).
No. 51. A double line, 4 f. 3.75 ch. long, from Tramway No. 50, along Lambeth Road to St. George's Road.
No. 52. A single line, 3.84 ch. long, from Tramway No. 51 in Lambeth Road.
No. 53. A double line, 2 f. 7.60 ch. long, from Tramway No. 52, along Lambeth Road, across St. George's Circus, along Borough Road into Southwark Bridge Road near Collinson Street.
No. 54. A single line, 4.10 ch. long, a continuation of Tramway No. 53.
No. 55. A double line, 3 f. 4.53 ch. long, from Tramway No. 54, along Southwark Bridge Road to Sumner Street.
No. 56. About 1 f. from Sumner Street to the terminus at the south side of Southwark Bridge.
No. 57. A double line, 1 f. 1.50 ch. long, from Keppel Street (Southwark Bridge) into Southwark Street.
No. 58. A single line, 7.50 ch. long, from Tramway No. 57 to Redcross Street.
No. 59. A single line, 1.90 ch. long, from Albert Embankment to Church Street (Lambeth Road).
No. 60. A single line, 0.87 ch. long, from Battersea Park Road into Victoria Road (Queens Road).
No. 61. A single line, 1.08 ch. long, from Battersea Park Road into Queens Road.
No. 62. A single line, 1.95 ch. long, from St. John's Hill into Falcon Road.
No. 63. A single line, in Queens Road, for depot access.

With the earlier dispute over the use of the "modified" rail still fresh in the minds of all concerned, Cameron asked whether it could be used where short connecting lines were required, to which both the Board of Trade and Wandsworth agreed. The lines, numbered 60, 61, 62 and 63 in the 1881 Act were dealt with in this way.

Once across the boundary from Wandsworth into Lambeth, the company had to use another type of rail. This time, it was the "Barker" section and fortunately, the Vestries of St. George, Southwark and St. Saviour, Southwark both agreed to its use. However, each insisted on a different arrangement when it came to paving!

123

More proposals were made in 1882, which were intended to complete the network, together with a re-numbering of some of the Tramways already authorised but not yet built. The **South London Tramways Act, 1882 (45-46 Vic. cap. cxcii)** authorised the following:-

No.1. A single line, 9.50 ch. long, in Wandsworth Road from Westbury Street to Pensbury Street.

No.2. A double line, 2.50 ch. long, from Tramway No.1 to Albion Road.

No.3. A single line, 1 f. 6.20 ch. long, from Tramway No.2 to Milton Street.

No.4. A double line, 2.50 ch. long, a continuation of Tramway No.3.

No.5. A single line, 1 f. 6.20 ch. long, from Tramway No.4 to Brookland Road.

No.6. A double line, 2.50 ch. long, a continuation of Tramway No.5.

No.7. A single line, 1 f. 6.20 ch. long, from Tramway No.6 to near Pascal Street.

No.8. A double line, 2.50 ch. long, a continuation of Tramway No.7.

No.9. A single line, 1 f. 7.20 ch. long, from Tramway No.8 to near Miles Street.

No.10. A double line, 5.85 ch. long, a continuation of Tramway No.9.

No.11. A single line, 1 f. 2.25 ch. long, from Tramway No.10 to near Clarks Place.

No.12. A double line, 3.35 ch. long, from Tramway No.11 to a point near Vauxhall Cross.

No.13. A single line, 1.40 ch. long, from Tramway No.12 to terminate at the commencement of Tramway No.45.(1881 Act).

No.19. A single line, 1 f. 3.45 ch. long, in Nine Elms Lane by a junction with the existing tramway, to near Wandsworth Road.

No.20. A double line, 1.40 ch. long, from Tramways Nos. 19 to 10.

No.21. A double line, 1.20 ch. long, from Victoria Road to the south-east gates of Battersea Park.

No.22. A single line, 9.20 ch. long, from Tramway No. 21 to Prince of Wales Road near Victoria Road.

No.22A. A single line, 0.90 ch. long, from Tramway No. 1 (1880 Act), to the termination of Tramway No. 22.

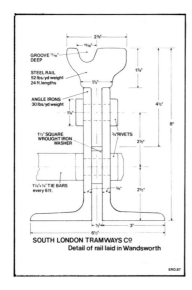

SOUTH LONDON TRAMWAYS C?
Detail of rail laid in Wandsworth

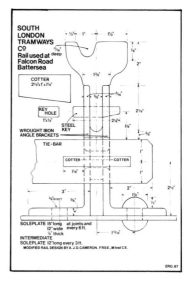

No. 23. A double line, 2.50 ch. long, from Tramway No. 22 to existing tramway in Battersea Park Road.

No. 24. A single line, 1 ch. long, in Battersea Park Road (passing place).

No. 25. A single line, 2 ch. long, a connecting line in Westminster Bridge Road near the Obelisk, terminating at Tramway No. 23 (1881 Act).

No. 26. A double line, 6.90 ch. long, between Southwark Bridge Road and Borough Road.

No. 27. A single line, 4.20 ch. long, from Tramway No. 26 to Southwark Bridge Road near Lancaster Street.

No. 28. A double line, 2.65 ch. long, from Tramway No. 27 to Southwark Bridge Road near York Street.

No. 29. A single line, 0.50 ch. long, from Tramway No. 28 to Southwark Bridge Road near York Street.

No. 30. A double line, 1 ch. long, from Tramway No. 53 (1881 Act) near Lancaster Street, to its junction with Borough Road.

No. 31. A single line, 8.45 ch. long, from Tramway No. 30, then along Lancaster Street to Southwark Bridge Road.

Additional capital of £40,000 was authorised, with extra borrowing powers up to £10,000.

Of interest is the purchase by the South London Tramways Company under Section 42 of the 1882 Act, of lines which were authorised by the terms of the **Tramways Orders Confirmation (No. 3) Act, 1881 (44-45 Vic. cap. clxiv)** whereby the City of London & Metropolitan Tramways Company Limited was empowered to construct and maintain:-

(a) A line from St. George's Circus, along Waterloo Road, 2 f. 8 ch. in length, double track except for 3 ch. at St. George's Circus.

(b) A line along St. George's Road from Lambeth Road to Nelson Place, 2 f. 3.60 ch. in length.

(c) A double line junction from Lambeth Road to St. George's Road, 1.40 ch. in length.

Terms of purchase were that in exchange for £1,500 in cash, the City of London & Metropolitan Company would hand over all rights to this line, together with £733. 3. 8d in a bank account. The South

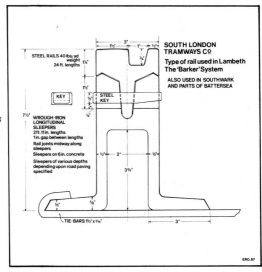

The three diagrams show the differences between the types of rail used by the company.

Car No. 55, seen in 1895, standing at Wandsworth, North Street. The top deck "knifeboard" seating was retained on these cars.

(Courtesy: P. J. Davis)

London Company agreed and formalities were completed on 23rd June 1882. As yet, nothing had been constructed.

Work eventually commenced on the outstanding sections of line in Wandsworth, much of it authorised by the three earlier Acts. As has been seen with the "modified" rail affair, the Wandsworth Board gave the appearance of not being the easiest of people to deal with. The position with regard to work in York Road was not made any easier by Wandsworth demanding £4,000 from the company as its share of the road widening costs, but which, after considerable objection, was reduced to £750.

On 10th June 1882, Maj. Gen. Hutchinson inspected the tramways along East Hill, Lavender Hill and Wandsworth Road as far as Westbury Street, and authorised their use. Services commenced on 13th or 14th June. There was then a break of some eight months before the lines in York Road and North Street, Wandsworth, together with those in Lambeth and Southwark were completed. On 24th February 1883, the Major General inspected the lines along Bridge Road (Battersea), from Plough Road to North Street Wandsworth, in Lambeth Road, Southwark Bridge Road and Borough Road. The lines in Wandsworth however, were not opened to traffic until 6th May, while the remainder had to wait until 29th May.

Due to delays that had occurred during construction of the lines, it became necessary for the company to obtain a "time and money" Act, in order that the powers obtained by previous Acts did not expire. The **South London Tramways Company Act, 1883 (46-47 Vic. cap. clxvii)** extended the time allowed to complete certain works and also authorised the raising of additional capital.

The next sections to be completed were those at the north-east end of Nine Elms Lane with its complex of railway level crossings, together with the lines at Vauxhall, the Albert Embankment and the short lengths in St. George's Road and Lancaster Street. All these were inspected by Maj. Gen. Hutchinson on 18th August 1883 and opened immediately. Finally, on 9th October 1883, Maj. Marindin inspected

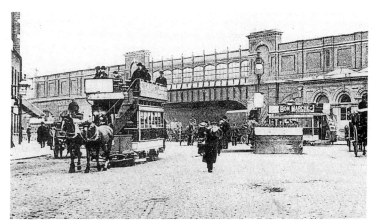

A car bound for Wandsworth passes Vauxhall Station. One of the London Southern Tramways Company cars can be seen in the background.

(Courtesy: P. J. Davis)

and authorised the use of the Wandsworth Road lines north of Westbury Street, those in Lambeth Palace Road to Westminster Bridge Road and a short line in Prince of Wales Road, Battersea.

In 1885, it appears that the company fortunes were at a rather low ebb. In addition to the financial problems being experienced, the Manager, Mr. Jaques, had been down-graded to that of a subordinate officer by the Chairman, as they had disagreed over Jaques' concern for the welfare of the conductors and drivers. Together with one of the directors, Mr. S. J. Wilde, he was also attempting to improve the general working conditions of the crews. All this came to a head when, partly as a result of the bickering, together with the fact that the revenue account was in debt to the sum of £12,995, the shareholders voted the Chairman, W. W. Duncan and one director off the Board. Wilde then became Chairman, while Jaques was restored to his former position. The rest of the Board members were Sir Charles Craufurd, D. P. Sellar, W. Pering Paige and G. F. Fry.

The company returns for 1890 showed an improvement over the 1889 figures, but not sufficient to pay the ordinary shareholders a dividend. The year 1891 was not much better. The first half year's accounts showed a loss, due mainly to continuous very bad weather, and extra expenditure on fresh horses, due to the stud being depleted by the incidence of disease. Traffic expenses were also up due to wage increases.

It will be recalled that the company purchased the Waterloo Road and St. George's Road lines several years earlier. Due however, to severe omnibus competition on the Waterloo Road line, this was running at a loss. The course of action decided upon was to lease it, at £150 per annum to the London Tramways Company, who were willing to connect it at their own expense to their lines in Westminster Bridge Road. The agreement took effect as from 24th July 1891.

Even though the Waterloo Road line had been leased away, it still did not improve the fortunes of the company and in view of the continued competition from omnibuses, it was also decided to abandon the Southwark Bridge Road line. During 1892, over 13½ million passengers were carried on the 13 miles of track owned and operated by the company. There were 86 cars and 715 horses, with which to undertake this task.

The Waterloo Road Line and the LCC

On 1st January 1899 at one minute past midnight, the London County Council became the owner of the assets and services of the London Tramways Company. The lease of the Waterloo Road line was allowed to continue in its original form for the remainder of the term, after which a new agreement, dated 28th July 1899, was concluded with the LCC Tramways for the continuing lease of the line at £600 per annum, payable in quarterly instalments. After one year, the Council purchased the line from the company for £5,276.

The LCC Takes Over

At an LCC meeting on 15th May 1900, the Council expressed its intention of purchasing the parts of the company's lines constructed under the terms of the 1879 Act, of a length of about 2¼ miles in Battersea Park Road and York Road (Nine Elms to Lavender Road). The necessary notice was served on 10th July. To meet this and other expenditure, the Council had set up an appropriation account consisting of £1,750,000 London County Consolidated Stock dating from 6th July 1899. Any additional expenditure would be met by the issue of London County Bills for Tramways for up to £40,000.

The company strenuously resisted this move by the LCC, suggesting that the two parties should instead negotiate for the sale and purchase of the whole undertaking as and when it was all due for consideration. The following year there was a repeat of the compulsory purchase intention, this time with respect to tramways authorised by the South London Tramways (Extensions) Act, 1880, when, at a special Council

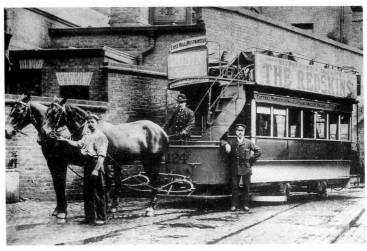

"Garden" seats were fitted on the upper deck of No. 124, seen in Jews Row depot yard in 1903.   *(London County Council)*

meeting held on Tuesday 23rd July 1901, it was resolved to purchase all of the tramways authorised under that Act, as permitted by Section 43 of the Tramways Act of 1870. The lines to be considered were those in Wandsworth Road, York Road, Queens Road and Falcon Lane, about 4¾ miles in all.

At this time too, the Council anticipated that the remainder of the company mileage would be available in 1902 and 1903. Meantime, it was attempting to come to terms with the company, but this was proving to be quite difficult. The directors again stated that they wanted the Council to negotiate for the whole of the assets, with the Council still trying to arrange to purchase the undertaking in a piecemeal fashion. To an outside observer, it might have appeared that both sides were playing for time!

Again, in 1902, the Council resolved to purchase the portions of line authorised by the South London Tramways Company Act of 1881, but the company again resisted this, suggesting - again - that terms be agreed for the sale of the whole undertaking. After further deliberation, the Council finally agreed, on 17th July, by resolution, that an agreement be constructed. This again, proved to be most difficult, as the company contested almost all the valuations put on lines, cars, buildings, horses and equipment. It took the services of an arbitrator, Edward Howard Martin, to finally get the parties to agree, his investigations taking several months. On 1st November 1902, agreement was reached, to which the Board of Trade signified its approval on 21st November.

The undertaking passed to the LCC at midnight on 21st November 1902. Total cost was £232,178.11 3d for 12.73 route miles of track, of which 8.29 miles were double line, 95 cars and 751 horses. Depots and stables were at Jews Row, Wandsworth; Falcon Lane, Clapham Junction; Queens Road, Battersea; Gonsalva Road, Wandsworth Road; Borough Road, Southwark and Clarence Wharf, Albert Embankment.

After the withdrawal of horse cars, some of the depots were disposed of. In this view, the empty Clapham Junction depot sports a poster advertising 900 tram horses for sale.

Routes on Takeover

Route	Colour	Distance mls	yds	Time (mins) (1895)	(1902)
East Hill & Hop Exchange	Brown	5	1188	65	54
East Hill & Westminster	Yellow	4	992	55	43
North Street & Hop Exchange	Green	5	1728	65	60
North Street & Westminster	Blue	4	1440	50	43
Lavender Hill & Chelsea Bridge	Red	1	440	10	12
Clapham Junction & Chelsea Bridge	Choc'te	2	130	14	20

A bank holiday service was operated between Westminster and Battersea Park Road (Prince of Wales Road). A horse bus service was also worked between Clapham Junction and Tooting via Trinity Road, but this was sold to Thos. Tilling on 2nd July 1899.

Other bus services which had been worked by the company were:-
Hop Exchange & Gracechurch Street, City.
Chelsea Bridge & Knightsbridge Road via Victoria Road.
Chelsea Bridge & Victoria Station.

On acquisition, the Council entered into an agreement whereby all employees were taken into its service, with the exception of the directors of the company, the secretary and the manager. All employees were put under the same terms and conditions as other LCC tramway operatives. The alternative weeks of six days (72 hours) and 7 days (80 hours) were replaced by a six-day week of 60 hours; wages, low by comparison with some other companies, were raised from 4d an hour to 6d; while the vicious system of fining employees for any minor beach of the rules was abolished.

The Cars

The first order for cars was fulfilled by the Lancaster Wagon Company Limited, who supplied 14 double deck and 14 single deck cars in 1881. The large cars had 6-window saloons and knifeboard seating on the open top decks, with a total carrying capacity of 42 passengers, while the smaller ones, of 5-window style, had seats for 18 passengers.

From available records, it has been deduced that the double deck cars cost about £190 each, with the small single deck vehicles about £130 each. A small fleet of double deck omnibuses, each seating 12 passengers inside and either 14 or 15 outside, were purchased for use as feeders to the tramways. The cost of these was also about £130 each. Subsequently, more cars were added to the fleet as new lines opened but, due to poor receipts from several of the sections, notably along Waterloo Road and on the Southwark Bridge Road route, a number of the single deck cars were eventually disposed of, some probably to the London Southern Tramways Company.

Car repairs, renovation and rebuilding were carried out in the workshops of the company at Queens Road depot, where comprehensive facilities were provided. During the spring of 1895, the workshop staff had the task of fitting a new type of brake, which had been invented by Mr. J. H. Betteley. With this arrangement, the brake blocks were applied to the rims of special "pulleys" mounted on the axles, instead of to the wheel tyres, which was said to save wear on the running surfaces of the wheels. (This was a forerunner of the disc brake, now in common use).

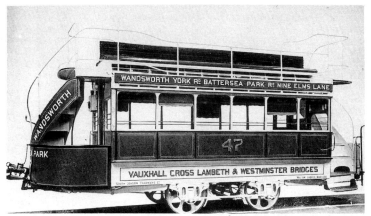

A Lancaster Wagon-built car when new. Before going into service, top deck decency panels were fitted.   (Tramcar Sponsorship Organisation)

Fares and Tickets

The early fares arrangement for the company was based on the common denominator of ½d a mile, but with a minimum of 1d being charged, except on Sundays and Bank Holidays, when the full throughout fare - or an agreed minimum - could be charged.

The first services provided used a weekdays fare structure based on this one penny minimum, which sum gave a ride of between 1½ and 2 miles.   As an example, just after through services commenced between Wandsworth Town and Hop Exchange on the "Bottom Road", the penny stages were:-

To or from:-	Wandsworth Town	and	"Princes Head"
	Plough Lane	and	"Brighton Rly Stn"
			(Battersea Park)
	"Princes Head"	and	"Rifleman"
	"Brighton Rly Stn"	and	Vauxhall Cross
	"Rifleman"	and	Lambeth Bridge
	Vauxhall Cross	and	St. George's Circus
	Lambeth Bridge	and	Hop Exchange

The 2d fare stages were:-			
	Wandsworth Town	and	Vauxhall Cross
	"Princes Head"	and	St. George's Circus
	"Brighton Rly Stn"	and	Hop Exchange

| The 3d fare:- | Wandsworth Town | and | St. George's Circus |
| | "Princes Head" | and | Hop Exchange |

The throughout fare was 4d.

There were some tickets used only for short journeys, such as a 1d fare to or from Lambeth Bridge and Hop Exchange, or Newington Causeway and Southwark Bridge, which were issued on the cars stabled at Borough Road depot, during the comparatively short time that these services operated.

Colours of tickets in use were:-
      1d, white; 2d, magenta; 3d, blue; 4d, chocolate.

131

On the opening of the line from Lambeth Bridge to Stangate in October 1883, the style of ticket used was altered to cater for the additional journeys being run on both the "top" and "bottom" roads, alternatively to Stangate and Hop Exchange. Some tickets displayed "UP" and "DOWN" stages, with others showing "UP" or "DOWN" stages. By this time, the local services around Southwark had been withdrawn due to lack of patronage, but the services between the "Falcon" and Chelsea Bridge and between Lavender Hill and Chelsea Bridge continued, with special 1d tickets covering these journeys.

The fare structure changed sometime in 1892 when the distance travelled for 1d and 2d was shortened, with consequent stage changes. On the Chelsea Bridge services, ½d fares were instituted for short journeys in addition to the 1d fares already in force, although the all-the-way fare for 1d appears to have been discontinued. The ½d tickets displayed four "UP" and four "DOWN" stages for these services. There was also a 1d omnibus ticket on issue for the journey between Chelsea Bridge and Buckingham Palace Road (Victoria Station), together with a set of transfer tickets, available for journeys where a change between tram and bus was necessary. This type of ticket was printed in two sections. A passenger would receive a ticket, punched in the top part and, on transferring to the second vehicle, would present the ticket to the conductor, who tore off the bottom section and issued an exchange ticket.

Workman 1d fares gave a longer ride than did ordinary 1d fares, and on the "bottom" road in the 1880s the stages shown were:-

"UP"	North Street	and	"Rifleman"
	"Brighton Rly Stn"	and	Borough or Westminster
"DOWN"	Borough or Westminster	and	"Brighton Rly Stn"
	"Rifleman"	and	North Street

Tickets were coloured white with red overprint, showing diagonally:-

WORKMAN'S
TICKET
ONLY

Chapter 12
The London Southern Tramways Company

Until the mid-nineteenth century, the districts lying to the south of Brixton and Camberwell had been quite rural in character, composed mainly of private estates interspersed with market gardens. Upon the heights above Low (later West) Norwood and Dulwich, was the area known as Beulah Heights with its Spa. Further to the east, upon the heights above Sydenham, the Crystal Palace, that glass masterpiece designed by Sir Joseph Paxton, was re-erected in 1854 after being used as the centrepiece of the Great Exhibition of 1851 in Hyde Park.

The Pimlico, Peckham & Greenwich Street Tramways Company (later the London Tramways Company) had constructed lines in the Camberwell area, connecting Kennington with Peckham and New Cross. Considerable development was taking place in Herne Hill, Tulse Hill and West Norwood, all in Surrey, and with this expansion, came the necessity for new and improved means of transport.

Early in 1880, the first proposals were being considered for the establishment of a tramway system in the area. A Bill was submitted to Parliament by the London Southern Tramways Company in 1882. The Act which was secured was entitled the **London Southern Tramways Act, 1882 (44-45 Vic. cap. cclvii)**, authorising the following tramways:-
No. 1. 1 ml. 7 f. 6.15 ch. long, from Vauxhall, along South Lambeth Road and Gresham Road to Cold Harbour (sic) Lane, with passing places.
No. 1A. 1.18 ch. long, at Vauxhall, a connecting line with Tramway No. 1.
No. 2 (part). 1 ml. 2 f. 7.65 ch. long, including passing places, from High Street, Camberwell and along Cold Harbour Lane to Brixton Road. A loop terminus to be constructed at Camberwell Green.
No. 3. 7 f. 4.60 ch. long, with passing places, from Cold Harbour Lane at Hinton Road then along Milkwood Road to Norwood Lane.
No. 4. 1 ml. 3 f. 4.10 ch. long, from the end of Tramway No. 3, along Norwood Lane and Thurlow Lane to West Norwood Cemetery.
It was stipulated that the roads were to be paved as directed by the local authorities, including the use of granite cubes of a specified size.
The capital sum authorised was not to exceed £90,000, issued as £10 shares. Borrowing on mortgage was not to exceed £22,500.
Fares were to be charged at the rate of 1d per mile, but a minimum sum of 2d could be charged. Parcels could be carried at the rate of 7 lbs for 3d; 14 lbs for 5d; 28 lbs for 7d; 56 lbs for 9d.
All cars were to show fare tables in a conspicuous position.
Special cheap fares and services for workmen were to be instituted.

Work was put in hand on the construction of Tramway No. 2 and the eastern part of No. 1, despite some opposition from Camberwell Vestry. Contractor for the work was Messrs. Westwood & Winby. A condition imposed upon the company was that along Stockwell Road

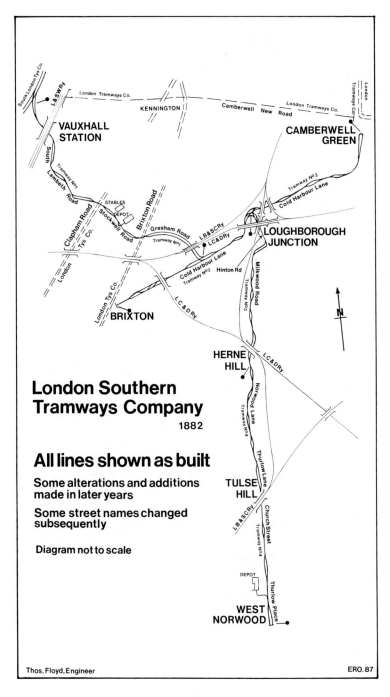

London Southern Tramways Company

1882

All lines shown as built

Some alterations and additions made in later years

Some street names changed subsequently

Diagram not to scale

Thos. Floyd, Engineer

ERO. 87

the whole width of the road was to be paved with jarrah wood blocks at the expense of the company. The sections from "The Swan" to Brixton and from Camberwell Green to Cold Harbour Lane and Gresham Road were completed at the end of November 1883. Both lines were inspected by Maj. Gen. Hutchinson on 4th December, the certificates being issued on 7th.

It was the intention of the company to obtain powers to construct a line along Acre Lane from Brixton to Clapham, to connect with the lines of the London Tramways Company. This line would have been an extension of the track in Cold Harbour Lane.

Meanwhile, construction of the section from Cold Harbour Lane into and along Hinton Road and Milkwood Road to Herne Hill was under way, involving the re-arrangement of road levels beneath the railway bridges spanning a large part of Hinton Road. Originally, the incline at its steepest part was 1 in 17 and the company reduced this to 1 in 30. By the spring of 1884, the line was completed and inspected by Maj. Gen. Hutchinson on 30th April. He was not satisfied that there was sufficient clearance under the lowest railway bridge in Hinton Road, and ordered that all cars be fitted with canopies above each staircase on the upper deck. After a further inspection on 28th May, the line opened on 30th, with conductors warning passengers to remain seated while passing beneath the bridge. The cars, however, by the fittings of these canopies, were made to look quite incongruous and were the subject of some ridicule.

The next section to be built was the northern part of Tramway No. 4 along Norwood Lane, from Herne Hill Station as far as Thurlow Park Road. Maj. Gen. Hutchinson inspected the line on 3rd July 1884 and it was opened on 10th. At the same time the London Southern Tramways (Extensions) Bill was passing through Parliament.

What emerged was a very much watered-down Act. The **London Southern Tramways Act, 1884 (47-48 Vic. cap. cxci)** did not give the company the additional mileage requested in the Bill, but granted the extra time necessary to complete the works still outstanding. The company was also authorised to enter into agreements with the London Tramways Company Limited and the South London Tramways Company regarding through working of car services. The Act also gave an extension of time (for one year) after completion of a new street (South Lambeth Road) for construction of the tramway from Stockwell Road to Vauxhall. It had originally been intended to use the old road alignment but, as the road was so narrow and tortuous a new cut was decided upon. It was the planning and construction of this new road that had been the cause of delay.

The line from Thurlow Park Road to West Norwood was inspected by Maj. Gen. Hutchinson on 3rd June 1885. The certificate was issued on 5th, although the line was opened in advance of its receipt, as the first car ran at 7.55 a.m. on 4th June.

At long last, in 1887, the final extension of the company's system, from "The Swan" Stockwell to Vauxhall Station was constructed, and was inspected by Maj. Gen. Hutchinson on 28th July. Sanction to operate was received by the company on 29th, but services did not commence until Sunday 21st August. On this section a more robust type of rail (90 lbs/yd) was used, being a variation of the Vignoles design. This extension also brought the total mileage of the company to 5 m. 6 f. 4 ch. and was quite small by comparison with other London companies.

An original car is seen here, fitted with the rather unsightly canopies, as required by the Board of Trade Inspector. (Tramway & Railway World)

The LCC Takes Over

The lines and assets of the company became purchaseable by the LCC in 1903, twenty-one years after the passing of the London Southern Tramways Act, 1882, but the LCC decided that, due to the condition of the tracks, the purchase should only take place if the lines were reconstructed for electric traction and some road widenings carried out. Lambeth Borough Council was asked to contribute one-third of the costs of widenings, but declined. The LCC in turn, decided not to purchase "for the time being". Even so, behind the scenes, the Council was attempting to arrange for the lines between Camberwell Green and Brixton and between Loughborough Junction and Herne Hill and on to West Norwood to be electrified on the overhead wire system, with only the section from Brixton to Vauxhall to have conduit track.

In the Parliamentary Session for 1905, the company introduced a Bill seeking to electrify its lines on the overhead wire system, at the same time asking that compulsory powers be deferred until 1924. This was opposed by the LCC but supported by Lambeth, even though it had since urged the LCC to reconsider its rejection of the scheme and suggesting that the number of street widenings could be reduced. The LCC meantime, was concerned that should the company electrify the lines, the overhead wire system would no doubt be used on the section from Cold Harbour Lane to Camberwell Green and, as it was preparing to build a new conduit line to Dulwich from Camberwell Green, both systems would be in use on the same length of line. This caused the LCC to reconsider the whole matter and, even though the company was still proceeding with attempts to get its Bill through Parliament and the LCC was still opposing it, agreement had been reached with Lambeth over the widenings issue and to the Borough Council subscribing £25,167 towards the cost of the work.

A busy scene at Norwood terminus, with one car having just arrived from Vauxhall, and No. 29 awaiting departure. (Commercial view)

Regarding purchase of the company, the parties agreed to go to arbitration, with Mr. L. L. Macassey of Belfast acting as referee. During his enquiry, the Council and company came to terms. The company had claimed £82,962, but indicated that £60,000 would be an acceptable figure. It was on this basis that Mr. Macassey made his award. In total, it cost the LCC £62,085.10. 9d. Operation was assumed by the Council on 2nd October 1906, but it was not until 16th November that the award was announced, with the Council finally becoming the legal owner on 20th December.

On takeover, all staff with the exception of the secretary, engineer and the foreman at Norwood depot were taken into Council employment, temporarily at first. Mr. Cloney, the Manager, was given the post of Traffic Assistant, South London (LCC) at a salary of £200 per year. Some members of the staff were transferred to other duties elsewhere. A change in the pattern of services was made when the through journeys between Vauxhall and Camberwell were replaced by short-working cars between Loughborough Junction and Camberwell. The service to Vauxhall was maintained by cars running through from West Norwood. This pattern was maintained for the next eighteen months, while preparations were made for the electrification of the line.

The Cars

The first cars operated by the company were standard seven-window double deck vehicles, each with a seating capacity of 22 inside and 24 out, which had been purchased from Falcon Works. All cars had knifeboard seating on the top decks, but due to the low-bridge restriction placed upon the company, end canopies were fitted at the head of the car stairs to protect any passengers who may have been walking over the centre part of the upper decks while the cars were passing

Upper
One of the new style cars introduced by the company in 1895.

Lower
In common with many other undertakings, the company made use of a water car as and when required, to assist in keeping the tracks as free as possible from dust.

beneath the bridges. In later years, some six-window, 42-seat cars were added to the fleet. Cost of these ranged between approximately £185 and £250 each during the years from 1881 and 1895. After about twelve years in service, it was decided to replace the rather unsightly cars with something "more modern" and elegant. In 1895, the manager, Mr. A. A. Tyler, introduced a new idea - a "lowbridge" car.

In order to utilise the more up-to-date arrangement of "garden" seating on the upper deck, the height of the car necessarily had to be lowered. This was done by letting the axleboxes and springs into the side sills and rocker panels, bringing the body of the car a total of 18 inches lower than on standard vehicles which stood at exactly nine feet from rail to top deck floor. This saving, making the maximum height to the top deck floor 7 ft. 6 in. was achieved by substituting 27-inch diameter wheels for the usual 30-inch ones, the other 15 inches being gained from lowering the body. The new cars, the first of which was built by Falcon, had a six-window body style, carried 20 passengers inside and 24 on the two rows of double seats on the upper deck and weighed 2 tons 2 cwts. After a thorough test of the new vehicle, the company decided to reconstruct the remainder of its fleet to the same standard in its own workshops.

There is some dispute over the car colours used by the company, but the following were those probably in use.

Norwood - Vauxhall	Red
Vauxhall - Stockwell - Camberwell	Blue (or Green)
Norwood - Camberwell	Brown (or Blue)
Brixton (Cold Harbour Lane) - Camberwell	Brown

Services on this basis were provided and, although shown as four distinct workings, it appears that after introduction, the main one became (Vauxhall) - Stockwell - Brixton - Herne Hill - Norwood. A secondary service was worked between Camberwell and Brixton, with passengers transferring as necessary at Loughborough Junction.

Depots and Stables

The first depot and stables to be opened by the company was on a site behind the "Old Queen's Head" public house, Stockwell Road near Stockwell Green, and taken on a 60-year lease as from 24th June 1882, at a yearly rent of £70. Another stabling block was erected on land leased from the London Tramways Company (which company had been the first to propose a tramway along Stockwell Road and had taken a 99 year lease on land at the rear of No. 105 Stockwell road on 25th March 1877) for the remainder of the term at £200 a year, as from 22nd November 1895.

There was also a number of railway arches rented from the London Brighton & South Coast Railway Company "at or near" Cold Harbour Lane as from 28th March 1893, at a total annual rent of £100 and numbered 269, 271, 272 and 273. Additionally, arch No. 23 was acquired on 28th September for £25 per annum and arch No. 268 was rented as from 1st December 1905 at £16 per annum. They were all used as secondary stables for sick horses, for a granary and works.

The other depot and stables was built on land to the rear of Nos. 8 to 20 Lansdowne Hill, West Norwood, taken on lease from 7th May 1894 at a yearly rent of £309. The buildings were reached by a spur line situated about 50 yards from the end of the main line. There was space for 15 or 16 cars, 147 horses, two loose boxes and a workshop for a farrier. In its busiest year, in 1901/2, the maximum fleet was 33 cars, which number was well within the capacity of the buildings.

Fares and Tickets

The original fares structure of this company was based upon the operation of several services, using a series of tickets, some of which were exclusive to one route, others with common stages printed thereon. In 1884 services were operated from "The Swan", Stockwell to Tulse Hill; "The Swan" to Camberwell Green and Tulse Hill to Camberwell Green, with 1d, 1½d, 2d and 3d fares to cover the services. On completion of the extensions to Norwood and Vauxhall, the maximum fare became 4d.

In 1896, the maximum fare charged between Vauxhall and Norwood was reduced from 4d to 3d, resulting in certain other reductions in the lesser fares, both by increasing the distance available and the general introduction of 1½d fares. Finally, in the late 1890s, the company joined in with the trend to introduce ½d fares; nevertheless, there were several separate ticket issues covering the various services, but all allowing about ¾-mile for the fare charged.

So far, no mention has been made of that short length of line in Cold Harbour Lane between Gresham Road and Brixton Road ("Brixton Church"). Services normally only operated on this section between Brixton and Camberwell Green, which attracted a fare of 1d. On the introduction of ½d fares, the stages on the main line became Camberwell Green - Loughborough Junction and Loughborough Junction and Brixton Road (Stockwell Road), but for some unusual reason the fare charged on the cars which ran between Camberwell Green and

"Brixton Church" was fixed at ½d.

The four possible alternative journeys which could be made on cars of this company were between; Vauxhall and Norwood, Vauxhall and Camberwell, Norwood and Camberwell, and Brixton Church and Camberwell, all via Loughborough Junction. It became obvious that at such a natural interchange point as Loughborough Junction, considerable use could be made of transfer working, thereby making savings in operational costs. The single transfer tickets used, all printed on white card were most unusual in that they were specially printed for specific journeys and, as well as carrying the necessary information regarding the fare payable, the journey authorised and the point at which a change should be made, were also overprinted in coloured ink with a series of code letters identifying the journey to be made. On presentation of the transfer ticket on the second car, it would be collected by the conductor, who would then issue an exchange ticket punched to destination.

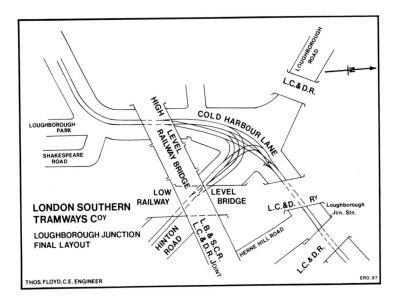

Chapter 13
Formation of the London County Council Tramways

Just before the Council became a tramway operator, consideration was given on how best to manage the new acquisition and also prepare for the huge works of electrification. Until this time, responsibility for tramway matters had rested with the members of the Tramways Sub-committee of the Highways Committee who, although they were keenly aware of their duties, were nevertheless unqualified in day to day operation of such an enterprise, and even less so in overseeing the reconstruction of the system for electric traction.

When the Progressives were returned to power in the election of 1898, Mr. (later Sir) John Williams Benn became Chairman of the Highways Committee. Honorary Secretary of the Progressive Party, Benn had served on the Highways Committee since the formation of the Council in 1889. Whilst he was the Council's chief spokesman on tramways and a keen advocate of the benefits of municipal control, his professional work was in the field of artistic design and publishing. His Vice-Chairman, Joseph Allen Baker, had supported Benn in the elections of 1889 and 1892 and had joined him on the Council in 1895. Of Canadian birth, Baker had come to Britain in 1876 to promote the sales of bakery machinery developed by his father. Baker's tramway experience was limited to developments in North America.

Both men were well aware of the Council's need for professional advice on such an important matter, and Baker had tried unsuccessfully to persuade his fellow members to appoint a Tramways Manager, the last rejection being at a meeting held on 23rd June 1898. Therefore, when the Council was making objection to the London United Tramways Bill for powers to electrify that system, it was Benn who appeared before the House of Commons Committee to present evidence on behalf of the LCC. Baker had prepared all the evidence and it is reported that he worked himself almost to the brink of a mental and physical breakdown, so conscientiously did he apply himself to the task. After discussion which included steam, cable, compressed air and the overhead wire system of electric traction, the report came out in favour of the electric conduit system.

Later in that year, Baker and Benn made another attempt at getting agreement to the appointment of a full-time manager, this time with more success. Due to the load about to fall on the officers of the committee, it was decided to advertise for the appointment of a Chief Officer of Tramways. On 29th November, the position was offered to John Young of Glasgow Corporation Tramways, who declined on learning that the Highways Committee were not prepared to employ an assistant to help him in the gigantic task of electrification.

The offer then went to Alfred Baker, Manager of Nottingham Corporation Tramways, who accepted at a salary of £1,000 a year. Baker had been at Nottingham since 1878 when the system had been owned and operated by a company. All his experience had been with horse tramways, as the Nottingham system had not by then been electrified. Yet, when he came to London he would, after taking charge of a horse-drawn and cable-operated system, have to set about arranging for the construction of an electrically worked conduit system. His appointment took effect from 1st February 1899, and with it the responsibility for the working of the ex-London Tramways Company.

After the transfer of the Company to the Council on 1st January 1899, all officials and employees, with the exception of the Secretary, Solicitor and Consulting Engineer were taken into Council service, being placed under the control of the Tramways Manager at their existing rates of pay and conditions for the time being. The Solicitor and Engineer were not employees of the company, as both received a retaining fee for their services, but the Secretary, who could have gone into the service of the Council, declined to do so.

The senior staff were:-

Alfred Baker, Tramways Manager, salary £1,000 per annum.
Capt. J. A. Ford, formerly General Manager for the Company, who became Principal Assistant and Horsing Superintendent, Tramways Department, salary £550 per annum, plus allowance for house, light and coal.
J. K. Bruce, Veterinary Surgeon, salary £550 per annum, plus allowance for house, light and coal.
G. A. Woolley, Superintendent of Works, salary £600 per annum, plus allowance for house, light and coal.
W. Scott, Traffic Manager, salary £550 per annum, plus allowance for house, light and coal.
G. Welling, Engineer, salary £430 per annum, plus allowance for house, light and coal.
Miss E. Penman, Superintendent of Women Checkers and Conductors, salary £400 per annum, plus allowance for house, light and coal.
H. Vorley, Accountant, salary £250 per annum.
H. Holland, Paymaster, salary £250 per annum.
J. McCarthy, Stores and Invoicing, salary £250 per annum.
J. Welling, Assistant Engineer, salary £220 per annum.
C. J. Johnson, Assistant Traffic Manager, salary £200 per annum.
J. Glover, Claims Clerk, salary £185 per annum.
G. Franklin, Assistant Paymaster, salary £180 per annum.
H. B. Taite, Manager's Clerk, salary £150 per annum.

Other employees taken over consisted of 25 foremen and 1870 tramwaymen. The routes taken over served the greater part of the southern and south-eastern suburbs running from the termini at Vauxhall, Westminster, Waterloo and Blackfriars Bridges out to Greenwich, Camberwell, Streatham and Tooting. There was also the isolated line from the north side of Vauxhall Bridge to Victoria. Total route length was 24 miles 3 furlongs served by 409 horse cars, 3,808 horses and 50 cable dummy cars. A further 45 omnibuses served to make connections with the trams from Westminster Bridge to Charing Cross, Waterloo Road to Strand and Blackfriars to Ludgate Circus.

Main tram services were:-

Westminster Bridge	- Clapham - Tooting
-do-	- Brixton - Streatham
	(Cable worked, Kennington - Streatham)
-do-	- Old Kent Road - New Cross - Greenwich
-do-	- Camberwell Green - Peckham - New Cross

Cars were washed, generally cleaned and the interiors disinfected daily. This view was taken at Peckham depot about 1900.

Waterloo Station	-	Clapham - Tooting
-do-		Old Kent Road - Greenwich
-do-		Walworth - Camberwell - Peckham
Blackfriars Bridge	-	Clapham - Tooting
-do-		Brixton - Streatham
-do-		Old Kent Road - Greenwich
Old Kent Road ("Lord Wellington")	-	St. George' Church - "Elephant" - Brixton - Streatham
Peckham (or Hatcham, New Cross)	-	Asylum Road (Old Kent Road) - St. George's Church - Camberwell Green
Vauxhall Cross	-	Kennington - Camberwell Green
Victoria	-	Vauxhall Bridge (north side)

The main works at Penrose Street Walworth, the wharf at Deptford and thirteen depots and stables were also included in the takeover.

Staff pay and conditions were decided at a meeting of the Highways Committee on 29th March 1899. The manager was to have responsibility for all aspects of operation, exclusive control of all staff directly and fully employed upon the cars, tracks, depots, works and stables and would, except for officials appointed by the Council have power to appoint and dismiss any person in the tramways service. The Council also regarded it as important that the wages paid should be at least equivalent to the best rates paid for similar work elsewhere in London and that the Council's rule with regard to one day's rest in seven should apply to all tramways staff. Prior to takeover, drivers and conductors were the only ones to have compulsory rest days, having been obliged to take one day off in eleven without pay. It was also decided that in order that no loss of pay was incurred by anyone, rates would be adjusted to ensure that all received in one year the same amounts as they would have received under the old system.

The Company had operated a system by which certain members of the staff received annual bonuses and in the re-adjustments made, it was decided to discontinue these, instead adding an equal amount to the pay rates so that no-one had cause to complain. Salaries of office staff were also increased. Details of the main changes were:-

GRADE	FROM	TO
Women checkers	12/- to 30/-	15/- to 30/- weekly
Drivers and conductors	4/6d to 6/-	4/9d to 6/3d daily

Horsekeepers	23/- to 25/-		26/- weekly
Washers and lampmen	20/- to 24/6d		25/- -do-
Track cleaners	20/- to 24/6d		25/- -do-
Horse shifters	18/- to 23/-	20/- to 25/-	-do-
Point shifters	15/- to 20/-	18/- to 24/-	-do-
Pole turners	15/- to 20/-	18/- to 24/-	-do-

Another change made was that drivers and conductors were to be provided with uniform clothing. Under company conditions, only conductors were supplied with jackets, but the Council decided that both sections of the staff should have the same consideration. In addition, brown "bowler" hats were issued to drivers, with caps for conductors. Lastly, the granary carmen, who delivered the products of the granaries to the stables, were to receive 5/- a day for the first six months' service, then 5/6d, instead of the 27/- a week for six days' work that they had previously received.

It had been estimated that the net profits of the undertaking during the year 1899-1900, after payment of interest and sinking fund charges would be about £52,400, allowing a sum of almost £31,900 to be used for rates relief or to be applied to such purposes as the Council decided.

Assets of the LCC Tramways
In the case of the London Tramways Company, the inventory of of assets handed over to the LCC shows how this important company was structured.

Vehicles: 409 tramcars, including 39 under repair.   3,808 horses.
45 omnibuses, including 5 under repair.
Eastlake Road depot (horse hospital) had 9 animals in care.
Cable line: 76 cars, 29 fitted with independent gripper gear.

Depot Allocations

Queens Road, Peckham	50 cars	Ewer Street	8 buses
Rye Lane	44 cars	Victoria	7 cars
Greenwich	39 cars	Chicheley Street	6 buses
Balham	35 cars	Lawson Street	7 buses
Old Kent Road	35 cars	Clapham	41 cars
Kennington Cross	13 cars	Streatham	43 cars
	19 buses		50 dummies
Bowles Road	35 cars	Penrose Street Works	39 cars
Camberwell	28 cars		5 buses

Distribution of Cars and Buses	Route	Colour
Queens Road Peckham Depot		
291, 825.	Greenwich-Blackfriars	Chocolate
141, 144, 152, 189, 208, 223, 244,	New Cross-Westminster	Green
251, 260, 293, 313, 321, 325, 347,		
358, 364, 366, 372, 388, 390, 391,		
814, 872, 884, 885.		
138, 139, 147, 160, 185, 233, 259,	New Cross-Blackfriars	Red
263, 268, 331, 333, 345, 355, 356,		
359, 376, 377, 391, 392, 396, 813,		
934, 955.		
Bowles Road Depot (Old Kent Road)		
284.	Greenwich-Waterloo	Lt. Green
157, 198, 199, 201, 204, 207, 235,	Camberwell Green -	
265, 271, 288, 301, 307, 309, 341,	"Lord Wellington"	White
349, 381, 859, 860, 865.		
212, 215, 217, 337, 397, 851, 898,	Streatham-Borough	Yellow

After the Council took control of the London Tramways Company, the initial letters "LCC" began to appear on the sides of the cars, but the old liveries were retained, as seen here on car No. 877, one of the self-propelled cable cars. *(Courtesy: C. Carter)*

Old Kent Road Depot (Leo Street)

241, 273, 277, 283, 285, 286, 295, 296, 299, 303, 305, 342, 352, 365, 824, 826, 936.	Greenwich-Blackfriars	Chocolate
161, 236, 240, 242, 264, 294, 302, 308, 314, 378, 839, 842, 843, 844, 848, 849, 850, 937.	Greenwich-Waterloo	Lt.Green

Greenwich Depot

179, 196, 228, 255, 262, 266, 276, 280, 281, 290, 292, 310, 317, 318, 330, 332, 336, 344, 354, 361, 379, 380, 382, 400, 818, 819, 820, 832, 833, 834, 835, 854, 855, 896, 899, 901, 935, 942, 943.	Greenwich-Westminster	Blue/white

Rye Lane Peckham Depot

136, 142, 168, 369, 370, 371, 374, 375, 389, 816, 845.	New Cross-Westminster	Green
137, 224, 229, 230, 231, 272, 327, 360, 393, 867, 956.	New Cross-Blackfriars	Red
150, 154, 159, 166, 186, 205, 206, 211, 220, 257, 278, 357, 836, 837, 383, 840, 852, 853, 929, 930, 931, 941.	New Cross-Waterloo	Yellow

Camberwell Depot

140, 353, 948.	New Cross-Waterloo	Yellow
203, 226, 238, 258, 297, 857, 861, 862, 863, 864.	Camberwell Green - "Lord Wellington"	White
368, 873, 878, 879, 881, 882, 883, 890, 893, 894, 895, 908, 932, 933.	Camberwell Green - Vauxhall (south)	Green

Victoria Depot

222, 886, 887, 888, 889, 891, 892.	Victoria-Vauxhall (north)	Green

Balham Depot

134, 158, 163, 229, 243, 246, 324, 351, 398, 817.	Tooting-Westminster	Brown
187, 191, 350, 383, 384, 385, 387, 823, 957, 958, 959, 960, 961, 962.	Tooting-Blackfriars	Dk. Green
151, 245, 248, 256, 269, 315, 870, 951, 952, 953, 954.	Tooting-Waterloo	Red

Clapham Depot

162, 170, 172, 184, 188, 190, 195, 214, 322, 326, 339, 362, 821, 822.	Tooting-Westminster	Brown
143, 164, 165, 167, 171, 181, 194, 298, 335, 386, 399, 830, 874.	Tooting-Blackfriars	Dk. Green
133, 148, 197, 247, 250, 253, 319, 346, 395, 827, 828, 829, 847, 946.	Tooting-Waterloo	Red

Streatham Depot

312, 320, 338, 902, 903, 904, 907, 911, 912, 913, 920, 921, 922, 941.	Streatham-Westminster	Red
153, 177, 192, 221, 232, 252, 329, 343, 831, 877, 900, 923, 926, 928.	Streatham- Blackfriars	Dk. Blue
156, 200, 210, 216, 218, 219, 261, 815, 897, 909, 915, 918, 919, 939, 946.	Streatham-Borough	Yellow

Dummies: Streatham Depot: 1-4; 6-16; 18-20; 22-50.
            No. 20 Brixton Road: 5, 17, 21.

Kennington Depot

316, 323, 871, 905, 940.	Streatham-Westminster	Red
234, 275, 394, 875, 876, 924, 925, 927.	Streatham-Blackfriars	Dk. Blue

Omnibuses

96, 97, 99, 101, 102, 112, 118.	via Westminster Bridge
132, 133, 136, 137, 138, 139, 140, 141, 142, 143, 145, 146.	via Waterloo Bridge

Chicheley Street Depot (Omnibuses)

98, 100, 113, 114, 115, 116.	via Westminster Bridge

Lawson Street Depot (Omnibuses)

95, 121, 122, 123, 129, 131, 147.	via Blackfriars Bridge

Ewer Street Depot (Omnibuses)

124, 125, 126, 127, 128, 130.	via Blackfriars Bridge
134, 135.	via Waterloo Bridge

Penrose Street Works. Tramcars

209, 270, 282, 300, 311, 340, 856.	Greenwich-Westminster
279, 287, 289.	Greenwich-Blackfriars
274, 373.	Greenwich-Waterloo
334, 348, 367, 369.	New Cross-Westminster
145, 227, 249, 866, 868.	New Cross-Blackfriars
135, 267, 304, 328.	New Cross-Waterloo
155, 183, 858.	Camberwell-"Lord Wellington"
237, 906.	Streatham-Westminster
182, 202.	Streatham-Blackfriars
146, 193.	Tooting-Westminster
213, 363, 841.	Tooting-Blackfriars
225, 254.	Tooting-Waterloo
Omnibuses, 93, 94.	via Westminster Bridge
119, 120.	via Blackfriars Bridge
144.	via Waterloo Bridge

146

Directory of Car and Omnibus Numbers

Cars, two-horse.
133-139, 140-148, 150-159, 160-168, 170, 171, 172, 177, 179, 181-189, 190-199, 200-209, 210-299, 300-399, 400, 813-819, 820-899, 900-962.
Omnibuses, Two-horse.
93-99, 100-102, 112-116, 118, 119, 120-129, 130-147.
Cars, one-horse and locations (all out of service).
Deptford Yard.
149, 176, 178, 402, 404, 405, 408, 410, 411, 601, 604, 607, 608, 802, 804, 806.
Clapham. 180, 407, 416, 603, 810. Streatham. 606. Queens Road. 609.
Omnibuses, one-horse and locations (all out of service).
Clapham.
41, 43, 48, 50-52, 56, 57-59, 60-64, 66, 67, 69, 71-75, 78, 80, 81, 83, 86, 87, 88.
Penrose Street Works. 44.

Miscellaneous Vehicles and Equipment

Under Penrose Street Control.
1 small trolley: 1 rail grinder;   1 p'way cart;   1 stores cart;
2 sand carts;   1 manure van;   1 phaeton;   1 van (one-horse)
1 van (pair-horse).

Advertisement lists.	Cars	Buses	Dummies
Painted wholesides	471	97	24
Bill wholesides	355	28	28
Enamel, whole (framed)	91		
Oval tablet stair-boards		57	
Painted end-boards			17
Sideboards for enamel plates			50
Endboards for enamel plates			42

Sandboxes (one on each car), 44.

Streatham Engine House.
Two pairs of compound non-condensing engines, each 500 h.p. with cylinders fitted with Proell's auto-expansion gear. All parts made to withstand a strain of 800 h.p. when the tandem cylinder is used.
The London cable with gear. The Streatham cable with gear.

Streatham Car Shed.
Top floor. One hand-powered traverser and winch.
Ground floor. One power traverser.
Electric lighting at 100 volts.
Cottages lit from main dynamo, 31 lamps.
Mr. Woolley's house lit from main dynamo, 23 lamps.

Of the 67 passenger cars allocated to the cable line, 29 were fitted with independent gripper gear. This was a patent fitting, the rights of which belonged to Mr. Woolley, the depot superintendent. He had made an agreement with the London Tramways Company regarding the use of the equipment, which was allowed to stand when the LCC took control.

All Night Services

Before the Council took possession of the tramways, consideration was being given to the need for all-night services of trams and of the omnibuses running in conjunction with them, but it was the Council who instituted the first, from New Cross Gate via both the Peckham and Old Kent Road route to Blackfriars on 12th February 1899, following this up on 19th with a service from "The Plough", Clapham to Westminster. The omnibus services working from the London tram termini to Charing Cross and to Ludgate Circus, were also operated throughout the night. The only times that the services did not run were early on Sunday mornings, Good Friday, Christmas Day, or on any Bank Holiday.

Due to the necessarily different arrangements applying to the cable line which closed down at night for maintenance work, a horse car service was put on to work over the line during the silent hours. This commenced early in 1890, running from Blackfriars to Water Lane, Brixton, operating at regular intervals throughout the night (except Saturdays), as is seen in an extract from the official timetable.

"ALL NIGHT CARS.
1. Blackfriars Bridge to New Cross Gate via Old Kent Road
   (from 12.2.1899). Every 20 minutes from 12 midnight till 7.18 a.m.
2. Blackfriars Bridge to New Cross Gate via Camberwell and Peckham
   (from 12.2.1899). Every 20 minutes from 12 midnight till 7.08 a.m.
3. Westminster Bridge to "Plough" Clapham (from 19.2.1899). Every
   20 minutes from 12.05 a.m. till 7.25 a.m.
4. Blackfriars Bridge to Water Lane Brixton (from early 1900). Every
   25 minutes from 12.03 a.m. till 7.08 a.m.

The cars, to and from Clapham and Brixton are timed to meet at Kennington, where passengers may make a transfer if required."

A development of the Blackfriars to Brixton service came shortly after its commencement, resulting in the following:-

Inward:-   All night horse cars;   Water Lane to Blackfriars, 12.43 a.m.
           and every 25 minutes until 5.18 a.m.
           Early morning cable and horse cars;   Telford Avenue to
           Blackfriars, 5.51 a.m.; 6.16 a.m.; 6.41 a.m.
Outward:- All night horse cars;   Blackfriars to Water Lane Brixton,
           12.06 a.m. and every 25 minutes until 4.41 a.m.
           Early morning horse and cable cars;   Blackfriars Bridge
           to Telford Avenue, 5.06 a.m.; 5.31 a.m.; 5.56 a.m.
           Early morning horse cars;   Blackfriars to Kennington Gate,
           6.36 a.m.; 7.01 a.m.; 7.26 a.m.

All these services operated at Workman fares, and this pattern was retained until after the lines were electrified.

The London Tramways Company omnibus services taken over and worked by the Council were almost immediately the subject of a legal battle, when certain omnibus proprietors decided to question the right of the LCC to operate omnibuses. After litigation lasting several years, with all judgements going against the Council, it finally gave up the struggle and, on 6th March 1902 the 'buses ran for the last time. Several of the "associations" of omnibus proprietors purchased about 40 of the vehicles and took into their employ a number of the conductors and drivers, all of whom had been dismissed by the LCC. A total of 503 horses were also sold, the whole transaction realising £19,292 in favour of the Council. The LCC never did own or operate omnibuses thereafter.

148

Car No. 821 passes new conduit track during the reconstruction of the Tooting lines.   This was aided by the use of temporary passing places.

Traffic Receipts, 1899

During the first complete year of operation by the LCC, receipts amounted to £439,310, compared with the £431,201 taken by the London Tramways Company in 1898, which had been the most successful year in the history of the company.   This was thought to be a most satisfactory result, the more so as large sums had to be set aside for the improvements made in the way of fare reductions and increased rates of pay to staff.   It was anticipated that after meeting all expenses and charges, receipts for the year 1900-01 would probably show a surplus of about £52,000 (including £13,000 brought forward from the previous year).   The cost of establishing the ten-hour day was expected to be about £10,120, which would leave a sum of approximately £42,000 for a reduction in the County Rate, or such other purposes as the Council might decide.

Tramway Scheme 1899

The only metropolitan tramway scheme to be introduced in the Parliamentary Session for 1899 was the London United Tramways Bill, by which power was sought, among other things, to repeal Section 37 of the company's Act of 1898, which restricted it to the use of the conduit system on its lines within the County of London and instead, giving the company freedom of action in the matter.   The LCC opposed, but later came to an arrangement with the company, allowing the use of the overhead wire system on the lines to be reconstructed in Uxbridge Road and Goldhawk Road.

Tramway Schemes 1900

Three Tramway Bills were deposited in Parliament for the 1900 Session.   These were:- The London County Tramways Bill
                              The London County Tramways (No. 2) Bill
                              The South-Eastern Metropolitan Tramways Bill

By the London County Tramways Bill, the Council sought powers to construct a number of lines, both on the north side and south side systems, and to double some of the existing lines.

No. 17. From the existing terminus at Streatham Hill, via High Road, Streatham, to the County boundary (a new line).

No. 20. Doubling of the line between Camberwell and the terminus at Vauxhall, via Camberwell New Road, Kennington Oval and Harleyford Road.

The Bill also provided for the reconstruction for electrical traction of the existing tramways between Westminster Bridge and the Tooting terminus and those from Blackfriars Bridge to "The Horns" public house, Kennington Park and for horse traction being used on the new extensions north of the river. In the case of the line at Streatham (No. 17), cable traction was proposed.

A provision was included for the acquisition of the freehold of a part of the existing Camberwell tramcar depot and adjoining property, upon which to build a generating station, and for the construction of a siding from the London, Chatham & Dover Railway line alongside the site, and for four of the tramway depots to be demolished to enable sub-stations to be erected on the sites.

The Bill was deposited, but owing to a few of the road authorities not having given their consents, its introduction was delayed. It was also found to be necessary to omit from the Bill the request to extend the cable line in Streatham, and for doubling the lines in Camberwell New Road, Kennington Oval and Harleyford Road, because of the refusal of Wandsworth District Board and Lambeth Vestry to consent to any of the proposals.

On 6th August 1900, the Bill received the Royal Assent, becoming law as **The London County Tramways Act, 1900 (63-64 Vic. cap. cclxx),** empowering the Council to reconstruct the Tooting route lines on the conduit system of electric traction and to build a power generating station at Camberwell.

The London County Tramways (No. 2) Bill was to enable the Council to reconstruct for electric traction the tramways already possessed, or which it would afterwards acquire. Included in the Bill was a clause

No. 827 works "wrong road" past new junction castings in place, and ready for completion.

requesting the repeal of the proviso in Section 24 of the North Metropolitan Tramways Act, 1897, prohibiting the use of electric traction on that part of the system worked by the company which was in the County of London. It also provided that no system of overhead wire traction should be used without the consent of each of the authorities through which the tramways passed. Considerable discussion on the Bill ensued, but in the end it was passed, receiving the Royal Assent on 6th August, and known as **The London County Tramways (Electrical Powers) Act, 1900 (63-64 vic. cap. ccxxxviii).**

By the South-Eastern Metropolitan Tramways Bill, the company sought to construct new lines in the County of London and to reconstruct its present lines for electric traction. The Council opposed the introduction of the Bill so far as the new lines were concerned, and these were struck out, it then being limited to the reconstruction of the existing lines for electric traction. As the lines of the company would not be liable for purchase by the LCC until 1909, the Council insisted that it be able to state which system of electric traction should be used in the event of the company obtaining its Act. In that way, the Bill proceeded, resulting in the company gaining **The South-Eastern Metropolitan Tramways Act, 1900 (63-64 Vic. cap. cxlvii).**

Light Railways in London

On 17th October 1899, the Council decided to apply for powers under the Light Railways Act, 1896 for authority to construct light railways, all to be worked by electric traction. That north of the Thames was:-
a) From the present tramway terminus near to the "Archway Tavern", to the County boundary.

South of the Thames:-
b) No. 1. From the present tramway at Clapham Common (south side), via Clapham Common, Battersea Rise, Wandsworth Common (north side) and East Hill.
   No. 2. From West Hill, via Kingston Lane to the County boundary.
c) No. 1. From the present tramway at Deptford Bridge, via Blackheath Road, Blackheath Hill and Shooters Hill Road to the Royal Herbert Hospital.
   No. 2. From the Royal Herbert Hospital, via Woolwich Common Road, to Beresford Square, Woolwich.
d) From the present tramway at New Cross Road, via Lewisham High Road, Loampit Hill and Vale, Lee High Road and Eltham Road, to a point near Wellhall (sic) Lane at Eltham.

The length of the proposed double line along Archway Road was about three furlongs, and it was intended that this would connect with the light railways of Middlesex, whose application was also before the Commissioners. The Vestry of Islington was asked to contribute a sum towards the cost of the widenings, but declined.

So far as the lines in Deptford and Shooters Hill were concerned, Railway No. 1 from Deptford to Shooters Hill, together with Railway No. 2 into Woolwich were together approximately 5 miles 4 furlongs in length.

Similarly, the total length of the proposed line from Clapham to Kingston was about 5 miles 3 furlongs, of which about half a mile was to be single line.

Dr. Kennedy, the Electrical Adviser to the Council had estimated that, on the basis of the construction work being undertaken in the manner as outlined above, the cost of construction on the conduit system would amount to about £15,000 per mile of single track or £12,000 for overhead wire traction. The cost of rolling stock, plant, power houses and mains was included in the price, but not the cost of the car sheds.

The Light Railway Commissioners heard the case on 26th April 1900, the objectors including Lewisham and Lee District Boards, the South Eastern & Chatham Railway, the South-Eastern Metropolitan Tramways Company, the Kent Waterworks Company and even the South Metropolitan Gas Company. At the end of the evidence, objection was made by Counsel for the opponents, by stating that the scheme was incomplete as, in their view the powers to acquire land for the necessary street widenings should have been included in the Order instead of in the London County Council's Improvement Act. The Commissioners sustained this objection, refusing the grant the necessary powers to the LCC to enable it to proceed. This experience cost £1,125.

The purpose of the presentation of an Improvement Bill was to enable the LCC to seek authority from Parliament to undertake certain public works, including, in this instance, the request for powers to purchase land and property under compulsory terms, for the purpose of road widening to allow the light railways to be laid with the standard clearance of 9 ft. 6 in. between the kerb and the nearest rail. Subsequently, in all Bills, the improvements called for were included as part of a Tramways and Improvements Bill.

As the Archway Road, Highgate scheme had not yet been before the Commissioners and, as in the mind of the Council it might be rejected when it was examined, it was decided to include the request for powers into the Tramways Bill then being prepared for the 1901 Session of Parliament. The LCC did not attempt to invoke the Light Railways Act again, even though several undertakings around the County of London were successful and built lines under this Act. In the case of the Metropolitan Electric Tramways, with part of its undertaking designated a Light Railway, connections were actually made to the LCC Tramways at several points. But it was not for the Capital. London was, indeed, "different".

The end of the line! A motley collection of horse cars dumped on waste ground at Balham, awaiting sale or scrapping.

Twentieth Century Purchases

The new century saw renewed efforts by the Council to purchase the assets of all the company undertakings which were working within its boundaries. As with earlier acquisitions, arrangements to purchase undertakings outright and complete were sometimes very difficult to finalise (as described in the company chapters). Purchases ranged over a period of about seven years from 1902 and the following table gives a precis of events which for completeness includes the London Street Tramways, the North Metropolitan Tramways and the London Tramways companies, which started it all.

London Street Tramways Company			
(Permanent Way & Buildings only)	1895/6	13mls 2f.	£225,572. 7. 5d
North Metropolitan Tramways Co.			
(Permanent Way & Buildings only)	1896	35mls 6f.	£580,307. 6. 1d
(Cars and Plant)	1906		£224,970.12.11d
(Compensation for Lease)	1906		£ 97,787. 7. 6d
London Tramways Company	1899	24mls 3f.	£882,043. 1. 8d
South Eastern Metropolitan Tys Co.	1902	2mls 4f.	£ 50,166.12. 4d
South London Tramways Company	1902	13mls 2f.	£232,178.11. 3d
London, Deptford & Greenwich T.Co.	1904	6mls 7f.	£ 96,327. 0. 3d
London, Camberwell & Dulwich T.Co.	1904	2mls 7f.	£ 6,543.19. 6d
Woolwich & S.E. London Tys Co.	1905	4mls 6f.	£ 49,930.11. 0d
London Southern Tramways Co.	1906	5mls 6f.	£ 63,256. 5. 6d
Bexley Urban District Council	1908	150yds	£ 1,189.17.10d
Lea Bdg, Leyton & W'stow T.Co.	1908	3f.	£ 8,188.18. 2d
Highgate Hill Tramways Company	1909	5f.	£ 13,216.11. 6d
Harrow Rd & Paddington (1st sec)	1909	1ml 5f.	* £ 40,631.13. 4d
(2nd sec)		1ml 1f.	** £ 52,000. 0. 0d
Totals:		113mls 2f.	£2,624,310.16. 3d

Notes: * Purchase of tracks only. Leased to MET.
       ** Approximation. Purchase of tracks only. Leased to MET.

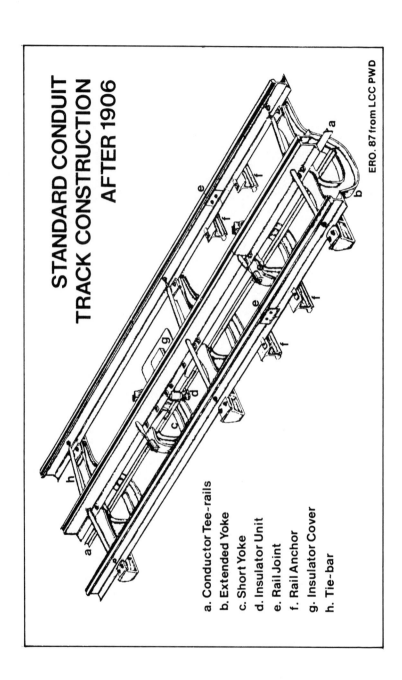

STANDARD CONDUIT
TRACK CONSTRUCTION
AFTER 1906

a. Conductor Tee-rails
b. Extended Yoke
c. Short Yoke
d. Insulator Unit
e. Rail Joint
f. Rail Anchor
g. Insulator Cover
h. Tie-bar

ERO. 87 from LCC PWD

154

Chapter 14
Electrical Construction

The senior management of the Tramways Department and members of the committee of the Council, spent some time visiting undertakings, both at home and abroad, collecting information in order to make the correct decision with regard to electrification. Even after the commencement of electric services, these visits continued from time to time in order to gain further experience and to be able to improve methods of operation and engineering. Exhaustive studies were made of several American undertakings which had all been electrified years before a start was made in Britain, and the Chief Officer of Tramways, A. L. C. Fell, who had replaced Alfred Baker in 1904, made many comparisons in his efforts to increase the efficiency of the undertaking. The Council had published its first dissertation on electric traction on 14th February 1901, which stated the policy to be adopted, together with the necessary action to be taken, and giving a description of the underground conduit system which it proposed to adopt, subject to Board of Trade approval.

The Council decided in June 1899 to undertake an experiment with the conduit system and the surface contact method. Using a "belt and braces" approach, its Bill for 1900 also included the proposal to reconstruct for electric traction all the tramways taken over in 1899 in the hope that the first section would be ready for working by Easter 1901. Authority was obtained in the LCC Tramways and Improvements Act, but the Council was not so successful in implementing the powers within the time limit it had set itself.

Meanwhile, the report made by J. Allan Baker had resulted in the Highways Committee appointing Dr. Alexander B. Kennedy as Consulting Engineer to advise the Committee on what he considered to be the best system of traction to be adopted by the Council and to advise where such a system should be tried. He again recommended that the slot conduit system be employed for the central areas of London with the probable use of the overhead wire for outer areas, employing a system of interchange which would allow a change-over from one method to the other to be effected in no more than a few seconds, provided that the lines and cars were "properly equipped". To try out the conduit system, the long busy route between Blackfriars and Tooting, with its branches from Kennington to Westminster and from St. George's Circus to Waterloo Station, was chosen as being the ideal lines to reconstruct.

The next stage was for the Council to arrange a demonstration of the conduit system. In July 1900, a conduit-plough equipped double deck open top bogie car, built for the British Westinghouse Electric Company was purchased, together with a short length of permanent way and associated equipment, which had been displayed at the 1900 Tramways and Light Railways Exhibition at the Royal Agricultural

Hall, Islington. The track was laid in a part of Camberwell depot, with the car placed upon it. A considerable number of local authority representatives were invited to Camberwell in February 1901 to witness working demonstrations of the line, with copies of a special descriptive brochure being made available to those assembled, who apparently received the information with some enthusiasm. The proposed surface contact experiment was not proceeded with at that time.

The Slot Conduit

The idea of using an underground tube or "conduit" from where to supply electric power to tramcars, came in an attempt to provide a safe method of collection, out of reach of the public and other road users, but not utilising all the equipment which an overhead wire system would involve. During the 1880s, experiments with this method were taking place in various cities and towns in America and Europe, with one notable example in England, at Blackpool, providing what has been termed as "The World's First Public Electric Street Tramway", which was constructed in 1885 under the guidance of Mr. Michael Holroyd Smith.

Development of the method in America, employing a fairly deep conduit, capable of being used for either cable-operated or electric traction, resulted in a very substantial and reliable arrangement, albeit a very expensive one. Basically, the structure consisted of a series of "yokes", fabricated from steel sections, which supported the track rails and, at the same time, provided a convenient housing for the power conductor bars, or "tee rails". Electric current to drive a car was collected by means of a device which came to be known as a "plough", carried beneath the vehicle, and which reached down into the conduit tube to make connection with the energised tee rails. Installation of such a system involved opening up large sections of road, into which the component parts of the new conduit tramway were to be laid, with all the disturbance, albeit temporary, that was entailed. It was this system that was chosen for London.

The Yokes

The curved or hollow pieces of wood placed over the necks of pairs of animals, usually oxen (thus coupling them together or "pairing" them) had chains or ropes attached in order that the animals could pull vehicles or, more usually, ploughshares. When inverted, this item, called a "yoke", looked like a pair of letters "u" joined together with wings, thus:- =u===u=. The metal items first used in Washington, New York and San Francisco, to support the rails and mechanisms of cable tramways, later to house the conductor bars of electrically worked tramways, because of their similarity in shape and because they connected the tracks, came to be known as "yokes". The similarity in terminology with "yokes" and "ploughs" is quite unusual, but in the case of tramways, the ploughs were drawn through the conduits, and hence the yokes, by the cars.

When it was decided that London should employ the conduit system, the question of what type of yoke to use was debated at considerable length, the result being that it was not considered necessary that such heavy items as seen in America would need to be used. A single "short" yoke was designed by Mr. A. N. Connett in conjunction with Dr. Kennedy which, in their opinion would be strong enough to take the loads imposed upon it, at the same time being considerably cheaper and more manageable than other types.

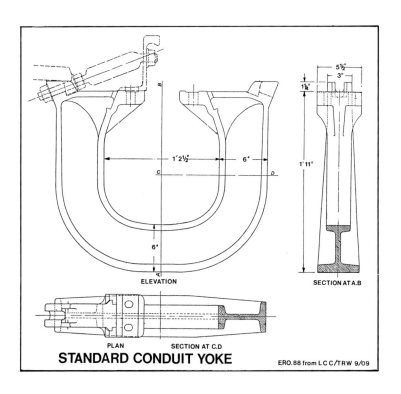

ELEVATION

SECTION AT A.B

PLAN   **SECTION AT C.D**

STANDARD CONDUIT YOKE

ERO.88 from LC C/TRW 9/09

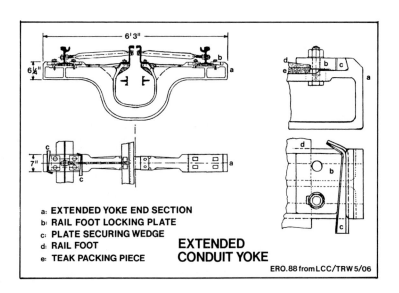

a: **EXTENDED YOKE END SECTION**
b: **RAIL FOOT LOCKING PLATE**
c: **PLATE SECURING WEDGE**
d: **RAIL FOOT**
e: **TEAK PACKING PIECE**

EXTENDED CONDUIT YOKE

ERO.88 from LCC/TRW 5/06

The cast-iron yokes, each weighing 153 lbs were placed at 3 ft. 9 in. intervals and the 61½ lbs/yd slot rails of Z-section were bolted to them. The inner edge of the slot rail was so designed that water dripping down would be harmlessly diverted from the conductor tee-rails. There were no fishplates used in conjunction with the slot rails, the ends being butted together midway between two yokes and held in place by short tie-bars bolted to lugs on the outside top edges of the yokes.

The "standard" or "short" yokes were used on several of the early conversions, but after hard usage, the design proved not to be as good as at first thought. In the first place, the width of the slot was only three-quarters of an inch and variations in temperature caused this to close up at times to just over half an inch, jamming ploughs, or worse, breaking them off from beneath the cars. Secondly, the exclusive use of short yokes did not give sufficient stability to the running rails, connected as they were to the noses of the yokes by tie-rods only, sometimes resulting in distortion to the whole assembly.

Consequently, after a further visit to the USA in 1905, specifically to study the New York and Washington systems, the Chief Officer came to the conclusion that extended yokes, upon which the running rails could be bolted, would have to be placed alternately with the short yokes in all future construction. This would give the additional strength needed to hold the rails to gauge, retain the track alignment more readily and minimise problems associated with slot closure due to extreme weather conditions. This proved to be a wise decision and all future work was undertaken in this way and, as the opportunity arose, some extended yokes were inserted into existing tracks. Conduit slot width was also increased to one inch.

Specially designed yokes were used at junctions and crossing points, many of them cast or otherwise made up for a particular location. These were used in conjunction with strategically placed gusset posts to support the assemblies at road level.

Original Construction

Construction of the conduit tube was carried out by digging a trench along the centre line of each track, of sufficient depth to accommodate the yokes which, when correctly aligned had concrete poured around and beneath them. Collapsible wooden formers known as "centering", consisting of two side pieces of the same contour as the insides of the yokes, were then fitted between them. Next, a wedge-shaped centre part was driven down between the side frames, jamming them tightly against the inside faces of the yokes. Concrete was then poured outside the centering to form the tube. When this had set, the wedges were withdrawn, releasing the formers and allowing them to be drawn along the tube to the open end, or to special openings where a piece of slot rail, 7ft. 6 in. in length could be removed. More concrete was then laid on either side of the tube to a depth of eight inches to form the base for the paving. Finally, a cement wash was applied to the insides of the tubes to give them a smooth finish.

The Running Rails

British Standard No. 4 rails were used, which were in lengths of 30 feet, weighed 102 lbs/yard for straight lengths and 104 lbs/yard for curved, all rails being seven inches high overall, with a base width of seven inches. Once in place, the rails were held to gauge by tie-bars bolted to them and to the noses of the yokes. Rails were fish-

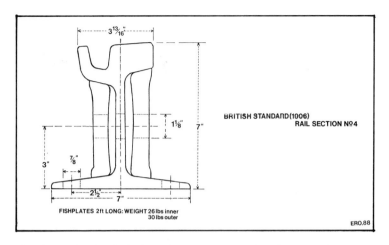

BRITISH STANDARD(1906)
RAIL SECTION №4

FISHPLATES 2ft LONG: WEIGHT 26 lbs inner
30 lbs outer

ERO.88

plated together by 20-inch long plates of special design, weighing 54 lbs per pair, to fit into cutaway sections at the rail ends, in order to present a continuous surface to the car wheels running over them. The four bolts used with each fishplate were made from special steel and were used in conjunction with locknuts of "helical" pattern. After the running rails had been laid, the inside of the conduit tube was "washed" with a 3-to-1 cement mortar, using a specially-shaped brush for the purpose.

The Slot and Tee-rails.

When working on the conduit system, the cars took their power at 550 volts d.c. from the fully insulated positive and negative conductor tee-rails, mounted in an open conduit or tube, the top of which was formed with specially manufactured Z-shaped slot rails. The tee-rails, shaped like a capital letter T, and mounted sideways, were made of a special soft steel with good electrical conducting characteristics, and were renewable. The contact faces were six inches apart.

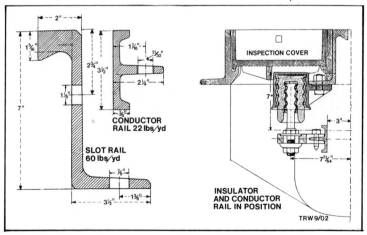

CONDUCTOR RAIL 22 lbs/yd

SLOT RAIL 60 lbs/yd

INSPECTION COVER

INSULATOR AND CONDUCTOR RAIL IN POSITION

TRW 9/02

The main conduit tube excavation has been dug and recesses for the yokes made. Yokes were then placed in the recesses, ready to receive the slot rails.

Slot rails were bolted to the nose-ends of the yokes and held fast to the yoke shoulders with short tie-rods. The concrete conduit tube was then formed and constructed.

Once the tube had been formed and mass concrete poured in, the running rails were placed and secured to the slot rails with tie-bars.

Next, the paviours completed their tasks, the road surface of granite setts being securely locked in place with hot tar supplied from the tar boilers. Lastly, the conductor tee-rails were installed and the insulator covers put into place. *(Courtesy: Tramway Museum Society, all views)*

The insulated hangers for the tee rails were fixed into place in the conduit tube, by being bolted at intervals of 15 feet, to the bottom edges of the Z-shaped slot rails. The conductor tee rail ends were then bolted to forked metal end-pieces suspended from the insulators and bonded together with two specially made stranded copper bonding wires, one end of which had previously been pressed into place by a hydraulic "bond compressor", using a pressure of 15 tons. In the tube, the other end of each bond was similarly treated by the compressor, the tool being mounted on a stand spanning the insulator entry hole.

To enable the conductor rails to be placed into, or removed from the tubes, they were manufactured in 30 feet lengths for easy handling, each length weighing 210 lbs. They could be removed and replaced by lifting short sections of the slot rails at intervals of about 220 yards, which provided sufficient room to manipulate the tee-rails in or out. They were then carried to their resting places with the aid of small trollies designed to run along the tops of the slot rails.

TEE-RAIL CARRIAGE

ERO 88

The renewal of tee-rails was usually carried out at night, so that services were not affected. Here, a new length of rail is seen being drawn into the conduit, where it was then fixed into place on the insulators. This procedure did not alter during the life of the tramways.
(Courtesy: L T Museum. U25265)

To maintain the specified distance of six inches between the tee-rail faces (three inches from the face to the centre line of the slot), special adjustable eccentric washers with a nut head on top were fitted at each end of the tee-rail forked clips so that precise adjustment could be made. A hand-hole was constructed at road level, above every insulator on either side of the slot rail into which a cover, 16 inches by 13 inches could be fitted and made in such a way that it was able to accept paving setts, wood blocks or macadam to the level of the road surface. It was then possible to inspect, clean and replace insulators, their mountings and the tee-rails as required.

At the end of every half-mile length there was a break in each conductor tee-rail to conform with Board of Trade Regulations, which required that the lines be electrically divided into sections. At these points the rail ends were flared so that the plough shoes could leave and enter the gaps without danger of damage. The end pieces were bolted to two insulators to strengthen the work, the positive and negative feed cables being also connected to the tee-rails at these points.

Removable hatches were provided above the tee-rail gaps to allow ploughs to be inspected or removed from the conduit. In order to enable a plough to be removed from the slot from inside a car, floor traps were fitted above the plough carrier and, by lifting these and disconnecting the plough leads, the suspect plough could be manhandled into the saloon of the car. Hatches were also placed near all crossovers and junctions in order that a damaged plough could be removed from the slot, but at these places the tee-bars were not always broken, the hatches being described as "live".

The conductor tees had of necessity to be "gapped" at crossings and points, in order that the car ploughs could pass unhindered through the pointwork and possibly (and quite likely) being reconnected to the next line of conductor bars whose polarity was opposite from the bars just left behind, with the longest break on any part of the system being 12 feet. Navigating a tramcar over sections of "dead" track was an art for which London tramwaymen were to become well known.

Drainage

With such a large and complex array of equipment beneath the road surface, efficient drainage was essential. Deep traps were constructed at 40 to 60 yard intervals beneath the insulator pits and connected by pipes to the track rails where, at these points special rails were laid which had drain holes incorporated in the grooves, allowing water to drain away harmlessly. The conduit tubes also drained into the traps and were connected together with 12-inch diameter pipes laid with a 1 in 10 fall away from, say, the "up" track to the "down" track. This fall continued through the floor of the "down" track trap and through another pipe to a sump about 5 feet deep, 3 feet long and 2 feet wide on the inside with a domed base or bottom, located outside the track margin. An outlet pipe, about halfway up the wall of the sump connected with the nearest rainwater sewer, allowing mud and debris to be trapped in the bottom of the sump, so facilitating its removal. A gas trap was provided in each sump over the outlet pipe to the sewer. Special gangs of men were employed whose sole duty was to keep the conduits, traps and sumps clean and healthy.

At busy points on the system, which coincided with town centres and like places, public toilets were often situated in subterranean positions in the centres of the roads. The tram tracks were specially laid out to give sufficient clearance to these edifices of Victorian

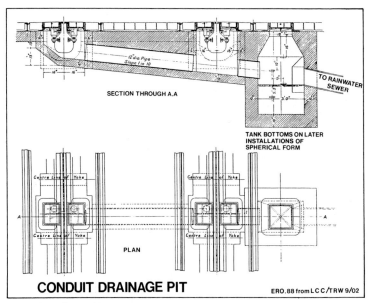

CONDUIT DRAINAGE PIT

ERO. 88 from L C C/T R W 9/02

and Edwardian splendour, which not only served their main purpose of attending to the needs of humanity, but provided outlets for rain water drains which could discharge from these places into the effluent sewers. An exception to this arrangement was, that on the Thames Embankments, the LCC were licensed by the Thames Conservancy Board (later the Port of London Authority) to discharge tramway conduit water into the river through sumps and tidal flaps.

The Overhead Wire System

After just a few years, even the LCC was tending to become a little overawed by the sheer cost of conduit construction. Electric tramways in almost all other parts of Britain - and in many other parts of the world - had been operating successfully with the overhead wire and trolley pole method, while around the edge of London, all other undertakings were using this system.

When the Woolwich and Plumstead line was being considered for electrification, the Council decided to use the overhead wire system because:-

a. Bexley had already brought the overhead wires into the Woolwich Borough with no objections.
b. The cost was about half that of conduit construction.
c. The same set of circumstances applied to the line being constructed in Hammersmith, where the LUT had succeeded in persuading the Borough Council, and the LCC, into allowing the use of the overhead wire as early as 1901.

Track Construction

Track centres for double lines built by the LCC when using the overhead wire system, were from 8 ft. 6 in. to 9 ft. apart, while the excavation in the roadway wherein to lay the tracks was 16 ft. 6 in.

wide. The foundation was of cement concrete upon which a bed of sand and cement one inch deep was laid. The rails were of grooved girder type of the same pattern as used on the conduit system tracks, of British Standard Section No. 4, weighing 105 lbs/yd, except on curves of 140 feet radius or under, where No. 4C rails were employed, having a weight of 111 lbs/yd. The rails were 7 inches deep with a 7-inch base and a $\frac{7}{16}$ inch thick web. The rail tread was 2⅛ inches wide, the groove 1⅛ inches deep by 1⅛ inches wide. On curves with a less radius than 140 feet, measured to the centre line of the track, the width of the groove was to be 1¼ inches, the lip of the rail being thickened to take account of the additional wear. Tie bars of ⅜ inch by 2 inch section with screwed ends were placed 7 ft. 6 in. apart. "Cooper" anchor joints were used with fishplates weighing 56½ lbs/pr. Cross-anchors were intermediately placed, 7 ft. 6 in. apart.

Both the "Cooper" anchors and the cross anchors consisted of lengths of standard rail, inverted and bolted to the foot of the running rails. The standard anchor was 2 feet in length, bolted to the underside of the rail at each joint and immediately beneath the fishplates, six bolts on either side of the anchor fixing it securely to the track. The cross anchor consisted of a 1 ft. 4 in. length of rail laid transversely beneath each rail and bolted by four high tensile bolts and nuts to special clips which held the rail in place. The anchors were embedded in concrete.

Double bonding strips were used at all rail joints in order to carry the return currents efficiently through the rails. Granite setts, 6 in. by 6 in. by 3 in. were used for paving the tracks, but alternatively, creosoted deal blocks of size 9 in. by 9 in. by 5 in. were used where required. If the road margins were of asphalt, a line of setts placed longitudinally on either side of the rails at the specified 18 inches would be used to strengthen the work. Setts could be either Aberdeen or Guernsey, while in addition to the use of creosoted wood blocks, Western Australian Jarrah or Karri wood blocks could be employed.

Suitable drain boxes were placed at regular intervals along the length of the tracks, consisting of special rail lengths with drain holes about six inches long in the grooves, which were connected to drain channels feeding into the sumps constructed beneath the road. These in turn, were connected to the main rainwater sewers.

The Overhead

The overhead wire equipment was constructed on the standard principle of using cross-span wiring with flexible suspension or, in a few places, making use of bracket arms. Swivel head trolleys were used on the cars, with a maximum outreach of five feet from the track centres.

Grooved trolley wire of 4/0 ("0000") s.w.g., with a breaking strain of 6,600 lbs. was used. Galvanised iron span wire of 7/12 stranded formation was employed to support the line ears and trolley wires, while guard wire was 7/15 stranded and galvanised. All overhead was suspended from spun steel poles placed at about 120 feet intervals, medium or heavy poles used where required. The trolley wire was usually suspended at a minimum height of 20 feet over the centre line of straight track and slightly to the inside of curved line, but deviations could be made where necessary.

In common with all tramway systems in Britain, the tracks were electrically divided into half-mile sections. On overhead wire sections this required the use of insulated section "breaker" ears. Each of these consisted of a length of specially shaped hard wood about 12

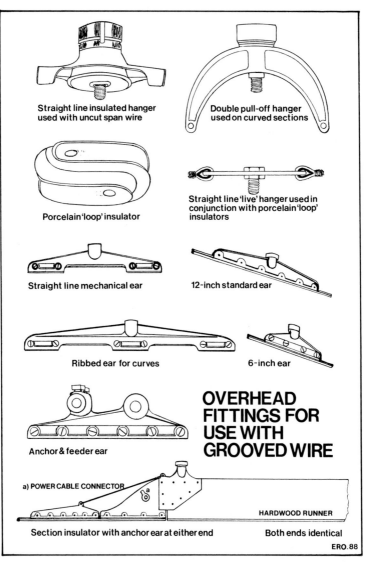

Straight line insulated hanger used with uncut span wire

Double pull-off hanger used on curved sections

Porcelain 'loop' insulator

Straight line 'live' hanger used in conjunction with porcelain 'loop' insulators

Straight line mechanical ear

12-inch standard ear

Ribbed ear for curves

6-inch ear

Anchor & feeder ear

OVERHEAD FITTINGS FOR USE WITH GROOVED WIRE

a) POWER CABLE CONNECTOR

HARDWOOD RUNNER

Section insulator with anchor ear at either end

Both ends identical

ERO.88

inches long, known as a "runner", fitted between two phosphor-bronze end castings into which the overhead wires were terminated on either side of the gap and to which the power supply cables were connected. An alternative to this was an all-metal fitting which employed an "air gap" which was, in reality a piece of metal of the same profile as a hardwood runner, insulated from the running wires by being bolted into an insulated frame, supported in line with the overhead wire and its terminating points. Special heavy poles and double span wires were used to suspend this weighty piece of equipment in its place in the overhead.

The First Ploughshifts

With the installation of overhead wires from 1908 onwards, there was a need for an efficient method of changing from conduit to trolley working. An easy way of removing the ploughs from the cars was found by running the plough out of its carrier from either side of the car. Normally situated midway between the running rails, the slot rail on the outbound track, was diverted into a short "dead end" siding placed on an "island" between the tracks, which guided the plough out of its carrier when a car left the conduit system, by then being powered from the overhead wire. A similar converging slot led back into the centre of the track on the inbound side, to allow an attendant to place the plough into a carrier of the car entering the conduit section. Officially known as "ploughshifts", these sites were more commonly known as change-points or, even - to imitate the American equivalent - change-pits. While in the vicinity of a plough-shift, all cars drew power from the overhead wiring, the conduit slots being electrically "dead", thereby protecting the attendant from the danger of electrocution.

In the case of the first two ploughshifts, which were at the Camberwell end of Coldharbour Lane and the Brixton end of Gresham Road, the ploughs were run out from the carriers and the plough leads disconnected by the attendant. Conversely, the attendant had to electrically connect a plough to a car before it could be run beneath it. This procedure was rather cumbersome and, with the prospect of the construction of several more ploughshifts at various locations, the LCC engineers evolved a method whereby the electrical connections beneath the car were made with sliding contacts.

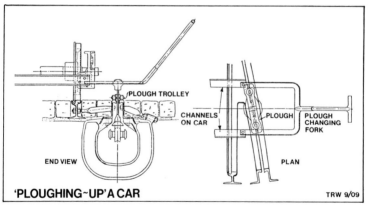

'PLOUGHING~UP' A CAR   TRW 9/09

Change-point Procedure

A car approaching the change-point on conduit working would be stopped before it, to allow the conductor to raise the trolley pole, and the motorman to operate the change-over switch which was fixed to the bulkhead panel beneath the stairs at one end of the car. This was carried out with the aid of the master controller key, which could only be removed when the controller was in the "off" position. The switch allowed only one circuit, either plough or pole, to be connected to the electrical system of the car.

In the opposite direction, a car would be stopped by the motorman at an exact place for the plough to be inserted. The attendant brought

*A typical scene at one of the many plough-shifts or "change-points"
on the LCC system, with a car being "ploughed-up" at Wandsworth.*
(The late Dr. Hugh Nicol, Courtesy: D. W. K. Jones)

up a plough from the "siding" slot and, sliding a large two-pronged
fork beneath it, lifted the fork ends on to holes drilled in the ends
of the guidebars of the plough carrier of the car. He then instructed
the motorman to move slowly forward. This movement, with the slot
rails being diverted to the centre of the track, guided the plough into
the carrier. Some yards further on, the car was again stopped where
the changeover procedure was carried out by the motorman operating
the switch. Meanwhile the conductor either stowed the trolley pole
beneath a hook fitted to the edge of the car roof at the back end,
or, in some cases, "ran" the pole round to the forward end of the car
and stowed it beneath the hook at that end, in readiness for use on
the return journey.

Plough Washing Equipment

The open conduit tubes were a "ready-made" receptacle for detritus
which laid about on the roads, much of this coming from the huge
numbers of horses then in use for various purposes. The problem was
particularly bad in wet weather, when large quantities of glutinous
mud would find its way into the tubes.

In an effort to overcome the electrical problems caused by mud
sticking to the ploughs, the Council agreed that an experiment with
a special plough washing plant be undertaken. This equipment consisted
of a number of powerful water jets which were permanently fitted
in the "plough washing pit" (which for safety was also in an electrically
"dead" section), and controlled by the passage of a car. The jets were
turned on by the action of the plough as it struck a lever at the beginning of the washing area, and were aimed at both sides of the plough
as it passed through the pit, being turned off as the plough struck
a second lever at the end of the pit. At the same time, any remaining
mud was removed by two fixed brushes, one on either side of the slot.

Believed to have been installed at New Cross Gate, the first washer
was evidently successful as, on 7th February 1911 it was agreed that
a further 13 be commissioned, sited on both southern and northern

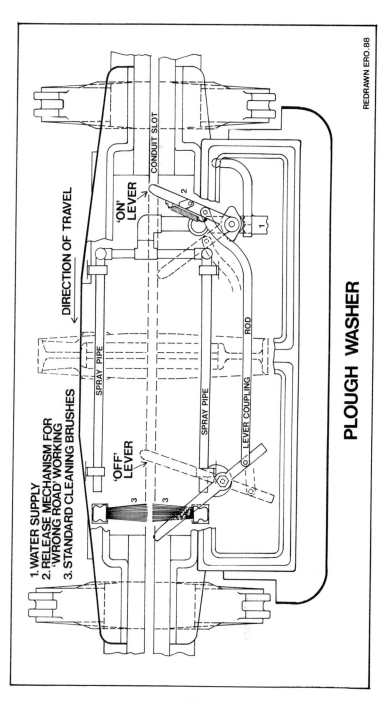

PLOUGH WASHER

DIRECTION OF TRAVEL

CONDUIT SLOT

'ON' LEVER

'OFF' LEVER

SPRAY PIPE

SPRAY PIPE

LEVER COUPLING ROD

1. WATER SUPPLY
2. RELEASE MECHANISM FOR 'WRONG ROAD' WORKING
3. STANDARD CLEANING BRUSHES

REDRAWN ERO. 88

systems. By the end of the Great War, there had been a considerable increase in the number of washers installed as, with a few exceptions, one was provided near each plough-shift, as well as those which had been installed in other places.

Track Maintenance

The Council maintained its system to a very high standard, with particular emphasis being placed upon the free operation of pointwork. Two-man parties were employed to keep the points and crossings in a clean and lubricated condition, with all points visited frequently - some daily. The tool kit used consisted of a couple of red flags, a point iron, brushes and an outsize oilcan. After carrying out their duties, the men would move on to the next junction, usually by travelling on the front platform of the first convenient car to come along.

It was necessary to ensure that the conductor bars were regularly inspected. Like the rest of the plant, they were beneath the road out of sight, and, to some, out of mind. As the tee-rails carried direct current at 550 volts, the necessity of regularly inspecting and maintaining the installation to a high standard was essential, a special staff under the control of the permanent way department undertaking the duty. Groups of five or six men made regular visits to all sections of track and, armed with flags and lamps and with each man carrying a long, thin, well-insulated rod with a mirror on the end, would walk the length of track under inspection. Each man would stop at regular intervals, push his mirror through the conduit slot, operate a handle to allow a thin rod or wire to move the mirror up or down to make his inspection of the rails, insulators and joints. His work done, he would walk to the head of the line and take up his station again to undertake his next inspection, each man reporting to the chargeman every time he passed him.

Another important, if unglamourous task was the removal of sludge and rubbish from the bottom of the conduit slots. Water was easily enough dealt with, as is explained elsewhere, but the removal of detritus required the services of another band of men who usually worked at night, coaxing any unwanted materials along the slots, aided by specially designed scrapers, until it was safely lodged at the sumps, there to be removed and carted away by contractors.

Rail replacement was another of the tasks usually carried out at night. Due to the intensive services operated on most of the system, it was virtually impossible - except for the most urgent of reasons - to take out lengths of rail during the working day. All preparatory work, as well as making good was dealt with in daytime, which left only the actual removal and replacement of rail lengths to be undertaken during the silent hours. Lighting was provided by the use of acetylene or paraffin flares mounted on long tubes, which were spaced out at intervals along the line of work, together with a liberal supply of paraffin oil lamps. In later years, these were supplemented by banks of floodlights supplied with power from the overhead wire or the conduit tee rails.

From the early days, the advantages of track welding were appreciated, special equipment being supplied by various manufacturers to enable this task to be carried out. A portable motor-generator set, to enable the welding current to be supplied at the correct voltage, was the centre piece of this assembly of equipment. The motor was energised by current drawn from the traction supply and collected from the overhead wire by means of a long bamboo pole with a metal hook at the top end, to which was attached a cable, being hung on to, or pressed up on to the overhead wire. The other end of the cable was connected to the motor set, the return current being conveyed to the running rail by a second cable connected to a device which looked rather like an oblong flat-iron, which was placed upon the rail.

When the welding set was used on conduit trackwork, the current had to be collected from below road level, for which a special type of connector was developed to enable this to be done easily and safely. In shape, it was rather like a plough, but shorter in length and lighter in weight. On top was an insulated handle which, when the "fore and aft" position, allowed the whole thing to be lowered down the slot at any convenient point, until the shoulders were resting on the slot rails. The handle was then turned through 90 degrees, this action extending a pair of arms equipped with electrodes which made contact with the positive and negative conductor rails in the slot, and by means of two cables connected to the electrodes, enabled current to be conveyed to the motor set of the welding plant. It will be appreciated that, should work be carried out while service cars were running, the connector would have to be withdrawn each time a car passed.

Overhead Wire Maintenance

With the introduction of overhead wires on sections of the Council's tramways, it became necessary to provide and maintain a fleet of special vehicles for use by staff to gain access to the overhead fittings. Three of these were located on the southern system, one for use in the Woolwich area, one for the lines between Camberwell, Brixton and Norwood and also for the short section between Streatham and Norbury, and one for the Hammersmith and Putney line, while a fourth was on the north side system for use in Poplar and Bow.

Known as tower wagons, these were horse-drawn by animals hired from local sources. The wagons were of quite simple construction, being virtually an adaption of the standard 4-wheeled cart then in common use, each with a two or three section tower permanently fitted to the cart floor. The tower was raised and lowered by means of a handle-operated screw mechanism.

The use of horse-drawn vehicles was, over the years, found to be slow and cumbersome in operation and so, in 1913, the Chief Officer recommended to the Council that these be replaced by motor vehicles, for which suitable towers could be supplied by Messrs. · Watlington at £75 each. The first two new motor lorry chassis were purchased but, just over a year later, were commandeered by the War Office, which forced the Council, once again, to have to rely on horse-drawn vehicles through out the war period.

Eventually, in 1919, the Council put out tenders for four electrically driven vehicles, which were to be powered by secondary batteries. The main contract went to Edison Accumulators Ltd. on 18th June 1920, but on 16th December 1920 was transferred to Electricars Ltd. with Edison supplying the batteries. The towers purchased in 1913 were then mounted upon the new vehicles.

Another battery powered tower wagon was called for in 1924. Electromobile Ltd. tendered for this on 14th October 1924 at a price of £1,097. However, the battery company went into liquidation before the job was completed, and on 17th November 1925 the LCC agreed to take over the wagon as it stood for £693, and purchase a new battery from Edison Accumulators Ltd.

Special Work

Construction of the many crossings and junctions on the system called for considerable skill, both in its design and operation. The main manufacturers in this field of engineering were Messrs. Hadfield Ltd. and the Lorain Steel Co. The method of operation of a set of conduit points was a considerable technical achievement, using complex linkages which had to switch the points and, at the same time being designed so that the car ploughs could pass unhindered through the work. The operating rods of a set of points were placed in a large pit constructed beneath the road and tracks. The LCC standard running rail points, 12 feet long were used, with the slot switch being formed by a leaf under each rail. The running rail points and slot rail leaves had to operate simultaneously and from one lever, usually placed at the outside of the point in the roadway, or in later years, remote from the track, on the kerb or footpath.

With the Lorain method of conduit pointwork, the two sides of the slot rail moved in a similar way to point blades, which unfortunately tended to become clogged with dirt, with consequent problems in moving the points. In the "Galbraith" system however, supplied by Messrs. Hadfield, the two slot leaves were concealed beneath the slot rails and remained free of dirt. The guides were connected together by vertical levers which in turn were connected together at the bottom by a horizontal rod within the conduit.

Independent levers and rods connected the two running rail point blades, both sets of levers being connected by horizontal shafts to the rocking arm which moved the points. This arm was pivoted, with the slot levers and rods joined up below the pivoted centre, while the running rail levers were coupled up above it. By moving the lever, an eccentric action was obtained, resulting in the running rail points being opened or closed, while the slot was actuated in the opposite direction. The pit containing the mechanism was covered with cast-iron boxes paved with setts.

At right-angled crossings, special yokes were used, consisting of sections bolted together to form rectangular "boxes" to which the track and slot rails were bolted. Once these were in place, heavy steel plates were laid in to form the foundation and support for the stone blocks of the road surface. Where the slot rails intersected, the conductor bars were broken to allow the ploughs uninterrupted passage.

Throughout the whole time that the Council operated the tramways in London, it was involved in considerable new works, much of it of a minor kind. Large numbers of additional crossovers were installed over the years; some junctions were re-arranged, added to or removed; and considerable doubling of single sections of track was accomplished. The list of improvements is so large that it is impossible to include them all in a work of this size, and it is hoped that the reader will understand this apparent omission.

There were, however, several schemes worthy of recording, among them the Nightingale Lane, South Side, Clapham loop;
The Harders Road, Peckham stub-end;
The Wickham Lane, Plumstead Corner third track lay-by;
The Forest Hill Station lay-by;
The provision of four tracks on Dog Kennel Hill;
The Blackfriars third track;
The provision of the second overhead wire at Beresford Square.

The layout at "The Plough", Clapham, with its third track lay-by, seen after completion, but still with horse cars working on the new tracks.

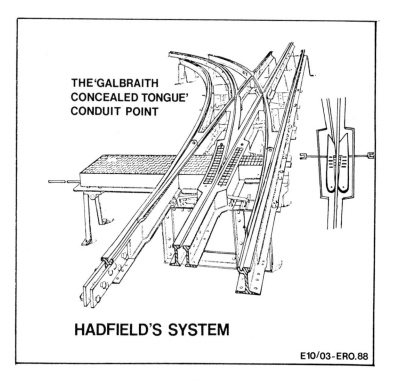

THE 'GALBRAITH CONCEALED TONGUE' CONDUIT POINT

HADFIELD'S SYSTEM

E10/03-ERO.88

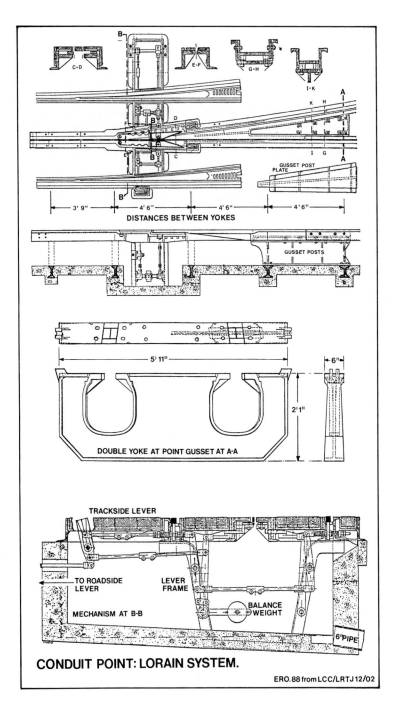

C-D

E-F

G·H

I·K

B

A

A

K H

I G

GUSSET POST
PLATE

| 3' 9" | 4' 6" | 4' 6" | 4' 6" |

DISTANCES BETWEEN YOKES

GUSSET POSTS

5' 11"

6"

2' 1"

DOUBLE YOKE AT POINT GUSSET AT A-A

TRACKSIDE LEVER

TO ROADSIDE
LEVER

LEVER
FRAME

MECHANISM AT B-B

BALANCE
WEIGHT

6" PIPE

CONDUIT POINT: LORAIN SYSTEM.

ERO. 88 from LCC/LRTJ 12/02

In September 1904, after a number of wilful attempts to cause disruption to services in the Elephant & Castle area, arrangements were made to provide extra switching pillars in the distribution network in order that sections could be individually switched off and on, to enable a service to be kept running in the event of further problems.

Another difficulty involved the use of point levers. On 4th July 1904, a complaint was made on behalf of the tramwaymen, that the positions of point lever boxes in the roadways were dangerous, especially where pointsmen had to be continually walking into the roads to operate the points. This was clearly recognised by the Chief Officer who stated "I am having them all removed to the pavements, except in the few cases where obstructions prevent this".

An unforeseen problem connected with the use of temporary flat-bottomed track to enable horse car services to continue during the period of reconstruction for electrification was that of alleged damage to the wheels of vehicles belonging to other road users. It had become most noticeable that the omnibus owners were making complaints about the state of the roads and about the effect it was having on their buses. In one case in 1905, Thomas Tilling Ltd. sued Dick, Kerr & Co. for alleged damage to their vehicles, caused when bumping over this type of track. The case was allowed to be heard because the LCC had not foreseen the problem when, making application for the Act authorising the reconstruction, and had not specifically requested that this type of rail could be employed on a temporary basis. To cover this, the expected use of temporary track had to be written into all future Bills.

On 27th December 1909 a great snowstorm lasting until 29th January 1910 swept across London, causing considerable dislocation of services. The conduit tramways were affected by powdered snow getting into the tubes, causing short circuits and earthing difficulties.

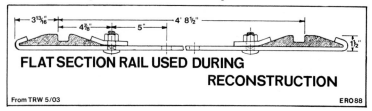

FLAT SECTION RAIL USED DURING RECONSTRUCTION

From TRW 5/03   ERO 88

Elephant & Castle Area, Complexities of Layout

A major difficulty facing the LCC Engineers and their staffs in 1902, was the construction of the extremely complex layout at the "Elephant & Castle", not only to cater for the Tooting-Bridges services, but also for subsequent routings, not yet electrified. In order to remove one obstacle, all of the horse-car services were diverted away from the area. Those from Kennington were re-routed along Kennington Road as far as Lambeth Road, and then into that road and along to St. George's Circus, where their normal routes were regained. All cars coming from New Kent Road and Walworth Road were diverted into Newington Causeway, where they then passed over the tracks of the South London Tramways Company in Southwark Bridge Road, then into Borough Road and on to St. George's Circus. Those on the service between Streatham and the "Lord Wellington", Old Kent Road were diverted to Waterloo Bridge. A special service was instituted between Camberwell Green and Asylum Road (Old Kent Road) via St. George's Church and Great Dover Street. These diversions involved

175

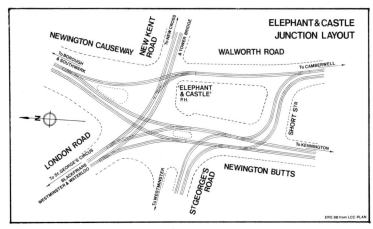

the provision of a considerable amount of temporary track, which was laid in a semi-permanent manner.

The "Inner South London Area", consisting of about two square miles of an intensely built-up maze of streets, with the "Elephant & Castle" and St. George's Circus junctions as its focal points, was the scene of considerable tramway activity in horse car days as services plied along the tracks laid in nearly every main road. Upon reconstruction, these roads and junctions had to be dealt with as one unit, in order that it would not be necessary to open the road surfaces again, when undertaking the vast works required when laying the conduit tracks and their associated electrical equipment.

In readiness for the replacement of horse cars by electric cars on services between Westminster, Waterloo Station and Blackfriars, all converging on St. George's Circus and the "Elephant", the special work for almost the whole of the subsequent routes was ordered and laid at one time. Regarding the "Elephant" junction, this entailed placing conduit tracks into the entrances to London Road, Newington Butts and Causeway, St. George's Road, New Kent Road, Short Street and Walworth Road, with all their connections into the layouts. The full length of St. George's Road, London Road, Newington Butts and the west end of New Kent Road were dealt with first and this included a length of single track, with its junctions and curves leading into Walworth Road from Newington Causeway.

At the other end of London Road at St. George's Circus, a similar programme was being carried out, with the junction special work for virtually the whole original layout being placed in one operation. This included the crossings and junctions between London Road and Waterloo Road, Blackfriars Road and Westminster Bridge Road, together with the special work which would make connection with the tracks to be laid from Borough Road and Lambeth Road.

The new electrified tracks along the full length of St. George's Road were provided basically for the Walworth Road to Westminster electric cars, but normally in the "up" direction only, to enable the Westminster-bound cars to avoid crossing the busy Elephant & Castle layout into London Road, and then across the complex of tracks at St. George's Circus into Westminster Bridge Road. In the "down" direction such a diversion was - apart from the importance of providing boarding facilities in the London Road - nowhere nearly as suitable to use, by reason of the difficult movements required to get into Short Street at the "Elephant" end, and so into Walworth Road.

The first sections of conduit track to be laid in the inner area included a number of complex junction layouts. Seen here at the Elephant & Castle, is a four-square crossing and a double junction layout being assembled. (Courtesy: Tramway Museum Society)

A double junction is seen in course of construction at the St. George's Circus end of London Road. The short ("standard") yokes used in all original construction are visible in the foreground.

(Courtesy: Tramway Museum Society)

The conduit track construction work in St. George's Road no doubt included the provision of point and crossing work at the junction of St. George's Road with Lambeth Road, ready for the installation of a single line curve leading from the "up" track in St. George's Road, across the "down" track towards the "up" Lambeth Road track (which was not reconstructed for electric operation until September 1906). This connection, combined with the relevant part of the complicated junction work at St. George's Circus, ultimately enabled electric cars to Blackfriars from Kennington and from Walworth Road to be diverted via St. George's Road, across St. George's Circus into Blackfriars Road. Except in weekday rush hour periods, such a diversionary facility was normally only used in emergency but even during the rush hours, such diversions were usually intermittent in that an attempt was always made to maintain as far as possible a frequent service - apart from cars coming from the Old Kent Road - of cars to Blackfriars calling at stops in the London Road.

Reconstruction work in Newington Causeway included the install-ation of double track points, crossing work and curves leading towards Southwark Bridge Road, and pointwork in the new single line south-bound track connecting with the "down" line in Walworth Road (after crossing the double track to and from New Kent Road, and the junction pointwork in London Road). Also included in the reconstruction work was a double track point and crossing layout, connecting new tracks in Borough Road (in the northbound direction), with the lines at the junction with Newington Causeway and Borough High Street.

The third important junction in this area was at St. George's Church at the point where Borough High Street, Marshalsea Road and Great Dover Street converged. This had been an important terminal point for the horse cars of the London Tramways Company, as well as being at the centre of a list of services working between the south-west and south-east suburbs. Conduit tracks on this section were laid as a result of the decision of the Council in December 1902, "to recon-struct for electrical working, some further short lengths of existing tramways in the Southwark and Bermondsey districts".

At St. George's Church there was, at first, only a reconstruction of the curves into Great Dover Street, with an electrified junction with the newly-laid tracks in Marshalsea Road and Great Dover Street, although the horse car services working from Streatham and Camberwell to Old Kent Road were not to become regular electric car services. The curve from Borough High Street into Marshalsea Road with its connecting junction came later.

In addition to the reconstruction of the main lines to Tooting and Greenwich, together with the Vauxhall to Camberwell line, a consider-able amount of horse car track within the "inner" south-east London suburban area was dealt with, together with some new work, with the object of making all the inner termini available to electric cars within the shortest possible time. The following table gives details of these.

SECTION	INSPECTOR	INSPECTION DATE	OPENING DATE
Junction, Camberwell Green, to bottom of Denmark Hill.	Col. Yorke	12th Jan 1904	24th Jan 1904
St. George's Road,	Col. Yorke	12th Jan 1904	30th Jan 1904
Southwark Bridge Road,	Col. Yorke	20th Jun 1904	1st Aug 1904
Marshalsea Road,			
Southwark Street (east)			

SECTION	INSPECTOR	INSPECTION DATE	OPENING DATE
Junction, Borough High Str. Great Dover Str. Lancaster Street, Newington Causeway.	Col. Yorke	20th Jun 1904	1st Aug 1904
Tower Bridge Road	Col. Yorke	20th Jun 1904	12th Sep 1904

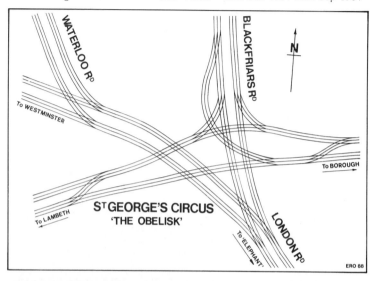

This section of interlaced double conduit track, showing the complexities of construction, was laid at Wandsworth, almost beneath the railway bridge spanning the road. (Greater London Photograph Library)

Some idea may be gained of the complications involved in laying conduit tracks in overcrowded conditions, usually in locations where nests of water or gas pipes had to avoided or diverted to allow construction to proceed. In the upper scene, sufficient clearance below the yokes was obtained without moving the pipes. In the lower view, taken on Victoria Embankment, main water pipes had to be diverted before construction of the tracks could proceed. The Metropolitan Water Board Inspectors kept watch on the proceedings.

(Courtesy: Greater London Photograph Library)

Chapter 15
The First Electric Line Opens

After the reported success of the conduit experiment, Dr. Kennedy was appointed Electrical Engineer for the reconstruction of the Tooting to the Bridges via Kennington lines at the rate of 4% on the cost of reconstruction plus 1% on the cost of buildings. To ensure that continuity could be preserved in the management and supervision of the electrification programme, the Council agreed that a permanent post of Electrical Engineer be created at a salary of £1,000 per annum. The holder was to be responsible to the Chief Engineer for all construction and reconstruction work (other than that being dealt with by Dr. Kennedy), for the efficient working of the generating station and all other electrical equipment of the tramways. Mr. J. H. Rider, who had been chief consulting and resident engineer for the electric lighting and tramways of Plymouth Corporation, took the appointment in February 1901, giving him sufficient time to make himself acquainted with the work in company with Dr. Kennedy.

Having made the decision to use the conduit system, the Council set to work with a will in making the first arrangements, and preparing specifications and plans. Unfortunately, the Metropolitan Borough Councils, so impressed with the original conduit demonstration, did not always respond with the same enthusiasm when it came to getting involved in the work and being expected to pay a share of the costs, although so far as the first reconstruction was concerned this difference of opinion was not too noticeable. As nothing could be done without the permission and goodwill of these authorities and, as they tended to take their time in coming to decisions, some of the work took longer to complete than originally anticipated. Parliamentary procedures also militated against any speedy work being undertaken by the Council.

Reconstruction was approved by the Board of Trade in April 1901, and it was expected that completion would be towards the end of that year. Apart from local difficulties with road authorities, however, a much greater problem was to be revealed. Power supplies for the lines should have come from a new generating station to be constructed at Camberwell, but this plan was scrapped in favour of a station to be built at Greenwich. Alternative arrangements had to be made to obtain power, which caused a further delay to the programme.

Initial financial approvals amounting to £644,350, later increased to £981,497, were authorised, which included new buildings and bridge construction, alterations to existing buildings, new lines, machinery, generating plant, rolling stock and electrical equipment. Tenders for all parts of the work were called for and contracts let. The proportion of the total estimated sum proper to the conversion of the 8 miles 1 furlong 9.30 chains total route length of the Tooting lines amounted to £440,120, comprising:-

£224,000 for rails and roadwork: Rate per mile, £13,660

£72,500 for cars (at a rate of 6.1 per mile)		£ 4,420
£74,000 for power stations and cables		£ 4,510
£20,600 for sub-stations		£ 1,255
£34,000 for car sheds and workshops		£ 2,075
£15,000 for salaries and incidentals		£ 915

working out at £26,835 per mile of single line inclusive.

Details of the contracts for the reconstruction of the Tooting lines were:-

Road and platelaying	J. G. White & Co. Ltd. London.	£171,145
-do- (additional)	-do- -do-	£ 8,230
Track rails and fastenings	Walter Scott Ltd. Leeds	£ 25,442
Slot rails, conductor tees and fastenings	-do- -do-	£ 25,334
-do- (additional)	-do- -do-	£ 2,085
Electric open top double deck bogie cars (100)	Dick, Kerr & Co. Ltd. London.	£ 71,754
Lowering carriageway beneath Clapham Rd railway bridge	Wm. Griffiths & Co. London.	£ 1,712
Laying stoneware cable ducts	J. G. White & Co. Ltd. London.	* £ 10,000

*Schedule of Prices basis of costing.

J. G. White sub-contracted Special Work to the Lorain Steel Co. and cast-iron work to the Anderston Foundry Co., Middlesbrough.

J. G. White took the sub-contract for ploughs and plough-carriers for the cars from Dick, Kerr and Co.

Dick, Kerr sub-contracted the car trucks to the J. G. Brill Company.

There was also a proportion of the cost of one million stoneware ducts for cables, a contract shared by three firms:-

G. Skey & Co. Ltd. Tamworth	500,000 for £9,125	
Stanley Bros. Nuneaton	250,000	£4,562.10s
H. R. Mansfield, Burton-on-Trent	250,000	£4,562.10s

Track laying commenced at the Tooting end of the line in April 1902 and the double line was completed throughout by 1st January 1903. There was an interesting if unusual three-track layout at the Clapham Common end of Clapham High Street, which was to provide for cars turning short at that point and also to act as a "holding" siding for the cars. Some delays had been brought about by a difference of opinion with Lambeth Borough Council over the method of paving to be used for some of the road surfaces, but after this problem had been resolved, completion of the roadwork was rapid.

In order that the horse car services could continue while the work of constructing the tracks was undertaken, temporary flat-bottomed grooved rails with flat steel tie-bars spiked into the roadway were laid alongside the existing horse car tracks at the many places where the work was going on, being connected to the existing, or relaid track by ramp rails. The temporary rails were laid in single track sections with passing places every 300 or 400 yards. Signallers were employed, complete with signal boxes and semaphore signalling apparatus, very similar to that used in railway practice. Signal arms painted red and white were used, augmented at night by red and white lights. The contractor, Messrs. J. G. White and Co. expected the LCC to pay for this aspect of the works which the Council declined to do but, under pressure from the contractor the Council after reconsideration decided to take over this responsibility with effect from 19th June 1902. By removing cars from the old tracks, the construction gangs could deal with an average of 700 feet of single line each day (the record on one day being 920 feet). In all, the total number of men employed varied from 500 to 600 under the control of the Chief Engineer to the contractor, Mr. A. N. Connett.

To break up the old track, a trench was cut on the outside of the rails. "Barratt Jacks" from the USA, each of 15-ton capacity were placed at 4-feet intervals along the trench, the heads of the jacks designed to fit under the rail webs. A long handle was fitted to each jack and operated by one man who, on raising and lowering the handle moved a ratchet and pawl device which pushed up the head of the jack, forcing up the rail and bringing up the setts and base concrete with it to a height of between 12 and 18 inches. Where this method could not be used (in places where old types of rail were still in situ) the more normal arrangement using wedges and sledge hammers had to be resorted to. After the removal of the old materials, a trench was dug along the length of the line to accommodate the yokes which were to carry the slot rails. The provision of the conduit tube, together with the associated drainage pipes and sumps, being at some distance beneath the roadway meant that the excavations would uncover a considerable number of pipes carrying water, gas and drainage. The cost of removing and resiting these was considerable and was included in the estimated charges to be borne by the Council.

It was, however to be another five months before services commenced, as there were many other matters to be attended to, such as electric cabling. Even this activity was delayed when a consignment of nine large drums of cable for the Clapham to "Elephant & Castle" section, being brought from Liverpool to London by sea aboard "S. S. Hopeful", was lost when the ship was sunk as the result of a collision off the south coast of England!

The jacking-out crew are seen here preparing to lift a section of horse car rail from the "up" line near "The Plough" Clapham.
(Courtesy: Tramway Museum Society)

In November 1902, the foundations were laid in a part of the cable depot at Streatham, for the provision of a temporary power generator to be driven from one of the cable-driving engines, for the purpose of obtaining sufficient current to drive one electric tramcar on the depot tracks for training motormen. The overhead wires, on top of which a special current collecting trolley was to stand, were in place by the middle of December. In January 1903, driver training commenced and continued at the depot for the next six weeks. In February, a start was made on cleaning out the conduits in preparation for electrical testing, after which the training of 250 motormen continued, using the completed conduit tracks between Clapham and Tooting, which was, by then, being supplied with power from the No. 1 engine at the temporary generating station at Loughborough Junction.

The Tooting Lines, Board of Trade Inspection

Once the track was complete and power applied to the conductor tee-rails, the first of the class "A" tramcars, assembled at Marius Road depot at Balham, ventured out on to the road on 7th April 1903 for test runs, followed by the others over the next few weeks. From then on, driver training continued, with electric cars running on lines which were also carrying a frequent service of horse cars. Driving tests were then carried out, in order that the motormen could be relicensed to allow them to drive the new cars in public service.

On 1st May 1903, all was ready for the official inspection of the lines, its associated electrical equipment and cars. The tracks and cars were inspected on 8th May by Col. H. A. Yorke, R. E., on behalf of the Board of Trade, while Mr. Trotter from the same department dealt with the electrical installation.

"Inspection by Col. Yorke of the lines between:-

Westminster and Tooting	5 mls 7 f. 3.4 ch.
Blackfriars and Kennington Park	1 ml 6 f. 3.5 ch.
Waterloo road	3 f. 3.0 ch.
Depot Line	9.4 ch.

and two short pieces of double line at "Elephant & Castle".

REPORT: Subject to speeds and stops named; to precautions at Railway Bridges and to raising the car railings (around the upper open deck) sanction may be given for electrical working. A slight alteration of the plough carriers to make them narrower is also suggested to meet the objections of the police. A ¾-inch slot rail groove width is agreed. The normal 15 inches between the widest parts of the cars generally met, except at a portion of the tracks which only allows 12½ inches. For this reason (it is) necessary for the Council to increase the height of the railings at the tops of the cars from 3 ft. 6 in. to 4 ft. 0 in. to protect the passengers. The road is in excellent condition. Mr. Trotter, the Electrical Adviser to the Board of Trade has reported on this. Beneath the two railway bridges, one at Balham and one at Clapham, the height is insufficient to permit of passengers standing up (on the top deck) with safety. All cars are to be brought to a halt before the bridges, then pass under at no more than 4 m.p.h. Notices are also to be affixed to the bridges warning passengers "KEEP YOUR SEATS" and conductors are to warn passengers verbally.

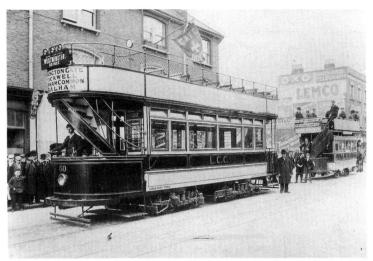

Prior to the opening of the electrified lines to Tooting, drivers were trained "on the road" while the horse cars were still running. In this view, the new and the old stand together.

(Courtesy: Tramway & Light Railway Society)

SPEEDS: Westminster to Tooting,
except Clapham Common,
South Side between
Clapham Park Road and
Nightingale Lane   12 m.p.h.
Clapham Common,
   South Side   10 m.p.h.
Kennington "The Horns"
to Westminster Bridge   8 m.p.h.
Blackfriars to Kennington
Park   8 m.p.h.
Waterloo Road line   8 m.p.h.
Through all facing points
and junctions and curves
into shed   4 m.p.h.

COMPULSORY STOPS: Either side of railway bridges at Clapham
and Balham;
Clapham Road - South Lambeth Road
crossing;
Clapham Road - Harleyford Road
crossing;
Lambeth Road - Kennington Road
crossing;

Stops in many other places, although many need not be compulsory.

CARS: Tidswell lifeguards, but with fixed steps there is some
danger.
If steps were made to fold up they would be much
safer.
The reversed-type stairs used are open to some criticism;
they do not allow the driver full observation all
round the car.

185

Plough Carriers. There is slight danger on sharp curves, they are too wide. The next batch of cars should carry slightly narrower carriers.

The conduit slot is wider at junctions, which could be a danger to cyclists, but this has been overcome by an ingenious arrangement of the points.

It is recommended that the lines may be opened.

(Signed) Col. H. A. Yorke, R.E.
8th May 1903."

The Board of Trade Certificate Number, R5380, was issued.

A Near Disaster

During his inspection of the tramways, Col. Yorke recommended that the railings round the top decks of the cars be made higher, in order to lessen the possibility of accidents occurring to passengers, through leaning over the sides. Resulting from this comment, the Commissioner of Police refused to license the cars for public service until his department was satisfied that the remedial work had been carried out.

The Tramways Manager, Mr. A. Baker, went personally to the office of the Commissioner on 13th May, in an attempt to explain that the Royal Opening had been set for Friday, 15th May, and that it was impossible for the modifications to be carried out before then. It had also been arranged for public service to commence immediately after the ceremony. The Commissioner, however, refused to see him. Baker then appealed to the Board of Trade to amend the Certificate, to give the Council six weeks to heighten the rails, in return, limiting the cars to a speed of 6 m.p.h. between Nightingale Lane and Tooting Terminus, until the work had been done. The reason for the recommendation was that between these points, the tracks were, in places, slightly less than the statutory distance apart, due to obstructions beneath the road making it impossible to properly align them.

This request was granted by Sir Herbert Jekyll, which gave the Commissioner no option but to issue the licenses, and so allow the Royal Opening Ceremony to take place and public service to commence afterwards.

Preparations for Opening

During the time that the finishing touches were being put to the pioneer conduit line, arrangements were being made for the opening of the system, and for this to be a festive occasion. Elaborate preparations were made for Their Royal Highnesses the Prince and Princess of Wales to attend the function, with the President of the Board of Trade together with his wife being invited as guests of the Council in joining in the celebrations. The following correspondence with the Board will illustrate the length to which the LCC went to ensure that the utmost prominence was attached to the occasion.

"I write to thank you for your letter of the 23rd instant stating that Mr. Gerald Balfour will have much pleasure in attending the inauguration by His Royal Highness the Prince of Wales of the Council's Electrical Tramways on the 15th proximo. The necessary arrangements have not yet been completed, but it is proposed that Their Royal Highnesses the Prince and Princess of Wales shall be received at the entrance of the pavilion in Lambeth Palace Road by the Chairman and several Members of the Council and will be conducted to the platform in the reception pavilion where the members of the Highways Committee and the past Chairman of the Council will be presented to His Royal Highness. The Chairman of the Council having presented to His Royal Highness a bound copy of the descriptive pamphlet of the Council's tramway system, the Chairman of the Highways Committee will make a statement in regard to the action taken by the Council in connection with tramways in London. His Royal Highness will then declare the electrical tramways open for use of the public. A vote of thanks to Their Royal Highnesses for honouring London by their presence on the occasion in question will then be moved and seconded.

It has occurred to the Council that as Mr. Balfour has taken such a great interest in the question of London locomotion and that, as the President of the Board of Trade, the plans of the tramways have been submitted to him and that the official inspection of the line by the Board of Trade will be made before the opening ceremony, Mr. Balfour may be willing to speak on the occasion. If Mr. Balfour would agree to assist at the ceremony in this manner, it occurs to me that the item be placed on the programme of proceedings immediately before His Royal Highness declares the tramway open, and stated in the following terms:-

'The President of the Board of Trade will state the views of the Board upon the Council's work'. The Council will be glad to learn that this proposal is agreeable to Mr. Balfour or (we) would alter the terms in any way which would meet Mr. Balfour's views.

After the ceremony, which will occupy about half an hour, Their Royal Highnesses will enter one of the electrical cars and will ride to Tooting and back, arriving back at Westminster at about 5.30 p.m.

The Council will be very pleased if Lady Betty Balfour can see her way to accompany Mr. Balfour on the occasion in question ...."

The extensive plans made for the accommodation of the large numbers of guests attending the Royal Opening Ceremony was the subject of considerable discussion in the Council chamber and with the Metropolitan Boroughs on the line of route, as well as with the management of St. Thomas' Hospital, who had made a large area available in front of the hospital upon which to erect a huge marquee for the occasion. The finer points of providing a covered walkway, with suitable carpet from the hospital grounds to the trams, generated much discussion. Special arrangements were made with the police in order to close the approach roads to all traffic on the great day and to deal with the crowds who were expected to come to view the proceedings.

The Ceremonial Pavilion

The huge pavilion which was set up in the grounds of St. Thomas' Hospital, close to Westminster Bridge, catered for the seated accommo- dation of 2,334 persons. The pavilion, 155 feet long by 75 feet wide was supported only by three centre poles. It was specified that the interior be "handsomely lined throughout with red and white decorative material and decorated with the Royal Arms and other suitable raised- design shields and trophies of national flags", and that a level wooden floor be laid on joists and sleepers.

A platform 45 feet long by 18 feet high was provided, which "was to project into the main pavilion", with steps at each end, the floor, front and ends covered with crimson baize with white ornamental balustrading at front and ends with necessary handrails for the steps. A Reception Room was constructed on the platform, with green and white decor, crimson carpet and matching crimson armchairs and draped with crimson silk plush curtains. Seventy-five superior gilt and upholstered chairs, with crimson cushions were provided for the platform, reception area and retiring rooms, together with suitable tables for each and for the Ladies' Cloakroom.

An annexe to the platform, 16 feet by 8 feet in area, was set aside as the Royal Persons' Retiring Room. This was substantially built and tastefully decorated with hanging red and white drapes, crimson carpets and rugs, and furnished with a number of "superior chairs and tables". A separate cloakroom area was provided, formed by a wooden framework divider, covered and draped to match the rest, with an additional area screened off with large heavy curtains, to form the private toilet accommodation.

Lastly, a covered way, complete with red carpet, 190 feet long, was provided between the pavilion and the tramway, so that the Royal Persons could have a comfortable walk to the cars after the ceremonial speeches were over.

All this was supplied and erected by John Edgington & Co., for a price of £243, while the total expenditure for the whole occasion was approximately £700.

The Royal Opening of the Tramway

The day set for the ceremonial opening of the Electrical Tramways of the London County Council was Friday 15th May 1903 at 2 o'clock in the afternoon. After the ceremonial speeches, the Prince of Wales, together with the Princess and their two sons were to travel upon the specially decorated car provided for the occasion. The Prince was also expected to start the car, the first of a long procession of fifty, on the journey to Tooting and back.

On the great day the weather was changeable but, suitably for the occasion, the rain held off. Invited guests included Mr. G. Balfour (President of the Board of Trade), Lord Monkswell (Chairman of the LCC), Mr. E. A. Cornwall (Vice Chairman of the LCC), Mr. J. W. Benn (Chairman of the LCC Highways Committee), the Members of the Council, the Tramways Manager and his senior staff, the representatives of St. Thomas' Hospital, together with all their Ladies. Ceremonial guards of honour and bands were present, while the ordinary citizens of London, who would probably gain most from the inauguration of the new electric tramways, were kept at a respectful distance from the Royal Persons.

After the arrival of the Royal Family and following the reception and speeches, each guest received a 32-page booklet giving the readers a short history of the origins of all forms of public transport in and around the metropolitan area, with emphasis on the tramways, leading to the eventual acquisition of the first lines and electrification by the Council. The Royal Family were then invited to take their places in the first car to run "in service", No. 86 of class "A". This had been specially painted in a livery of white and was decorated with evergreen and fern. Armchairs, upholstered in pale blue and pink material were provided in place of the more usual wooden benches in the lower saloon, while blue and white curtains and blue carpets completed the scene. The first duty of the Prince in starting the Royal car having been completed, the Royal Tram Driver went to the open top deck with his two sons, where the wooden seats remained in situ, taking his place at the front while the General Manager drove the car the rest of the way. The conductor for the occasion, Mr. J. Williams Benn,

A commemorative souvenir, issued on the occasion of the Royal Opening of the tramways, displays in a light-hearted way the progress from Thames to Tooting. (Courtesy: L T Museum. 1677C)

dutifully collected the Royal halfpennies for the fares, issuing special tickets printed in blue and gold on white in exchange for the coins.

On arrival at Tooting, the Royal Family left the car and were taken to the Totterdown Fields Estate where several of the cottage-type houses built by the Council were visited, thereby setting the seal of approval on the Council's programme of building homes in healthy surroundings for a number of that great cross-section of the community, known at that time as "working class". After this visit, they returned to the special car and travelled back to Westminster on the front top deck seats, to the delight of all concerned. The celebrations of the afternoon gave way to public service in the early evening when large numbers of people paid their halfpennies to have their first experience of riding on an electric car.

An Extract from "A Victorian Diarist 1895 - 1909".
Dated Friday 15th May 1903. This is from the pen of Lady Monkswell, describing the Royal Visit to the LCC Electrical Tramways upon the Opening on that Day.

"I went with Bob (Lord Monkswell!) to the ceremony of the opening of the Tramway from Westminster to Tooting, where the County Council have built some 200 Workmens' Dwellings. The Prince and Princess of Wales opened them and they and the two little boys, Edward and Albert, took the first "ride" in them to Tooting where they inspected the Dwellings and then "rode" back again to Westminster. The stir and excitement to meet Their Royal Highnesses was very great and to me very amusing. An immense tent had been set up in the yard of St. Thomas' Hospital, big enough to hold 3,000 people. The Royalties and we and some 20 of the County Council and their wives were on

It was a proud day for the LCC when the Prince and Princess of Wales opened the electric tramways. The Prince is seen starting the first car to leave Westminster. (Courtesy: Tramway & Light Railway Society)

the platform. Bob as Chairman had to order the proceedings. Mr. Benn, as Chairman of the Tramways Committee made a most excellent, brilliant speech, then Gerald Balfour spoke, also very well, then they were conducted to the trams, got in, the Princess, Lady Lamington and me inside, the Prince and the two little boys outside, and off we went five miles to Tooting. What amused and delighted me were the great importance and excitement of the County Councillors and their wives, all in their best clothes. Bob and I and some four others stood at the entrance to receive our Royalties. Captain Wells of the Fire Brigade came up in his uniform and brazen helmet and reported officially to Bob. "Sir, there are 12 Officers and 100 Firemen on duty".

A very strong, clever, foreign-looking man, very well dressed, came and looked round; this was the Prince's Private Detective.

On the stroke of 3.30 (p.m.) the big carriage with brown horses and servants in red liveries drove up and out got the Prince, looking very smart and very tired, the Princess the picture of health in a grey suit and rather small toque and the two dear little boys, Edward and Albert, in sailor clothes. Bob solemnly introduced us all, and they shook hands with us. I made the regulation deep curtsey and had the honour for the first time in my life of touching the hands of our future King and Queen, the second greatest people in the whole world. Lady Lamington, a fair, pretty woman and I walked into the tent after the Royalties and sat down behind them, the two boys being on either side of their parents. The speeches over, they all four signed their names in a book, the little boys taking the greatest pains. The Prince said to Prince Albert, "don't take too much ink". The Princess invited me to sit down and when we were in the tramcar together she spoke to me several times.

The Prince stood in the front of the car, and afterwards went on the top with the little boys, Bob and the others. The tramcar was very nicely arranged with blue chairs and pink cushions. What almost overcame me - it was so moving and also to me so novel, were the hundreds of thousands of people, also school-children without number, who lined the route, and the continuous cheering.

The Royal couple alighted at the Tooting end of the line, but the two princes appear not to want to leave their grandstand seats on the top deck of the car. (Courtesy: L T Museum. U15127)

The interior of a class A car used on ceremonial occasions. The comfort of the Royal Persons has been assured. (Tramway Museum Society)

The tramway runs sometimes along streets, then it cuts into the houses and crosses the bottoms of numberless small yards and gardens. Here would stand family groups, the stout middle-aged middle-class parents, their children of all ages, with the family dog, and these groups would be smiling from ear to ear so delighted to see first the Princess and then they looked up at the little boys who had taken up a good position on the roof and then the smiles redoubled. The Princess was so well used to this that I noticed that she did not turn a hair. Lady Lamington and I pinned up the little blue curtains so that she could be seen as clearly as possible. She is a very fine woman with a splended figure, broad shoulders, deep chest, upright. I wonder that the little boys are not bigger. On arriving at Tooting, they were met by Lord Carrington, who made them the most lovely bows and then, with others, conducted them over the Workmens' Dwellings (this move had been Bob's happy thought) very nice little houses, each with garden and yard for 10/6d and 12/6d per week and less. This took about half an hour, then we all returned in the same order, only on top of the tram as the wind was behind us. On arriving at Westminster, the gorgeous carriage again awaited them, the Princess shook hands with me and off they drove amid much cheering from the crowd. The poor Prince, who has not much hair, had to hold his hat three inches above his head nearly the whole way to Tooting and back. These kind, good Royalties took such trouble to do everything as well as possible".

(Courtesy of C. S. Smeeton)

As a result of the electrification of the Tooting lines, 854 horses were sold at £39 per head at which the Council expressed satisfaction as, in the valuation, horses were standing at an average of £30 per animal. Later, the selling price dropped to about £35 each as greater numbers of animals became surplus to tram and 'bus requirements. But it was different story with regard to the disposal of the cars. Nobody was interested in buying old horsecars. Consequently, as the companies were purchased, any cars which were sub-standard were replaced in service with an equal number from the surplus stock, the faulty cars then being scrapped. For a time this work was undertaken at a temporary site at Balham, then on Council land at Charlton, finally at the Central Repair Depot at Charlton for south side cars and at Union Road Works, Leytonstone, for north side cars.

Further South Side Conversions and New Construction

Only one extension was made to the electrified system in 1905, this being a short length of double track from Tooting, Totterdown Street to Defoe Road (now known as part of Garratt Lane). Constructed by Messrs. J. G. White & Co., it was inspected by Col. Yorke and sanctioned for use on 3rd August, being opened to traffic on 8th.

Even at this early stage in the reconstruction programme, voices were being raised at the stupendous sums of money needed to pay for the work. The immense sum of £26,835 per mile of single line was the figure most often used but it must be remembered that this first cost included many parts of the undertaking that would be common to other routes, in the use of track, depot space and power plant. But, it seems, this was not appreciated at the time (or if it was, it was not mentioned). A favourite comparison was between this line in London and the cost of the overhead wire system built in Manchester which worked out at about £6,800 per mile of single line; or of an estimate of what the Greenwich and Peckham lines would cost if reconstructed on the overhead wire system, viz; £7,496 per mile of single line. In later years the cost of track settled down to a little over double that of overhead, at between £15,000 and £18,000. It was a high price to pay and the Council knew it but, as frequently pointed out, the aesthetics of the case were, to most of the Borough Councils, as indeed they were to the County Council a most important part of the decision not to use overhead wires, especially in the inner areas of the County. Even so, the LCC was making discreet overtures about overhead wiring to the outer borough authorities, and would be doing the same thing to several of the inner ones in a few years.

The new cars had not been running very long when problems were experienced by mud on the roads being swept into the conduit slots by local authorities' employees (as a nice, easy way of getting rid of it). So great was the quantity of this glutinous muck that it caused power supply problems on some sections of line until the Tramways Department was able to convince the authorities concerned that the conduits were not there for that purpose. At the same time, difficulties arose over the design of the ploughs used, resulting in a number of breakages with accompanying delays to services. Remedial work was carried out under the supervision of Mr. Connett.

Another difficulty concerned wilful damage to the conduits and power tee-rails of the tracks in the Elephant & Castle area. During the first year of operation, deliberate attempts were made to bring services to a standstill, by people dropping metal objects into the slots, which caused short-circuits with the ensuing chaos. Rewards were offered for the apprehension of wrongdoers and over a period of several months four persons were imprisoned for their parts in offences of this nature.

Not so easy to eradicate was the problem of children with metal hoops who, in pursuing their pastime, sometimes allowed these articles to roll into the roads and, if one of these things slipped into a conduit slot, it would be likely to invoke the same level of mayhem as a deliberate attempt to cause a short-circuit. This problem was never really overcome although with the vast increase in road traffic, mainly motor omnibuses before the 1914-18 war and general motor traffic afterwards, it proved to be exceedingly dangerous for children to attempt to roll these play-things along main roads.

The introduction of class E cars on the Clapham and Tooting services was the cause of considerable interest. Car No. 413 is seen standing at the Defoe Road terminus. (Commercial view)

Chapter 16
Electrification, South East London

Although it had been stated that the conduit lines from the Bridges to Tooting were to be considered as experimental, plans were being made in 1902 to convert the lines from the Elephant & Castle to New Cross and Greenwich via Old Kent Road and via Walworth Road and Peckham to conduit working. This brought a spate of public comment and pro- and anti- debate in local council chambers, some of it quite acrimonious, including a broadside from Deptford over the purchase by the Council of land at "Fairlawn", New Cross upon which to build a car shed. Despite opposition, however, the LCC was not to be put off. Powers had been obtained to make the conversions; a compulsory purchase order had been secured for the part of "Fairlawn" required, and the Council intended to use these powers to the full.

Camberwell & Vauxhall

Work started on the reconstruction of the line from Camberwell Green to Kennington and Vauxhall, resulting in the horse car service being suspended as from 1st April 1903 as, with a single track and narrow roads, it was not possible to maintain a service whilst the road widenings were being carried out. The contractor for the lines, Messrs. J. G. White & Co., had the double track section between Camberwell Green and Kennington completed by mid-June; it was inspected by Col. Yorke for the Board of Trade on 25th and opened on the same day. The section between Kennington and Vauxhall was complete by the middle of July, being inspected by Col. Yorke on 1st August. Both sections were provided with a through service on 2nd August.

Greenwich via Old Kent Road: New Cross via Camberwell

Contracts for the reconstruction of the Old Kent Road, New Cross and Greenwich sections were let in January 1903, work being divided between Messrs. J. G. White & Co. Ltd. and Messrs. Dick, Kerr & Co. Ltd., on "an amicable basis" with Dick, Kerr dealing with the special work from the "Bricklayers Arms", along Old Kent Road, New Cross Road and Greenwich Road to the terminus at East Greenwich; White's dealing with similar work on the northern section of the Old Kent Road, along New Kent Road, at the Elephant & Castle, along Walworth Road, Camberwell Green and Peckham Road to New Cross. The tenders of:-

> J. G. White at £218,005.12. 4d (using Lorain special work)
> and £216,630.10. 4d (using Hadfield special work)
> Dick, Kerr at £208,218.19. 5d (using Lorain special work)
> and £211,985. 0.11d (using Hadfield special work)

showed that this "amicable arrangement" would also ensure that both "special work" manufacturers got their share of the contracts.

There were several sub-contractors involved, all being under the superintendence of Mr. Maurice Fitzmaurice, the Chief Engineer to the Council and Mr. J. H. Rider, the Chief Electrical Engineer.

Some examples of quantities of materials ordered can be seen from the following:-
Rails, 2,245 tons; slot rails, 1,470 tons; conduit tees, 705 tons; all from P. W. Maclellan, Glasgow, at a cost of £33,876.19. 8d.

Stoneware cable ducts for the New Cross and Greenwich sections were to be supplied by Reid Bros. London, for £24,363.17. 9d; 150 tons of soleplates by Cooper Anchor Patent Rail Joint Co. for £1,786.14s; uniforms for car crews from H. Lotary & Co. London, £2,556. 5s; and for the provision of new lamp standards and alterations to existing ones on which to put stop signs, £250.

One important change in the structural details of the tracks was that the rail length had been altered from 30 to 45 feet. This was to reduce the number of rail joints which, it was considered would reduce wear on the car wheels and car trucks. In conjunction with the use of longer rails, the special fishplates as used on the first lines were replaced by ordinary ones, two feet long, having six bolts - three in each rail end. Changes were also made to the shape of the drain sumps and their positions beneath the tracks.

On a short piece of single track at Greenwich - the first on the system - special arrangements had to be made for the cars to pick up power when moving in either direction, this being accomplished by using two conduit slots side by side, the inner tee-rails supported by insulators mounted between the track on specially cast double yokes, while those on the outsides were supported in the usual way.

A major problem encountered in connection with the reconstruction of these lines was the need to completely rebuild two railway bridges carrying the road over the tracks of the London, Brighton & South Coast Railway near New Cross Gate, and over the South Eastern & Chatham Railway at New Cross Road, about half a mile east of the first-named bridge.

A busy scene in New Cross Road as class D car, No. 353, with enclosed top deck but still sporting reversed stairs, heads a line of cars towards New Cross Gate early in 1907. (Courtesy: A. D. Packer)

The Greenwich terminus for electric cars was to be at the same place as that used by the horse cars, outside the "William IV" public house, Trafalgar Road. It was here that the line of the Woolwich & South East London Tramways Company was met head-on, and where a change of gauge was encountered, the Woolwich company line being 3 ft. 6 in., which was to cause some problems in later years, when it came to the conversion of it and the extension of standard gauge conduit tracks towards Woolwich.

At the beginning of January 1904, the work was complete. After trials, the Board of Trade inspection took place on 11th January, when Col. Yorke visited the line. Public services from the Bridges, via "Elephant", Old Kent Road, New Cross Road and Greenwich High Road commenced on Sunday, 17th January. On the following Sunday, the 24th, electric car services began running to Greenwich via Camberwell, Peckham and New Cross.

Cars of all four classes are to be seen in this view, taken at New Cross Gate during the summer of 1906.   (Courtesy: A. D. Packer)

New Cross, Lewisham & Rushey Green

Remaining in the south-eastern suburbs, the first sections to be completed during 1906 were the new lines between New Cross, the "Marquis of Granby" and Lewisham Obelisk, together with reconstruction of a standard gauge horse tramway onwards to Rushey Green, Catford. In both sections, considerable bridgeworks and road widenings had to be attended to where the railway tracks of the S. E. & C. Railway crossed over both Loampit Vale and High Street, Lewisham, before track laying could begin. The bridge carrying Loampit Vale over the River Ravensbourne also had to be rebuilt, both to widen the road and to accommodate the conduit tracks.

During the course of construction of the lines in Lewisham High Road by Messrs. Dick, Kerr & Co. Ltd., the junction work was inserted at Malpas Road and Shardeloes Road in advance of the construction of the lines to Brockley and Forest Hill in order to avoid further disturbance to the tramway traffic and ordinary traffic in Lewisham High Road. The same course of action was taken at the junction with the horse tramway at the Obelisk. The Board of Trade inspection was taken by Col. Yorke on Saturday 27th January 1906, sanction to operate being given on 29th, the lines opening to traffic on 30th. This was followed by the inspection of the Lewisham to Rushey Green line by Col. Yorke on 6th June 1906, after which the whole line was opened to traffic on 10th, by extending the service between Vauxhall and Lewisham to Rushey Green.

A rare view of a horse car and an electric car standing together at Rushey Green. This combination of services only lasted for five days.

The South Street Line to Lewisham

This section of the South Eastern Metropolitan Tramways Company line, which was more or less half the length of the company's tracks, was about seven furlongs in length; all single line with passing places, and all worked through narrow streets.

After the acquisition of the company by the LCC, the horse car service continued to run as it had always done. Despite the insertion of a conduit junction at the South Street end of the line when the New Cross to Greenwich section was electrified in January 1904, the horse cars never worked beyond the original terminus in South Street. Upon electrification of the Lewisham to Rushey Green section, the horse car service was maintained between Lewisham and South Street until the decision was taken late in 1907 to close down the service in order to expedite reconstruction on the conduit system. During the time that the cars were off the road, Messrs. Thomas Tilling & Co. provided a special horse omnibus service between Greenwich and Lewisham on behalf of the LCC.

Reconstruction was carried out by the LCC Works Department at a cost of £50,500 for road works, with extra costs for rails and special work, plus approximately £10,000 for cables and ducts. A considerable quantity of special work was required as there were originally seven sections of single track, each requiring two sets of points and the associated mechanical linkages, etc. This was eventually reduced to six sections, at which number it remained throughout the whole of the tramway era.

Another expense incurred was in the virtual reconstruction of the road bridge over the Greenwich Park branch railway line in Lewisham Road, together with a considerable sum spent in lowering the road beneath the railway bridge at the Lewisham end of Lewisham Road, so that top-covered double deck cars could negotiate this section.

Col. Yorke inspected the line on the same day as he visited the South Lambeth Road line on 3rd April 1908, and it was opened for public services on 4th April.

Class C car, No. 240 seen soon after the opening of the electrified line between Lewisham and Greenwich. *(Courtesy: Lens of Sutton)*

Tooley Street & Bermondsey to Deptford & Greenwich

The tramways belonging to the London, Deptford & Greenwich Tramways Company passed to the LCC in July 1904 and almost at once there was discussion about electrification of the lines. It was, however, to be some years before this materialised. In the meantime, the main line of the ex-company system between Deptford, "Noahs Ark" and Tooley Street continued to be worked in much the same way as before, while services on the branch lines were improved somewhat.

During the latter half of 1909, reconstruction of the London Bridge to Deptford route commenced with the rebuilding of Blackhorse Bridge (the bridge over the Surrey Canal) and incorporation of new conduit track as the first part of the work. Shortly afterwards, the road bridge spanning the Metropolitan District Railway line at Deptford Road Station (later renamed Surrey Docks) was similarly dealt with.

Roadwork commenced on 10th August 1910, the contract for this being awarded to Mr. A. N. Coles of Paddington, with an original estimate of £123,675, later increased to a final figure of £133,997 due to extra works requiring execution. The work was undertaken in five sections; from Lower Road, Rotherhithe "Red Lion" to Dockhead; from Dockhead to Tooley Street at the same terminus as used by the horse cars; from Rotherhithe, "Red Lion" to the west side of Creek Bridge, which included just over a quarter of a mile of new extension; from the east side of Creek Bridge to Greenwich, which was also new work, and lastly across the bridge itself.

Col. Yorke next inspected the sections between "Red Lion", Dockhead and Tooley Street (Bermondsey Street), 2 miles 2 furlongs in length, together with a short junction line at the head of Tower Bridge Road in the direction of London Bridge on 22nd February 1911, after which it was opened to electric cars on 25th. This was followed on 20th June 1911 by his inspection of the line between "Red Lion" and Creek Bridge, one mile long which opened to traffic on 22nd. The line from the east side of Creek Bridge to Greenwich Church, 3 furlongs, including the junction layout at Greenwich, was opened to traffic on 5th August 1911 after inspection by Col. Yorke on the previous day.

There were three sections of single track between Rotherhithe Tunnel and Dockhead, two in Union Road, the other in Parker's Row, where the roads were quite narrow and effective widenings could not be carried out. One other short section of single line was placed beneath the railway bridge spanning the north end of Creek Road, where it was found to be impossible at that time to carry out widening work.

When the first sections of conduit track were laid, a double junction layout was inserted into the track at the "Red Lion", Rotherhithe in anticipation of eventual reconstruction of the horse tramway running through parts of Rotherhithe New Road and Southwark Park Road to Tower Bridge Road. Due to delays in obtaining the necessary authority to carry out the work and the ultimate onset of the Great War, this was never undertaken and, after cessation of horse car services in 1915, the whole project was abandoned and the pointwork taken out.

Creek Bridge, spanning Deptford Creek required total rebuilding to be able to accommodate a double deck tramway, and the opportunity was taken to reconstruct it as an electrically operated bascule bridge. Messrs. Dick, Kerr & Co. Ltd. laid the conduit tracks and provided the electrical equipment for raising and lowering the bridge. After completion, the bridge and tramway were inspected by Col. Von Donop on 2nd October 1912, and both were opened to traffic on 3rd.

A short extension of the tramway from its terminus at Bermondsey Street to Duke Street Hill, Tooley Street, in all about 200 yards long was constructed by Messrs. Dick, Kerr & Co. Ltd. at a cost of £7,796; was inspected by Col. Yorke on 22nd November 1912 and then opened in two sections, firstly as far as Cotton's Wharf, Stanier Street on 28th November and throughout to Duke Street, London Bridge on 9th December 1912. The terminal arrangements were quite unusual at this end of the line, there being a section of single track about 50 yards long from Stanier Street towards the end of the line, after which it opened out to double line for the remainder of the route, with a standard trailing crossover about two car lengths from the end of the line. It had been intended that the line should be extended along Duke Street Hill to join up with the tracks in Southwark Street but, like so much else that the Council wished to do, was not allowed for one reason or another.

E/1 class car No. 1422 being driven towards Deptford through the single track section in Union Road, Rotherhithe, while another car, bound for Tooley Street waits to use the section. (Courtesy: A. D. Packer)

The Greenwich & Woolwich Line and
Greenwich to Blackwall Tunnel

Once the conversion of the narrow gauge line, lately belonging to the Woolwich and South East London Tramways Company, had been decided upon in the summer of 1905, it was dealt with in two distinct parts. The west end of the line butted up to the conduit tracks which terminated at the "William IV" public house, Trafalgar Road, East Greenwich and the Council were determined to reconstruct as soon as possible the section as far east as Tunnel Avenue, a distance of about three-quarters of a mile. On 27th November 1905 the section between East Greenwich and Blackwall Lane was closed, to be followed a couple of weeks later by the length between Blackwall Lane and Tunnel Avenue. Reconstruction took about six months, with electric cars being given trial runs over the new line in May 1906. The Board of Trade inspection was undertaken by Col. Yorke on 6th June, and public service started on 10th. This pattern of closing sections of the narrow gauge horse tramway to enable reconstruction work to proceed was the only practical way in which the LCC could cope with the situation.

Concurrently with the reconstruction of the short length in Woolwich Road, a new section of conduit tramway was being constructed from a junction with that line, along Blackwall Lane and the northern end of Tunnel Avenue, to end almost at the mouth of Blackwall Tunnel. This double track line, built by Messrs. Dick, Kerr & Co. Ltd., was inspected by Col. Yorke at the same time as the remainder, but was not opened to traffic until 18th June 1906.

Meanwhile, the new Central Repair Depot of the Tramways Department was taking shape. This installation, conveniently placed next to the Angerstein Wharf branch line of the South Eastern & Chatham Railway Company, had access from Woolwich Road and a branch tramway line was planned to connect with the conduit lines in Woolwich Road - when they were built.

The first section of the Works was expected to be ready for use in March 1909 and, in order to connect it into the growing network, it became imperative to extend the Woolwich Road line at least as far as Rainton Road, a distance of 308 yards. After considerable difficulties in obtaining agreement with Greenwich Borough Council over road levels were overcome, arrangements were made for this short length to be reconstructed and be available as soon as possible after the opening of the Works and, if possible, to attempt to extend the conduit tracks even further eastwards. Due this time to difficulties in coming to terms with frontagers, the further extension proved to be impossible, the Council having to be content for the time being with having got as far as the Central Repair Depot.

At the eastern end of the horse tramway, considerable work had been going on with the reconstruction of the section between Plumstead and Woolwich, which resulted in the narrow gauge horse cars working only as far east as Beresford Square, Woolwich. The stables and horse car depot at Plumstead were therefore no longer available and premises in Tunnel Avenue were provided on a temporary site. Corrugated iron sheds were erected to serve as an office and stables, and a couple of storage tracks laid in, upon which the cars, covered in tarpaulin sheets, could stand when not in use. A connecting line, about 150 yards long, was laid between the depot and Woolwich Road. Cost of this temporary work was approximately £300 for the buildings and £350 for the tracks.

Class C car No. 257 standing at the Blackwall Tunnel terminus, almost outside the tunnel entrance. *(Commercial view)*

The reconstruction of the length between Tunnel Avenue and Rainton Road was undertaken by Messrs. Dick, Kerr & Co. Ltd., the roadworks for which cut off the temporary depot from the horse tramway. Arrangements were made for accommodating the horse cars in the CRD for a short time and, in order to provide a track, an extra rail was laid outside the standard gauge branch line which had been constructed from Woolwich Road to the Works, at a distance of 3 feet 6 inches from the conduit slot.   Thus, for the time that the temporary car stand was in the Works, the "dual gauge" track was in use, but did not last for very long.   When the conduit track extension in Woolwich Road had been completed, an extra rail was laid outside the electrified track (as at the CRD) to enable the horse cars to be taken back to the temporary depot in Tunnel Avenue when not in service.   The horses continued to be stabled at Tunnel Avenue throughout this period.

The Central Repair Depot was ceremonially opened on 5th March 1909; while the conduit track extension from Tunnel Avenue was inspected by Maj. Pringle on 17th July 1909 and opened to traffic on 22nd. Electric cars were extended over this short piece of track, while the horse cars now worked between Woolwich Road, Rainton Road and Beresford Square.

As mentioned, the LCC had high hopes of extending the conduit tramway into Charlton and Woolwich, but were delayed by the problems associated with the purchase of frontages.   These difficulties were overcome towards the end of 1909, when preliminary works connected with duct laying and drainage re-arrangements commenced, and massive works in connection with the relocation and rebuilding of a wall at the west end of Woolwich Dockyard were undertaken to enable the road to be widened.   The horse car service continued to operate from Rainton Road until 22nd August 1910, when it had to be closed progressively to enable track work to commence.   The section between Rainton Road and Church Lane was the first casualty, and the cars which were still in use were moved to a temporary siding at Anchor & Hope Lane, with the horses still stabled at Tunnel Avenue.   For three weeks a service was maintained between Church Lane and Woolwich

Ferry (by now a westwards extension of the overhead wire line had been completed as far as the Ferry), but on 29th August the section between Church Lane and Trinity Street was closed, to be followed three days later by the closure of the line as far as Chapel Street. By this time, the horses and cars had again been moved back to Plumstead depot.

Track reconstruction between Rainton Road and Chapel Street was rapidly carried out by Messrs. Dick, Kerr & Co. with a trial car being run over the new extension on Wednesday 22nd March 1911. Col. Yorke inspected the line on behalf of the Board of Trade on 30th March and it was opened to traffic on 1st April. The greatest difficulty of all then confronted the LCC Engineers on surveying the remainder of the horse car route as, in order to be able to lay even a single line of conduit track, huge construction works had to be undertaken, which included the provision of a new section of road.

An interesting side issue arising from the use of this very short section of narrow gauge horse tramway, concerns the employment of a specially built flat truck fitted with standard gauge tramway wheels, which was used to convey the narrow gauge horse cars to and from the depot in Plumstead to the isolated section of line. This wagon was equipped with a folding ramp and narrow gauge rails upon which a horse car could be carried and in this way the cars required for the service were taken from or to the depot to the narrow gauge track at Woolwich Ferry, there to be let down or taken up as required.

A rare photograph showing the unusual standard gauge trailer with a narrow gauge horse car standing upon it, about to be unloaded at Woolwich Ferry. When the ramps were positioned, the car was let down with the aid of a hand-operated winch. The reverse procedure was carried out at the end of the day when the car was taken back to the depot at Plumstead. (Courtesy: Tramway Museum Society)

Car No. 202 of class C and class D car No. 366, both in covered top, open balcony condition, pass in Greenwich Road. No. 366 is held up by the slow-moving horse-drawn dray. *(Courtesy: A. D. Packer)*

During the course of one of these early morning excursions, an incident occurred which is worth recording, being taken from an article by E. F. E. Jefferson, entitled "Woolwich and the Trams", reported in the Proceedings of the Woolwich and District Antiquarian Society Vol. XXX, and reproduced from "The Tramways of Woolwich and South East London" (LRTA/TLRS, 1963).

"At 4 a.m. one very wet morning in November 1911, very wet, even for November - a certain Mr. Jago and his confederates had brought the outfit from the yard and, having reached Nile Street, and unhitched the horses from the trolley, took shelter from a particularly heavy downpour in the doorway of a corner shop, Streatfield, Cornchandler. For some unknown reason, the tram, aloft, on the trolley, began to move forward. Before the crew could do anything, the front wheels bumped to the ground, the horses suddenly took fright and ran off along the High Street in the direction of St. Mary's Church. The dragging traces and clanking bar, only incited the horses to swifter movement, as they galloped on in the murky darkness, up the steps leading to Church Passage and full tilt into the plate glass window of the Mitre Public House. Both horses were seriously injured, in one case fatally, but the staff were exonerated of all blame.."

Eventually, on 23rd November 1913, this rather novel car transporter and its unusual load was taken out of service when the short section of narrow gauge line was closed for reconstruction to enable the all-conquering electric cars to take the road. Five months later, dream became reality when, on Wednesday 1st April 1914 the first trial runs took place on the new line, the Board of Trade inspection taking place two days later when Maj. Pringle visited the line.

Finally, on Sunday 5th April 1914, the section was opened to traffic, even though parts of it were single track. A conduit/overhead wire change point was installed just east of Nile Street, Woolwich Ferry to enable through working to take place. Woolwich was isolated no longer. The horses and their unusual narrow gauge cars passed into oblivion. It had taken the LCC 8 years and 5 months to reconstruct just over six miles of tramway. A record surely!

The Woolwich & Plumstead Tramway

Under the provisions of the London County Tramways (Electrical Powers) Act, 1900, clause No. 3, the Council was empowered to reconstruct the existing horse tramways in Beresford Square, Plumstead Road and High Street for electric operation and, under the provisions of the London County Council (Tramways & Improvements) Act, 1904, the Council was authorised to construct new tramways in Beresford Square (Nos. 15A & 15B), and in High Street and Bostall Hill, Plumstead, and McLeod Road and Knee Hill, Abbey Wood (No. 16). The Council had been in negotiation with the Metropolitan Borough of Woolwich and the Board of Trade, regarding the use of overhead wires on this route and, as Bexley UDC had already brought its electric tramway into Plumstead, terminating at Plumstead Church, traversing the last mile or so on roads within the County of London and employing the overhead wire to provide power for the cars, the Woolwich Borough Council could not very well refuse to allow the LCC to do the same.

In an Act of Parliament obtained in 1903, the Urban District Council of Erith had obtained powers to build a tramway from the LCC boundary at Abbey Wood, along Knee Hill, McLeod Road, Basildon Road and Bostall Hill to connect with the Bexley Council line at Wickham Lane Corner (Tramway No. 7) and to provide a junction line into Wickham Lane (Tramway No. 7A), but these were not to be built except with the consent of the Metropolitan Borough of Woolwich and the LCC. A further clause was added preventing Erith opposing the LCC if it should decide to build the line itself. The object of Erith was plain enough; the tramways of that Council would undoubtably become more profitable if a through service to Plumstead and Woolwich, with a connection into the London system could be obtained. To this end, Erith made overtures to the LCC from time to time, but to no avail. Meantime, the LCC, by an Act of Parliament obtained in 1904, received powers to build the line itself, thus thwarting the plans of Erith who nevertheless still hoped that the line to Abbey Wood would be connected to the UDC system. But it was not to be, even though the two lines were only about 20 yards apart. After several attempts to obtain an agreement and several threats of unilateral action including one to run omnibuses from Abbey Wood to Woolwich, the matter rested.

Reconstruction commenced at the Plumstead end of the horse tramway when, on 21st November 1907, the section between Plumstead Church and Bannockburn Road was dealt with. Two days later, the horse car service was cut back to Lakedale Road to enable new standard gauge tracks to be laid into the depot. On 10th January 1908, a further section between Lakedale Road and Heverham Road was closed, to be followed at intervals of between about four to seven days of other short sections until, by 3rd February the whole line was being dealt with.

However, some sort of service resumed on 27th February, with horse cars running between Plumstead Church and Plumstead Station on the reconstructed tracks. The LCC had evidently brought in several standard gauge cars "from retirement" for this. The decision to resume horse car working was taken to ensure that the road was re-opened at the earliest opportunity and, even though the journeys were quite short, provided the means of transport for large numbers of people who were employed in Woolwich Arsenal and other establishments in the area.

Due to the narrow roads, much of the track between Plumstead Church and Orchard Road, just east of Plumstead Station, was single

Very early days of electric traction in Plumstead. Car No. 185 stands at the stopping place at Lakedale Road, bound for Woolwich.

(Commercial view. Courtesy: P. J. Davis)

with passing places. From there, along Plumstead Road to Burrage Road, the line was predominantly double, but for the last quarter of a mile, two more sections of single line were laid. At Beresford Square, two single stub-end tracks were provided, one for use by the LCC cars, the other for the Bexley cars.

Early in April 1908 the work was complete and a physical connection had been made with the Bexley UDC tracks. Trial running with one of the specially adapted class "B" cars took place as from 15th April, to be followed by the Board of Trade inspection by Col. H. A. Yorke on 16th, with public service commencing on the following day. The 150 yards of Bexley UDC track in Plumstead High Street was purchased for £1,189.17.10d. on 7th June; a junction was installed at Wickham Lane Corner and new track laid from the junction to Abbey Wood. Apart from a long single line section between Wickham Lane and the top of Basildon Road, the remainder was all double track. This was inspected by Col. Yorke on 25th July 1908 and opened for public service on the following day.

Overhead equipment was supplied and erected by Messrs. Dick, Kerr & Co. Ltd., who sub-let the contracts for line ears and hangers to Messrs. Brecknell, Munro & Rogers; trolley and other wire to F. Smith & Co.; poles to John Spencer; insulators to Johns, Manville & Co.; pole-straps to B. C. Barton & Co. Total cost of the Woolwich - Plumstead section was £2,323. 4. 2d. for the overhead, while points and crossings supplied by Messrs. Hadfield cost £967. 5s. Roadworks cost £19,241.14. 7d, with rails, section feeder pillars and the like supplied from bulk order stocks as required. The Council laid the tracks.

The Plumstead to Abbey Wood section added another £23,280 to the cost of this, the first LCC line to use overhead wires. Power was supplied at 550 volts d.c. by Woolwich Borough Council Electricity Department, from its generating station in White Hart Lane, Plumstead, at a contract rate of 1d (one penny) per unit.

As Bexley tramcars were already serving Plumstead and, as the UDC had come to terms with the LCC, it was not surprising that Bexley pressed for running rights to Woolwich. This commenced on the 26th July and was the first instance of a through running arrangement being made between the LCC and another undertaking. Bexley however, had to pay dearly for the privilege; it cost the UDC the gross receipts earned on the section less working expenses, plus a rent of 6d per car mile, the agreement to stand for an initial period of seven years.

The next stage in the extension of this isolated line was the reconstruction of the half-mile length from the western terminus at Beresford Square, along Beresford Street to Nile Street, Woolwich Ferry which was still in use by the narrow gauge horse tramway to East Greenwich. Due to the narrow streets, the decision was taken to lay a single line of tramway with three passing loops at suitable places. In July 1909, Messrs. Dick, Kerr & Co. contracted to reconstruct this section on the overhead wire system as an extension of their contract for the Lewisham Road line at an expected additional cost of about £6,150, with the overhead work costing an extra £650.

Eight cars of class B were modified and specially adapted to work on the isolated Woolwich, Plumstead and Abbey Wood line in 1908. No. 118 stands at Beresford Square soon after the line was opened.

An interesting problem occurred in the construction of this section. Messrs. John Mowlem & Co. Ltd. had the task of pole planting along the half-mile route, but had great difficulty in avoiding obstructions beneath the footways, resulting in the use of a number of cantilevered or "bent" poles to avoid the obstacles. The Admiralty also became involved, as the west end of the extension was just three miles from Greenwich Observatory and in the view of that body, its permission was required before the line could be reconstructed using overhead wires. Eventually, after "dragging their feet", the necessary authority was received from the Admiralty on 29th September.

Another "difficulty" encountered concerned the attitude of the War Office, for which it was stated that, in the opinion of the Department, cars should not be allowed to stop anywhere in the vicinity

Although fitted with the equipment for a "Venner" type service number stencil, car No. 1566, seen at Abbey Wood early in 1913 still retains the original type of number plate.   *(Commercial view)*

of the main Arsenal Gate, nor should the tracks be removed to new positions. The question of the position of the tracks had been settled at the time of the initial electrification and, in the opinion of the Chief Engineer to the Council, Mr. Maurice Fitzmaurice, should not be raised again, even though there was to be some re-arrangement in Beresford Square. In his view, the matter had nothing at all to do with the War Department; the tramways were in the public streets. Regarding stopping places, it was his opinion that this was not an insurmountable problem. No more was heard of this.

This extension was almost all single line, including one length which rounded the corner at the west end of Beresford Street into High Street, at which point an automatic signalling system was provided in order to control the passage of the cars on this awkward section. Two sets of signal lamps were mounted on a traction pole on the corner, one set facing in each direction, and each controlled by the passage of the trolley wheel of a car when entering or leaving the single line.

Operation of the signalling equipment was by means of special contacts screwed to the overhead line ears, one at either end of the section, on both "up" and "down" wires. When the line was clear, the contact would be struck by the trolley head of a car proceeding beneath the contact, actuating the signal lamp facing the other end of the section, giving a "line occupied" (lamp lit) indication. Once clear of the single line, a second contact restored the signal to "line clear" (lamp extinguished). Signals were of the "Simplex" pattern, operated from the overhead line power supply and manufactured by the Equipment & Engineering Co. London, to patents of Schofield & Tickell. The signal wires consisted of uninsulated aerial wires carried on porcelain insulators between the two ends of the section.

The line was inspected by Col. Yorke on 26th November 1909, after which he authorised its use. Service commenced on 30th as an extension westwards of the Plumstead line. The Bexley cars however, continued to terminate on a short stub-end track at Beresford Square.

For the next four and a half years this line worked in isolation until, eventually on 5th April 1914 with the completion of the last stretch of conduit track eastwards from Chapel Street Woolwich and the installation of a ploughshift on the hill just east of Nile Street, the final connection was made and the line to Abbey Wood was isolated no longer. It was fortuitous that this connection had been completed, albeit with much difficulty and several problems, as the clouds of war were gathering but at the time were not very noticeable. The new connection was to prove to be a most important link in the transport chain for the many thousands of people who were eventually to be employed in Woolwich Arsenal and other factories in the Woolwich and Charlton areas. But, in April 1914, all that was a long way off.

The Woolwich & Eltham Line

Arising from the Bill seeking powers for the construction of a light railway from Greenwich to Shooters Hill and Woolwich and its subsequent failure, but followed by the success of the tramways Bills of 1902 and 1904, the Council determined to consider the construction of a tramway from Woolwich to Eltham by way of Woolwich Common and Well Hall Lane (as it was then known) and to construct the line on the overhead wire system. This brought an objection on 19th December 1902 from the Astronomer Royal, W. H. M. Christie, and the Lords Commissioners of the Admiralty stating that, in their opinion, the insulated conduit system should be used in order to avoid any possibility of interference to the instruments at Greenwich Observatory. When it was pointed out that East Ham Tramways were built on the overhead system, Christie said that there were "special circumstances" which tended to reduce disturbance to the magnetic instruments and in any case the nearest point on the East Ham Tramways to Greenwich was more than three miles away from the Observatory. What was apparently overlooked was that West Ham Corporation were in the process of obtaining powers for tramways, all to be worked on the overhead wire system, some of it less than three miles from Greenwich.

On 31st March 1904, with the first sections of conduit track in use, the Council again approached the Board of Trade, the Admiralty and the Woolwich Borough Council, this time for permission to use what they called "the three wire system". This consisted of "down" and "up" wires spaced 18 feet apart by the use of short bracket arms on either side of the road ("open sky" method) or by the use of fully insulated span wires. Each wire would be fed at 550 volts, one positive to the centre-tapped running rails (at earth potential), the other at 550 volts negative to the running rails which, in the opinion of the Council would cause no problems at the Observatory. At Woolwich, long section insulators, each consisting of an eight-foot length of wire connected to earth between two normal section insulators would separate the balanced system from the more usual 550 volt positive feed around the proposed turning loop at Beresford Square. The line would be fed by two 550 volt d.c. machines in series, centre tapped to the running rails.

However, the Admiralty would not agree to the use of any uninsulated system, insisting that an all-insulated arrangement must be used on any line within a three-mile radius of the Observatory. This discussion continued for several years on ways and means of overcoming the objections and in 1909 the LCC tried again, but to no avail; the Admiralty would not countenance anything other than an all-insulated system. The Council was also concerned about the possible unsatisfactory financial results which would be likely to occur if this line was constructed as a conduit tramway as, for a few years at least, it was expected that traffic would be sparse, thereby possibly sustaining considerable losses, and it was keen to find a cheaper solution to the difficulty.

Finally, on 16th November 1909 the Council was advised that an all-insulated method, using the overhead wires over each track, would satisfy the conditions imposed upon it. On 30th November a recommendation was submitted for the use of a "four-wire" system to be used between Eltham Church and Thomas Street Woolwich, with normal positive wire working round Beresford Square, as that piece of track was more than three miles from the Observatory. The LCC measured the distances involved to the last inch! The change from twin-wire to single-wire working was to take place at Anglesea Road near the Post Office, which would be convenient for running the cars round Beresford Square and also for allowing cars to run through to and from Abbey Wood for service and depot workings. As a short length of the line (just a few yards at Shooters Hill) was to be in the Borough of Greenwich, that body was advised as well as the Woolwich Council. The Admiralty agreed to the proposals on 1st January 1910 with the two borough councils following on 6th January and, as the Board of Trade had already agreed, the necessary proposals were incorporated into the London County Council (Tramways & Improvements) Bill for 1910.

Trackwork for the "four wire system" was as for all other overhead wire lines in London, standard No. 4 rails being used, except on curves of less than 140 feet radius, where No. 4C were to be used. The only departure from normal was that electrical bonding strips were not specified. Regarding the overhead wiring, this all-insulated system had a positive and negative wire above each track, the negatives to be placed side by side at a nominal distance of six feet apart with the positive wires hung outside the negatives at a distance of three feet from them. The "up" and "down" wires were to be insulated from one another by globe insulators placed in the cross-spans between the negatives, further insulators being let in between the positive and negative wires and outside the positives. The line voltage was to be the standard 550 volts between positives and negatives, with the negatives at approximately earth potential. Section insulators and feeders were to be at the usual distance of about half a mile apart, all four wires to be section switched.

Where the four-wire system came to an end, the positive "up" and "down" wires would continue to feed the cars at 550 volts but with the return current being fed through the car wheels to the rails. At this point, it was stipulated that normal electrically bonded joints be made, using two copper bonds each of a sectional area of 0.166 sq. in. The rails of each track were also to be bonded together at intervals not exceeding 40 yards and, where the track was double, by inter-track bonds at intervals of not more than 80 yards. Efficient bonds were to be applied at all points and crossings. As most of the track around the Woolwich loop was in different streets, cross bonding was carried out at New Road near Anglesea Road where the two tracks came together and in Beresford Square where the loop line was connected to the Abbey Wood line.

In view of the special arrangements required regarding electrical switching on the cars, each of the 10 class M four-wheeled double-deck covered top cars to be used carried two trolley poles mounted side by side, 3 feet apart at mid-point on the roof, requiring the fitting of a four position switch allowing the use of pole 1 with earth return;

pole 2 with earth return; double pole (positive and negative insulated); conduit. A switch was designed that could be turned by the master controller key and fitted on an end panel beneath the stairs at one end only.

After confirmation by the Council on 16th November 1909, work commenced on roadworks and platelaying by Messrs. Stark & Sons of Glasgow for £32,528. British Insulated & Helsby Cables Ltd. supplied and erected the overhead equipment at a cost of £5,760. Finally, on 21st July 1910, Col. Yorke inspected inspected the completed work on behalf of the Board of Trade, and it was opened to traffic on 23rd July, a through service of cars working between Eltham and Abbey Wood via Woolwich.

The Eltham Tramway Saga, 1911

An article in the Light Railway & Tramway Journal for 24th November 1911 gave an interesting account of the application of the regulations framed by the Board of Trade, at the insistence of the Admiralty, regarding the use of the twin overhead wire system on the Woolwich and Eltham tramway.

The article headed "The Control of a Tramcar" goes on:-
"A point in the law affecting London's tramway service was raised at Woolwich, before Mr. Hutton when Harold Vincent Dimon was summoned for driving a tramcar on the Woolwich - Eltham system without two overhead conductors being in use. Mr. Barber, for the police, said that an accident had occurred and Dimon was tried at the Sessions on a charge of causing bodily harm, but was acquitted". (The police then brought the lesser charge, outlined as above).

Mr. Jenkin, defending, argued that the Council, not Dimon were responsible, because the regulation read "any person using electrical power ..." and the Council answered to the "person" in this case. The magistrate ruled against this view, but himself questioned whether the man at fault might be the conductor, whose business it was to put up the second trolley pole.

Class M car No. 1436 crosses Woolwich Common on the Eltham service, specially fitted with two trolley poles to work on the twin-wire route.
(Commercial view)

Mr. Barber submitted that the driver was in charge of the tramcar, and the conductor could not put up the pole unless the driver stopped the car. Mr. Hutton fined Dimon 5/-, saying that he did so on the ground that the defendant drove the car without the second trolley pole or conductor being in use!

When the incident was reported to the Board of Trade, Mr. Gordan said that "it was an interesting case", but argued that the ruling of the magistrate was open to question. The County Council and not a "person" was using the electric power, etc. and an action it would seem should have been taken against them for negligence on the part of their servant, leaving the man to be dealt with on a matter of discipline. This statement was rebuffed by his superior, Mr. Elliott, who said "that it is not for us to question the magistrate's decision, I think", but asked that Mr. A. P. Trotter, the Electrical Inspector for the Railway Department see the case and express his views. Comment from Mr. Trotter was that "this is a very interesting case, but it would have been more interesting if a single wire had been used for a week and an inspection made of the magnetic records at Greenwich to see if there had been any appreciable disturbance. I mentioned this case to the late Astronomer Royal, who was pleased to learn 'that the police are looking after the welfare of the Royal Observatory' ..."

The real point made by Mr. Trotter was a very relevant one, as it appeared to be his view that the Admiralty, together with the Royal Observatory senior staff had made a great issue out of an alleged problem in the first place, by demanding that no earthed return circuits on tramways should be used within an arbitrary three-mile limit of Greenwich; that no proper tests had been conducted to see whether the Woolwich and Eltham tramway would have been the likely cause of interference to the Greenwich instruments; that no apparent notice was taken of the fact that both West Ham and East Ham Tramways were worked on the single overhead wire system. It also appeared that the police were only interested in obtaining a conviction against the motorman, the more so as he was cleared of the original charge, of which there are no details recorded in the report.

The Woolwich Track Layout

There was a most unusual track layout at the Woolwich end of the line where, for the last two hundred yards, the "down" and "up" lines formed a large single track loop line. The roads through which the rails were laid were, with the exception of Beresford Square itself, all quite narrow. Where the line turned from Beresford Square into New Road at the northern-most point of the loop, the restriction placed upon the LCC was such that, in order to connect the line to the one in Plumstead Road to allow the cars coming from Abbey Wood to get into New Road, a rather complex set of curves and trailing points was installed.

To enable cars to leave the loop line to travel towards Abbey Wood an equally unusual arrangement was resorted to. A junction was installed just before the beginning of the curved track into New Road, which allowed cars to run on to the "up" line of the double track loop of the Plumstead - Woolwich Ferry tracks and, after running "wrong road" for a few yards, were able to get on to a section of single line, after which they regained normal working for the remainder of the journey.

The movements necessary to get the Bexley UDC cars to their terminal stand were also quite contrary to normal practice. From the west end of the single line section in Plumstead Road, the cars would then be run "wrong road" to Beresford Square, where a special siding was provided for their exclusive use.

From the opening date, the method of working round the single track loop line was that cars were driven on the standard single trolley pole with earth return, the second pole being lowered before taking the loop track, and raised again on regaining the double track opposite Anglesey Road, where the necessary switching was carried out. This state of affairs persisted for about eleven years, when the Chief Officer was advised that it would be more economical and easier for service reasons to extend the second wire round the loop track. As the negative wires on the "up" and "down" roads were on the offsides of the positives, there would be no difficulty in transferring cars to or from the tracks along Plumstead Road for depot or through workings. Construction commenced early in January 1922 and was ready for inspection by Maj. A. Mount on behalf of the Ministry of Transport on 16th February 1922. The facility was brought into use immediately after the inspection. The 325 yards of additional overhead cost approximately £165, and the work was carried out by the Tramways Department.

Lewisham to Lee Green

Completed during 1907, the 1 mile 8.7 chain double track conduit line between Lewisham Clock Tower and Lee Green, was constructed by the LCC Works Department, the first time that direct labour had been employed on such work. Standard methods were employed, using the one-inch conduit slot, alternate short and extended yokes and 45-feet long track rails. There were no outstanding features or problems, except that the bridges carrying the road over the River Quaggy at either end of Lee High Road had to be practically reconstructed. Cost of this new construction was approximately £40,700. Col. Yorke inspected the completed line on 25th April 1907, after which public service commenced on 4th May.

The Board of Trade inspection of the Lee Green line was evidently a great local event, especially for the children of the area! Car No. 497 of class E is being driven slowly past the police station.

(Commercial view)

Lee Green & Eltham Extension

When the line was laid from Lewisham to Lee Green and opened to traffic on 4th May 1907, it was not intended that this should be the ultimate terminus. Powers were gained in 1915 to construct an extension on the conduit system to meet the line from Woolwich at Eltham Church and the work was planned for that year, the contract for track laying being let to Mr. W. Manders of Leyton for £57,025. Because of restrictions placed upon the Council by the government due to war conditions the contract had to be cancelled, with Manders gaining compensation for lost work.

As all the proposed track between Lee Green and Eltham was within the three mile restricted area surrounding Greenwich Observatory, it was incumbent upon the LCC to provide an all-insulated system when the line was eventually built. The section of "double overhead" track between Eltham and Woolwich was quite successful and it therefore became Council policy to equip the new line in the same way.

Following the Great War, the decision was taken to build the 1 mile 6 furlongs 160 yards of line as soon as possible. The roadwork and platelaying went on contract to Messrs. Dick, Kerr & Co. on 27th April 1920 for £83,461.3.10d. but was subsequently transferred to the Consolidated Construction Co. Ltd., at the same contract price, plus a further £11,500 for supplementary work. Overhead work was undertaken by Messrs. Clough, Smith & Co. Ltd., for £8,650.2.1d., cabling work was undertaken by the Western Electric Co. Ltd., for £23,803.9.1d. and the ducts for the cables were supplied and laid by Messrs. Mowlem & Co. Ltd. for £8,522.2.8d.

The line was completed in two sections; Lee Green to Eltham Road, Lyme Farm was attended to first, inspected by Col. Pringle on 4th November 1920 and opened to traffic on 29th; and Lyme Farm to Eltham Church inspected by Maj. Hall on 19th March 1921 and opened to traffic on 22nd March, completing the connection between Woolwich, Eltham, Lewisham and London. Service 46, which had been extended from Lee Green to Lyme Farm was further extended to Eltham and Woolwich daily.

The Royal Observatory was moved away from Greenwich in 1926, the Astronomer Royal and his staff having given up against great odds, not because of the tramways, but due to many other factors affecting observations, such as air pollution, noise and the threat of a comprehensive electrification programme by the Southern Railway, as well as by the vastly increasing use of electricity for all purposes. which was alleged to be the cause of considerable electrical interference. The special arrangements made by the LCC Tramways to ensure that there were no problems due to the working of the Lee Green - Woolwich route were no longer necessary, and at the earliest opportunity the line was converted to the normal single wire and earth return system, which made it necessary to electrically bond the rail joints to provide a path for return currents. The old positive wires were removed, and the inner wires were electrically switched to become the positive wires. This meant that the "up" and "down" wires were closer together than standard and remained so throughout the life of the line.

The final re-arrangement took place in July 1928 when the overhead wires were extended westwards from the Lee Green change-point for a distance of about 200 yards at a cost of £500, in order to make it easier to effect the conduit-overhead change.

The Westhorne Avenue Line

A new housing estate was constructed by the Woolwich Borough Council in the 1920s, between Well Hall Road at its junction with Rochester Way (which had been built in the early 1920s) and Eltham Road at the foot of Eltham Hill (later to be known as the "Yorkshire Grey" junction). The main road through this estate was named Westhorne Avenue with the section of it between these two points being just under one mile in length. The LCC resolved to incorporate a tramway into the construction of the road, both as a very desirable transport feature and as a means of providing work for many people in this time of great unemployment. For this, the LCC would qualify for a special government grant to assist in financing the road-making part of the project. Authority to lay the tramway was obtained in the **London County Council (General Powers) Act, 1929, (19 & 20 George V. Ch. lxxxvii).**

One of the conditions imposed by the Unemployment Grant Scheme was that 12½ % of the labour force should be unemployed men in the London area, and a further 12½ % drawn from men residing in a depressed mining area. In order to take the fullest advantage of the terms of the grant regulations, it was decided to sub-contract the track and roadwork to the Woolwich Borough Council, the LCC itself undertaking the job of pole planting and overhead wire stringing to its own standard.

Work was carried out in two stages, the section from Well Hall Road to the railway bridge (which was under construction over the road about halfway along its length) being dealt with first. The tracks were laid in advance of the programme to construct the road in order to conform with the terms of the grant, this work commencing in November 1929. Total cost of this section, including the length of track to go beneath the bridge was expected to be £18,000. Construction time was about two years; on comnpletion, the line was opened to traffic on 1st October 1931 in advance of an official inspection which, by agreement with the Ministry of Transport, would be undertaken on completion of the whole line. Service was provided for the time being by a diversion of part of service 44.

The southern section of the work was completed early in June 1932 at a similar cost to that of the northern half, plus a further £10,000 for exigencies. It was inspected by Col. Trench on 29th (together with the first section) and opened to traffic on 30th. Service 72, hitherto working between Victoria Embankment and Forest Hill, was diverted at New Cross to run via Lewisham and Westhorne Avenue to Woolwich on a daily basis, its route between New Cross and Embankment being via Camberwell, Kennington and Westminster.

It had been the intention of the Council to extend the line southwards along the remainder of Westhorne Avenue and then along Baring Road to Grove Park Station, there to join up with the overhead wire line which had been constructed in the late 1920s. Although the LCC obtained powers for this, they were never implemented. The LPTB, on taking over the tramways, abandoned the project in 1934.

Chapter 17
Electrification, South London

Over Vauxhall Bridge

At the London end of the Camberwell and Vauxhall line, the first connection across the River Thames was nearing completion. During the whole period of operation of horse tramways in London there had never been any service working over a Thames bridge, although many attempts had been made to gain authority, especially for lines over Westminster and Vauxhall bridges. The nearest that the London Tramways Company got was a line to either side of Vauxhall Bridge, which they connected together by an omnibus service. On the reconstruction of these lines, coupled with the rebuilding of Vauxhall Bridge, powers were obtained to lay a double track tramway over it. In view of the peculiarities of conduit construction, a clear depth of two feet was essential, into which the yokes could be placed. It was necessary in this case to incorporate supporting steelwork, specially designed to carry the plate flooring of the bridge in such a way that the plates beneath the tramway were fixed at a lower level than for the remainder of them. This steel trench supported the specially-shaped yokes, set at the standard distance of 3 ft. 9 in. apart. The yokes, of cast iron, were 2 ft. 4 in. wide as against the more usual 2 ft. 2 in., having a maximum thickness of ten inches across the flat base. Extended lugs on either side allowed for the yokes to be bolted to the bridgework. The conduit tubes were also of a different design.

The depth from the surface of the paving to the steel decking was 2 ft. 5 in. Sole plates were used for anchoring the track running rails, these being directly fixed to the slot rails between yokes, while at the yokes, the slot rails were bolted to the yoke shoulders. Tee-rail insulators were suspended in the usual way.

The bridge and tramway were engineered to the design of the Chief Engineer to the Council, Mr. Maurice Fitzmaurice. The tramway was laid by Messrs. John Mowlem & Co., slot rails and conductor tees were supplied by the Frodingham Iron & Steel Co., and cast-iron yokes by the Anderston Foundry Co. The contract price for construction work, which included the reconstruction of the lines in Vauxhall Bridge Road, was £16,523, with an additional £5,300 being the cost of the rails, which were taken from LCC stock.

All works were completed early in May 1906, and a ceremony was arranged to formally open both on 26th May. To this end, the Council had asked the Board of Trade Inspector to visit the installation before this date. The LCC had, however, overlooked the fact that parliamentary powers would be required before the line on the bridge could be used by electric cars. Thus thwarted, the inspection by Col. Yorke on 22nd May, resulted in him giving his permission for the operation of horse cars only, until authority was gained in an addition to the current Bill for 1906, which was proceeding through Parliament at that time. Opening of electric services had to wait until the position was legalised, when a fresh inspection by the Board of Trade was then to take place. Col. Yorke visited the line again in the morning of 31st July 1906, giving the Council permission to open the line to electric cars as soon as the Act of 1906 was passed.

At last, on 4th August the Council obtained its Act and armed with legal powers, arranged that electrical operation should commence on the following day when a considerable re-arrangement of south side car services took place, running through to the terminus at the Victoria Street end of Vauxhall Bridge Road.

It had been the intention, so far as the isolated line on the north side of the bridge was concerned, once it was reconstructed, to equip the horse car shed temporarily for the use of electric cars and lay a single line curve of 60 feet radius from the depot to the nearside "up" track in the southerly direction, but this was not followed up. Instead, for the remainder of the time that the line was isolated, and during the period that the horse car service worked over the bridge to Vauxhall, the horse cars were dragged across the roadway when being taken into or out of the depot, the LCC having agreed in May 1906 to pay to the City of Westminster sufficient money to compensate for any damage done to the road surface whilst this operation continued.

Along Vauxhall Bridge Road

The three-quarter mile long line along the length of Vauxhall Bridge Road between the north side of the bridge and Victoria Street, although reconstructed as a conduit tramway at the same time as the one on the bridge, continued to be worked by the horse cars, which were extended over the new tracks to the south side of the bridge. This situation remained until, on 4th August 1906, the horse cars ran for the last time, being replaced by electric cars on 5th.

A line of cars at Victoria terminus are waiting to turn on the stub-end single track. *Courtesy: A. D. Packer)*

The Victoria Embankment Tramway

The second tramway to be constructed over the Thames was the one across Westminster Bridge. Several attempts had previously been made by the London Tramways Company to allow it to lay a tramway in the usual position in the centre of the road, across the bridge and along Victoria Embankment, but without success. A further attempt had been made on behalf of the London Tramways Company by the London County Council (Westminster Bridge & Embankment Tramways) 1898, Bill, in which it was still intended that the tracks would be laid in the usual position, but this met with stiff opposition and fell on the second reading, by 248 votes against to 129 in favour.

Upon acqusition by the Council of the lines of the company and the electrification of the line at the east side of the bridge in 1903, the Council tried again, but without success. It continued to press during 1904 and 1905, but to no avail. However, on 4th July 1905, the Council received a letter from Mr. J. A. Hunter suggesting that, should the Council be successful in its quest, the tracks could be laid on the downstream side of the bridge instead of in the centre of the road, and be continued along the side of Victoria Embankment nearest the river. Thus, when an extension could be made over Blackfriars Bridge, this too could be laid to one side, the only two points of contact and confliction with all other traffic being on the Surrey side of the bridges, where certain widenings would no doubt overcome the difficulty at these points.

An acknowledgement was sent to Mr. Hunter, together with an expression of thanks for his interest and a comment that the idea would be seriously considered. That it was, became evident when, in 1906 Parliament finally relented and gave the necessary powers to the Council to construct a double line of tramway in the positions suggested.

In 1908, electric traction was still overshadowed by horse-drawn traffic as seen here with a class A car crossing Westminster Bridge.

(Commercial view)

The first of the powers obtained would only allow the tracks to be laid along the Embankment as far as the City of London boundary, although by mutual consent the LCC and City authorities agreed that an extension would be permitted at a later date when Blackfriars Bridge had been widened to accommodate the tracks. John Carpenter Street was to be the nominal terminus, but in fact the tracks were extended a little into the City area where crossovers were provided for turning the large number of cars which were to use the new tracks. A junction was also to be formed with an extension southwards from Aldwych of the Kingsway Subway line, which was under construction.

Messrs. Dick, Kerr & Co. had successfully tendered for the whole job in the sum of £45,836.14. 2d for the 1 mile 5 furlongs of double line, and construction commenced on the Embankment on 3rd September a few weeks after bridgework had been started. Some difficulties were experienced with tracklaying on Westminster Bridge, but with the knowledge gained in building the new line across Vauxhall Bridge, these were quickly overcome. The method employed was similar to that used at Vauxhall, with special yokes being bolted to the bridge structure, which had to be altered to accept them. The cross bracing between the arch ribs had to be partly removed, flat girders being substituted to make room for the yokes. Because the arch ribs were partly in the way, the conduit slot on the up-stream track was off-centre from the running rails. Other special measures were necessary to accommodate the drains and mud pits, which had to be designed specifically for this section.

On the Embankment itself, the more normal construction methods were once again used, with the exception of the complex situation which developed near the entrance to the extended Kingsway Subway at Waterloo Bridge. Here, the roof of the District Railway tunnel had to be remodelled and a girder roof installed, as the clearances were insufficient with the original roof arches in place. There was also a junction layout to be constructed at this point, connecting the Embankment lines with the Subway tracks, a double junction running off the Embankment into the Subway from both directions. (Details of the Subway will be given in Volume 2 of this work).

A double junction was constructed between the entrance to Kingsway Subway and Victoria Embankment, which involved some complicated track and road works.

Although roadworks were in progress on Victoria Embankment when this view was taken in 1907, the tramcars passed by unimpeded.

(Commercial view)

The only other problem was with drainage as, due to the almost flat roadway on the Embankment, a considerable number of extra sumps and pits had to be provided to ensure that all sections of the tracks and conduits would be well drained. Although it could not be called a problem, the difference in levels between the roadway after the tram tracks had been laid, and the footpath to the riverside of it were quite unusual. At some points, the pathway was as much as three feet higher than the one on the other side of the road. However, all these difficulties having been overcome, the tramway, when completed was inspected by Col. Yorke on 12th December 1906, opened ceremonially on 14th, with public services commencing on 15th. This section of the LCC Tramways proved to be of great benefit to the travelling public, but unfortunately tended to arouse much comment and criticism from a number of people, some of whom were quite openly hostile to its construction and operation. It was several years before the tramway became accepted as a normal part of the scene.

One criticism of the way in which the construction of the line could unwittingly be the cause of some "inconvenience" to the public was made by the Inspecting Officer, when he stated that "as things stood, persons wanting to get on a car 'from the Strand' would have to walk across the whole width of the road to the tram". This same comment was made by one Lewis Jones of Peckham, to the Board of Trade when, on 19th December 1906, he penned a forthright letter on the subject, but was rather more forceful than the Inspector had been.

He pointed out that ... "These cars coming over the Bridge from the Surrey side discharge their passengers on the off-side to the mercy of any traffic which may be coming right or left, and they have to reach the other side of the road, perhaps endangering their lives. I would suggest that proper landing stages be erected at reasonable distances, say at the foot of the bridges, Charing Cross and otherwise, whereby ladies and children are not likely to be mowed down by some, not all, ruthless motors and other scum of the roadway. To land passengers to the mercy and dangers as now might be considered as absolutely disgraceful by many, in fact I must confess that I cannot see how matters will go on in time to come ... Certain temporary landing stages, or refuges, with granite kerbing and wooden framework could be erected at little cost as an experiment, to obviate the danger ... and (would ask) ... Kindly give this prompt attention as lives may be lost".

Resulting from this plea, the Council made arrangements to provide a number of refuges at stopping places on the eastbound side of the track, throughout the length of the Embankment.

On completion of the junction to and from Kingsway Subway, services were provided via both Westminster and Blackfriars. Subway car No. 587 waits its turn to pass on to the Embankment, bound for Blackfriars and Tower Bridge. *(Courtesy: LT Museum. H14406)*

Blackfriars Bridge & Tramway

In conjunction with the construction of the Embankment tramway, the authorities of the City of London and the London County Council agreed in 1905 to the extension of the conduit lines from the south side of Blackfriars Bridge, over the bridge, there to turn westwards to join up with the proposed Embankment line, which was to be built almost as far as the northern approach to the bridge. The problem was that the bridge was not thought to be wide enough to accommodate a double track tramway on the 75-feet wide carriageway. The decision was taken to add another 30 feet to the width of the structure on the upstream or western side, so that the tracks could be conveniently laid on that side of the bridge and connected to the Embankment lines. Finance was made available from the funds of the Bridge House Estates, administered by the City Corporation which, with ample resources, could meet the commitment without call upon the City ratepayers. When completed, this section of the tramway was to be leased to the LCC by the Corporation at a rent of £500 per annum, with a small extra payment for running rights over the tracks.

Contracts for widening the bridge went to Sir William Arrol & Co.; that for the tramway to Messrs. Dick, Kerr & Co. for £13,225 for trackwork and £1,200 for pipework; while a third contract went to Perry & Co. of Bow, London for construction of a footway subway beneath the north end of the bridge, for which the LCC was to pay all costs, amounting in all to just under £30,000.

Work started on the widening of the bridge early in 1907 and was expected to take three years. The first task was to sink caissons upstream of the four piers, in order to provide the working environment necessary for placing the foundation piles. Sadly, during the course of this operation, one of the 200-ton caissons collapsed, killing four men and injuring others. This setback, which occurred on 28th November was, understandably, the cause of some disquiet, but did not make for any delay to the work.

In order to form the foundations for the tramway, three sets of arched ribs were placed on the west side of the bridge, laid on the new piers. The supporting bridge girders on to which the conduit troughs were placed were of such dimensions that when the tracks were laid, the conduit tubes were 9¾ in. out of centre of the running rails. Special extended yokes were required for this work, being cast as shown in the accompanying diagram.

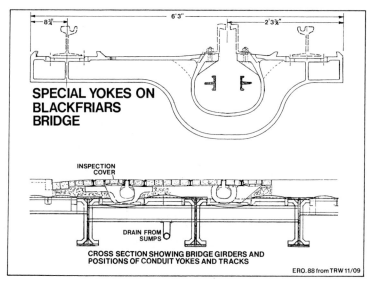

SPECIAL YOKES ON BLACKFRIARS BRIDGE

INSPECTION COVER

DRAIN FROM SUMPS

CROSS SECTION SHOWING BRIDGE GIRDERS AND POSITIONS OF CONDUIT YOKES AND TRACKS

ERO. 88 from TRW 11/09

The remainder of the trackwork was to standard design, short yokes being laid alternately with extended ones, the only difference being that the depth of the conduit was 1 foot 9 inches instead of the usual 2 feet. Rails were supplied from LCC stock, being of British Standard Section No. 4 for straight lengths and No. 4C for curves, these weighing 105 lbs/yd and 111 lbs/yd respectively. Two rainwater sumps were provided, one in pier No. 1 (on the north side), the other in pier No. 4 (south side) and connected together by a 6-inch cast-iron pipe which took the water from No. 1 to No. 4 where it was discharged into the rainwater sewer.

On the northern side of the bridge, the tracks were joined to the existing lines on the Embankment by means of a great curve, which had a minimum radius of 67 feet 6 inches as measured at the centre point of the inner track. As the angle between the bridge (south to north) and the Embankment (southwest to northeast) was only 55°, this necessitated a total arc through which the cars were to travel being covered by a curve involving a change of direction of 125°. This very severe curvature was dealt with by designing a complex spiral which had the effect of easing the cars round the bend in either direction, only the centre part of the arc being of minimum radius. To complicate matters even further, a pedestrian subway was being constructed immediately beneath the northern half of the curve, with a pipe subway also impinging upon the works at the Embankment end, together with the south-side retaining wall of the District Railway. In all, a daunting set of parameters upon which to superimpose a conduit tramway.

Completion of the task was ahead of schedule; the lines being inspected by Col. Yorke on 30th August 1909, after which the bridge and the tramway were ceremonially opened by the Lord Mayor of London, Sir George Wyatt Truscott on 14th September 1909. The Bridge tramway of some 130 yards in length together with the 300 yards of track on the Embankment constituted the first of three short sections of conduit line to belong to the City Corporation.

In conjunction with this work, a new line was constructed along Southwark Street from a junction with the existing tramway in Blackfriars Road to a junction to be formed with the existing lines in Southwark Bridge Road and the east end of Southwark Street. Messrs. Dick, Kerr & Co. obtained this contract additionally to the works on the bridge, at a cost of £14,964 and which was inspected and opened at the same time as the Blackfriars Bridge line.

An interesting development occurred just south of Stamford Street, with the extension of the tracks on to Blackfriars Bridge. The Council had commenced construction of a three track layout from a point about 60 yards south of Southwark Street, with the intention of continuing it right to the foot of Blackfriars Bridge with access from the "up" and "down" tracks at either end to the centre track, in order to give a measure of flexibility of working, in part due to the congested traffic conditions which prevailed between Stamford Street and the bridge. In the event, road widening was carried out between these two points, making it unnecessary to complete the scheme.

A specially decorated class E/1 car was used to open the tramway across Blackfriars Bridge. The Lord Mayor of London is seen at the controls.

The southern section of the layout had been constructed and was allowed to remain, with the centre track as a stub-end, to be used as a terminal point for cars when required, at the same time allowing through cars to continue running unhindered. Due also to the considerable number of Official Processions which progressed through the City of London each year, the terminal point at Stamford Street was used quite regularly during the times when cars were unable to proceed over Blackfriars Bridge.

Crossing Southwark Bridge

Almost from the early days of electric tramways in London, the County Council attempted to gain the goodwill and assistance of the City of London Corporation, to enable tracks to be laid into and across the City of London but, except for a couple of short lengths laid in 1909 over Blackfriars Bridge and in 1913 between Norton Folgate and Liverpool Street, the City authorities steafastly refused to have tramways within its boundaries.

Eventually, however, towards the end of 1924, permission was given to the LCC to lay a double track extension from the Southwark Bridge terminus on the south side of the Thames, across the bridge and into Queen Place to a point a few yards short of Cannon Street, a distance of just over two furlongs. Estimated cost of the trackwork was £33,500 plus £200 for cables and ducts, which would all fall to the LCC. Other conditions imposed by the Corporation were:-

That the exact site of the terminal point be decided by the City Corporation.

A license to work the line to be issued to the LCC and to be limited to an initial period of 21 years.

An annual wayleave payment of £1 to be made by the LCC.

No shelters or other structures to be erected within the City.

Full indemnity to be given to the City authorities for any eventuality of whatever kind.

The line to be worked by the LCC on the basis of termination of operation on 12 months' notice being given by either side.

Track construction was completed early in 1925, and was inspected by Maj. Hall on behalf of the Ministry of Transport on 9th July. After a ceremonial opening by the Lord Mayor of London, Sir A. Bower, at 12.30 p.m. on 14th July 1925, public service commenced with the extension of all cars which had terminated at the southern approach to the bridge.

The construction arrangements were, by now, well known and no unusual methods were necessary. The main problem, once the tracks had been laid, was that rainwater entering the conduits on the bridge approach caused some difficulties through leakage into premises located in the arches beneath the approach, this trouble taking some time to locate and eradicate.

The Camberwell & Dulwich Lines

This new tramway was the only other one to be built during 1906. Construction between Camberwell and Dulwich, Lordship Lane by Crystal Palace Road was authorised by the Act of 1902, while the short extension to Barry Road (Dulwich Library) was authorised by the Act of 1904. A short section of this line in Lordship Lane, between Crystal Palace Road and Barry Road was, in fact a reconstruction of the moribund ex-London, Camberwell & Dulwich Tramways Co. tracks.

The LCC had hoped that it could get permission to use the overhead wire on part of this line, especially the section in Lordship Lane, but the Metropolitan Borough of Camberwell blocked this scheme in favour of conduit working, to which the Council had to acquiesce.

This part of south London has some very steep hills and gradients for much of the length of the new tramway were quite severe. Denmark Hill has a mean gradient of about 1 in 63, with the steepest part being 1 in 31; the junction of Denmark Hill with Champion Park is at about 1 in 19; in Grove Lane the gradients vary* between 1 in 22 and 1 in 50 and still climbing, then with a short length of 1 in 11 near the top of Dog Kennel Hill downwards, where this grade is maintained for about 500 feet, before easing gradually to about 1 in 30 for the remainder of the quarter-mile length of the hill. Once beyond East Dulwich Station, the road levels out for about half a mile, but then climbs again at varying gradients, the steepest being 1 in 14 towards Crystal Palace Road. Prior to the construction of the lines, extensive street widenings were necessary, as was the raising of the road by about twelve inches over the railway at Champion Hill and the lowering of the road beneath East Dulwich Station railway bridge by two feet.

The junction lines from Camberwell Green and Camberwell New Road had been laid in some time before, as part of an earlier reconstruction, while a new junction and crossover was provided at the Denmark Hill and Coldharbour Lane intersection, in order to allow the horse car service to continue to run to and from Loughborough Junction, until such time as that line was reconstructed for electric traction. Another junction layout was provided in advance of its use at a point where East Dulwich Road met Grove Vale and Lordship Lane, so that when the proposed tramway to Peckham Rye was built, no further disturbance to the tracks would be necessary. Construction was undertaken by Messrs. Robert W. Blackwell & Co., at a cost of £82,620. Standard conduit components were used throughout, alternate standard and extended yokes being used.

Inspection of the line by Col. Yorke for the Board of Trade took place on Saturday 10th November 1906, with a service of 4-wheeled cars commencing on 19th November as far as Crystal Palace Road, to be followed on 20th December by the opening of the last 200 yards

Class C cars Nos. 235 and 236 pass on Dog Kennel Hill soon after the first pair of tracks opened late in 1906. (Commercial view)

to Barry Road, which remained the terminus for the next two years.

Dog Kennel Hill Track Quadrupling

Services using the 380 yards of track on Dog Kennel Hill were severely restricted by the regulations imposed by the Board of Trade, who insisted that only one car should be on either the downhill or uphill track at any time. In order to ease the problem, the Council obtained powers in its Act of 1911 to lay duplicate tracks to both lines.

Early in 1912, Messrs. Dick, Kerr began laying the additional tracks by the side of the existing lines. Work commenced on 16th March on connecting one of the new lines to the existing "down" track, with a trial car being driven over the new section at 5.25 a.m. on 21st March, followed by the first service car at 5.58 a.m. In order that regular services were maintained during the course of the work, the Board of Trade and Metropolitan Police had authorised the Council to operate the cars over sections of the new track prior to inspection.

Alterations to the "up" track connections were carried out during the weekend of 13th April, following which a special programme of services was operated over the lines by permission of the Board of Trade. Finally, on 20th April, a full trial run was made over the entire work, while on 23rd April, normal working was resumed. Col. Yorke carred out an official inspection of the whole installation on 6th May, authorising use of the four tracks immediately afterwards. Final cost to the LCC to double the capacity of the tracks on this very steep hill was £9,227.

The Peckham Rye Branch

It had been the intention of the Council to lay a tramway from the junction with the Lordship Lane line at Goose Green, along the side of Goose Green and Peckham Rye as far as Stuart Road where, it was hoped a connection would eventually be made with the proposed lines to Brockley Cross. As described above, the junction and crossing had been installed at East Dulwich in preparation for this.

Mr. W. Manders of Leyton gained the contract for the construction of the double track section between Grove Vale and the top of Peckham Rye, a distance of 7 furlongs 5 chains 16 yards at a cost of £31,800, plus the cost of rails, etc. and commenced work in mid-1907, completing it early in November. The Board of Trade Inspector, Col. Yorke paid a visit to the line on 22nd November, authorising its use, and services commenced on 28th November.

Even though attempts were made from time to time to extend the line eastwards towards Brockley, it was never built, in the main due to the considerable costs which would be involved in widenings and also to the opposition to the scheme from many quarters.

Extension to Forest Hill

In the same way that the Council had hoped that the overhead wire system would be used on the Dulwich section of the line, it had made preliminary plans to adopt the same system on the projected extension to Forest Hill, London Road near Forest Hill Station and a hoped-for line to Crystal Palace via Upper Sydenham. The same difficulties occurred as with the recently-opened line to Dulwich Library, resulting in the conduit system being employed for the 1 mile 1 furlong 3.2 chains of double track.

The line to Forest Hill terminated almost end-on to the railway station. The track was laid to allow for an unfulfilled extension to Sydenham. Car No. 242 stands at the terminus. (Commercial view, T. Smellie)

Mr. Manders undertook the construction of this line also, at a cost of £27,431 for roadwork, plus the cost of rails, pipes, etc. The line was completed early in December 1908. After trial cars had been run, Col. Yorke inspected the line on 16th December 1908 and, being satisfied that all standards had been met, authorised its use. Regular services began on 19th December by an extension of the cars onwards from Barry Road.

So far as the proposed extension to Crystal Palace was concerned, the obstacles placed in the way of the Council eventually caused the abandonment of the plan, along with similar proposals for tramways in other parts of Forest Hill and Sydenham.

Heading for Forest Hill on the Brockley route, E/1 class car No. 1388 stops for passengers outside Crofton Park Station on a summer's evening in 1911. (Commercial view)

New Cross & Forest Hill via Brockley

The first indication from the Council that it was interested in providing an electric tramway in the Brockley area came in 1905, when proposals were made for a double track line to be constructed in Malpas Road, which would require considerable road widenings and the consequent demolition of a large number of houses.

Following lengthy discussions with members of Deptford Borough Council and, after considering a proposal to lay the lines in Shardeloes Road instead of Malpas Road to avoid the widenings, the Council finally proposed that the "down" track be in Malpas Road and the "up" line in Shardeloes Road, which would avoid any disturbance to frontagers in either road. Temporarily, the terminus was to be just short of the railway bridge crossing Brockley Road, a few yards past the spot where the two tracks converged.

In the London County Council (Tramways & Improvements) Act, 1906 authority was given for the construction of tramways (Nos. 20A and 20B) to run between Lewisham High Road and Brockley Lane Station (known as "Brockley Tips"), the "up" and "down" tracks to be in the two roads as outlined above. Messrs. Dick, Kerr & Co. obtained the contract for tracklaying in the sum of £12,799, using standard conduit tracks, and work to commence in late autumn, 1909. On completion, the lines were inspected by Col. Yorke in January 1910, but some remedial work resulted in a re-inspection on 23rd February. Public service commenced on 26th February 1910.

It had also been the intention of the Council to construct a number of tramways in the Forest Hill and Sydenham districts and, as part of this programme, authority was obtained in the Council's Act of 1904 to lay a double track line, Tramway No. 11 (part) from Forest Hill, just east of the station, via Sunderland Road, Stanstead Road and Brockley Rise to Brockley Road, a distance of 6 furlongs 5.09 chains, the remainder of No. 11, of 7 furlongs 8 chains long to continue along Brockley Road to meet the lines just north of Brockley Lane Station.

Due to the northern end of Brockley Rise being very narrow in places, the Council suggested that the line should be diverted to run through Stondon Park instead, making an end-on junction with the Brockley Road section. After much agitation, the LCC got its way, but the re-alignment required the authority of Parliament, which was obtained in 1906 as Tramway No. 19 of the Act of that year. Also included in this Act was permission to extend Tramways Nos. 20A and 20B at Brockley for a distance of just over 17 yards, which enabled the two sets of line to be connected together.

Another problem, involved the reconstruction of the railway bridge at Brockley, so that the road could be widened, at the same time lowering the level to give sufficient headroom to allow double deck covered top cars to safely run beneath the bridge. There was also the bridge over the railway at Crofton Park to be rebuilt.

Eventually, in January 1910, the final arrangements were made to begin work. The roadwork contract was let to Messrs. John Mowlem & Co. in the sum of £39,792, plus £200 for steelwork for the bridge over the railway at Crofton Park. To this was added £3,000 for contingencies, while a provisional sum of £7,000 had been included to allow for alterations to pipes, mains, etc. Construction took about a year to complete and, on 22nd January 1911, Col. Yorke carried out his inspection. Services commenced on 25th February.

The Forest Hill Link

So that a through connection could be given to passengers on the services working to either side of Forest Hill Station, the Council resolved to construct this link, which had been authorised as Tramway No. 10 in the Act obtained in 1911. At the same time, alterations to the terminal layout at the east side of the railway were required, resulting in the construction of a single track lay-by in Park Road, just south of Waldram Road.

Track work was carried out by Messrs. John Mowlem & Sons, in conjunction with similar work being undertaken at Wandsworth. Cost of this, based on a schedule of prices, amounted to approximately £12,500, plus £2,300 for the lay-by, together with special work. The installation was inspected by Col. Von Donop on 10th August 1915 and opened to traffic on 13th.

After the problems thrown up by the Great War had subsided, the decision was taken to increase the capacity of the lay-by at Forest Hill by the addition of another crossover and doubling of part of the track which was to cost the Council just over £3,000. This layout then remained in use and unaltered for the remainder of the time that the Council operated the tramways.

Brockley Rise to Rushey Green and Catford to Grove Park

There were two other sections of proposed line which were in the sphere of influence of the Brockley and Catford tramways, these being the one which was eventually constructed from a junction with the Forest Hill tramway at Brockley Rise, Cranston Road, along Stanstead Road, Catford Hill and Road to Rushey Green; the other from Rushey Green to Southend at Bromley Road, Beckenham Lane. The Council received powers in its Act of 1911 to construct the first line (Tramway No. 11), length 1 mile 5.89 chains double and 0.67 chains single, together with 2.01 chains of single line in Rushey Green, known as Tramway No. 7 (part) of the 1912 Act, which short length was the first part of the extension southwards of the Lewisham - Catford tracks. A junction layout was also included in the work.

Construction of the tracks on the Stanstead Road tramway cost £29,830, the roadwork being undertaken by Messrs. Wimpey for £19,943. The tracks were inspected by Col. Yorke on 27th May 1913 and public service commenced on 29th.

The other line, from Rushey Green to Southend, consisting of 1 mile 2 furlongs 5.85 chains of double line and 1.25 chains of single line was constructed by Messrs. J. Mowlem & Co. Ltd. as part of a contract which included the line from Chapel Street, Woolwich to Nile Street. On completion, the line was inspected by Maj. Pringle on 3rd April 1914 and opened to traffic in two sections, the first as far as Bellingham Road on 5th April, the remainder on 9th April.

An extension of this line, partly conduit and partly overhead wire was planned in the early years of the 1920's in order to serve a large, new housing estate then being built on behalf of the LCC. The first section, as far as Valeswood Road, 7 furlongs 2.60 chains double and 1.25 chains single line, with a conduit/overhead wire change-point in Downham Way, about halfway along the route was inspected by Maj. Hall on 27th September 1926 and opened on 28th.

Ten months later, on 26th July 1927 the next 3 furlongs 0.26 chains of double line, ending at Southover was inspected by Col. Mount and opened on 28th, to be followed by the last 3 furlongs 9.98 chains to

Service 50 initially worked between Forest Hill and Greenwich via Catford. Class M car No. 1427 is seen at Catford Bridge Station.

its final terminus at Grove Park being inspected by Col. Trench on 12th November 1928 and the extension opened on 15th.

The whole of the extended line had cost approximately £33.875 for trackwork and associated roadworks and had taken just over two years to build. It was not intended at that time that Grove Park should be the end of the line, and powers were obtained for an extension to Eltham. But it was not to be - the new masters, after 1st July 1933, had other ideas.

The tramway extension through fields in what was to become Downham Way was built at the same time as the Council's Downham Estate. The limit of construction, seen here in 1927, provides a playground for local children. (Courtesy: A. H. Spring)

Under The Wires From
Camberwell & Brixton to West Norwood

The reconstruction of the lines between Camberwell Green and Brixton, from Loughborough Junction to West Norwood via Herne Hill and from Brixton via Effra Road to Herne Hill, in the Metropolitan Boroughs of Camberwell and Lambeth was the first example of inner borough authorities agreeing to the use of the overhead wire. The reasons for this apparent change of heart are quite interesting and are bound up with the purchase and operation of the horse tramways formerly belonging to the London Southern Tramways Company.

The lines and assets of the company became purchaseable by the LCC in 1903, but the Council decided that due to the condition of the tracks, the purchase should only be effected if the company were to reconstruct the tramways for electric traction and certain widenings were carried out. Lambeth Borough Council declined to contribute one-third of the cost of widenings, whereupon the LCC decided not to carry out the purchase "for the time being". Nevertheless, the Council was attempting to arrange for the lines to be electrified on the overhead wire system, with only the section between Brixton and Vauxhall using conduit.

In the Parliamentary Session for 1905, the company introduced a Bill into Parliament seeking to electrify its lines on the overhead wire system and for the date of compulsory purchase by the Council, due in 1910 to be deferred until 1924. This was opposed by the LCC, even though Lambeth decided to support the issue and suggest to the LCC that it reconsider its rejection, at the same time stating that the number of street widenings called for could be reduced. On the other hand, the Council stated that should the company electrify the lines, overhead wires would be most likely strung along Denmark Hill to Camberwell Green. As the LCC was preparing to build a new conduit line from Camberwell Green to Dulwich, it was feared that both systems could be in use on this section of line.

Meantime, the 1905 Bill was rejected by the Select Committee of the House of Commons, which caused the Highways Committee to have second thoughts over the whole affair, but nevertheless the Council opposed the Bill again when it was presented in 1906. Behind the scenes however, the LCC and Lambeth had come to terms over the widenings issue, even agreeing that a number of footpaths could have their widths reduced in order to get sufficient clearance for double track working; had agreed to the use of the overhead wire on all sections except that from Brixton to Vauxhall and had agreed to subscribe one-third of the cost of those widenings that were essential, which would amount to £25,167.

In view of this, the company again approached the Council with a view to the sale of the lines as from 2nd October 1906, in accordance with Section 44 of the Tramways Act of 1870, but on terms under which tramways were compulsorily purchaseable, subject to the appointment of an arbitrator to settle the price to be paid, to which the Council agreed on 10th July 1906.

Plans for electrification were drawn up, with overhead wires being specified between the east end of Coldharbour Lane, Camberwell and the west end of Gresham Road by Brixton Road via Loughborough Junction, and from Loughborough Junction to West Norwood via Herne Hill. The tortuous curves and difficulty with low bridges in Hinton Road, Loughborough Junction were avoided by taking a diversionary route along a short section of Herne Hill Road and into Wanless Road,

Class E/1 car and another stand at the original West Norwood terminus. Although a trolley reverser is available it appears to have been little used. *(Commercial view)*

which allowed the use of standard double deck bogie cars. The original line was regained in Milkwood Road, where a single track section was laid until the junction with Poplar Walk Road was reached. At this point, the tracks diverged, the southbound line following Poplar Walk Road and Lowden Road, at the south end of which it met the north-bound line, which had been laid in Milkwood Road all the way from Herne Hill.

A complex junction layout was installed at Loughborough Junction, Herne Hill Road with tracks turning out from Coldharbour Lane from both east and west. The one from the east side was so severe that only a single line could be laid, resulting in cars travelling from Camberwell to Herne Hill having to run "wrong road" for a few yards before making the turn (also "wrong road") into the foot of Herne Hill Road. There was also one short single track section of line in Norwood Road, just to the south of Brockwell Park by Trinity Road (sic), where it was not possible to obtain the necessary statutory clearances for double line.

Track construction for the whole line between Camberwell, Brixton and Norwood was undertaken by Mr. W. Manders, at a cost of £63,776, the overhead work between Camberwell and Brixton supplied and erected by Messrs. Dick, Kerr & Co. as an extension of work at Woolwich, for an additional £3,160, and between Loughborough Junction and Norwood by Messrs. R. W. Blackwell for £5,490. Two ploughshifts were installed, one at the Denmark Hill end of Coldharbour Lane, the other at the end of Gresham Road by Brixton Road, which enabled through services to operate to Herne Hill and West Norwood from Vauxhall via Stockwell and from London termini via Camberwell Green. The changepoints were the first to be used in the capital, the attendants at both being required to unplug or replug the plough connector leads from and to the cars, as the sliding contact plough had not by then been introduced.

The South Lambeth Road conduit section, described elsewhere, was opened to traffic on 4th April 1908. The overhead wire lines however, were dealt with several months later in sections, beginning with the Coldharbour Lane and Gresham Road route, 1 mile 2 furlongs in length, reconstructed during the autumn of 1908, inspected by Col. Yorke on

17th November and opened on 21st November 1908. On 26th May 1909, Col. Yorke inspected the remainder of the installation from Lough-borough Junction to Herne Hill and West Norwood, 2 miles 2 furlongs 3 chains long, the section from Loughborough Junction to Herne Hill opening to traffic on 28th May, and on 30th May between Herne Hill and West Norwood. As constucted, the overhead wiring incorporated a trolley reverser at West Norwood, but apparently it did not remain in use for long, probably due to the fact that the conductor of a car would need to "nurse" the trolley rope throughout the whole of the movement, this activity being seen as rather unnecessary and possibly more time consuming than turning the pole in the normal way.

The Effra Road Line

An alternative route between Brixton and Herne Hill via Effra Road and Dulwich Road was proposed by the LCC as part of a more comprehensive plan for that area. Other proposals did not materialise, but authority was obtained in the Council's Act of 1910 to construct the line from Brixton Road, via Effra Road, Morval and Dalberg Roads (southbound) , Water Lane (northbound) and Dulwich Road, to a junction with the existing line at Herne Hill, a distance of 6 furlongs 6.5 chains double and 3 furlongs 0.53 chains single line, using the overhead wire system, with standard equipment being used throughout. The only problem was that the bridge carrying the road over the River Effra had to be rebuilt to obtain sufficient depth to lay the tracks.

Junction special work was laid in at Brixton to allow cars to get to the new tracks and, what may not be so well known is that full junction and crossing work was also laid in towards Acre Lane to enable to be run via Acre Lane to Clapham when authority was forthcoming. That it was not, was always a "thorn in the side" of the LCC and resulted in the eventual removal of the unused trackwork, which was stored away to be used - presumably - elsewhere. A conduit to over-head change-over point was installed about 50 yards into Effra Road from the junction with the Brixton Road tracks.

Track and roadwork was contracted to Messrs. Kirk & Randall of Woolwich, and overhead wire construction to Messrs. Dick, Kerr & Co.,

Class E/1 car No. 845, having just turned out of Water Lane, is seen in Effra Road, bound for Brixton and Victoria. *(Commercial view)*

232

work commencing at the end of 1911. Total costs amounted to £24,370, and all work was completed at the end of March 1912, the inspection being carried out by Col. Yorke on 3rd April. The new line was opened to traffic on 5th April 1912, resulting in the service between Brixton, Herne Hill and West Norwood being diverted away from Loughborough Junction to run over the new route.

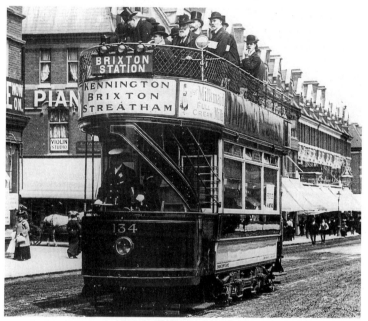

The Board of Trade inspection of the reconstructed tramway between Kennington and Brixton took place on 20th May 1904. Class B car No. 134 was used to convey the official party over the line.

(Courtesy: LT Museum. 20163)

Chapter 18
Electrification, South West London

Conversion of the Kennington & Streatham Cable Line

It had not been the intention of the Council to convert the cable line to an electrically operated tramway until the remainder of the ex-London Tramways Company lines and some new work had been dealt with. The Board of Trade had authorised retention of the line for a further three years as from 18th November 1902, and in order to obtain some of the benefits of electrification, it was decided to use some four-wheeled double deck open top electric cars on a through service. The first 80 of an eventual class of 100 of these cars, to be known as class B, were on order, and it was some of these which were to be modified to allow them to work electrically between London and Kennington, then to be attached to the cable for the rest of the journey to and from Streatham.

A device had been developed to enable the car plough to be wound up from its position in the plough channels to a resting place just beneath the floor. After removal of the plough from the slot at the change-point, an attendant pushed the gripper gear beneath the car at the "country" end, the lifeguards and gates being divided to allow the gear free access into and out from the vehicle. When the gripper gear control rods had been connected to the car controls, the driver was then able to take up the cable and continue on the journey to the suburban end of the line at a sedate 8 m.p.h.

One of the first cars to be delivered was taken to Telford Avenue cable car depot, towed there by a Fowler steam traction engine. At the depot, the car was experimentally fitted with gripper gear and tests carried out. To enable the car to be moved in and around the depot, a length of double trolley wire was erected, upon which stood a four-wheeled trolley power collector, to which was connected a length of jumper cable with a plug on the lower end which was plugged into a socket beneath the canopy of the car. In this way, power was fed to the car. Acetylene gas lamps were fitted into the lower saloon of each car, one in either end bulkhead, which acted both as interior lighting and as signal lamps. Reversible destination route boards were fitted instead of the more usual indicator blind boxes.

The experiment commenced on 2nd August 1903, but from the outset was something of a failure. The class B electric cars were about double the weight of the horse cars which had been in use on the line, with the result that the greatly increased load imposed upon the cable machinery almost brought the operation to a standstill. There was also an accident involving one of the cars during this period when apparently it jumped the rails at New Park Road (at the top of Brixton Hill), ran back down the hill and collided with another car coming up, which incident, coupled with the lack of power from the cable engine, brought the whole experiment to an untimely end.

Almost immediately, arrangements were made to convert the line to electric conduit operation and on 5th April 1904 it was closed to traffic, the contractor's men moving in on the following day.

Arrangements had been made with Messrs. William Griffiths & Co. that the work would be carried out under contract by them in the sum of £86,623.19.11d, the line to be ready for use by the end of June 1904. Griffiths & Co. were already carrying out the reconstruction of several sections in Southwark and Bermondsey (about 8 track miles) and short lengths in Tooting. The supply of special work had been sub-let to Messrs. Hadfield, with yokes, roadboxes and covers to the Anderston Foundry. Just before work was due to start, Griffiths withdrew, and it was left to Messrs. J. G. White to take over the contract at a new price of £95,005.

The problems involved in tearing up over three miles of well constructed double track with its cable conduits was a task of considerable magnitude and, so that this could be dealt with in the shortest possible time, jacks were employed to remove the old tracks. The conduits were split with wedges, four men to a wedge wielding sledge hammers, the rubble cleared away and only then could the work of excavation commence in order that the conduit yokes could be placed in position. At the end of the first week's work, about 1,600 men were employed and such was the rate of progress that the line was complete as far as Water Lane, Brixton, 1¾ miles from Kennington, in time to allow a car to be electrically worked on 18th May, with Col. Yorke inspecting the line two days later. Services to Brixton Station commenced on 21st May and to Water Lane on 30th. The remainder of the line to Streatham was complete by 13th June, the Board of Trade inspection by Col. Yorke took place on 15th, with services commencing on 19th June 1904, seventeen days ahead of schedule. A service between Streatham Library and St. George's Church was provided.

Several important improvements in design and construction had been applied on the line. Rail lengths had been increased to 45 feet as on the Greenwich section; rail anchor joints were used and anchoring was also employed between joints; the positions of sumps were changed, these being placed between the tracks instead of in the margins as on previous lines; the number of sumps was increased, being placed at 140 feet intervals instead of 180 feet as previously used.

In conjunction with the extension of the Streatham tramway to Norbury in 1909, a plough change-point was established at Gleneagle Road. Class E/1 car No. 1082, London bound, has just received a plough.

From Streatham to Norbury

The Streatham terminus of the tramway, situated almost outside the Tate Library, had by the end of 1908 proved to be totally inadequate for two reasons. Firstly, due to the increase in traffic on the line the terminus fell short of the demands placed upon it and secondly, by this time considerable development of housing had taken place well beyond the end of the line. In fact, apart from the open land of Streatham Common, housing was taking all the remaining available land out as far as the LCC boundary and beyond into Croydon. The Council decided to extend the line southwards, along Streatham High Road as far as Hermitage Road, Norbury at the County boundary, just a few yards short of the tracks of the Croydon Corporation Tramways.

Use of the conduit system for the proposed extension was seriously considered, but this time due to the suburban nature of the southern end of the route, agreement was reached to use the overhead wire on the outer part of the line, the change-point to be sited at Gleneagle Road, about ¼-mile south of the junction of Streatham High Road with Mitcham Lane. By then, the overhead wire was in use at Woolwich and Hammersmith. It had also been employed between Brixton and Camberwell and with it an efficient form of conduit/overhead wire changeover arrangement.

The Norbury extension line was constructed under the authority of the London County Council (Tramways & Improvements) Act, 1908. Messrs. Dick, Kerr & Co. were the main contractors for the roadworks, while Messrs. R. H. Blackwell undertook pole planting and overhead wire erection. Total cost of the work, including all incidentals, was £35,537. On completion, the line was inspected on behalf of the Board of Trade by Col. Von. Donop on 29th July 1909 and public service began two day later.

Mitcham Lane & Southcroft Road

Having made the decision to extend the line from Streatham to Norbury, the Council then resolved to provide a route from Streatham via Mitcham Lane as far as the County boundary, there to make a sharp right turn into what had until then, been open country, but was to be developed into a housing estate. The line was then to continue in a westerly direction, following the County boundary, along the new road to Tooting, Amen Corner, a total distance of 1 mile 5 furlongs 3.7 chains, of which 6.53 chains was single track, in two short sections in Mitcham Lane. It was also intended that as well as installing a junction into the Mitcham Road line, facing Tooting Broadway, the Council would arrange to lay another curve and junction from Mitcham Lane into Mitcham Road in the Tooting Junction direction, but this was never built.

The London County Council (Tramways & Improvements) Act, 1909 gave authority for the line to be constructed, and the contract for trackwork went to Messrs. Kirk & Randall in the sum of £38,575 (which also included the cost of a short line in Wimbledon Road). At the end of October 1910 work was complete and, on 2nd November an inspection was carried out by Col. Yorke, after which he expressed his satisfaction with the work. The line opened on 5th November.

At the Streatham end of Mitcham Lane, almost as soon as the lines had left those in Streatham High Road, there was a short section of single track by St. Leonard's Church, for which standard special work and a single conduit was used. The other single section was at a narrow

Class D car No. 313, is seen at the Tooting end of Southcroft Road on its way to Wandsworth late in 1912. (Commercial view)

length of road near Thrale Road, about halfway along Mitcham Lane. This area was quite built up by then, in total contrast to what was to be seen when the tracks finally left Mitcham Lane to turn right on to undeveloped land.

"The Prairie", "Klondyke" and other pseudonyms were given to this new length of double track, which was laid in what was to be known as Southcroft Road. A few houses had been constructed at the Mitcham Lane end, with a few more at the other end at Tooting, Amen Corner, but in between was nothing but the tram tracks and their foundations - not even made-up roads or footpaths. And this is how it stayed until after the Great War when, finally, the whole area was developed.

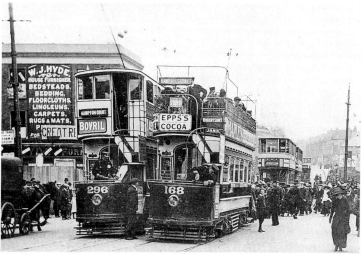

On the extension of the Tooting tramway to Merton, the tracks met those of the LUT end-on, but were not connected at the time. It really was "all change here"! (Commercial view)

The Tooting Extensions

Two new, short lengths of conduit line were constructed between Tooting, Defoe Road and the County boundary at the south end of Tooting High Street, a distance of 575 yards, and between Defoe Road, via Mitcham Road to the County boundary by Tooting Junction Station, a length of 1,172 yards, both of which were double track throughout. The contractor for both lines was Mr. W. Manders at a cost of £20,720.

Construction of both lines was completed early in October 1907, and after tests and trials, both lines were inspected by Col. Yorke on 11th October. The certificate was issued on 12th and services over both lines commenced on 13th.

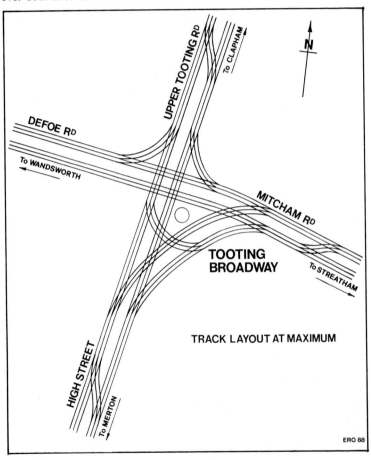

TOOTING BROADWAY

TRACK LAYOUT AT MAXIMUM

ERO 88

The Tooting, Wandsworth & Battersea Tramways

On 5th August 1906, the same day as the new tramway across Vauxhall Bridge was opened to traffic, another new line was put into service. The London County Council (Tramways & Improvements) Act, 1901 authorised the construction of a new conduit tramway in Garratt

Lane, from Tooting to Wandsworth, there to meet the existing horse tramway in York Road, part of which was also to be reconstructed. The contract was accepted by Messrs. Dick, Kerr & Co. at a price of £96,242, to build the new double track line and to reconstruct the horse tramway between Wandsworth and Plough Road, Battersea.

As usual, some road widenings had to be effected, to be able to obtain the statutory 9 ft. 6 in. clearance between the outer rails of the tramway and the kerbs. This was obtained in all places except for a short distance beneath the railway bridge at York Road, where an unusual piece of interlaced track was laid in, with the "up" and "down" rails incorporated into two specially made steel sections. Between these, two separate conduits were placed, in a similar way to that used at Greenwich and Stockwell. There were several other places where tracks were permitted to be laid closer to kerb lines than normal, particularly beneath railway bridges, where widening was impossible.

The Board of Trade inspector, Col. Yorke visited the line after inspecting the Vauxhall line in the morning of Tuesday 31st July 1906 agreeing to its use. New class E cars were in course of assembly at Clapham car shed for use on the service, but in the meantime, class A and class D cars were used, some of these in their open-top condition. As the car shed at Jews Row was not yet available, the cars used on this service worked out of Clapham shed, gaining access to or from Defoe Road over a double track curve laid in for the purpose. The south to west curve was replaced by one from south to east in 1907.

Jews Row shed became available on 12th October, the Garratt Lane cars running into it at the end of the day's work. These joined additional class E cars which had been brought in to extend the Garratt Lane service northwards from Plough Lane as far as Battersea Park Station, and between "Princes Head" and Clapham Junction via Falcon Road, both extended services commencing on the following day.

These sections, reconstructed by Messrs. J. G. White & Co., of a total mileage of 3 furlongs 8.41 chains of double track in Falcon Road, together with 1 mile 3 furlongs 2.83 chains double and 2.51 chains of single line in York Road and Battersea Park Road just west of the "Princes Head" public house, were inspceted by Col. Yorke on the afternoon of 10th October 1906.

Meanwhile, considerable reconstruction had been undertaken at the London end of the ex-South London Tramways lines in Lambeth Road, from St. George's Circus to Lambeth Bridge, and in Stangate, Lambeth Palace Road and Albert Embankment as far as Vauxhall, totalling about 1 mile 5 furlongs in length. All this work, including some complex junction layouts, was undertaken by Messrs. J. G. White & Co. within the same contract as for the the lines in Battersea. There was only one short section of single track in Lambeth Road, which was between Lambeth High Street and Norfolk Row and which was to be doubled when the road was widened. Col. Yorke inspected all these on 4th September 1906, the Vauxhall to Stangate section, which included a double junction curve into Harleyford Road, opening to traffic on the 8th and the Lambeth Road section on the 24th. Cars were shedded at Camberwell for the short, temporary services which were to work over these lines until they were connected to further reconstructed sections.

The final lengths of line along Battersea Park Road, Nine Elms Lane and Wandsworth Road to Vauxhall Cross were reconstructed by Messrs. J. G. White & Co. and inspected by Col. Yorke on 21st December 1906. A service of electric cars began running to Stangate the next day. It had been hoped that the lines in Stangate would have been connected

On the "bottom road", otherwise Battersea Park Road, car No. 314 on service 12, is seen on a journey to Tooting Junction. (Commercial view)

to those in Westminster Bridge Road, to allow cars to travel over the newly-opened Westminster Bridge and Embankment tramway, but due to the intransigence of Parliament at that time, in refusing to allow such a connection to be made, the formation of the junction had to wait until 4th February 1907, when the parliamentarians relented.

Total route length was about 1 mile 3 furlongs, all double track. Included in this reconstruction was the provision of a double junction from Wandsworth Road, which turned in a westerly direction to connect with the tracks leading to Vauxhall Bridge from Upper Kennington Lane. There was another at the Nine Elms Lane and Wandsworth Road intersection, which had been laid in advance of the reconstruction of the horse tramway in Wandsworth Road. Total cost of all these works was £199,245.

An interesting and unusual feature of the tramway in Nine Elms Lane was that seven sets of railway tracks used in connection with the Goods Depot of the London & South Western Railway crossed the road on the level, not far from the junction with Wandsworth Road, and special trackwork had to be supplied for each crossing. Road widenings were also necessary, and two bridges carrying the road over railways had to be partially reconstructed in order to obtain sufficient clearance for the conduit yokes.

Along Wimbledon Road

Powers for the construction of this double track line, 1 furlong 5.73 chains in length were obtained in 1903 as Tramway No. 6 of that Act, along with Tramway No. 6A, a double junction of 2.3 chains length, to connect the line to those in Garratt Lane, in order to be able to work cars into Wimbledon Road from both directions.

Construction was undertaken by Messrs. Kirk & Randall as part of the contract for the Southcroft Road line, and was completed at the same time as the main work. Col. Yorke inspected it after his visit to Southcroft Road on 2nd November 1910, the line opening to traffic on the 5th November, at the same time as Southcroft Road and sharing a new car service put on cover the roads.

This short line, of no topographical significance ended at the County boundary at what is described by the late Mr. A. W. Morant as the "no-mans land in Wimbledon Road at Summerstown". There, the line met, but was not connected to the overhead-wire equipped line of the London United Tramways Company, on which a shuttle service was worked between High Street, Colliers Wood and Summerstown. Its only claim to fame, if that is the right term, was that in later years a greyhound racing stadium was erected at Summerstown, which was the source of considerable traffic on the occasions when dog-racing took place.

The line was eventually joined up to the LUT company's tracks in 1931, with a conduit to overhead wire change-point being installed at the County boundary, to enable a through service of cars to be worked through between Wimbledon and London, so replacing the short working service provided by the LUT.

The Battersea Bridge Road Line

The LCC had resolved from time to time to construct a network of tramways in south-west London north of the Thames and in the neighbouring west London districts, but were always thwarted by the objections of one or more of any number of bodies such as the railway companies, the London General Omnibus Company, the local authorities and the Metropolitan Police.

Eventually, in 1909 an Act of Parliament was gained, authorising the Council to construct Tramway No. 8, a double line 7 furlongs 7.3 chains long, from the junction with the existing tramways in Battersea Park Road, along Battersea Bridge Road, over Battersea Bridge and along Beaufort Street, to terminate in that street at its junction with Kings Road, Chelsea. This, the Council decided, was the beginning of a successful end to a long struggle. But this was not to be the case, as it could get no further and the new line remained as a rather unremunerative "fag-end" to the tramway system, although in later years, business did pick up considerably.

Battersea Bridge had a roadway only about 24 feet wide, which was the cause of much concern, particularly to the Metropolitan Police, who suggested that a single line be laid in the centre of the carriage-way. The Board of Trade, however, agreed with the LCC that a double line could be constructed, with the tracks close to each kerb, leaving a ten-feet wide section in the centre of the roadway for the use of other vehicles if required.

Certain structural alterations were necessary to enable the conduit tracks to be laid across the bridge, these and the trackwork being carried out by Messrs. Dick, Kerr & Co. at a cost of £21,630. Upon completion, the extension was inspected by Col. Yorke on 20th June 1911 and opened to traffic on 22nd. A short branch line was laid into the LCCT wharf and permanent way yard, which was situated on the west side of Battersea Bridge Road, on the riverside.

During the life of the tramways, the bridge was not altered in any way, but as an interesting tailpiece to its history, although not strictly within the sphere of this account, the bridge was closed in 1950 due to being damaged by a passing vessel, just a few months before the proposed closure of the tramway service. For this period, the terminus of service 34 was at a crossover by the entrance to the sand-yard, on the south side of the bridge.

Vauxhall & Brixton via Stockwell Road

Originally part of the London Southern Tramways Company's system, the line between Vauxhall Station and Brixton, Gresham Road via South Lambeth Road and Stockwell Road became the only part of it to be reconstructed on the conduit system. It was reconstructed at a cost of £58,995, which included £4,900 for ducts and cables and £7,900 for rails, in the early months of 1908. Junction work at Vauxhall had already been installed, but the crossings at Clapham Road and Brixton Road were put in as part of the main work.

The line had one single track section in its 1 mile 5 furlongs length, this in Stockwell Road between Stockwell Green, Conference Road and Rumsey Road, which was equipped with double conduit. After completion at the end of March 1908, Col. Yorke inspected it on 3rd April and it opened to traffic on the following day.

Vauxhall & East Hill via Lavender Hill
Lavender Hill & Chelsea Bridge via Queen's Road

Using the words of the tramway historian, C. S. Dunbar, the "bottom" road of the ex-South London Tramways Company had been electrified in 1906, still leaving horses and their yellow cars dominant in the more residential areas of the "top" road, which situation was to remain until the end of 1908.

Prior to the reconstruction of the "top road", the first section to be converted to electric conduit working was the short line along the length of Queen's Road, from Lavender Hill to the Surrey side of Chelsea Bridge, a distance of about one and a half miles. This route, which was bedevilled by having to pass beneath several low railway bridges at the Battersea Park end of the southern half of Queen's Road, was constructed throughout with double track by the LCC Works Department at a cost of £30,282, the last major work of this type that the Department undertook.

This line was ready for use at the end of 1908, complete with a double track crossing over the "bottom road" tracks and a double line curve connecting the Battersea Park Road tracks from the Vauxhall direction to the Queen's Road tracks in the Lavender Hill direction. The tracks at the other end of Queen's Road terminated just a few yards short of Lavender Hill in a double track stub-end. At Chelsea Bridge, the rails ended in a length of single track.

A class C car just emerging from the dark depths of the very wide railway bridge spanning Queen's Road Battersea. (Photographer unknown)

The other route to Wandsworth was via Lavender Hill. Car No. 348 is seen in 1911, bound for Hop Exchange via Westminster.

After the usual trials and tests the line was inspected by Col. Yorke on 20th January 1909. Being satisfied, the Inspector authorised its use, subject to the usual restriction regarding speeds. The LCC began operations on 25th January with a service of single-deck cars of classes F and G (shedded at Jews Row), as the height of the bridges over the road prevented the use of anything else at that time. The opening of this route enabled the Council to provide some sort of electric car service between Lavender Hill, Vauxhall and Westminster during the time that the "top road" was under reconstruction by routing some cars through from Kingsway Subway over the top end of Battersea Park Road and the Queen's Road curves to Lavender Hill terminus.

The first section of Wandsworth Road to close to horse cars, after all preliminary pipe and drainage works had been completed for the new electrification, was between Nine Elms Lane and Wandsworth Road Station during the spring of 1909, to be followed soon afterwards by the lines between Wandsworth Road Station and Queen's Road. During reconstruction of this section, substantial roadworks were required at the junction of Lavender Hill with Queen's Road and Cedars Road, in order that a right-angled double track crossing could be laid in, to connect the tracks in Queen's Road to new lines to be laid along Cedars Road for an authorised extension to Long Road, Clapham Common and "The Plough", Clapham, together with a double junction curve from the Clapham Junction direction of Lavender Hill, turning into Cedars Road.

The 1 mile 5 furlongs 4 chains of double line between Nine Elms Lane and Queen's Road was completed at the beginning of September 1909, inspected by Col. Yorke on 21st and opened to traffic two days later. The next six furlongs of track onwards to Clapham Junction, Falcon Road was completed about three weeks later and was inspected by Col. Yorke on 6th October and opened on 9th.

Meanwhile, the final three-quarters of a mile of line to Wandsworth, East Hill, had been completely reconstructed by early December 1909, being inspected by Col. Yorke on 14th. Electric cars began running through to the new terminus on 15th. No further extension of the line was made until 1921. Contractor for all the work between Nine Elms Lane and East Hill was J. Mowlem & Sons, and cost £97,503.

Class D car No. 323 picks up passengers near the railway bridge at Wandsworth Road Station. The bridge is of interest with its clutter of advertisements. *(Courtesy: A. D. Packer)*

The Cedars Road Line

The London County Council (Tramways & Improvements) Act, 1906 gave authority for the construction of a double track tramway (Nos. 15 and 15A) from a junction at Lavender Hill into and along Cedars Road and Long Road, Clapham Common to a new junction with the Tooting tramway at South Side, Clapham Common. As described elsewhere, a section of the line had already been laid in Cedars Road in advance of the main work, as part of the crossing and junction layout at that point.

The Council had estimated a total sum of £32,500 for the complete reconstruction of this line including pipeworks, cabling and other items. Messrs. Dick, Kerr & Co. gained the contract in the sum of £20,177 for track and roadwork, which were commenced in the late autumn of 1909 and completed in 1910. Col. Yorke for the Board of Trade, carried out his inspection on 23rd February, authorising its use and services commenced on 26th February.

Cedars Road had a severe down gradient leading to Lavender Hill, which required all the skill which the tramwaymen could muster in controlling their cars on this section, both in the "up" and "down" directions. There were several reports of accidents occurring through cars running out of control on the hill, and usually ending up embedded in one or other of the premises in Lavender Hill opposite the junction.

The High Street Wandsworth & Garratt Lane Link

The isolated line working between Harlesden, Hammersmith and Wandsworth (Putney Bridge Road) became connected to the rest of the southern system when, by authority of the Act of 1910, the Council constructed part of Tramway No. 8 between the termination of the line at High Street, Wandsworth and Garratt Lane, a distance of 2 furlongs 1.36 chains, including the junction layout in Garratt Lane. An overhead wire/conduit change-point was installed at the extreme southern end of Putney Bridge Road, just before the tracks turned into High Street Wandsworth.

Messrs. J. Mowlem & Sons carried out the work as part of a number of disconnected jobs, all based on a schedule of prices formula, at a cost of £24,707, which included special work. Final costs, including work done by the LCC amounted to £25,815. The completed section was inspected by Col. Von Donop on 13th July 1915 and it opened for traffic on 16th.

The East Hill Extension

The final link in the network of tramways in the Wandsworth area was forged by the construction of a line from the terminus at East Hill, to connect with the junction layout at the York Road/Garratt Lane crossing, a distance of 414 yards and which included the provision of a four-square crossing at the Garratt Lane intersection. This was constructed by Mr. W. Manders, who successfully tendered for the work in July 1920 in the sum of £64,279. The completed lines were inspected by Maj. Mount on 2nd August 1921, and opened to traffic on 4th.

The LCC and Croydon Corporation tracks were joined early in 1926 in preparation for a through service of cars between London, Croydon and Purley, which commenced on 7th February. In this view, short lengths of rail are being welded in to close the gap across the boundary. The class E/1 car is standing at the original terminal point.

(Courtesy: LT Museum. 13131)

Chapter 19
Electrification, The Hammersmith Lines

Although this area for tramway purposes was originally considered to be part of the Northern Division of the LCC Tramways, there was always a strong affinity with south London and, in fact, some years after the introduction of electric car services, the area was placed under the control of the Southern Divisional Offices, due in the main to the connection at Putney with the south London tramways and the fact that the car services were numbered into the south side scheme.

The London County Council had obtained powers in 1902 to construct a line from Putney to Hammersmith, to be built as a conduit tramway, but this was to take second place in the scheme.

Hammersmith to Harlesden

About two weeks after the line in Woolwich was opened for electric traction, the first part of a new line, which had never been a horse tramway, was completed in the area centred on Hammersmith and built under powers obtained by the London County Council (Tramways & Improvements) Act, 1903. The double deck tramway between Hammersmith and Harlesden, opened on 30th May 1908, was just three miles long and planned as part of a line connecting the Harrow Road tramway at the northern end of Scrubs Lane with Hammersmith and Putney, and with a view to extending further southwards and connecting into other proposed lines in the western suburbs.

A great exhibition was due to be staged in the summer of 1908 at a site on the west side of Wood Lane, then known as the Great White city, where a joint Franco-British enterprise was expected to attract large numbers of visitors. This caused the LCC to expedite the work on this section in an effort to cull a proportion of the expected traffic. Arrangements were made with the exhibition authority to place a double-track lay-by in the grounds of the site, enabling passengers to have direct access to the turnstiles.

A contract was placed with the Hammersmith firm of Geo. Wimpey & Co. in the sum of £42,800 for the construction of the track, including a single track accesss line across Hammersmith Broadway to the car shed at Great Church Lane. The overhead wire equipment was erected by Messrs. Dick, Kerr & Co. for an estimated £8,000, while special work at junctions, etc. was supplied by Hadfield of Sheffield. Standard No. 4 rails, weighing 105 lbs/yd were used throughout, joined together with two-feet long fishplates and strengthened by the use of inverted rail anchor plates, also two feet long, while intermediate inverted rail anchors were placed transversely beneath the rails at intervals of 7 ft. 6 in. Trackwork was to the standard adopted by the LCC as has previously been described. The overhead trolley wire was of the grooved type, having a breaking strain of 6,600 lbs. This was supported by grip ears held up with 7/12 stranded span wire. Medium and heavy traction poles were used where necessary, spaced out at the standard average distance of 120 feet.

An unusual feature of this line was that it crossed the tracks of the London United Tramways Company at two places, Goldhawk Road and Uxbridge Road Shepherds Bush. At both crossing points, the whole of the overhead wiring was isolated from the rest of the two systems by means of section insulators placed in each wire on each side of each crossing place, a distance in each case of about 40 yards. These isolated crossing sections could be fed with power from either the LCC or LUT systems, two-way changeover switches being provided for the purpose in boxes at the bases of the traction poles supporting the section insulators.

After inspection by Col. Yorke on 28th May 1908, who pronounced the line fit for public use, a service was begun on 30th just a few days after the opening of the exhibition, with 25 cars of class E/1 of Hurst, Nelson construction being available for use. These cars, which were numbered mainly in the 900 series, were housed in Hammersmith car shed. It had been hoped that passengers could have been carried across Hammersmith Broadway as far as Great Queen Street but, due to the many problems in widening the north side of the Broadway, as well as to other widening work to the south of it, there was only a sufficient width of road to lay a single line to enable the cars to obtain access to the car shed.

At the time of the inspection of the line, the representative of the Metropolitan Police complained to the Board of Trade Inspector that, in the opinion of the police, the "trolley standards" used on the LCC cars were considered to be "unsafe", as the rolled steel longitudinal bearers for the bases were "only fixed to the roofsticks with wood screws, and should a trolley be wrenched, it could fall off and do injury or worse, could cause serious damage by the 550 volts being transmitted through the fallen pole"!

Class E/1 car No. 996, seen passing the Great White City exhibition grounds soon after the line between Hammersmith and Scrubs Lane was opened in 1908. The ornate entrance to the grounds was a notable feature in the district. *(Commercial view)*

247

To this, Col. Yorke and Mr. Trotter said " ... This is a false alarm. The risk involved is exceedingly remote. There is no trolley standard in the ordinary sense. The pole end is attached by a hinged joint and bearing plate directly on the roof. There is no leverage. The strains and pressures are distributed over a length of 10 feet and a width of 1 foot 8 inches, which equals about 16 square feet area, and the bearers are fixed with 40 screws". There was no reply from the police to this comment.

The lay-by at the entrance to the White City consisted of a double track layout, connected at both ends to the main line and was provided with two scissors crossovers, one at either end of the siding. In essence, it was a four track layout, two in the street, the others within the exhibition grounds.

The scissors crossovers were of the standard 60 feet length, with a 200 feet length of double track between them, providing standing space for five cars on each track.

It had been intended that the lay-by was to have been a permanent feature of the exhibition ground but, due to the exhibition management deciding to re-arrange the entrances to the site, the Council was asked in 1911, to remove the layout. Being on private property, there were no grounds upon which it could refuse, resulting in the removal of the installation at a cost to the Council of £1,900.

Hammersmith to Putney

After completion of the line northwards from Hammersmith, the Council resolved to construct the section southwards through Fulham, to and over Putney Bridge and to terminate for the time being in Lower Richmond Road. Powers obtained in 1902 authorised the Council to construct this line on the conduit system, but as the Hammersmith tramways, both LCC and LUT, were using the overhead wire system, it was logical to continue with the use of the overhead, the more so as this line, when completed, would be connected to the Harlesden section. To this end, the LCC sought and obtained a variation of its powers in the 1908 Session of Parliament, to allow it to use overhead wires between Hammersmith and Putney. The route length of about 2½ miles was constructed in a similar way as for the northern part of the line, with the exception that rail joints on the westerly (or north-bound) of the two tracks were welded throughout, using the "Thermit" process. This was done to evaluate the welding system as against the more usual way of joining rails together with bolted fishplates. There were no other unusual problems, except for considerable street widenings near the southern end of Fulham Palace Road, where several houses were demolished.

Track and roadworks were carried out by Messrs. Geo. Wimpey & Co. with the overhead wiring being entrusted to Messrs. R. W. Blackwell & Co. Rails were supplied from LCC stock, traction poles by Messrs. James Russell & Co. and grooved trolley wire by Messrs. Frederick Smith & Co. Cost of all the work, excluding the provision of rails and cables was approximately £34,700.

The southern terminus of the line in Lower Richmond Road was almost immediately next to the south side of the bridge on the west side of the road. A double track curve led into the terminus, which was a double track stub end with a crossover at a suitable distance from the end of the line. A trolley reverser was also installed but, as at West Norwood, it appears to have been very little used.

248

The original southern terminus of the Putney tramway was in Lower Richmond Road. Here, the crew of car No. 1000 are just about to turn the trolley pole by means of the trolley reverser. (Commercial view)

It was the intention of the LCC to obtain further powers to extend the line westwards towards Roehampton, but this scheme was later abandoned. Instead, the terminal tracks were to remain, even though several years later, an extension of the line was constructed towards the east, to Wandsworth.

Across Putney Bridge

The only other part of the work which required special consideration was the section on Putney Bridge, which at that time was quite narrow. The bridge then in existence was of granite construction, with several inset parapets at equal distances from each other on either side of each footpath. The total width of each carriageway was approximately 24 feet, with a six feet wide pavement on either side. Due to the restriction imposed by the width of the road, the tram tracks were laid near the kerb on either side, leaving a ten feet wide centre section clear of obstruction, which could be used by other traffic if required, for instance, to allow a tram to pass a horse-drawn wagon.

As the bridge was of quite massive construction, there was no need for special arrangements to be made regarding the laying of rails. It was also convenient that the parapets were suitably spaced, allowing all the traction poles to be planted as close to the sides of the bridge-work as possible, leaving the footways clear of all obstructions. In later years (the 1920s) the bridge was practically rebuilt, the width of the carriageway being virtually doubled, allowing the tracks to be positioned in the centre of the roadway. The line from Hammersmith to Putney was opened to traffic on 23rd January 1909, after an inspection by Col. Yorke on 20th.

The Putney Bridge Road Extension

Due to the inability of the Council to obtain authority to extend the line westwards from Lower Richmond Road, it obtained powers in its Act of 1910 to extend the line eastwards along Putney Bridge Road to a point just short of Wandsworth High Street, a distance of just under a mile, using the overhead wire system.

The Putney line, when extended along Putney Bridge Road, terminated quite close to Wandsworth High Street. The last few yards of track were constructed for conduit working, complete with change-point.

Construction of the track was undertaken by Messrs. Geo. Wimpey of Hammersmith, while overhead work was carried out by Messrs. Clough, Smith at a total cost to the Council of £26,409. The completed line was inspected by Col. Yorke on 26th January 1912 and opened to traffic on 30th.

One feature to be seen on this section was the very low railway bridge over Putney Bridge Road just east of Fawe Park Road. To enable standard class E and E/1 double deck trolley equipped cars to pass beneath it, the road had to be lowered to a considerable depth before the lines could be laid. Due to this restriction, the original cars of classes A and D, when fitted with trolley poles, could not safely negotiate this section of track.

The footpaths on either side of the roadway, which were left in their original positions, were almost ten feet above the road under the centre portion of the bridge, level with the upper decks of the cars.

Crossing Hammersmith Broadway

The inability to come to terms with Hammersmith Borough Council, both in obtaining consent to place the tracks in an agreed position and to construct lines in the Broadway to connect with the lines of the LUT, caused severe delay in joining up the two sets of track in order to run a through service between Harlesden and Putney. The Borough authorities wanted considerable and expensive roadworks to be effected before allowing the tracks to be laid, including the resiting of a public toilet, while the Metropolitan Police requested that the tracks be laid in a different position from that agreed by the Councils.

In an effort to overcome the difficulties, the LCC finally obtained agreement which allowed the use for public services of the west, or northbound track across the Broadway. This arrangement, brought into use on 30th January 1912, while to the advantage of the County Council, was operated with some difficulty, as the two ends of the

The double track connection across Hammersmith Broadway was opened to traffic in May 1912. Car No. 1358 is seen on a through journey soon after the opening. (Courtesy: A. D. Packer)

track were not in direct line of sight. It was possible that the service arrangements required the use of a hand-held "staff", or of a human "travelling token". Finally, after very extensive and expensive work of demolition and rebuilding, both to the roads and buildings, the second track was laid and opened to traffic on 23rd May 1912, just four years after the opening of the first section of the line to Harlesden!

The Harrow Road Connection

Under the terms of an agreement made between the LCC and MET in 1909, the Council had the right to run up to one-third of the number of cars operated by the MET between Scrubs Lane and Edgware Road. It had been decided to hold a Coronation Exhibition at the White City ground in May 1911 and the Council arranged to take advantage of this by running a through service of cars between Putney, Hammersmith, Scrubs Lane, Harrow Road and Edgware Road. As the tracks in Harrow Road were in Middlesex, it fell to the MET to provide the necessary junction layout, which was installed and ready for use by 25th April 1911.

In conjunction with the new service, the Council offered a combined tram and exhibition entrance ticket for the sum of 1/1d, the LCC getting a 5% commission in respect of the admission charge. Similar arrangements had been made for the Franco-British, Imperial International and Japan-British exhibitions held in 1908, 1909 and 1910.

The through service, however, was reported as being something of a failure through lack of patronage, the Council deciding to withdraw from it early in August, even though Paddington and Hammersmith Councils asked for it to be retained. But there was another reason for the withdrawal. The Board of Trade and LCC has insisted that the MET cars to be worked on the line be specially rebuilt to come within a width restriction of 6 ft. 9 in., as the tracks were only at eight feet centres. As the LCC cars were wider, the Council was technically in breach of the Regulations. After this experiment, no other LCC services were ever run into London via the Harrow Road. (A detailed history of the Harrow Road Tramway is given in the LRTA/TLRS publication, "The Metropolitan Electric Tramways" by C. S. Smeeton).

In 1924, the British Empire Exhibition was staged at Wembley, and the Council arranged to work a service northward from its terminus at Scrubs Lane, into MET territory to Wembley and Sudbury. An agreement was concluded with the MET for the construction of a junction into the MET tracks, the Council to pay 6% per annum on half the installation costs, and to continue the payments for as long as the junction remained in use. The LCC was also to provide an exclusive through service of cars between Putney and Wembley, or between such points "as may be agreed by the managers". This commenced on 23rd April 1924, as described in the chapters dealing with routes and services.

The London United Tramways in Hammersmith

The lines of the London United Tramways in west London first came up for consideration for purchase by the LCC on 6th July and 8th August 1909. The Council decided on 6th April to start proceedings and notified the company. This was to begin a series of arguments that were to continue until well after the Great War. The LUT had also been in dispute with Hammersmith Borough Council since 1907 because of the alleged poor state of the tracks and pavings, and on 3rd June 1909, Hammersmith asked the Board of Trade to nominate an arbitrator to deal with the matter. Mr. W. Worby Beaumont took the appointment on 8th October.

It was arranged for the hearing to take place on 16th December, and by then, the list of complaints included the alleged bad condition of some of the cars. However, on 9th December, Hammersmith withdrew its arbitration request, as the LUT had carried out some track repairs. This resulted in the hearing being suspended for the time being. The repairs, however, appeared to have been minimal, resulting in the LUT, the LCC, Hammersmith Borough Council and the Board of Trade all getting involved in the issue, which was still being discussed in February 1911.

Returning to the affairs of 1909, the action of the LCC caused the General Manager of the LUT, Sir James Clifton Robinson to appeal to the Board of Trade to intervene, stating that the company was to the fore in providing good and cheap facilities for its passengers. He also commented adversely on the activities of the LCC in the Tooting area, in not making an effort to connect up with the lines of the company, thereby giving better facilities to passengers. Robinson also stated that the company would expect the sum of £414,234 for the 5 miles 3 furlongs 7 chains of line, together with 45 cars, Chiswick depot and the power station which the LCC did not want.

A Bill was then presented to Parliament by the company proposing that the purchase by the LCC should be deferred; that the lines in Tooting be connected up; that clauses in previous LUT Acts referring to the use by the company of conduit construction for new lines be removed; that extra time be allowed for the construction of other lines authorised by earlier Acts. It particularly sought to gain an extension of time for the implementation of compulsory purchase by the LCC.

The General Manager then took his case to local councils and well-known personalities of the day. Chiswick UDC arranged for a petition to be raised and presented to the Board of Trade, stating its opposition to the LCC proposal for compulsory purchase. Great play was made of the supposition that if the LCC did purchase the lines, passengers would have to change cars at boundary points (even though the LCC had repeatedly pointed out that this need not be the case). A comment from Sir F. J. Hopwood (Colonial Office) to Mr. Winston Churchill (President of the Board of Trade) stating "that, to break the facilities existing and make 20 million (sic) passengers 'get out' at the LCC boundary would be simply monstrous" was certainly one to fuel the flames. Nevertheless, at a meeting held on Tuesday 6th April 1909, the Council resolved "to purchase such lines of the London United Tramways which lay in the County of London".

Sir James next stated that the notice had been prematurely served and that, in any case, six months may elapse while the Board of Trade reconsider the position. He then decided to depart for the Continent "under doctor's orders", letting it be known that he would not return until the end of September at the earliest, when he would then take the matter up once again.

Upon his return, further correspondence ensued with the Board of Trade, expressing the hope that the LCC would not be permitted to purchase the lines, and asking for a public enquiry into the question. This drew the response from Mr. W. F. Marwood of the Board of Trade, that Sir James must have known that the LCC would be legally able to purchase the lines when it resolved to do so, and pointed out that he (Robinson) had made no mention of the fact that there was every possibility of agreement being reached with the LCC on working arrangements. The Board considered that a public enquiry was not necessary and suggested that the company try to come to terms and adopt a more reasonable attitude to the matter. Mr. Churchill agreed to this, and asked that he "be kept informed of each step, as he was anxious to safeguard the facilities".

The LCC in the meantime, informed the Board of Trade that it had the statutory right to purchase the lines in question and still wished to do so. Regarding the comments made on fares and of passengers changing cars at boundary points, these did not affect the issue, and the Council was prepared "at the proper time" to discuss the issues and enter into agreements. So far as making a connection between the two systems was concerned, this was quite possible and, indeed, the Council was anxious that it should be done. At the same time, the Council said that it had decided to notify the House of Lords that it intended to submit a petition to the House of Lords against the LUT Bill.

Winston Churchill arranged for a meeting to take place on 25th November 1909 in an effort to get the two sides together, at which Messrs. A. Shirley Benn and Sir H. Llewellyn Smith represented the LCC, with Sir J. Clifton Robinson and Albert Stanley spoke for the LUT. Resulting from this, it became clear that Robinson and Stanley wanted a comprehensive agreement to be struck with the LCC before purchase - not afterwards. They both commented on the "harsh terms" imposed upon the MET with regard to the Harrow Road line after purchase which in their eyes proved the point about the intentions of the LCC, and Sir James said that he would not tolerate that. For the LCC, Mr. Benn commented that he would suggest that the Council would try to be agreeable, although there was no promise, only that if agreement could not be reached, arbitration could be resorted to.

The Board of Trade found itself in a rather difficult position. On the one hand, Mr. Marwood was rather sceptical of the attitude of the LUT when he said, referring to the fact that the Board could not refuse the demand of the LCC " ... the (Sir. J.) Robinson tactics no doubt will be to make out a strong case of public inconvenience and then obstructing any method by which such inconvenience can be overcome ... ". On the other hand, it was proving to be almost impossible to get the Council to state what its "reasonable terms" were likely to be. Eventually, the Board agreed on 21st December 1909 to the LCC purchase proposal, but matters went no further for a considerable time. During the early part of 1910, Sir James Clifton Robinson died, leaving Albert Stanley more deeply involved as General Manager of the LUT for the time being.

The farcical situation dragged on into 1911; by the beginning of June there was still no agreement, but this time it was the price to be paid for the line that was in dispute. This resulted in the LCC asking the Board of Trade to appoint a referee to resolve the difficulty. The name of Robert Elliott-Cooper was mentioned by the LUT as being a suitable person, the company also making it known that Messrs. Stanley & Co. were acting as Solicitors on its behalf. To this, the Board of Trade retorted "We make recommendations and appointments - not them. We appoint R. Elliott Cooper ... ". The LCC (already advised that by the LUT that Cooper would be a likely candidate) agreed. He was offered the appointment on 26th July and accepted it on 3rd August 1911.

It was announced on 2nd November 1911 that the arbitration hearing would take place "next week" but, before "next week" the Board of Trade was advised that Mr. Stanley "who is now General Manager of these tramways as well as the Metropolitan District Railways and Allied Tube Railways, has hinted that he would have to come to some arrangement to take passengers on into London by omnibus"! Mr. Marwood (Board of Trade) commented that he did not know "then that a scheme was afoot" to get the LGOC into an alliance ... under Stanley's management. This series of statements was to be the cause of more delay, while the Board tried to unravel the truths and fictions.

On 15th February 1912, R. Elliott-Cooper made his award, that the LCC should pay a total of £248,653 plus costs, for the Hammersmith lines, which included £33,974 for the tracks and £127,249 for Chiswick depot and power station. The Council immediately appealed against the award, which was to be the cause of more delay.

Meantime, the suspended 1909 arbitration hearing regarding the condition of some of the lines in Hammersmith was resumed, with the award of the arbitrator, Mr. W. Worby Beaumont being announced on 3rd May 1912. He stated that he found that "the LUT had always rectified defects in the track when asked, and Hammersmith Borough Council had not found it necessary to repair the paving in December 1909". A request by Hammersmith to reconstruct the track "was not reasonable" and Hammersmith was ordered to pay the costs of the arbitration and award.

However, despite the award of the arbitrator, the Board of Trade and the LCC had become convinced that some track reconstruction was necessary, and Hammersmith Council agreed to inspect all track and report details of wear, bad joints and other defects, which was carried out in the last week in May. As for the cars, the company reported on 20th June that all were in good condition and perfectly safe.

The company at this time was in some financial difficulty, which appeared to be worsening. The LCC still aimed to take over, and voted £16,100 on 1st February 1913 to pay for the reconstruction of the tracks in part of King Street and Goldhawk Road. The LUT undertook to carry out the work, which started on 21st May. On 17th July, the LCC Highways Committee recommended that arrangements be made with the company to reconstruct other sections of Goldhawk Road, King Street and the Hammersmith loop at an agreed total cost of £19,700.

The rest of 1913 passed by, as did the first half of 1914, with the whole matter still charting its weary course. On 11th July, the Board of Trade reported that agreement was close at hand, but had reckoned without the forces working against the whole nation. One month later, the country was at war!

Post War Purchase by the LCC

On 18th May 1917, the parties announced that final agreement in principle had been reached under the following terms:-

"The LCC to pay the LUT £235,000, its own costs of £10,000 and LUT costs of £12,000. The agreement to be exchanged as soon as possible, but not completed 'until up to one year after the Declaration of Peace'. Meantime, the company is to continue to work and maintain the lines, with the LCC entitled to run cars to any point on the tramways of the company in the County of Middlesex, and the company to be able to run over the purchased lines."

Due to the continuation of the war until November 1918, together with post-war difficulties, the Declaration of Peace on 2nd May 1921 and the official end of the war on 31st August 1921, it was not until 31st January 1922 that the Council decided to implement the terms of the 1917 agreement. By this time, the management of the company had changed again, with Christopher John Spencer as General Manager. It became his responsibility to attend to the details of the transfer.

The LUT lines in Hammersmith and Shepherds Bush were finally added to the LCC mileage on 2nd May 1922. The LUT line between Longley Road, Merton and Wimbledon Hill was also included in the transaction, giving the LCC through running rights over this section, for which a plough change-point was laid in at the County boundary. Supplementary agreements were arranged regarding through running between the two undertakings on a mileage balancing basis.

From that date, cars of the LUT continued to work on the lines in Hammersmith, a connection was made between the two systems at Hammersmith Broadway, LCC service 26 was extended to Kew Bridge via Chiswick High Road from its terminus at Hammersmith, services 2 and 4 were extended from Merton to Wimbledon Hill, while each party agreed that the LCC should fix fares on the Wimbledon line and the LUT should do likewise on the Hammersmith lines, and each was to retain fares taken on its own cars.

One other effect that the sale and purchase had, was that the company was entitled to convert part of the generating station into a transforming station for its own use for a period not exceeding 21 years. In return, it was to provide a supply of direct current to the LCC free of charge up to 1,800,000 units a year, with the County Council paying for any excess power at a rate to be agreed by arbitration.

In addition to the tracks, depot and power station, forty-five cars and a horse-drawn tower wagon were included in the sale. The cars were:-
Type X: Nos. 101-106, 109-116, 119-124, 126-136, 139-147.
Type T: Nos. 319-323.

Upon receipt of the cars, the LCC advertised them for re-sale, as it was considered that they would not be up to the standard required by the Council, neither would they meet traffic requirements. Receiving no enquiries from the advertisements, negotiations were entered into with the LUT, who eventually took them all back in return for a sum of £2,000, plus the Chiswick tower wagon for an additional £450.

The final conveyance for the sale of and transfer to the London County Council of the lines, power station and cars, together with the agreement regarding through running was approved and sealed on 12th October 1922. It had taken nearly fourteen years to complete and had been the cause of much unnecessary discussion and argument.

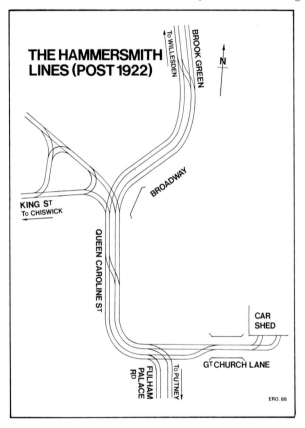

Chapter 20
Rolling Stock
Classes A, B, C, D & E

Britain has always been the home of the double deck tramcar. In horse tram days the double deck car was not uncommon abroad but in the electric era, double deck cars were largely confined to Britain and its Empire. The earliest electric cars were based upon the horse car design of the period and had quite light bodies with uncanopied open top decks and "garden seats", which were pairs of wooden slatted seats with reversible backs, placed on either side of a central gangway, although some were built with the early traditional "knifeboard" seats, which consisted of two longitudinal benches mounted back-to-back along the centre line of the car body. Before long, all body builders were turning out cars of this type, and with this body came the vogue for "reversed stairs". On uncanopied cars, the lower end of the stairs had to start near the dash, while the top would be by the end of the saloon, but on extended canopy cars, there was the choice of this arrangement or the alternative of having the stairs start next to the saloon off-side bulkhead and finish above the motorman's head. The advantage of the latter arrangement was that the entire length of the top deck was uncluttered by the two staircase wells and more garden seats could be packed in. The disadvantages were that both upper and lower deck passengers tended to use the side of the platform nearest to the saloon door when boarding and alighting, together with the fact that the motorman's vision to the nearside of the car was obscured by the staircase.

Car body construction of the first of the LCC electric cars was to some extent a follow-on from the methods used in horse car building, but with the use of considerably heavier section timbers as was shown in the cars of classes A, B, C and D, strengthened as necessary with steel sections. Those in classes E, E/1 and M, while having wooden bodies, had the underframes made of steel. The class F and G cars, built especially for use in Kingsway Subway, were of all-metal construction, while the cars of classes E/3 and HR/2 were of composite construction, with all-steel lower saloon bodies and aluminium and steel section upper decks. Only the top deck roofs were made of timber. The American influence was also to be seen in the types of trucks used on LCC cars. The Brill 21E trucks on the B and C class cars, and the Brill 22E trucks of the A class were of imported design, while the McGuire trucks used under the class D cars, although designed and built in Britain, owed some allegiance to American ideas. Only the trucks used under the M and HR/2 cars were totally British in concept, although the E/3 trucks were developed far enough away from the original design that they could be considered to be a "home product".

The regulations of the Metropolitan Police, the authority which licensed all the LCC cars individually under the authority of the Metropolitan Carriage Act, 1869, bore quite heavily upon all aspects of LCC

Tramways operations. The reversed staircases were soon condemned by the police as being an obstruction to the vision of the motormen, resulting in the Council indulging in some "horse trading" with the police and the Board of Trade and eventually instituting a replacement programme for those fitted to the A, B, C and D class cars.

It was the same with vestibule screens. In other parts of Britain, this item was in use very early in the century, but in London, the Metropolitan Police would have none of it! In the eyes of that body, the use of glass to protect the drivers of passenger carrying vehicles was dangerous in the extreme and this ban lasted until 1931, when, at last, it became acceptable to use them. Many "experiments" were conducted in the late 1920s in an effort to circumvent this rather peculiar regulation.

The LCC operated well tried traditional equipment relying on superb maintenance to give optimum efficiency. By 1903 most of the problems involved in electric tramway operation had been resolved and almost all the equipment used by the Council had been tried under service conditions on other systems for several years. The initial rolling stock was built to well established designs, while the later cars of class E/1, several of which lasted almost to the end of operations, were highly functional vehicles in all respects. Under the management of A. L. C. Fell, modernisation and visual improvement were subjugated to the quality of maintenance and it was left to his successor, J. K. Bruce, to introduce the "pullmanisation" programme, consisting of replacing the wooden benches in the lower saloons with transverse upholstered seats, brightening up the interior paintwork and applying a new livery to all but the oldest cars in the fleet.

Livery

The livery colours consisted of a combination of the "Preston" style Midland Red (or "Purple Lake" as it was sometimes described) and Cream (or "Primrose" as the LCC called it), with the red being used on the waist panels, dashplates, stair stringers and truck sides, while cream was used on the remainder of the exterior. Gold lining shaded black and red was applied to the Midland Red colour, while the parts painted Cream were embellished with burnt sienna and black lining-out.

Stair treads and risers were elaborately painted in red, primrose and black. The upper deck window frames and destination boxes were varnished natural wood, while trucks, plough carriers and lifeguards were usually painted black, although on occasion, cars appeared with these items sporting red oxide paint.

Over the years, repeated coats of paint and varnish, together with the effects of the weather took their toll on the original colours. They gradually became "Deep Chocolate Brown and Dirty Buff", the more so on the cars of classes A, C and D as, during the mid-1920s, the Council decided, after the new General Manager had advised that a new image should be presented to the public, that a new, distinctive livery of crimson and cream should be applied to all cars with the exception of those in the original classes. Thus doomed, the old cars carried on in their old livery until, by 1931, all had gone.

In 1926, cars began to appear in liveries of red and cream of various shades and styles. Even orange was used. However, the standard new colours of Crimson and Cream were finally decided upon. The first cars dressed in the new livery appeared soon afterwards.

When the question of an identification symbol was discussed by the Council in June 1902, consideration was given to using the design of the Council Seal, oval in shape, placed centrally on the waist panels of the cars, with the full title "LONDON COUNTY COUNCIL TRAM-WAYS" in large block capitals over the length of the rocker panels, or of simply using the initials "L.C.C." in gold or yellow on the waist panels, with, as required by law, the owners' name and manager's name painted in small lettering at the bottom ends of the rocker panels. With the economics of the work in mind, the Council decided that the second, simpler arrangement would be used.

The First Conduit Electric Car (No. 101, later No. 110)

This car was actually the first to be purchased by the LCC, after having been used for demonstration purposes by Messrs. Westinghouse at the Tramways Exhibition held in the Agricultural Hall, Islington, London in 1900. The body of this open-top four-window bogie car with short canopies was constructed by G. F. Milnes & Co. Ltd., and was carried on Brill 22E maximum traction bogie trucks, with Westinghouse electrical equipment. Open half-turn direct staircases at either end led up to the top deck "garden" seating.

The purchase price paid by the Council for the complete car was £900, in addition to which the LCC paid another £175 for the running rails and conduit equipment. In order to be able to operate the car on the track, which was relaid in Camberwell horsecar depot, the company loaned a gas-engine and d.c. generator set for a rental of £75 for six months.

It does not appear that the car was used very much in passenger service in the early years of electrification, if indeed, at all. However, after the Great War it was cut down to form a single deck body, fitted with extended canopies and renumbered 110, the class B car of that number having previously been renumbered 101. This unique vehicle was easily distinguishable from the other single deck cars, because of its near-flat roof and four-window body. After the Great War, it worked on service 32 from time to time until it was taken out of service in 1926 and stored. The body was finally broken up at the Central Repair Depot, Charlton in 1931.

The bogie car displayed at the 1900 Tramways Exhibition appeared to have been the centre piece of the show and well patronised.

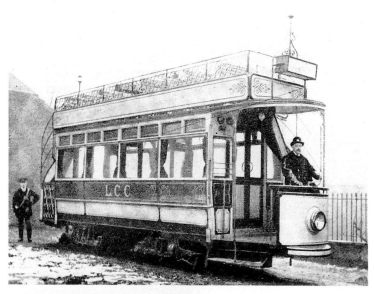

Top.
Car No. 101 after purchase by the LCC. It was used at Camberwell depot to demonstrate the conduit system of power collection.
Centre.
A view of the rather ornate interior of car No. 101.
    (Courtesy: P. J. Davis)
Bottom.
A pen-and-ink drawing of the car after it had been cut down to single deck and renumbered 110.
    (The late W. Gratwicke)

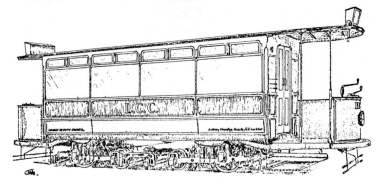

Class A Cars (Nos. 1-100)

The order for the first 100 cars was intended to provide sufficient vehicles with which to open the first electric services on the routes from London to Clapham and Tooting, together with several short services within the areas of the first conduit electrification. These were supplied by Messrs. Dick, Kerr and Co. Ltd. at a total contract price of £71,754 or £717.10. 9d each, and were built on what was then known as the "Preston" style or pattern, with bodies constructed by the Electric Railway & Tramway Carriage Co. Ltd., of Preston, Lancs. and carried on a pair of Brill 22E motorised bogie trucks. Electrical equipment was supplied by Messrs. Dick, Kerr and Co. Ltd.

These 8-wheeled open top double deck cars had 4-bay bodies, the windows of each end bay being divided into two opening drop lights, together with a row of eight opening ventilator lights above the main windows on each side of the body.

Carrying capacity of the class A car was 66 passengers, 28 in the lower saloon and 38 on the open upper deck. The 28 passengers in the lower saloon were seated on either side of the central gangway, on longitudinal wooden benches. Each bench, seating 14, was divided at the centre of the car by a timber framed glass screen which had the effect of providing seating for seven passengers in each section, which was done - so it is said - to give the conductor better control over passenger seating. The upper deck passengers were provided with "garden" seating.

The underframe followed "Preston" practice, being constructed of teak, strengthened at the side sills by angle irons (flitch plates) six inches deep, running the whole length of the body. Main structural members were of ash, while panelling was of mahogany for the main body and canary white wood for subsidiary sections. The roof, which was double skinned, consisted of an inner boarding of pine, covered with millboard, the exterior surface being protected from the elements by waterproof sheeting, securely fixed over its entire area. Inside bodywork was of quartered oak.

Each car was mounted upon two bogie trucks which, when new, each carried a type 3A4 Dick, Kerr motor rated at 30 h.p., controlled

Class A car No. 18, showing the half-drop end windows, advertisement panels and waist height route boards. (*Courtesy: LT Museum U40088*)

by DK DB1 Form D controllers, one at either end of the car. One truck carried a plough-carrier on extended castings. Lifeguards of the "Tidswell" pattern were specified.

The new cars were delivered to Balham (Marius Road) and Clapham car sheds, where the outside seats and other furniture items were fitted, the bodies then being mounted on to their trucks. As at 15th January 1903, all 42 cars scheduled for Balham had been delivered to and assembled at Marius Road. Six of these had to be stored outside the depot, protected by tarpaulin sheets, due to the inability of the Council at that time to place any of the cars in the as yet uncompleted Clapham electric car shed. By 29th January, another six had arrived, also to be temporarily stored under tarpaulin sheets, after which Messrs. Dick, Kerr & Co. were prevailed upon to store some of the bodies until the remaining 52 could be brought to London for completion in the new premises at Clapham High Street. As at 19th February, 49 cars had been delivered, with a further 26 arriving in the following month and the remaining 25 following as soon as accommodation was available for them. On completion, all cars were thoroughly tested, after which some of them were used for driver training purposes. The class A cars entered public service immediately after the Royal Opening Ceremony.

Class B Cars (Nos. 102-201)

Due to the fact that the cable tramway was in operation between Kennington, Brixton and Streatham, and was not expected to be converted for electrical working for several more years, the decision was taken to provide through services between the London termini and Streatham, using specially adapted electric cars. Due also to the steep hill to be climbed between Brixton and Streatham and the undulating roads from thereon, the Council decided that 4-wheeled cars, weighing some two tons less than those of class A would be suitable. A second consideration was that smaller cars would be available for working on the route from Kennington to Camberwell Green, which was not expected to attract very heavy traffic (at that time).

From tenders received, it has been revealed that the successful bidder was not the one to have offered the lowest price. Due to the insistence of Dr. Kennedy, the Consulting Engineer to the Council, that Dick, Kerr / Brill vehicles were best, and because a reduction on the original tender price was obtained from the company, 80 cars with bodies built by the Electric Railway & Carriage Co. Ltd., of standard "Preston" three-window design were ordered. Each car body was carried on a Brill 21E single truck with a plough carrier set midway between the wheelsets. Dick, Kerr DB1D controllers and DK 25A motors of 25 h.p. were specified, and the cars were designed to carry 22 passengers inside and 34 on the open top deck. Seating was similar in style to that used on class A cars, but there was no central division in the lower saloon. To all intents and purposes the class B body was a shortened version of the class A, even to similar platform layout and reversed staircases. The tender was accepted on 29th July 1902 and deliveries of the cars, known by the LCC as class B, commenced in April 1903.

In the provision of lifeguards for these cars, it was decided that the Council itself would manufacture these at its Penrose Street works at a cost of £4.10s per car set. Ploughs were also to be manufactured by the LCC from bought-in parts, although these were still to be known as the "J.G. White" plough. Cost of the 80 cars was £47,686, excluding

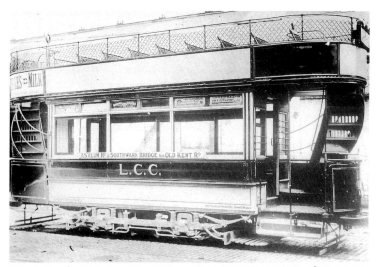

The cars of class B were really only shortened versions of the bogie cars of class A, but were without the half-drop windows.　　*(LCC Photo)*

lifeguards, but including conduit plough carriers and ploughs. A further 20 cars were subsequently ordered from Dick, Kerr to complete the class, this being dealt with as a follow-on job at the price of £11,312, making a total cost of £58,998 for the 100 cars of the class.

One car, reputed to have been No. 126 of class B, was cut down in 1905 to single deck form and modified for driver training purposes, which included the provision of special seats on either platform for the use of trainee motormen. The late Walter Gratwicke made a pen and ink drawing of the car in this condition, which is reproduced here. The car worked at and from Streatham car shed for a time, after which it was restored to double deck, covered top condition. It was eventually sold to Sheffield in March 1917.

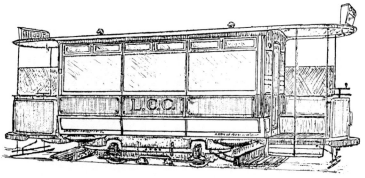

The cut-down class B car, with seats fitted on the platforms, which was used for driver training for a time.

Class C Cars (Nos. 202-301)

It is interesting to note that in February 1903, the then General Manager of Tramways, Alfred Baker, when discussing the provision of new electric tramcars for the New Cross and Greenwich tramways, had decided to order 200 cars by a contract divided into two parts, one for an order of 100 single-truck cars "similar to those on order for the Streatham lines" and the other for 100 double-bogie truck cars "similar to those for the Tooting lines". He said that it was felt desirable to divide the order in this way so that large double bogie cars of greater carrying capacity would be available at busy periods, with smaller cars to be used when the traffic was lighter.

The specification also divided each 100 into two batches of 50, in order that earlier delivery dates might be possible, but it was also recognised that, even though 200 cars were to be ordered, there would only be room in temporary accommodation for 160 of them. The contractors were to be urged to store all or any of them until they were required. This course of action was adopted by the Council on 7th April 1903 and was to cause problems for a time.

On the same date it was also agreed to award the contract for the four-wheel cars, to be known as class C, to British Westinghouse. For each car, the electrical equipments consisted of two Westinghouse 200 motors, each of 30 h.p., mounted into Brill 21E single trucks and two Westinghouse 90M controllers. Bodies built by the Brush Company were to be supplied. Reyrolle ploughs and Tidswell lifeguards were specified.

Body outline was similar to the class B cars, but with a more pronounced curve to both the waist and rocker panels, and with subtle differences to body-end beadings and corner brackets of the distinctive Brush design. Seating capacity was for 22 passengers inside and 34 outside. After several years of service, the cars proved to be much more robust than those of class B.

Contrary to the initial intention of Mr. Baker, this class of 100 cars was all constructed in one batch at a total cost of £53,012, which

Generally similar in design to class B cars, those of class C proved to be more substantial. No. 296 is seen in 1907 condition. (LCC photo)

was the second lowest tender. By accepting this, the Council considered that a better timescale for deliveries would be achieved than was offered by the lowest bidder.

The original intention to use single truck and bogie cars selectively as traffic demanded did not last for very long. As the demand for cars increased when further sections of electrified track were opened, it was concluded that the class C cars would be admirably suited to working over the hilly route to Dulwich when that opened to traffic on 19th November 1906. These, by then being fitted with covered tops with balcony ends, were eventually fitted with magnetic track brakes, the controllers being suitably modified to work with these.

Class D Cars (Nos. 302-376; 377-401)

The last of the manufacturers' standard cars as epitomised by the class A tramcars, was to be seen in the 100 class D cars, which were originally intended to be used during busy hours on the New Cross and Greenwich routes.

As stated above, the contract for the 100 cars was to be divided into two batches of 50 cars each, but in the event the whole contract went to British Westinghouse, who supplied all the type 220 motors and 90M controllers, sub-contracting the side-bearing maximum traction bogie trucks to Messrs. European McGuire. Regarding the bodies, however, 75 were built by the Brush Electrical Engineering Company at Loughborough, the remaining 25 by the British Electric Car Company. Total order value was £65,968. Ploughs for all 100 cars were to be supplied by Messrs. Reyrolle, while watt-meters (for checking the economics of drivers' methods of working) were to be supplied by the British Thomson-Houston Company.

The 75 Brush-built bodies Nos. 302 - 376, although generally similar in style to the class A cars, had subtle differences incorporated into the design, in much the same way as with the distinctions between cars of classes B and C. They also proved to be much more robust than the class A cars. Conversely, the last 25, Nos. 377 - 401 were

Cars of class D were quite similar in many respects to those in class A. The McGuire bogie trucks were, however, unique. (L T Museum U37267)

very much more like the cars of the A class, and did in fact, incorporate parts manufactured at Preston and supplied to the British Electric Car Co. In each of the two batches, seating capacity was for 28 inside and 38 outside on the open top deck, with all other general details as for class A cars.

Although the rather unusual McGuire bogie trucks were used on these cars, no spare trucks were ordered. The LCC works was able to cope with most repairs and replacements when spare parts were available. However, after a number of years, with the emphasis now on flow-line maintenance, the lack of spare trucks was to prove to be the cause of some difficulty. In an effort to ease the problem, two of the cars, Nos. 388 and 392 were fitted with Brill 22E trucks in 1915 or 1916, along with Dick, Kerr 3A motors and Westinghouse T2A controllers. The McGuire trucks were then made available as spares for maintenance purposes.

Long Wheelbase Four-Wheeled Trucks

In the early years of the first decade of the century, considerable efforts were being made by individuals and companies to devise tramcar trucks which would be economical to operate and maintain, and yet be robust and simple in design. Some used the 4-wheel single truck as the basis for variations in design, such as "radial" and "pivotal".

The LCC turned its attention to the possibility of making use of the long-wheelbase 4-wheel truck and its variants as an alternative to the, then, almost standard bogie truck of Brill or McGuire design which were used on their larger cars of classes A and D.

A popular idea was to "stretch" the standard 6 ft. or 6 ft. 6 in. wheelbase of a single truck to an 8 ft. 6 in. base as on the Brush version, or to 8 ft. as was achieved by Brill. Both of these were used experimentally, using a class D car, but the long overhang of the body outside the wheelbase made the car unstable and was soon rejected.

By far the most unusual 4-wheel long-wheelbase arrangement was to be seen in the Simpson & Park radial truck of 1905/6 and a similar item by Brush of about the same period. This arrangement allowed the wheelsets an element of flexibility in that they could move independently out of the normal parallel configuration, one to another, to take account of curves in the track. The theory was good - but in practice there were many difficulties, not least that the truck only worked with any degree of success when everything was in good condition.

One class D car was fitted up with a long wheelbase Simpson & Park radial truck assembly. It was soon removed. (Courtesy: R. Elliott)

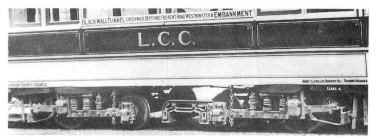

Brill 22E trucks, as used on class A cars.

Brill 21E truck, as used on classes B and C cars.

McGuire trucks as used on class D cars.

Mountain & Gibson type-4 trucks as used on class E cars.

Trucks as fitted to classes A, B, C, D and E cars.

Common Equipment: Classes A-D

Having decided to invest in electrification, the Council arranged to purchase the first 400 cars from two manufacturers as described above. There were, however, many features in common between the four classes. None of these cars were originally equipped with trolley poles, although provision was made for plugging in cables from separate over-running trolleys, these being originally used in Streatham, and later in Rye Lane, Old Kent Road and Greenwich (Hoskins Street) depots. There were also a number of items of equipment which were common to all cars. Destination indicator boxes, made of metal and each incorporating a three-lamp colour light display, were supplied by the British Electric Car Co. Ltd., while all cars had "reversed" staircases installed.

Passengers in the lower saloon were seated on either side of the central gangway on longitudinal wooden benches, which when new were provided with carpet covers. Floor carpets were also supplied on all new cars, but these, along with the seat covers, were removed in 1904 at the request of the Chief Officer, A. L. C. Fell, due to "vermin infestation".

The reversible "garden" type outside seats were of the "Never Wet" pattern, with the seating made from woven wire, while the seatbacks incorporated "pickpocket-proof" suspended panels. Provision was made to accommodate the passengers on two rows of double seats together with a single seat at each end opposite the stairs. As these cars carried no trolley masts and poles, there was no necessity to arrange the seating specially in order that passengers could avoid such an obstacle.

An electric bell system was devised, operated from the platforms by bell pushes, in order that the conductor could give starting and stopping signals to the motorman. Power for the bells came from a wet primary battery, situated beneath the seats. This system did not last for very long, probably due to the difficulties associated with this type of battery on a moving vehicle. It was replaced by a cord-operated arrangement, with a bell being provided at each end of the car, worked by separate pull-cords running the full length of the car, including the platforms. In practice, the bell cord on the left-hand - or nearside - of the car, according to the direction of travel, was the one used. To assist passengers, a notice was displayed on each cant rail advising that:-

"When Travelling in Direction of Arrow, ≫--------≫ Pull This Cord To Stop Car".

No bells were provided on the upper deck, it being left to the conductor to give whistle signals to the motorman to stop or start the car. Passengers were not allowed to give the starting signal under any circumstances.

One of the niceties decided upon when the class A and B cars were put into service, was that the Council considered that it would be a good idea to enhance the interiors by installing photographs of "scenic beauty" and by the placing of advertisements of "good taste only"!

Electric lighting in the lower saloon of each car was provided by a number of 20-watt lamps, each shaded and mounted on a swan-neck brass fitting. Each platform was illuminated by one lamp, while the upper open top deck had an "oyster" pattern lamp mounted on a column at the head of each staircase. A single dash-mounted headlamp at either end, provided the necessary illumination for the benefit of the motorman. A change-over switch was provided which ensured that only one of these lights and the platform light at the other end of the car was illuminated at any one time. A red light was shown to the rear of the car at night, by means of adjustable spectacle glasses mounted inside each bulkhead panel above the windows nearest to the entrances, which were illuminated from the lamps inside the car.

Each car was equipped with a comprehensive kit of tools, contained in an oak tool chest which was fixed on the platform floor in front of the spare plough bracket. The tool kit consisted of a W A G lifting jack; one 2-lb hammer; one 12-inch screwdriver; a pair of pliers; two Clyburn adjustable spanners; one chisel. In addition, there was a pair of India Rubber gloves and a padded wooden case containing two spare electric lamps. Each article was prominently marked "L C C".

Class E Cars (Nos. 402-426; 427-551; 602-751)

The Chief Officer of Tramways, published a report on 6th December 1904 concerning the construction of new standard bogie tramcars which he stated would, among other things, afford economy in maintenance charges and cut down on the stores capital account. The Highways Committee agreed that the Council should have a full range of drawings and patterns covering every detail of the proposed new rolling stock. Castings would be supplied direct from a foundry to be finished in the Tramways Department workshops. An allocation of £350 was made for the preparation of drawings and patterns for the new cars. The overall height of the totally enclosed top covers of the new cars was also to be such that they could pass beneath the two low railway bridges at Clapham and Balham.

Messrs. Hurst, Nelson & Co. were entrusted with building the bodies of the first 150 cars, while British Westinghouse supplied the electrical equipment. Messrs. Mountain & Gibson provided an improved design of centre-bearing maximum traction bogie truck, which was a development of the Mc.Guire design. The combined result was to be known as the LCC class E car.

It is of great credit to the design team that 76 passengers could be accommodated in the new cars, affording a 20% increase in carrying capacity over that of the class A and D cars. By 4th July 1905, the draft specification had been drawn up, and a decision was taken to order 150 cars for use on new and improved electric car services in south London.

The new design marked a complete departure from that previously used in London. The predominantly wooden body structure of the A to D class cars, was replaced on the class E with a main underframe of steel girders, strengthened with heavy flitch plates. Body styling was redesigned; non-opening main windows were used throughout the lower saloon, instead of the drop-type half-width windows fitted in the earlier cars. The ventilator lights above them opened outwards, facing towards the ends of the car from the centre window pillars. The stouter construction of the body allowed the central partition in the lower saloon to be dispensed with.

Lower saloon seating followed the traditional pattern, with two benches, one on either side of a central gangway, each occupying the full length of the car body. Fifteen passengers could be accommodated on each bench. Slatted wooden sections were used to form the complete

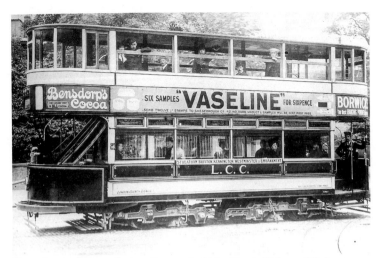

Three hundred cars of class E were built by Hurst, Nelson, 150 for use on south side services. This car is standing outside Streatham shed.   (LCC)

seats.   Interior woodwork was finely grained and varnished, which gave a high quality finish. Interior lighting was to the same standard as that employed on the Class A and D cars. Bell ropes were provided for signalling purposes.

A totally enclosed top deck was fitted, capable of accommodating 46 passengers, mainly on "two by two" reversible transverse seats. Seating for 12 additional passengers was obtained by utilising the space above the "direct" pattern stairs at either end of the car. The first 150 of the class E cars as delivered, were not fitted with stairhead draught screens.   It can be imagined what the "fresh-air" conditions must have been like on one of these cars, when travelling during a howling gale in winter!   Draught screens and stairhead doors were included in the order for the second batch of 150 cars.

The design of the top deck cover of the class E cars originated from the "Magrini" - Milnes, Voss arrangement, which it was intended would be used on the A and D class cars, described later. An agreement, concluded between the LCC and Milnes, Voss on 13th February 1905, covered the use of the patent design on the older cars.

While the E class cars were being built, Milnes, Voss made a request to Hurst Nelson for royalty to be paid in respect of the top covers. which, it was claimed, fell within the terms of the patent rights. At first, Hurst Nelson denied this, but as the window mechanism was an improvement on the original design, Milnes, Voss persisted with their demand.   In November 1907, however, the patentee was seen to have a case, which was subsequently recognised by the LCC in an out-of-Court settlement.   In order to extinguish future royalty payments, the sum of £2,250 was paid to Milnes, Voss by the Council, who also paid all legal costs surrounding the case.

The trucks used under the E class cars were a development of the McGuire type 3 bogie truck. Late in 1904, Messrs. Mountain & Gibson acquired the business of the European McGuire Company, along with manufacturing rights of the McGuire type trucks. Although the LCC had purchased a number of the earlier type of truck for use under D class cars, they wanted something more advanced to use with the new standard tramcar. Fortunately, McGuire had developed a swing-bolster centre-bearing maximum traction truck, which was in use successfully by several operators. As this was the only design that met the specification of the Council, 150 sets were ordered.

A feature of the truck was a central bolster, which had a "floating" action that allowed the car body to move in all three planes, giving a smoother ride. The bolster carried a fixed pivotal seat and two side-bearing pads. The trucks supported the body frame on the swing bolsters, while a series of pins and links connected the two together. Each set of equipment consisted of two trucks, one of which had a plough carrier extension fitted. The manufacturer's classification for this bogie was type 3, but the LCC referred to it as Class 4. Component parts for the trucks were sub-contracted to other specialist firms. Wheels were supplied by Messrs. Hadfield of Sheffield, while axle forgings were supplied by Cammell Laird and Glasgow Engineering.

Construction costs of the 150 cars, which were to be numbered by the LCC in the series 402 - 551, were:-

Bodies, Hurst Nelson:	£ 63,525	(£423.10s per car)
Trucks, Mountain & Gibson:	£ 18,000	(£120)
Electrical equipments, British Westinghouse:	£ 32,950	(£219.13. 4d)
Ploughs, LCC assembly, (2 per car):	£ 1,800	(£12)
	£116,275	(£775. 3. 4d)
Magnetic brakes (as and when fitted), British Westinghouse:	£ 8,550	(£57)
	£124,825	(£832. 3. 4d)

The order was placed on 12th August 1905, the contract requiring that 40 cars were to be delivered by 15th January 1906, 40 more by 15th February, 40 by 15th March and the remainder on or before 15th April 1906. It was stipulated that the contractor was to be responsible for maintenance of the cars for a period of six months after delivery. Completed cars were conveyed from the Hurst Nelson works at Motherwell, using specially adapted well and flat wagons, the upper and lower decks on alternate trucks. The block trains were worked to London, New Cross (LB&SCR) Goods Station, from where the body halves were conveyed to New Cross car shed for assembly and completion.

For operation on the first sections of electrified lines on the north London system, the Council purchased another 150 cars of class E. This was undertaken as an extension of the original contracts, the same price being quoted for each item except for the magnetic brake equipments, which were to cost £8,475 (£56.10s per car), a reduction of 10/- on each set. The electrical equipments for this batch were identical with those of 427-551. Numbered 602-751, these cars were ordered on 8th March 1906 and were to be delivered at the rate of 40 per month, commencing in July, with the final 30 scheduled to arrive in London by 10th October 1906. The extended contract retained the manufacturer's responsibility to maintain the cars for a period of six months from delivery.

It is evident that the delivery dates were not being kept to, as on 4th October, Mr. Fell reported that cars were not arriving on time, as required in the contract. He then said that even if the builder was working to schedule, there was insufficient accommodation available

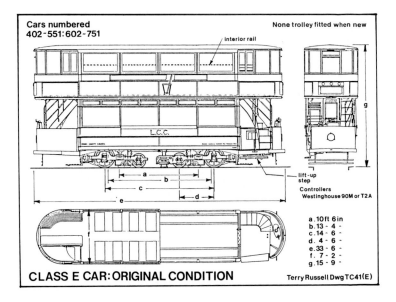

Cars numbered
402-551:602-751

None trolley fitted when new

interior rail

L.C.C.

a

b

c

d

e

lift-up step

Controllers
Westinghouse 90M or T2A

g

f

a.10ft 6in
b.13 - 4 -
c.14 - 6 -
d. 4 - 6 -
e.33 - 6 -
f. 7 - 2 -
g.15 - 9 -

CLASS E CAR: ORIGINAL CONDITION

Terry Russell Dwg TC41(E)

in which to house them. At that time, the first sections of the car sheds for the north London fleet were under construction at Poplar and Stamford Hill, but work was not advanced enough to hold all the cars. As there was a penalty clause in the contract for late delivery, this statement was possibly made in order that a penalty would not be imposed.

It is recorded that magnetic track brakes were not fitted to the first 25 cars delivered (Nos. 402-426), but were provided within a few months of delivery. The same record shows that the original electrical equipment consisted of two Westinghouse class 200 motors, each rated at 35 h.p., together with Westinghouse 90M controllers. The other 125 cars had Westinghouse type 220 motors, rated at 42 h.p., together with Westinghouse T2A controllers. However, photographic evidence reveals that in c 1907, car No. 407 had T2A controllers, while at the same time, Nos. 433 and 445 carried 90M controllers.

Similarly, it has always been understood that only the first 150 cars of class E were delivered without stairhead draught screens. Again, photographic evidence shows that this may not have been the case. In an accident suffered by car No. 744 on New Years Day, 1908, one end of the car was badly damaged, and a photograph taken from inside the upper deck clearly shows the original open stairhead. Due to this apparent discrepancy, it cannot be stated with any degree of certainty which cars were in either condition at any time before 1912, when all upgrading work on stairhead screens was recorded as being complete.

Chapter 21
Improving the Rolling Stock

Not long after the introduction of electric car services, it was realised by the Council that, as all cars in use were of double-deck open top construction, they were not able to provide the kind of service envisaged by the Tramways Department, or required by the public. The use of cars without roof covers had the effect of limiting the number of passengers who were prepared to travel in the open air, particularly when weather conditions were less than comfortable, which they were for much of the time in the capital. The first consideration therefore, was to find a suitable design of top cover which could be fitted with a minimum of disturbance to the existing bodywork of the cars.

Other improvements were to follow as technical development, finance and the demands of the Metropolitan Police permitted. In association with the installation of top covers was the eventual provision of direct stairs, stairhead draught screens and stairhead doors. The Council also arranged for the provision of more efficient methods of braking, strengthening of car bodywork, fitting of overhead wire trolley poles and the installation of modified plough carrying gear which, together, would enable the Council to provide a better service to the public.

Top Covers

Early in 1904, the General Manager made enquiries about providing top covers for some of the cars then in service, and for others about to enter service on the routes between London and Greenwich, after having convinced the Council that passengers would be more inclined to travel on the top decks during cold or inclement weather, if some measure of protection was given to them.

After studying the success of the "Magrini" Patent Roof Cover, manufactured by Messrs. Milnes, Voss & Co. and in use in Liverpool, it was recommended that a sample cover be experimentally fitted to "D" class car No. 310. After fitting, the car went into service on the London, Peckham and Greenwich route on 20th July 1904, when it was hoped that the income per car mile would be 12.50d as against 10.82d for open top cars.

Claimed to be an advance on previous ideas, the cover was of the "balcony" type and had several new features. The roof extended over the whole length of the car, but only the main body of the upper deck was totally enclosed. Access to the enclosed section was given by means of sliding doors made from ash, fitted in a central position at either end of the structure. The roof over the balcony ends was supported by polished brass stanchions and brackets, while the supports for the roof cover above the enclosed parts were fabricated from metal strips, two being used at each upright, one behind the other, so leaving a clear space between for the operation of the window mechanism. The sides of the cover consisted of the waist panels, those externally being of figured oak, while internally they were of ash, and above which were sets of windows. Polished brass "hit and miss" ventilators were provided in the top portion, above the windows. The underside of the roof was panelled with papier mache, or with alternate light and dark oak strips, finished with oak and ash mouldings. Four "bulkhead" type electric lamp fittings were mounted upon the ceiling within the body of the cover, two on either side of the central gangway.

The Magrini Patent Window Mechanism was used with the Milnes, Voss top cover, which allowed the side windows to be opened or closed as required. It consisted of a rack and pinion winding mechanism, driven at one end by means of a removable revolving handle, which was placed into a socket in the recessed centre of a gearwheel. All four windows on one side of a bogie car, or three on a four-wheeled car, were fitted into a long, one-piece frame and, when the mechanism was operated, were lowered or raised together in the space between the exterior and interior panels. One problem with this early type of equipment was its tendency to be unable to hold the windows squarely, once the mechanism became worn.

Anticipating the success of the top cover, the Council arranged with Messrs. Milnes, Voss on 26th July 1904 to provide 50 covers at an estimated £80 each. Ten more covers were manufactured by the Council under license at its Penrose Street Works, a royalty payment of £4.10s being made to Milnes, Voss for each cover made. In fact, the total cost for the 61 covers was £5,560 (or £91. 2. 6d each), which exceeded the estimate by £500.

By 1st December 1904, Milnes, Voss had delivered 15 of their order, while the LCC had delivered eight (with two already in use). Assembly and erection of all of these was undertaken at Rye Lane Peckham depot.

On the 13th December 1904, Mr. Fell sought the authority of the Council to go ahead with the manufacture of another 100 covers. All of these were to be built to the Magrini pattern, with a royalty payment as before. Six of these were to be of the "small type" (low

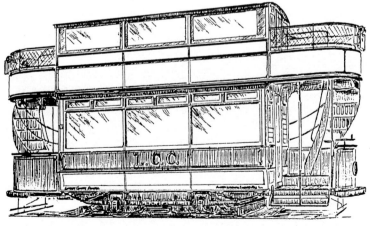

The experimental "low height" top cover fitted to a class B car.

height), of which one was to be fitted to a single truck car for use on the Balham route. As cars with the standard height cover were unable to pass beneath two bridges on that route, the single truck car was fitted up in an effort to overcome this problem.

With an estimate of six cars a week to be dealt with, the Council agreed, on 20th December, to expend £8,500 on this work. The manager decided that this batch of covers should also be manufactured at Penrose Street works, thus keeping the staff there in full employment, and also to enable the Council to "have better control" on production. The first of the covers was expected to be available about four weeks after commencement of the work.

Class D car No. 371, showing the top cover with open balcony, but still with reversed staircases. (LCC Photo)

By 31st January 1905, with assembly of the covers proceeding, the men from Milnes, Voss working at 8½d an hour alongside LCC staff getting 9d an hour, complained about the discrepancy in pay rates. The Council complained to the company, resulting in the extra ½d an hour being paid to the contractors.

It was announced on 1st June 1905 that, of the 161 covers made, one hundred had been fitted to the cars. For the time being, the rest were to remain in store as, due to cars being shedded for the most part in temporary accommodation, it was not possible to get them into the buildings when fitted with covers. These would have to wait until New Cross shed and the first sections of Camberwell and Streatham sheds were available for use. Income per car-mile appeared to settle down to about 11.93d for the top-covered vehicles as against 10.92d for open-top cars.

Despite the accommodation problems, it was agreed by the Council on 11th June 1905 that another 150 covers should be constructed at Penrose Street works at a cost, including royalty, of £13,500. It was disclosed at the same time that no more cars would be fitted with "low" roof covers, as cars of a new design (class E) were to be ordered.

The height of these new top-covered cars was to be such as to permit their use on the Tooting route. The class A cars so displaced could then be top covered and transferred for use elsewhere.

Given the extra weight of the top covers and the heavier passenger loadings, it soon became apparent that the extra weight per car might impose an unbearable strain on the available power supply. Until sufficient output was available from the new generating station at Greenwich, it was thought to be inadvisable to attempt to overload the temporary supplies by demanding too much additional power. The top cover programme had to be arranged with this factor in mind.

With the closure of Penrose Street works in July 1906, the work of cover construction was moved away temporarily to the assembly site at Rye Lane depot, while later, on 14th May 1907, the Council decided that the staff at Leytonstone, Union Road (ex-North Metropolitan Tramways Co.) works should become involved in the manufacture of these.

It was also agreed on 30th November 1909 that, as the tenancy of the Union Road works could not be terminated until April 1911, the 90 covers still required, would be manufactured there for £10,238 (£113.15s each). Timber purchased as part of the sale to the LCC of the North Metropolitan Tramways Company would be used, together with additional supplies bought-in to a total value of £1,490.12s. In this case, the type of cover built was of the totally enclosed arrangement and included draught screens and doors at the heads of the staircases. The total appeared to include the original experimental car No. 101 (although this car, which is not to be confused with the "B" class car which was renumbered 101 in September 1911, was never top-covered).

Draught Screens

Shortly after the completion of the first order for the class E cars, most of those of the second order then under construction, were fitted with stairhead draught screens and suitable entrance doors as standard. Meantime, the Council had decided to install screens and doors of similar pattern on all the cars not fitted. A further advance made in design, produced cars of class E/1 from 1907 onwards, which were fitted with draught screens and doors during manufacture.

By January 1908, roof covers had been fitted to 311 of the 400 cars of classes A to D, while the 600 cars of classes E and E/1 then in the fleet already had them. Of these 911 cars, 423 had no draught screens at the tops of the stairs, so arrangements were made to institute a programme to instal these at an estimated £5 each, or £10 per car. However, these screens could not be fitted on the original vehicles until the "reversed" staircases had been replaced by those of the "direct" pattern.

It was at this point that, due to the increasing complexities of accounting involved with all the relatively small improvements being carried out on the 400 original cars, the Council decided to amalgamate the financial estimates and votes for roof covers and draught screens. During the remainder of the 1907/8 financial year, 50 cars were top-covered, 150 in 1908/9, 133 in 1909/10 and the last 90 in 1910/11, while by 10th May 1910, there were still 133 cars which required draught screens.

To give some indication of the quantities of timber used for the draught screens, this example for the 133 cars dealt with in the year

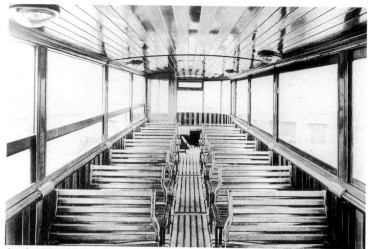

An interior view of the upper saloon of a class E car, showing the slatted wooden seats and the draught screen at the stair-head.

(Courtesy: Greater London Photograph Library)

1909/10 will suffice. 600 ft. of 3-inch of oak (in 13 ft. lengths)
3,500 ft. of 2-inch oak
5,500 ft. of 1¼-inch oak
1,500 ft. of ½-inch oak
3,000 ft. of 1-inch satin walnut
3,000 ft. of 1-inch whitewood

at a cost of £304.15. 4d, giving a unit cost of £2. 5. 10d per car.

It was intended that the screen doors would have simple latching arrangements, both when open or closed. The Metropolitan Police, however, would have none of this, insisting that a special double latching device be designed and fitted to each door, in order to safeguard the passengers under all conditions. The latches, costing 6/10d each, were ordered in batches as required and fitted by direct labour.

Eventually, by summer 1911, the provision of top covers and draught screens were complete. A period of seven years had elapsed since the first car had been attended to, and it had cost the LCC £43,600 to do the work. As this expenditure had been approved over a period of seven years, the total estimated cost of £41,746 was exceeded by £1,146 due to wage increases and an extra £714 for the double-acting locks on the upper saloon doors.

Stairs

The original fleet of 400 cars purchased by the Council were traditional, commercially built vehicles, using the "reversed" type of staircase which was in vogue at the time to gain access to the open top deck. During the first two years that they were in service, there did not appear to be much objection made to this type of staircase, but, as recorded elsewhere, when the LCC sought authority to raise the maximum permitted speeds at which the cars were allowed to be driven, the Metropolitan Police immediately put up a case that the cars were not constructed in accordance with the terms of the

"London" bye-laws. These stated that "... no owner of a vehicle ... shall drive ... or cause to be driven on any highway ... any vehicle ... whereby the driver does not have an uninterrupted view forward ...".

In the opinion of the police, the reversed staircases did not allow motormen to have "an uninterrupted view forward", and were therefore illegal. This put the Council in breach of the law and liable to a summary fine of 40/- for each and every infringement. As the LCC was the largest user of this type of staircase in the Metropolitan Police District, it was imperative that something be done about the problem, the more so as the police were making comments directly to the Council on the matter.

The other users of this type of staircase in the Metropolitan District, including Ilford, Croydon and Bexley, did not seem to be much bothered by this edict. This was possibly because, as they were all operating on outer routes at that time, they were not so much under police scrutiny.

A series of experiments was carried out, using several different types of staircase, in an effort to decide which was best to use. A class D car had a pair of staircases installed which were quite similar in style to the "Robinson" stairs used by the London United Tramways. One class C car received spiral stairs of a very unusual pattern, the outside stringer twisting through 170°, while a class B car, No. 167, was fitted with a pair of direct staircases, of a slightly different design to that subsequently adopted for use as standard on all cars.

On 18th July 1905, the Council stated that the first 27 cars would be attended to by replacing the reversed stairs with those of "direct" pattern, this in the normal course of maintenance where staircases needed to be renewed. It was stated that a staircase could normally be expected to last up to about five years in service. Cost of replacement would be £10 per car, or £5 per staircase.

Meantime, reverting to the application of the bye-law, the Home Secretary, who was nominally in control of the Metropolitan Police,

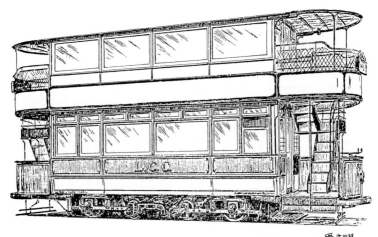

A class D car experimentally fitted up with "Robinson" type stairs.
(The late W. Gratwicke)

let it be known that, if the Council agreed to replace the reversed staircases with those of direct pattern and made every effort to expedite the work, he would trust the Council to do its best and, so long as the Home Office was kept informed of progress, no police action would be taken against the LCC. This statement gives ground for thinking that the reversed stairs were not so dangerous as the police imagined.

The speed limits imposed on the cars of the Council by virtue of the LCC Tramways Statutory Rules and Orders, 1904 were:-

12 m.p.h.:-	Clapham Common, between Clapham Park Road and Nightingale Lane.
	Old Kent Road and New Cross Road between Surrey Canal and Greenwich Borough boundary.
	Queen's Road, between New Cross Gate and Kender Street.
	High Street Peckham between Pomeroy Street and Asylum Road.
	St. George's Road.
	Brixton Hill between Acre Lane and Streatham Library.
8 m.p.h.:-	Kennington Road between "Horns" Kennington and Westminster Bridge Road by Stangate.
	Kennington Park Road and Newington Butts.
	London Road, St. George's Circus, Blackfriars Road, Waterloo Road, Trafalgar Road, Walworth Road.
6 m.p.h.:-	Westminster Bridge Road, London Street, High Street, Peckham opposite Rye Lane.
4 m.p.h.:-	Through facing points, on all curves less than 66 feet radius, under Balham and Clapham Road railway bridges.
10 m.p.h.:-	All other places.

An agreement with the Board of Trade was also being sought, to allow the Council to increase the authorised maximum speeds of the cars in conjunction with the installation of magnetic track brakes. To this, the police again demurred on the grounds of the visibility problem allegedly thrown up by the use of the reversed stairs. In an attempt to overcome this "difficulty", the Council, in August 1906, arranged for the risers on two treads of the stairs of one car to be cut away, so improving vision to the lefthand side. The comment of the Commissioner of Police, Sir. E. Henry was, to say the least, surprising. "Female passengers would be likely to object and the press would take it up ..." and, almost as an afterthought, "the motormen would not get much in the way of improved vision, either"!

Col. H. A. Yorke, the Board of Trade Inspector, was in agreement with the LCC claim that an extra 2 m.p.h. would cause no major problems, whichever type of stair was in use, and that he could see no good reason to with-hold an increase in speed, merely because of the rather intransigent attitude of the police. As the Council wanted this increase as much as anything else to attempt to protect motormen from the constant threat of alleged law breaking, they both wished to see the matter cleared up. On 10th October 1906, Col. Yorke authorised an increase of 2 m.p.h. to 14 m.p.h. for cars not fitted with direct stairs and an extra 2 m.p.h. to 16 m.p.h. for those that were.

The police, however, were adamant. They insisted that no rearrangements should be made until and unless all cars were fitted with direct stairs. After a series of meetings at which Col. Yorke accused the police of being obstructionist and awkward, a compromise "agreement" was suggested by the Commissioner which would give the LCCT the increased speeds required, if it would arrange to convert all 360 cars still fitted with the old type of stairs, at the rate of 120 per year.

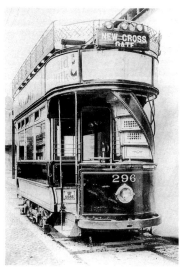

These two view of class C cars show the progression made through several modifications from the original to final condition. The left hand photograph of No. 296 shows the car in its 1906-07 condition, only having had the stair risers drilled to improve visibility for the motorman, while No. 284 is seen in final condition in 1928. The sub-class C3 was not used after all cars had attained this condition.

(Left, LCC: Right, The late Dr. H. Nicol, courtesy: D. W. K. Jones)

At this point, the Board of Trade Inspector reminded the police that an agreement had already been made with the Home Office by the LCC Tramways on the question of alteration of the cars. Nevertheless, the Council did acquiesce and agreed that 120 cars per year could be dealt with. At the end of November 1906, the Board of Trade again authorised the Council to increase car speeds to those agreed on 10th October.

On 10th December 1906, Capt. Hemphill, Sir John Benn and Mr. J. A. Baker of the LCC met the Home Secretary, Mr. W. E. Gladstone, to discuss the position regarding the LCC and reversed stairs, the renovation of cars, car speeds and the use of trailer cars again, in a further attempt to obtain the goodwill of the police. There was still some concern that motormen were in some danger of prosecution by the police for allegedly exceeding the speed limits and, as much as anything, this was a further attempt to give a little more latitude to the men in their efforts to maintain a service, and was really a "hands off" exercise.

One of the side effects of the programme of fitting new stairs and other works was that, to quote the words of the Tramways Manager in December 1908, "We think that, with a view to continuing in employment as long as possible the men at present engaged on this work, arrangements should be made for the work of alterations to be accelerated, and we propose therefore, to deal with an additional 52 cars during the current financial year." Extra expenditure involved by these alterations was £370, which worked out at £7. 2s per car.

The fitting of direct stairs to the 400 cars of classes A to D was undertaken in a programme which lasted from 1906 to 1911 and which, in conjunction with other improvements carried out on these cars, resulted in them all being brought up to an "LCC" standard condition, similar to the cars of later classes.

Secondary Classifications, Car Classes A to D

During the initial period of fitting top covers and altering staircases, the cars in these four classes were given secondary classifications to denote the stage of modification that had been reached on each car. By 1914, when they had all been top-covered and fitted with direct stairs, these sub-classes were abandoned. Only one car was placed in class A 1, while none were classified B 1, A 4 or C 4.

Original Class	A	B	C	D
Balcony top covers reversed stairs	A 1	- -	C 1	D 1
Enclosed top covers, reversed stairs	A 2	B 2	C 2	D 2
Enclosed top covers, direct stairs and draught screens	A 3	B 3	C 3	D 3
Open top, direct stairs, trolley poles	- -	B 4	- -	D 4

Brakes

The braking system employed on the early cars, while generally satisfactory when these were new and working in their open top condition, nevertheless left something to be desired after a short period in service. It consisted of rheostatic retardation, backed up with a hand-operated wheel brake system.

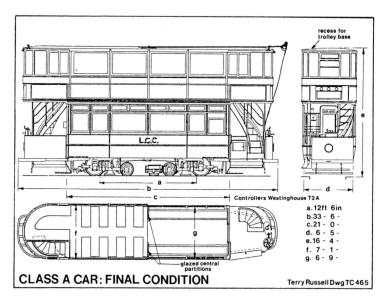

CLASS A CAR: FINAL CONDITION   Terry Russell Dwg TC 465

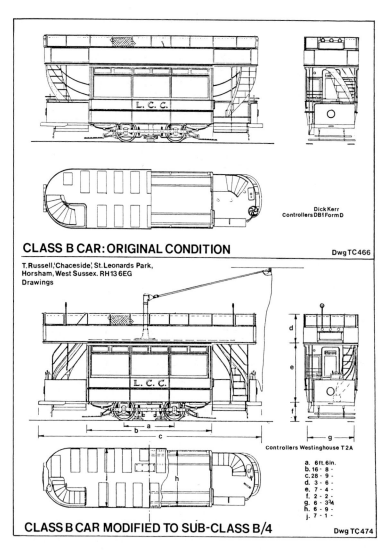

CLASS B CAR: ORIGINAL CONDITION

Dick Kerr
Controllers DB1 Form D

Dwg TC 466

T. Russell, 'Chaceside', St. Leonards Park,
Horsham, West Sussex. RH13 6EG
Drawings

Controllers Westinghouse T 2A

a. 6ft, 6in.
b. 16 - 8 -
c. 28 - 9 -
d. 3 - 6 -
e. 7 - 4 -
f. 2 - 2 -
g. 6 - 3¾ -
h. 6 - 9 -
j. 7 - 1 -

CLASS B CAR MODIFIED TO SUB-CLASS B/4

Dwg TC 474

*The drawing of a class A car as shown on page 281 depicts it with
a side-mounted trolley pole and in the condition that many were in
when finally withdrawn. The two drawings above show a car of class B
in new condition, and of the unusual form that eight of them were
modified to when working in Plumstead in 1908-1910. One, No. 106,
has been restored as a class B/4 car, and is now in working at the
National Tramway Musemu, Crich, Derbyshire. (Drawings: T. M. Russell)*

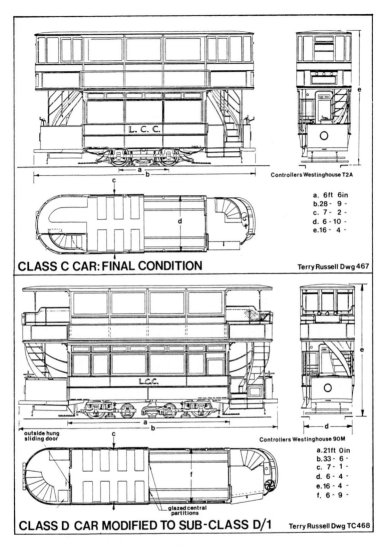

CLASS C CAR: FINAL CONDITION

Controllers Westinghouse T2A

a. 6ft 6in
b. 28 - 9 -
c. 7 - 2 -
d. 6 - 10 -
e. 16 - 4 -

Terry Russell Dwg 467

CLASS D CAR MODIFIED TO SUB-CLASS D/1

outside hung sliding door

glazed central partitions

Controllers Westinghouse 90M

a. 21ft 0in
b. 33 - 6 -
c. 7 - 1 -
d. 6 - 4 -
e. 16 - 4 -
f. 6 - 9 -

Terry Russell Dwg TC468

Cars of classes C and D went through several changes. Initially, all were delivered as open top cars, but soon received roof covers of the balcony-end type as shown in the lower drawing. Eventually, all the balcony ends were fully enclosed and direct stairs were fitted, as seen in the drawing of the class C car.

Reference to the drawing of a class E car at page 272 will show the considerable improvements that were made in design, as compared to the cars of classes A to D.   (Drawings: T. M. Russell)

In the days of horse traction, the handbrake was a sufficient means of bringing a car to a halt. It consisted of a set of iron blocks which could be screwed on to the wheel rims of the car by turning a handle situated at either end of a car. Each handle was at the top of a vertical staff, with a chain fixed to the bottom of it, connected at its other end to a sway bar which, in turn, pulled the brake blocks into position when either handle was turned in a clockwise direction and the chain wound round the staff and tightened up. It was this type of mechanism that was provided on the early electric cars, albeit with a rather more effective system of winding mechanism, levers and sway bars.

To provide rheostatic braking, it was only necessary, when a car was travelling at a reasonable speed, to short-circuit the motor windings for a very quick, albeit rather dramatic way of stopping the vehicle and doing no good to the motor(s). In order to harness the braking effect of the current output from an electric motor, a graduated resistance replaced the short-circuit, which had the effect of slowing down the car, without damaging the motor windings.

When travelling at low speeds, the rheostatic brake became ineffective, sole reliance then being placed upon the efficiency of the handbrake. This was the cause of some concern, as many low speed collisions occurred and, as the Council had decided to equip a number of the cars with top covers, the resultant greater weight of a vehicle and its extra passengers decreed that a more efficient form of braking was essential.

It had been reported to the Council as early as 25th July 1905 that the Board of Trade would be prepared to raised the speed limits imposed upon the cars if the LCC were to fit brakes of the magnetic type, but this later became dependent upon the replacement of reversed stairs by those of direct pattern, as described.

Early in January 1906, a paper was delivered by A. L. C. Fell to the Tramway and Light Railway Association in which he advocated that electro-magnetic track brakes should be fitted to all LCC cars. One Class D car had been fitted with this type of brake some months before and used on overnight trials. These were undertaken on Saturday nights and Sunday mornings out of traffic hours, using different lines in varying weather conditions. The car was fitted with special test instruments consisting of:-

1. Boyer speed and distance recorder.
2. Recording voltmeter.
3. Recording ammeter.
4. A time relay clock (5-second pulses marking the instrument charts).
5. A special controller contact which indicated on the speed/distance recorder when the brakes were operated.
The record chart papers were driven by clockwork gramophone motors.

Exhaustive tests were undertaken on two types of magnetic brakes:-
Type "A". Track shoes on the rail only.
Type "B". Track shoes coupled to and acting in conjunction with ordinary brake shoes on the wheels (This arrangement had been developed by Mr. Fell and his engineers).
In the event, type "B" was fitted to all cars.

Mr. Fell pointed out that the tests were necessary in order to obtain the agreement of the Board of Trade Inspectors, to enable the speed limits to be raised as, with only hand and rheostatic brakes, cars were restricted to a maximum speed of 12 m.p.h. He had also arranged for the re-inspection of practically the whole of the tramways, prior to the request for increased maximum speeds.

An electro-magnetic track brake unit of type "B" consisted of two track shoes, rigidly connected together by a cross-bar placed between the side frames of the truck and supported by a pair of tongue-shaped steel brackets bolted to the truck frame and arranged to take the thrust of retardation. These were interconnected with links and levers, for simultaneously transmitting the downward pull and resultant drag of the magnetic track brake into lateral pressure upon the wheels through the ordinary wheel brake blocks. A set of spiral springs was provided to support the shoes clear of the track when not in use. One unit was fitted to each of the bogie trucks on class A and D cars, while two sets were fitted - one on each side of the centrally-mounted plough carrier - on class B and C cars.

Each shoe was a simple form of magnet 18 ¾ inches long, consisting of two steel plates connected by a yoke carrying the exciting coil of the electro-magnet, which was electrically connected to the braking notches of the controller. The lower edges of the plate were planed and fitted with wearing shoes, shaped to the rail profile and made to gauge. The coils of each magnet were completely enclosed in water-tight metal cases. The magnets were energised by electric current produced by the motors acting as generators, which created a very powerful magnetic field, and strongly attracted the magnet shoes to the running rails.

The type of magnetic brake decided upon required seven brake notches on the controller for gradual application, with the brake connections entirely disconnected from the power circuit. Controller connections had also to be arranged so that when one motor was cut out, the brake winding would not be short-circuited. It was acknowledged that the one disadvantage of the magnetic brake was that it did not function efficiently upon manganese steel rails and special castings, where these were used at junctions and crossings.

Whilst the Council was examining other systems of braking, including air, it was decided to fit an initial batch of 60 cars with magnets

One car of class C was experimentally fitted up with a set of magnetic brakes which included the use of extended guards. This arrangement was not made a permanent feature of the brake. (Courtesy: P. J. Davis)

as an experiment, for operation on the Streatham route, which had a rather steep hill south of Brixton. Total cost of the equipment and its installation was £3,330, with British Westinghouse contracted to supply 50 sets at £57 each, and BT-H ten sets at £48 each. The price included the necessary alterations to the car controllers. An estimate of £26,000 was expected to cover a similar conversion of the remaining 340 cars of classes A to D. Although all this was agreed during the summer of 1905, it was to be nearly a year before the 60 cars were equipped.

In April 1906, it was agreed to purchase another 170 magnetic brake sets. By November, the decision was taken that 100 sets were to be supplied by British Westinghouse and fitted to the D class cars, 20 sets by the same manufacturer for A class cars and 50 BT-H sets to B and C class cars. The cost varied according to which type of car they were fitted. Most expensive were the A class, at £59 per car, followed by the D class cars at £56.10s, while the single truck cars cost £32 per car set. Total cost of these improvements was £8,430.

At the same time, it was decided to fit the 150 class E cars, then under construction for use on additional south side services, with similar braking equipment at £57 per car. Of the 170 older cars which had still to be fitted, arrangements were made on 5th February 1907 with British Westinghouse for the supply of the remaining sets of equipment. The total cost, including fitting to the cars, was £8,485. Subsequent deliveries of all new LCC cars included magnetic brakes as standard.

Meantime, as mentioned above, Mr. Fell had designed a special linkage which actuated the wheel brakes in conjunction with the magnets, but could also be operated by the hand brake handle. After the Board of Trade inspector, Col. A. H. Yorke had approved the device, it was fitted to all cars. Once the cars had been equipped, they were ready to be run at higher speeds - or so the manager thought!

As previously described, the police were in dispute with the Board of Trade over the maximum speeds at which the cars should be allowed to travel, and had lost the argument. Nevertheless, they continued to keep up the pressure, as the following extract from Council records shows. On 10th December 1906, at the meeting of members of the Council with the Home Secretary, the LCC complained that police officers boarded cars to "test the brakes". It was noted that the constabulary had no technical knowledge of the braking systems employed, and also that this placed Council employees, particularly the motormen, under some stress. To "assist" the police, the LCC offered suitable training for police inspectors at the Tramways Department motor school, but it seems that this offer was not taken up. It is also understood that the "brake testing" ceased.

The Mechanically Operated Auxiliary Track Brake

Cars of class C, together with a few of class B, operated on the services working over Dog Kennel Hill on the route between Camberwell and East Dulwich. Severe restrictions were placed upon the car crews, both as to the maximum speeds permitted and the manner in which they were allowed to operate on the hill, and for this, the motormen received a small extra sum for each day that they drove cars on this route. Although the cars had been equipped with magnetic braking, the Chief Officer considered that there should be an additional braking system introduced, purely for safety reasons.

In April 1909, three designs of secondary braking were inspected, two of which, incorporating "screw-operating equipments" were discarded in favour of a "spindle and twisted chain" device. This required the installation of a hollow spindle or tube, with a handwheel at the top and connected to a heavy chain at the bottom. The normal handbrake spindle was fitted inside the additional, new brake spindle.

The original type of handwheel used for operating the normal mechanical brakes had to be replaced by a cranked handle of brass, beneath which the new handwheel was located. When the motorman turned the handwheel in a clockwise direction, the chain was wound up on to the spindle, in turn tightening up the linkage and pressing the shoes of the magnetic brakes on to the track.

After approval by the Board of Trade Inspecting Officer, Col. Yorke in February 1909, the contract for the equipment for 65 car sets was let in April to Messrs. Hurst, Nelson & Co. Ltd. at a cost to the Council of £2,600, the work being completed by the end of the year.

The "Non-Run Back" Brake

An accident occurred on Dog Kennel Hill early in August 1926 when car No. 226 ran back down the hill and derailed. The traditional way of controlling a "run-back" was for the motorman to place the controller key in the "reverse" position before applying the magnetic brake. In the case of the run-back of 226, the motorman, through some oversight, did not carry out the procedure in the correct manner.

The comment of the Ministry of Transport Inspector, Maj. Hall during his enquiry, was that "it is possible to obviate the necessity for changing over the reversing key before applying the magnetic brake (in the case of a run-back) by an alteration in the standard connections between the armatures and fields of the motors. The Council's officers are aware of this alternative method of connection, but consider that it introduces other drawbacks so serious, as to outweigh any advantage which it possesses in the direction of avoiding the necessity for this change-over in order to check a run-back".

Mr. J. K. Bruce, the acting General Manager countered this by commenting that the manufacturers of controllers had indicated that such an arrangment was impracticable, and by taking the operation of the controller out of the motorman's hands in an emergency such as the recent one, by means of an interlock which might easily get out of order, it would be dangerous and could not be advised. He also pointed out that only experienced men were allowed to drive over this route and, in order to ensure that the highest standards were being maintained, "each man will receive actual testing on Dog Kennel Hill on early Sunday mornings, before the commencement of services".

Despite these comments, the Manager did agree to conduct an experiment, for which finance was made available up to the sum of £100. The result was that a "non-runback" brake was devised and fitted to car No. 235. The design was submitted to the Ministry of Transport for consideration and, after an informal inspection had been made by Major Hall on 26th August 1926, an extended trial of the device was authorised. On 12th May 1927, after studying the results of the trials, it was agreed to continue the experiment and to equip five more cars at a cost of £75 each.

No further information has become available regarding either the fleet numbers of the other cars used in the trials, or whether the experiment was again extended.

Bodywork Trussing
Car Classes A and D

On 21st November 1911, the Chief Office of Tramways advised the Highways Committee of the Council, that a more substantial method of trussing the body frames of the bogie cars was required. Structural weaknesses had occurred, caused by the additional weight of the top covers and, as a consequence, greater passenger loadings.

The traditionally accepted way in which car bodies were stiffened - or "trussed" - was for stiffening rods to be fitted between the two ends of the body, one on either side of the car, the ends of the rods being bolted into the timber members of the framework, or being either bolted or welded to steel corner plates which were bolted to the framework. The rods could be adjusted to the correct tension by turning screwed ferrules (or "turnbuckles") inserted between two sections of each rod.

By this time, the Council had 875 cars of classes E and E/1 trussed during construction, in what was termed a "new" way. This method employed "deep rolled trussing plates" made of steel, two feet deep and three-eighths of an inch thick, tapered at the ends, extending the full length of the car body, and rivetted vertically on to the longitudinal steel solebars on each side of the car frame. Pressed steel brackets or "gusset knees" connected the transverse members of the underframe to the truss plates and main frame of the car body.

It was a modification of this arrangement that was to be used on the class A and D cars, which were mainly constructed of timber. The plates, 19 ft. 11 in. long and of the same height and thickness as those used on the newer cars, were to be bolted to the main frame members, with additional strength provided transversely by each plate having three "gusset knees" rivetted to it, each of which was 14 ½ inches high and 8 inches deep.

The contract for the supply of the first 50 sets of plates went to Messrs. Hurst, Nelson & Company. Installation was undertaken at the Central Repair Depot, Charlton by LCC staff, during the annual overhaul of selected cars at a cost of £31 per car set (£1,550 for the whole work). Mr. Fell also stated that he intended to arrange for the remaining 150 cars of classes A and D to be dealt with at the rate of 50 or more a year, as a continuation of the original programme.

Car Classes B and C

Body weakening was also being experienced on the 200 cars of 4-wheeled type. In this case, due to the way in which the bodies were constructed, it was impossible to employ the same trussing arrangement as was used on the bogie cars. Instead, the corner pillars of the bodies were strengthened with triangular steel segments, bolted to the bulkhead pillars and sole bars. The ends of the truss rods, already in position along the body sides, were welded to the steel segments for added strength. A total price of £5 per car, including labour charges was quoted. This work was also undertaken by LCC staff during the annual overhaul of the cars.

Seating
Classes A to D cars

When new, cars of these classes were fitted with steam-formed bent and polished plywood seats and seatbacks in the lower saloons.

A rather complex, but pleasing effect was introduced, by drilling a series of perforated patterns into the wood, presumably to enable the seats to "breathe". At first, seating carpets were also provided but, after a short time, the Council decided to have these removed, as they quickly became soiled and a haven for various kinds of unpleasant insects. Seating capacity was for 28 passengers in the lower saloon of the bogie cars and 22 in the single truck cars.

On the open top decks, basic wooden "vertically-slatted" double transverse seats were provided, with the thin edges of the slats, suitably strengthened, forming the seat. The reason for this was to assist in the rapid drainage of rain water. Each seat was fitted with a turn-over back, consisting of a backrest supported on two metal rods, between which was suspended a "pickpocket-proof" panel. When the cars were top-covered, this seating was retained. There were however,

The upper view shows the lower saloon of a class D car in original condition, with plywood seat backs and fitted seat carpets. In the lower view, the enclosed top deck of a balcony-end car depicts the rather spartan conditions experienced by passengers.
(Upper, LT Museum U 49665: Lower, Greater London Photograph Library)

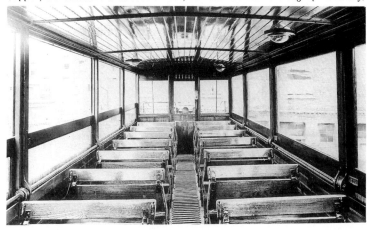

minor differences in detail between the upper deck seats of the four classes of car, which were retained.

Outside seating capacity was originally for 38 passengers on cars of classes A and D and 30 on the cars of the B and C classes. When top covers and draught screens were installed, this number was increased in each case by six or eight, depending upon the formation of the additional seating in the upper saloon canopies, which differed between cars in each class.

By the mid-1920s, J.K. Bruce came to the conclusion that better seating would attract more passengers. This aspect of travel was becoming particularly important, as some of the omnibus companies had already improved their standards of passenger comfort, while the other main tramcar operators in the metropolitan area were also carrying out experiments in improving the seating in certain of their cars.

A plan had been approved by the Council to improve the general standard of comfort in its cars, and several experiments were carried out to ensure that the best idea was adopted. It was realised that the older cars with a relatively short life expectancy, could not be economically dealt with in the same way as those of the newer classes. Therefore, to cater for this, two programmes were arranged.

Class A car No. 5 was fitted experimentally with "pad cushions" on the longitudinal seats in the lower saloon. This merely involved the installation of thin wooden retaining bars to the fronts of the seats, which served to prevent the seat pads from being displaced once they were fitted into position.

This trial was evidently a success as, on 5th February 1925, an allocation of £2,600 was made on a capital account to provide cushion seats on 120 class A and D cars, which included No. 5. These were supplied by G.D. Peters & Co. of Windsor Works, Slough at a total cost of £2,355. Installation of the new seating was carried out by the Tramways Department, at an additional cost of £225, giving a grand total of £2,580, or £21.10s per car. The rest of the cars of these classes were to be fitted with wooden seats of "improved" type in the lower saloons, which were quite possibly the ones recovered from the class E and E/1 cars when they were reconditioned, as mentioned below. The wooden upper deck seats on all cars were retained, as was all seating on the remaining cars of classes B and C, although it is recorded that these were also to receive the "improved" type of wooden seating in the lower saloons. A minor improvement, but none-the-less important, was the provision in the upper saloons of grab rails, suspended by brackets from the ceilings.

Class E cars

In contrast to the arrangement adopted for the older classes of cars, a very much more comprehensive renovation programme was agreed to for the cars of the E, E/1 and M classes. In March 1926, the Council decided to introduce a modernisation programme, whereby the lower saloons of all cars were to be provided with reversible, transverse two-and-one cushioned seating, together with other improvements, while the upper saloons were also to be improved, mainly in the provision of leather-padded sprung seats in place of the transverse wooden seating, but still retaining the horizontal-bar seat backs. Upon implementation of this programme, total seating capacity per car was reduced by five in the bogie cars and by two in the single truck M class cars.

The first cars to be dealt with were 100 of those of class E/1, which were eventually followed by the cars of class E. A full description of this work, known as the "Pullmanisation" programme, will be given in Volume II of this history.

The installation of fabric covered seats required special cleaning facilities, mainly to remove the dust which was likely to accumulate in the material. This was provided for by the installation of "Sturtevant" suction cleaning equipments in the car sheds and depots.

Post-war Controller Changes
Provision of Higher Powered Motors.

On 3rd January 1923, the General Manager made a recommendation that new electrical equipments and 60 h.p. motors be purchased from various manufacturers, in order to re-equip 200 class E/1 cars working on south side services. The 42 h.p. motors and British Westinghouse type T2A and T2C controllers released, were to be used to replace the remaining type 90M controllers still in use on cars of classes A, D and E. The old equipment, to be sold as scrap, was expected to realise about £1,700. It was estimated that total cost of this work would be £144,000, consisting of £142,000 for the new equipment and £2,000 as the cost of re-equipping the classes A and D cars. It was also anticipated that a "saving" of some £34,690 could be made annually on operating expenses and maintenance.

Even though the programme was aimed mainly at the class E/1 cars, the benefit obtained by upgrading the class A and D cars would be well worth while, as it was expected that these cars would be in service for several more years from 1923. There was no mention, at that time, of re-equipping any of the four-wheeled cars which had not, so far, been dealt with and no arrangements appear to have been made. In 1924, however, a second batch of 200 sets of new equipment was ordered, which resulted in the cars of class C being brought into the programme. Eventually, all of the older cars had controllers of type T2C or T2A, with the exception of the remaining 41 class B cars. Of these, all that were converted to snowbrooms received 42 h.p. motors and T2A controllers.

CAR CLASSES A TO E.   ROLLING STOCK WHEN NEW AND WHEN FIRST TOP COVERED

	FLEET Nos. & CLASS		YEAR	BUILDER	TRUCKS TYPE & CLASS		MOTORS	CONTROLLERS CLASS & TYPE		SEATS LS	US	LENGTH	WIDTH	HEIGHT COVERED TOP
A	1–100	100	1903	ER&TCW	2 x Brill 22E	1	2xDK3A	1	DK DB1D	28	38	33 ft. 6 in.	7 ft. 1 in.	16 ft. 4 in.
Ex	101	1	1900	G. F. Milnes	2 x Brill 22E	1	2xW.B49	3	W 90M	28	36	32 ft. 6 in.	7 ft. 1 in.	—
B	102–201	100	1903	ER&TCW	Brill 21E	2	2xDK25A	1	DK DB1D	22	34	28 ft. 9 in.	7 ft. 1 in.	16 ft. 4 in.
C	202–301	100	1904	Brush	Brill 21E	2	2xW200	3	W 90M	22	34	28 ft. 9 in.	7 ft. 1 in.	16 ft. 6 in.
D	302–376	75	1904	Brush	2 x McGuire	3	2xW200	3	W 90M	28	38	33 ft. 6 in.	7 ft. 1 in.	16 ft. 4 in.
D	377–401	25	1904	B E C Co.	2 x McGuire	3	2xW200	3	W 90M	28	38	33 ft. 6 in.	7 ft. 1 in.	16 ft. 4 in.
E	402–426	25	1905	Hurst Nelson	2 x M&G	4	2xW200	4	W 90M	30	46	33 ft. 6 in.	7 ft. 2 in.	15 ft. 9¾ in.
E	427–551	125	1906	Hurst Nelson	2 x M&G	4	2xW220	4	W T2A	30	46	33 ft. 6 in.	7 ft. 2 in.	15 ft. 9¾ in.
E	602–751	150	1906	Hurst Nelson	2 x M&G	4	2xW220	4	W T2A	30	46	33 ft. 6 in.	7 ft. 2 in.	15 ft. 9¾ in.
T	1–8	8	1913	LCC	Framed Single					20	28	27 ft. 2 in.	7 ft. 1 in.	
T	9–158	150	1915/6	Brush	Framed Single					18	30	27 ft. 2 in.	7 ft. 1 in.	
P	1–3	3	1913	LCC	Framed Single					20	28	27 ft. 0 in.	7 ft. 1 in.	

	WHEELBASE TRUCK	TOTAL	WEIGHT OPEN TOP T	C	Q	COVERED TOP T	C	Q	NOTES
A	4 ft. 0 in.	13 ft. 6 in.	11	5	e	13	14	2	a
Ex	4 ft. 0 in.	13 ft. 6 in.	9	15	-	—			
B	6 ft. 6 in.		8	15	e	10	19	1	b
C	6 ft. 6 in.		8	5	e	10	16	2	b
D	4 ft. 0 in.	13 ft. 6 in.	10	15	e	13	5	3	a
D	4 ft. 0 in.	13 ft. 6 in.	10	15	e	13	5	3	a
E	4 ft. 6 in.	14 ft. 6 in.	—			14	8	0	c
E	4 ft. 6 in.	14 ft. 6 in.	—			14	8	0	c
E	4 ft. 6 in.	14 ft. 6 in.				14	8	0	c
T	6 ft. 9 in.		2	10	e				
T	6 ft. 9 in.		2	15	e				
P	6 ft. 6 in.		2	15	e				

ER&TCW Electric Railway & Tramway Carriage Works
Exp Experimental
Brush Brush Electrical Engineering Co.
BECCo. British Electric Car Co.
HN Hurst, Nelson & Co.
LCC London County Council
DK Dick, Kerr & Co.
M&G Mountain & Gibson
W Westinghouse Electric
McG McGuire Engineering

a. Top deck seating increased to 46 with totally enclosed top cover.
b. Top deck seating increased to 38 with totally enclosed top cover.
c. Saloon seating reduced to 25 when "pullmanised".
e. estimated.

Chapter 22
Electrical Equipment on the Cars

Controllers

The type of controller used on electric tramcars, was designed to allow for the smooth and efficient operation of the electric motors on the car. A controller was fitted at each end of a car, allowing the vehicle to be driven from either end. The controller handle operated a shaft or spindle, upon which a cylinder or "drum" carrying a number of insulated and inter-connected copper segments was fixed. These made contact with a number of fixed contacts called fingers, to which the motors, resistances and power supply were connected. No connections could be made, however, until the controller master key was switched into the "forward" position from "off".

All LCC cars of classes A to E were fitted with two motors, with the bogie cars having one in each truck. In order to obtain the maximum tractive effort when starting a car from rest, the controller connections were arranged in such a way that the two motors were connected in series. After moving the controller handle through the several notches of the series section, which progressively cut out the starting resistances, the handle would be moved over a transition quadrant which caused the motors then to be connected in parallel, but with the resistances again connected into the motor circuit. Moving through the parallel notches, the resistances were again switched out until, on "top notch", the motors were each receiving maximum current at full line voltage.

With the controller key in the "reverse" position, a second drum was brought into use which connected the motor windings to the power supply in such a way that the motor armatures revolved in the opposite direction, thereby allowing the car to be driven "backwards". It was not accepted practice to use this method of control to move a car, unless there were special and very good reasons for so doing.

The controller master switch and reversing handle was interlocked with the driving handle, and provided for switching out one motor of the pair, allowing the car to be driven on a single motor if necessary. Keyways in the top of the controller also prevented either handle being removed unless they were both in the "off" position. An arc-blowout device was also incorporated into the circuitry, which was wired in such a way that it provided for the almost instantaneous destruction of any electrical arc which tended to form across the contact fingers or mechanism.

As there was no earth return circuit for electric currents and, as the polarity of the conduit tee-rails could be reversed, two canopy main switches and circuit breakers were provided, one in each side of the circuitry. One pair was mounted side by side on the ceilings of the canopies at either end of the car, by the bulkheads nearest to the entrances. Provision was also made for the inclusion of a watt-meter into the power circuit, in order to monitor the amount of current used to propel the car.

Another innovation was in the arrangement of the controller notches to allow for rheostatic braking. With the state of technology at that time, it had always been difficult to provide for a suitable number of power and braking notches within the dimensions of early controllers. In the case of the Dick, Kerr type DB1 controllers used on classes A and B cars, this was overcome by arranging that the three power notches used for parallel working should also be made to do duty for the braking function when approached from the opposite or "wrong" direction, i.e., the braking side. A similar system was employed on the Westinghouse 90M controllers installed on classes C and D cars.

Rheostatic braking was applied by turning the controller handle into the "off" position and then moving it in the opposite direction to that used to supply power. This switched the motor windings - now generating current - into parallel and in connection with several sections of a resistance grid, which were progressively switched out as the handle was moved round through the braking notches, causing the motors to be forcibly slowed down. In addition to the three parallel power notches, two more braking notches were provided, which, on the power side were merely transition, or change-over notches. The resulting arrangement gave four power series, three power parallel and five braking notches.

The decision to use magnetic braking coincided with the construction of a large part of the order for class E cars. The Westinghouse T2A controllers with which these cars were fitted, were found to be well suited to this task. The controller had seven braking notches entirely separated from the power side. Equipped with full mechanical inter-locking, it was a more effective unit than those used earlier.

After having gained experience with this type of controller on the class E and, later E/1 cars, the Council agreed, on 15th November 1910 to purchase 200 in order to re-equip 100 cars, mainly from the A and D classes, but including a few of the first of the class E cars as well. The cost of £6,490 included cabling and installation charges, with an allowance from British Westinghouse for the return of the old, discarded equipment. A further consignment was obtained in 1912, to be used for maintenance replacement purposes.

Until about 1910, it had been the practice to detach the controller handles from the spindles, thereby only needing one per car. Given that the controllers were in constant use, any wear on the handle was compensated for with the aid of an adjustable screw clamp. Possibly to overcome this problem and also to avoid the need for motormen having to carry a controller handle in addition to the master control key necessary to activate the controller, the LCC decided to make controller handles a permanent fixture. On 23rd February 1910 an order was placed with Messrs. Buller Ltd. for 325 handles, of which 150, to Drawing No. 459 were to cost 3/10½d each, and 175 to Drawing No. 460 to cost 2/1d each. Total cost, including the special patterns and tools required was £54. 2. 4d.

Conduit Plough Collectors - Long Lead Type

The conduit system of current collection on tramcars called for the use of an item which, fitted beneath a convenient point on the car, reached down through a slot in the road, either midway between the running rails or as an intergral part of one track rail, to make contact with electrically charged wires or metal bars conveniently fitted in the open tubes. It was to the USA that the credit went for the design and application of the standard conduit in which the current collecting apparatus became known as a "plough".

When the first lines in London were reconstructed for electric traction, the conduit system was used exclusively. Following the practice of Mr. A. N. Connett, who had used such an item in Paris, the plough was connected to the power feeds of the car by flexible cables and could, if necessary, be removed and replaced by unplugging or plugging the plough leads to the car leads. This version became known as the "long lead plough".

Supplied by Messrs. J. G. White & Co. Ltd., the first ploughs gave considerable trouble after several months of use. They were made mainly of wood and treated with gutta-percha insulation, which proved to be inefficient in extremely wet conditions. This caused a breakdown in electrical insulation between the cables within the plough shank, which in turn led to many fires. The predominantly wooden construction also proved to be mechanically weak. Fuses were fitted into both sides of the electrical circuit of the plough itself and, when actuated, would disconnect the line power. Due to the design of the fuse carriers, there was considerable trouble with accidental disconnections from the supply.

Things became particularly bad on the Greenwich routes soon after the commencement of electrical operation in January 1904. The LCC called in Mr. Connett to investigate the problem and, during his work on this, he visited Paris. From this and other investigations, he designed a much-improved plough, greatly strengthened by metal plates. He also recommended the use of hard india-rubber covering for the cable which would considerably improve the standard of insulation. In return for his work, he received a fee of 50 guineas (£52.10s) and £42.10s as expenses.

For a number of years, use was made of moulded, tough india-rubber plough bases supplied by J. Ingram & Sons, Ltd., Hackney at 45/- each. The special contractual arrangements specified that the Council would supply all metal parts for enclosure by the contractor. The assembled plough bases were returned to the LCC for completion. On 10th December 1907, it was agreed that 600 rubber bases were to be supplied by the India Rubber, Gutta Percha & Telegraph Works Co. Ltd. at 56/- each and 1,200 leads at 4/3d each, a total cost of £1,935.

The ploughs were subject to great stress, which inevitably was the cause of some damage and failure. For example, in December 1913 it was noted that 200 damaged rubber bases would need to be repaired by Ingram & Sons at a cost of £206.

It was becoming clear that wood and rubber were, at that time, not the real answer to the problems facing the Council and, in its search for a more durable alternative to rubber, a contract was entered into with Messrs. Doulton of Lambeth in 1912, for the supply of 400 cream coloured earthenware plough bases for £170 (8/6d each). A year later there was a further order for 500 bases, together with 1,000 covers for plough leads, at a total cost of £231.11. 3d. Even these, apparently, were not totally satisfactory, as a return was contemplated to the use of timber, when, in 1917 it is recorded that the Council was exploring sources of supply of English or American Ash for plough bases.

Sliding Head-Contact Ploughs

When the first cars were fitted with trolley poles to enable them to be used on routes where both conduit and overhead wire sections were in use, the long-lead ploughs were at first retained. At that time, the only two change points in use were at Gresham Road, Brixton and Coldharbour Lane at the Camberwell end, and at these points the attendants had to physically connect or disconnect the plough cables to or from the car connections.

In 1908, the sliding head contact plough was developed, which made the changeover procedure easier and safer. Instead of external cables, the top of the plough was fitted with two copper "shoes", which were connected to the plough cables, and transmitted electric power to collector bars which had been installed above the channels of the plough carrier on the car.

This modification was at first restricted to cars of class E/1 and later, some from class E, the older cars being confined to conduit-only working. However, on 21st July 1914, approval was given to equip 150 cars of classes A and D with carrier collector bars and trolley poles. British Westinghouse agreed to supply the plough carrier parts at a cost of £1,181. 5s. With the beginning of the Great War, this programme was at first severely disrupted and then curtailed.

After the war, arrangements were once again made to continue the work, but even so, 47 cars of class A and 76 of class D were never modified. Most of them retained the original long-lead equipment for a number of years, some until they were withdrawn. None of the class B or C cars were included in the programme.

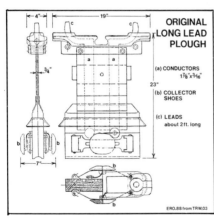

ORIGINAL LONG LEAD PLOUGH

(a) CONDUCTORS
1⅞" x ³⁄₁₆"

(b) COLLECTOR SHOES

(c) LEADS
about 2ft. long

ERO.88 from TRW.03

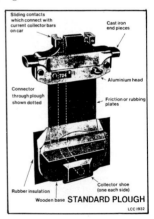

Sliding contacts which connect with current collector bars on car

Cast iron end pieces

Aluminium head

Connector through plough shown dotted

Friction or rubbing plates

Rubber insulation

Collector shoe (one each side)

Wooden base STANDARD PLOUGH

LCC 1932

Fire Precautions

Should a fire occur in a long-lead plough or its cables, or in the connections to the car, the first priority was for the car crew to isolate the power supply from the car cables. If it was possible for the car to be driven to the nearest "dead" point in the track, the rest of the procedure, which was to unplug the plough from the car connections after lifting floor hatches to obtain access, was reasonably safe to undertake. If such a move was not possible, the crew, using heavy rubber gloves, were to take such action as they could to prevent the fire from spreading.

In the case of a sliding head contact plough taking fire, there was a different procedure to be gone through. Instructions stated that "..the hinged bus-bars above the plough contacts should be moved out of contact, using rubber gloves and wooden battens (provided in the toolbox of the car). Access to the bus-bars is obtained through a sliding door in the top of the wooden cover enclosing the collector gear. The cover should not be smashed, except in case of emergency.."

The Plough Workshop

The Council set up a temporary but comprehensive workshop in part of the still incomplete New Cross car shed. One of its first tasks was the construction of 300 ploughs, authorised on 21st November 1905 at a cost of £1,800, for the 150 class E cars then on order. By May 1906 nine men were fully employed assembling all new ploughs from parts bought in, and repairing existing ploughs. The plough workshop was moved to the Central Repair Depot when it opened in 1909, after which all component parts were made and serviced under the direct control of the LCC.

Plough Allocation

Initially, each car was allocated two ploughs, one in use in the carrier, the other on a special bracket fixed beneath the stairs at one end of the car. Ploughs were designed to a common standard which permitted their use under any car fitted with a suitable carrier. With the introduction of plough-shifts, the ploughs became truly "common user" in that one being shed from a car entering an overhead wire section, would be used shortly afterwards beneath a different car moving on to the conduit system. It is probably a tribute to that design that the system worked so efficiently for upwards of 45 years.

As the number of cars in service increased, together with the introduction of a considerable mileage of overhead wire supply, and the implementation of through running with other operators on the north side system, the decision was taken to increase the number of ploughs to three per car. Gradually, over about three years, this programme was carried through, but it did not reach the three per car ratio.

In a memorandum dated 13th March 1913 to the Highways Committee, the Chief Officer recommended that an additional 50 ploughs be provided at a cost of £6. 6s. each (total of £315) for use with cars of other authorities working into Central London. He also anticipated that the maintenance charges for these would be about £24 per year, but it was not expected that the costs would be passed on to the users.

On 17th November 1914, a capital estimate valued at £1,250 was raised to pay for the manufacture of 605 additional ploughs to put the matter right. This figure was arrived at in the following way.

Total fleet, 1725 cars,
    of which   120 were on overhead sections
    and   120 in workshops
        leaving 1,485 for which ploughs needed to be constantly available.
On this basis, a total of 4,455 ploughs, at 3 per car were required,
        of which 3,850 were available,
            leaving 605 short.
These were all made in the Council's workshop at CRD.

After the Great War, a further increase in the number of through conduit-overhead workings, together with joint operation with other undertakings, both south and north of the river, again caused the Council to increase the number of ploughs in service. In all, at its maximum extent in 1932, the LCC had upward of 6,000 ploughs in circulation, with facilities for overhauling up to about 1,000 a week at the Central Repair Depot.

In the 1920s, the LCC continued to be much troubled by broken ploughs, deciding that it was probably due to the "hunting" movement of the bogies when running at speed, which threw the ploughs about in the carriers. Furthermore, if a car had a "flat" on one of the pony-wheels of the truck to which the plough-carrier was bolted, the plough was subjected to excessive lateral and vertical movement. In 1929, class E/1 car No. 1565 had its plough carrier fixed to the underframe of the body on brackets of suitable length. Following this successful experiment, all E and E/1 class cars were fitted with modified plough carriers bolted to the car underframes, almost midway between the bogies. All cars of classes E/3 and HR/2, together with the 50 "Reconstructed Subway Cars" of class E/1, were put into service with the new type of carrier already installed. The remainder of the older cars, together with those of class M, retained the truck-mounted carriers.

On any car which had been modified, the inner end of the bogie which had originally carried the plough-gear could be easily identified, as it was more substantial and shaped differently to the other bogie.

The original type of truck-mounted plough carrier and its variations (left), put considerable strain on the ploughs. Eventually, a body-mounted carrier (right) was designed which eased the problem considerably.

Overhead Wire Trolley Poles

The first use of trolley poles by the LCC was when the short line between Woolwich, Plumstead, and later, Abbey Wood was electrified and 12 cars were fitted with trolley masts and poles. These were the only LCC open-top cars to be so equipped. This was soon followed by the opening of an overhead wire route from Hammersmith to Harlesden, where 25 cars were fitted with trolley booms and bases. Next came the introduction of trolley booms and change-over switches on the 14 cars working via Loughborough Junction.

Cars of classes A to D were not originally built with any provision made for current collection other than by conduit plough. On the open-top cars used in the Plumstead area in 1908, power was collected by trolley poles mounted upon Watlington trolley masts, in the same manner as on most open-top cars of other undertakings. The mast was bolted into the floor of the upper deck and carried the tensioning spring which kept the pole up. Electric current was taken from the overhead wire by a free-running wheel mounted in a swivel head at the top end of the pole. Current was then conveyed to a slip-ring attachment fitted inside the base of the mast, by an insulated cable inside the pole and mast. This enabled the cable to be divided, allowing the trolley pole to be turned in either direction. The lower cable then passed through cavities in the car bodywork, to terminate at the control equipment.

To protect persons from the possibility of electric shock, the cast-iron mast was electrically connected to the metal undergear of the car, so that in the event of a failure of insulation, etc. the stray current would be "earthed". Attached to the head of the pole was a rope which was used for turning the trolley at reversing points. The rope was also used to tie down the pole if and when required. The modified cars were Nos. 104, 118, 124, 150, 175, 178, 185 and 196 of class B and Nos. 350, 354, 393 and one other (343 or 373) of class D, being re-classified as B/4 and D/4 respectively. All 12 were replaced by cars of classes M and E/1 in 1910/11 and returned to CRD to receive totally enclosed lightweight top covers without trolley poles.

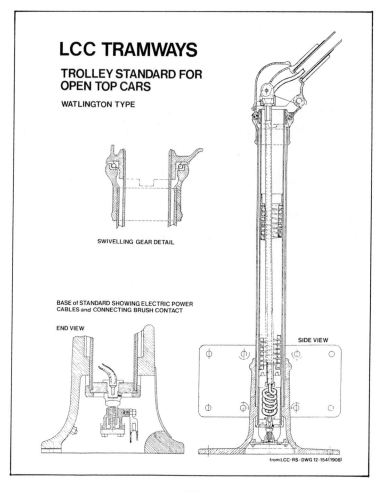

LCC TRAMWAYS

TROLLEY STANDARD FOR OPEN TOP CARS

WATLINGTON TYPE

SWIVELLING GEAR DETAIL

BASE of STANDARD SHOWING ELECTRIC POWER CABLES and CONNECTING BRUSH CONTACT

END VIEW

SIDE VIEW

from LCC-RS-DWG 12-154 (1908)

On top covered cars, the situation was quite different. Each car was fitted with one trolley pole and head, which was attached to a spring loaded trolley base mounted on the roof of the car, the assembly being known as a "dwarf trolley standard". The base contained a slip ring mechanism to convey the current to a cable for transmission to the control equipment. This cable was laid in troughing within the roof structure, window pillars and bulkheads of the car body.

In the case of the cars working on the Woolwich to Eltham line however, each was fitted with two poles, bases and cables, as were a number of other cars in later years. Special changeover switches were installed in these cars, to provide for two-wire working.

When not in use, the pole was stowed beneath a securing hook, one of which was fitted to the roof at either end of the car. The pole was raised, lowered and manoeuvred with the aid of a rope attached to the trolley head. In order that the rope did not billow out while the car was in motion, a rope restrainer was fixed to the roof panelling at each end of the car, or to the upper deck end panelling above the indicator boxes.

To enable the changeover from the conduit to overhead working to be effected, a two-position master switch was installed at one end of the car, where all cabling terminated. This switch could only be operated with the motorman's controller key, ensuring that the changeover was made with the controllers in the "off" position. The changeover switch prevented the car from drawing power from both conduit

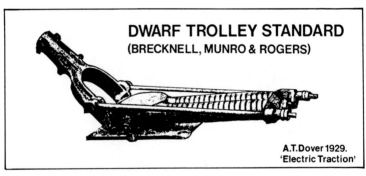

DWARF TROLLEY STANDARD
(BRECKNELL, MUNRO & ROGERS)

A.T.Dover 1929.
'Electric Traction'

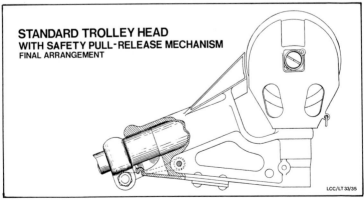

STANDARD TROLLEY HEAD
WITH SAFETY PULL-RELEASE MECHANISM
FINAL ARRANGEMENT

LCC/LT 33/35

and overhead wire at the same time. While the conduit system had an all-insulated power system, the use of the single overhead wire required that return currents be deployed through the running gear of the cars, and then through the rails.

The original top covers fitted to the cars of classes A to D had no provision made for the installation of trolley poles. A considerable amount of work was needed to adapt the car bodies to take the additional fittings. This may have been one of the reasons why not all cars in these classes were fitted. Trolley poles were never fitted to any top-covered cars of classes B and C, except for those of class D which had them installed immediately prior to being sold to other operators during the Great War. The six class B cars hired to Bexley between 1917 and 1920 were only trolley fitted for the duration of the loan, whilst the plough gear was also removed during this period.

When cars of classes A and D were fitted with poles, the overall height of the cars was 16 ft. 4 in., which prevented their use on some routes where the clearances beneath certain railway bridges were insufficient. Cars which were fitted had trolley bases of foreign design, and were known as the "shallow type". They were placed on one side of the car roofs, above the centre pillars of the upper deck windows. During the course of the trolley fitting programme, it became obvious that there were a considerable number of class E/1 cars already fitted (total height 16 ft. 1⅜ in.), thereby reducing the need for all the class A and D cars to receive them. Even so, there remained two bridges at Clapham and Balham which prevented the operation of any trolley fitted car until 1922, when the roadways were lowered beneath them to allow cars of classes E and E/1 to be worked on the route, but not those of classes A and D. There were other places where a similar prohibition applied and, in order to inform car crews of the restrictions, a route availability notice was displayed on the insides of the dashes of the relevant cars.

When it was decided to fit class A and D cars with trolley poles for use on the newly extended line to Woolwich and Abbey Wood as from 5th April 1914, these cars would not have been able to pass safely beneath the Angerstein Wharf branch railway line bridge at Woolwich Road, Westcombe Hill. As a result, arrangements were made with the railway company on 28th October 1913 to raise the bridge by about 4 inches at a cost to the LCC of £200.

The Council had to authorise considerable expenditure on equipping cars for dual working. For example, in 1913, it was decided to fit 150 cars, requiring a total expenditure of £5,250 (£35 per car). Items to be purchased under this proposal included 150 trolley heads with booms from Brecknell, Munro & Rogers for £195 (£1. 6s. each); 150 two-way changeover switches from Johnson & Phillips for £262.10s. (£1.15s. each); 150 trolley bases from Alfred Clare & Co. Ltd. for £525 (£3.10s. each). The intervention of the Great War severely delayed the programme, resulting in its total suspension in 1915. On the resumption of the work in 1921, total cost had risen by £2,450 to £7,700.

A total of 51 class A and 24 class D cars were recorded in 1923 as carrying trolley poles. All were allocated to New Cross or Abbey Wood car sheds and were:-
Nos. 1-5, 7-11, 14-16, 18-20, 22, 23, 25, 27, 29-31, 34, 37, 39, 42, 44, 50, 51, 53, 55, 56, 58, 59, 61, 66-68, 70-72, 75, 77, 78, 81, 83, 86, 88, 91, 100, 328, 334, 337, 344, 350, 354, 357, 360, 361, 366, 371, 378, 379, 382, 384, 385, 388, 393, 395 and 397-401.

Trolley poles when fitted to cars of class E posed less of a problem. Once the car roofs had been strengthened, the lower overall height allowed the installation of standard equipment, which still left the cars 2⅝ inches lower than those of earlier design. The programme for fitting poles to these cars began in 1920 when 25 (402-426) were dealt with for an increase in services to Abbey Wood. Another 50 (427-476) received poles in 1922 while at New Cross, after which all of this batch (except No. 476) were transferred to Hammersmith in 1924. In 1925, No. 477 received a pole and also went to Hammersmith.

Opening of the Amhurst Park Tramway in 1924 brought a further requirement for cars fitted with trolleys. Of those at Hackney shed, 40 (Nos. 640-679) were fitted to work the additional services. Improvements to service 49 from Stamford Hill resulted in 10 more cars being fitted (742-751) in 1926. Another 62 cars at Stamford Hill were fitted in 1928 (680-741), whilst at the same time, 34 cars at New Cross (478-511) and 29 at Hampstead (602-611, 621-639) received poles. Lastly, in 1931, seven cars (545-551) were trolley fitted, and then transferred from Hampstead to Holloway. The remaining cars of class E (512-544, 612-620) were never fitted.

A birds-eye view of the roof and trolley mechanism of a class E car, showing the "dwarf mast", and of the roof of a class E/1 car fitted with two trolleys.   *(Extract from LT Museum U21203)*

Chapter 23
Subsequent History
Car Classes A to E

After all the additions and re-arrangements had been completed, it could have been expected that the cars on the system were to be destined to give a reasonable number of years of good service. While this was true for those of classes A, C and D, it would seem that class B cars, however, were not in the same category.

Classes A and D

From their introduction in 1903/4 until they were disposed of between 1929 and 1931, these two batches of cars were in almost continuous use. By 1913, after completion of the many improvements carried out upon them, they worked mainly from New Cross and Jews Row, Wandsworth car sheds.

None of the cars were withdrawn from service to carry out other non-passenger duties, as occurred in the case of cars of classes B and C. It is understood, however, that a few of them were used from time to time to convey employees to and from the CRD. Class A car No. 82 was severely damaged by fire in 1927, followed by No. 2 in 1928, resulting in their being withdrawn and scrapped.

When the time came for their withdrawal from service, replaced by new cars, many of the bodies were sold off as allotment and garden sheds, some ending their days in the Abbey Wood locality. Others were purchased by speculative builders in the Sidcup and Blackfen districts, where they were used as accommodation for construction workers, together with their tools and supplies. The bogie trucks and electrical equipments were removed by the LCC and disposed of or used again as required.

Class B Cars

After about ten years in service, the cars of class B appeared to be regarded as being structurally weaker than the others. This, together with the preferable use of the larger bogie cars, resulted in a number of them being relegated to rush-hour workings only, and mainly confined to New Cross and Streatham sheds. However, prior to the introduction of class M cars, several class B cars had been in use on the services to and from Forest Hill and Peckham Rye via Dog Kennel Hill.

In a spectacular accident in 1911, No. 110 was severely damaged when, under the control of a learner motorman, it overturned when turning from Shardeloes Road, New Cross into Lewisham High Road. After it had been repaired, the car was given the number 101, while the original No. 101 (the prototype electric car) eventually became No. 110.

Two cars of the class, Nos. 184 and 187, together with one car

The last resting place for the remains of this class A car, seen on 6th July 1952 on Abbey Wood Marshes, was doing duty as an allotment garden shed. *(Courtesy: J. H. Meredith)*

of class C (No. 277) were each fitted with a special type of slot brake beneath the centre of the trucks and put to work on the newly-opened Highgate Hill line in March 1910. In order to carry the plough collector gear, a special carrier was fitted to an extension, 2 ft. 8 in. long, on one end of the truck frame of each car. This was a temporary measure until the cars of class M, which had been ordered for this line were delivered and commissioned, after which the older cars were returned to normal service on the south side system. Movement of these cars between the south and north sides must have presented some problems, but no reference has yet been found to describe how it was carried out.

By August 1914, many of the class B cars were stored out of service. During the four years of the war, a number of tramway undertakings elsewhere suffered car shortages. By agreement with the Board of Trade and Ministry of Munitions, the LCC sold a total of 59 cars to various undertakings, and also loaned six more to Bexley during 1917 and 1918. The cars were all fitted with trolley poles and had the plough carriers removed. The first batches were sold during 1917, ten going to Sheffield, five to Bexley, ten to Rotherham and six to Newport at an agreed price of £450 each, while Bexley had another twelve on loan which it wished to purchase.

The cars for Bexley were towed to Woolwich, from where they continued their journeys under their own power. The remainder were dispatched from New Cross car shed, to be taken by railway to their destinations. Those which remained in LCC ownership were in use fitfully during the years following the war, but gradually their numbers dwindled. Several were dismantled for various reasons. The remainder went into store during 1924 and 1925, after which none ran again in passenger service.

One of the great difficulties experienced by the operating department occurred during periods of severe weather, when snow clogged the conduit slot rails to varying degrees. Clearance was effected,

Two that got away! These class B cars were sold to Newport, Mon. during the Great War and saw many more years' service in that town.
(Photographer unknown)

as far as was possible, by using rotary brooms drawn by Foden steam lorries, in conjunction with the use of "arrowhead" brooms fitted beneath a number of the service cars. The arrangement was only partially successful.

Early in July 1926, the Rolling Stock Engineer suggested that 14 of the class B cars could easily be adapted to work as snow sweepers at a probable cost of about £160 per car. Tenders were called for and, on 13th October 1926, it was reported that the contract had been awarded to the Kilmarnock Engineering Company for 14 snow sweeping equipments at £120 each. Additional preparatory work undertaken by the Council at the Central Repair Depot was expected to cost about £40 per car.

Eventually, it was decided to convert 21 of the stored cars, the first one being completed just in time to be severely, and successfully tested with the heavy snow of the winter of 1926/7. Final cost of this work was £172 per car. All of the snowbrooms remained available for use for many years, some of them lasting almost to the end of tramway operation in 1952.

One car, however, is still extant in 1988. Snowbroom No. 022 was preserved by London Transport in 1952 as it stood, with the intention of restoring it to its original open-top 1903 condition as class B car No. 106. Due to a lack of finance this was not done, and a number of people, all members of the various societies interested in tramways, formed themselves into the London County Council Tramways Trust and took on the task. To enable it to run again as a passenger carrying vehicle on the line of the National Tramway Museum at Crich, Derbyshire, it was necessary to provide it with a trolley pole. Fortunately, eight of the class were so fitted in 1908 when they were converted to open top "class B/4" cars and operated in Woolwich in 1908/1910. With a trolley mast similar in style to a Watlington, a trolley pole and, additionally, conduit plough gear, No. 106 now has a third "life".

An unusual accident was reported as having occurred during 1923, when class B car, No. 138, which was in the process of being overhauled at the CRD, fell from the accommodation truck upon which it had been placed. The assembly was standing on the traverser at the time, with the result that it fell into the traverser pit and was severely damaged, with the top deck destroyed. Now reduced to a "single-deck" car, No. 138 was put aside for a time.

Some years before, car No. 110 was badly damaged and, after repair was re-numbered 101. The decision was taken that this car, also due for overhaul at about the same time as No. 138, should replace the stricken vehicle and, after work had been completed, the numbers were exchanged. The "new" No. 101 was stored away for the time being, still with no upper deck. It was eventually selected for conversion into a snowbroom and, after the work had been carried out was given the number 030 in the works fleet. Meanwhile the car now identified as No. 138 remained in service until 27th June 1924, when it was finally delicensed and eventually scrapped.

The car which had been the subject of the experiments in 1901 and 1902 and numbered 101 in the fleet, had been renumbered 110, and worked for a short period on the Clapham and Chelsea Bridge service. It was withdrawn in 1926 and scrapped in 1931.

Class C Cars

Cars of class C appeared to fare much better than those of class B, and were considered to be more robustly built. Many of them worked on the services to Dulwich and Forest Hill via the notoriously steep Dog Kennel Hill, in which duty they were joined in 1910/11 by some of the new class M cars. As more of the new cars were allocated to the hilly routes, many cars of the C class were transferred to other duties, some being transferred to New Cross car shed, from where they worked on services in that area.

During 1906, 60 cars of the class were fitted with additional mechanical track brakes for use on Dog Kennel Hill. These were:-
202-204, 206-211, 213-220, 222-226, 229, 231-241, 245, 246, 249, 251, 253, 257, 259, 266, 267, 269-271, 278-280, 283, 284, 286, 289, 290, 292, 296, 297, 299, 330, 301.

After almost twenty years in service, these cars were beginning to show signs of obsolescence, and were being unfavourably compared with later vehicles, both for the standard of comfort and riding quality. These features even provoked public complaints, as shown by a letter from a Brockley resident to the Council in July 1924, in which the complainant observed that up to 30% of the Brockley service was still operated by four-wheeled cars. The answer from the Council was that the cars would remain on the route for as long as they were required to maintain the service, and certainly until the remotoring programme, then being undertaken on many of the other cars in the fleet, was completed.

These cars were also well known for their rolling and pitching motion when travelling at speed, sharing this phenomenon with the newer four-wheeled cars of class M. It was on a number of these that an experiment was carried out in 1924.

The Houdaille Hydraulic Suspension Apparatus was basically a shock absorber as used on motor cars of that period. The Council, on 26th June 1924 decided to use it as an "anti-sway device" in an effort to reduce the oscillations of the car bodies. A class M car was fitted with the apparatus as an experiment, at a cost of £8. 8s for the equipment and £2. 2s for labour charges. This was followed by fitting the apparatus to another six of the cars working on Highgate Hill, and six working on the Dog Kennel Hill services. One class C car, No. 250 was also fitted in April 1926. Although swaying was somewhat reduced, the equipment soon showed signs of wear, examination of the components indicating that the device was unsuitable.

In the meantime, the Tramways Department Rolling Stock Engineer had developed a device to control vertical oscillation, which was tried out in October 1925 on one car of class M, No. 1690 and on two class C cars, Nos. 278 and 276 (or 226). After several months in service, the experiment appeared to have proved its worth, resulting in 12 more sets of equipment being fitted, six to class C cars, the others to class M.

Finally, on 18th February 1926, the decision was taken to install this device to all of the remaining cars of both classes. A provisional estimate of £5,250 was drawn up, which included £455 for the wages of Council staff, who were to fit these to the cars. A tender was accepted on 20th July 1926 from Messrs. Kilmarnock Engineering for the supply of the 188 units for £2,560, with Messrs. Hurst, Nelson supplying certain parts for the sets for £816, a cost considerably less than the estimate allowed for. By the end of March 1927, about 100 cars had been dealt with and by the end of the year, the work had been completed.

It has been recorded by the late Frank E. Wilson that cars Nos. 293 and 294 were fitted with trailer couplings to enable them to shunt trailer cars into and out of Streatham car shed. No dates are given, and so far, no additional information has been forthcoming.

Car No. 256 was the subject of an experiment in May 1926 when it was reported that an improved type of sanding gear was tried out.

All the class C cars remaining in passenger service were withdrawn by 1930, being replaced (either directly or indirectly) by the new cars of HR/2 and E/3 classes. It is known that some of the C class cars withdrawn during 1929 were taken to the former L.U.T. depot at Chiswick where their bodies were offered for sale at £5 each. One survived until as recently as 1986 doing duty as a watchman's hut in a Hertfordshire factory, but the fleet number is unknown.

Snowploughs

Following on from the successful conversion of certain B class cars as snowbrooms, it was decided to provide a number of snowplough equipped cars for use in addition to the snowbrooms. Eighteen cars of class C were converted in a similar fashion to their Class B counterparts by having their top decks and stairs removed. Each car was then fitted with a snowplough mounted under each platform. The snowplough was placed at an angle which swept snow to the nearside of the tracks.

Cars Taken Out Of Service, Final Dates   Class A

Car No	Date Delicensed	Last MSCNo	Notes	Car No	Date Delicensed	Last MSCNo	Notes
1	24.10.31	3392	a. b.	51	11.02.31	3280	a. b.
2	12.05.28	9221	a. b.	52	20.10.31	2410	
3	04.05.29	5184	a. b.	53	20.10.31	1653	a. b.
4	21.08.29	5155	a. b.	54	11.10.30	5337	
5	30.05.31	9949	a. b.	55	20.10.31	5423	a.
6	21.07.30	886		56	10.01.31	3737	a. b.
7	08.03.30	9333	a. b.	57	07.05.31	2610	
8	08.01.31	7671	a. b.	58	04.03.31	3291	a. b.
9	20.10.31	1481	a. b.	59	18.08.30	7189	a. b.
10	24.10.31	9670	a. b.	60	04.11.25	2873	
11	28.03.29	4344	a.	61	02.04.27	4279	a. b.
12	27.08.28	4968		62	04.02.31	2837	b.
13	10.06.30	9065		63	10.03.31	8481	
14	08.08.31	5951	a. b.	64	25.02.31	5442	b.
15	20.09.30	6014	a.	65	08.09.30	9091	
16	21.08.29	6379	a. b.	66	10.01.31	309	a.
17	14.02.31	2239		67	26.01.27	8700	a. b.
18	05.01.29	6368	a.	68	24.10.31	494	a.
19	06.10.30	1481	a. b.	69	22.10.27	5584	
20	08.08.31	7216	a. b.	70	20.10.31	8566	a. b.
21	18.09.31	2780		71	08.08.31	3268	a. b.
22	14.07.31	4588	a. b.	72	20.10.31	7730	a. b.
23	08.08.31	7087	a. b.	73	**.06.31	828	
24	10.05.30	9384	b.	74	20.10.31	5309	
25	10.01.31	8430	a. b.	75	19.11.30	5904	a. b.
26	05.12.30	2852		76	17.09.30	475	
27	12.06.30	332	a. b.	77	27.11.30	6895	a.
28	28.09.29	6789		78	24.01.31	5392	a. b.
29	08.08.31	1065	a. b.	79	03.09.30	3299	b.
30	03.09.30	8566	a.	80	12.05.31	5757	b.
31	20.02.31	5246	a. b.	81	20.10.31	475	a. b.
32	24.01.31	9361		82	24.09.27(?)	1730	b.
33	22.05.31	6833		83	19.11.30	6882	a.
34	15.12.30	5989	a. b.	84	29.10.30	5267	b.
35	27.11.30	979		85	18.07.31	1101	b.
36	24.06.31	9384		86	08.08.31	7985	a. b.
37	15.08.31	6004	a. b.	87	29.06.29	1554	
38	09.10.31	745		88	04.04.31	1602	a.
39	14.12.29	441	a. b.	89	30.05.29	418	b.
40	13.10.30	7215		90	13.11.29	483	
41	08.08.31	7375		91	24.10.31	4647	a.
42	08.08.31	4366	a. b.	92	18.08.30	895	b.
43	04.02.31	1961		93	23.12.30	610	b.
44	12.08.31	8460	a.	94	19.10.31	7170	b.
45	11.03.31	180		95	31.08.29	8820	b.
46	13.09.30	7122		96	03.11.28	1796	
47	16.10.31	306		97	12.06.29	7080	
48	06.12.30	314		98	20.10.31	1134	b.
49	20.03.30	1359		99	15.10.31	5217	
50	13.07.27	7315	a. b.	100	24.10.31	7671	a. b.

a. Pole fitted
b. "LCC" top cover

Cars Taken Out Of Service, Final Dates   Class B

Car No	Date Delicensed	Last MSCNo	Notes	Car No	Date Delicensed	Last MSCNo	Notes
101	03.10.24	4228	d.	151	19.04.15	5754	f.
102	11.03.25	9397	Sb 032	152	12.05.15	976	g.
103	01.08.14	2325	g.	153	09.05.24	4192	Sb 017
104	05.11.24	4857	a.	154	01.04.18	5365	k.
105	02.01.15	6843	h.	155	26.01.25	681	a.
106	11.03.25	475	Sb 022	156	08.07.14	4064	g.
107	21.03.25	7087	b.	157	04.03.16	202	f.
108	06.05.14	3694	g.	158	30.10.24	2423	b.
109	15.06.15	5462	f.	159	08.05.15	4037	h.
110	—	—		160	28.03.14	5267	g.
111	21.10.15	5584	f.	161	25.10.16	856	k.
112	03.06.16	639	f.	162	22.05.15	2081	j.
113	28.05.24	79**	a.	163	14.08.24	2217	Sb 031
114	23.06.15	2205	h.	164	22.01.16	3994	h.
115	03.05.13	1193	h.	165	28.02.25	6019	Sb 019
116	10.04.15	5264	g.	166	10.06.18	6888	g.
117	22.10.24	3887	a.	167	23.11.12	3524	f.
118	01.07.15	4356	c.	168	01.04.25	7084	Sb 021
119	28.11.14	4175	g.	169	17.06.24	8963	Sb 034
120	23.01.25	7360	Sb 028	170	21.10.15	5477	g.
121	18.04.14	6820	g.	171	01.06.18	2057	g.
122	18.09.24	1649	a.	172	02.12.14	6758	j.
123	20.03.15	1762	f.	173	05.06.18	2067	g.
124	18.09.24	9252	a.	174	11.04.14	5199	j.
125	29.08.24	662	Sb 025	175	02.02.25	3516	a.
126	29.05.15	3711	g.	176	19.11.21	6894	a.
127	30.05.14	6078	h.	177	07.11.24	2825	a.
128	11.06.15	649	f.	178	10.08.14	2423	f.
129	18.11.24	9162	a.	179	01.02.16	5369	g.
130	06.07.15	3374	f.	180	21.01.16	2722	f.
131	17.11.24	5371	a.	181	01.11.15	4055	g.
132	16.07.24	7970	Sb 036	182	25.02.25	3737	Sb 020
133	14.01.25	3251	a.	183	18.11.24	8217	Sb 026
134	13.09.22	5888	Sb 029	184	06.03.15	5777	f.
135	09.03.18	1575	k.	185	24.07.18	5435	g.
136	04.03.16	1002	h.	186	11.07.18	4907	g.
137	08.07.15	3783	h.	187	29.05.15	5259	f.
138	27.06.24	1948	e.	188	02.09.14	3524	g.
139	13.01.15	2521	f.	189	16.07.24	2800	Sb 024
140	19.04.15	5809	f.	190	10.07.15	6850	j.
141	09.05.24	7079	Sb 023	191	02.01.15	3***	j.
142	09.09.14	3306	h.	192	01.04.18	3227	k.
143	16.07.24	3227	a.	193	05.06.18	6013	g.
144	09.09.24	3942	Sb 035	194	23.12.22	2873	Sb 033
145	03.02.23	3559	a.	195	09.09.24	8926	Sb 018
146	26.06.15	4077	h.	196	14.04.15	356	f.
147	04.11.24	1928	a.	197	19.04.15	2579	j.
148	13.09.22	5083	Sb 027	198	01.04.18	2722	k.
149	13.07.18	356	g.	199	18.11.24	610	a.
150	01.04.25	4366	Sb 016	200	01.05.18	2908	k.
				201	08.07.15	407	f.

All cars top covered
None trolley fitted for use in London
Sb = snowbroom
a. Scrapped in London
b. Staff car, 1927/31
c. Sand car
d. Was 110. Renumbered 138
      Scrapped in London
e. Renumbered 101
      Became snowbroom 030

59 class B cars sold out of service.
f. Sold to Bexley
g. Sold to Sheffield
h. Sold to Rotherham or Newport
j. Sold to Rotherham
k. Sold to Southampton

Cars Taken Out Of Service, Final Dates   Class C

Car No	Date Delicensed	Last MSCNo	Notes	Car No	Date Delicensed	Last MSCNo	Notes
202	11.07.30	9146		252	08.03.30	7370	Sp 047 (1)
203	30.08.30	9253		253	06.01.31	6918	Sp 054
204	10.10.25	4481		254	04.09.29	2832	
205	01.06.27	2586		255	20.09.28	7738	
206	31.10.25	3800		256	18.08.30	2172	Sp 041 (2)
207	12.07.30	7529		257	17.04.30	9***	
208	24.11.27	5771		258	13.09.30	4501	Sp 048 (1)
209	29.10.30	6776	Sp 044	259	02.12.30	4679	
210	08.01.30	7547		260	25.03.22	3182	
211	19.05.28	3893		261	31.05.30	1198	
212	28.06.28	895		262	16.05.25	8010	
213	25.07.30	5415		263	**.03.31	314	
214	13.09.30	7442		264	10.09.30	5280	
215	02.12.30	11935	Sp 045	265	03.07.30	2331	
216	16.10.30	4074	Sp 037 (1)	266	29.10.30	7255	Sp 042 (1)
217	21.12.29	704		267	28.04.28	5366	
218	20.06.25	2140		268	31.01.25	4914	
219	04.05.29	710		269	02.10.29	2032	
220	02.12.30	1913		270	02.12.30	10476	Sp 049
221	16.11.27	7122		271	25.07.30	5809	
222	23.04.27	5907		272	05.09.25	8580	
223	01.12.26	5177		273	09.10.29	7647	Sv 015
224	20.10.30	11972	Sp 038 (2)	274	09.10.29	6019	
225	25.05.29	33		275	26.04.30	4228	Sp 050
226	19.09.28	7158		276	07.07.28	6151	
227	17.01.24	6874		277	21.03.30	2228	
228	07.12.28	8442		278	12.02.27	6604	
229	01.10.30	5412	Sp 040 (1)	279	03.11.30	4785	
230	09.07.30	449		280	09.07.30	4980	
231	15.06.27	6011		281	04.05.27	2052	
232	04.06.27	5054		282	21.08.29	7189	
233	02.12.30	11926	Sp 053	283	13.04.29	2619	
234	02.12.30	5913		284	04.04.30	6219	
235	23.06.30	4190		285	14.10.25	8771	Sp 051
236	20.08.30	78**		286	11.09.24	6604	
237	29.04.25	1253		287	03.10.25	7306	
238	16.09.25	6885		288	28.02.30	5843	Sp 052
239	18.05.27	425		289	06.01.31	5852	
240	06.09.29	407		290	23.06.30	4914	
241	20.08.30	11956	Sp 043 (1)	291	25.02.28	2841	
242	12.12.25	7124		292	29.08.25	1788	
243	08.02.28	7370		293	16.01.26	7375	
244	18.08.28	7965		294	16.10.29	3373	
245	27.07.27	33		295	21.08.29	1058	
246	19.06.30	3796		296	31.10.29	1938	
247	23.06.28	3861		297	03.07.26	2070	
248	07.08.30	7306	Sp 039	298	19.07.30	7363	
249	26.05.30	3641		299	21.08.29	6655	
250	03.03.30	1117	Sp 046	300	22.10.27	1788	
251	13.11.30	4991		301	20.10.30	7449	

Cars not otherwise accounted for,
scrapped by LCC

Sp = snowplough

(1) Later became snowbroom
(2) Later became stores van

Cars Taken Out Of Service, Final Dates   Class D

Car No	Date Delicensed	Last M S C No	Notes	Car No	Date Delicensed	Last M S C No	Notes
302	23.04.31	1117		352	06.11.31	6776	
303	31.07.31	7383		353	07.07.30	1457	
304	23.05.31	8651		354	12.12.30	1774	a.
305	27.10.30	6749		355	27.09.30	4630	
306	19.02.31	7357		356	21.10.31	675*	
307	14.11.29	1077		357	31.10.31	5485	a.
308	25.11.31	1961		358	19.10.79	4759	
309	20.08.30	4555		359	26.11.30	2713	
310	03.01.31	6669		360	30.04.27	1034	a.
311	15.02.30	3164		361	06.11.31	3709	a.
312	18.05.29	7383		362	07.10.30	3734	
313	13.10.31	414		363	31.07.31	3066	
314	13.01.31	3699		364	29.01.31	6734	
315	07.11.31	4675		365	31.07.31	4550	
316	11.10.30	15**		366	13.03.29	4337	a.
317	30.03.31	918		367	09.05.31	5106	
318	21.06.30	8973		368	01.09.28	7215	
319	15.07.30	7666		369	27.09.30	4625	
320	18.02.31	2202		370	09.04.30	7112	
321	23.06.30	1445		371	29.04.30	3516	a.
322	04.11.31	863		372	05.07.30	5900	
323	26.11.30	3104		373	31.07.31	5328	
324	04.11.31	5324		374	03.05.30	3127	
325	31.07.31	7776		375	05.12.31	6107	
326	31.07.31	4634		376	21.12.29	461*	
327	29.01.31	6738		377	05.12.31	8211	b.
328	03.10.31	7738	a.	378	31.07.31	6804	a. b.
329	26.03.31	2478		379	12.08.31	2761	a. b.
330	18.06.27	3844		380	29.11.30	4749	b.
331	26.12.30	8484		381	03.10.29	5022	b.
332	17.06.30	5328		382	20.10.30	3630	a. b.
333	13.07.29	4938		383	23.03.29	4967	b.
334	08.08.31	5516	a.	384	04.11.31	8090	a. b.
335	08.02.30	2370		385	24.01.31	4318	a. b.
336	14.12.29	5324		386	11.01.30	2067	b.
337	31.10.31	1744	a.	387	31.07.31	5123	b.
338	12.03.31	4604		388	08.08.31	6884	a. b.
339	22.12.30	4221		389	04.04.31	3781	b.
340	08.08.31	4488		390	25.09.30	6653	b.
341	31.07.31	7663		391	04.11.31	4504	b.
342	30.04.30	5350		392	25.10.30	8820	b.
343	25.11.31	2905		393	24.01.31	5058	a. b.
344	30.03.29	4318	a.	394	14.10.30	2683	b.
345	06.11.31	583		395	10.03.31	7363	a. b.
346	28.07.30	4504		396	15.11.30	8811	b.
347	26.02.31	2677		397	11.07.31	8005	a. b.
348	22.10.30	5981		398	12.08.31	6015	a. b.
349	31.07.31	334		399	08.08.31	9936	a. b.
350	09.10.31	4501	a. b.	400	12.10.31	7398	a. b.
351	17.06.31	4300		401	01.05.30	3985	a. b.

a. Pole fitted
b. "LCC" top cover

Class E Cars

A limited upgrading or equipments was undertaken in 1912, when several of the cars which had 90M controllers were re-fitted with type T2A controllers and type 220 motors of 42 h.p. rating. No. 415 certainly had controllers of this type in 1917. Nevertheless, it was not until a comprehensive re-equipping programme was undertaken in 1923, that the last of the 90M controllers and their associated type 200 motors were taken out of service.

In common with the rest of the fleet, all cars of the class were fitted with service number equipment in 1912/13, while in 1922/23, side indicator number boxes were installed which incorporated adjustable red aspects. Uncommonly, a number of the 402-551 series received trailer drawgear subsequent to 1914, retaining this until no longer required in the early 1920s.

In 1921, the LCC had on order 125 new cars of class E/1, to be delivered to the southern system. The first of these arrived towards the end of the year and, with the prospect of a large new fleet of cars being made available, together with extension and alteration to existing services, a considerable re-arrangement of existing stock was undertaken. This included the transfer of 40 cars from the southern to northern system, when class E cars Nos. 512-551 were moved from Clapham car shed to Hampstead.

There has always been speculation as to how the cars were moved from south to north, the most popular idea being that they were taken via Hammersmith and the M E T lines north of Willesden Junction. However, despite protracted research, no evidence of any kind has been found to substantiate this, not even an exchange of letters between the Tramways Managers of the L C C and M E T Ltd.

On information received from Mr. R. Elliott, the operation was dealt with by one of the C R D Foremen, whose responsibility it was to oversee the move. After the close of normal services at night, each car would be driven to the nearest convenient point south of Tower Bridge where its plough was removed, the trucks disconnected, the body lifted on jacks and the motor and brake cables disconnected. After the trucks had been run out, the body was lowered on to a flat trailer, to be hauled by a steam tractor wagon across the bridge to the most convenient point on the northern system at Leman Street (London Docks). The trucks, meantime, had been loaded on to another wagon and brought across to be re-united with the body, after which the cables and linkages were re-connected, the plough inserted into the carrier through the floor hatch, and the car driven away to Hampstead. It is understood that this operation was so arranged that one car was dealt with each night.

Provision of Heaters

On 1st September 1924, the Council decided to instruct the General Manager to investigate the provision of heaters in the lower saloons of the cars. Additional resistances were to be provided, which could be switched in or out as required in cold weather. A sum of £187.10s was allocated to cover the cost of sufficient equipment to be fitted to five cars. This work had been completed by February 1925.

During the summer of 1925, it was agreed to extend the experiment. On 8th July, it was reported that eight sets of heating equipment had been provided, which had been assembled on six class E cars at Hampstead, Nos. 629-632, 638 and 639, and two class E cars at New

Cross, Nos. 507 and 508. Four sets had been supplied by the Rheo-static Co. Ltd., Slough, and fitted to cars 507, 630, 631 and 639, the other four sets supplied by Messrs. E M B Co. Ltd., West Bromwich.

By all accounts, the tests proved to be inconclusive. It had been anticipated that there would have been a rise of 8.5 degrees F. in the ambient temperature of the saloons on a cold day. From reports and records taken, it seemed that in some cases the passengers complained of excessive heat, others complained of variation in temperatures, while some said that the heaters appeared to make little difference. Nevertheless, the Council persevered and, on 4th December 1925, decided to extend the experiment until the spring of 1926, when the trials were discontinued.

Car No. 420

In its early days this car operated from Clapham shed and at one time was fitted with trailer couplings. When the line between East Hill, Wandsworth and Putney Bridge Road was opened, No. 420 was transferred to Hammersmith. In 1930, it was involved in an accident, after which both saloons were completely rebuilt. The LCC was experimenting with metal alloy upper deck framing at the time, and 420 was fitted with a new type of top cover which incorporated large, externally hung service number stencil plates. In 1936, it was experimentally fitted with new controllers and high power motors removed from a scrapped M E T car. As a result, No. 420 survived the tram to trolleybus conversions, which took place prior to the Second World War. At the end of 1938, E/1 No. 1597 suffered an accident at Balham and was scrapped. No. 420 was fitted with the English Electric equipment from No. 1597 and took its number. It was subsequently fitted with vestibule screens, and remained in service until 1950. (Parts of the service number equipment are still in use, fitted at one end of preserved class HR/2 car, No. 1858, which is in operation at the East Anglia Transport Museum, Carlton Colville, Lowestoft, Suffolk).

Experiments

In 1925, an experiment was conducted on class E car No. 511, when the existing electrical equipment was replaced with BT-H 504A motors and B521A controllers. On 30th November 1927 the Tramways committee reviewed the experiment and after 75,000 miles of operation it was agreed to purchase the equipment (at the request of BT-H) for the sum of £610.

Tailpiece

Although the cars of class E were only five or six years younger than the original four classes, they were more substantially built and capable of many more years of service. All were modernised during the 1920s and all passed to the L P T B in 1933.

The LCC had always maintained the fleet to a high standard, and to attain this, had used quite sophisticated methods of overhaul, even prior to the opening of the Central Repair Depot in 1909. It is likely that there is some ground for thinking that a simple flow-line method of overhaul was employed from the beginning of electric traction. This may have involved the use of replacement units, or else to have had at least one spare car available to replace the one due for overhaul, and may have resulted in some car renumbering. Although this cannot be confirmed, the authors suggest that it may have occurred.

Chapter 24
The Petrol-Electric Cars (P1-3)

In 1912, the Council was contemplating the electrification of the line between West India Docks and South Hackney, Cassland Road and had asked that it be allowed to erect overhead wires along this rather lightly loaded route. This however, was rejected by the local authorities and, in an effort to provide a service of mechanically propelled cars without going to the expense of laying conduit track, the Council suggested that self-propelled petrol-electric cars might suffice, and wrote to the Board of Trade on 24th June 1912 asking for consent to carry out this work. It was also stated that "the service could easily be met by the use of an internal combustion engine coupled to a generator driving traction motors, with electrical control, and carried on specially adapted horse car bodies. The system is practically silent".

The bodies concerned were several of the later batches of horse cars purchased, of the same vintage as those being adapted for use as trailer cars. Many of the features as seen on the trailer cars were also adopted, such as standard car platforms and direct staircases, open top decks and fitments, together with standard LCC destination boxes and other accessories.

In his reply to the Council on 6th July, Major Pringle, the Inspecting Officer for the Board of Trade, said that there was no objection in principle to the proposal, but as there were some narrow sections of road on the route, special arrangements would have to be made regarding speed restrictions 'after he had gone over the route'. His recommendation after his visit was that, provided the track was relaid and repositioned in several places, he would not oppose the proposal. Meantime, a discussion had developed within the Board of Trade with regard to the definition of the term "electric traction" as applied to the operation of the proposed new cars. The outcome of this was that it was agreed that the LCC was covered by its Electrical Powers Act of 1900.

The LCC then decided that the Woolwich to Abbey Wood line would be ideal for carrying out working tests, using one car, before investing in considerable expense. To this, the Board of Trade replied that if passengers were not to be carried, a formal letter of authority would suffice, but otherwise, the LCC must obtain the consent of Woolwich Borough Council and the Metropolitan Police. Woolwich agreed to the experiment, as did the Board of Trade on 9th October 1912. The police, however, stated that the LCC had not applied for a license to operate a petrol-electric car in public service and could not comment until it did.

Although one report states that a car ran in the Woolwich area on or about 17th March 1913, there is no further evidence seen to confirm or deny this. Nevertheless, it appears that the police did

Car No. P1 is seen standing in the yard at the Central Repair Depot soon after completion in 1913.

inspect a car, and that tests were carried out on it. On 26th May 1913, a letter from the Commissioner's Office to the Board of Trade pointed out that, in the opinion of the police, additional braking would be required on a car operated in public service, as Car No. P 1 only had a handbrake. As the car could reach a speed of about 20 m.p.h. on level track and could not be stopped within three car lengths, an additional brake would be required. To this comment, the Board noted that "as the car could be electrically braked by short-circuiting the motors" and, as the route proposed was almost level, they saw no reason to alter the braking arrangements. Different conditions would apply, however, if hilly areas were likely to be served by the cars.

Criticism was also made by the police regarding the construction of the stairs, the fact that an unusual type of lifeguard fitting was employed, of the way in which the unprotected exhaust pipe was carried down the outside of the body and, as it pointed directly towards the ground, raised a continuous cloud of dust from the surface of the road. With regard to the exhaust pipe, the recommendation was made that it be repositioned and then heavily lagged with asbestos from the engine to the silencer.

At that time, the petrol-electric omnibus was being developed, the power units for which were supplied by Messrs. W. A. Stevens of Maidstone, Kent. The Council decided to entrust Stevens with the job of providing the power units for the three tramcars at a total price of £1,651. 4s. An additional £750 was allocated by the Council for the alterations and modifications which would have to be made to the three horse car bodies before they could be adapted for the experiment.

The power unit on each tram, a petrol engine with a bore and stroke of 4¾ in. by 5½ in., capable of developing about 40 b.h.p. at up to 1,000 r.p.m., was coupled to and mounted with the electric power generator on a pressed steel frame which was suspended on the platform bearers at one end of the car beneath the staircase. The main cooling

The engine was fitted beneath the stairs on one platform, with the petrol tank immediately above it. The exhaust pipe was fixed to the outside of the bodywork. *(All views courtesy of K. C. Blacker)*

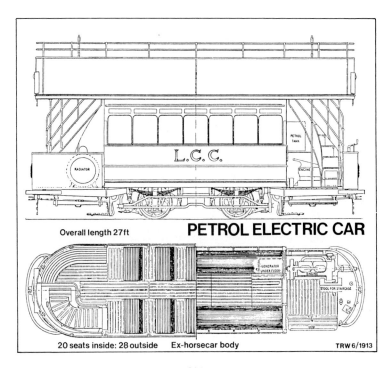

Overall length 27ft   **PETROL ELECTRIC CAR**

20 seats inside: 28 outside   Ex-horsecar body   TRW 6/1913

radiator, water circulation pump and other ancillary items were placed on the other platform, also beneath the stairs. An additional small radiator and fan were fitted near the generator, to assist in cooling when required. Waste gases from the engine were carried away by an exhaust pipe to a point beneath the car, where they were discharged into the atmosphere.

On each car, electric current was generated by a shunt-wound interpole dynamo, working at 350 volts d.c. An engine throttle, used in conjunction with the car controllers, fed power to the two series-wound motors through resistances, while a reversing switch allowed the car to be driven in either direction. While magnetic braking was not provided, the General Manager said that this could easily be applied by making a slight modification to the controllers.

On 7th May 1913, trials using one car were carried out on the track between Greenwich and Woolwich Dockyard. On 21st May, the first car was tested and approved by the Board of Trade and put on to service No. 70 on the Greenwich to Tooley Street line, being followed by Car No. 2 on 23rd October. The experiment was short-lived however, as on 9th December 1913, both cars were withdrawn. By all accounts they were not very successful. They were allegedly noisy, suffered from the emission of large quantities of fumes, and from loss of power due to overheating. None of the vehicles were placed in service where it was originally intended they should go - the horse cars on the Victoria Park line continued to run. For the time being they were stored away pending a decision on their future. That came on 22nd December 1914, when the Council agreed to spend £40 on each of the three cars and convert them into tractor units. The bodies were removed and replaced by flat flooring and short bulkheads and, at the same time, coupler gear was fitted to each one. They ended their days shunting trailer cars at Marius Road depot, Balham.

The above information has been extracted from original notes kindly supplied by, and with permission of K. C. Blacker, Esq.

"Winding-up" No. P 1. The fussy petrol engine no doubt required much coaxing before it started.

Chapter 25
The Trailer Cars

by M. J. D. Willsher
with additional notes by E. R. Oakley & C. S. Smeeton

A series of articles by M. J. D. Willsher entitled "The LCC Trailers" was published some time ago by the Light Rail Transit Association in "Modern Tramway", these being eventually collected together in a booklet of the same title. Mr. Willsher and the LRTA have kindly consented to the use of extracts from his work, for which the authors are extremely grateful.

Legislation and Experiment

The use of trailers was not common on British tramways, although there were some experiments. In the years preceding the Great War there was also much discussion in sections of the technical press on the merits, or otherwise, of trailer working in conjunction with, or opposed to, the use of the double deck tramcar. The Board of Trade appeared to be somewhat undecided. As there was no general regulation which permitted or prohibited their use, the Board treated each case separately, except for certain provisions and requirements. One of these was that each trailer should be staffed with a minimum of one crew member at all times. By 1909, however, 28 tramway undertakings had been given powers to operate trailers, but many of these operations did not survive for very long.

Interest was expressed by the London County Council in running trailer cars, and in operating coupled power cars as well in an effort to provide sufficient seating, particularly in the rush hours when services were stretched to such an extent that it was difficult to cope with the crowds. This problem was made worse by the adamant refusal of the police to allow standing passengers on any public service vehicle running on the streets. There was also a difficulty regarding the operation of services through Kingsway Subway which, at this time, could only accommodate single deck cars, each carrying no more than a maximum of 36 passengers. Due to the method of signalling employed, the service was restricted to some extent and the only way that the Council could overcome the problem was by operating trains of two cars, or by the use of trailers.

Powers had been obtained by the LCC to enable trailers to be operated for works purposes only between the hours of 10 p.m. and 6 a.m. and this was written into the LCC Tramways Statutory Rules and Orders, 1907 (No. 646) for the Northern System. There were, however, no powers to use trailers in any other way on any other part of the system.

The Coupled Cars Experiment

In early correspondence between the LCC, the Board of Trade and the Metropolitan Police in January 1906, it was made clear that the

Police had a rooted objection to the working of trailer cars of any kind in London, stating "... the amount of space occupied on the roads ... is too great ... . Exceptionally, the subway trailers would be acceptable, but in this case, street running through the districts served would be necessary, which would cause problems".   The Chief Commissioner, Sir. E. N. Henry, then went on to say "... that the police will not license any vehicle more than 23 feet long or 7 feet 2 inches wide.   This includes tramway multiple unit operation.   It is suggested that the matter be referred to the Advisory Traffic Board which is just being constituted by Bill in Parliament".   An aside from Col. Yorke of the Board of Trade Railway Inspectorate reads "... in my view, the LCC have made a great mistake in not building the (Kingsway) Subway to take double-deck cars".

The discussion went on all through 1906, with the police still putting up objections, even though the Commissioner agreed that it was the Board of Trade who had the last word.   To this, Col. Yorke commented that "the police claim to have no control, but in view of their comments, (this is) unlikely".

Almost three years later, on 3rd March 1909, there was another meeting between the interested parties, at which the LCC again put forward the proposal of operating trailer cars, stating that these should not run between 10 a.m. and 4 p.m. and would only be used as rush-hour extras.   Rather surprisingly, the Commissioner agreed that, if the LCC made an application to run trailers on an experimental basis, he would be pleased to give it his consideration.

Following this, Mr. Fell reported to the Highways Committee on the design of a "trailer" car.   This was, in fact a two-car multiple unit, the motors and magnetic brake equipment of the leading car being controlled manually as usual, while those of the rear car (or "trailer") were controlled by means of electro-magnetically operated switches.   Quotations were obtained to enable one set of equipment to be ordered, the British Thomson-Houston Company Ltd. providing a suitable specification and fulfilling the order.

The Council made its application to the Board of Trade.   The comment of Col. Yorke on 3rd April is interesting; "Agreed (to the request). It is noted that the LCC say nothing about limiting the use of trailers to single deck cars.   I do not advocate the use of trailers where either car is double deck.   But when both are double deck, (this) might be allowed (experimentally at first) during rush hours - say - before 10 a.m. and after 5 p.m.

When the police were finally persuaded to reply, which they did on 25th May, they again objected on the grounds of congestion, adding also "... unless the number of cars is increased, the service provided would only be half as frequent.   Would also it be desirable to operate trailers if a speed of 16 m.p.h. was authorised?" (The LCC at that time were attempting to have the maximum spped raised).   The reply from Col. Yorke was quite sharp and to the point, when he said "... speed has nothing to do with it.   If anything, their use would seem to point to higher speeds, so that the obstruction element, suggested by the police, should be removed as quickly as possible".

Meantime, the Council had suggested that powers should also be given to run a double deck trailer on the Woolwich - Eltham route, as well as the experimental operation of a two-car single deck unit of the self-propelled type on the Tooting - John Carpenter Street route.   Quite unexpectedly, the police agreed, but stated (regarding the Tooting route) "But ... speeds of cars are very high and magnetic

brakes are liable to failure in damp or greasy conditions.." to which
Col. Yorke replied "not so, not as much as when mechanical brakes
are used .." After more protracted discussion, the experiment was
moved away from south London, when the Board of Trade authorised
and the police agreed, on 14th January 1910 that a two-car self-propelled
trailer set could be used on the Euston Road - Hampstead route via
Camden Town and Chalk Farm Road. The police however, declined
to take any responsibility for the decision, merely stating that, as
the Board of Trade had authorised the experiment, the Board must
be responsible for it, meaning of course, that the Board take all responsibility for any accidents which may occur.

An order was placed with the British Thomson-Houston Company
Ltd. in March 1910 for "control apparatus for subway cars 572 and
573", for which the company had provided the specification for a "con-
tactor control scheme for subway cars" to the LCC in February 1909.
In this system, both the cars took their traction supply independently,
so that each car had to have its own plough. This could have presented
problems, as the motorman would have had to have coasted long distances
through junction layouts and through "deads" in the track, or to have
switched off his controller twice when crossing any break in the conduit,
to avoid the likelihood of arcing at the plough collector shoes.

By December 1910, the two G-class single deck cars had been
fitted with the BT-H equipment for use as a coupled two-car set,
with brakes and all four motors able to be controlled from either end
of the set. The Westinghouse T2A controllers, suitably modified, were
retained. The cars were satisfactorily inspected by Col. Yorke on behalf
of the Board of Trade on 13th January 1911. They were put into service
between Euston Road and Hampstead on 17th January 1911, but not
for long as, on 1st February, the police refused to re-license car No. 572,
which had been in collision with a motor-bus on 27th January, when
the 'bus driver stopped his vehicle suddenly to avoid some children
who were playing in the roadway. The police claimed that the unit
was unable to be stopped quickly in such an emergency, and again
stated that, in their opinion, these vehicles should not be allowed on
the roads.

This argument continued right through March and well into April,
with the police still trying to coerce the Board of Trade into refusing
to authorise another experiment, which the Board declined to do, the
comment of the Board of Trade Inspector on the whole affair being
"... (it is) strange that the police should object to coupled cars when
traction engines towing two wagons each are commonplace ...". Col. Yorke
also commented that "the police seem determined to do all they can
to hamper the LCC Tramways traffic. I have just spoken to Mr. Fell
on the telephone and I understand that some members of the Highways
Committee have had an interview with the Commissioner (Sir. E. Henry)
on Wednesday last (5th April 1911) and after prolonged discussion,
agreed that a further experiment of one month should be made. I do
not know how the 'unit of co-efficient of obstruction' (stated by the
police as being introduced by the Board of Trade, but refuted by that
body) is arrived at by Sir. E. Henry, but I do not think that a compara-
tive table can be accepted as giving a correct view of the case so
far as tramcars are concerned".

"The Unit of Co-efficient of Obstruction" table was supposedly constructed by the Road Traffic branch of the Board of Trade but, as
stated, was rejected by the Railway Inspectorate. That it was used
by the Commissioner of Police as a yardstick for his purposes, there
can be no doubt and it is recorded that on one occasion he asked "that

it be treated as confidential, as it would be liable to some misunder-
standing otherwise". It was more than likely used as a measure to
enable the police to make comparisons for prosecution purposes.

The Unit of Co-Efficient of Obstruction Table

Trade Vehicles:		Passenger Vehicles:	
One-horse, fast	3	Electric Tram	10
One-horse, slow	7	Omnibus, Horse	5
Two horse, fast	4	Omnibus, Motor	3
Two-horse, slow	10	Cab, Horse	2
Motor, fast	2	Cab, Motor	1
Motor, slow	5	Carriage, Horse	2
		Carriage, Motor	1

No mention was made at all of Steam Traction Engines!

Resulting from the meeting of 5th April 1911 between Council representatives and the Commissioner of Police, a further period of
operation was agreed to. The cars were put back into service on 15th April
for one month, and ran daily excepting Sundays and Easter Monday,
until 13th May, when they were once again withdrawn. The LCC meantime, continued to press for a further extension, but it was not until
5th June that a reply from the Board of Trade was received. A further
three months operation was agreed to, but only between 7 and 9 a.m.
and after 7 p.m. The terms were so restrictive that it would have
been impossible for the LCC to do more than one journey each way
in the mornings, while the evening operations would have been such
that full use could not have been made of the car-set. The Council,
therefore, requested that running should be allowed up to 10 a.m.
and after 5 p.m. as before, and additionally between 12 noon and 3 p.m.
on Saturdays, but this was refused. Thus disheartened, the Highways
Committee came to the conclusion that the Board of Trade did not
appear to be favourably disposed to the operation of the coupled cars.
It is probably nearer the truth to say that the Board of Trade was
disenchanted with the attitude of the police, and was working behind
the scenes, in order to push the Council into taking the whole matter
to Parliament.

The Commissioner, meantime, was restating his views. He considered the results of running the coupled cars far from satisfactory.
He again said that the LCC Tramways were "classed by the Board
of Trade as the most obstructive vehicles in London"; to double the
length by coupling was liable to intensify congestion; the greater
weight would also render brake failure far more serious. For the same
reasons, he was also against the use of double-deck trailer cars. However, the LCC was still of the opinion that the operation of trailer
cars could be beneficial, especially in dealing with very heavy peak
loads at rush hours, deciding that, in the face of general hostility,
the only course was to seek Parliamentary powers in an effort to allow
the operation of trailers in London.

Throughout the period from 1911 until the summer of 1915, there
was almost continual dialogue between the police and the Board of
Trade and between the police and the London County Council over
this question, with the police always at odds with the other two, even
after Parliamentary sanction had been given to the Council to legally
allow the use of trailers. The police attitude only changed when the
problems associated with the Great War diverted their attention to
far more important matters, and after it was clearly seen that the
trailers were quite useful in safely moving the crowds. There was
no further mention of 'the unit of co-efficient of obstruction', either.

The London County Council (Tramways & Improvements) Bill, 1912
The Relevant Clause

The application for permission to run both trailer and coupled cars was contained in one clause of the London County Council (Tramways & Improvements) Bill, 1912, which read: "Notwithstanding anything to the contrary contained in any Act, Order, Bye-law or Regulation the Council may provide, maintain, work, and use trailer carriages and coupled carriages on any of their tramways". The Bill came before a Committee of the House of Commons under the chairmanship of Sir Luke White on 10th and 11th June 1912, when a number of witnesses were called by the promoter to support the case for trailer operation. The Council concentrated on the fact that trailer operation was more effective, economical, safer and a less obstructive method of dealing with rush hour traffic than running extra single cars.

Major Pringle, the Inspector for the Board of Trade, said that the Board was not opposed to the proposal within certain limits. They were not, however, in favour of running more than two cars in a coupled train, nor were they in favour of both cars being powered, but that there should be only one tractor car, with the trailer of lighter construction and preferably single decked. In the opinion of the Board, trailers should not be used on routes which had severe gradients or curves, or where the roadway was particularly narrow.

The Tramways Chief Officer, Mr. Fell gave evidence on behalf of the Council, in which he stated his arguments in favour of trailer working. These were that loading and unloading would be more rapid than with electric cars as, in the absence of a motorman, both rear and front platforms could be used for the purpose; the amount of road space occupied would be less for a car and trailer than for two electric cars, while obstructions at street crossings would be less pronounced; accidents would be fewer than with two separate cars as most accidents involved front-end collisions with other vehicles or with pedestrians; a crew of three would be required instead of four, while the maintenance and accommodation costs for trailers would be less than for an equal number of electric cars.

Mr. H. E. Blain, General Manager of West Ham Corporation Tramways and President of the Municipal Tramways Association described the brake test, which had been carried out on Dog Kennel Hill, Dulwich with the aid of a converted horse-car coupled to an M-class car. He said that "when the coupling had been slipped ... the car stopped absolutely within a foot or two ...". The ex-horse car, No. 585 had been reconstructed as an open-top double deck trailer at the Central Repair Depot during the winter of 1910/1911 and was brought out from the Depot after completion by car No. 1700.

The main opposition at this time came from the Omnibus Association, but to no effect as the Committee approved the clause, although this was subject to the design of the trailers being approved by the Board of Trade; that not more than two cars be run as a coupled unit (unless specially approved by the Board); that the motor unit be on the front car only; that routes and times of operation of the trailers be approved by the Board.

Having been accepted by the House of Commons, the Bill then went to the Lords. Opposition now came mainly from the Roads Improvements Association, which sent a letter to all Members of the House putting its objections to trailer operation. It mentioned the problem of shunting at termini, which had not so far been discussed. Lord Montagu of Beaulieu, a member of the Council of the Roads Improvements

Association, attempted to obtain the withdrawal of the trailer clause at the third reading of the Bill, but was not successful.

The London County Council (Tramways & Improvements) Act, 1912, (2 & 3 Geo. 5, Ch. cvi), Section 29 gave the Council powers to use trailer cars and coupled cars, of types approved by the Board of Trade. However, additional restrictions were included, among them the power of the Board of Trade to refuse or revoke approval for the use of trailers. Operation was only to be on the southern system, which included the lines across Battersea, Vauxhall, Westminster and Blackfriars Bridges and lines north of the Thames between Vauxhall and Victoria, along Beaufort Street to Kings Road, Chelsea and along Victoria Embankment. Their use was restricted to specified times and on such routes as approved by the Board, and that cars and trailers should not stop directly outside railway station entrances except for picking up or setting down passengers, and then for the absolutely minimum time required. Lastly, the trailers and tractor cars were to be fitted with special brakes to a design approved only by the Board of Trade.

The First Trailer Cars

Despite the continuing obstructive attitude of the Metropolitan Police who, even though the Act of Parliament gave clear authority to the Council to operate trailers, were still arguing over the terms of the Act, the Council was actively pursuing the planning policy it had formulated with regard to obtaining a fleet of trailer cars and operating them to the best advantage.

One horse car had been adapted, as previously mentioned, and this became the basis for the conversion of another seven of the last series of horse cars purchased by the North Metropolitan Tramways Company at the turn of the century. Agreement was reached on 13th October 1912 that work should proceed on these cars, at an expected cost of about £1,400, which was to include further modifications

One of the original eight trailer cars stands outside Clapham car shed in December 1913. The picture shows the truck detail and the open platforms at each end of the car. *(Courtesy: LCC/LT Museum)*

to the prototype car. At the same time, another £200 was allocated for design work for a series of purpose-built trailer cars. All work was to be carried out by the Tramways Department at the CRD. It was also agreed to fit towing equipment to 25 electric cars to act as tractors for the trailers.

The horse car bodies, after a thorough overhaul, were equipped with standard electric car fittings, such as route indicators, electric light fittings, etc. Extended canopies were provided, fitted with higher decency panels and safety rails all round the open top deck. The platforms were lengthened and the direct staircases mounted moved forwards to allow for passenger entry and exit at both ends. The bodies, numbered T 1 to T 8 were then mounted upon light, strong underframes made up of standard rolled steel sections, these being extended right through to support the platforms. The four-wheeled truck frame assembly carried standard electric car axles in SKF ball-bearing axleboxes, the whole unit supporting the car body through elliptical spring-packs. Specially shaped fenders were fixed to the whole length of the frame and carried round both ends of the car at roughly the shape of the body outline.

The automatic brake gear, which had been specially designed, was used on the eight converted horse cars and, proving to be successful, was subsequently used on the 150 purpose-built trailers, which are later described. This mechanism was built with the prime object of ensuring the safety of the trailer and its occupants, should the coupling break while the unit was travelling on an up gradient. A set of inside-hung brake blocks was fitted which were normally forced on to the wheels by the action of a pair of powerful springs in compression, carried directly between the two beams.

When the tractor car exerted a pull on the spring-loaded extensible drawbar, the movement was transmitted through a chain fixed to its end, and anchored to a cast-iron drum keyed to a rotatable shaft at its other end, upon which a smaller chain drum carrying a double purchase chain was fixed. The movement actuated this drum and chain, which in turn moved a sway bar which, when rotated through a small arc of a circle, drew the two brake beams together by means of an equalising chain, thereby releasing the brake blocks from the wheels. The greater the pull on the drawbar, the further away the brake blocks were moved away from the wheels.

Conversely, when the tractor car slowed down, the effort exerted on the drawbar was reduced, allowing the bar to resume its normal position slowly. This, in turn, allowed the trailer car brakes to be progressively applied, preventing "snatching" of the braking gear and, at the same time, helping to prevent the trailer from making contact with the motor car at the buffing beams.

To enable the car to be moved, such as in a backing operation, or when it was necessary for service reasons in the car shed, provision was made to release the brakes by inserting an ordinary point lever into a socketted quadrant mounted beneath the platform, through a special slot in the platform floor. Movement of the lever towards the body of the car served to release the brakes by rotating the chain drum shaft of the brake gear. In order that the car should not be operated in service with the brakes in the "off" position, the shape of the lever slot was so arranged that the lever could only be withdrawn when the releasing quadrant was in the normal, "brake on" position; and, as the lever when in its "brake released" position obstructed the entrance to the car, it was most unlikely that it would be allowed to remain there. When in this position, the lever was held by a detent, and could only be released by momentarily pressing forward on the lever, and at the same time, depressing a pedal-operated pawl, which released the detent. Once in the normal "brake on" position, the lever could then be lifted out of its socket.

The springs between the brake beams were enclosed in cast-iron spring boxes consisting of a cylinder and plunger. The relative position of the two parts indicated the pressure being applied on the brakes, while calibrated index plates were attached to each side of each cylinder, so that the pressure could be read. The initial pressure, which would need to be sufficient to hold the trailer on the steepest of gradients could be pre-set, and periodic adjustments could be made to compensate for wheel and brake block wear. In deference to Board of Trade Regulations, the standard tramcar handbrake was also fitted, which operated on a second set of brake blocks fitted in the customary position around the wheel treads.

Automatic couplings designed by Walter Ingram and made by the ABC Coupler Co. Ltd. were fitted. The trailer portion of the coupling contained a shackle which engaged a rotating disc-hook in the tractor portion. As the shackle entered the tractor portion of the coupling, the disc-hook was rotated into the locked position, in which it was held by a spring-loaded locking bar. To uncouple the car, the locking bar was pulled, allowing a gravity latch on the disc-hook to fall, keeping the locking bar in the uncoupling position while the motor car moved away from the trailer. As the shackle was withdrawn, it pulled the disc-hook back into its uncoupled position ready for the next coupling operation.

Simple collapsible side gates were provided to prevent the passage of pedestrians between the two vehicles. These removable accessories were provided with two hooks at either end, which fitted into suitable lugs mounted on posts bolted to the platform dashplates of both tractor and trailer cars. They proved to be quite unsuitable for heavy duty and were very soon replaced with a more substantial item, of the "Bostwick" pattern.

In December 1912, it was stated that extra expenditure on the horse-car conversion had been £458 on the capital account and £426 on maintenance, mainly brought about by having to replace parts of the cars found to be not up to standard.

The First Operations

Board of Trade approval was required for the routes upon which trailers would be allowed to work, sanction for operation on the Abbey Wood, Woolwich and Eltham routes being given to the Council on 20th March 1913 for a three-month trial period, the hours of working to be 6 to 10 a.m. and 4.30 to 11.30 p.m. on Mondays to Fridays; 6 to 10 a.m. and 12 noon to 2.30 p.m. on Saturdays and 4 p.m. to midnight on Sundays and public holidays.

There is the possibility that these routes were used to conduct the experiment, as they were easily accessible from the Central Repair Depot at Charlton. As the lines were also still totally isolated from other standard gauge lines of the Council and, as the Eltham route had a convenient turning loop at the Woolwich end, all phases of operation could be undertaken, including the use at Abbey Wood of a stub-ended trailer shunt which was being provided at the extreme end of the line.

After the first trial period, with the first of the trailers in service on the Eltham route from 20th March and the second from 24th March, the Council asked the Board of Trade for an extension. This was granted for a period of three months up to 11th July. The third trailer was put into service on 10th May, where it joined the other two working on the Abbey Wood to Woolwich route. Subsequently, with a further extension until 31st October, these three cars worked in and around Woolwich before being transferred away to Clapham.

The Chief Officer, reporting on the experiment said that it was extremely satisfactory, stating that "the cars proved very useful in dealing with traffic in busy periods". When the Woolwich Borough Council was approached, the reply was that the Council had not observed any undue interference with other road traffic on either route. The whole operation was however, the subject of police objection. The extension of the experiment, agreed to by the Woolwich Borough Council, was also objected to by the police. The Highways Committee recorded that it was not impressed with the police attitude.

Trailers on the Merton Services

On 5th May 1913, the LCC applied to the Board of Trade for permission to run trailers on the Merton and Victoria Embankment circular services Nos. 2 and 4, feeling that experience should be gained by working over conduit track and on a pair of long, busy trunk routes. As at Woolwich, there was only need to uncouple trailers for reversing purposes at one end of the line. At the same time, authority was given to equip another ten electric cars with trailer coupling gear.

Approval was given on 7th June 1913, to allow operation for a period of three months, the hours of working to be 6 to 10 a.m. and 4.30 to 11.30 p.m. on Mondays to Fridays; 6 to 10 a.m. and 12 noon to 12.30 a.m. (midnight) on Saturdays; 4 p.m. to midnight on Sundays and 10 a.m. to 12.30 a.m. (midnight) on Bank Holidays. The trailers were brought into service on 27th July 1913. At the beginning of October, the LCC asked that the experimental period be extended, which again was granted, as from 11th November "for the present".

Next, on 29th October 1913, the Council asked the Board of Trade for authority to work trailers over the whole of the south side system. Again, on the 18th November the police objected. The Council followed this up on 18th December 1913 with a request for authority to operate all-night and workman cars, using trailers, but the police objected, as they did when the LCC asked to be allowed to use trailers at all times except on Mondays to Fridays between 10 a.m. and 4 p.m., and Sundays between 12.30 a.m. and 10 a.m.

When Major Pringle discussed the police objections on 27th March 1914, he stated that, in his opinion:-
1. The existing traffic "difficulties" were exaggerated
2. The complaints about (a) Complicated terminal shunting,
   (b) Increase in obstruction and danger and increase in weight causing "difficulties" were nothing new and not substantiated.
One month later, on 27th April, the police objected to the wording of Major Pringle's letter to the Commissioner!

The original eight trailers continued to operate on services 2 and 4 until 1915, when they were joined by the first of the 150 new purpose-built vehicles on 25th January and five more by 29th March, together with three more shedded at Abbey Wood, two of which were destined to

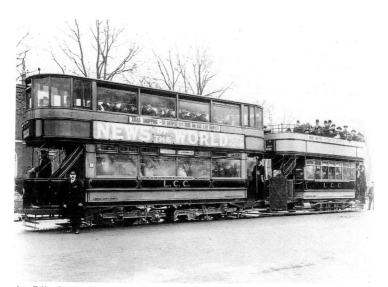

An E/1 class car, towing one of the original trailer cars, seen in a posed picture. The trellis safety gate between the two cars can be clearly seen. (Courtesy: L T Museum, U13564)

work on the service to Waterloo Bridge (Savoy Street Strand), the other on the Eltham service.

It has been stated that when the Brush-built trailers were put into service, the ex-horse cars were transferred to Evelyn Street depot for use on service 70, but this cannot be substantiated, although it is quite feasible, as this depot was specifically opened to house trailer cars on 31st August 1916. Prior to that date, they would either have remained at Marius Road, where all trailers for the Clapham services were then housed, or they would have been taken to Camberwell to work on the circular service 84 between New Cross Gate and Victoria Embankment, or else once again to Abbey Wood.

The Brush Trailers

In the closing weeks of 1913, Mr. Fell was considering whether to convert more horse cars into trailers to the same standard as was achieved with Nos. T 1 to T 8, or whether to recommend the purchase of new purpose-built vehicles. In December, he reported on the cost of ordering a fleet of 150 new cars which, it was estimated would cost £67,500 for normal heavy construction or £75,000 for specially made light weight vehicles. Additionally, a further £5,250 was estimated for equipping 200 electric cars with drawgear for towing the trailers. He was then asked by the Highways and Finance Committees of the Council, whether horse cars should be used, to which he replied that, out of the remaining vehicles of this type, only eleven had been found to be sound enough to be re-used, eight for trailers and three for petrol-electric cars. So far as the economies of operation were concerned, he said that a trailer car would show considerable savings over an electric car during its life, quoting an approximate figure of £335 to £340.

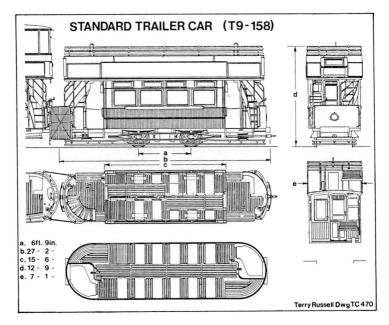

STANDARD TRAILER CAR   (T9-158)

a. 6ft. 9in.
b. 27 - 2 -
c. 15 - 6 -
d. 12 - 9 -
e. 7 - 1 -

Terry Russell Dwg TC 470

Tenders for the supply of 150 trailer cars and 200 sets of towing gear for electric cars were called for and considered by the Highways Committee in July 1914.   The Brush Electrical Engineering Company Ltd. quoted the lowest price at £74,200, which was accepted.   Brush in turn sub-contracted the complete undergear to Hurst, Nelson & Company Ltd., who, incidentally, had tendered the next lowest bid at £80,750.

The new cars, numbered T 9 to T 158 were also of double deck open top design, but with more substantially built bodywork, including heavier section end pillars, between which were fitted four equally spaced full-drop windows on either side of the car, each of which had a single opening ventilator light above.   The body sides were of vertical matchboard construction, which gave sufficient width inside for transverse seating to be installed.   Large destination blind boxes, with space for two-line blinds in the lower half and service numbers above were also installed.   Seating accommodation was for 18 passengers inside, on six sets of two- and-one transverse seats, and 30 upstairs on six sets of two-and-two transverse seats, together with end benches, each seating three, above each nearside rear entrance.   Portable collapsible side gates as later employed on the original cars were supplied, in order to prevent people walking between the car sets.   There were also some minor differences in undergear design, particularly with regard to the positions of several of the components.   Axleboxes, as specified for the original batch were of SKF ("Skefko") double ball-bearing pattern.   ABC Couplers were again used on all cars.

Main dimensions were:-

Length over the couplings	28 ft.	10 in.
Length over the fenders	27 ft.	2 in.
Length of body	15 ft.	6 in.
Width over the guard rails	6 ft.	10 in.

Total height	13 ft.	2 in.
Height from rail level to floor of upper deck	9 ft.	
Height inside the car	6 ft.	2 ¾ in.
Wheelbase	6 ft.	9 in.
Diameter of wheels	2 ft.	7 ¾ in.

Electric lighting was provided to the trailer by means of a "jumper" cable, which was plugged into a suitable socket, one of which was fitted at each end of the tractor car. Communication between trailer car conductor and his counterpart on the motor car was by means of bell signals. On the experimental vehicles, the bell on the trailer was used at first (later modified) as the signal to the conductor on the electric car, but on the main fleet, an extended bell rope, connected between the front of the trailer and the back bell of the tractor, gave more positive information to the conductor of the electric car, who then would give the appropriate signal to the motorman on the front bell. The trailer car conductor was also provided with a special whistle shaped rather like a miniature hunting horn, which gave a distinctive sound, in order that the tractor car conductor and the motorman, would be aware that the other conductor was on the upper deck of the trailer.

In order to comply with Police Regulations a large oil lamp was installed at each end of the trailer car, mounted above the rear nearside bulkhead window at either end. In this case, because of this Regulation, the Council was able to assist itself and the Brush Company, by supplying 300 pairs of burners and collars for signal lamps at the rate of 3/- a dozen pairs, plus 10%, together with 300 lamp glasses for the trailer cars at 12/6½d per gross plus 10%, all from surplus ex-horsecar stock parts.

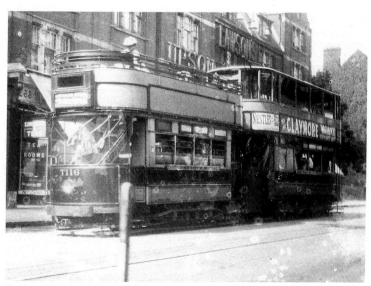

Trailer T116 behind an E/1 tractor car on service 18 in Streatham High Road, just north of St. Leonard's Church, photographed in 1917.
(The late O. J. Morris, courtesy: Lens of Sutton)

Delivery of the new trailer cars should have commenced in December 1914 but, due to the increasing problem of the supply of materials brought about by the Great War, together with the emphasis on war work for which the factories of Britain were becoming involved, and the inability of the railways to carry ever-mounting goods traffic, it was inevitable that delays would occur.

The first one, T 9, made its appearance in January 1915, to be followed by several more during the next couple of months, but soon afterwards an unforeseen problem occurred when operating in crushed conditions. A large number of passengers standing near or on the back platform of a trailer whilst awaiting to alight tended to cause the front end to rise and the fender plate to attempt to ride up over the rear buffer of the tractor car, occasionally causing damage to the vehicles. To overcome this, each trailer had extended steel plates fitted in front of the original buffers. Each was affixed by means of three strong springs in compression which were fitted inside simple cages welded to the backs of the fenders. The extended plate was high and deep enough to prevent over-riding and, at the same time being sprung, acted as a more efficient buffing device.

Delays in deliveries of the new vehicles continued into 1916 when, by March of that year, only 112 out of the 150 were in service in London. This was increased to 130 in August, and by October it is believed that all had been delivered. The Board of Trade Annual Return from the LCC shows that by March 1917 all were accounted for.

Operations

During the period of trailer-car working, the vehicles saw service on certain selected routes only. The largest number of them operated on the car services between Tooting and Victoria Embankment (2/4), some on the Norbury and Streatham to Embankment services via Brixton (16/18), a few on the various services which worked at times between New Cross Gate and the Embankment (64 and/or 84), several on the Greenwich to London Bridge service (70), and the remainder on the Abbey Wood to Embankment (40) and Woolwich to Eltham (44) services. A reference dated 27th April 1915, shows that authority was specifically granted by the Board of Trade to the Council, to allow the operation of trailers at all times between Rainton Road Charlton and Abbey Wood during the continuance of the War, also that trailer cars be allowed out all day on the other south side services.

Accommodation for the trailers was provided at Marius Road Balham for those working on the Clapham services, where specially adapted petrol-electric tractor cars were used to haul the trailers in and out of the depot. A section of Streatham car shed was used for the Streatham services, where two C cars, Nos. 293 and 294 were employed to undertake shunting duties, while at Camberwell, for use in that area, the tractor cars dealt with depot movements. For the Woolwich and Eltham services, the electric cars at Abbey Wood could conveniently deal with the shunting. The ex-horsecar depot at Evelyn Street Deptford was specially re-opened for trailers on 31st August 1916, and to get the cars in and out of this depot, two horses were provided by Messrs. Thomas Tilling to undertake the task, at a cost of £145 per horse per annum. In June 1917, this was reduced to £127, being again reduced to £102 in 1919. Forage for the two animals cost £78 per annum. During the spring of 1919, the depot was equipped with twin overhead wiring to enable an electric tractor to be used instead of the horses, although it is still not clear what type of vehicle was employed.

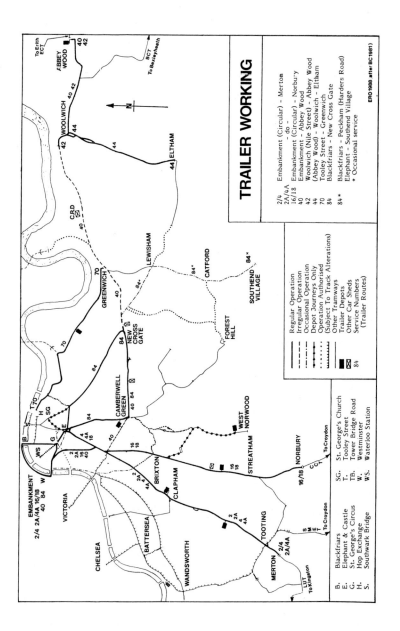

TRAILER WORKING

2/4	Embankment (Circular) - Merton
2A/4A	- do -
16/18	Embankment (Circular) - Norbury
40	Embankment - Abbey Wood
42	Woolwich (Nile Street) - Abbey Wood
44	(Abbey Wood) - Woolwich - Eltham
70	Tooley Street - Greenwich
84	Blackfriars - New Cross Gate
84 *	Blackfriars - Peckham (Harders Road)
	Elephant - Southend Village
	* Occasional service

ERO 1988 after BC 1981

Regular Operation
Irregular Operation
Occasional Operation
Depot Journeys Only
Operation Authorised
  (Subject To Track Alterations)
Other Tramways
Trailer Depots
Other Car Sheds
Service Numbers
  (Trailer Routes)
84

B. Blackfriars   SG. St. George's Church
E. Elephant & Castle   T.   Tooley Street
G. St. George's Circus   TB. Tower Bridge Road
H. Hop Exchange   W.   Westminster
S. Southwark Bridge   WS. Waterloo Station

331

At the beginning of 1922 the LCC took delivery of the first of 125 new cars of class E/1, 50 of which (Nos. 1727-1776) were by Messrs. Hurst Nelson/MetroVick, the remainder (Nos. 1777-1851) by Brush/English Electric. The Brush cars (Nos. 1777-1851) were eventually to take up residence at Clapham shed, working on the long route to Wimbledon on services 2 and 4, while the Hurst Nelson batch went to Streatham to work on services provided from that shed.

The 1922 Report of the Tramways Manager to the Highways Committee referred to the fact that in May 1922, there were 35 trailers in use on the Merton rush hour services numbered 2A and 4A. On the Norbury services in rush hours there were 36 trailers, pulled by all cars on the services.

On 18th May 1922, Mr. Fell was asked to report on the general use of trailer cars. He commented that, on the through services to Tooting, Merton and Wimbledon, which had been recently introduced, trailers were only used as far as Longley Road, and then only in rush hours on services 2A and 4A, due to the refusal of the members of Wimbledon Council to allow trailer working in their area. Thus, the first seeds of doubt as to the real economy in the opeation of trailers was sown in the minds of the Highways Committee of the LCC.

Decline and Disposal

In order to determine whether the use of trailer cars was as cost effective as the use of electric cars alone, a number of tests were undertaken on the route to Tooting during November and December 1922. During the six days, 13th to 18th November, a close watch was kept on the class E/1 cars hauling trailers, after which, on 20th, the trailers were withdrawn. Sufficient powered cars to convey a similar number of passengers to that carried by cars and trailers were then put into service and, on 6th December a further series of tests commenced which lasted another six days, which produced quite startling results. During the second period, 21,093 more passengers were carried than during the trailer test period, with a corresponding increase of £164. 7.10d in receipts. Moreover, the journey time, using cars without trailers was six minutes less than when using them, while the time entailed in cars standing at Longley Road to wait for a short-journey car to turn, was reduced to under 15 seconds from the considerably higher time of something in excess of one minute.

Resulting from this, Mr. Fell recommended that trailers be withdrawn from the services working on both the Tooting and Norbury routes. So far as the Tooting route was concerned, an all-electric car service had already commenced on 20th November, and trailers were never re-instated. He also said that serious reconsideration should be given generally to this type of operation.

Further tests took place between 8th and 14th March 1923 on the Streatham and Norbury route, when trailers were used and between 22nd and 28th March, when they were replaced by an all-electric car service. The result was a conclusive victory for electric car-only operation, as it was shown that during the test period with trailers, 178,386 passengers were carried with receipts at £1,431. 3. 9d, while in the period when no trailers were run, 192,534 passengers travelled and £1,521. 5. 3d was taken in fares. The trailer cars were not re-introduced upon the Streatham lines. The secondary effect of this withdrawal was that all services working along these lines of route were also speeded up to some degree.

On 19th April 1923, the Council announced that as an experiment, all trailer services were to be withdrawn from any service using Victoria Embankment, which can only really mean that it was quite feasible that some were still in use on the New Cross and Camberwell services to the Embankment.

A special new car shed for housing trailers was under construction on a site at the top of Brixton Hill, about half a mile north of the car shed at Streatham. Due to the change in policy, it was decided that the building was to be used to accommodate electric cars, the General Manager implying that the additional room could be put to good use. Meantime, some of the trailers taken out of service were housed temporarily in the, as yet, incomplete building, with the remainder at Balham, Camberwell and Evelyn Street, Deptford depots.

The one problem, however, in housing electric cars in the new shed was that the rails had not been electrically bonded, and no conduit track had been installed. So that electric cars could use the facilities, double overhead wiring, with one wire electrically positive and the other negative, was installed. Cars of the 1922 series, which were fitted with two trolley poles and the necessary change-over switches, were eventually allocated to Brixton Hill, commencing service from there on 6th March 1924.

In the LCC Annual Report dated 31st March 1921, it was stated that 119 trailers were in stock, while in the 1922 Report, this figure was down to 107.

The last stronghold of trailer working, between Greenwich and London Bridge via Rotherhithe, finally succumbed to total working with electric cars on 17th April 1924. By this time, there had already been considerable discussion on ways and means of disposing of the fleet, none of them very promising. The General Manager had considered whether it would be a worthwhile project in converting the trailers into electric cars, but decided against this step.

It is known that trailers Nos. T139, 140, 148 and 155 were at Camberwell shed in 1923, and Nos. T94, 133, 143, 146, 154 and 156 were there in 1924. However, Nos. T143, 146 and 156 were transferred to New Cross sometime in 1924. Similarly, Nos. T66, 86, 89 and 90 were at New Cross in 1923, while T98, 109, 111, 114 and 115 were there in 1924. In the case of the New Cross cars, it may have been that they were actually shedded at Evelyn Street depot, Deptford, but came under the control of the New Cross Superintendent. All these cars were de-licensed from either Camberwell or New Cross.

In May 1924 it was decided to put them all up for sale and advertise in various journals, both at home and abroad, and also to send particulars of the vehicles to about 50 possible purchasers, which however, met with virtually no response. In the meantime, the Council decided to dispose of as much of the spare parts stores as was possible, followed on 17th July by the Highways Committee authorising Mr. Fell to dismantle parts of the cars in order to obtain some spare parts for the electric car fleet, and to make the remainder of the bodies, etc. available to the Chief Officer for Stores for disposal on the best terms. The depot at Evelyn Street was nominated as disposal point. Again, advertisements were placed in certain journals, which resulted in the sale of some of the material, including 45 complete "Skefco" wheel bearings, which went back to the manufacturer for £4. 10s per bearing, less reconditioning costs, if any, with some more of these going to the LCC Chief Engineer for £3. 10s each, for use in another department within the Council. Several complete bodies were sold in October, one at £4.10s and four others at £5 each, but it was left to Messrs. Fielder Bros. of 189 Balham High Road, to make an offer for the rest of them at £4 each, which was accepted.

A number of the Hurst Nelson trailer bodies have survived, with one, T 131 now in "kit" form, preserved by the London County Council Tramways Trust, while another has been acquired by the East Anglia Transport Museum with the intention of eventually restoring it. A third, T 86 is still in existence and it is hoped that it might be restored by the LCCTT, using the running gear from T 131 to complete the work. The whereabouts of several more are known, and it surprising that any of these unusual wooden bodied vehicles have lasted for so long.

Regarding the fate of the ex-horse cars, little is known of the movements of these after the purpose-built vehicles were brought into use. It is believed that these, together with a few of the main series were transferred to Evelyn Street depot at Deptford, where they may have been used on the local service between Greenwich and London Bridge. It is known that one or two were broken up in Rye Lane depot in 1920-21, and there may have been more. On the other hand, it is understood that a few remained at Abbey Wood and were used from time to time on services in that area. It is recorded that one, T8 was kept at Abbey Wood car shed, in use as a store.

"The Marius Road Shunt"

The following description of the method of dealing with the trailers as they were brought into and taken out of service at Marius Road Depot, Balham was witnessed and recalled by Frank E. Dix and published as part of the text of the L R T A booklet.

Marius Road depot had been originally built to house horse cars but, as described elsewhere, was brought into use as an electric car shed for a time in 1903-05. For a number of years afterwards, it was used as a store, but the tracks and traverser pit remained. On the introduction of trailer operation, and with minimal re-arrangement of the tracks in the depot yard, the depot was again brought into use on 1st September 1915.

The shed had six roads, each of a length to take seven or eight trailers, making a total potential capacity of up to 48 vehicles. As two of the tractor "tugs" (of the P1-P3 series, adapted for the purpose) occupied spaces, there were in reality, probably no more than 44 or 45 trailers housed in the depot. A seventh track ran along the outside of the building on the south side, extending from the traverser (which had been re-erected) alongside the depot wall.

There were two passing loops on the entrance road, one round the traverser, the other about half-way between the traverser and the gates. The traverser loop had spring-loaded points, but the other had loose tongues, which remained in the place that they were set by a passing vehicle. In this way, the road was set for the return of the tractor and trailer.

The "tug" driver always operated his charge from the end nearest the road, irrespective of which way he was travelling, which no doubt enabled him to keep an eye on the trailer coupling as well as looking out for other traffic on the road. Other staff consisted of the traverser driver, one man in the depot, together with the trailer conductor and the part-time services of the tractor-car crew.

On a typical summer Saturday afternoon in 1916, just after one o'clock, the first of the rush-hour trailers would be coming off service, to be followed by many of the others at about two-minute intervals for the next hour or so. The two "tugs" were usually positioned side by side on the "halfway" loop, while the traverser was standing at the entrance track waiting for its first trailer.

The first to come in were attached to cars returning from Merton and, as soon as the car and trailer set appeared, one of the "tugs" would move off the loop and move down to the edge of the pavement. Exit tracks were trailing to the main line and had spring-loaded points which were always set for the depot. The unit would over-run the depot connection and stop with the back end of the trailer about one car length past the points, the trailer conductor applying the brake immediately the unit came to a stand. He would then get down from his platform, ready to couple the trailer up to the "tug", which had moved out as soon as the trailer had passed.

At the same time, the crew of the tractor car were busy uncoupling the trailer safety gates and swinging them into the trailer platform, after which the motorman went to his controls, while the tractor car conductor operated the release handle of the towing bar and advised the "tug" driver (usually with a wave of his hand) that the trailer was free from the tractor. By this time, the trailer conductor had released the handbrake of his car and, almost immediately the "tug" and trailer disappeared into the depot, leaving the tractor car to be driven on its journey to London. As soon as the "tug" and trailer had passed through the half-way loop, the second "tug" moved out to the pavement, ready for the next unit to arrive.

When a "tug" and trailer reached the traverser, the conductor un-coupled the vehicles and the "tug" was driven away to the end of the outside track where it was reversed, being then driven, via the outside loop, to its standing place on the half-way loop to await the return of the other "tug" with another trailer. Meantime, the traverser man had moved the machine sideways to the required depot road, where he, the trailer conductor and the depot duty man pushed the vehicle to its resting place in the depot.

To bring the trailer cars out for service, the reverse procedure was enacted, with the selected trailer being pushed to the traverser, the "tug" then coupling to it when it arrived at the end road, pushing it to the half-way loop, to stand until required. It was then pushed out to the road, where it was coupled to its tractor car, after which the "tug" returned to collect the next trailer, The whole operation took less than a minute to perform.

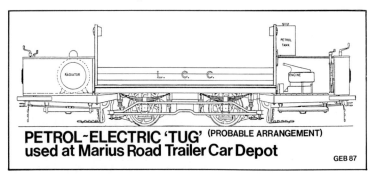

PETROL-ELECTRIC 'TUG' (PROBABLE ARRANGEMENT)
used at Marius Road Trailer Car Depot

GEB 87

Trailer Cars Taken Out Of Service, Final Dates

Trailer No.	Date Delicensed	Last Known M S C No.	Trailer No.	Date Delicensed	Last Known M S C No.
1	22.03.19	64	56	20.03.17	4481
2	26.03.19	5140	57	23.04.21	3058
3	25.03.16	3315	58	13.01.23	4775
4	29.10.15	2422	59	20.12.19	2052
5	05.10.18	1983	60	Not Known	****
6	26.07.15	1127	61	18.04.23	5091
7	29.03.19	5744	62	16.12.22	5476
8	26.03.19	91	63	25.11.22	7220
9	04.06.21	5083	64	26.05.22	4884
10	21.01.22	6851	65	13.01.23	4394
11	14.01.22	3796	66	12.04.23	5184
12	26.05.22	6863	67	27.03.20	2391
13	02.07.23	4298	68	18.04.23	5328
14	02.12.22	6089	69	06.01.23	407
15	18.04.23	4476	70	18.04.23	6862
16	18.04.23	6758	71	18.04.23	1204
17	12.09.17	2780	72	13.01.23	6844
18	21.10.22	4221	73	07.02.20	5287
19	03.06.22	6824	74	18.04.22	6883
20	18.04.23	6447	75	06.03.21	326
21	18.02.22	6436	76	01.01.23	705
22	26.05.22	5544	77	18.04.23	525
23	21.01.22	1938	78	16.10.20	1719
24	26.05.22	2215	79	01.12.22	2796
25	02.06.22	1119	80	16.04.21	279
26	24.01.20	3097	81	20.10.22	6827
27	02.04.23	4334	82	21.01.22	72
28	20.12.19	2072	83	07.01.22	6151
29	02.06.22	4229	84	28.01.22	4379
30	18.04.23	6812	85	28.01.22	4394
31	02.06.22	4276	86	12.02.23	6021
32	25.09.20	319*	87	03.09.23	5754
33	18.04.23	3248	88	01.03.23	1879
34	18.04.23	6808	89	19.04.23	3768
35	25.11.22	4854	90	12.02.23	6342
36	02.06.22	4594	91	11.06.23	1390
37	12.02.23	4122	92	03.09.23	2616
38	02.12.22	4106	93	Not Known	****
39	09.01.20	1127	94	23.04.24	6814
40	Not Known	****	95	01.02.23	5457
41	21.10.22	3401	96	19.04.23	4985
42	18.04.23	5669	97	25.07.23	3220
43	26.05.22	1472	98	23.04.24	7372
44	17.12.21	3796	99	Not Known	****
45	01.02.23	6452	100	23.04.24	****
46	24.11.22	3121	101	26.06.20	594
47	26.05.22	1951	102	05.03.21	4122
48	13.06.19	3307	103	08.04.22	4122
49	23.04.21	829	104	09.07.23	6436
50	18.04.23	4379	105	01.03.23	5234
51	18.04.23	5545	106	17.04.20	4316
52	01.03.23	3097	107	18.03.22	5105
53	08.03.23	6183	108	16.05.23	279
54	18.04.23	5105	109	23.04.24	7369
55	01.01.23	72	110	16.07.22	3397

Trailer No.	Date Delicensed	Last Known M S C No.	Trailer No.	Date Delicensed	Last Known M S C No.
111	23.04.24	7370	135	21.11.23	1446
112	26.02.22	2011	136	18.02.22	5234
113	05.03.21	2032	137	18.08.20	1467
114	23.04.24	7368	138	04.09.20	1651
115	23.04.24	6020	139	05.06.23	829
116	12.07.23	1648	140	21.11.23	6814
117	04.03.23	2386	141	14.08.20	1979
118	01.10.23	806	142	24.06.23	1759
119	10.05.22	1537	143	23.04.24	2103
120	26.01.17	1286	144	26.06.20	2327
121	01.01.24	304	145	Not Known	****
122	14.05.22	5243	146	23.04.24	9597
123	10.06.23	1266	147	01.04.22	16
124	Not Known	****	148	02.07.23	704
125	08.07.22	5738	149	03.07.20	2053
126	08.10.23	4146	150	Not Known	****
127	06.09.23	1788	151	08.07.22	5398
128	21.08.20	704	152	04.03.23	5412
129	13.05.22	3326	153	01.07.22	2049
130	21.03.22	5526	154	23.04.24	1983
131	01.12.23	6897 (1)	155	05.11.23	2032
132	17.10.21	6758	156	23.04.24	2245
133	23.04.24	4980	157	08.07.22	1651
134	02.07.23	1481	158	22.02.22	1651

(1) Dismantled and preserved by the LCC Tramways Trust

Trailer cars Nos. 1 to 8, which were the original converted horse-cars, were disposed of by dismantling them at Rye Lane Depot. Many of the remainder were sold for other purposes, such as summer houses, sports ground pavilions and even living accommodation. Some of these were disposed of complete with underframes and wheelsets.

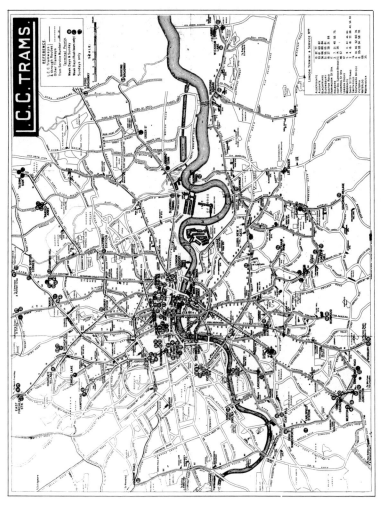

Chapter 26
Routes and Services
South, pre-1913

One of the difficulties in dealing with descriptions of routes and services, is the blurred distinction between the two when attempting to define the differences. In the case of tramways, the routes over which the cars travelled were clear enough, being from one end of the tracks to the other. However, on these routes there could be superimposed any number of services, working between various points on the routes.

Contrary to the practice adopted by the London Passenger Transport Board in 1933, who defined both the way and the means as "route" (and which is in common use today), the policy of the LCC Tramways was very different and was inherited from the tramway companies who provided services along "lines of route". Therefore, the terminology used in this work will reflect the methods used by the LCCT. The term "service" is used to describe the provision of the cars to run along the lines and designated by colour or number, while "route" will describe the place of a car in the service. In London, the tramway-mens' jargon declined "route" into "rowt" (as described by Mr. C. S. Dunbar as rhyming with "shout"), the "route" or "rowt" being identified by the use of a number displayed in white on a dark blue background on a small metal plate hung on the side of the car. As an example, a car taking route 3 on service 36 meant that the car worked on the Abbey Wood to Victoria Embankment via Blackfriars service and that it was in position No. 3 in the service, which determined its place in the duty schedule for the day and where the turning points would be during the course of its day's work.

The earliest electric car services covered the same routes which had been worked by horse cars and advantage was taken of using the same methods of identification on the new services that had previously prevailed. The main method used in daylight was that, in addition to new roller destination blinds installed at each end of the cars, the passing points were displayed around each end panel below the destination boxes. The same information was also provided on long wooden boards which were at first fitted into brackets mounted above the lower saloon windows, but soon found new resting places by being slotted into brackets fitted along the side panels of each car.

Indications given during the hours of darkness were quite different from the daylight arrangements, combining the destination blind indications with a system of coloured lights mounted above the indicator boxes. Unlike the horse car method, the new display made use of three lamps, each one mounted in a brass carrier and having a clear glass aspect covering it. By inserting coloured lenses behind the clear glass, a system of coloured indications was devised which it was considered would be sufficient to enable both the passengers and the pointsmen along the route to see clearly where the car was bound for. Four distinct tints were used, being Amber (A), Green (G), Ruby (R), Blue (B), and were augmented with Clear (W) and Blank (x).

339

Before long it became apparent to the management that the system had serious limitations, but nevertheless was retained until 1912. In the meantime, a numbering of "routes" had been published in 1908 in conjunction with the Official Tramways Guide issued on behalf of the Council in that year and again in 1909 and 1911, but so far as is known, the numbers were not displayed anywhere on the cars.

After a meeting of the Tramways Management Committee of the LCC on 9th July 1912 it was agreed that a numbering scheme was to be adopted which would be based on "services" rather than "routes". Arrangements were being made at this time to distribute free maps and guides of the system to the public and the numbering of services would make it easy to present a simple plan to intending passengers. Numbers were allocated in two blocks, odd for services north of the Thames and even for those on the south side, but even here, two departures were to be seen. The Subway Services were allocated north side numbers, although they travelled into the southern area, while the one service operating between Putney, Hammersmith and Scrubs Lane was allocated an even number, even though most of its route lay north of the river. The short sections of routes crossing the Thames bridges from the south side were all considered to be part of the southern system to be used only by south side services.

The first issue of the Map and Guide appeared in December 1912, with all the new numbers displayed in the text and on the map itself, this being the pattern which was to be followed thereafter at about three monthly intervals. Another publicity handout was distributed during the summer of 1913, giving information about the popular pastime of Band Performances at the many LCC Parks and Open Spaces. These free handbills were a feature of the public relations section of the LCC Tramways, in taking every opportunity to bring attention to the tramways services provided. Except for the period from the end of 1915 until the end of the Great War, a considerable amount of this material was made available. With the re-introduction of the issue of maps and guides after the war, the Council decided to issue them each Spring and Autumn (usually May and October or November), which arrangement continued for the remainder of the time that the LCC was the operator.

The occurrence of the Great War did not at that time reduce the level of service given to the public to any great extent, although a number of men left to join the military services. Expansion and extensions were still being considered, with the hope that "all will be well - the war will be over by Christmas". Of course, it was not, and some re-arrangements were made during 1915, including the withdrawal of several services, which are described in the following chapters.

Routes and Services, South Side, 1899-1913

Between 1st January 1899 and 2nd October 1906, six company owned systems were absorbed into the undertaking known as the London County Council (Southern) Tramways, with horse car services covering the area from Plumstead in the east to Wandsworth in the west. Details of all these are given in chronological order of acquisition with the service numbers subsequently allocated to them being shown in parentheses, even though, by the time that the numbers were brought into use, the electric services had been considerably altered and/or rerouted.

London Tramways Co. Ltd., absorbed 1st January 1899.
(2) Tooting - Westminster via Kennington
(4) Tooting - Blackfriars via "Elephant"

(16) Streatham - Westminster
(18) Streatham - Blackfriars
(24) Streatham - Old Kent Road "Lord Wellington" via St. George's Ch.
(30) Tooting - Waterloo Station
(36) East Greenwich - Blackfriars via Old Kent Road
(38) East Greenwich - Westminster via Old Kent Road
(40) New Cross Gate - Westminster via Walworth Road
(46) Rye Lane Peckham - Waterloo Station via Walworth Road
(52) Camberwell Green - Asylum Road via St. George's Ch. and
     Old Kent Road
(54) Camberwell Green - Vauxhall Bridge (south side)
(54) Vauxhall Bridge (north side) Victoria Station
(64) East Greenwich - Waterloo Station via Old Kent Road
(66) New Cross Gate - Blackfriars via Camberwell and "Elephant"

South Eastern Metropolitan Tramways Co., absorbed 1st April 1902.
(50) Rushey Green, Catford - South Street, Greenwich

South London Tramways Co., absorbed 22nd November 1902.
(12) North Street, Wandsworth - Hop Exchange via Battersea, Vauxhall
     and St. George's Church
(14) North Street, Wandsworth - Westminster via Battersea and Vauxhall
(26) East Hill - Westminster via Clapham Jcn and Vauxhall
(28) East Hill - Hop Exchange via Clapham Jcn, Vauxhall
     and St. George's Church
(32) Lavender Hill - Chelsea Bridge via Queens Road
(34) Clapham Junction - Chelsea Bridge via Battersea

London, Deptford & Greenwich Tramways Co., absorbed 7th July 1904.
(70) Deptford "Noah's Ark" - Tooley Street via Rotherhithe
(88) "Bricklayers Arms" - Rotherhithe "Red Lion" via Southwark Park
(90) Canal Bridge, Old Kent Road - Raymouth Road
     via Rotherhithe New Road
(92) "Bricklayers Arms" - St. James' Church via Spa Road

Woolwich & Southeast London Tramways Co. Ltd., absorbed 1st June 1905.
(40) Plumstead - East Greenwich via Woolwich and Charlton

London Southern Tramways Company, absorbed 2nd October 1906.
(78) West Norwood - Vauxhall via Herne Hill, Loughborough Jcn,
     Brixton and Stockwell
(80) Loughborough Jcn - Camberwell Green via Coldharbour Lane

Due to the rather complex order in which the first of the south
London horse tramways were reconstructed for electric operation,
in the main by the Council having taken the decision to convert whole
routes rather than concentrate on specific areas, the authors decided
to describe the services instituted in conjunction with early conversions
in the order in which they occurred rather than in a geographical manner,
but this arrangement would only hold good for the first conversions.
For subsequent descriptions, the area has been divided into "Inner South
London", "South-east London" and "South-west London". It will be
appreciated however, that some overlapping of this arrangement will,
of necessity take place. In all, it took the London County Council
something over eleven years to complete the electrification of the
horse tramways it inherited during the last years of the nineteenth
and first years of the twentieth centuries.

The reconstruction programme for tramways on the south side of the Thames became very complex from about the end of 1905, with work being progressively dealt with, both in the south-west and south-east suburbs. In order to make it easier to follow, the south-west districts will be dealt with first, followed by the south-east and the remainder of services which crossed the imaginary boundary between the two.

The Bridges to Tooting & Merton

With the commencement of electric working on 15th May 1903, three services were provided, working from Clapham and Balham sheds:-

a) Westminster Bridge and Tooting, Totterdown Street
   via Kennington Road and Clapham (2)
b) Blackfriars Bridge and Tooting, Totterdown Street
   via Elephant, Kennington Park Road and Clapham (4)
c) Waterloo Station and Tooting, Totterdown Street
   via Elephant, Kennington Park Road and Clapham (30)

On 28th August 1904, Balham shed closed and all cars were transferred to Clapham. Resulting from this, a staff car was put into service between Clapham and Tooting as from 3rd September. On 19th September, a new service was introduced between Southwark Bridge and "The Plough", Clapham via Southwark Bridge Road and "Elephant" (6) on weekdays only, but this was withdrawn between 9.55 a.m. and 4 p.m. as from 10th October 1904.

The first extension to the line occurred on 6th August 1905, when a short length of track was laid from the existing terminus at Totterdown Street, across the road junction at Tooting Broadway and for about 100 yards into Tooting High Street. This was done in conjunction with the insertion of the first part of a junction layout and crossing between Defoe Road and Mitcham Road, in advance of a new tramway to be laid in Garratt Lane. The three original services were extended to the new terminus.

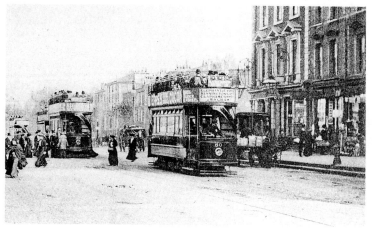

In this scene, taken shortly after the opening of the electric tramway, cars of class A pass at "The "Swan", Stockwell, each carrying goodly numbers of passengers.

When the Victoria Embankment line opened on 15th December 1906, the service terminating at Westminster Bridge Road (2) was extended over the new tracks and along Victoria Embankment to Blackfriars, John Carpenter Street.

The next extension took place on 13th October 1907, when new lines were opened between Tooting High Street and the County boundary, known in LCC parlance as Merton (Longley Road), and the Blackfriars service (4) was extended to the new terminus. This was followed on 5th December 1907 by the extension of the Southwark Bridge to "Plough" Clapham service (6) to Nightingale Lane, Clapham Common and, on 6th April 1908, again extended to Tooting.

On 30th May 1908, the Waterloo Station and Tooting service (30) was extended on Saturdays and Sundays to Merton. Six weeks later, on 11th July, an additional service was introduced between Victoria Station and Tooting via Stockwell (8), on Mondays - Fridays except between 10 a.m. and 4 p.m., and all day on Saturdays and Sundays. During the early summer of 1909, it was extended to Merton on Mondays to Saturdays. By May 1911, it had once again been altered to terminate at Tooting, and was working as a daily, all-day service, this change possibly having taken place when Blackfriars Bridge opened to tramway traffic.

A further change occurred on 11th May 1909, when the Westminster service (2) was extended to the County boundary on a daily basis, while on 14th September 1909 the new line across Blackfriars Bridge was opened, giving a through connection to services terminating at Blackfriars Road and John Carpenter Street. This was the beginning of the "circular services" around the Embankment loop (2/4).

The crew of class A car No. 91 pose for the camera in Tooting in 1904-05. The end destination plates were soon to be dispensed with in the interests of greater operational flexibility. (Courtesy: E. R. Oakley)

The Streatham and Tooting routes converged at Kennington Gate. An E class car gives way to a London-bound car of class C, despite the wrong destination display. *(Courtesy: A. D. Packer)*

THE INNER SOUTH LONDON AREA

Co-incidentally with the construction of the Tooting lines, crossing and junction special work was installed at Kennington Gate and Camberwell New Road. On the completion of trackwork in Camberwell New Road, a service commenced on 26th June 1903 between Camberwell Green, Kennington Gate and Blackfriars via "Elephant" (76). This was followed on 28th June by the commencement of another service from Camberwell Green to Westminster via Kennington Gate and Kennington Road (72). The reconstructed lines in Westminster Bridge Road, between the junction with Kennington Road and St. George's Circus had also been made available to electric cars as from 7th July, but horse cars continued to work between Westminster Bridge and Greenwich via Old Kent Road, until the services on that route were converted to electric traction early in 1904. This was one of the short lengths completed as part of the main contract, and used as required until a regular service was run upon it.

On the completion of track reconstruction in Harleyford Road and Kennington Oval between Vauxhall Bridge and Kennington Church, and with provision of a connection into the junction work at Kennington, a new service was introduced on 2nd August 1903 between Vauxhall and Camberwell Green (54). On the same date, with a short extension of the conduit tracks from the junction into Brixton Road as far as Handforth Road, a new electric/cable service was started, working between Westminster and Streatham Library via Kennington Road, Brixton and Brixton Hill (16), to be followed on 11th September by a service from Blackfriars, via "Elephant" and Kennington Park Road to Brixton and Streatham (18). The services to Streatham were, however, a failure, as described elsewhere, only lasting until 14th October when, once again the cable cars were brought out to work between Kennington and Streatham, while electric cars worked short services between Kennington (Handforth Road), Westminster and Blackfriars.

The next change came on 17th January 1904, when the long route between the Elephant & Castle and East Greenwich via New and Old Kent Road, New Cross Road, Deptford Broadway, Greenwich High Road and Trafalgar Road saw electric cars. Three services were

344

provided, replacing exactly the horse cars which had hitherto plied between Westminster Bridge (38), Waterloo Station (64), Blackfriars Bridge (36) and East Greenwich, all travelling by way of St. George's Circus and "Elephant & Castle", and all as daily services. This was followed on 24th January by the opening of electrified tracks between Camberwell Green and New Cross Gate via Peckham, so allowing a new through service to commence between Westminster Bridge and New Cross Gate via "Elephant", Walworth Road, Camberwell Green and Peckham (40) on a daily basis.

During February 1904, several more changes took place, the first being that the short journeys between Camberwell, Kennington and Blackfriars were replaced on 11th February by a new electric car service between New Cross Gate and Blackfriars via Peckham, Camberwell and "Elephant" (66), which itself had replaced a horse car service. One week later, on 18th February, the horse cars working between Waterloo Station and Rye Lane, Peckham (46) were replaced by a new electric car service which was extended to New Cross Gate. On 25th February, it was the turn of the horse car service working between Asylum Road, Old Kent Road, St. George's Church and Camberwell Green to be replaced by horse cars running between Old Kent Road "Lord Wellington", St. George's Church and Southwark Bridge (52H), and between Camberwell Green, St. George's Church and Hop Exchange via Southwark Bridge Road (60H). On 30th April 1904, the New Cross Gate to Westminster via Walworth Road and London Road (40) service which had commenced on 24th January, was diverted at the "Elephant" to run via the whole length of St. George's Road, thus avoiding the busy St. George's Circus junction.

Returning to the inner area, electric car operation was able to commence on the following sections as from 1st August 1904:-

St. George's Circus - Newington Causeway via Borough Road
"Elephant & Castle" - St. George's Church via Borough High Street
Newington Causeway - Southwark Bridge via Southwark Bridge Road
Hop Exchange - Southwark Bridge Road via Southwark Street

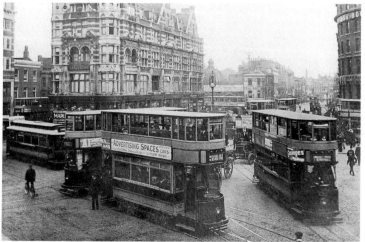

This animated scene at the "Elephant & Castle" illustrates the great importance of this junction as the hub of the south London network.
(Courtesy: LT Museum H16496)

Completion of these allowed the electric cars to use the whole length of track between the "Bricklayers Arms" and Southwark Bridge, resulting in a new service replacing the horse cars between Southwark Bridge and Asylum Road, Old Kent Road (52), together with one between Camberwell Green and St. George's Church via Walworth Road (60/1). Another service commenced running between Camberwell Green and Southwark Bridge via Walworth Road and the full length of Southwark Bridge Road (60/2) on 19th September.

Meanwhile, on 5th September, a service had commenced working between Water Lane, Brixton Hill and Southwark Bridge (10), while the service working between Southwark Bridge and Asylum Road, Old Kent Road, had been extended to New Cross Gate on 8th September. After a period of just over two months, the extension was withdrawn during slack hours as from 27th November.

Concurrently with the reconstruction work mentioned above, the tracks in Borough Road and Lancaster Street were dealt with, a new extension along the east end of Borough Road completing the links between all sections of the "inner area" around Newington ("Elephant & Castle") and St. George's Circus. It can therefore be seen from the foregoing that there were several sections of track upon which both horse and electric cars worked for a time, most noticeably the horse cars of the late South London Tramways Company, which served Wandsworth, Vauxhall, then Lambeth Road, St. George's Circus, Borough Road, Southwark Bridge Road and Southwark Street, to terminate at Hop Exchange and which continued to run for about another two years.

The reconstructed tracks in the west end of Borough Road, together with a junction and curves into Southwark Bridge Road were, as just mentioned, in constant service use. The new extension eastwards to Borough High Street and the double tracks in Lancaster Street however were, in the main, used as "escape routes" for the services using London Road in congested rush hours or in case of emergency, such as a break-down on the main lines. As an example, using the former route, it could allow cars running from Blackfriars Road into Old Kent Road to make a diversion, via the curve into Borough Road, then along that road and Borough High Street, the east-to-south curves at St. George's Church, Great Dover Street and so into Old Kent Road. In the "up" direction, a similar route was available, but subject to a most difficult turn across a complex array of tracks from Borough Road, across St. George's Circus and into Blackfriars Road. On the other hand, the double tracks in Lancaster Street were easily negotiable, giving an almost direct link in the "down" direction between Blackfriars Road and Newington Causeway, so enabling considerable relief to be given to the heavily-loaded "down" London Road track.

Bearing in mind that once the services to and from Blackfriars and Streatham had been taken over by electric cars (first as far as Brixton in May 1904), there were about 85 cars an hour running towards the Elephant & Castle junction, and more in rush-hour periods, (40 an hour from Blackfriars, 20 an hour from Westminster and at least 25 an hour from Waterloo Station), it was probably the case that from almost the beginning of electric operation, cars bound from Blackfriars to Walworth Road were diverted during the rush-hour periods at St. George's Circus to proceed via Borough Road and Lancaster Street into the southern end of Southwark Bridge Road, then across to the single line track at the Elephant & Castle end of Walworth Road. This diversion became quite regular, the practice lasting virtually until the end of electric tram operation in south London. Conversely, cars proceeding from Blackfriars to both Brixton and Clapham (and in the

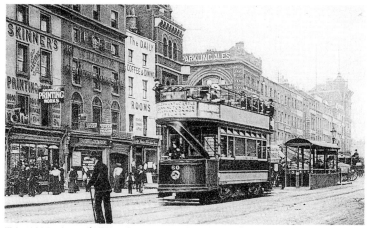

This 1904 view of the original terminus in Blackfriars Road by Stamford Street, shows car No. 60 standing by the covered "queue" which was erected to control passengers waiting for cars. (Commercial view)

opposite direction) were not often diverted through Lancaster Street, this routing usually being used only in case of emergency.

The Lancaster Street link after September 1906, became a vital part of what can only be described as a "tramway roundabout", but in one direction only. It consisted of the "up" track in St. George's Road from the "Elephant & Castle", the single line junction and curve connecting the "up" track with the reconstructed "up" track (formerly belonging to the South London Tramways Company) in Lambeth Road, along to St. George's Circus to cross the complex of lines into Borough Road and then via the "down" track into Lancaster Street, Southwark Bridge Road to Newington Causeway, near the Elephant & Castle junction. This facility enabled cars to take a circular routing round the St. George's Circus complex from either Kennington or Walworth, and which was used for reversing cars in emergency. Looking forward somewhat, this routing was used during one summer period in the 1920s to turn cars with trailers on a Saturdays-only service numbered 84 which worked between Southend Village, Catford and "Elephant" via Lewisham, New Cross, Peckham and Walworth.

The next electric car service to be introduced was made possible by the completion of the reconstruction of a short length of the horse car line in Tower Bridge Road from the "Bricklayers Arms" to Grange Road, then by a new length of track as far as the Tower Bridge approach road at the junction with Tooley Street. On 12th September 1904, a daily service was instituted between Westminster Bridge and Tower Bridge via St. George's Circus, "Elephant", New Kent Road and Tower Bridge Road (68).

Camberwell horse car depot, part of which was in use as temporary housing for electric cars, had to be closed to enable it to be rebuilt as an electric car shed. On 5th December 1904, cars working on the services to Southwark were transferred to Rye Lane shed. One week later, the depot was cleared when the remainder of the cars working on services between Camberwell and Vauxhall and those to Westminster were transferred to Clapham.

347

During the early months of 1905, the only route information of any consequence was, that on 25th January and 2nd February, statutory horse cars were run over the disused ex-London, Camberwell & Dulwich Company lines as required by the Board of Trade and Parliament, otherwise the Council would have given up the right to either work them again or reconstruct them for electric traction and, as sections of these were required again, it was essential that the right to them be maintained.

Heavy tramcar traffic was building up around the Elephant & Castle area, which was of concern to the Council, as timetables and schedules were not being adhered to in the manner thought necessary. The only way of avoiding the area altogether was by using the route from Camberwell to Westminster via Camberwell New Road and Kennington Road. On 3rd April 1905, the service between Greenwich and Westminster via Peckham and Walworth Road (40) was diverted to run via Kennington in an effort to improve workings to and from the south-eastern suburbs.

There was a re-arrangement of depot accommodation when the first section of "Fairlawn", New Cross car shed was opened on 15th May 1905, resulting in the cars housed in the temporary depots at Leo Street and Bowles Road being transferred to the new premises. The Greenwich and Waterloo via Old Kent Road cars were transferred on 16th May, while Bowles Road depot closed on 20th May and Leo Street on 28th May. Also on 15th May, the cars used on the Camberwell to Vauxhall service were moved to Rye Lane shed from Clapham, where they had been housed since 12th December 1904. Finally, the cars working on the Old Kent Road route between Greenwich and Westminster and still housed at Hoskins Street, Greenwich depot, were moved into New Cross shed on 16th June 1905.

Reconstruction at Vauxhall and Re-arrangement of Services

In view of the massive conduit electric tramway crossing and junction work being undertaken at Vauxhall Cross, the ex-South London Tramway horse car services to and from Wandsworth Road/Battersea Park Road and Stangate/Hop Exchange were split at Vauxhall, isolating the cars and horses required to work the truncated services to and from Vauxhall, Stangate and Hop Exchange. Furthermore, the small depot and stables at Borough Road having been closed, the ex-London Tramways Company horse car depot and stables in Kennington Road at Kennington Cross were re-opened to house, for the time being, some of the cars and horses required, the cars having to be "jumped" at Lambeth Baths Corner to and from the Lambeth Road tracks and the electrified lines in Kennington Road. Finally, to facilitate the completion of the work of reconstruction, the remaining horse car services were withdrawn from Lambeth Palace Road and Lambeth Road in May 1906.

The reconstruction work involved the installation of a double track junction, crossing and pointwork on the Albert Embankment at Lambeth Bridge, to connect with the new tracks in Lambeth Palace Road and Lambeth Road (the third side track horse car track connection between Lambeth Road and Lambeth Palace Road outside Lambeth Palace, was not replaced by conduit track). In Stangate, the new lines ended for the time being in a trailing conduit-equipped crossover. In Lambeth Road, outside Lambeth Parish Church, a short length of single line track was laid in the narrow section outside the "Bell" public house, with the associated pointwork providing reversing facilities when required. From this point, the road, in which double tracks were laid, became

348

quite wide, with the "up" and "down" lines being on either side of the centrally situated brick-built support for the multi-track overbridge belonging to the London & South Western Railway Company. At the points where Lambeth Road crosses Kennington Road and St. George's Road, double track right-angled crossings had already been installed as part of the original Clapham/Tooting reconstruction work, whilst at the latter road crossing, conduit junction and crossing special work was installed into the "up" track in Lambeth Road to complete the connection with the "up" line in St. George's Road. Another trailing crossover was provided in Lambeth Road, just short of the St. George's Circus tracks, to which the new Lambeth Road lines were eventually connected.

With the opening of these lines for electric traction, the Tramways Department was able to dispense with horse traction in the "Inner South London Area". Although the installation of the complex set of junctions, crossings and curves in the vicinity of Vauxhall Cross had also been completed, in readiness for the opening of the new lines across the bridge, and the re-opening of tram services to Battersea, together with the completion of the new purpose-built car shed at Jews Row, Wandsworth, there was still a considerable amount of work to be done on the reconstruction of the Battersea Park Road tramway. Until this was completed, the new junction layout could not be used to the best advantage.

A shuttle service of electric cars replaced the horse cars on the sections from Vauxhall Cross to Stangate and Vauxhall to Hop Exchange via Lambeth Road, Borough Road and Southwark Bridge Road on 8th and 24th September 1906 respectively. Five cars were provided for the time being by Camberwell car shed, and making use for approach purposes of the junctions and curves at Vauxhall Cross which connected the conduit tracks in Harleyford Road (already in use by an electric car service from the Camberwell direction) with the newly constructed tracks on Albert Embankment. When the rebuilt lines in Battersea

Rush hour on a summer evening at Vauxhall Cross, probably in 1912. The covered top programme for the older cars appears to be complete.
(Courtesy: L T Museum H16498)

Park Road became available for electric operation in December 1906, through services, provided by Jews Row, commenced working between Hop Exchange and Tooting via Lambeth Road (12) and between Stangate and Clapham Junction via Battersea Park Road (34/86), horse cars continuing to work along Wandsworth Road (26H) on a truncated service between Vauxhall Cross and East Hill, Wandsworth.

The cessation of horse car services on the ex-South London Tramways routes through the "Inner South London Area" saw the end of the "each route having its own livery" era, and the long-standing colourful tramway scene was ended with the LCC's replacement of horse cars by electric cars wearing a standard livery of "chocolate and cream". But even the new cars provided a little colour at night by the use of individual route colour codes shown by illuminated "bullseyes".

Vauxhall and Victoria

The isolated horse car service operating between the north side of Vauxhall Bridge and Victoria Station was withdrawn on 28th February 1906, to allow the contractor to have unrestricted access to the tracks during the period of reconstruction. This task was completed at the same time as the new Vauxhall Bridge tracks, but due to an official "oversight", the powers necessary to allow the Council to work electric cars over the new lines on the bridge were overlooked, which resulted in the resumption of a horse car service between Vauxhall and Victoria from 26th May, until the electric cars working on the Catford, New Cross, Kennington and Vauxhall (54) daily service were at last allowed to cross the bridge from the south side, and run right through to Victoria Station as from 5th August.

Westminster Bridge and Victoria Embankment

It had always been the aim of the LCC Tramways to gain access to Central London via both Westminster Bridge and Blackfriars Bridge but due to the intransigence of Parliament, together with continual objections by the Metropolitan Police and the omnibus companies to any proposals made by the LCC, this "advance" into Westminster was thwarted for a number of years. At last, however, in 1906 an Act of Parliament was obtained authorising the extensions and on 15th December 1906 the tracks, joined at the foot of Westminster Bridge on the Lambeth side, were opened to public service. All cars which previously terminated at York Road were extended over the bridge and along the Embankment.

The services from Tooting (2), Streatham (16) and Dulwich (62) ran through to a new terminus at John Carpenter Street (near Blackfriars Bridge), with those from Tower Bridge (68), Woolwich Road or Blackwall Tunnel via Old Kent Road (38) and Greenwich via Peckham (40) running as far as Waterloo Bridge (Savoy Street). Probably as the result of congestion at Savoy Street, the Tower Bridge service cars (68) were curtailed at Charing Cross as from 25th December 1906.

An extension of the lines from Stangate to join those in Westminster Bridge Road was delayed, by the necessary powers not being included by Parliament in the LCC Tramways Act of 1906. After considerable argument, Parliament relented and the Council lost no time in making the connection, points and junction work for which had already been laid in earlier, in anticipation of permission being granted to make this obvious extension. On 4th February 1907, the daily service from Clapham Junction to Westminster Bridge (Stangate) via Battersea Park Road (34/86) was extended to John Carpenter Street.

Class D car No. 400 is seen passing class E car No. 492 near Waterloo Bridge during the winter of 1906-07.   *Courtesy: C. Carter)*

Included in the track construction work on Victoria Embankment was a three-way junction layout, sited at the point where the Kingsway Subway tracks would emerge on to the Embankment when its extension was completed.   On 10th April 1908 this extension was opened and single deck cars run through from Highbury on services to Kennington Gate via Kennington Road (35) and to Tower Bridge via "Elephant & Castle", New Kent Road and Tower Bridge Road (33).   The last-mentioned replaced the service running between Charing Cross and Tower Bridge (68).

The lines of tramcars moving to and from Westminster Bridge and Victoria Embankment illustrates the level of service given to travellers in the 1910-11 period.   *(Courtesy: L T Museum H16494)*

Blackfriars Bridge and Southwark Street

Blackfriars Bridge stands within the boundaries of the Corporation of the City of London, an authority with great powers and privileges. The Corporation decided that the bridge was too narrow to allow a tramway to be laid across it, but arranged for a considerable widening to be effected, as is described elsewhere. The new tracks over the bridge from John Carpenter Street to join those in Blackfriars Road and also to form a junction into Southwark Street were opened to traffic on 14th September 1909, resulting in the merging of services from both John Carpenter Street terminus, and from the terminus in Blackfriars Road. This marked the beginning of the renowned Embankment Circulars which, with many revisions and variations over the years, became an accepted part of the London tramway scene, with services such as "Merton" and Embankment via Westminster and Blackfriars (2/4), or Blackfriars and Westminster (4/2); Streatham (later Norbury) and Embankment via Westminster (16) or via Blackfriars (18); and (intermittently) Greenwich and Embankment via Westminster (38) or via Blackfriars (36) operating over these lines. Services working round the Embankment were by now generally "circular" in pattern, with the main terminal point being described as Waterloo Bridge, although in reality, most cars on many services travelled along the full length of the Embankment in both directions.

The new tracks in Southwark Street as far as Southwark Bridge Road, in conjunction with the existing lines eastwards to Hop Exchange, allowed an initial short service to be instituted between Hop Exchange and Embankment, Northumberland Avenue (Charing Cross) (26) on 14th September 1909 on a daily basis, which was extended on 23rd September along the Embankment, over Westminster Bridge, then via Lambeth Palace Road, Vauxhall and the reconstructed tracks in Wandsworth Road as far as Queens Road, Battersea. An extension to Clapham Junction was effected on 9th October, with a final extension to East Hill, Wandsworth on 15th December, which was to remain the suburban terminus of this service for the next twelve years.

A single-deck car service from Bloomsbury to Hop Exchange via the eastern curves of the Subway/Embankment junction began on 2nd December 1909 (33A), but not being remunerative, was withdrawn on 22nd January 1910.

Southwark and Lambeth

On 30th September 1909, a new junction layout linking Borough High Street with Marshalsea Road at St. George's Church in a northerly direction was made available for use, but the first record of a service running over it is dated 14th December, when the rush hours only cars between Streatham and Southwark Bridge (10) were diverted to run through Newington Causeway, Borough High Street, the new junction, Marshalsea Road, and then the original route in Southwark Bridge Road.

In subsequent years, other services working through the full length of Southwark Bridge Road (avoiding St. George's Church) were gradually re-routed via St. George's Church. Records show that the last of these was service 6 which forsook Southwark Bridge Road at a date as yet unknown in 1917.

A new double track junction layout between Kennington Road and Lambeth Road in a north-to-east direction was made available for use on 28th August 1912, but was not used regularly until 23rd October when the lightly loaded morning "down" and evening "up" cars of the rush hours service between Tooting and Southwark Bridge via Clapham and Kennington (6) were diverted over this route, travelling by way of St. George's Circus and Borough Road, so avoiding the congested Elephant & Castle junction.

SOUTH-WEST LONDON

The Battersea Park Road Line

Reconstruction work in the Wandsworth area commenced in August 1905, resulting in the closure of Jews Row depot on the 8th. The horses still required for services in the area were moved to the ex-London Tramways Company depot at Balls Yard, Kennington. It is most likely that the cars were temporarily housed at the ex-South London Tramways Company works yard in Queens Road, Battersea. Between 2nd February and 6th March 1906, services were progressively cut back between Wandsworth and Latchmere Road to allow track reconstruction to go ahead. The remainder of the route between Latchmere, Vauxhall and Lambeth continued to be worked by horse cars until 30th April 1906, when massive reconstruction works commenced at the Vauxhall junction, resulting in all services to and from the Battersea and Wandsworth area being divided into four sections:-

1. Latchmere and Vauxhall
2. East Hill and Vauxhall
3. Westminster (Stangate) and Vauxhall
4. Hop Exchange and Vauxhall

Fourteen horsecars were moved to Kennington Cross depot on the same day in order to supply the sections still running north of Vauxhall. These only survived for another week as, on 7th May the services along Lambeth Palace Road and Lambeth Road were withdrawn to allow for the reconstruction of those sections and a junction layout at the foot of Lambeth Bridge. A short shuttle service, using three cars, was maintained between Lambeth Bridge and Vauxhall with a similar service working along Lambeth Road until 30th May, when that too was closed for reconstruction, the 14 cars being dispersed elsewhere or disposed of. The horses were still stabled at Kennington, in order to provide for the service from East Hill which was to resume for a time after the completion of the Vauxhall junction layout. Queens Road yard, having served its purpose, was closed on 7th July, to be followed on the 9th by withdrawal of services along Battersea Park Road and Nine Elms Lane.

During the time that reconstruction was under way on the Battersea "bottom" road, a new line was under construction between Wandsworth High Street and Tooting Broadway via Garratt Lane and Earlsfield. This was opened to traffic 5th August 1906, a service being introduced between these two points and extended over the newly reconstructed tracks to Plough Road, Battersea (12). The cars for this were provided by Clapham car shed until 12th October when the rebuilt car shed at Jews Row opened, the Garratt Lane service vehicles running in there on completion of the day's work.

The next sections of the electrified tracks between Plough Road, Battersea and Queens Road via "Princes Head" and between Clapham Junction and Queens Road via Falcon Road, were brought into use as from 13th October 1906, these being covered by an extension of the service from Tooting (12) and, for the time being, by a new service from Clapham Junction (86) to Queens Road. Finally, the short section between Queens Road and Vauxhall Cross via Nine Elms Lane was completed and, on 22nd December the service from Tooting to Queens Road (12) was extended to Hop Exchange via Lambeth Road.

Class D car No. 302, operating from Jews Row car shed, leaves Tooting Broadway on the Tooting Junction via Battersea service.

On the same day, the cars on the Clapham Junction service (86) were extended to Westminster (Stangate), being further extended to John Carpenter Street as from 4th February 1907, working in this way for exactly five years until, on 4th February 1912, it was withdrawn north of Vauxhall outside busy hours on weekdays, while on Sundays, the service worked between Clapham Junction and Vauxhall until 2 p.m., when it was then extended forward to Stangate for the rest of the day. This was short-lived however as, on 17th June it was withdrawn completely, being replaced by an extension through to Clapham Junction of the "Angel", Islington and Vauxhall service (35).

A new service between Earlsfield Station and John Carpenter Street via Nine Elms Lane and Westminster (14) commenced running during weekday busy hours only as from 7th September 1910. It was extended on 27th February 1911 from Earlsfield Station to Wimbledon Road, Summerstown. (See also the Streatham services for further details of car workings to Summerstown.) On Saturdays the service worked between Battersea, "Princes Head" and Tooting Broadway. It is believed that on 17th June 1912, certain cars were extended to Tooting Junction during weekday rush hours and that it operated in the afternoons on Sundays.

The Wandsworth Road Route

Reconstruction of the lines from Vauxhall Cross, through Wandsworth Road to East Hill commenced at the beginning of 1909, working from the Nine Elms end of the route. The horse car service in this instance was not maintained during the course of the works. The first section to close was between Nine Elms Lane and Wandsworth Road Station on 17th February, followed by the closure to Queens Road on 6th March and finally to East Hill on 3rd May. Electric cars commenced working on 23rd September when the short service between Hop Exchange and the Embankment (26) was extended over Westminster Bridge, then via Lambeth Palace Road, Vauxhall and the reconstructed tracks in Wandsworth Road as far as Queens Road, Battersea. The extensions to Clapham Junction and East Hill, Wandsworth took place on 9th October and 15th December respectively, at which point the suburban terminus of this daily service (26) remained for the next twelve years.

Another class D car, No. 341, stops for passengers in St. John's Hill, Clapham Junction. Compare this with the view in the horse car section.
(Commercial view)

Just over three weeks later, on 3rd January 1910 a new daily service was inaugurated between East Hill, Wandsworth and Victoria (28) via Wandsworth Road, which operated until 5th Octiber when it was withdrawn outside busy hours on weekdays. On Saturdays the cars ran every six minutes between 11.28 a.m. and just after midnight. Sunday service was every twelve minutes until about 10 a.m. and then 8 minutes during the rest of the day, the last car running in just after midnight. The service ran in this way until, on 10th July 1912 it was again made a regular daily working.

Work also started on the replacement of the horse car tracks through the length of Queens Road, Battersea as from 25th August 1908, and the new work was made available for electric cars on 25th January 1909. Single deck cars, shedded at Jews Row, were put into service, running between Chelsea Bridge and Lavender Hill (32), to be joined on 28th January by diverting the Subway service (35) away from Kennington and re-routing it along Albert Embankment, Nine Elms Lane and Queens Road to Lavender Hill. A further change was made as from 1st May 1910, when this service was withdrawn between Vauxhall Cross and Lavender Hill.

A new connection between the line at the "Plough" Clapham and the Wandsworth Road tracks was constructed along Long Road, Clapham Common and Cedars Road, the contractors commencing work at the Clapham end in November 1909. The new tracks were brought into use on 26th February 1910, when the service working between Waterloo Station and Tooting via Clapham was diverted at the "Plough", to work along Long Road and Cedars Road, then into Lavender Hill to Clapham Junction and East Hill, Wandsworth (30). This was augmented by an extension of the Chelsea Bridge and Lavender Hill cars (32) to "The Plough", Clapham as from 1st May 1910, but this lasted for only eight days, when half of the cars were re-scheduled to work between Chelsea Bridge and Lavender Hill only, while the remainder reverted to a similar arrangement on 5th October 1910.

Clapham Junction to Kings road Chelsea, via "Princes Head"

The opening of the tramway from Battersea Park Road to Kings Road, Chelsea via Battersea Bridge on 22nd June 1911, was covered by the introduction of a new daily service between Clapham Junction and Kings Road via Falcon Road (34). It continued to operate in this way until many years after the introduction of service numbering, details of which are given elsewhere.

The Hammersmith Lines

The tramway between Brook Green Road, Hammersmith and Scrubs Lane, Harlesden had been planned by the LCC as far back as 1903 but, due to many factors, it was 30th May 1908 before the line was opened. A car shed was built at Great Church Lane, Hammersmith, to which cars going into or coming off service had to cross the Broadway.

Upon opening, the LCC was able to provide a service (82A) to and from the Franco-British Exhibition, due to be staged in the summer of that year together with the Olympic Games, at the White City Exhibition Ground at Shepherds Bush. In an effort to cater for the crowds expected at this event, special arrangements were made to provide a double-track siding within the entrance area of the exhibition site. It continued to be used regularly each summer for several years during the staging of international events, with the tramway providing special services to and from the several railway stations in the area, to the London United Tramways at Hammersmith and the Metropolitan Electric Tramways at Harrow Road.

The car service between Hammersmith and Scrubs Lane was extended to Paddington via Harrow road (82EX) on 3rd June 1911, over a junction layout which had been installed by the Metropolitan Electric Tramways some time during April or May 1910, (Metropolitan Electric Tramways, Vol. I by C. S. Smeeton), or by 25th May 1911, (LCC Signed Minutes) in conjunction with the Coronation Exhibition staged at the Great White City, for which special combined admission and tram tickets were issued costing 1/1d, the LCC receiving 5% commission on the sales.

On 1st September, the extended service reverted to its original working due, as recorded in the Official Minutes of the LCC, to unsatisfactory receipts owing to poor patronage and the fact that the LCC were paying 7d per car mile to the MET. In November 1911, Paddington Borough Council asked that the through service be re-instated, but the Highways Committee would not consider this. Another of the stated reasons was that the Council still hoped that powers could be obtained for a direct tramway to be built between Hammersmith and Marble Arch, which would have the effect of providing a much shorter link into the West End of London.

There was, however, another reason why the service may have been short-lived. When the line between Paddington and Harlesden, much of which was inside the boundary of the County of London, was constructed by the MET, the two tracks were laid closer together than was the case with LCC lines. After representations to the Board of Trade by the County Council, the MET was forced to specially adapt a number of its cars by decreasing the overall width by several inches. Therefore, when the LCC ran class E/1 cars on the line, they were, by the Council's own standards, too wide to be "safely used" and it is quite possible that the MET saw an opportunity to even the score by complaining to the LCC.

It had been anticipated that the whole line between Harlesden and

Putney and probably beyond would have been constructed as a continuous process but this was not to be. Due to problems with the width of the road at Hammersmith Broadway, it was not possible to connect the two projected sections for some years. However, the Hammersmith to Putney line was complete and open to traffic on 23rd January 1909, with a service of cars terminating at its northern end just south of Hammersmith Broadway and in Lower Richmond Road at the Putney end (82B).

Public service commenced throughout from 30th January 1912, when one track across Hammersmith Broadway was brought into use, together with an extension from the south side of Putney Bridge to High Street Wandsworth. This resulted in a through service operating between Harlesden (nr Willesden Jcn) and High Street Wandsworth (82). This remained the southern terminus until, on 16th July 1915 it was extended over new conduit construction into Garratt Lane, Wandsworth, and on to Tooting Junction, by then bearing the number 82 and unusually for the LCC, providing a long, totally suburban through service.

Car No. 993 standing at the terminus in Lower Richmond Road during the period that the service was working between Hammersmith and Putney only.   *(Commercial view)*

The Streatham/Norbury, Stockwell Road and Southcroft Road Lines

All services of electric cars using Brixton Road, Brixton Hill, Streatham High Road and Stockwell Road grew out of the three-mile long cable line which operated between Handforth Road, Kennington and Streatham Library.

An experiment took place as from 2nd August 1903 in which electric cars were conveyed over the cable line, using a complex change-over arrangement at the Kennington cable terminus. From the opening date, this service worked between Westminster and Streatham Library, (16) to be augmented as from 11th September (18) by a service terminating at Blackfriars at the London end, but these were unsuccessful, due to problems with the weight of the cars. This was shown to its full effect in a spectacular incident which occurred early in September 1903 when an electric car stalled on the uphill journey to Streatham. Despite the efforts of the driver of the following "dummy", which were used to convey some of the horse cars still working between Blackfriars and Streatham, the failed electric car pushed the other backwards down the hill, into the front of a third car coming up. The three of them continued to run back down the hill, until stopped by the action of the driver of yet a fourth car who, apparently, "saved the situation". Several passengers on the cars were said to have sustained slight injuries. The decision was taken to re-instate the original cable cars between Kennington and Streatham, and to provide transfer facilities for passengers wishing to make through journeys. This change took place on 14th October 1903. On the night of 5th April 1904, the cable line was closed down to allow for its reconstruction to conduit electric working.

Electric traction began on 21st May 1904 when the Westminster (16) and Blackfriars (18) cars which terminated at Handforth Road, Kennington, were extended to Brixton Station. Nine days later, on 30th May these services were further extended to Brixton, Water Lane. The final extension came on 19th June, when reconstructed tracks were opened throughout to Streatham Library, which then remained as the southern terminus of the line for several years. A few days later, on 27th June, an all-night service of cars was introduced, running at half-hourly intervals between John Carpenter Street, Blackfriars and Water Lane, Brixton.

A new service was instituted between St. George's Church and Streatham Library (10), probably on 1st August 1904, to be followed on 5th September by another between Southwark Bridge and Water Lane (24). The through services to Streatham were worked by Camberwell car shed staff while the service to Water Lane from Southwark was operated by Clapham staff and cars. This situation changed as from 3rd February 1906, when all cars on these services were transferred to the newly-opened car shed at Streatham, Telford Avenue.

The Water Lane and Southwark Bridge (24) service was extended to Streatham on 27th September 1906, together with the extra cars which worked between Westminster, Blackfriars and Water Lane. Five additional cars were worked out of Camberwell yard on the Southwark

An early view of class B car No. 193 in Brixton Road on the Brixton Station- Westminster service. The end destination board on the curved end panel is of a different style to those seen in other views.

Another early view of a car on the Streatham route, this time, outside Streatham Library. By now the end signboards have been removed as shown on class C car No. 228. *(Commercial view)*

service. The next change came when the tracks across Westminster Bridge and along Victoria Embankment to John Carpenter Street were opened to traffic on 15th December 1906, as previously described.

Another service commenced on 4th April 1908 when the conduit tracks in Stockwell Road and South Lambeth Road were brought into use. Cars began running between Victoria Station and Brixton Station (20). These were extended on 24th May to Streatham Library.

In 1909, the first alteration for several years affected the services between John Carpenter Street, Blackfriars and Streatham (16) and between Victoria and Streatham (20), when these were extended on 31st July over new tracks to Norbury at the County boundary, on conduit as far as Gleneagle Road, just south of the junction of Streatham High Road with Mitcham Lane, then on the overhead wire for the remainder of the route.

A new junction layout between Borough High Street and Marshalsea Road was brought into use on 14th December 1909, when cars working between Streatham and St. George's Church (10) were extended to Southwark Bridge on Mondays to Fridays (late evenings excepted), and Saturdays until about 2.30 p.m. while the service between Streatham and Southwark Bridge via Southwark Bridge Road (24) was reduced to busy hours only. On 27th February 1911 this service was withdrawn between Telford Avenue and Streatham Library and was also re-routed via St. George's Church and remained so until its withdrawal on 27th November 1913.

There were a number of short working services operating between Water Lane and the London termini which from time to time were extended to Streatham, either Telford Avenue or Streatham Library. No details of these are given.

Mitcham Lane and Southcroft Road

With the opening of the new lines in Mitcham Lane and Southcroft Road, together with those in Wimbledon Road, the Southwark Bridge,

St. George's Church and Streatham Library service (10) was extended to Summerstown via Tooting Broadway on 5th November 1910. This did not last for long however, as on 27th February 1911, the service was withdrawn between Tooting Broadway and Summerstown, but extended from St. George's Church to Southwark Bridge on Saturdays until late evening.

The Charing Cross and Telford Avenue short working rush hours only service (16/22) was also extended at both ends on 27th February 1911. At the London end, Victoria Embankment (Waterloo Bridge) became the new terminus, while at the other end, it was extended from Telford Avenue to Mitcham Lane, Southcroft Road (22/16).

Norbury and Streatham

Another re-arrangement took place on 5th September 1911 when the Waterloo Bridge, Blackfriars and Norbury service (18) was withdrawn between Norbury and Streatham Library during Monday to Friday midday periods and evenings after about 9 p.m.; and on Saturdays between 10 a.m. and 1.30 p.m. On and from 29th October 1911, the service was cut back to work only between Blackfriars and Streatham on all days of the week. However, by December 1912, it was once again working to Norbury on a daily basis.

SOUTH-EAST LONDON

The Woolwich Road Services

The first services to work in south-east London were those between Westminster, Blackfriars and Waterloo via Old Kent Road and New Cross to East Greenwich (36/38/64) on 17th January 1904. One week later, on 24th the line from Camberwell Green to New Cross Gate was opened with a service operating between Westminster Bridge and New Cross Gate via Walworth Road and Peckham (40). The delay in providing the service via Peckham was due to difficulty in finding sufficient accommodation in which to house the electric cars for the service. On 4th May 1904, the Peckham service was extended to New Cross Gate and the "Marquis of Granby", and then onwards to East Greenwich on 9th June. This was followed on 21st November with the service running between Waterloo Station and East Greenwich via Old Kent

Seen in 1904, not long after the opening of the electric car service between New Cross and Blackfriars via Walworth Road, car No. 239 stops for passengers at High Street, Peckham. *(Commercial view)*

Class C car, No. 257 is seen just leaving New Cross (SE&CR) Station, bound for Greenwich. *(Courtesy: A. D. Packer)*

Road (64) only working between 4.30 p.m. and 9 p.m. on weekdays. Lastly, on 3rd April 1905, the Westminster and Peckham service (40) was diverted away from Walworth Road to run via Kennington Road and Camberwell New Road in an attempt to alleviate the continued congestion which was occurring at the Elephant & Castle junction.

The LCC took over the operation of the Woolwich & South-East London Tramways Company on 1st June 1905 and immediately set about making arrangements for electrification of the first sections of the line, working from both the Plumstead and East Greenwich ends. Dealing with the extension eastwards from Greenwich, the Westminster and East Greenwich via Peckham service (40) was extended to run as far as Woolwich Road, Tunnel Avenue, a distance of about half a mile, on 10th June 1906. At the same time as the tracks were being reconstructed along Woolwich Road, a new line was being laid along Blackwall Lane as far as Blackwall Tunnel entrance. On 17th June 1906, the service from Blackfriars via Old Kent Road was extended to Woolwich Road, Blackwall Lane (36), to be followed the next day by the service working from Westminster via Old Kent Road being extended to Blackwall Tunnel (38). On 10th September, the Blackfriars to Blackwall Lane (36) service was extended to Woolwich Road, Tunnel Avenue, and finally, both services terminating at Westminster Bridge (38, 40) were extended over it and along the Victoria Embankment to John Carpenter Street, Blackfriars on 15th December 1906.

During the next three years there were several changes involving the position of the London termini of the cars serving Greenwich and Woolwich Road, details of many of which are obscure. It seemed that the terminus at John Carpenter Street on Victoria Embankment may have been severely overloaded at times, resulting in the cut-back of some services to one of the crossovers nearer to Savoy Street, Strand, until the opening of the Blackfriars Bridge tramway on 14th September 1909 allowed a general re-arrangement to be effected.

One such alteration which was recorded, occurred about ten days after the opening of the Victoria Embankment line, when the service via Kennington (40) was withdrawn between John Carpenter Street and Waterloo Bridge on 28th December 1906, to be followed by the Old Kent Road service (38) on 1st January 1907.

All three sides of the triangle at New Cross Gate are in use in the 1912 view. Class B car No. 189 is seen working on a journey from Waterloo to Lee Green, while No. 149 heads for Forest Hill.

Courtesy: A. D. Packer)

A comprehensive repair works was under construction on a large site on the north side of Woolwich Road, just to the east of the bridge carrying the branch line of the South Eastern & Chatham Railway to Angerstein Wharf, Charlton. The installation was opened ceremonially on 5th March 1909, but was still not connected into the electric tramway network that was developing. At last, on 22nd July 1909, the 308 yards of reconstructed track between Tunnel Avenue and Rainton Road was opened, with the Westminster via Peckham service (40) being extended this short distance on a daily basis, and with part of the service via Old Kent Road (36/38), being extended in rush hours.

The next extension eastwards to Chapel Street, Woolwich was opened to traffic on 1st April 1911, with the Westminster and Peckham service (40) working to the new terminus. For ten days as from 3rd July 1911, there were no through services operating via Greenwich due to the installation of new pointwork at Greenwich Church, which was to connect the lines in Nelson Street to those which had been constructed from Greenwich Church to Deptford and London Bridge. Cars were turned on either side of the works for the time that the obstruction remained, the road east of Greenwich Church being served by a shuttle service of 16 cars, which were housed temporarily at the Central Repair Depot.

With the completion of the installation of the new junction layout, a service working between the east side of Creek Bridge and Chapel Street via Greenwich Church (70-1), commenced on 5th August 1911, resulting in the withdrawal of the rush hour extension of the Old Kent Road service between Blackwall Lane and Rainton Road. The Creek Road service however, lasted less than a year, being withdrawn on 26th June 1912, in favour of a shuttle service worked by two cars between the east side of Creek Bridge and Greenwich Church (70-2).

From the opening of Blackfriars Bridge on 14th September 1909, the Woolwich Road via Kennington service worked from Chapel Street via New Cross, Kennington and Westminster to Waterloo Bridge, then on to Blackfriars, Elephant and Walworth Road to terminate at New Cross Gate on the return journey and vice versa. The dividing line was shown on the indicator blinds as "Waterloo Bridge", even though the cars were not turned at that point. From 6th November 1911, however, the service was divided, the Westminster section via Kennington (40) operating only as far as Waterloo Bridge and that via Blackfriars, from John Carpenter Street, then via Walworth Road to New Cross Gate (66). At the suburban end the Old Kent Road services had reached Chapel Street, Woolwich on a daily basis by 31st May 1912.

The Plumstead, Woolwich and Eltham Lines

The horse car service working between East Greenwich, Woolwich and Plumstead Church was, as just described, progressively replaced by electric cars between East Greenwich and Chapel Street, Woolwich over a period of several years. The Plumstead and Woolwich end of the line was being dealt with in the same way, with short sections being reconstructed, beginning at Plumstead Church and working westwards to Beresford Square.

A service of six electric cars, which were housed in the ex-horse car depot, now a temporary electric car shed, commenced working on 17th April 1908 between Plumstead and Beresford Square, Woolwich (42). This service, augmented with additional cars, was extended over brand new track to Abbey Wood on 26th July. On the same date, cars of the Bexley UDC Tramways, which had terminated at Plumstead Church since their introduction in 1903, were extended over LCC metals to Beresford Square.

Plumstead High Street in 1911, with E/1 car No. 1351 coming towards the camera, just entering one of the several single track sections, bound for Abbey Wood. No. 1505, on the other track, shows "Middle Gates" as the destination. (Courtesy: Greater London Photograph Library)

The next extension of the line on 30th November 1909 took it as far as Woolwich Ferry, Nile Street, a distance of about half a mile, which was to remain the terminus until, on 5th April 1914, the final connection was made with the system from the London end, the services resulting from this being later described. Additional short workings occurred on Monday-Friday mornings between Wickham Lane and Nile Street, with evening and Saturday extras between Wickham Lane and Beresford Square (42 EX). As from 31st July 1911, all extras worked to Nile Street.

Class C car No. 280, on the short-lived Creek Bridge service, is seen at Woolwich Dockyard terminus, the interchange point for the narrow gauge horse cars to Woolwich. (Commercial view, Molyneaux, Woolwich)

For a few days, from 13th to 15th June 1910, the service was curtailed at Beresford Square to allow the installation of pointwork to be used in conjunction with working the new tramway to Eltham (44), which was in the final stages of construction. This line, running via Woolwich Common and Well Hall Road, was brought into use on 23rd July 1910, the Council using new class M cars for the purpose, which were housed at the new car shed at Abbey Wood. The basic service worked between Beresford Square and Eltham Church, but it is known that there were several excursions during the day with extensions from Woolwich to Wickham Lane, Plumstead and Abbey Wood. There were also depot runs in both directions during each day and these always carried passengers.

Double trolley operation is demonstrated in this view, with class M car No. 1433 on the Woolwich & Eltham service. (Commercial view)

"The Marquis of Granby" to Lewisham and Catford

The line between New Cross "Marquis of Granby" and Lewisham Obelisk via Lewisham High Road opened to traffic on 30th January 1906. A service was provided over the new construction by extending the Westminster and Rye Lane via Walworth Road cars to New Cross Gate and Lewisham (48-1), which in turn resulted in the Waterloo Station and New Cross Gate via Peckham (46) service being cut back to Rye Lane.

Coincidentally with the construction of the tracks in Lewisham Road, reconstruction was going ahead between Lewisham and Catford. The horse car service working between Catford and Greenwich (50H) was affected by the work, all cars having to be removed from the depot at Rushey Green on 1st November 1905 to allow track work to proceed. It is almost certain that the horse cars were run in to and out from Deptford Granary Yard, Greenwich Road from then until 1st February 1906, when once again Catford Yard was opened and some of the cars were sent back there, the remainder staying at Deptford for another five weeks. On this date also, the horse car service was divided at Lewisham, one part working between South Street, Greenwich and Limes Grove, the other betweeen Ladywell Road and Rushey Green. The probable reason for this was to allow major work on the raising of the railway bridge over Lewisham High Street to be carried out, together with considerable road widenings. On 5th March 1906, the horse car service resumed operation throughout and Deptford Yard was closed as a running depot.

Electric car service to Rushey Green commenced on 10th June 1906, when the Westminster and Lewisham via Walworth Road cars (48-1) were further extended. The horse car service continued to run between Catford and Lewisham until 15th June 1906, when it was cut back to work between Lewisham and South Street, Greenwich only, the cars once again being moved into Deptford Granary Yard in Greenwich Road. In conjunction with this change, the cars working between Vauxhall and New Cross (54), and which had been extended to Lewisham on 12th June, were extended to Rushey Green three days later, replacing the horse cars.

The crew of class E car No. 486 prepare to take their car back from Rushey Green to Victoria, sometime in 1908-09. (Commercial view)

Messrs. Thomas Tilling & Co. Ltd., had been horsing the cars working between Catford and Greenwich, and had also been providing omnibus services in the area, mainly between Peckham and Lewisham. The management of that company must have felt that, with the introduction of electric cars to Catford and the loss of business in horsing the tramcars, the services provided by them were under threat, as it is recorded that a five-minute service of motor omnibuses was put on by that firm between Peckham and Catford via Lewisham. The LCC however, was not to be easily outdone. On 16th July 1906, the Southwark Bridge and New Cross via Old Kent Road service (52) was extended to Catford on a daily basis, but on Sundays the London terminus became Elephant & Castle. This special Sunday working was seasonal in nature, and over the years suffered winter truncation or withdrawal, usually between November and May of each year.

The lines across Vauxhall Bridge were finally opened to electric cars on 5th August 1906, the car service between Catford and Vauxhall being extended to Victoria (54), resulting in a number of short service extra cars running between Lewisham and Catford being withdrawn. The official record also states that the Catford and Westminster (48-1) cars were withdrawn between Catford and New Cross Gate in the midday period as from 10th September 1906. This service was extended over Westminster Bridge and along Victoria Embankment to Waterloo Bridge on 4th February 1907, working in this way until 4th May, when it was withdrawn between Rye Lane, Peckham, and Catford. In fact, what happened was that the service was diverted at Lewisham Clock Tower to run along the newly completed tracks to Lee Green, described below.

The remaining cars working on the short service between Rye Lane and Waterloo Bridge (later Charing Cross) via Walworth Road continued in this way for just over two more years, the service being diverted via Camberwell New Road and Kennington as from 28th May 1909 (40-1, ex 48-1), in conjunction with the opening of a new service between Waterloo Bridge and Norwood via Westminster and Walworth Road.

Another re-arrangement affecting the area was on 27th April 1908 when the Catford - Southwark Bridge via Old Kent Road (52) daily service was relegated to rush hours only working on Mondays to Fridays, but retained its all day operation on Saturdays. An additional short service of cars between Southwark Bridge and Asylum Road, Old Kent Road (72) was extended on weekdays and Saturdays to New Cross Gate from 31st August 1908, being followed on 6th December by the Sunday service.

By the spring of 1909 a short working service had been instituted between Victoria and Rye Lane, Peckham on Monday to Friday morning and evening, Saturday morning rush-hours and Saturday afternoon and evening. This was considered to be part of the main working of the Victoria - Catford service (54), even though part of it was eventually extended to Lee Green in 1912, as described in the following section.

A rather unusual extension to services commenced on 24th May 1912 when afternoon and evening cars between New Bridge Street, Blackfriars and New Cross Gate via Walworth Road (66) were extended to Catford, only to be cut back to New Cross again on 27th June.

Lewisham to Lee Green

Another new service was introduced on 4th May 1907, with the opening of new tracks in Lee High Road. The service working between Waterloo Station and Rye Lane, Peckham via Walworth Road (46) was extended to New Cross, Lewisham and Lee Green, 19 cars being used.

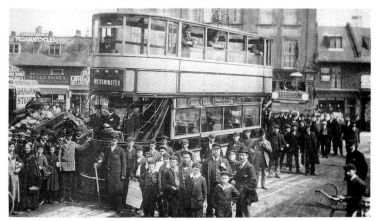

Car No. 497 of class E, being used for the Board of Trade inspection of the Lewisham - Lee Green line, 4th May 1907. (A. D. Packer)

Three years later, on 6th May 1910, three cars began working a shuttle service between Lewisham Obelisk and Lee Green. It is not known for how long this lasted, or why it was instituted.

Lee Green continued to be provided for in this way until, on 24th May 1912, an additional service between Victoria and Lee Green (48-2) began operation by an extension of part of the Victoria and Rye Lane, Peckham service (54), at first on an all-day basis on Monday to Friday, with p.m. service only on Saturdays. This was, in fact a diversion at Lewisham of the service to Catford, as mentioned above. On 21st June however, it was upgraded to become a weekday all-day working, and on 23rd June, Sunday service commenced. 18 cars were in use.

The Lewisham and Greenwich Tramway

The last section of the Lewisham horse tramway to be reconstructed was between Lewisham Obelisk and South Street, Greenwich. The road was closed to traffic after the end of the schedule of 1st September 1907, the horse cars working on this route being finally withdrawn. A replacement service of horse omnibuses, run by thomas Tilling on behalf of the Council filled the gap for the next seven months until, on 4th April 1908, a new electric car service began working daily between Rushey Green and South Street, Greenwich (50).

On 18th May 1912, a short extension was made to this daily service, the new terminus being at Greenwich Church. It was again extended to London Bridge, Tooley Street on 25th November 1912, by which time it had officially received the number 50. Variations in the terminal points at Tooley Street are covered in the section dealing with the main service to work between Greenwich and London Bridge (70).

Lewisham High Road, Brockley and Forest Hill

On 26th February 1910, a new length of line was opened between Lewisham High Road and Brockley Cross (also known then as "Brockley Tips"), outbound cars working via Malpas Road, inbound via Shardeloes Road. The Southwark Bridge and New Cross Gate service via Old Kent Road (72) was extended to Brockley Station on a daily basis. This was to remain the terminus until 25th February 1911, when a further extension over new tracks took the cars to Forest Hill Station, Park Road.

Due to increased passenger loadings, three cars working on the St. George's Church and New Cross short working evening rush hours service were extended to Crofton Park as from 10th June 1912, to be followed on 15th June by an extension of cars working on the Southwark Bridge and Asylum Road short working service.

Information extracted from the official reports of 1911 and 1912 indicate that some Sunday workings were subject to variation in summer and winter. As mentioned above, an example of this is that the Catford and Elephant & Castle via Old Kent Road Sunday service (52) was withdrawn on 22nd October 1911, restored on 19th May 1912, but in this case, absorbed two weeks later on 2nd June by an extension of the Waterloo Station and New Cross via Old Kent Road service (64) to Catford.

The reconstruction of Malpas Road junction at Lewisham High Road, between 24th October and 6th November 1912 caused a division of the services to Brockley and Forest Hill to be made, with cars working to either side of the works.

From Camberwell to Peckham Rye, Dulwich and Forest Hill

An interesting group of services commenced operation on 19th November 1906 with the opening of new tracks between Camberwell Green and Lordship Lane, Dulwich (Crystal Palace Road) via Dog Kennel Hill, with a service of cars running between Victoria, Camberwell Green and Dulwich (58) on a daily basis. On 26th November, this service was joined by one from Southwark Bridge (60), a rush-hours only working on weekdays, which was extended to Dulwich from Camberwell Green. Both these were extended on 20th December to Dulwich Library, a matter of about 200 yards. Sunday service between Dulwich Library and St. George's Church commenced on 14th April 1907 as an extension of the St. George's Church to Camberwell Green workings.

The next date of importance is 15th July 1907, when a new daily service commenced between Dulwich Library and John Carpenter Street via Camberwell, Walworth Road, Elephant & Castle and Westminster (62). This was followed by the opening on 28th November 1907 of a new extension from Goose Green to Stuart Road, Peckham Rye, with daily services being provided to Blackfriars, John Carpenter Street via Walworth Road and Westminster (56) and Victoria via Vauxhall (94).

Upon a reorganisation of services in the area on 2nd November 1908, the Peckham Rye to Victoria slack hours service was withdrawn, as was the slack hours service between Dulwich and John Carpenter Street via Westminster. Passengers making through journeys were able to obtain transfer tickets to allow them to change cars at Camberwell Green, but this was altered to Goose Green on 22nd November.

The Peckham Rye and Victoria service, by the end of 1908 a rush hours only working, became something of an enigma. According to the LCC Official Tramways Guide for 1909-1910, there was no service, but in 1911 it was again listed as a weekday rush hours and Saturday afternoon working. As, in 1911, cars were listed as running at irregular intervals and were time-tabled, it is probable that it was only intended to provide a sufficient service to cater for a relatively small number of passengers between Peckham Rye and Goose Green, a distance of just over a mile. It is also probable that it continued to work throughout the years between 1908 and 1911, but by 1912 it had been discontinued,

On 20th July 1909, King Edward VII opened King's College Hospital at Denmark Hill. Car No. 269 passes through the gaily decorated streets at Camberwell Green. *(Commercial view, the Card House)*

with a through transfer fare being made available, passengers changing cars at Goose Green.

A new extension of the tracks from Dulwich Library to London Road, Forest Hill, just to the west of the railway station, was opened to traffic on 19th December 1908, the service from Victoria (58) being extended to the new terminus on a daily basis. The terminus of the rush hours service to Westminster, however, remained at Dulwich until 4th July 1910, when it too was extended to Forest Hill during the afternoons. Sunday services were generally of a frequency of between 4 and 10 minutes depending upon the time of day, but this varied from time to time, as did the operation of additional short workings, some probably seasonal in nature.

Camberwell and Brixton to West Norwood

Upon the opening of the Coldharbour Lane and Gresham Road lines for electric traction on the overhead wire system on 20th November 1908, a conduit/overhead wire change point was installed about 50 yards along Coldharbour Lane from Denmark Hill, with another in Gresham Road just east of the Brixton Road crossing. A service was provided along the new route by extending the short working service between St. George's Church and Camberwell Green (via Walworth Road) along Denmark Hill and into and along Coldharbour Lane to Brixton (74). On 8th December, the service was further extended across the junction at Brixton Road, along Stockwell Road and South Lambeth Road to Vauxhall and Victoria Station.

New tracks were laid from Loughborough Junction via Herne Hill Road and Wanless Road to rejoin the reconstructed lines in Hinton and Milkwood Roads, these being opened to traffic on 28th May 1909 as far as Herne Hill, and on 30th May throughout to West Norwood. A new service was provided between Victoria Embankment, Waterloo Bridge and West Norwood via Westminster, Elephant, Walworth Road, Camberwell Green, Loughborough Junction and Herne Hill (80). On the opening of Norwood car shed on 10th October 1909, cars working this service were transferred from Camberwell shed and cars working to Victoria and St. George's Church were transferred from Camberwell and Streatham sheds.

On 22nd November 1909 the Norwood and Embankment service (80) was withdrawn between Camberwell and Embankment at all times except weekday busy hours. The short working slack hours service which remained, only lasted until 7th February 1910 when it too was withdrawn. It was replaced by a new all-day daily service between Victoria Station and West Norwood via Vauxhall, Stockwell, Brixton and Loughborough Junction (78).

This also resulted in the St. George's Church and Victoria Station via Coldharbour Lane service (74) being curtailed on the same day at Gresham Road from the Camberwell direction, the service being totally withdrawn between Brixton and Victoria.

The Norwood-Embankment service (80) was re-introduced on Sundays, beginning on 1st May 1910, but from 28th September, the Sunday service was withdrawn between Camberwell and Embankment. It was again extended for the summer of 1911.

On 5th April 1912, a new tramway was opened between Brixton and Herne Hill via Effra Road, the Victoria and Norwood service (78) being diverted along the new route. The road between Herne Hill and Loughborough Junction was covered by the re-introduction of a weekday slack hours service between Norwood and Camberwell (80). By 1st November 1912, a new weekday rush hours only service was working between Herne Hill and Blackfriars, John Carpenter Street via Effra Road, Brixton, Kennington and Blackfriars Bridge (76).

A quiet urban scene in the 1910 period, with car No. 1081 travelling along Milkwood Road, Herne Hill. On this road between Herne Hill and Loughborough Junction, the roads were quite narrow, resulting in the "up" track being laid through the whole length of Milkwood Road, while the "down" line made a deviation for part of the way along Poplar Walk Road and Lowden Road. (Commercial view)

The Tooley Street Line

The tramway between Deptford and London Bridge was one of the last to be electrified, the first section being opened to traffic between "Red Lion" Rotherhithe and Tooley Street, Bermondsey Street (70) on 25th February 1911. On the same date, subway service (33) was extended from Tower Bridge Road at the junction with Tooley Street, along Tooley Street as far as Bermondsey Street. On 22nd June 1911, the service terminating at "Red Lion" (70) was extended eastwards to the west side of Creek Bridge.

Meanwhile, new tracks were being constructed from the east side of Creek Bridge to Greenwich Church and these were opened on 5th August 1911, with a service (previously mentioned) between Creek Bridge and Woolwich Road, Chapel Street. Creek Bridge was opened to traffic on 3rd October 1912 at 12 noon, which resulted in the two isolated sections being linked across the bridge. The main service provided worked between Catford, Greenwich and Tooley Street (50), with a second, short working service between Greenwich and Tooley Street (70).

A short extension westwards from Bermondsey Street as far as Stainer Street (only about 100 yards), took place on 28th November 1912, with the final length to Duke Street, Joiner Street opening on 9th December 1912. This resulted in the services (70/50) being extended beyond Bermondsey Street, but only during certain hours on weekdays and all day on Sundays and Bank Holidays, due to a restriction placed upon the LCC by the Board of Trade and Metropolitan Police, who were concerned about the congestion that tramcars might cause on this length of track during the periods when the wholesale produce markets in the area were in operation.

This view, taken sometime in 1911, shows class E/1 car, No. 1178 on a journey to London Bridge, Tooley Street, standing at a stopping place opposite the "Black Horse" public house, Lower Road, Deptford. After leaving the stop, the car would have climbed up to and crossed over the Surrey Canal by way of Black Horse Bridge.

(Commercial view)

371

Chapter 27
Routes and Services
South, 1913-1933

In complete contrast to the way in which the development of routes and services has been described so far, an entirely different approach has had to be taken with regard to events which occurred from about the middle of 1912. Great changes to the image of the LCC Tramways were taking place, in the main, due to the introduction of service numbering for cars on all routes.

In the years before 1912, the public had been offered a London Tramways Guide for one penny. This included a map of the system, but only referred to the lines worked as "routes", giving information on one or more services at a time, to some extent dependent on where on the route it operated. There had also been "6d maps" on sale, but apparently these were not successful. Ultimately, on 15th October 1912, the decision was taken to provide the travelling public with all this information, which would also include details of the service numbering scheme, in a comprehensive map and guide of the system, to be issued free to all who required it. The first known issue appeared in December 1912, printed by the Tramways Department.

By that time, the situation in the Southern Division of the LCC Tramways network was vastly different from that in north London. There were only three minor sections of horse tramway to be electrified, two of which were in the Bermondsey area, the third in Woolwich. The two lines in Bermondsey had not been converted, as there were problems, both operational and otherwise, which will be discussed when dealing with that area. The short section in Woolwich was in the process of conversion and was opened to electric cars early in 1914.

The method of allocating service numbers in south London also differed from that applying to the north side. Even numbers were used, but instead of numbering in an orderly manner from west to east as was the case in north London, the allocation was made in a somewhat haphazard way, with Clapham car shed receiving the lowest numbers, possibly in deference to the fact that Clapham services were the first to be electrified. A further complication was that although Hammersmith car shed was at that time placed in the Northern Division for operational purposes, the one service then working was given an even number in the southern series. However, on 16th August 1921, control of Hammersmith was transferred to the southern division in preparation for considerable interworking with cars from other south side sheds.

In order that a logical description can be given, it is proposed to deal with the south side by groups of services in car shed order where possible but, as some did not remain the responsibility of one shed at all times, certain deviations from this arrangement will be necessary. Another difference between the two divisions was the operation of circular services, mainly along the Victoria Embankment, but common in later years in the Streatham and Tooting areas, all of which had an effect on the service numbers allocated. The following table gives the complete list of numbered services, as presented in the map and guide for December 1912.

2   Merton, Tooting, Clapham, Kennington Road, Westminster, Embankment.

4   Merton, Tooting, Clapham, Kennington, Elephant, Blackfriars, Embankment.

6   Tooting Broadway, Clapham, Kennington Park Road, Elephant, Southwark Bridge Road, Southwark Bridge.
      Monday to Saturday rush hours only.

8   Tooting Broadway, Clapham, South Lambeth Road, Vauxhall, Victoria.

10   Tooting Broadway, Streatham, Brixton, Kennington, Elephant, St. George's Church.
      Extended Monday to Saturday until 9 p.m. to Southwark Bridge

12   Tooting Junction, Garratt Lane, Wandsworth, Battersea Park Road, Vauxhall, Lambeth Road, Borough Road, Southwark Bridge Road, Hop Exchange.

14   Tooting Junction, Garratt Lane, Wandsworth, Battersea Park Road, Vauxhall, Westminster, Embankment, Blackfriars (John Carpenter Str),
      Monday to Saturday rush hours only.
      Tooting Junction and Westminster (St. Thomas' Hospital),
      Sunday afternoons and evenings.

16   Norbury, Streatham, Brixton, Kennington Road, Westminster, Embankment.

18   Norbury, Streatham, Brixton, Kennington, Elephant, Blackfriars, Embankment.

20   Norbury, Streatham, Brixton, South Lambeth Road, Vauxhall, Victoria.

22   Southcroft Road, Streatham, Brixton, Kennington Road, Westminster, Embankment (Waterloo Bridge),
      Monday to Saturday rush hours only.

24   Streatham (Telford Avenue), Brixton, Kennington, Elephant, St. George's Church, Southwark Bridge,
      Monday to Saturday rush hours only.

26   East Hill, Clapham Junction, Wandsworth Road, Vauxhall, Westminster, Embankment, Blackfriars, Southwark Street, Hop Exchange.

28   East Hill, Clapham Junction, Wandsworth Road, Vauxhall, Victoria.

30   East Hill, Clapham Junction, Cedars Road, Clapham Common, Kennington, Elephant, Waterloo Station.

32   Lavender Hill, Queen's Road, Chelsea Bridge.

34   Clapham Junction, Falcon Road, Battersea, King's Road Chelsea.

36   Blackwall Tunnel, Greenwich, New Cross, Old Kent Road, New Kent Road, Elephant, Blackfriars (John Carpenter Street).
      Some cars started from Chapel Street Woolwich.

38   Chapel Street Woolwich, Greenwich, New Cross, Old Kent Road, New Kent Road, Elephant, Westminster, Embankment (Waterloo Bridge).
      Some cars started from Blackwall Tunnel.

40   Chapel Street Woolwich, Greenwich, New Cross, Peckham, Camberwell, Kennington Road, Westminster, Embankment (Waterloo Bridge).

42   Abbey Wood, Plumstead, Beresford Square, Free Ferry Woolwich.

44   Beresford Square Woolwich, Woolwich Common, Well Hall, Eltham Church.

46	Lee Green, Lewisham, New Cross, Camberwell, Walworth Road, Elephant, Waterloo Station.
48	Lee Green, Lewisham, New Cross, Camberwell, Vauxhall, Victoria.
50	Catford, Lewisham, Greenwich, Creek Road, Rotherhithe, Tooley Street.
52	Catford, Lewisham, New Cross, Old Kent Road, St. George's Church, Southwark Bridge, Monday to Saturday rush hours only.
54	Catford, Lewisham, New Cross, Peckham, Camberwell, Vauxhall, Victoria.
56	Peckham Rye, Goose Green, Camberwell, Walworth Road, Elephant, Westminster, Embankment (Waterloo Bridge).
58	Forest Hill (London Road), Dulwich, Goose Green, Camberwell, Vauxhall, Victoria.
60	Dulwich Library, Goose Green, Camberwell, Walworth Road, Elephant, Southwark Bridge Road, Southwark Bridge, Monday to Saturday rush hours only.
62	Forest Hill (London Road), Dulwich Goose Green, Camberwell, Walworth Road, Elephant, Westminster, Embankment (Waterloo Bridge). Monday to Saturday p.m. rush hours only.
64	New Cross Gate, Old Kent Road, Elephant, Waterloo Station Sundays: cars extended from New Cross Gate to Catford via Lewisham. No evening service on Mondays to Saturdays.
66	New Cross Gate, Camberwell, Walworth Road, Elephant, Blackfriars (John Carpenter Street).
68	Rye Lane Peckham, Camberwell, Kennington Road, Westminster, Embankment (Waterloo Bridge). Monday to Saturday rush hours only.
70	Greenwich Church, Creek Road, Rotherhithe, Tooley Street.
72	Forest Hill (Park Road), Brockley, New Cross, Old Kent Road, St. George's Church, Southwark Bridge.
74	Brixton Road, Coldharbour Lane, Camberwell, Walworth Road, Elephant, St. George's Church.
76	Herne Hill, Effra Road, Brixton, Kennington, Elephant, Blackfriars (John Carpenter Street). Monday to Saturday rush hours only.
78	West Norwood, Herne Hill, Effra Road, Brixton, South Lambeth Road, Vauxhall, Victoria.
80	West Norwood, Herne Hill, Loughborough Junction, Camberwell Extended Monday to Saturday rush hours to Walworth Road, Elephant, Westminster, Embankment (Waterloo Bridge).
82	Harlesden (Harrow Road), Shepherds Bush, Hammersmith, Fulham Palace Road, Putney Bridge, Wandsworth High Street.
84	Rye Lane Peckham, Camberwell, Walworth Road, Elephant, Blackfriars (John Carpenter Street). Monday to Saturday rush hours only.
86	Greenwich Church, New Cross, Old Kent Road, St. George's Church. Monday to Saturday only.
88	Rotherhithe "Red Lion", Raymouth Road, Grange Road, Tower Bridge Road. (Horse car service).
90	Raymouth Road, Rotherhithe New Road, Canal Bridge (Old Kent Road). (Horse car service).

Subway Services

33   Highbury Station, "Angel" Islington, Bloomsbury, Kingsway Subway, Westminster, Elephant, Tower Bridge Road.

35   "Angel" Islington, Bloomsbury, Kingsway Subway, Westminster, Vauxhall, Battersea Park Road, Falcon Road, Clapham Junction. On Sundays, extended from "Angel" via Essex Road to Mildmay Park (St. Paul's Road).

Night Services

Tooting Broadway, Clapham, Kennington Road, Westminster, Embankment (Waterloo Bridge).

Water Lane Brixton, Kennington, Elephant, Blackfriars, (John Carpenter Street).

New Cross ("Marquis of Granby"), Old Kent Road, New Kent Road, Elephant, Blackfriars (John Carpenter Street).

New Cross Gate, Camberwell, Walworth Road, Elephant, Blackfriars, (John Carpenter Street).

Battersea ("Princes Head"), Battersea Park Road, Vauxhall, Westminster, Embankment, Blackfriars (John Carpenter Street).

These services did not operate on Saturday nights/Sunday mornings.

The Clapham and Tooting Route

The first group to be considered consisted of the four services to Tooting and Clapham, receiving the numbers 2, 4, 6 and 8 in 1912. Services 2 and 4 were always circular in nature around the Embankment and both terminated at the County boundary at Longley Road, Tooting. This terminus was also shared by the London United Tramways, whose lines butted on to those of the LCC but did not connect. The descriptions used by the two operators for the same terminus were totally different, the LCC calling it "Merton", which was at least one mile further on. The LUT, on the other hand, called it "Tooting", a little nearer the truth, as Tooting Broadway was only half a mile away.

During the early part of 1922 the two systems were connected and trial runs were made by LCC cars to Wimbledon Hill on 24th April. These being successful, services 2 and 4 were extended to Wimbledon Hill as from 2nd May 1922. LUT service 71 from Hampton Court was withdrawn between Longley Road and Wimbledon, Ely's Corner. (This change was part of a re-arrangement of operations agreed to by the LCC and LUT, which mainly affected services in west London).

Kingston as a shopping centre, and Hampton Court as a summer weekend pleasure resort attracted fairly heavy traffic on Saturdays and Sundays, and the LCC agreed to take part in handling it. A trial run over LUT metals was carried out on 12th March 1926, resulting in the extension of part of services 2 and 4 to Hampton Court on Saturday afternoons and evenings, all day on Sundays and Bank Holidays, although during the winter months the extension was made on Saturday afternoons and evenings only. Commencing on 22nd May 1926, the arrangements were as follows:-

1926:	From Sunday	22nd May	until	26th September (incl)
1927:		23rd April		2nd October
1928:		13th May		30th September
1929:		12th May		6th October
1930:		20th April		28th September
1931:		17th May		30th August

The summer extension of services 2 and 4 to Hampton Court is shown here by E/1 car No. 1780 in Wimbledon. The signal controlling the single track section is mounted on the traction post to the left of the view. (Courtesy: P. J. Davis)

Due to the conversion from trams to trolleybuses of the Hampton Court and Wimbledon services worked by the LUT, the Saturday service ran for the last time on 29th August 1931. From 16th May 1931, LCC cars worked alongside both LUT trams and trolleybuses as the new vehicles gradually replaced the old.

According to LCC records, an entry was made in the account books showing an apparent service to Hampton Court as having operated on Tuesday 1st September 1931. The mileage allegedly worked was recorded as being 6,984, and was credited to "Mr. Black's Parties". It is a matter of conjecture as to who and what "Mr. Black" was, and given the practicalities of providing this concentrated service on what was a normal weekday, it is more likely that it was an accounting device and that such a service did not operate.

Trailer operation on services 2 and 4 is shown here as trailer T24 waits behind its class E tractor car at John Carpenter Street, Victoria Embankment in 1916. (Commercial view)

Following the extension of services 2 and 4 to Wimbledon, the workings from London to Longley Road, Tooting continued to operate with cars towing trailers in rush hours and bearing the numbers 2A and 4A. Sunday operation of services 2A and 4A did not last long, being withdrawn as from 4th June 1922. It is therefore possible that any Sunday short workings after this date carried the numbers 2 or 4. Trailer operation was finally withdrawn from the Tooting services as from 20th November 1922. (A full account of the operation of trailer car services is given in the LRTA Publication "The LCC Trailers" by M. J. D. Willsher, B.Sc., A.L.A.).

Services 2A and 4A continued to run to Longley Road until 6th October 1927, when they were diverted at Tooting Broadway via Southcroft Road and Mitcham Lane to Streatham Library. In reality, the cars would show 2A or 4A until reaching the junction of Southcroft Road and Mitcham Lane, where the numbers would be changed to 22 or 24, and the cars would continue to London via Brixton.

The country terminus of services 2 and 4 then remained at Wimbledon Hill until the trolleybuses were extended from Ely's Corner to Wimbledon Town Hall on 15th December 1932, when the trams from London were also cut back to that point.

The plough of car No. 953 is just about to leave the car as it approaches the "plough shift" at Tooting Junction on a journey to Mitcham.

(The late Dr. Whitcombe)

Service 6 in 1912 worked on weekday rush hours only between Tooting Broadway and Southwark Bridge, running from the Elephant & Castle via Southwark Bridge Road. From 10th January 1917, the afternoon and evening journeys in the "up" direction were diverted via Kennington Road, Lambeth Road, Borough Road and Southwark Bridge Road, presumably to relieve pressure on the traffic at the Elephant and Castle. At an unknown date in 1917, it was diverted to run via Borough High Street and Marshalsea Road, which became the normal route for all cars between the Elephant and Southwark Bridge. On 10th March 1919, a midday service was introduced on weekdays, but after 3 p.m. on Saturdays the service did not work north of St. George's Church (Borough). The 1919 map and guide, which was probably issued in May, shows a Sunday afternoon and evening service working between Merton and St. George's Church, but the date of introduction is not known.

At Tooting, a new junction layout connecting Upper Tooting Road and Mitcham Road was laid in and received Board of Trade approval on 6th November 1919. Service 6 was extended to Tooting Junction and became a daily working as from 24th November, although the London terminus on Saturday afternoons and Sundays remained at St. George's Church. There matters rested until 16th June 1921, when the cars were diverted at Amen Corner, Tooting to form a new circular service with 10 (Tooting - Southwark Bridge via Brixton). A weekday evening service now began operating as far as St. George's Church and the Sunday service, which also turned at that point, began working on an all-day basis. Cars on 6 displayed this number as far as Tooting, returning to Southwark Bridge via Brixton as 10. Similarly, cars on 10 became 6 at Tooting Broadway. This practice lasted until 24th November 1924, when the changing of numbers at the country end ceased and 6 ran outwards via Clapham, returning via Brixton, with 10 working in the opposite direction.

A trial run took over the new tramway across Southwark Bridge on 8th July 1925, followed by the Ministry of Transport inspection the next day. The tramway was then left idle until 14th July, when the Lord Mayor of London, Sir A. Bower, drove a tram across the bridge at 12.30 p.m., after which sevices 6 and 10 were extended to the new terminus on Mondays to Fridays all day and on Saturdays until 3 p.m. It is possible that the new terminus generated extra traffic as, from 21st December, the daily service operated all day to the City. A re-organisation of routing took place in the Tooting area on 19th July 1928, when service 6 was detached from its circular operation at Amen Corner and diverted to run to Mitcham, Cricket Green in place of 8. Incidentally, for a matter of three months between 11th January and 23rd April 1923, a supplementary service numbered 6A ran between Southwark Bridge and Tooting Broadway on weekdays.

Service 8 began working daily in 1912 from Victoria to Merton, Longley Road, which it continued to do until 23rd November 1919. The following day it was diverted over the new curve at Tooting Broadway to run via Mitcham Road to Tooting Junction, where it met the metals of the South Metropolitan Tramways and Lighting Company, Limited, who operated a small system based on termini at West Croydon, but also had a short spur line in Mitcham stretching from the Fair Green to the Cricket Green, a distance of just over a quarter of a mile. This had been laid in anticipation of the company obntaining powers to extend to Sutton and Belmont, a scheme which did not materialise. A shuttle service was worked from Tooting Junction to the Cricket Green until the early part of the First World War, but from then on the line fell into disuse.

The LCC suggested to the SMET as early as March 1923, that the tracks of the two undertakings should be connected at Tooting Junction to enable the Council to provide a through service to Mitcham but, despite meetings between the two bodies in 1924 and early in 1925, no agreement was reached. In June 1925, the Ministry of Transport remarked that the spur line to the Cricket Green had not been used for some time and asked the company to remove it. This encouraged the SMET to resume negotiations with the LCC, resulting in service 8 being extended from Tooting Junction to the Cricket Green on 1st September 1926, working to that terminus until 19th July 1928, when it changed places with service 6, the 8 then becoming a "circular" with 20. The operations of 8, 20 and 10 will be discussed with the Streatham group.

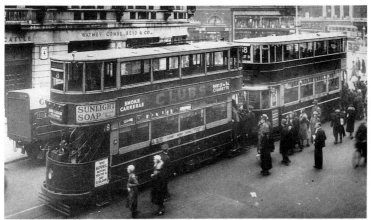

E/1 car No. 1100 loads passengers at Victoria terminus, before leaving on the long circular journey round south London on service 8 in 1932.

The Wandsworth and Battersea Areas

Both of these districts were served from Jews Row car shed, with the Wandsworth area being additionally served from Hammersmith. The services involved were 12, 14, 26, 28, 30, 32, 34, 82, 86, 31, 35 and 89.

In 1912, the number 12 was allocated to the service working between Hop Exchange and Tooting Junction via Lambeth Road, Vauxhall, Nine Elms Lane, Battersea Park Road, York Road and Garratt Lane. Only one minor change is recorded whilst under LCC management. This occurred between 8th November 1931 and 20th January 1932, whilst an approach road to the new Lambeth Bridge was under construction, closing the junction between Albert Embankment and Lambeth Road. During this period, service 12 was operated in two separate sections, with cars turning on either side of the obstruction.

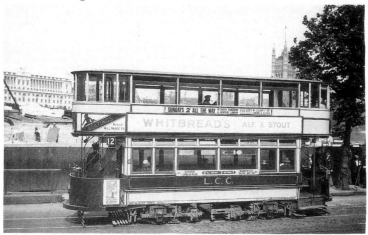

Car No. 314 of class D on service 12, passes the working site of the new Lambeth Bridge during the summer of 1930. (P. J. Davis)

Service 14, working from Jews Row shed was, at the commencement of numbering, running between Tooting Junction and John Carpenter Street, Blackfriars on weekdays until 8.12 p.m. In addition, a service was provided on Sundays between Tooting and St. Thomas' Hospital from 3 p.m. until 10.33 p.m., in both cases following the route of service 12 all the way from Tooting to Lambeth Bridge. On 9th June 1913, the service was re-arranged with quite complex routings. The Map and Guide for June 1913 describes it as follows:-

Weekdays:
Early cars (until 9.30 a.m.):- Tooting Junction - Blackfriars.
9.45 a.m. until 4.30 p.m.:- Streatham Library - Wandsworth High Street.
4.30 p.m. to 8 p.m. (noon to 3 p.m. on Saturdays):-
Streatham Library - Blackfriars.
8 p.m. to last (3 p.m. to last Saturdays):-
Streatham Library - Wandworth High Street.

Sundays:
Until 4 p.m.:- Streatham Library - Battersea, "Princes Head".
After 4 p.m.:- Streatham Library - New Scotland Yard.

It is not likely that the travelling public understood very well these complicated workings; and yet the timetable was to become even

Westminster Bridge and class E/1 car No. 798 on service 14, bound for Wimbledon, seen in 1930. (LCC Tramways)

more difficult to follow. Minor alterations were made on 30th June 1913 when the slack hours weekday service was extended from Wandsworth High Street to "The Princes Head", Battersea, whilst the Sunday cars ran from Streatham to Latchmere Road until 4 p.m. when they were then extended to Westminster (New Scotland Yard). By December 1913, weekday workings had become extremely complex and are quoted here in detail.

Mondays - Fridays:

First car until 9.16 a.m.	:- Wimbledon Road - Blackfriars.
9.16 a.m. to 4.24 p.m.	:- Streatham Library - Latchmere Road.
4.24 p.m. to 7.09 p.m.	:- Tooting Junction - Blackfriars.
7.09 p.m. to last car	:- Tooting Junction - "Princes Head".

Saturdays:

First car until 9.18 a.m.	:- Wimbledon Road - Blackfriars.
9.18 a.m. to 10.54 a.m.	:- Streatham Library - Latchmere Road.
10.54 a.m. to 1.57 p.m.	:- Tooting Junction - Blackfriars.
1.57 p.m. to 4.09 p.m.	:- Tooting Junction - Vauxhall.
4.09 p.m. to last car	:- Streatham Library - Vauxhall.

Sundays:

First car until 3.10 p.m.	:- Streatham Library - Latchmere Road.
3.10 p.m. to last car	:- Streatham Library - Queen's Road.

Things then settled down for a while, but the advent of the Great War resulted in some alterations being made to services. From 15th September 1914 service 14 was withdrawn between Tooting and Streatham Library and while morning journeys on weekdays up to 9.18 a.m. continued to operate between Wimbledon Road and Blackfriars, for the rest of the day the service was from Tooting Junction to Blackfriars (John Carpenter Street), while on Sundays it worked between Tooting Junction and Savoy Street. The extension of 82 to Tooting Junction on 16th July 1915 had an immediate effect on 14, which was cut back from Tooting to Wandsworth High Street.

On the issue of the Spring 1918 map, 14 is shown as running between Blackfriars (weekdays) or Savoy Street (Sundays) and Wandsworth High Street, with an extension from Wandsworth to Earlsfield Station during weekday rush hours. On 13th January 1919, the service was extended from Blackfriars to Hop Exchange on weekdays, but was withdrawn on Sundays.

An interesting working was introduced with the football season of 1921-1922 when on 3rd September 1921, cars on service 14EX operated from the Embankment to Kings Road, Chelsea via Battersea Park Road, utilising a new junction laid in from the easterly direction at Latchmere Road. This extra service was operated whenever Chelsea F.C. were at home.

The map and guide for May 1925 shows a Saturday afternoon and evening projection of service 14 onwards from Wandsworth to Tooting Junction. This may have happened on 15th November 1924 when official records indicate that a change occurred to the Saturday schedule with the curtailment of the p.m. service at John Carpenter Street. It is also likely that early morning services to Summerstown, which also made an initial appearance in the guide for May 1925, had probably been working since 16th July 1915.

A Sunday service numbered 14 was re-introduced in 1926, working between Tooting Junction and Savoy Street. This was achieved by reducing the frequency of service 12 from 16th May, thereby saving nine cars, these being worked on service 14 with five others. The winter service on 12 was restored from 24th October when the 14 was again withdrawn on Sundays. The summer augmentation in subsequent years was confined to service 12.

The London United Tramways Company's line from Summerstown ("The Plough"), through Haydons Road to Merton High Street, became isolated from the rest of its system when LCC cars began to work through to Wimbledon, which meant that a car had to be brought from Fulwell each day to work over it. Having successfully introduced trolley-buses in 1931, the company could no longer supply this car and negoti-ated with the LCC to make an exchange of mileage, whereby LUT cars would again make an appearance on service 89 in the Putney area. From 16th April 1931, the Council took over the working of the Haydons Road line, resulting in weekday service 14 being extended all day via Summerstown to Wimbledon Hill Road, providing the people of Haydons Road with through facilities to London for the first time. In addition, a Sunday service was re-introduced, to work this time between Wands-worth and Wimbledon Hill Road.

The final change came on 15th December 1932 when the Wimbledon terminus was re-located at Wimbledon Town Hall, consequent upon the short extension of the LUT trolleybus service.

Service 26 was working between East Hill, Wandsworth and Hop Exchange via Wandsworth Road, Vauxhall and Embankment when it was numbered in 1912, a duty which it was to perform for another eight years without change, apart from a short period in 1917 during the reconstruction of St. John's Hill Bridge. Between 12th May and 20th July the service was divered at "Arding & Hobbs Corner", Clapham Junction to run via Falcon Road and York Road to Wandsworth High Street, reversing in Battersea Park Road.

The link down East Hill to Wandsworth High Street was opened to traffic on 4th August 1921, resulting in the service being extended to Putney High Street. A few weeks later, on 10th September, at the commencement of the football season, service 26 was extended to Hammersmith Broadway whenever Fulham F.C. played at home, whilst on 9th October, the Sunday service joined those of the 28 and 82 to Harrow Road (Scrubs Lane). On 1st December, it was extended to Hammersmith Broadway on a daily basis.

In 1922, the LCC purchased the London United Tramways Company lines in and around Hammersmith within the County of London and,

County Hall, the administrative headquarters of the erstwhile London County Council forms the backdrop for this view in which car No. 437 is seen just about to cross Westminster Bridge sometime in 1930.

to balance the mileage to be run by the LUT over their former tracks, service 26 was extended to Kew Bridge via Chiswick High Road on 2nd May as a daily working, the London terminus remaining at Hop Exchange, thereby giving the cars the distinction of crossing the River Thames three times on their journeys, via Blackfriars, Westminster and Putney bridges, beginning and ending their journeys almost at the south side of London Bridge and at the north side of Kew Bridge. In conjunction with the purchase of the LUT lines in London by the Council, the Chiswick depot of the company also passed to the LCC. An allocation of cars from Chiswick was worked on service 26 until 5th May 1932, when the depot ceased to be used for operational purposes.

Traffic on this route became very heavy on Bank Holidays, resulting in extra cars being run between Kew Bridge and Clapham Junction. For the Whitsun Bank Holiday of 1926, these extras were extended to the "Plough", Clapham via Cedars Road, being further extended on the August Bank Holiday to Camberwell Green via Stockwell and Brixton, providing the only example of a tram service going through two complete overhead to conduit changes on one journey by working the first section between Kew and Wandsworth on the overhead wire, then on conduit for the section between Wandsworth and Brixton, back again to overhead from Brixton (Gresham Road) to Denmark Hill, then on conduit again for the last 300 yards of the journey to Camberwell Green. This special working continued until 1935, when the LPTB converted part of the route to trolleybus operation.

The number 28 was allocated to the service from East Hill, Wandsworth to Victoria via Clapham Junction and Wandsworth Road. The first alteration to the service was between 12th May and 20th July 1917, when the closure of St. John's Hill Bridge curtailed the service at Clapham Junction. The next change was made on 4th August 1921 when the service was extended to Scrubs Lane, Harrow Road via Putney and Hammersmith, after the link between East Hill and Wandsworth High Street had been opened. The new terminus was quaintly described on the destination blinds as "near Willesden Junction via Putney". The service was worked from Jews Row and Clapham sheds until 5th May 1932, when Hammersmith also provided some cars. This was another of the results of the closure of Chiswick depot.

On the allocation of service numbers, 30 was given to the service operating between East Hill, Wandsworth and Waterloo Station via Clapham Junction, Cedars Road, Clapham, Kennington and Elephant & Castle. Official records show that on 13th June 1915, service 34 was extended daily to "Plough" Clapham, with a further extension during July in busy hours to Waterloo Station via Kennington and Elephant & Castle. These extensions may well have replaced the 30, as the service did not appear in the October 1915 map and guide. It is possible that it was withdrawn during or after the tramwaymens' strike, which began on 15th May.

At this point it is pertinent to introduce to the reader a west London service numbered 82, which in 1924 was to be linked to the re-introduction of the number 30. Upon numbering, 82 was allocated to the isolated service running between Scrubs Lane and Wandsworth High Street, working from the small car shed at Hammersmith. The connecting line from Putney Bridge Road, along Wandsworth High Street to Garratt Lane was laid in the early part of 1915, resulting in the service being extended on 16th July 1915 to Tooting Junction. This pattern of service continued throughout the Great War years and afterwards until 1922 when, on Sundays between 15th October and 5th May 1923, a short working service numbered 82A ran between Shepherds Bush Green and Tooting Junction. On 23rd December 1923 the number appeared again on Sundays, but on this occasion the service worked between Harrow Road and Tooting Junction. As it was not mentioned in the May 1924 map and guide, it can only be assumed that it was not a financial success.

The number 30 was used on 23rd April 1924 for a weekday service from Putney High Street to Wembley Hill Road via Hammersmith, Scrubs Lane and Craven Park. This new service, which did not operate until after the morning busy hour, catered for the traffic to the British Empire Exhibition at Wembley and was worked by Hammersmith crews. Official records show that from 25th May, the service on Thursdays did not commence until 1.12 p.m., in contrast to a 9 a.m. start made during the rest of the week.

The crew of class E/1 car No. 1362 pose outside Hammersmith car shed in this rare photograph of the car on service 82. (Courtesy: A. D. Packer)

The Wembley terminus was in Harrow Road just south of the junction with Wembley Hill Road, where road traffic left the Harrow Road for the Exhibition Grounds. In addition to LCC 30, a short working service of the MET, numbered 58, also turned there, impeding through cars to Sudbury on regular MET services. In an effort to ease the congestion, LCC 30 was extended to Sudbury, "The Swan" as from 2nd June 1924. At the same time, half the cars working service 82 were re-allocated to service 30, which was then extended on an all-day basis to Tooting Junction.

Official records note that Whit Monday 1924 occurred one week after the alteration, and 82 was extended to Sudbury for one day only, as service 30 was suspended for that day, but on August Bank Holiday Monday, a special timetable was in use for service 30. The Exhibition closed on 1st November, but service 30 continued to operate between Tooting Junction and Sudbury on weekdays only, with 82 providing a daily service as far as Harrow Road.

The Wembley Exhibition opened daily throughout the summer of 1925, necessitating the daily working of service 30 from 12th April. When the Exhibition finally closed on 31st October, service 82 was withdrawn on Mondays to Fridays and drastically reduced on Saturdays, being replaced by extra cars on service 30, which itself had been withdrawn between Craven Park Junction and Wembley.

On 17th July 1926, the 30 was again extended to Sudbury on Saturday afternoons and Sundays, in order to supplement MET service 62. This ceased on 23rd October, and at the same time service 82 was completely withdrawn. In 1927, the Sudbury extension was re-introduced between 21st May and 8th October, with the 82 also making a brief re-appearance between 21st May and 23rd July only. Documentary evidence, in the shape of the account books, suggests that the service worked on Bank Holidays until 1932.

Greyhound racing was introduced at Wembley Stadium in the latter part of 1927, and 30 was extended to Wembley Hill Road on Thursday evenings and Saturday afternoons as from 10th December to assist the MET in moving the crowds attending this pastime.

As from 26th April 1928, service 30 incursions into MET territory were confined to weekday rush hours workings to Craven Park Junction, with the main service from the south terminating at Harrow Road, Scrubs Lane. In 1929, the 30 was once again extended to Wembley Church in afternoon rush hours on weekdays as from 6th June, and morning rush hours and all day on Saturdays from 24th October. The final change during LCC ownership occurred on 5th May 1932 when cars on the service, operating outside rush hours on weekdays were again extended to Craven Park, continuing to Wembley during rush hours and on Saturdays as before.

The short service which worked between Chelsea Bridge and Lavender Hill via Queens Road, Battersea (later Queenstown Road) received the number 32 in 1912, and was worked by single deck cars until the road beneath the low railway bridges spanning Queen's Road was lowered, which then allowed the use of double deck cars as from 3rd May 1926. From 6th November 1927, the service was once again extended to "The Plough" Clapham via Cedars Road after an absence of 17 years. Jews Row car shed provided both the single deck and double deck cars for this service until 5th May 1932, when Clapham assumed responsibility for it.

Dealing next with service 34, on numbering it worked only between Kings Road, Chelsea and Clapham Junction, using 4-wheeled cars of

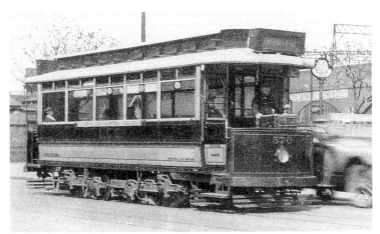

Operation of service 32 was confined to single-deck cars until 1926, and class G car No. 570 is seen here in Queens Road, Battersea.

class B or C drom Jews Row. It is probable that, using the new curve at Clapham Junction from Falcon Road into Lavender Hill, it was extended to "The Plough", Clapham via Cedars Road on 13th June 1915. From 22nd July, during busy hours, it was further extended to Waterloo Station via Kennington and Elephant & Castle, these extensions replacing service 30 as discussed above, while also from the same date, Clapham cars and crews took over from Jews Row.

By October 1915, the Waterloo extension was being worked until approximately 9 p.m. on weekdays, and all day on Sundays, but on 5th March 1916, it was withdrawn, the service reverting to its June 1915 form. No further alterations occurred until 22nd January 1922, when a new junction layout was brought into use between Clapham Road and Stockwell Road, which resulted in the 34 being extended to Southwark Bridge via Stockwell, Brixton and Camberwell Green, replacing service 74 over the section eastwards from Brixton. In common with other services in the area, 34 was extended over Southwark Bridge on 14th July 1925. On 14th May 1931, alterations were made to the pattern of services in the Camberwell area, one result being that service 34 only ran beyond Brixton to Camberwell and the City on Sundays. To prevent congestion with cars reversing in either Stockwell Road or Brixton Road, it ran up Brixton Hill as far as Water Lane on weekdays. This arrangement did not last long, as from 4th June 1931 the service was again routed along Coldharbour Lane as far as Camberwell Green on weekdays, settling down to this pattern until after the advent of the LPTB, when further changes were made.

It is likely that Jews Row ceased to take part in the service from January 1922, being replaced by the provision of Camberwell cars which had previously operated service 74. Participation by Camberwell appears to have ceased during the later years of the 1920s, but records show that Camberwell cars and crews again began to share the Sunday service with Clapham as from 15th May 1931, and with a weekday involvement commencing on 28th January 1932.

Operationally, services 35 and 86 were closely interlinked in the Wandsworth district. Early in 1913, service 35 was working between Clapham Junction and "The Angel", Islington via Falcon Road, Battersea

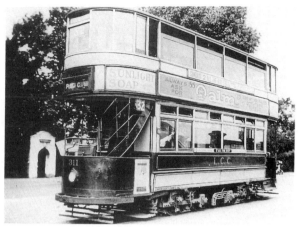

Double deck car working on service 32 is represented by this view of class D car No. 311 standing at Chelsea Bridge terminus.

Park Road, Vauxhall, Westminster and Kingsway Subway, being diverted on Sundays via Essex Road to St. Paul's Road (Balls Pond Road). Despite the fact that double-deck cars were working along Battersea Park Road on services 12 and 14, the single deck cars of service 35 could not cope with the traffic offered, in part due to cars on service 14 not running beyond "The Latchmere" during certain times of the day. To ease the problem, service 35 was replaced on 28th November 1913 by double-deck cars bearing the number 86, working daily between Clapham Junction and Waterloo Bridge. This became a wartime casualty on 15th September 1914 when operation became Mondays - Fridays rush hours only and all day on Saturdays, with no service on Sundays. It was completely withdrawn in October 1915, never to re-appear. The subsequent history of service 35, together with 31 and 33 is dealt with in the section covering the Kingsway Subway group of services.

The reconstruction of Putney Bridge during 1932-33 resulted in the re-siting of the tram tracks. Class E car No. 402 is seen crossing the bridge on its way to Acton, on service 89.   *(Courtesy: D. W. K. Jones)*

The last service to consider was the one numbered 89. This was originally worked solely by the London United Tramways Company, between Acton and Hammersmith. The tracks of the two undertakings were connected in 1922, which allowed the subsequent extension of the service to Putney on weekdays only from 28th November 1928. At first, this extension was a joint working of LCC and LUT cars until 30th January 1930, when the LUT ceased to work south of Hammersmith. This re-arrangement was made in order to adjust the mileage worked by both undertakings to a previously agreed figure. For the same reason, LUT cars worked to Putney between 16th April and 30th July 1931, 28th October 1931 and 16th February 1933 and finally from 20th April 1933. From 18th June until 24th September 1932, and from 24th June 1933, the service was further extended to Tooting Junction on Saturday afternoons. LCC cars were provided by Hammersmith shed, while extra cars for the Saturday service to Tooting came from Jews Row.

The Streatham Group

Streatham car shed, always known in the familiar term as "Telford Avenue", was the home base for six services, numbered in 1912 as 10, 16, 18, 20, 22 and 24. This was joined on 6th March 1924 by the opening of Brixton Hill car shed, which operated in conjunction with Telford Avenue. Service 10 worked between Tooting Broadway and Southwark Bridge via Southcroft Road, Streatham, Brixton and Elephant & Castle on weekdays, terminating at St. George's Church (Borough Station) after 9 p.m. and all day on Sundays. A new curve and junction from Mitcham Road to the southern half of Tooting High Street was opened on 12th July 1914, and service 10 was extended to the LCC terminus at Longley Road, Merton, a working that was to last until after January 1916, when it was cut back to Tooting Broadway. By April 1916, operation at the London end between St. George's Church and Southwark Bridge was confined to weekday rush hours only.

As previously stated, services 10 and 6 were combined on 16th June 1921, and as a result the operation of service 10 to Southwark was restored during midday hours Mondays to Fridays, and on Saturday mornings

This view, taken during the Great War, shows class E car No. 542 standing at Streatham Library on service 10.

The Streatham change-point attendant retrieves the plough from car No. 1012 as it proceeds to Norbury on service 16 during the summer of 1916.

between the rush hours. Initially, the cars changed service numbers at Tooting, but from 24th November 1924, this practice was superseded when the number 6 was used for the service operating in an anticlockwise direction via Clapham and Streatham, with the number 10 being used in the other direction.

The next change came on 15th July 1925, when the 10 was extended over Southwark Bridge to a new terminus in the City and, as from 31st December, the service operated all day to that point. This lasted until 19th July 1928, when 10 became separated from service 6, to once again work only between Tooting Broadway, Streatham and City via Southwark. The last change of note occurred on 3rd October 1931, when the Saturday afternoon service was once again curtailed at St. George's Church, a duty that it was to perform for the rest of its existence under LCC control.

Services 16 and 18, like the Clapham services 2 and 4, worked around the Embankment loop for the whole of their existence. From 31st July 1909 until 6th February 1926, the outer terminus for both services was at Hermitage Bridge, Norbury. From the first day of operation, through tickets were issued to and from the cars of Croydon Corporation to various farestages in both the LCC and Croydon areas, passengers changing cars at the boundary point. Encroachments into this considerable traffic were made by the LGOC in 1912 when omnibus service No. 59 began working between Oxford Circus and South Croydon, to be followed in the early part of 1913 by a service from Shepherds Bush to Thornton Heath, which competed with the LCC trams from Streatham and also with the Croydon cars along Brigstock Road. A further blow came during the summer of 1914 when through Sunday 'bus services began to such places at Reigate, Godstone and Whyteleafe, skimming off some of the traffic that the trams had carried at weekends to the countryside around Purley.

Before the two tramway authorities could conclude an agreement to make a connection between their systems, the Great War had started. One effect of this was to reduce the numbers of omnibuses working in the Croydon and Norbury districts, resulting in the two tramways having their hands full in coping with extra passengers, a situation which remained until after the war. In February 1921, the Ministry of Transport in a letter to Croydon Corporation mentioned the desirability of through running between Purley and London and negotiations to this end commenced in 1922, with agreement being reached on 12th November 1923. Due to many factors, including the relaying of the Croydon tracks to conform to LCC standards, and a chronic shortage of suitable rolling stock in the Croydon area, which is fully discussed in "Tramways of Croydon" (by G. E. Baddeley, LRTA/TLRS), operation did not commence until 7th February 1926, when services 16 and 18 were extended to Purley. Apart from minor adjustments, the two services remained virtually unaltered while being worked by the LCC.

The numbers 16A and 18A were first used on 15th March 1923 for rush hour workings between St. Leonard's Church, Streatham and Victoria Embankment, when the use of trailers on services 16 and 18 ceased. Just over a month later, on 23rd April, both these were withdrawn, the main services taking over the workings under their numbers. After the extension of LCC cars into the Croydon area, short workings in rush hours in the London area between Norbury and Embankment were classified as 16EX or 18EX, and may have been given the numbers 16A and 18A for a short time.

Car No. 1101 is seen here on service 18A during the evening rush hour on the Embankment. *(The late R. B. Parr, courtesy: T & L R S)*

In 1912, service 20 was running between Victoria Station and Norbury via Brixton, but by October 1915 the weekday late evening service was withdrawn between Streatham Library and Norbury. At the beginning of January 1916 it was working only between Victoria and Streatham Library, but on 12th October 1917 it was extended to Tooting Broadway via Mitcham Lane in the afternoons and evenings. By spring 1918, it was working between Victoria and Mitcham Lane, Southcroft Road in weekday rush hours, and between Victoria and Tooting Broadway on Sunday afternoons and evenings. However, on 30th November, it became an all day service on weekdays. On 27th January 1919, the Sunday service was withdrawn and the weekday operation transferred from Telford Avenue to Norwood shed in order to make room for a number of trailer cars, some of which had been working from Abbey Wood car shed.

E/1 class car No. 1143 passes Acre Lane, Brixton on its way to Victoria.

A strike of coal miners commenced at midnight on 31st March 1921, lasting for many weeks. Due to a shortage of coal, power output was reduced at the generating station, with some consequent reductions in tram services. Service 20 was withdrawn from 9th April and transfer tickets introduced, passengers changing to and from cars on services 10 and 22 to those on 78 at Brixton. In order to save printing special tickets, those applicable to service 20 were carried by conductors on 10, 22 and 78 and were accepted as being transfer tickets when presented to conductors on the second car boarded. The miners' strike ended on 4th July, but service 20 was not restored until 3rd October 1921, when it returned to work daily between Victoria Station and Southcroft Road, extended on Saturday afternoons and Sundays to Tooting Broadway.

The operation of service 20 (together with 22 and 24) was returned from Norwood to Streatham on 23rd April 1923, as a result of the withdrawal of trailer cars leaving sufficient space at Telford Avenue to once again accommodate the cars. Extension to Tooting after 8 p.m., Mondays to Fridays commenced on 27th October 1924 while, as from 30th September 1926, it was also extended during the midday period on weekdays. A rush hour working to Tooting Broadway began on 30th December 1926, making the extension an all day daily operation. From 19th July 1928, the 20 became a full circular service from Victoria Station back to Victoria Station, outwards via Brixton and Streatham, returning via Balham and Clapham, the working the other way round the circle being carried out by service 8, which had formerly been running to Mitcham from Victoria via Clapham.

Referring now to service 22, it was always a rush-hours-only working, except for a short period in the early 1920s. In December 1912, it was running between Southcroft Road, Mitcham Lane and Waterloo Bridge via Streatham, Brixton, Kennington and Westminster, while the 24, also a rush-hours only service, was operating between Telford Avenue and Southwark Bridge, which continued until November 1913. During March 1914 the Council decided that another circular service should be worked round the Embankment, with 22 and 24 taking on the role, cars on 22 changing number to 24 in Westminster Bridge Road, then proceeding via Embankment and Blackfriars, with 24 doing the same thing in Blackfriars Road and travelling in the opposite direction. This arrangement lasted until October 1915, by which time the 24 had been withdrawn and 22 once again became a rush-hours-only service between Southcroft Road, Mitcham Lane and Waterloo Bridge via Kennington and Westminster.

For a short period after the war, from 26th January 1920, service 22 became a full weekday working between Waterloo Bridge, Savoy Street and Tooting Broadway via Westminster and Brixton. Sunday service commenced on 2nd May 1920, while circular working around the Embankment was resumed on 16th June 1921, again in conjunction with 24. This, however, was only a "flash in the pan" as, with the resumption of service 20 on 3rd October after its withdrawal due to the miners' strike, services 22 and 24 were once again relegated to weekday rush hours only operation between Southcroft Road and Embankment. At this time, Norwood shed was involved with the operation of this service, which ceased after 23rd April 1923, as mentioned above.

However, on 6th October 1927, both services were once again extended to Tooting Broadway, this time combined with 2A and 4A, to form a circular service. The numbers on the cars were changed both at Tooting and at the London end, and to give an example of this, a car entering the Embankment loop at Westminster as a 2A might leave as a 22 or remain unchanged as a 2A, subject to operational requirements. Similarly, at Tooting, a car arriving from London via Brixton as a 22 or 24, may have had its number changed to become either 2A or 4A, as required. Given the rush hour nature of these four services, it is unlikely that an individual car would have its numbers changed more than twice.

The Norwood Group

This area is the one that was covered by the cars operated from Norwood, the smallest of the south London sheds. In December 1912, it catered for three services which were numbered 76, 78 and 80. Of these, the 78 remained unchanged for the whole of the period under review, working between West Norwood and Victoria Station via Herne Hill, Effra Road, Brixton and Stockwell. The other two were interlinked to such an extent that it is thought desirable to study them together.

At the beginning of numbering, service 76 was working between Herne Hill Station and New Bridge Street, Blackfriars via Brixton, Kennington and Elephant, in weekday rush hours only. At the same time, service 80 was working daily between West Norwood and Camberwell Green via Loughborough Junction, extended on Mondays to Fridays in rush hours and all day on Saturdays to Waterloo Bridge via Walworth Road, Elephant and Westminster. Sometime between July and September 1913, service 76 was extended to West Norwood, while the Sunday workings on 80 were extended from Camberwell Green to Waterloo Bridge. This arrangement was not to last long, as from 4th November 1913, the 76 became an all-day weekday operation, but with Sunday workings commencing at 4.30 p.m. Conversely, from the same day, service 80 was altered during weekday slack hours to work between Herne Hill Station and Waterloo Bridge.

This situation was reversed on 24th August 1914 when service 76 on Mondays to Fridays was confined to rush-hours only and service 80 became an all-day daily working between West Norwood and Waterloo Bridge via Westminster, which lasted until 19th December 1915, when it was withdrawn on Sundays between Camberwell and Waterloo Bridge. By January 1916, service 76 had been withdrawn.

The South Eastern & Chatham Railway had two stations between Loughborough Junction and Elephant & Castle, these being Camberwell New Road and Walworth Road. Due to operational difficulties brought

Car No. 1545, looking rather careworn during the Great War, stands at Blackfriars on service 80.

about by the Great War, train services had been progressively reduced, and these stations were finally closed to traffic as from 3rd April 1916, together with a considerable reduction of services between the stations still open. These changes were no doubt considered by the LCC when, on 27th March 1916, tram service 80 was diverted at the Elephant and Castle to run to Blackfriars (New Bridge Street) to cater for displaced railway passengers, the former frequency of service from Walworth to Westminster being maintained by the augmentation of service 62. From 26th November 1916, service 80 was curtailed on Sundays to work only between Norwood and the Elephant & Castle.

Examination of available records, show that by the spring of 1918, the weekday service beyond Camberwell Green to Blackfriars, John Carpenter Street had ceased after 9 p.m. A year later, the map and guide shows an all-day daily service working between West Norwood and Blackfriars. The next relevant entry in the official diary records that service 80 was extended to Blackfriars after 9 p.m. on Saturday evenings from 13th December 1919, but this is at variance with the information given in the previous sentence.

Service 76 returned in a different guise on 16th June 1921, when it started running between West Norwood and Waterloo Bridge via Brixton, Kennington and Westminster on an Embankment circular working in conjunction with number 80. The numbers on the cars were changed on the inward journey at Westminster (76 to 80) or Blackfriars (80 to 76), the cars returning to Norwood via the Embankment and either Blackfriars or Westminster bridges as appropriate. This arrangement continued until 10th December 1925, when the services were re-arranged to work around the Embankment without changing numbers during the journey. Service number 76 was shown on cars working inwards via Brixton and Westminster, and outwards via Blackfriars and Camberwell, with 80 being displayed on cars travelling in the opposite direction.

The Sunday service from 3rd October 1926 was reduced before 3 p.m. to work only between West Norwood and Blackfriars via Camberwell, cars running inwards to Blackfriars as service 80 and returning with the number 76. This unusual feature became an all-day Sunday operation as from 26th June 1927, but by the early part of 1929, the whole Sunday working had received the number 80.

393

The 76 disappeared for ever after the last journey on 13th May 1931, being replaced the following day by a daily service numbered 33, working between West Norwood and Highbury Station, subsequently being diverted to Manor House as from 8th October 1931, the cars for which were provided by both Norwood and Holloway sheds. As a result of the loss of the 76, service 80 became a daily working between West Norwood and Blackfriars via Camberwell Green.

The Camberwell Group

There were seven services operating from Camberwell car shed in 1912, which received the numbers 56, 58, 60, 62, 68, 74 and 84. The Dulwich route, embracing services 56, 58, 60, 62 and later, 84 was to remain the principal one.

On numbering, service 56 was working between Waterloo Bridge and Peckham Rye, Stuart Road via Westminster and Walworth Road on a daily basis and continued to do so until 16th June 1921, when a balancing weekdays service via Blackfriars was introduced, bearing the number 84. These two services were linked, with the numbers being changed as described in the section dealing with the Tooting route. Service 56 continued to run on Sundays without change, thus there was no service between Savoy Street Strand and Peckham Rye via Blackfriars on that day.

The practice of changing numbers on the Victoria Embankment services ceased on 12th November 1923, consequently 56 worked inwards via Westminster and outward via Blackfriars, with 84 working in the opposite direction. Yet again the Sunday service on 56 remained unaltered, working between Peckham Rye and Savoy Street, Strand (Waterloo Bridge) via Westminster, with cars showing this number in both directions across the Bridge. No further change occurred in subsequent years.

The number 58 was given to the service which worked between Victoria Station and Forest Hill Station via Dog Kennel Hill and Dulwich. At Forest Hill, it reversed in London Road, until the connection was eventually made on 13th August 1915 with the tracks which ended on the other side of the railway. Service 58 was then extended to Blackwall Tunnel via Catford, Lewisham and Greenwich, absorbing service 50 which had worked between Forest Hill and Blackwall Tunnel. On 6th March 1917, service 58 was altered to run between Victoria and Catford only, and service 50 was re-instated. However, some workman cars on 58 were sent through to Greenwich. It is unclear how long this state of affairs continued, but by the spring of 1918, service 58 was working between Victoria and Catford on a daily basis. From 10th September 1922 on Sundays only, it was extended once again to Blackwall Tunnel, with service 50 being again withdrawn on that day. Details of service 50 are to be found in the section dealing with operations from New Cross car shed.

On 19th April 1928 a re-arrangement of services 50, 58 and 62 took place, with 58 working between Victoria Station and Forest Hill (daily), extended to Blackwall Tunnel during weekday rush hours, evenings and all day on Sundays. Although service 50 was not finally withdrawn until 15th January 1931, full daily working between Victoria Station and Blackwall Tunnel began on service 58 from 25th April 1929 and no further alterations were ever made.

Service 60 was always a rush hours only working. It operated between Dulwich Library and Southwark Bridge via Walworth Road, and between 2nd June 1913 and the end of 1915 the afternoon service was extended to Forest Hill. Until 28th November 1913, it approached its London

Two new cars of class HR/2 pass on Victoria Embankment, both working on the Peckham Rye services 56 and 84. (Courtesy: London Transport)

terminus via the full length of Southwark Bridge Road, but from that date was diverted via St. George's Church and Marshalsea Road. In common with the other services operating to Southwark Bridge, it was extended to the new terminus in the City on 14th July 1925.

The number 62 was allocated to a weekday rush hours only service working between Waterloo Bridge and Dulwich Library via Westminster and Walworth Road, with an afternoon extension to Forest Hill. From 2nd June 1913, the whole of the afternoon working was withdrawn. Sometime during the years of the Great War, and certainly by the spring of 1917, the afternoon service had been reinstated, but only between Dulwich Library and the London terminus. By the summer of 1919, an afternoon extension to Forest Hill had been re-instated and later in the year, on 8th December the service between Waterloo Bridge and Dulwich Library became an all-day weekday operation, this being extended to Forest Hill a week later. Extension to Catford followed on 16th June 1921, and to Blackwall Tunnel via Lewisham on 14th August 1922, but still the service only operated on weekdays.

A new double track curve was laid in at Catford between Catford Road and Bromley Road, and 62 was diverted on 19th April 1928 over this route to Bromley Road, Downham. Extension along Downham Way to Southover took place on 23rd July 1928 and, after the completion of the tracks to Grove Park Station on 15th November 1928, the service was extended to that point.

Traffic on the new extension was probably adequately catered for by the frequent cars on services 52 and 54, resulting in 62 being withdrawn between Grove Park and Bellingham Road as from 3rd April 1930. However, on 3rd July 1930 it had been extended again as far as Southend Village (Beckenham Lane), but on 15th January 1931 it resumed its earlier route, being diverted at Catford to work once again to Blackwall Tunnel, where the suburban terminus was to remain. Regarding the service frequency, it was noticeable that the headway during the middle

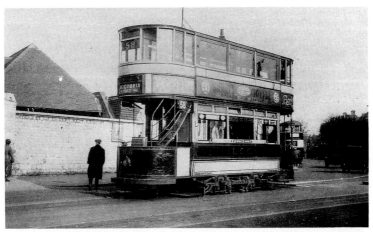

Class C car No. 296 on service 58, shows its age in 1929 as it stands alongside the Fire Station in Catford Road (the site of the present-day Lewisham Concert Hall). In the background can be seen one of the unique NS type omnibuses of the LGOC which worked through Blackwall Tunnel. *(Courtesy: A. D. Packer)*

day hours in 1923 was nominally one of 6 minutes, whereas in the rush hours it was every 8 minutes. This situation was reversed with the diversion to Grove Park, when the midday service became of a frequency of 9 to 10 minutes, with the rush hour headway remaining unchanged at 8 minutes. Overall, the 62 appeared to have been one of the less-frequently worked services.

One of the unusual aspects of the working of services 58 and 62 was that there were runs between Camberwell car shed, Lewisham and Greenwich via New Cross instead of the normal route, offering a considerable saving in staff time and mileage costs.

Late in 1914, a set of tickets was printed for the Camberwell shed routes, which included the number 90. It has always been assumed that this number was to have been allocated to a service between Peckham Rye and Victoria. However, evidence has come to light which shows that 90 was allocated to a service between Dulwich Library and New Bridge Street via Walworth Road and Blackfriars. This may have explained its appearance on the tickets, as the latter service is shown in the 1914-15 copy of the Fares and Services Manual issued to staff by the LCC Tramways. This may have worked in conjunction with 62 until, according to a reference in the Official Diary of Events, 27th March 1916, when a re-arrangement of services using the Walworth Road would have permitted the withdrawal of 90. Uncertainty still surrounds the operation of this service, as it does not appear in any of the issues of the map and guide for 1914 or 1915.

Services working from Camberwell car shed in the direction of Peckham and New Cross, covered three phases in the years between 1913 and 1933. The first, between the commencement of numbering and the end of 1914, involved 68 and 84; the second during the period between 1916 and 1919 involved services 64 and 84; whilst the third and longest phase covered the operation of Subway service 35, which is discussed elsewhere.

Service No. 62—WATERLOO BRIDGE and DULWICH LIBRARY
Via Westminster Bridge, Elephant & Castle, Walworth Road, and Denmark Hill

Service 90—NEW BRIDGE STREET and DULWICH LIBRARY
Via Blackfriars Bridge, Elephant & Castle, Walworth Road, and Denmark Hill

---

½d. Stages (WORKMEN'S AND ORDINARY)

Waterloo-bridge to York-rd., Westminster-bridge-road
New Bridge-street to Stamford-street
York-road, Westminster Bridge-road to Elephant & Castle
Stamford-street to Elephant & Castle
Elephant & Castle to Camberwell-gate
Manor-place to New Church-road

Camberwell-gate to Camberwell-green
Camberwell-green to Denmark Hill-station. S.E.& C.R.
Denmark Hill-station, S.E.& C.R. to East Dulwich-station, L.B.&S.C.R.
East Dulwich - station, L.B.& S.C.R. to Whateley-road
Whateley-road to Dulwich-library

1d. Stages—

Waterloo-bridge to Camberwell-gate .
Westminster-stn. District Railway to Camberwell-grn
New Bridge-street to   „
Elephant & Castle to Denmark Hill-station, S.E.& C.R.

Camberwell-green to Whateley-road
Denmark Hill - station, S.E.& C.R. to Dulwich-library

1½d. Stages—

Waterloo-bridge to Camberwell-green
Westminster-station District Railway to Denmark Hill-station, S.E.& C.R.
New Bridge-street to Denmark Hill-station, S.E.& C.R.

Elephant & Castle to East Dulwich-station, L.B.& S.C.R.
Camberwell-gate to Whateley-road
Camberwell-green to Dulwich-library

						Single	Return
Waterloo-bridge to East Dulwich-station, L.B.& S.C.R.		...	...			2d	3d
Westminster-station District Railway to Whateley-road		...	...	...		—	3d
New Bridge-street	„		...	...	...	—	3d
Westminster - station District Railway to Dulwich - library		...	...	...		2d	—
New Bridge-street	„		...	...	...	2d	—
Elephant & Castle	„		...	...	...	—	3d
Waterloo-bridge	„		...	...	...	2½d	4d
	„		...	...	(WORKMEN'S)	1d	2d
New Bridge-street	„		...	...	(„)	1d	2d

THROUGH FARES
Change cars at Goose Green or Camberwell Green

					Single	Return
New Bridge-street to King's Arms. Peckham-rye	...	...	...		2d	3d
Camberwell-gate to Lordship Lane-station, S.E.& C.R.		...	...		2d	3d
Dulwich-library to Westminster-station District Railway	...	...			2d	—
Whateley-road	„	„	...	...		—	3d
„ , Southwark-bridge		...	...	...		—	3d
New Bridge-street to Lordship Lane-station, S.E.& C.R.		...	...		2½d	4d
„ „ Stuart-road, Peckham-rye		...	...		2½d	4d
Elephant & Castle to Forest-hill	...	...	...	...		2½d	4d
Dulwich-library to Waterloo-bridge, via Westminster		...	...		2½d	4d
New Bridge-street to Forest-hill	...	...	...		3d	5d
Waterloo to Forest-hill ...	...	...	...	...	...	3d	5d

Extract from LCC Fares & Services Tables, August 1914

Turning to the first phase, the number 68 was given to a weekday rush hour service operating between Rye Lane, Peckham and Charing Cross via Kennington and Westminster, extended to Waterloo Bridge from November 1913. This working lasted until early June 1914, when it was withdrawn.

Meanwhile, 84 was the number allocated to another rush hour service working between Rye Lane and Blackfriars, New Bridge Street via Walworth Road and Elephant & Castle. This survived the May/June 1915 cuts (the result of a strike of drivers and conductors), having by then been extended at the outer end for about a quarter of a mile, to a new lay-by constructed at Harders Road, Peckham and opened on 16th April 1915. On 3rd April 1916, 84 was extended and joined by 64 in a peculiar circular routing which involved some use of trailer cars, but still in rush hours only. Both started from New Cross Gate, the 64 proceeding via Old Kent Road and Blackfriars and returning via Westminster in the morning busy hours, the reverse direction being followed in the evenings. 84 also ran from New Cross Gate via Peckham and Walworth Road, then inwards via Blackfriars and outwards via Westminster in the mornings, the reverse direction being followed in the evenings. To prevent cars and trailers having to stand at New Cross Gate, a 64 approaching New Cross would change its number to 84 and, using the western link junction line at New Cross Gate, would return to London as an 84. The 84 used similar tactics, returning to London via Old Kent Road as a 64.

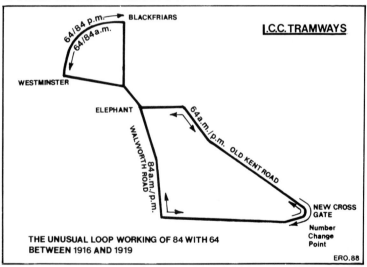

The unusual loop working of services 84 and 64 between 1916 and 1919

This unusual working was altered as from 10th February 1919, when service 64 was withdrawn, and the 84 reverted to its original working from the lay-by at Harders Road, Peckham to Blackfriars, via Walworth Road and Elephant. This continued to be a rush-hours-only working until it was withdrawn on 2nd February 1920. The final appearance of 84 came on 16th June 1921 when it was paired with 56 on a circular service as described above. A more detailed account of service 64 appears in the New Cross and Abbey Wood section.

Operation of service 62 to Grove Park only lasted from November 1928 until April 1930, and here, class M car No. 1684 is seen standing at the terminus. Courtesy: Tramway & Light Railway Society)

On the introduction of service numbers, the cars working daily between Brixton and St. George's Church via Coldharbour Lane, Camberwell Green and Walworth Road were allocated the number 74. Extension to Southwark Bridge via Marshalsea Road commenced on 28th November 1913, but by March 1914, the Sunday service was again terminating at St. George's Church. This lasted until 26th June 1921, when it was again extended to Southwark Bridge on Sundays as well as weekdays. The service was withdrawn on 22nd January 1922, being replaced by an extension of 34 from "The Plough", Clapham to Southwark Bridge via Stockwell, Brixton and Camberwell.

A new service was provided by Camberwell cars from 14th May 1931, when 48 began working between Victoria Station and City, via Stockwell, Brixton, Coldharbour Lane, Camberwell, Elephant and Southwark Bridge, replacing 34 on weekdays between Brixton and City. From 13th August 1931, the section between Brixton and Victoria was only worked during rush hours and for the remainder of the day, cars only worked between Brixton and City. After 14th April 1932, operation between Brixton and Victoria had ceased, with extra cars working on service 78 to cover the deficiency. No further changes were made until after the LPTB took control of the tramways.

Another interesting working from Camberwell was that of service 92 (the highest number actually used and displayed by the LCC Tramways). This was introduced on 28th November 1913 on weekdays only between Brixton Road and Blackfriars, New Bridge Street, via Coldharbour Lane and Camberwell. From 24th August 1914, the Monday-Friday service became rush hours only, with all day running on Saturdays, whilst from December of that year, a Sunday evening service was also provided. Sunday operation, however, was short-lived, having been withdrawn by April 1915, after which the weekday service carried on until it too, was withdrawn in the autumn of 1915.

The New Cross and Abbey Wood Group

The massive group of services worked from New Cross and Abbey Wood car sheds is being considered jointly, as there was an appreciable amount of shared operation on some of them after 1914. The services concerned were 36, 38, 40, 46, 48, 50, 52, 54, 66, 70, 72 and 86, later joined by 64 and 68, at New Cross, and 36, 38, 40, 42, 44 and 46 at Abbey Wood. New Cross car shed was the largest on the south side system, capable of housing over 300 cars, while Abbey Wood shed, tucked away in Abbey Wood Road, at the extreme end of the line, held 86 cars after the building was extended.

Services 36, 38, 40 and 46 were worked by both Abbey Wood and New Cross crews in the later years of LCC ownership, but in 1913 the story was very different, as Abbey Wood had not been connected with the main LCC system. Leaving out 46, as it did not commence working from Abbey Wood until 1921 and which will be described later, each of the other three had separate existences.

In December 1912, 36 was operating between Blackwall Tunnel and New Bridge Street, Blackfriars via New Cross Gate and Old Kent Road on a daily basis, which it continued to do until 3rd May 1914, when service 50 was extended to Blackwall Tunnel and 36 was curtailed at the Woolwich Road end of Blackwall Lane, although some cars continued to run through to Blackwall Tunnel for the shift workers at the large gasworks and other factories in the vicinity.

The connection between the Woolwich lines and the rest of the system had been made in April 1914, enabling service 36 to be extended to Woolwich Ferry from 3rd May after 5.30 p.m. on Mondays to Fridays and 1.30 p.m. on Saturdays, but the Sunday service only worked between New Bridge Street and Blackwall Lane. By December 1914, the slack hours service had been further curtailed to work between New Bridge Street and Greenwich Church, whilst the rush hour service had been extended from the Free Ferry to Plumstead, Wickham Lane, to which point the cars also ran on Sundays after midday. By January 1916, the slack hours service had deteriorated still further, only running between New Bridge Street and New Cross Gate.

The spring 1918 map and guide shows the main service of 36 as still running between New Bridge Street and New Cross Gate only, with a weekday rush hours extension to Wickham Lane, Plumstead, and the Sunday service after midday running right through to Abbey Wood, but by the early part of 1920 this extension did not commence to run until 4.50 p.m. The extension to Abbey Wood on a regular daily basis occurred on 19th April 1920 when Abbey Wood car shed took an allocation of cars. On 17th January 1921 the service was paired with 38 around the Victoria Embankment loop, 36 in by Blackfriars and 38 in by Westminster, making the round trip from and to Abbey Wood one of the longest continuous journeys on the system. One result of this arrangement was that, in common with other services working along the Embankment, the practice of changing numbers during the journey ceased after 12th November 1923.

Service 38 worked on a daily basis in 1912 between Waterloo Bridge, Savoy Street and Woolwich, chapel Street via Westminster, Old Kent Road, Deptford and Greenwich. Between Chapel Street and Woolwich Ferry there was a short length of horse-hauled tramway and this was finally reconstructed and opened for electric traction on 5th April 1914, when 38 was extended to Beresford Square daily, and to Wickham Lane from 4.30 p.m. to 9.30 p.m. on Mondays to Fridays. On 3rd May, 38 was extended to Wickham Lane daily, whilst the Saturday afternoon and Sunday service was further extended to Abbey Wood.

The Bexley Council Tramways made use of the LCC tracks between Plumstead Corner and Beresford Square from the introduction of electric car services by the LCC in 1908, and it was inevitable that at some time the question of through running would be raised. Negotiations took place, with the result that in the first instance, through fares were instituted between London and Bexleyheath Market Place, followed by through running at weekeds when, on 11th July 1914, some cars on service 38 were diverted on Saturday afternoons and Sundays along Wickham Lane and through Welling to Bexleyheath Market Place. Due in part to war conditions, but aggravated by the strike of LCC tramwaymen which commenced on 15th May 1915, the service to Bexleyheath was officially withdrawn on 6th June 1915. The through transfer fare with passengers changing cars as Wickham Lane Corner, continued until 1st March 1917, when it too, was withdrawn.

By January 1916, service 38 was working between Waterloo Bridge and Plumstead, Wickham Lane, with the Monday to Friday rush hours and Saturday and Sunday service extended to Abbey Wood. Running to Abbey Wood on a daily basis commenced on 19th April 1920 and, as mentioned above, 38 became linked with 36 as from 17th January 1921.

From the time that these services were extended eastwards from Blackwall Lane, certain early morning cars always worked between London and Blackwall Tunnel both as 36 and 38, in order to convey passengers to and from the many factories and works in that area.

The general pattern of operation on services 36 and 38 remained constant from 12th November 1923 until the end of tram services. There was however one exception to this, when on Bank Holidays the basic services were supplemented by one numbered "EX" which operated between Abbey Wood and Waterloo Station via Old Kent Road. This was possibly intended to augment services working to holiday attractions at Greenwich Park and Abbey Wood.

Service 40, like 38, was working between Savoy Street and Chapel Street, Woolwich, but via Westminster, Kennington, Peckham and New Cross, with all cars being provided by New Cross car shed. Certain early morning and late night journeys operated via Walworth Road, a practice that lasted at least until the end of LCC operation, but in later years, was confined to one late night journey on weekdays. When the final section of the horse tramway in Woolwich was electrified on 5th April 1914, service 40 was extended on a daily basis to Abbey Wood, part of the car allocation then being taken by Abbey Wood shed. Service 40 then remained unchanged until after the formation of the London Passenger Transport Board.

The number 42 was given to the service working between Abbey Wood and Free Ferry, Woolwich and with 44 were, at that time, the only two worked by Abbey Wood shed crews. When the final section of electrified track was opened between Chapel Street and Free Ferry and the cars from London were brought into Woolwich, 42 became less important, but still continued to work until, in April 1915, the Sunday service was withdrawn. By October of that year, the complete withdrawal of the service took place, although many cars worked short journeys in Woolwich under the guise of EX. The number 42 was not used again in LCC days.

Once the through services between London and Abbey Wood had been established, it could have been expected that a settled pattern would have emerged. Due to the outbreak of war on 4th August 1914

*A rather rural scene at Abbey Wood around 1920, as E/1 car No. 1694
waits its turn to be taken to the terminal crossover and the return
journey to London on service 40.   (Courtesy: A. D. Packer)*

and the strategic importance of Woolwich Arsenal and other factories
in the area, all of which became vital to the manufacture of warlike
equipment, the thousands of persons employed in these establishments
had to be conveyed from and to their homes in all parts of London.
It was then that services 36, 38, 40 and 44, service 42 until it was
withdrawn in 1915, together with the Bexley UDC service of cars,
took on a role that was probably unequalled anywhere else in London.

In the first place, the numbers 36, 38 and 40, although applied to
the basic services, were not always displayed on many of the extra
cars - up to 200 - which visited the district each day, some from as
far away as Norwood and Streatham.   Considerable use was made of
the indication "EX" and it is understood that there were, at times,
up to seven EX cars to one numbered service car.   This also applied
to the service which operated between Woolwich and Eltham under
the number 44, which is the next to be described.

The service number 44 was given to the cars shedded at Abbey
Wood, which worked between Eltham Church and Woolwich, Beresford
Square via Woolwich Common, with certain cars being extended to
Plumstead and Abbey Wood.   There were also depot workings from
and to Abbey Wood.

After the war, things slowly returned to what was described as
"normal", which meant for the people of Woolwich and district a degree
of hardship, with many of them being out of a job, due to the Arsenal
and other establishments not now needing to make guns and other items
associated with war.   For the tramways, things settled down to give a
more orderly pattern of services, beginning with the extension of service
46 from Lee Green to Eltham and Woolwich on 22nd March 1921.

By November 1921, service 44 had ceased to operate on Saturdays
and Sundays, and it was to be another two years before the next change

was made. As from 10th December 1923, it was extended to Lewisham Obelisk via Lee Green during midday hours. The additional service between Lewisham and Woolwich on Saturdays was provided by New Cross shed cars, working as extra (EX) to 46. The Lewisham extension, however, ceased as from 8th August 1928, when it was withdrawn outside rush hours, being confined to work as a supplementary service to 46 between Woolwich and Eltham.

As from 5th February 1931, service 44 was out all day on Mondays to Fridays, replacing extra cars on service 46, but there was still no Saturday service. In the meantime, work had been proceeding on the first part of the tramway that had been authorised along a new road named Westhorne Avenue, between Well Hall and the route of service 46 at the foot of Eltham Hill, with the proposal (which was never implemented) that it should be carried on to Lee and Grove Park. Once this line had been sufficiently completed to enable part of it to be brought into use, half of the cars on service 44 were diverted at Well Hall as from 1st October 1931, to run on the new line as far as Briset Road, a distance of about half a mile. The Saturday service on the new extension was catered for by diverting half of the extra cars provided on the 46.

The Westhorne Avenue portion of 44 was further extended, when the rest of the tramway between Briset Road and Eltham Green was opened to traffic on 4th February 1932. From 30th June 1932, however, service 72 was diverted away from Forest Hill to work between Savoy Street and Woolwich via Kennington, New Cross, Lewisham and Westhorne Avenue, resulting in the short workings on 44 being withdrawn. From the same date, the extra Saturday cars on service 46 were withdrawn and 44 was re-instated on that day between Woolwich and Eltham Church. No further alterations were made to the service for the rest of the time that it was working under LCC Tramways management.

It appears from documents researched, that a pattern of short workings between Woolwich and Eltham emerged, in which cars operating from Abbey Wood showed 44 and those provided by New Cross shed showed EX. This is borne out in the period between 1921 and 1927, in which records show that the 44 did not operate on Saturdays, being replaced by extra cars on 46, which were worked from New Cross shed.

In 1912, the number 46 was allocated to the daily service working between Waterloo Station and Lee Green via Walworth Road, Peckham and New Cross, for which class "C" cars were provided by New Cross car shed. Like most other services, the Great War had an adverse effect on it, as in January 1916 it is recorded that it was only running between Lee Green and Lewisham Obelisk on weekdays, with a Sunday extension to New Cross Gate in the mornings and Waterloo Station after 3 p.m., although the Sunday service was withdrawn after 30th April, leaving it as a weekdays-only operation, shuttling between Lee Green and Lewisham. A further change on 17th July 1917 saw the service running between Lee Green and New Cross on weekdays, extended via Old Kent Road to Southwark Bridge in rush hours. On 7th November 1917, the service to Southwark Bridge operated throughout the day, while from 10th March 1918, a Sunday service appeared once again between Lee Green and New Cross Gate to replace service 48.

As from 29th November 1919, part of the service on Saturday after-noons was diverted at "Bricklayers' Arms" to run to Elephant & Castle, with the remainder continuing to operate to Southwark Bridge. The only difficulty then seemed to be that the cars, on turning on a crossover in New Kent Road, held up other cars in the process, causing the Council to extend the service on Saturday afternoons as from 17th January 1920 to Waterloo Station, but still working via Old Kent Road.

The next change came at the country end. Extension of the line from Lee Green to Eltham via Eltham Road had been authorised in 1914-15, but was postponed until post-war conditions allowed work to proceed once again. On 29th November 1920, work was sufficiently advanced to allow service 46 to be extended as far as "Lyme Farm", approximately halfway along the route. A weekdays-only service was provided, with Sunday cars continuing to terminate at Lee Green.

Extension to Eltham High Street, just a few yards short of Eltham Church, took place on 25th February 1921, the service east of Lee Green now running on Sundays also. Saturday afternoon service was to Waterloo Station, while on Sundays it terminated at New Cross Gate.

The final connection round the corner from Eltham High Street to Well Hall Road was made on 22nd March 1921, resulting in 46 becoming a through service between Woolwich, Beresford Square and Southwark Bridge, Mondays to Saturdays; part service between Woolwich and Waterloo Station on Saturday afternoons; Woolwich to New Cross Gate on Sundays. This pattern was to last until 25th June 1921, when the Waterloo journeys were withdrawn, and the Sunday service was extended from New Cross to Southwark Bridge. In common with all services working to Southwark Bridge, 46 was extended across the bridge to the City side as from 14th July 1925.

The allocation of cars, so far, had always come from New Cross, but on 7th November 1927, several cars were transferred from New Cross shed to Abbey Wood, thereby improving the early and late services between Lewisham, Eltham and Woolwich.

Service 48 made two separate appearances when at New Cross under LCC control. The first, in 1912 was from Lee Green to Victoria Station via New Cross, Camberwell and Vauxhall. This ran on a daily basis at first, but from 24th August 1914 was altered to run during rush hours only on Monday to Friday, but continuing with the Saturday and Sunday service. By July 1915, the Saturday service was confined to rush hours, but still working all day on Sundays. By October 1915, it was running on Sundays only. It was finally withdrawn on 10th March 1918, when 46 again commenced Sunday workings.

The daily short working cars on service 46 between Lee Green and Lewisham were extended to Greenwich and Blackwall Lane via South Street and renumbered 48 on 27th September 1920. A rush hours extension to Blackwall Tunnel commenced on 4th October 1920. The Sunday service was withdrawn a month later, on 7th November. The weekday service remained in being until 9th April 1921 when an announcement was made that it would be withdrawn temporarily to save power during the long-drawn-out strike of miners but, unlike service 20, which did ultimately return, 48 disappeared entirely from the Lewisham area. It re-appeared at Camberwell in 1931 as previously described.

The number 50 was given to the service working daily between Tooley Street and Catford via Dockhead, Rotherhithe, Surrey Docks, Greenwich and South Street, when service numbering was introduced. As from 15th February 1913, it was curtailed to work between Greenwich Church and Catford only. Shortly after this, the tracks through Catford Road and Stanstead Road to Forest Hill were opened to traffic, which resulted in service 50 being extended to Forest Hill, Waldram Road on 29th May 1913. Extension of the 50 from Greenwich Church to Blackwall Tunnel occurred on 3rd May 1914, replacing most journeys of service 36 along Blackwall Lane.

Operation of service 50 in later year was very limited. The declining years for both the service and class A car No. 45 can be seen in this view, taken at Blackwall Tunnel in 1929. *(Courtesy: P. J. Davis)*

The first withdrawal of 50 occurred on 13th August 1915, when the connecting link at Forest Hill between London Road and Waldram Road was opened, and service 58 began running right through to Blackwall Tunnel in place of it. Due to wartime exigencies, service 58, after running a through service, was cut back to work between Catford and Victoria Station on 6th March 1917, resulting in service 50 being re-instated between Blackwall Tunnel and Forest Hill.

No changes took place for the next five years, when a through link was re-established on 14th August between Dulwich, Catford and Greenwich by a weekday extension of service 62 to Blackwall Tunnel. On this occasion however, service 50 was kept in being as a Monday to Friday rush-hour working, and an all-day service on Saturdays and Sundays, but not for long. Just over three weeks later, on 10th September 1922, the Sunday service was the first to go, its place being taken by an extension of service 58 to Blackwall Tunnel. Early in October, the weekday service of 50 was altered to become Monday to Friday rush hours only, and on Saturday until early evening.

On 19th April 1928, service 62 was diverted to run to Downham and 50 once again became an all day weekdays service, being assisted in rush hours by an extension of 58 from Catford. The Downham extension of 62 lasted until 15th January 1931, when it was diverted at Catford to again serve Blackwall Tunnel, and service 50 finally closed.

One of the weekday rush hours only services which provided a useful, if uneventful function was that worked between Southwark Bridge and Catford St. Laurence's Church and which received the number 52 in 1912. It did not suffer a great deal of change and, indeed, the first alteration did not occur until 30th March 1922 when it was extended at the country end from Catford to Southend Village (Beckenham Lane). Like all other Southwark Bridge services, this one was extended over the bridge to the City terminus on 14th July 1925. The extension to Downham and Grove Park took place in two stages, the first on 29th November 1926 to Bromley Road, Downham Way, with the second, to Grove Park taking place on 15th November 1928.

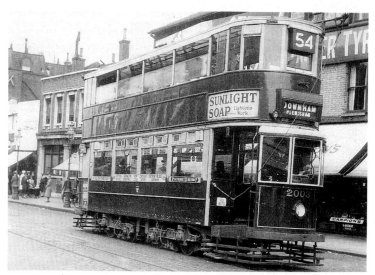

No. 2003 of class E/3 is seen at the "Marquis of Granby", working from New Cross car shed. It was delivered in 1930, prior to the re-opening of the reconstructed Kingsway Subway. (Courtesy: P. J. Davis)

The number 54 was given to the daily service working between Victoria Station and Catford via Kennington, Camberwell, Peckham, New Cross and Lewisham and, apart from extensions at the outer end, suffered no other changes. The first such extension, on 5th April 1914 took it along Bromley Road as far as Bellingham Road, with a further extension to Beckenham Lane (Southend Village) four days later.

Twelve years were to pass before any other changes were made. In that time the Downham Estate had been planned and was under construction, with the major road through it, named Downham Way, being made sufficiently wide to accommodate a double track tramway, with adequate clearances on either side of the tracks. This was opened as far as Valeswood Road on 28th September 1926; to Southover on 28th July 1927, and right through to Grove Park Station on 15th November 1928, with service 54 being extended on each occasion to its new terminus. It became the main daily service over this route, being supplemented at various times by rush-hour service 52, weekday service 62 and, on Saturdays and Sundays by 74, together with the extension of service 35 to Valeswood Road for a short time.

Service 64 had two periods of operation from New Cross car shed. With numbering, 64 was given to a service then running during weekday rush hours between Waterloo Station and New Cross Gate via Old Kent Road, and which also ran as a Sunday service between Waterloo Station and Catford. By April 1914, the Sunday service did not commence until 4.30 p.m. whilst, by November of that year it had been curtailed to run between Waterloo Station and New Cross Gate. By October 1915, the complete service had been withdrawn.

Its operation as a circular service in conjunction with 84, working out of Camberwell car shed has already been described and, after that was withdrawn, a period of about eighteen months elapsed before the

This rare photograph of a car on service 64, shows No. 277 travelling along the Embankment towards Blackfriars and New Cross Gate.
(Courtesy: Tramway Museum Society)

number 64 again appeared, this time working from New Cross car shed as a weekday rush hour service, a duty it was to perform for the rest of its existence. Commencing on 20th September 1920, it worked between New Cross Gate and Blackfriars, running inwards via Peckham and Camberwell and returning via Old Kent Road. Records show that on 10th January 1921 the service in both directions was diverted via Walworth Road, but the suburban terminus became Harders Road lay-by in the mornings and New Cross Gate in the evenings. This seems to have been a "trial-and-error" service as, on 7th February 1921 the working became New Cross Gate to Embankment via Blackfriars and Westminster in the mornings and via Westminster and Blackfriars in the evenings.

This method of working lasted until 20th February 1922, when the service officially became Camberwell Town Hall to Embankment, but still with the morning and evening changes in direction round the Embankment. It appeared in this form on the map for some years, but the guide on the reverse of the map was at variance in showing that service commenced at New Cross Gate. As it was provided by New Cross cars, there was every probability that there was a regular working to and from New Cross Gate. In later years, some journeys were worked inwards via Kennington and Westminster, returning via Blackfriars and Walworth Road, with others running the opposite way. There were also journeys projected beyond New Cross Gate to Crofton Park, with official records showing, on 12th June 1930, a further extension of these to Forest Hill. The only way it seemed to many, to treat the destination and routing of a 64 tram, was to take a good look at the destination indicator before boarding the car, otherwise one could find oneself going the wrong way! All these "delights" disappeared when services 35, 66 and 72 were re-arranged on 30th June 1932 and 64 was renumbered 66EX.

Authors' Special Note:-   In connection with the operation of service 64 and its somewhat tenuous links with 84, the authors are prompted to include some notes penned by the late A.W.Morant, based on first-hand knowledge in his observation of the services concerned.

"The number 64 was first allocated, as from 1st January 1913 to the daily service from Waterloo Station to New Cross Gate via Old Kent Road, a service of electric cars which, in 1904 replaced (in part) the Waterloo Station to East Greenwich via Old Kent Road horse car service. The electric car service was subsequently extended on Sundays to Catford. This version of a 64 service was one of those withdrawn in May 1915, following the termination of the tramwaymens' strike.

"The number 84 was originally allocated to the weekdays only rush hour service from Rye Lane, Peckham to Blackfriars via Walworth Road.   This survived after the May 1915 cuts (having by then been extended slightly southwards to a new lay-by at Harders Road, Peckham).

"So far as I am aware, the position remained much the same during the war years, i.e., no service 64, but a weekday rush hour 84 from Harders Road to Blackfriars via Walworth Road.

"LCC tram services soon began to revive generally after the war, but surprisingly (to me) the Spring 1918 issue of the pocket folder "Map & Guide to Car Services" shows service 64 as:-

New Cross Gate - Savoy Street Strand
  Morning - via Old Kent Road, Blackfriars and Westminster
  Afternoon - via Old Kent Road, Westminster and Blackfriars
  Service suspended midday
  This service does not run on Sundays
The same pocket folder shows 84 as:-

New Cross - Savoy Street Strand
  Morning - via Peckham, Walworth Road, Blackfriars and
               Westminster
  Afternoon - via Westminster and Blackfriars
  Service suspended midday
  This service does not run on Sundays

"The 1919 issue of the pocket folder (which, by my deduction must be pre-November 1919, probably Spring) does not show 64 at all, but it does show 84 as a weekdays only service from Harders Road to John Carpenter Street.

"The next issue I hold of the pocket folder is nowhere dated but clearly relates to services running in 1921 and by deduction must relate to the position post-March 1921 but pre-August of that year.   This issue shows neither 64 or 84 as running. (Authors' Note: As a result of researches into other aspects of the subject matter, the edition referred to by Mr. Morant was very likely issued before September 1920).

"In doing tentative researches into LCC Tramway services generally in post-First World War days I came up against contradictions between my memories of services provided and those mentioned above.   For example, it was with surprise that I noted the position revealed in the Spring 1918 folder which seems to point to 'circular' services being operated from Embankment to New Cross Gate via both Walworth Road and Old Kent Road.

"Admittedly, I was not around much at that time, being away from London and serving in the RAF, but once back to civil life, in February 1919 and getting around again on my beloved LCC trams, I have no recollection of seeing such 'circular' services in operation.   But in

1922, I do remember that following the withdrawal of trailers from the 2/4 Embankment-"Merton" circulars, the reversals at Longley Road of the rush hour motor cum trailer cars interspersed with the new through to Wimbledon cars, had caused a most frustrating position operationally that some of the trailers plus some class "E" motor-cars fitted with trailer connecting gear were transferred from Clapham to Camberwell to start what I had always understood to be "new" circular services operated by tram and trailer whereby:-

(i) the number 64 appeared once more for the first time since its disappearance in May 1915 on a service operating in the morning rush hours from New Cross Gate to Blackfriars via Old Kent Road, returning via Westminster Bridge and Old Kent Road, this arrangement being reversed in the evening rush hour; and

(ii) 84 operated in the morning rush hour from New Cross Gate to Blackfriars via Peckham and Walworth Road, returning via Westminster Bridge and Peckham, this arrangement being reversed in the evening rush hour.

"No reversals at New Cross Gate were involved for these two services because the cars (and their trailers) used the third (double track) side of the triangular junction at New Cross Gate - thus a 64 car (plus trailer) arriving at New Cross Gate from the Old Kent Road direction, proceeded round the "third" side and went back to Embankment as 84 and, similarly, a set-up on the 84 arriving via Peckham proceeded round the "third" side and on as 64 to Embankment via Old Kent Road.

"My recollection is that the 64/84 circular services with their trailers did not last very long and that both numbers disappeared from the list for a time until 84 appeared again later in 1922 as the "Blackfriars" part of a new 56/84 Embankment circular service from Peckham Rye via Dog Kennel Hill."

The number 66 was given to a service which worked between New Cross Gate and Blackfriars via Peckham and Walworth Road. On 5th April 1914, it was extended on weekdays to Forest Hill via Brockley, in which form it remained until 17th July 1917, when it became a daily service. About four years later, on 16th June 1921, it became an Embankment circular service in conjunction with service 72, the 66 going round via Blackfriars and Westminster, the 72 running in the opposite direction. From 3rd June 1928 however, 66 ran on weekdays only, leaving the 72 to work a new type of circular service on Sundays, which will be discussed under another heading.

With the 35, 66, 72 reshuffle mentioned under the section dealing with service 64, the 66 was to remain a weekday service from Forest Hill to Blackfriars and, apart from an extension along the Embankment to Somerset House on 1st September 1932, there were no further changes until after the LCC relinquished control of the tramways.

Service 68 re-appeared as from 6th September 1915, working between Tower Bridge and Waterloo Station via Elephant & Castle, with class C cars from New Cross shed. It may have been a replacement for the single deck Kingsway Subway service 33, which worked between Highbury Station and Tower Bridge. In May 1915, service 33 was withdrawn south of the river, leaving a residue service of short-working single deck cars between Tower Bridge and Elephant & Castle, which were housed at Camberwell shed. At the Elephant, the reversal of tramcars may well have caused operating difficulties, which would have been eased by their extension to Waterloo. This formed the new service 68.

At the Tower Bridge terminus, the lines continued with a left-hand

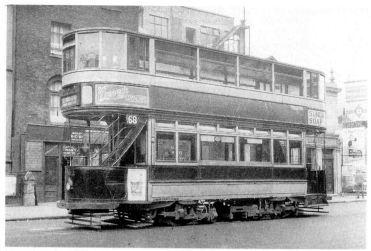

Waterloo Station terminus on a quiet Sunday morning about 1925, with class D car No. 392 on service 68, standing at the terminus.

curve towards London Bridge, which had been used by the subway service in the days before service numbers, when it ran for a short period from Highbury to Tooley Street, but no move was made to use this link for the 68.

The west-facing curve and junction layout was removed during 1923, being replaced by one leading eastwards from Tower Bridge Road, which allowed cars on service 68 to be extended via Rotherhithe to Greenwich Church from 22nd October. From then on, the service remained unchanged.

When it was numbered in 1912, the 70 was working between London Bridge, Tooley Street and Greenwich Church and was effectively a short working of service 50 (Catford and Tooley Street), with additionally, an extension to Woolwich Dockyard in rush hours and at weekends. By February 1913, however, the map and guide indicates that service 70 was working only between Tooley Street and High Street Deptford. However, on 15th February, service 50 was withdrawn between Greenwich and Tooley Street, while the 70 was once again extended to Greenwich and the service frequency increased. From 26th April 1913, the service was extended to Woolwich Dockyard on Saturday and Sunday evenings, but by December 1913, the workings to Woolwich Dockyard had been withdrawn, after which the service always worked between Greenwich and Tooley Street.

With regard to operation of the service, three features are noteworthy. Firstly, cars were provided by New Cross shed, resulting in access to the route being obtained either via Old Kent Road and Tower Bridge Road or via Deptford Broadway, which arrangement also applied to service 68. Secondly, the timetable of services 70 and 68 indicate that the cars were noticably slower than on many other services in south London, at an average speed on Mondays to Fridays of about nine miles an hour (service 70 was 9.67 m.p.h. in the busy hours, with 9.34 m.p.h. at other times). This was undoubtably due to the irregular but frequent lifting of Creek Bridge, the single track sections between Rotherhithe Tunnel and Tower Bridge and chronic road traffic congestion at the London Bridge end. Lastly, due to conditions imposed by statute upon the LCC, the terminal point in Tooley Street varied between Bermondsey Street and the end of the line just west of Joiner Street according to the time of day.

The daily service between Forest Hill, Waldram Road and Southwark Bridge via Brockley, New Cross and Old Kent Road, the main stay of services in the Brockley area, received the number 72 in 1912. It worked in that way until, on 5th April 1914, with a comprehensive re-arrangement of services in south-east London, together with an addition to the Brockley services by an extension of 66 on weekdays to Forest Hill, 72 became a Monday to Friday rush hour service, but still working all day on Saturdays and Sundays. Due to wartime conditions, with its consequent staffing difficulties and the fact that there was not so much pleasure traffic, the Sunday service by January 1916 had been curtailed to work only between Forest Hill and New Cross Gate. On 17th July 1917, the service was further reduced to work on weekday rush hours only, while at the same time, 66 became the daily service in its place. Finally, on 7th April 1919, service 72 disappeared altogether.

It re-appeared on 16th June 1921 on a new daily service, when it was paired with 66 to work on an Embankment "circular", running inwards via Walworth Road and Westminster. After almost seven years of operation in this way, the next change came when 66 was withdrawn on Sundays as from 10th June 1928 and 72 was re-arranged to terminate on Sundays at Savoy Street, Strand. In reality, however, on arrival at Savoy Street, the service number was changed to 74, the cars running back to Forest Hill via Blackfriars and Old Kent Road. This method of working resulted in a 72 starting from Forest Hill and finishing its journey at Forest Hill (later Grove Park) as a 74, there to be turned to repeat the whole sequence in the opposite direction.

This form of Sunday working ceased on 30th June 1932, when the 72 was re-routed away from Brockley and Forest Hill to run to Woolwich via Lewisham, Lee and Westhorne Avenue. This replaced the cars, numbered 44, which had provided a temporary service along the newly-opened Westhorne Avenue, and also those on service 46EX, working between New Cross Gate/Lewisham and Woolwich. On the same day, the routes of services 35 and 72 were transposed between Lambeth North Station (Christchurch) and Camberwell Green, the 72 now running via Kennington Road and the 35 via Walworth Road. The 72 was also replaced between New Cross and Forest Hill by service 35.

The first use of the number 74 has been described in the section dealing with Camberwell car shed, being withdrawn from that area as from 22nd January 1922. After lying dormant for about 10 months, the number was used again from 13th November on a weekday rush hours only service between Blackfriars and Forest Hill via Old Kent Road and Brockley, after which, on 2nd September 1926 the service began working all day on weekdays. Sunday service was added from 10th June 1928, when it was paired with service 72, as described above.

The installation of new junction layouts at Brockley Rise, Cranston Road and St. Laurence's Church, Catford, resulted in the diversion of service 74 away from Forest Hill, to run along Stanstead Road, then Bromley Road to Grove Park on a daily basis as from 3rd April 1930. Just over a year later, on 14th May 1931, the service was withdrawn between Beckenham Lane and Grove Park on Mondays to Fridays and Saturday mornings. However, from 2nd August 1932, it was extended again to Downham Way, Bromley Road.

A number mentioned previously in south-west London, was used for a short time working from New Cross car shed. In December 1912, a service was operating on weekdays only between Greenwich Church and St. George's Church via Deptford, New Cross and Old Kent Road, and the number 86 was allocated to it. However, this service did not appear in the map and guide for February 1913 and it must be assumed that it was withdrawn very early in that year.

It now only remains to describe the two Bermondsey horse car services which were in operation in 1913 and one other little-known service which may have worked for a short time in 1914. The two horse car services were the remnants of the London, Deptford & Greenwich Tramways Company lines and were operated from a small depot in Evelyn Street, Deptford. The number 88 was allocated to the service working between the "Red Lion" Rotherhithe and "Bricklayers Arms" via Southwark Park Road and Tower Bridge Road, while 90 was given to one, or maybe two cars shuttling back and forth along Rotherhithe New Road between Raymouth Road and St. James' Road, Old Kent Road. It had been the intention of the LCC to electrify the route via Southwark Park Road but, due to the outbreak of the Great War, the plans were shelved, never to be revived. Both services were withdrawn, the 90 on 12th July 1913, followed by 88 as from 1st May 1915.

The three remaining service numbers (94, 96 and 98) do not appear to have been used by the LCC. There has been speculation over many years of a service 96 working between Victoria and Abbey Wood via Camberwell, New Cross and Greenwich but, apart from one mention in the May 1914 map and guide and the issue of one set of tickets bearing the number, no more is known.

The Kingsway Subway Services

Although administered mainly from the Northern Divisional Office, the Kingsway Subway group of services will be discussed both from the southern and northern system points of view in Volumes I and II respectively, as they formed a significant part of the operations of both divisions.

Upon the 1912 allocation of service numbers, 33 and 35 were given to the single deck cars working daily services through the Subway and via Westminster Bridge. The former was operating between Highbury Station and Tower Bridge, whilst the latter ran between the "Angel" Islington and Clapham Junction via Battersea Park Road. On Sundays however, there is evidence that 35 was extended from the "Angel" via Essex Road to St. Paul's Road, Mildmay Park.

On 28th October 1913, with the introduction of a new service 86 between Clapham Junction and Waterloo Bridge, worked by double deck cars, service 35 was effectively withdrawn, being covered north of Westminster by extra cars on service 33 between Westminster Station and Southampton Row. Further strengthening of the services north of the subway was provided by extra cars running on services 39 and 51, which parallelled the 33 and erstwhile 35 as far as "The Angel". The map and guide for December 1913 shows that the service number 35 was no longer in use.

The single deck cars may well have proved to have been inadequate for the heavy traffic on offer and these changes permitted the use of more double deck cars over the unrestricted sections of line on either side of the subway, passengers being able to obtain transfer tickets for through journeys which were now no longer possible. The withdrawal of service 35 was short-lived however, as during January

Class F car No. 560 emerges into the sunshine from the south portal of Kingsway Subway on its journey to its Elephant & Castle terminus in St. George's Road. *(Courtesy: E. R. Oakley collection)*

or February 1914 it had re-appeared, running all day on weekdays and on Sunday evenings between "The Angel" and Westminster Bridge.

By October 1915, service 33 had been withdrawn and 35 extended to Highbury Station on a daily basis. No further changes were made until 24th October 1921, when 35 was extended from Highbury Station to Highgate, "Archway Tavern". From the same day, additional cars were operated during the busy hours between Westminster and Highbury, and from 14th November these received the service number 33. Both were extended over Westminster Bridge to County Hall from 24th July 1922, where they reversed on a crossover at Stangate. Following the installation of a new crossover at the end of St. George's Road near Newington Butts, the service was extended to the Elephant & Castle via Westminster Bridge Road and St. George's Road on 27th June 1924.

No more changes occurred until the subway was closed for reconstruction on 2nd February 1930, to enable it to take double deck cars. Service 33 was withdrawn, while 35 worked between Bloomsbury and Highgate with double deck cars, some of which had new bodies mounted on the trucks of the old single deck cars. During the seven months that the subway was closed, there were many rumours spread regarding the routes to be taken and services to be operated when it re-opened.

New Cross car shed had been allocated some of the E/3 class cars which were destined to work the subway services, and which were mainly being used for the time being on 46, 52 and 54. There were others at Telford Avenue, mainly used on services 10, 16 and 18. The New Cross crews working on services 36, 38 and 40 were sure that 40 was going to work from Abbey Wood to either Stamford Hill or Manor House, whilst staff from Telford Avenue were equally sure that they were going to work from Norbury to Highgate. Rumours also went round Camberwell depot to the effect that 62 was going to run from Catford to Highgate Village. As it turned out, the New Cross and Camberwell prophets were wrong, whilst those at Telford Avenue were only partially right. When the subway re-opened on 14th January 1931, three services were provided, numbered 31, 33 and 35.

Service 31 was totally new, being put to work between Wandsworth and Hackney and extended on Saturday afternoons and evenings to Tooting Junction. Sunday service was first provided from 19th April, when 31 began running from Tooting Junction to Leyton, "Bakers Arms", giving the longest one way journey on one car in London, a situation which lasted until October 1931, when it settled down to the following:-

Wandsworth - Hackney Station (weekdays)

Tooting Junction - Hackney Station (summer Sundays)

Wandsworth High Street - Leyton "Bakers Arms" (winter Sundays)

The summer Sunday service in 1932 returned to the 1931 pattern from 8th May until 25th September, when the winter service reverted to working between "Bakers Arms" and Wandsworth. The last month of LCC control saw service 31 again extended to Tooting as from 4th June 1933. This time, however, the service to "Bakers Arms" was retained, giving a run of over 16 miles.

The second of the new Subway services, numbered 33 followed the same route as it had done prior to the Subway closure. Starting at Highbury Station, it ran beyond its former terminus at Westminster, to Brixton, Water Lane via Kennington Road during weekday rush hours, the cars being provided by Holloway shed as before and additionally, some from Telford Avenue, Streatham. It is interesting to note that the single and ordinary return tickets carried fare stages as far as Norbury Station, whilst the workman returns carried stages only as far as Streatham Library. In actual fact, the main service terminated at Water Lane, and only isolated journeys ran as far south as Streatham Library.

This arrangement was not to last long, as from 14th May the service was diverted at Brixton, to work to West Norwood via Effra Road and Herne Hill on a daily all-day basis, while the Streatham allocation of cars was replaced by one from Norwood. The diversion to Norwood covered the same route as service 76 (Victoria Embankment and West Norwood via Westminster), which was withdrawn. A further change took place on 8th October, this time at the northern end, when it was diverted at Islington Green to run to Manor House via Essex Road and Green Lanes, instead of to Highbury Station. This change resulted in the diversion of service 51 between Bloomsbury and Muswell Hill, to run instead between Aldersgate and Muswell Hill, and the withdrawal of service 37 (Aldersgate and Manor House).

The third service, numbered 35, which had been running from Highgate to Bloomsbury whilst the subway was closed, was extended to New Cross Gate via Kennington Road, Camberwell and Peckham, replacing some cars on service 40. With this extension into South London, additional cars to work the service were provided by Telford Avenue, Streatham shed. On 14th May 1931, the Streatham cars working on the service were transferred to Camberwell car shed, and the service was extended to Brockley Rise, Cranston Road at the same time.

From 30th August 1931, it was extended on Sundays to Downham Estate, Valeswood Road, to be followed, as from 10th October by a Saturday evening extension to Downham. This ceased on 5th March 1932 when it was curtailed once again at Brockley Rise. On 30th June 1932 the service was extended daily to Forest Hill, and was re-routed via Walworth Road instead of running via Kennington. This diversion trans-posed the routings of 35 and 72 between Lambeth North Station and Camberwell Green, while service 72 was displaced between New Cross and Forest Hill by its diversion to Woolwich, as described elsewhere.

A final change was made on 1st June 1933, by the addition of extra Monday to Friday midday workings between Elephant & Castle and Highbury Station, bearing the number 35A.

The Victoria Embankment

One of the unusual features of operation of the LCC Tramways on the southern system was the method of "loop" working around Victoria Embankment, which became possible when the tracks were extended across Blackfriars Bridge to meet those at John Carpenter Street and opened on 14th September 1909. This resulted in services from Tooting, Streatham, Peckham, Greenwich and Woolwich Road being paired up for operational purposes.

Changes to these arrangements were made periodically, some of the first casualties being the Woolwich Road and Peckham services which, by the time numbering was introduced were working separately again. Two pairs of services, from Merton and Streatham were then operated in a circular style, trams working inwards via Westminster returning via Blackfriars and vice-versa, but by December 1912, a third service to and from Norwood had been added to the group. Those inward via Westminster were numbered 2 from Tooting, 16 from Norbury and 80 from Norwood, with their Blackfriars counterparts being 4, 18 and 76 respectively. The Woolwich Road services, numbered 38 via Westminster and 36 via Blackfriars were not however, officially reclassified as "circulars" until 17th January 1921. By contrast, the Peckham services, numbered 64 and 84 in 1912, did work "circulars" from time to time. For a period during the last year or so of the Great War until 10th February 1919, these two worked to a rather unusual pattern as has been described elsewhere.

The use of numbers on the circular services created its own problems, which the LCC solved by advertising these as terminating at Waterloo Bridge, although in practice the cars continued under a different number. A car from Merton on service 2 would cross Westminster Bridge, continue around Victoria Embankment and, on crossing Blackfriars Bridge be displaying the number for service 4 for its return to Merton. The precise place where the numbers were to be changed was also laid down by the Council, with cars coming in via Westminster having their indications changed in Westminster Bridge Road, while those coming in via Blackfriars, being changed in Blackfriars Road.

Circular workings of the Norwood service had ceased by January 1916 when the Blackfriars section was withdrawn. This left the remaining "circulars" to carry on working for several more years in the manner described above. On 17th January 1921, the 36/38 was made "circular", to be followed on 16th June 1921 by the addition of four more. Existing service 22, running between Tooting and Savoy Street, Strand, via Streatham and Westminster was given a twin, numbered 24, which worked via Blackfriars. The Peckham Rye, Westminster and Savoy Street service, numbered 56 was joined by its Blackfriars counterpart numbered 84, but only worked in this way on weekdays. The Sunday operation of 56 remained unaltered.

Service 66, working between Forest Hill and John Carpenter Street via Walworth Road and Blackfriars was balanced by a new daily service via Westminster, numbered 72, but also running via Walworth Road. The fourth additional service saw the return of the number 76, again working from and to Norwood, this time via Brixton and Westminster, having 80 as its counterpart, which had been working to Blackfriars since 1916.

Given the practicalities of changing the service numbers on cars running round the Embankment loop, it is perhaps surprising that the LCC persisted with the practice for so long. On 23rd November 1923, the changing of numbers was abolished on all services, except for 76 and 80. This resulted in the numbers being displayed on cars entering the loop being retained throughout the remainder of the journey around the Embankment.

Although services 76 and 80 were not included in these changes, their turn came as from 10th December 1925. Existence in this form only lasted five years as, from 14th May 1931, the 76 was withdrawn in favour of an extension to subway service 33. In much the same way, circular services 66 and 72 were divided as from 30th June 1932, the Forest Hill portion of 72 being taken over by a diversion of service 35. At the end of LCC control, there were six pairs of services working round the Embankment loop. Three of these, 2/4, 16/18 and 36/38 were regular daily workings, 56/84 operated on Mondays to Saturdays only, and the other two, 2A/4A and 22/24 only worked during weekday rush hours.

All Night Services
The Horse Car Era

In response to a widely expressed desire, the Council, shortly after the transfer to it of the London Tramways Company's undertaking, had established all-night horse-car services between:-
1. New Cross Gate and Blackfriars Bridge via Peckham
2. New Cross Gate and Blackfriars Bridge via Old and New Kent Roads
3. Blackfriars Bridge and Water Lane, Brixton
4. Westminster Bridge and "The Plough" public house at Clapham

Each of these services operated at intervals of about 30 minutes, except in the early morning of Sunday, Good Friday, Christmas Day and Bank Holidays, when the demand was not sufficient to justify the continuance of the services. Workmen's fares, with the usual half-penny stages were charged on the all-night cars. Prior to the discontinuance of the omnibus services on 6th March 1902, these were run over the bridges in connection with the night services.

Electric Cars.

The electrification of tramway services in the capital invariably meant that large numbers of cars would be run for all sections of the community, from the earliest in the morning rush hours, through to the evening busy times, and then thinning out during the late evening, to eventually finish the day's schedule sometime after midnight, after which all-night services worked, usually at half-hourly intervals on the principal routes, from about 11.30 p.m. until 4.30 a.m. Mondays to Saturdays.

The use of electric cars on night services appeared to have been introduced in a rather haphazard way, but in reality the unreliable power supply militated against operating electrical services during the silent hours. It was not until after the Council had had sufficient operating experience with normal daytime working, that it was decided to convert the all-night services and then only after making special arrangements with regard to power supplies. Both the Peckham and Old Kent Road night services were electrified on 28th March 1904, the Clapham and Brixton routes (worked out of Clapham shed) on 27th June 1904.

A wet night-time scene on the Victoria Embankment near the Kingsway Subway entrance, with its line-up of trams.   (Courtesy: C. S. Smeeton)

The Old Kent Road night service was extended from New Cross Gate to "the Marquis of Granby" on 18th October 1904, and to Catford, Rushey Green via Lewisham on 18th April 1914, which only lasted until 17th October 1914, when the extension was withdrawn for the whole of the Great War period.   The service was again extended to Catford on 20th November 1922, being further extended to Downham, Bromley Road on 29th April 1928, where it remained.   As from the opening of the Blackfriars Bridge tracks, it is most probable that the services terminating at Stamford Street were extended to John Carpenter Street. On 9th October 1913, the two services from New Cross were further extended to Savoy Street.

Dealing next with the service to Brixton, this was transferred from Clapham to Streatham shed on 3rd February 1906 when Streatham shed opened.   On 17th May 1920, the suburban end of the line was extended to Streatham, St. Leonard's Church, but cut back again to Water Lane again on 14th March 1921.

The Clapham and Westminster night service was extended to Charing Cross upon the opening of the Westminster Bridge and Embankment lines on 15th December 1906.   There was also a Clapham to Blackfriars service introduced on 16th May 1903, but it was withdrawn on 2nd March 1908.   On the withdrawal of this service, transfer tickets were made available to passengers between the Brixton to Blackfriars and Clapham to Westminster services.   The Clapham service was extended to Tooting Broadway on 21st December 1908.

On 1st February 1922, the Water Lane, Brixton and Blackfriars service was re-arranged to work inwards via Kennington Road and West-minster, along Victoria Embankment and outwards via Blackfriars, while the Tooting and Clapham service was routed inwards via Blackfriars, along the Embankment and out via Westminster and Kennington Road. The next change came on 18th July 1928, when the service terminating at Brixton, Water Lane was extended to Tooting Broadway via Mitcham Lane and Southcroft Road.   Cars arriving at Tooting via Streatham would then return to London via Clapham and Blackfriars, while those arriving at Tooting via Clapham were extended along Southcroft

Road and Mitcham Lane to Streatham, Brixton and Westminster via Kennington Road. This, in conjunction with the changes made to the inner ends of the service in 1922, resulted in complex circular working, which continued throughout the tramway era and for many years with the replacing buses, surviving until 1984. Night cars were never given service numbers during the time that they were operated by the LCC.

On the Nine Elms and Battersea route, a night service began working between Earlsfield and John Carpenter Street via Westminster as from 8th November 1909. This was followed on 6th December by the introduction of an early morning run from Earlsfield to Waterloo Bridge via Westminster, commencing its journey at 4.10 a.m. Fourteen months later, on 2nd January 1911, the night service was withdrawn between "Princes Head", Battersea and Earlsfield Station. Battersea was to remain the night service terminus for the next twenty years until, in the autumn of 1931, the route between "Princes Head" and Tooting Broadway was once again provided with an hourly service of night cars.

Staff cars were also worked over the system during the night hours, many of which were available for passenger use, in addition to the very early and late cars of the daily schedules. The exceptions were on Saturday nights, when no "all-night" cars were run, but the day schedules still provided for very late and early workings on Saturday evenings and Sunday mornings, ensuring that there were still very good services available for those who wanted them.

List of car services as at 30th June 1933.
All services operated daily, unless otherwise shown.

2   Wimbledon Station, Tooting, Clapham, Kennington Road, Westminster, Embankment. Return via Blackfriars.
4   Wimbledon Station, Tooting, Clapham, Kennington, Elephant, Blackfriars, Embankment. Return via Westminster.
2A   Streatham Library, Tooting, then as service 2 to Embankment Monday to Saturday rush hours only. See also services 22/24
4A   Streatham Library, Tooting, then as service 4 to Embankment Monday to Saturday rush hours only. See also services 22/24
6   Mitcham (Cricket Green), Tooting, Clapham, Kennington, Elephant, St. George's Church, City.
8   Victoria, Vauxhall, South Lambeth Road, Clapham, Tooting, Streatham, Brixton, South Lambeth Road, Vauxhall, Victoria.
     One direction only. See also service 20.
10   Tooting Broadway, Streatham, Brixton, Kennington, Elephant, St. George's Church, City.
     Saturdays: no service after 3.40 p.m. St. George's Church and City.
12   Tooting Junction, Garratt Lane, Wandsworth, Battersea Park Road, Vauxhall, Lambeth Road, Borough Road, Southwark Bridge Road, Hop Exchange.
14   Wimbledon Station, Merton, Haydons Road, Garratt Lane, Wandsworth, Battersea Park Road, Vauxhall, Westminster, Embankment, Blackfriars, Southwark Street, Hop Exchange. Monday to Saturday only.
     Mondays - Fridays after 9.04 p.m. and Saturdays after 3.14 p.m.: no service between Blackfriars (John Carpenter Str) and Hop Exchange. Sundays: no service between Wimbledon Station and Wandsworth.

16   Purley, Croydon, Thornton Heath, Norbury, Streatham, Brixton, Kennington Road, Westminster, Embankment.   Return via Blackfriars.

18   Purley, Croydon, Thornton Heath, Norbury, Streatham, Brixton, Kennington, Elephant, Blackfriars, Embankment.
Return via Westminster.

20   Victoria, Vauxhall, South Lambeth Road, Brixton, Streatham, Tooting, Clapham, South Lambeth Road, Vauxhall, Victoria.
One direction only. See also service 8.

22   Tooting Broadway, Streatham, Brixton, Kennington Road, Westminster, Embankment. Return via Blackfriars.
Monday to Saturday rush hours only.   See also services 2A/4A

24   Tooting Broadway, Streatham, Brixton, Kennington, Elephant, Blackfriars, Embankment. Return via Westminster.
Monday to Saturday rush hours only.   See also services 2A/4A

26   Kew Bridge, Hammersmith, Putney, Wandsworth, Clapham Junction, Wandsworth Road, Vauxhall, Westminster, Embankment, Blackfriars, Southwark Street, Hop Exchange.

28   Harrow Road (Scrubs Lane), Shepherds Bush, Hammersmith, Putney, Wandsworth, Clapham Junction, Wandsworth Road, Vauxhall, Victoria.

30   Tooting Junction, Garratt Lane, Wandsworth, Putney, Hammersmith, Shepherds Bush, Harrow Road (Scrubs Lane).
Extended on Monday to Saturday to Craven Park Junction, and Monday to Friday rush hours and all day Saturday to Wembley.

32   Clapham "Plough", Queen's Road Battersea, Chelsea Bridge.

34   King's Road Chelsea, Battersea, Falcon Road, Clapham Junction, Clapham Common, Stockwell Road, Coldharbour Lane, Camberwell Green.
Sundays: extended via Walworth Road and St. George's Church to City.

36   Abbey Wood, Plumstead, Woolwich, Greenwich, New Cross, Old Kent Road, New Kent Road, Elephant, Blackfriars, Embankment.
Return via Westminster.   Some cars started from Blackwall Tunnel.

38   Abbey Wood, Plumstead, Woolwich, Greenwich, New Cross, Old Kent Road, New Kent Road, Elephant, Westminster, Embankment
Return via Westminster.   Some cars started from Blackwall Tunnel.

40   Abbey Wood, Plumstead, Woolwich, Greenwich, New Cross, Camberwell, Kennington Road, Westminster, Embankment (Savoy Street)
Some cars started from Blackwall Tunnel.

44   Beresford Square Woolwich, Woolwich Common, Well Hall, Eltham Church.
Mondays to Saturdays only.

46   Beresford Square Woolwich, Woolwich Common, Eltham Church, Lee Green Lewisham, New Cross, Old Kent Road, St. George's Church, City.

48   Brixton Road (Gresham Road), Coldharbour Lane, Camberwell, Elephant, St. George's Church, City.
Mondays to Saturdays only.

52   Grove Park Station, Catford, Lewisham, New Cross, Old Kent Road, St. George's Church, City.
Monday to Saturday rush hours only.

54   Grove Park Station, Catford, Lewisham, New Cross, Camberwell, Kennington, Vauxhall, Victoria.

56   Peckham Rye, Goose Green, Camberwell, Walworth Road, Elephant, Westminster, Embankment. Return via Blackfriars.
Mondays to Saturdays. See also service 84

Sundays: Peckham Rye and Embankment (Savoy Street) via Westminster.

58 Blackwall Tunnel, Greenwich, Lewisham, Catford, Forest Hill, Dulwich, Goose Green, Camberwell, Kennington, Vauxhall, Victoria

60 Dulwich Library, Goose Green, Camberwell, Walworth Road, Elephant, St. George's Church, City.
Monday to Saturday rush hours only.

62 Blackwall Tunnel, Greenwich, Lewisham, Catford, Forest Hill, Dulwich, Goose Green, Camberwell, Walworth Road, Elephant, Westminster, Embankment (Savoy Street).
Mondays to Saturdays only.
Mondays to Fridays: no service after 8.13 p.m. between Blackwall Tunnel and Greenwich Church.

66 Forest Hill Station, Brockley, New Cross, Camberwell, Walworth Road, Elephant, Blackfriars, Embankment (Savoy Street).
Mondays to Saturdays only.

68 Greenwich Church, Creek Road, Rotherhithe, Tower Bridge Road, Elephant, Waterloo Station.

70 Greenwich Church, Creek Road, Rotherhithe, Tooley Street.

72 Beresford Square Woolwich, Woolwich Common, Westhorne Avenue, Lee Green, Lewisham, New Cross, Camberwell, Kennington Road, Westminster, Embankment (Savoy Street).

74 Downham (Bromley Road), Catford, Brockley, New Cross, Old Kent Road, New Kent Road, Elephant, Blackfriars (John Carpenter Street).
Extended on Saturdays p.m. and Sundays from Downham (Bromley Road) to Grove Park Station.
Extended on Sundays from Blackfriars to Embankment (Savoy Street).

78 West Norwood, Herne Hill, Effra Road, Brixton, South Lambeth Road, Vauxhall, Victoria.

80 West Norwood, Herne Hill, Loughborough Junction, Camberwell, Walworth Road, Elephant, Blackfriars (John Carpenter Street)

84 Peckham Rye, Goose Green, Camberwell, Walworth Road, Elephant, Blackfriars, Victoria Embankment. Return via Westminster
Mondays to Saturdays only. See also service 56.

89 Acton, Askew Road, Hammersmith, Putney High Street.
Mondays to Saturdays only.
Extended on Saturday afternoons to Wandsworth, Garratt Lane and Tooting Junction.
Joint service with London United Tramways, who also operated a Sunday service between Acton and Hammersmith.

Subway Services

31 Hackney Station, Shoreditch, Bloomsbury, Kingsway Subway, Westminster, Vauxhall, Battersea Park Road, Wandsworth.
Extended on Sundays from Hackney Station to Lea Bridge Road and Leyton "Bakers Arms". Also extended on Sundays from Wandsworth to Garratt Lane and Tooting Junction.

33 Manor House, Green Lanes, Essex Road, "Angel" Islington, Bloomsbury, Kingsway Subway, Westminster, Kennington Road, Brixton, Effra Road, Herne Hill, West Norwood.

35 Highgate "Archway Tavern", Holloway Road, "Angel" Islington, Bloomsbury, Kingsway Subway, Westminster, Elephant, Walworth Road, Camberwell, New Cross, Brockley, Forest Hill Station.

35A Highbury Station, then as service 35 to Elephant.
Monday to Friday midday hours only.

Night Services

Blackfriars, Elephant, Kennington, Brixton, Streatham, Tooting, Clapham, Kennington, Elephant, Blackfriars, Embankment, Westminster, Kennington Road, Clapham, Tooting, Streatham, Brixton, Kennington Road, Westminster, Embankment, Blackfriars.
The whole double journey was then repeated as above.

Downham, Bromley Road, Catford, Lewisham, New Cross, Old Kent Road, New Kent Road, Elephant, Blackfriars (John Carpenter Street).

New Cross Gate, Camberwell, Walworth Road, Elephant, Blackfriars (John Carpenter Street).

Tooting Broadway, Garratt Lane, Wandsworth, Battersea Park Road, Vauxhall, Westminster, Embankment, Blackfriars (John Carpenter Street).

These services did not operate on Saturday nights/Sunday mornings.

Certain day services had late night and early morning journeys throughout the week, which could be considered as providing almost an all-night service. On Sunday mornings, when the official all-night cars did not operate, early cars (displaying service numbers) worked on daytime services. An example of this was the service 40 car which worked from Elephant & Castle to Blackwall Tunnel via Walworth Road and Peckham.

Chapter 28
Destination Equipment

The traditional nineteenth century method used to inform intending passengers of the destinations of public service vehicles was by signwritten boards. These were fixed to external parts of the vehicles where they could be easily seen. On horse-drawn tramcars, they were placed prominently at both ends of the cars above the platform canopies, as used almost everywhere in Britain. In London, the routes served were also identified by the colours of the car liveries.

When the LCC opened the first electric car services, this arrangement was varied to some extent. A standard livery was adopted for all cars, which made it necessary for clearer written information to be displayed. The terminal points of a car on the Tooting services was displayed on a roller destination blind housed in a glass-fronted box. These were fitted, one at each end, in front of the flat profile wire mesh surrounding the open top deck. At night, this information was supplemented by the use of up to three coloured lights, each lamp mounted in a separate box above the destination boxes. Places served along the line of route however, were shown as signwritten information placed on the curved end panelling of the open top deck of the car.

With the introduction of electric car services to New Cross and Greenwich, it was realised that the permanent lettering restricted the use of cars to certain lines of route. With the growth of the network, the necessity to operate some cars on other services, led to the provision of signwritten information on thin boards. Shaped to the contour of the car-panel fronts, these were displayed according to the route being served, but were cumbersome, and their use was short-lived. They were replaced by horizontal wooden boards, fitted above the lower saloon windows, which gave route information in a single line of lettering. Some of these boards were painted in the colours of the erstwhile horse-car services, as shown below.

	Westminster	Blackfriars	Waterloo
Clapham & Tooting	brown	dark green	red
Streatham	red	dark blue	-
Greenwich via			
Old Kent Road	blue	dark brown	light green
New Cross Gate			
via Peckham	green	red	yellow

After about two years, the side route boards were moved down to waist level and fitted into brackets, where they could be more easily seen by the public. This position also made them more readily accessible to tramway staff. A standard uniform colour scheme of white with black lettering (or in one or two cases in east London, red lettering) was introduced.

This view shows the original destination displays used, which included the signwritten route information on the upper deck end panels.

(LCC official view)

Single line route boards were in use on all cars until just after the beginning of the "pullmanisation" programme in 1926, when the refurbished cars began to appear with double-height mahogany boards. This became the new standard for route information, and was eventually used on all cars. In September 1928, there was difficulty in obtaining supplies from Honduras, resulting in Lagos mahogany being supplied at a reduced price of £46. 6. 8d per 100 boards. Certain single line boards for special workings however, such as the Bank Holiday service between Abbey Wood and Waterloo Station, survived for several years after the cessation of LCC operation.

With the introduction of cheap midday fares in 1920, their availability was advertised on the boards. It became the practice to show the legend "Cheap Midday Fares - 2d All the Way - 3 Sections 1d" in the middle area of one side of the board, in white on a red background, together with the places served at the extremities of the route. On the reverse of the board, the full display of places served was used at all other times. Additional information boards, positioned on either side of the main route boards were also to be seen from about 1926, when the first cars were reconditioned to the new "LCC Pullman" standard.

Side route boards soon replaced their rather cumbersome predecessors which were used or the upper deck end panels of the original cars.

(LCC official view)

Publicity boards were also fitted on the upper deck side panels above the advertisements, which were mainly used to provide information about connecting services of other tramway operators. Such an example was "Change cars at Merton for Wimbledon, Raynes Park, Kingston and Hampton Court", as shown on cars working services between London and Merton via Clapham. In later years these boards were used to display additional information regarding cheap fare facilities.

Coloured Lights at Night

During the hours of darkness, a system of coloured lights was used. Where the horse cars displayed a single coloured light, the new electric cars used three lamps, each one mounted in a separate carrier, with a clear glass "bulls-eye" aspect covering it. These were fixed to the tops of the destination indicator boxes. By inserting coloured lenses behind the clear glass, a system of indications was devised which, at that time, was sufficient to enable both the intending passengers and the pointsmen along the route to see where the car was bound for. Four distinct tints were used, Amber, Green, Ruby and Blue, being augmented with Clear and Blank.

The original arrangement for lamp indication was that on the inward journey it was the **number** of lamps that decided which way the car should be sent by the pointsmen along the route, with one lighted lamp indicating Westminster Bridge; two for Waterloo Station via Waterloo Road; three for Blackfriars Bridge. On the outward journey it was the **colour** that was important, with green for Clapham and Tooting; ruby for Streatham; amber for East Greenwich via Old Kent Road; blue for New Cross Gate via Peckham. Therefore, it was not necessary to change either the colour or the number of lamps showing during the time that the car remained on, say, the Greenwich and Blackfriars service, which would show three amber lamps at both ends of the car, the three to indicate Blackfriars on the inward journey, while the amber aspects indicated that the car was travelling outwards to East Greenwich via Old Kent Road. Although the coloured lenses were easy to change, the signwritten information displayed at the ends of the cars presented more of a difficulty. It was therefore unlikely that a car would be transferred between services whilst on the road. Any changes were made in the car shed.

Very soon after the inauguration of electrical operation, it became obvious that cars would be required to work on different services and routes, and that it might be necessary for them to be moved from one car shed to another, which would result in the colours of the lamp lenses having to be changed as required. With the open top cars this did not present too much of a problem, but with the coming of totally enclosed top-covered cars of classes E and E/1, followed later by cars of the A, B, C and D classes as they were fitted with top covers, the lack of flexibility was more pronounced, as it was not possible to change the spectacle glasses easily from inside the cars. To do this, a ladder was necessary to gain access to the indicator box to carry out the necessary work. The illumination of the destination blind and coloured lenses came from the same lamps. This meant in practice that cars were still confined to one service, particularly during the hours of darkness, but with the ability to "turn short" if required.

The colours used were outstandingly clear, but before long there were problems. Additional London termini were soon to open at Vauxhall (later Victoria), Hop Exchange, Southwark Bridge, St. George's Church and Tooley Street. New outer termini were served at East Hill Wandsworth, Forest Hill, Lee Green and others. New routings were made via "Elephant & Castle" and Old Kent Road, "Elephant" and Walworth Road, Nine Elms Lane and Battersea Park Road, Lavender Hill, Kennington, Camberwell and many others. Routes and services were lengthened, shortened, altered and re-arranged. The original routings did retain their "old" colours, for example on the Victoria Embankment "circulars" which developed after 1909. On these, the indications held good as it was the colour that was important on the outward journey and not the number of lamps. However, the pointsmen eventually had a lot more to memorise, as most of the additional indications required combinations of colours and numbers of lamps that bore little resemblance to the original concept.

The whole process had to be undertaken again with the opening of the north side electric services. With the exception of the cars travelling through Kingsway Subway, there was no need for concern about the way in which the colours were allocated, as none of the other services connected with those south of the Thames.

There was one other ingredient in the mixture that must have caused difficulty on many occasions. In those pioneer days, traction lamps were invariably manufactured with carbon filaments. These were notorious for giving unpredictable service, although "if you got a good one" it would last for years. It was also the case that the lamps did not give a white light except when the voltage of the supply was at the maximum for which they were designed, and on tramways it often was not. Therefore the light source could, and almost certainly did, range from somewhere near white, through yellow and orange to light red. What that did to the colours displayed to the passengers and pointsmen is anyone's guess.

The known, but incomplete, list of lamp colour codes, together with all relevant information about services operated between 1903 and 1913 on both the south and north side systems, is shown below. This list does not take account of local alterations which may have been used from time to time.

Official designations of coloured lenses were:-
W - white or clear; A - amber; G - green; R - ruby; B - blue; x - blank. (Note: There are references in other works to "violet", "purple" and "yellow", but these are misrepresentations of ruby, blue and amber.

Tooting - Embankment via Westminster	x G x	
Blackfriars	G G G	
Waterloo Station (in later years from East Hill)	G x G	
Clapham - Southwark Bridge (from Tooting in evening rush hours)	R W G	
Tooting Junction - Hop Exchange	G G x	
Earlsfield - Embankment	G x x	
East Hill - Victoria	R R x	
- Hop Exchange via Westminster	x R G	
Clapham Junction - Embankment via Battersea Park Road	R G x	
Norbury - Embankment via Westminster	x R x	
Blackfriars	R R R	
- Victoria	R R G	
Streatham - St. George's Church (occasionally Waterloo)	R x R	
Water Lane - Southwark	W W W	

West Norwood - Victoria	R G G	
Dulwich - Embankment via Westminster	G W R	
- Southwark Bridge	B W R	
- Victoria	W x W	
Peckham Rye - Embankment via Westminster	G R R	
- Victoria	R x W	
Camberwell - St. George's Church	W W W	
(as from 5th August 1906)	A A A	
Brixton Road - St. George's Church via Camberwell	A A G	
Catford - Embankment via Walworth Road	G B G	
- Southwark Bridge	x R x	
- Victoria via Lewisham	W W x	
		or W W B
Rye Lane - Embankment via Walworth Road and Westminster	R G R	
Blackfriars	B B B	
- Waterloo Station via Walworth Road		
(in later years from Lee Green)	B x B	
South Street, Greenwich - Catford	R R G	
Blackwall Tunnel - Blackfriars via Old Kent Road	A A A	
(as from 5th August 1906)	W W W	
East Greenwich - Westminster via Old Kent Road	x A x	
(as from 5th August 1906)	x W x	
New Cross - Waterloo Station via Old Kent Road	A x A	
(as from 5th August 1906)	W x W	
Woolwich Road - Embankment, Waterloo Bridge via		
Kennington	x B x	
Beresford Square Woolwich - Plumstead - Abbey Wood	W x W	
Woolwich - Eltham	W x W	
Highgate - Holborn	R G R	
- Aldersgate	G G G	
- Moorgate	x R x	
Highbury Station - Tower Bridge	R G R	
- Kennington	x G x	
Stamford Hill - Moorgate	W x W	
- Holborn	x W x	
- London Docks	W W W	
- Norton Folgate	x B x	
Kings Cross - Moorgate	R x G	
- Holborn	x R x	
Cambridge Heath - Bloomsbury	x G x	
Poplar - Bloomsbury	R R R	
		or R x R
- Aldgate	x R x	
Palmers Green - Euston Road	W G G	

Two examples of services that carried colour codes, but for which there are no known records are:-
The Hampstead group of services to Euston Road, Holborn and Moorgate:
The Tooley Street service to Deptford.

The official LCC description of the coloured spectacles used, extracted from the Master List of Stores as held at the Central Repair Depot and the quantities held is:-

Description	Code	Max Held	Min Held
Amber	5472	250	100
Blue	5473	750	250
Green	5474	1500	500
Ruby	5475	750	250
Zinc Blank	5471	288	72

Glass Bullseye 4 15/32" ext. dia.	5466	200	50
Frame for Bullseye, Brass	5465	48	12
Spring Slide, Retaining	5470	432	72
Holder, Cast Brass for Slide	5468	100	25
Casting Zinc	5468Z	100	
Holders, Zinc for Spare Slides	-----	72	12
Key, Operating (Indicator Blind)	5501	Not known	

Service Number Stencils

Service numbers began to appear on cars during the summer of 1912. Small plates, painted black with figures in white, were fitted into back plates screwed on to the canopy bends above, and just to the left of the drivers' heads. An estimate of £1,754 was raised for the implementation of this work, which was to be dealt with by the Council's own tramways staff. After this had started, the Highways Committee had a change of mind as, due to the position in which the plates were fixed, they could not be seen very well at night.

It had been brought to the notice of the Council, that a more efficient method of displaying service numbers had been devised by the Venner Sign Company of London. Employing metal plates, 26 ½ inches wide by 8 ½ inches deep, the numbers were drilled out in a series of holes which were then filled with glass beads. The plates, enamelled black, had the numbers picked out in white and were fitted inside the upper deck front windows. These were backed with white-enamelled plates, two electric lamps being fitted between them, making the service numbers easily visible in daylight or by night. Over the years, most of the beads either fell out or were taken out, but all the same, the service numbers could always be clearly seen.

It was agreed to re-equip the fleet with the Venner type number stencils at a cost of £1,570, to which was added further expenditure of £481. 6. 2d for installation work on the cars. In conjunction with the costs of the earlier abortive work, the Council spent a total of £3,805. 6. 2d. This was for 1,675 pairs of plates for double-deck cars, together with 200 additional pairs, which took account of the cars travelling around the Embankment "loop", and for 50 special sets of illuminated number boxes and plates to equip single deck subway cars. All work was completed by the summer of 1913.

Wear and tear took its toll on the original Venner stencils and, combined with the introduction of more frequent services, it became necessary for the LCC to obtain additional number plates. These were manufactured by the Council at the CRD, but were somewhat different in appearance to the original batches, having the figures completely cut out from the sheet metal.

A "modified set" of number stencils was displayed at Hampstead depot in July 1923. The General Manager recommended that, for the time being at least, the idea should not be pursued as the likely cost per car would be £3.15s. including labour charges.

On 24th January 1924, the Chairman of the Highways Committee issued an order in respect of a new design of end service number fitting, which was inspected by the Committee at Camberwell depot on 14th February 1924. Early in 1925, this type of equipment was fitted to car No. 1235, which then operated on service 34. With the reported success of this experiment, the Council decided, on 18th June 1925, that a total of five cars should be equipped with the experimental design of number plate at a total cost of £81. Those used for the experiment, in addition to 1235 were 1056, 1547, 1688 and either 1236 or 1578 (as both were fitted, but that on 1578 was as a result of body damage). From this, it was decided that the ten-inch metal number plate would be used on all new cars, but none would be fitted to existing cars, except when top decks were replaced for any reason.

Illuminated Side Number Indicators

Although the service number was painted on to the side route boards of the car, there were difficulties, particularly at night, for intending passengers in observing the number. On 1st August 1922 the Council discussed the provision of some kind of illuminated indicator which would overcome the problem. It was decided that a box-type indicator, internally illuminated and incorporating a front and/or rearlamp aspect would be required. Suspended from the canopy adjacent to the stair-case, the box carried detachable metal stencil plates, about eight inches square, one on either side.

The General Manager proposed that a sum of £4,475 be made available to equip 1,790 double deck cars (£2.10s. per car set of two boxes and four stencils), the manufacture and installation to be carried out at the CRD. This estimate also included the provision of spare stencils, to allow for service numbers to be changed during journeys (e.g. the Victoria Embankment services).

The Council, however, decided to invite outside manufacturers to tender for the supply of the new indicators. There was a poor response with only two firms offering to carry out the work (out of seven who expressed an initial interest). The General Manager again asked that the LCC idea be pursued and this was finally agreed by the Council on 7th December 1922 when the decision was taken to equip one car.

By the 1st February 1923, the General Manager reported that the CRD was unable to carry out the manufacture of the boxes, adding "that there were now 1,851 cars to be fitted". It was still expected that the cost of fitting each car would be in the region of £2.10s. Again, the manufacture of the indicator boxes went out to tender, the bid of Benjamin Electric Ltd. being accepted by the Council on 15th May 1923, for 3,602 indicator boxes and associated stencil number at £2,845.18s. 6d (£1.10s. 6d per car set). An additional 1,988 stencils were also to be supplied at a cost of £99. 8s. (1/- per stencil). Fitting of the indicator boxes to the cars was still to be carried out at the CRD at a cost of £1,755.19s. 6d (19s. 6d per car). The boxes were to be delivered eight to twelve weeks after the 15th May 1923 at the rate of 250 per week.

The left-hand view shows a standard "Venner" type stencil, while the right-hand photograph shows a side number box and stencil.

428

With the coming of the new cars of classes E/3 and HR/2, together with the "reconstructed subway cars" of class E/1 in 1929/1930, the arrangement was modified. The box carried only one stencil, displayed on the outside, at the same time it was moved to a position adjacent to the bulkhead. The inward-facing plate was hung from a new sheet metal backplate, secured in front of the staircase at head height.

Destination Blind Boxes

The first type of indicator box, as originally fitted to cars of classes A to D, was supplied by the British Electric Car Company and was of the "two line" style, although there was barely room in the display window for two lines of information, when use was made of 4½-inch high letters.

With the arrival of the class E cars, a new type of indicator box was introduced. The destination roller blind equipment was still placed below the signal lamps, but the whole assembly was contained inside a wooden box, fitted into the curved front panel of the upper saloon. This type of box then became the standard for the LCC Tramways for a number of years, even after the use of coloured signal lamps ceased after 1912. The clear external glasses were left in place, but blanking-out plates replaced the coloured lenses.

A standard destination display box is seen on the left, while on the right is to be seen a box of "K-Ray" design.

Until the Great War, the wooden blind boxes were varnished, but with post-war refurbishing the opportunity was taken to paint the boxes in the "Deep Purple Lake" (or the alternatively-named "Midland Red") colour, the lamp glasses also being painted. As breakages occurred, either by collision damage or other accident, wooden plugs sometimes replaced the glasses. By the mid-1920s, when replacement was required, it became common to insert plain wooden strips in place of the original fitments.

It is interesting to note that the two experimental cars of classes HR/1 and HR/2 when new in 1929, were fitted with "flat" destination boxes of the standard LCC type. However, with the coming of the "reconstructed subway cars" of class E/1 and the main batches of both HR/2 and E/3 cars, the opportunity was taken to introduce a new and improved box, incorporating the "K-Ray scheme of reflected light illumination", whereby the three lamps were above the roller blind, instead of behind, which was said to give a clearer display. This type of box was 41 inches wide, had the top section, seven inches deep, sloping outwards towards the bottom, while the glass covering the main display sloped inwards from the top, the hinged panel of which was 13 inches from top to bottom, while the total depth of the box was some 7½ inches. The main glass panel was 34 inches wide and 10 inches deep.

The last important change came in 1931, when new cars of class E/3 began working on the Kinsgway Subway services. In order to emphasise this fact, the top panels of the new-style boxes were fitted with glass inserts 34½ inches wide and 4½ inches high, inscribed with the words "via Kingsway Subway" in relief on a red background. These could be covered by wooden panels when the cars were working on other services, and were normally fitted or removed by depot staff.

Indicator Blinds

White linen was used by the Tramways Department for the manufacture of destination roller blinds. The necessary information was either printed on to paper labels which were then pasted on to linen, or printed directly on to the material by the use of the silk-screen method. In both cases, the reverse image was displayed, the destinations appearing in white lettering against a black background.

With the early examples of destination box, there was barely room in the display window for two full lines of information. Regarding the use of standard style alphabets, there were up to four variations in the size, particularly where a second line of lettering was required, such as in the destination,

WESTMINSTER
BRIDGE

After some years, the standard finally decided upon was that the main display had 4-inch letters, with subsidiary lettering 2½ inches in height.

To assist conductors in identifying destination information shown on the blinds, a "tell-tale" indication was stamped on the back of each display. In order to make this easy to see, a white space was left within each display so that a copy of the indication could be printed on the reverse of the blinds. Size of this panel was approximately four inches wide by 1½ inches high.

Experimental Car No. 1.

With the construction of this entirely new car, the opportunity was taken to make a complete departure from the traditional methods employed in giving destination and route information to the public. A three-line roller blind at each end was used to give the destination, while another roller blind mounted above it carried the service number. In place of the usual route boards, a large roller blind was fitted into each side of the car body giving route information, with another above it giving the service number.

Car No. 1 of 1932, had all destination information displayed on roller blinds, which gave neat and precise displays.

Chapter 29
The Great War, 1914-1918

A history of a tramway system should not be the vehicle wherein to describe war and military paraphernalia, but in the case of south London, the two were very much interlinked in the years between 1914 and 1918. It was almost like a phantom that the threat of a ghastly war crept up on the population of Britain in 1914. There had been rumblings of a conflict involving several nations of Europe for a couple of years, but no-one seriously thought that, by August of that fateful year, almost half the countries of the world were about to embark on the bloodiest and most terrible war that, so far, had been suffered by humanity.

War means armaments, which, in turn mean that arsenals are required to manufacture and store them. The town and Metropolitan Borough of Woolwich, in south-east London, boasted (if that is the right word) the greatest arsenal in what was then the British Empire. Woolwich Arsenal was vast in the geographical sense and potentially so in the amount of material which was capable of being turned out. In all, it covered an area of about four square miles, from the centre of Woolwich almost to Erith at Crossness. It had its own electricity generating station, gas works, water supply, railway system and even a residential village within its walls. On the northern flank it was bounded by the River Thames, while on its southern side a huge brick wall stood at its boundary for a distance not far short of four miles. The "Main Gate" of this emporium of war was at Beresford Square, Woolwich, where an imposing archway, topped by a large clock, stood guard. At regular intervals along the Plumstead Road, which followed the wall eastwards for a distance of about three-quarters of a mile, as far as Plumstead Station (SE&CR), were what were known as the "Middle Gate(s)", "Third Gate" and "Plumstead Gate". Eastwards from Plumstead Station, the boundary wall of the Arsenal struck out along the north side of the railway line and, with entrances at Church Manor Way (Plumstead) and Harrow Manor Way (Abbey Wood), finally met the Thames near Crossness.

To the south of Woolwich, upon the heights of Woolwich Common, were the barracks occupied by the Royal Regiment of Artillery, the Royal Engineers and other branches of the British Army. It was, of course, due to the presence of the military that the Royal Arsenal was founded in the first place, being greatly enlarged over a period of almost two centuries.

Into this concoction of military barracks and the Arsenal was sprinkled a large part of the population of the surrounding districts. The manufacture of armaments meant employment for a great number of people, who travelled to and from Woolwich and Plumstead by what public transport was available at the time. On 5th April 1914, the LCC Tramways in Woolwich, Plumstead, Abbey Wood and Eltham were

The lunchtime break at Woolwich Arsenal.   As many of the workers lived locally, they journeyed home for a meal.   Two class M cars on service 44 and an E/1 on 42 await their passengers.   (Commercial view)

connected to the remainder of the electric tramway network of London, just in time to take the brunt of an invasion of people who were called upon to undertake war work in the Arsenal, and in surrounding factories mainly sited along the road through Charlton and Greenwich, leading to London, and in similar establishments in Erith, Crayford and Dartford, just across the County boundary, in Kent.

The Woolwich and Eltham Line

Prior to the Great War, the double track tramway between Woolwich and Eltham was almost rural in character for a large part of its length. At the Woolwich end, it passed along roads lined with military barracks until Woolwich Common was reached which, although belonging to the military, was nevertheless quite open in aspect and available for use by the public.   Once across the Common and past the foot of Shooters Hill, there was very little in the way of housing until Well Hall was reached about 2½ miles south of Woolwich.

The Great War was to change matters considerably.   The Royal Arsenal was being filled to capacity and workers came to Woolwich from all parts of the Kingdom.   Homes had to be found for them, with the result that the Progress Estate, a large cottage-type housing project, was built in 1915 at the bottom of Well Hall Road on the west side and along the east side of Well Hall Road between the south side of Eltham Common and the Corbett Estate houses at Well Hall.   A considerable number of wooden bungalows were also built at the upper end of Well Hall Road on the west side in 1915, by the direction of the War Department, who also provided the necessary materials and labour to erect them.   Many hundreds more of these wooden bungalows were erected in the East Wickham, Welling and Abbey Wood districts. In addition to this, the fact that people travelled to the tramway by train and omnibus from outlying areas, caused the 4-wheeled cars of class M which were used, to become greatly overloaded.   The LCC had obtained powers in 1913 to operate trailer cars on this line to a limited extent, and these were renewed.

The Woolwich, Plumstead and Abbey Wood Line

When the extension of the conduit tracks from Woolwich Dockyard to Woolwich Ferry opened to traffic, much of this half-mile length was single track, due to the narrow sections of road in Church Street and High Street. Most of the line already in use between the Ferry and Plumstead was also laid through narrow roads, and lengthy sections of it were also of single track formation. This restriction was not of too much consequence in more peaceful times, but when war loomed not long after the beginning of through working, the situation was to dramatically alter.

During the early summer of 1914, the Council decided that there was already sufficient traffic being generated to extend some cars on service 38 through to Plumstead, Wickham Lane. At this point the road was wide enough to allow for a third track, three cars in length, to be laid as a siding, to accommodate cars turning there. The decision was taken on 30th June 1914 by the Highways Committee to go ahead with this work at an estimated cost of £1,115, the whole job to be undertaken by the Tramways Department.

With the build-up of services brought about by the war and the load added to by the superimposition of Bexley cars upon the already - by now - overcrowded single track sections, Mr. Fell decided that conditions were becoming intolerable with constant traffic congestion. At the end of November 1915, after putting up with great difficulties for over a year, and with there being no sign that the war would be over in the foreseeable future, the first moves were made by the LCC to obtain authority to double considerable lengths of the line.

Meanwhile, the housing programmes initiated by the War Department at East Wickham and Abbey Wood in 1915 had the effect of saturating the services to such an extent that at times they were almost brought to a standstill, and clearly, something had to be done to ease the situation. In December, the Metropolitan Police suggested that, "as an expedient", a re-arrangement of stopping places might be effected at Beresford Square, to which the Council agreed. This, however, was only the first step.

On 23rd December 1915, the LCC made a formal request to the Board of Trade for authority to double a number of sections of single track as a first move to solving the problem once and for all.
1. From the west side of Beresford Street, at the Salvation Army Citadel to No. 84 Beresford Street (The Wesleyan Tabernacle).
2. From No. 84 Beresford Street to Beresford Square.
3. Along Plumstead Road from Beresford Square to Parry Place.
4. In Bostall Hill near Woodhurst Road.
It was anticipated that, without undertaking extensive widenings, it would cost approximately £5,500 to do the work, which would ultimately allow up to an extra 1,000 passengers an hour to be carried.

Woolwich Borough Council, however, would only agree if extensive and expensive widenings were carried out, to which the LCC replied that this course of action was undesirable and, in war conditions, totally inconvenient to war workers. After much discussion, the Borough Council, on 6th April 1916 did agree to the construction of the passing place at Bostall Hill. Work started on 10th April and was completed in 10 days. In the meantime, the LCC had added further proposals for track doubling to the original list.
5. From Nos. 170 to 208 High Street, Plumstead.
6. From Nos. 183 to 219 High Street, Plumstead.
7. From Nos. 231 to 255 High Street, Plumstead.

8. Across Beresford Square.
9. From No. 103 High Street, Woolwich to No. 50 Beresford Street.

Once again, the Woolwich Borough Council proved to be very difficult to deal with, insisting on extensive widenings and, in lieu of some widenings, imposing other onerous conditions upon the LCC. These were "that any additional lines laid in Beresford Square and Plumstead Road be removed and single lines restored within six months after the war if Woolwich Borough Council so requires", and attempting to extract a promise that all the sections of the road where the doublings were placed, would be widened not more than one year after the declaration of peace. It took the combined efforts of the War Department, the Ministry of Munitions and the Board of Trade to convince the Borough Council that the attitude being adopted was, to say the least, selfish and not helpful to the war effort.

Once the "difficulties" with Woolwich were overcome, the work was carried out quite quickly. The first section to be doubled, between Nos. 170 and 208 High Street (also mentioned in another document as No. 165 to Bannockburn Road School) was put into use at the end of August 1916 before completion; next was between Nos. 183 and 219 High Street, completed on 25th September; then between 231 and 255 High Street, already in use on 30th October, the completion date. The section between 103 High Street Woolwich (at Market Hill) and 50 Beresford Street, which included an almost right-angled curve at the west end of Beresford Street, was first used by cars on 11th November 1916. None of these were inspected by the Board of Trade, a formal letter sent by Lt. Col. Pringle, R.E. to the LCC on 20th November giving full approval for their use.

At long last, the two sections of track in Beresford Street, Beresford Square and in Plumstead Road to Parry Place were doubled and brought into use by 2nd August 1917, being officially sanctioned for use by Lt. Col. Pringle for the Board of Trade, by formal written authority and without inspection. It had cost the LCC upward of £10,000 to provide the extra sections of double line, with the Ministry of Munitions accepting liability for one-quarter of this sum, plus another £5,000 if the Council completed the Beresford Square widenings within three years of the conclusion of the war. Thus, after 2½ years of discussion, argument and aggravation, the doublings were complete. There were, however, still five sections of single line between Plumstead Station and the top of Basildon Road, and these were to remain until the end of tramway operations in July 1952.

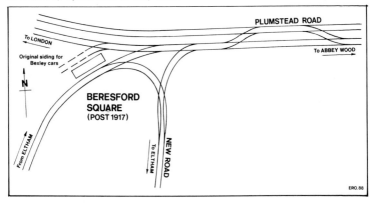

434

The track doublings along Plumstead High Street between Bannock-burn Road and No. 255, and along Beresford Street, Woolwich, resulted in the eastbound track being only two to three feet away from the kerbline in both cases. In order to give a measure of flexibility of working on these sections, a considerable number of facing and trailing crossovers were installed so that, should the track nearest the kerb at any point along the roads be blocked by, say, a household removal van, cars could be worked through the affected sections on a "single line and staff" arrangement, with, usually, a Traffic Regulator or an Inspector in charge of the operation.

One thing which may have assisted the London County Council in its battle to enable it to undertake the doublings, or at least most of them was that, under the terms of the Munitions of War Acts of 1915 and 1916, the LCC Tramways, together with those of the other municipalities, were certified by the Minister of Munitions as being of national importance, by carrying out its duty in conveying munitions workers to and from their places of employment. This qualification carried with it the conditions that strikes and lock-outs were prohibited, and that staff were unable to leave their jobs without the Ministry giving its consent, which, in the circumstances, was not forthcoming without good reason. This was made clear in a communication sent to the LCC and other municipal authorities from the the Minister on 17th October 1916.

Electric Power Problems

Almost immediately after the outbreak of war, the Council realised that great problems were to arise in the Woolwich area with regard to the supply of sufficient power from its sub-station in New Road to serve what was to become one of the busiest sections on the system. On 30th March 1915, a building works programme was initiated to enlarge the station at a cost of about £2,000. Once this part of the work was complete, extra switchgear was installed at a cost of £440, while the installation of additional main and distribution cables was to cost another £11,260. The additional rotary machines required were brought from Forest Hill and Hackney sub-stations.

At the same time, arrangements were made between the Council and the Underground Electric Railway Company of London Limited for that company to supply power to Woolwich sub-station in addition to that coming from Greenwich. Cables for this were supplied and laid by the Western Electric Company Limited. Bearing in mind that there had been power failures at Greenwich from time to time and that the planned extensions of plant there had not all been realised, this alternative supply was seen to be essentially a "back-up" as well as being available for "topping-up" purposes when required.

The station was again extended in June 1916, by the addition of a 500 kW machine taken from another station, while in March 1917, the installation of special control equipment and additional cabling from Greenwich generating station was put in hand, after the decision was taken by the LCCT and the Ministry of Munitions that power should be supplied to Woolwich Arsenal from Greenwich generating station. This was done in order to enable increased production of armaments to be effected, the cost of this work being borne by the Ministry. Two more rotary machines were transferred from Greenwich to deal with the output. Finally, so far as war service was concerned, the power feeder cables between Woolwich and Eltham were augmented in February and March 1918, to allow more cars to be run on this section.

The following table shows how the traffic build-up affected the number of cars in use and the car miles worked, both for the whole of London and for the Woolwich area.

Month & Year	Car Miles		% in Woolwich	Total Cars	Cars in Woolwich	% Cars in Woolwich
	System	Woolwich				
July 1914	174,827	10,745	6.15	1,465	101	6.89
July 1915	139,289	12,015	8.63	1,247	130	10.43
July 1916	139,746	14,910	10.70	1,369	158	11.54
July 1917	143,883	16,426	11.40	1,448	186	12.85
July 1918	140,733	19,361	13.76	1,377	207	15.03

Co-ordination Discussed

During 1915, it had come to be realised that there was wasteful competition on the part of the various undertakings in the Metropolitan area, not least between the activities of the London General Omnibus Company and the LCC Tramways. In an effort to get the two parties to work together in providing transport for war workers, Parliament decided to approach both in order "to avoid waste and duplication in providing competing services". While the Council was in favour, no such response came from the management of the omnibus company. In fact, it seems that they were looking in other directions in order to maintain their traffic, and even build it up to higher levels.

Secret Dealings

During the spring of 1918, a revelation was made that was to begin a searching enquiry into into the way financial subsidies had been dealt with, particularly with regard to certain omnibus services working in the Woolwich area. It began towards the end of 1915, when the LGOC was apparently approached by a representative of the Ministry of Munitions, who suggested that the company might work additional omnibuses for carrying war workers to and from Woolwich Arsenal. An agreement, later referred to "as having been made in secrecy" was then struck between the two parties, giving the company the right to operate vehicles on hire to the Ministry, with services to be worked in conjunction with the Royal Arsenal Authority, but with the 'buses remaining under the control of the company. Mr. Frank Pick of the LGOC then stated that in his opinion, extra journeys would be required on the following services:-

101, North Woolwich - Manor Park;   101A, Blackwall Tunnel - Erith;
75, Lewisham & Lee - Woolwich;   21 & 21A, Lewisham - Eltham;
53, West Hampstead - Plumstead Common.

Col. Wedgwood of the Ministry of Munitions suggested that an additional 10,000 people would be likely to be brought to Woolwich, which was translated by Pick into "areas from which people will be drawn". Following this, a committee was formed in June 1916, which consisted of Mr. Pick; Col. Wedgwood and Mr. Self of the Ministry of Munitions; Miss Gardner and Miss Stopford of the London Divisional Offices for Labour Exchanges. There were no representatives from the tramway undertakings. It was then considered where many of the women, who would form the majority of potential passengers would be likely to live, which was:-

Blackheath - brought into Woolwich by 'bus service 75.
Deptford - brought in by 'bus 53.
Brockley and Lewisham - brought in via Eltham on 'bus service 21.

Bromley - brought in by special 'buses via Beckenham and Eltham.

Tooting - brought in by special non-stop 'buses.

Camberwell - these could come in by tram but, if so, argued Pick, all trams should go via Peckham and 'bus service 53 should be free to work the Old Kent Road.

Special garages were to be made available at Farnborough and Crayford.

Resulting from the meeting and the decisions taken, Mr. Pick then pressed Col. Wedgwood to make contact with the LCC Tramways, in an effort to clear the Old Kent Road of trams working to Woolwich, which it seems, the Colonel was not very keen to do. In July, Pick asked "whether you have come to any arrangement with the LCC over cars via Peckham, as we now have a small number of 'buses available to work between Camberwell and Woolwich via Lewisham and Eltham". The answer from Col. Wedgwood, as may have been expected, was noncommittal. The LGOC was also attempting to introduce a Brockley, Lewisham and Woolwich service, but had reckoned without the influence of the ladies, particularly Miss Gardner, who had obviously impressed Col. Wedgwood when he reported that ".. she (Miss Gardner) did not consider it to be necessary"! Nevertheless, a "munitions" service was instituted between these points before the year was out!

On 4th July 1917, an Assistant Financial Secretary to the Ministry of Munitions challenged the fuel allocations which had been made and the payments which were about to be paid to the LGOC, which was to signal the beginning of an investigation, which went on for another year, ending in an enquiry on 16th May 1918. The result suggested that this was a personal semi-secret arrangement between Pick and Wedgwood, and had just been allowed to go on. Finally, the matter was aired in Parliament, when J. D. Gilbert, M P (LCC) tabled a Question on behalf of the LCC Highways Committee, the answer to which was, to say the least, vague ".. The main trouble has been that no definite agreement existed, and it has not been possible to arrive at a satisfactory working arrangement".

The Secretary of the Metropolitan Municipal Tramways Association, T. B. Goodyer commented "we are not disputing the accuracy of LGOC accounting, but the principle of the whole thing is questioned. The tramways were, and are, capable of carrying much of what was creamed off to the LGOC. Some of the services which received subsidies never went anywhere near Woolwich. The MMTA should have been consulted. It was not".

In the end, it was Col. Wedgwood who was held to be theoretically responsible for the affair. The Ministry of Munitions then offered to withdraw the subsidy from 'bus service 53, if the LCC could take the total load on the Old Kent Road route. But it was too late. The war had finally collapsed. The subsidy was stopped two days after Armistice Day.

Bexley Cars in Woolwich

The service of cars worked into Plumstead and Woolwich by Bexley Council Tramways played an important part in the pattern of operations in the area. It provided the first service of electric cars in the district, gave an early example of a through working agreement and, during the Great War, became tied to some extent to the activities of the LCC. Bexley obtained running powers through to Woolwich upon the electrification of that line by the LCC. The track along Wickham Lane, which was within the London area, was owned by Bexley, but the junction at Wickham Lane Corner was owned by the LCC.

When through running was instituted between London, Woolwich and Abbey Wood, the LCC negotiated with the Bexley Council Tramways for a through service of LCC cars, numbered 38, to work between Victoria Embankment (Waterloo Bridge) and Bexleyheath Market Place on Saturday afternoons and all day on Sundays, beginning on 11th July. On Mondays to Fridays all day and on Saturday mornings a through transfer fare was on offer for the same journey, passengers to change cars at Wickham Lane Corner. When, with the onset of war on 4th August, some other facilities began to be curtailed, this one remained for the time being, probably with the pious but forlorn hope that the war would not last very long.

It was early in 1915 when Bexley UDC realised that, with a total fleet of 16 open-top 4-wheel cars and with the increase in traffic in the conveyance of munition workers to and from Woolwich and their homes in Welling and Bexleyheath, it was becoming increasingly difficult to cope. An approach "in the strictest confidence" was made to Mr. Fell by the Bexley Tramways Manager, for the loan of several cars of the E/1 class, to assist in carrying the extra loads. After long negotiations, an agreement was concluded for an intial period of one year under the following conditions:-

1. The LCC would loan cars, exactly as those working on the Bexley system on Saturdays and Sundays.
2. Bexley UDC would undertake all running repairs.
3. Bexley would be expected to pay all sinking fund charges and interest on the capital cost. This would be £64 per car per annum "and in addition, an amount to be agreed between the Managers which shall cover the annual renovation of the cars, so as to comply with Metropolitan Police requirements. In general, a cost of about £100 per car per annum".

Two class E/1 cars, Nos. 823 and 827 were sent to Bexley at the beginning of July 1915, only a few weeks after the weekend workings on the through LCC service was discontinued.

With regard to the operation of the through service on Saturdays and Sundays, it was made known that as the route was a "difficult" one, with one very long, steady climb along Upper Wickham Lane towards Welling, the motormen would be required to take a test run along it. On 17th April 1915, a class E/1 car, No. 822 stalled on its way up the hill, and then ran back for about 200 yards. Before the motorman managed to stop it, a lady passenger, apparently in panic, jumped off and died as a result. The outcome of this incident was that the motorman was taken off driving duties, it being stated at the enquiry that he apparently "could not get to grips" with dealing with a crisis.

When the first car was run through to Bexleyheath in July 1914 it was found that it could only just get beneath the railway bridge at the Welling end of Upper Wickham Lane. To ease the problem, the overhead wires were moved to positions outside the roof width of the cars and, in the summer of 1915, with the prospect of regular workings by E/1 cars, it was decided to lower the rails of the single track beneath the bridge. While this was going on, the use of bogie cars was temporarily curtailed, services with these being resumed early in September.

Disagreement, Enquiry and Arbitration

Meantime, the Bexley Council Tramways were in conflict with Erith UDC over through running across the Bexley/Erith boundary at Northumberland Heath, which argument had been going on since 1913, and which was the cause of passengers having to change cars at the boundary. Similarly, Erith was at loggerheads with the LCC over the long-standing half-promise made by the LCC to connect the tracks of the two undertakings at Abbey Wood, which were separated by a distance of about 20 yards!

By November 1915, the Ministry of Munitions, War Department and the Board of Trade were all becoming rather tired of the constant bickering among the three and arranged for Mr. J. M. McElroy, Manager of Manchester Corporation Tramways, to undertake an enquiry and adjudicate on the problem. He was only partly successful in resolving the Bexley/Erith problem and the LCC/Bexley difficulties and totally unsuccessful in resolving the LCC/Erith difficulty.

With regard to the shortage of rolling stock suffered by Bexley, which had reached serious proportions, Mr. McElroy approached the LCC with the request that three more class E/1 cars be sent to Bexley. The reply from Mr. Fell on 5th November was surprising ... "instead of borrowing cars from the LCC, Bexley should cease running cars over LCC lines (to Woolwich)". Mr. McElroy retorted that this was no solution; people should not be expected to change cars just for reasons of non co-operation. The Ministry of Munitions entered the argument and helped to "persuade" the LCC to let Bexley have three more cars, together with motormen and depot staff and to provide them with "War Workers' Badges". Enough spare parts were to be purchased by Bexley from the LCC to maintain the vehicles up to LCC standards. This was agreed to on 25th November 1915, resulting in E/1 cars Nos. 1376, 1378 and 1380 being sent on loan.

So far as the LCC/Erith connection was concerned, the arbitrator was less than successful. The Chief Officer explained on 27th November 1915 that "in April 1913, first arrangements were made with the (then) manager at Erith, Mr. Coveney, for a connection to be made at Abbey Wood. The special work necessary for the job was ordered, then stored, and is still available. Mr. Coveney then resigned his position, Mr. Williams taking over. Since then, the only subject has been discussion over the weight and capacity of the LCC cars on Erith metals. No progress has been made on a connection. Since the start of the war, it is not now practical to do the work. The line between Abbey Wood and Woolwich, with much single track is very congested. Bexley cars add their weight to the congestion between Plumstead and Woolwich. When power supplies are increased at the Woolwich sub-station, London services will be increased ... . Sorry ... I cannot be more helpful ..."

In reply to this, Mr. McElroy suggested to Erith on 25th February 1916 that it apply for powers to run 'buses to cover the break of track. Before anything could be done to implement this the LGOC commenced running a service along the lower roads to Belvedere. In an almost instant act of retaliation, Mr. McElroy castigated the LGOC, almost ordering them "to take the 'buses off and let the trams do their job". After much bitter discussion and the suggestion that the company run their 'buses over the upper route to Belvedere and Erith via Bostall Heath, together with the LCC threatening to block the LGOC in its request to operate other services, the company withdrew and complied. In turn, Erith withdrew the application for an Order to enable them to run 'buses. This incident may have been a direct signal to the LGOC to alter its tactics - at least for the time being - and not show its hand with regard to other activities recently discussed. It is also probable that the LCC did not realise the full implication of its actions, or what was going on elsewhere. Had it have done so, the tracks may well have been connected. In the event, the break in the tracks at Abbey Wood remained and, in fact the connection was never made by the LCC, it being left to its successor to complete the job in December 1933.

The Dartford Involvement

Another ingredient in the rather complicated situation was the fact that, at Crayford, about two miles east of Bexleyheath, a large factory owned by Messrs. Vickers-Armstrong had turned over to war production and, in a similar way to what was happening at Woolwich, required the services of a large number of people. At this time, the cars worked on behalf of Dartford UDC and known as Dartford Light Railways ran between Horns Cross and Bexleyheath Market Place via Dartford and Crayford and, although the tracks of the Bexley and Dartford undertakings were connected, there were no through workings by either.

Long negotiations had been going on between the two regarding extending the working of Bexley cars to Crayford, in order to get employees of Vickers to their place of work, but to no avail. In desperation, a service of "chars-a-banc" (motor coaches) was put on for these people, which spurred the two tramway undertakings to come to terms. Eventually, on 7th July 1915, the basis for an agreement was formulated, to be followed one week later by the announcement that Bexley UDC was to pay Dartford 1/6d per car for the return journey between Bexleyheath and Crayford when using the 4-wheeled cars of Bexley UDC Tramways, but if LCC bogie cars were used, the fee was to be 2/6d per car for each return journey made. The "chars-a-banc" were also to be taken off.

Power Problems

The section of Bexley Council Tramways track in Wickham Lane was within the area of the London County Council, but, so far as Bexley was concerned, was at the extreme western end of its system. The power supply for Bexley Tramways was generated at 550 volts d.c. at the Electricity Department generating station at Bexley (known locally as "Old Bexley" as distinct from the upper area of Bexleyheath) and employed no sub-stations.

The feeder cables serving the Wickham Lane sections were about five miles long, giving rise to problems involving voltage drop due to the ohmic resistance of the network. This was sometimes as low as 350 volts at the Plumstead end. With the use of comparatively light 4-wheeled open-top cars, this problem was not acute, but with the introduction of very heavy totally enclosed double deck bogie cars, coupled with the greatly increased services the Council was called upon to provide, the problem of lack of power soon asserted itself.

Despite pleas from Bexley to the LCC for assistance, that body was unable to help and, in an attempt to overcome the difficulty, the Council on 17th January 1917 installed a "petrol driven motor racing car engine of 150 horsepower" coupled to a d.c. generator in a temporary building (a corrugated iron shed) sited at the southern end of Wickham Lane, which was to be used to supplement supplies in busy hours. This attempt at boosting the power supply was, unfortunately, only partly successful, due to the temperamental nature of the machine employed. After a year in service, the Council gave up, recovered the engine and its generator and, as the class E/1 cars had been returned to the LCC, reverted to relying on the original power arrangements, with the probability of the occasional cable fire at the Plumstead end of the line.

Later LCC/Bexley Loans

Hire charges for the cars on loan to Bexley for the period up to 31st March 1916 amounted to £142. 7. 6d, while sundry spare parts cost another £34. 4.10d. Towards the end of 1916, Bexley Council asked the LCC for the loan of four more class E/1 cars in an attempt to be able to have sufficient vehicles available to deal with the vast increase in the numbers of passengers travelling. Fell responded on 10th January 1917 by saying that it would be extremely difficult to comply with this request for cars "similar to those already on loan to Bexley", proposing instead to hire five or six cars of a different type. He also said that the hire and interest charges for these would be the same as for four E/1 cars. The Bexley manager was also advised that the five cars offered "were about ten years old" and had not been used for six years, but the class B cars on offer were actually 14 years old. In order to assist Bexley further, the LCC would pay all charges in fitting trolley poles to the cars at an estimated cost of about £25 per car and then deliver them to Bexley free of charge. The five cars, Nos. 157, 167, 178, 187 and 196 were placed in service on the Bexley route early in February 1917.

Then came calamity. On the night of August Bank Holiday, 1917, the whole of the Dartford Light Railways' fleet of tramcars was destroyed by fire; 13 cars were lost. The LCC immediately came to the rescue by equipping six more class B cars with trolley poles and sending them to Bexley on loan. Nos. 112, 128, 130, 139, 151 and 180 were put to work immediately by Bexley on behalf of Dartford, and using Dartford men to staff them.

As a result of the disastrous Dartford Tramways fire in 1917, the LCC loaned Bexley some cars of class B. In this view, two of these, seen in Dartford, were numbered 34 and 35 by Bexley UDC. (Commercial view)

Having got 11 cars of class B at work on its system, Bexley Council Tramways Manager reported on 16th September 1917 that the LCC had requested the return of the five E/1s and would, in exchange, replace them with six class B cars at the same hiring charge as for the five E/1s. Bexley had no reason to refuse this and asked at the same time for the hire of another six on the same terms as previously, but with a view to ultimate purchase. During the period of delivery of these, the E/1 cars were all sent back to the LCC, the last at the end of December 1917. By 9th January 1918 the delivery of the class B cars was complete, the twelve cars being Nos. 109, 111, 123, 140, 184 and 201, which were subsequently purchased, Nos. 101, 120 and 194, which were returned to the LCC in December 1919 and Nos. 131, 133 and 169, which were returned to the LCC in February and March 1920.

Woolwich, 1919 and After

At the end of the war it was time to take stock. A phenomenal amount of time, effort and money had been expended by the LCC Tramways to rise to the occasion to carry the vast numbers of people who came to be employed in armaments work in the Woolwich area. Great obstacles, many of them untimely and unnecessary, had been put in the way of the LCC while carrying out this vital duty, but equally, the Council was in some measure responsible for some of the problems, particularly with regard to its relations with Bexley and Erith. But the fact remains that, in the main, the Council did succeed in its task, which reflects great credit upon that body. The bones of contention regarding the demand by the Woolwich Borough Council, that the LCC widen the roads where track doubling had taken place during the war, were allowed to remain quietly buried in the vaults - no widenings were ever carried out.

During the 1920s, a programme of rehabilitation was carried out on many sections of line in the area. Track doubling was carried out in Woolwich High Street, while, between Woolwich and Wickham Lane, many of the traction posts were replaced and a considerable amount of the overhead wiring with it. Long lengths of running rail were replaced in conjunction with a complete road reconstruction programme undertaken by the Woolwich Borough Council. The overhead wiring leading to the long-defunct Lakedale Road depot was removed in 1929, during the course of this reconstruction, with the running rails into the depot and those in the lay-by track near Wickham Lane following shortly afterwards.

As in the Woolwich area, the LCC were busy "picking up the pieces" in the remainder of the southern district after the very difficult period of the Great War. Apart from essential work, nothing else had been attended to for several years and, although actual damage to tracks was not of too much importance, there was a considerable backlog of rail renewals, due to wear and tear.

Wartime Generally in London
Railway Station Closures

With the diminishing supplies of coal with which to fire railway locomotives, and the lack of operating and station staff, the railway companies operating in the London suburbs made the decision to close several of the inner London stations, as it was felt that there were sufficient alternative facilities available to convey the comparatively few passengers using these stations, which were in easy reach of the

LCC Tramways. Restricted services were operated on suburban lines by many companies for large parts of each day, which left intending passengers to find other means of transport.

In order to assist with the conveyance of the displaced passengers, the LCC re-arranged certain car services, as is described in the chapter dealing with routes and services.

Track Doubling

In addition to the eventual doubling of tracks in the Woolwich area, similar work was carried out elsewhere on the system. An example of this was the single line junction from Falcon Road into Lavender Hill, Clapham Junction which was doubled in June 1915 and opened to traffic with the agreement of the Board of Trade Inspector, but without inspection. On Sunday, 13th June, service 34, working between Kings Road, Chelsea and Clapham Junction was extended to "The Plough" Clapham.

Wartime Lighting Restrictions

Shortly after the war started, arrangements were made for car lighting to be restricted by dipping the electric lamp bulbs in a white paint wash. It was not long before reports were being made to the management and the police that some cars were seen at night with either no shading on canopy lights, or that the paint had been scratched off the glass of the bulbs, in order that conductors could get a better light. Dire consequences were threatened if any member of the staff was caught interfering with the lighting arrangements.

With the introduction of lighting restrictions, it became necessary for the LCC to considerably reduce the amount of light coming from the headlamps of the cars. In the first place, the glasses covering the lamp bulbs were given a coat of whitewash on the insides, in order to diffuse the output from the lamps. This was soon altered, the new arrangement showing the fleet number of the car through the painted glass, giving a kind of reversed stencil effect, and was retained throughout the war.

Early in October 1914, an accessory known as a "Blue Dot Shade" made its appearance. This item was apparently an outer cover for lamp bulbs, which was "dipped" in blue dye, in order to severely restrict the amount of light shed by the lamp. It was the duty of the "Light & Power" attendants employed at each car shed to ensure that these items were in good order and efficient.

It was at the beginning of January 1915, that the first of a new type of shade was to be seen on the cars. A contract had been entered into with the Nestlé & Anglo-Swiss Milk Co. Ltd. for the supply to the Council at 2/6d a dozen of up to 6,000 lamp shades, each carrying the Nestlé advertisement, but at the same time, limiting the amount of light emitted into the car saloon. These too, were fitted and inspected by the Light & Power staff.

Early in May 1917, new lighting restrictions came into force, which reduced even further the amount of light that could be emitted from any fitting in a public service vehicle. Messrs. Nestlé again rose to the occasion by introducing a new pattern of shade to comply with the regulations, but still bearing the company advertisement. A supply of these was made available to the Council on payment of £72.10s as part cost of producing the shades. The restrictions remained until almost the end of the war in November 1918.

Diminished lighting, both in the cars and in the streets outside, was to throw more responsibility on conductors to ensure that passengers boarded the correct cars, and alighted at their proper destinations. A regulation was framed in 1915 instructing conductors to announce all stops, points, routes and destinations, in addition to carrying out their more normal duties. This instruction was re-issued from time to time in order to remind the car crews of their obligations.

Due to air raids which occurred from time to time, regulations were drafted by the Home Office which set out clearly the action to be taken by tram and omnibus crews on receipt of a warning. All lights were to be extinguished and motormen were instructed to avoid electrical sparking from the ploughs or trolley poles as much as possible. Even when there was no warning, a standing instruction stated that all car lights had to be extinguished when cars were crossing any of the Thames bridges, in order that there would be no reflection of lights in the river, which might be seen by the crew of an unsuspected raider.

The method of warning car crews of an air raid was by means of the illumination of electric lamps mounted on the feeder pillars and at other key points on the system. There were three lamps in each signal display, which could be seen through green glass windows. Responsibility for switching the warning lamps on and off lay with the sub-station charge engineer, who also had to arrange for these circuits to be regularly tested. The cost to the Tramways Department for the installation of this special plant was £624. Belatedly, in 1917, the colour of the lamps was changed from green to red!

It is interesting to note the different arrangements made by other authorities with which the LCC had through running agreements. In the territory where the Metropolitan Electric Tramways operated, a green lamp was placed at junctions and other suitable points whenever an air raid was expected. In East Ham, the line voltage was reduced, remaining so until it was thought to be safe enough to resume normal service, while in the neighbourhood of West Ham, green lights were used, backed up by verbal instructions from tramway officials.

The arrangement employed by Leyton however, was totally different from all the others, and it was the most complex. The instruction stated that "the current will be cut off three times in succession, the lights being out approximately 10 seconds between each operation. Immediately power is cut off, the motorman must place the controller in the 'off' position and note the action of the lamps before proceeding. The conductor must immediately draw the motorman's attention to the current being cut off. When approaching section insulators the motorman must call the attention of the conductor by one ring on the gong, and the conductor must put the lights out when passing under section insulators".

In conjunction with all this, a printed notice was issued to all motormen. "Overhead system - Flashing at Section Insulators. In connection with the danger during air raids of flashing from overhead wires, motormen must bear in mind that the trolley head is **behind** the car. After shutting off power at a section insulator, the power must not again be put on until the trolley head has passed the section insulator". Additionally to all this, motormen must, when in Leyton, observe that ... "if, during the time in which cars are being operated under air raid conditions, searchlights 'are thrown into the sky', motormen will then immediately bring their cars to a standstill, show a light at each end of the car and remain stationary until notice to resume normal control is given. Conductors must co-operate with motormen and notify them of searchlights when observed ... Motormen must carefully examine the condition of their trolley heads, as anyone working with a defective trolley head which causes excessive flashing will be liable to punishment".

There was probably good reason for the authorities in that District Council to be concerned over problems of this nature, as that area tended to get more than its fair share of "hit and run" air raids during the Great War, and the Tramways Department, backed up by the police and military, were not prepared to take what they saw as undue risks.

One of the minor changes made as a result of the threat of bombing from hostile aircraft, was that motormen were instructed to "place the controller in the 'off' position when passing beneath section insulators, frogs and crossings. For the guidance of motormen operating cars on the overhead system, a portion of the poles carrying section insulators, have been painted white immediately above the base ...". Eventually, this band of white paint became the standard mark for a section insulator pole, but it was repositioned to appear just above the first welded joint, about eight feet above the ground.

Bombs and Distress

There were a number of bomb incidents involving the tramway system but, in the main, there were comparatively few fatalities among the tramway staff. One such incident on the night of 24th September 1916 caused the sad loss of Conductor Charles Boys, aged 35, Motorman John Gaymer, aged 46, and Ticket Inspector Elijah Wade, aged 54, when car No. 1145, working on Streatham Hill, received a direct hit by a bomb dropped from a hostile airship. Mrs. Boys was left with five children to support, while Mrs. Gaymer, with one son in the armed forces, had one other child to support. It was also reported that Mrs. Wade, with no family (and with reasonable means of support), was of great assistance in helping to ease the distress of the other two ladies.

This view of car No. 1517, together with the happy-looking conductress, shows how the headlamps of the cars were "dimmed out", by placing a reversed stencil inside the glass of each lamp, which only allowed enough light through to show the car number.
(Courtesy: D. W. K. Jones)

Almost immediately, the Council resolved to pay the widows the full wages for one year that their husbands would have received. This was to be followed by payments, up to £300 each to both Mrs. Gaymer, who was to receive this at the rate of £1 per week, and to Mrs. Boys at the rate of £1. 7. 6d per week.

Another such incident, but one which was to be the cause of much more publicity than the unfortunate incident at Streatham, occured on the 4th September 1917, when a bomb dropped from an enemy aeroplane landed close to Cleopatra's Needle on the Victoria Embankment, severely damaging class G car No. 596, killing Motorman Alfred Buckle and one lady passenger, while severely injuring Conductor John Carr. The bomb also caused the fracture of a 30-inch gas main, at the same time badly damaging the Needle and one Sphinx.

Resulting from this incident, more stringent regulations were published, whereby car crews were instructed to seek shelter on each occasion when there was enemy activity overhead. Until that time, there had been a measure of freedom of choice by crews, whether to stop their cars or not, and it appears that in most instances, they did not.

Killer 'Flu in 1918

At the beginning of October 1918, Britain was beset by a severe influenza epidemic, the like of which had not appeared for many years past. This scourge caused the deaths of many people, and laid low many thousands of others during the time that it was active. It affected the services of tramways in the London area to a marked degree, as hundreds of staff, both operational and supportive, were forced to take to their beds.

On one day, the 29th October, it was reported that 197 motormen and 410 conductors were off duty through sickness, which was to cause the cancellation of many cars, resulting in reduced services on all routes. It was the same in the generating station and sub-stations, where staff levels were seriously affected. Several of the sub-stations were only kept going by the few who remained on duty not going home for several days. At Hammersmith, one of the smaller ones, the staff was down to two members only!

The LCC came in for some criticism from several of the local borough authorities for the way in which they were - or were not - dealing with the epidemic. In the case of Islington, the members of that council insisted that the cars be "thoroughly ventilated" in order to remove the "foul air" which collected when large numbers of people used the cars at any one time. In order to placate this authority, an Order was issued to car crews in the area that, whatever the weather, both doors of the saloons should be kept open for the last 100 yards of every journey, in an effort to blow the "foul air" away!

Police on Strike

For two days, the 30th and 31st August 1918, there were very few police on duty in London. Most of them had gone on strike!

A report on 18th October by the General Manager, Mr. Fell stated that "the recent strike, caused the withdrawal of Police Regulations from practically all, except for one or two most important points. Arrangements were made immediately for assistance to be given to the Tramway Regulators and for Officials to be placed at busy junctions, where normally there were no Regulators. Almost without exception, it was found that Traffic Regulation was quite good, and in some instances better than when the Police had control."

Extracts from reports of District Traffic Superintendents and District Inspectors state:-
"During the strike, we had no difficulty with the traffic, (and) in my opinion we got on better without them, but still they are useful at times."
"At New Cross Gate, Bricklayers Arms, Elephant & Castle, St. George's Church and Stamford Street, congestion was less than when the police are in charge."
"The absence of Police at Vauxhall was not noticed, in fact traffic did better without them."
"Except for slight congestion at Aldgate terminus, the cars got through at all points better without police than with them. We were able to regulate our cars at Gardiners Corner, a thing we were not in a position to do when the police - all four of them - were on duty ..."

Chapter 30
Power Generation

Before Greenwich

In order to supply the huge quantity of power necessary to operate an electric tramway network as large as that envisaged by the London County Council, it was decided that, rather than contract with power companies for the necessary supplies, the Tramways Department would generate and distribute its own. It had been the intention, once electrification had been decided upon, to build a generating station at Camberwell in south-east London, on a site adjacent to the existing horse car depot and stables, from which to supply the south side tramways, with another station north of the River Thames providing power to that part of the system, when operation of it reverted to County Council ownership.

To enable the Council to use electricity at all and to authorise the reconstruction of its expanding system, two Bills were deposited with Parliament in 1900; the first known as the London County Tramways Bill, seeking authority to extend and double existing horse car lines, together with the reconstruction for electrical traction on the conduit system, of the horse tramways between Tooting and the Thames Bridges. The London County Council (No.2) Bill sought powers to reconstruct "for some system of electrical traction" other tramways already in its possession, together with any that it might acquire thereafter, and to enable it to generate its own electricity supplies. The Bill also included the proviso that the Council should in no case make use of the overhead wire system of electric traction without the consent of each of the road authorities concerned through which the tramways ran. The London County Tramways Act, 1900 and the London County Tramways (Electrical Powers) Act, 1900 gave the Council the authority it needed, with powers to build a generating station and other plant.

It was intended that direct current generators working at a line pressure of approximately 550 volts would supply power to the tramways in the vicinity of Camberwell, thus obviating the need for sub-stations. There would, however, also be high-tension three-phase machines generating power to be fed to sub-stations situated in the outer areas. Approximately 20,000 kilowatts of power was seen as being necessary to supply the whole of the system.

At the time of the appointment of Mr. John Hall Rider as Electrical Engineer to the LCC Tramways in February 1901, plans were well advanced for the construction of the station, with some prospective works out to tender. Mr. Rider, however, was concerned that the station as planned would not be in the best interests of the Council, nor of the local population. As there would be no supply of cooling water, the station would have to be equipped with non-condensing engines or be provided with cooling towers. All coal, amounting to an estimated 150,000 tons annually, would have to be conveyed to the station by rail and would require a sizeable transfer yard to offload it, to which the management of the South Eastern & Chatham Railways was said to be not very enthusiastic. Ash and debris would have to be disposed of in the same way. As a result, it was decided that this would not be an economic proposition.

Fortunately, the Council had a riverside site at Hoskins Street, East Greenwich which was in use as a car depot and stables. After agreement in July 1901, the electrical engineering staff drew up designs and plans for a large station to be built on the site, which would be capable of supplying power at an economical rate to the whole of the future tramway network on both sides of the river. The buildings were designed by Mr. W. E. Riley, F.R.I.B.A., Architect to the Council.

In order to provide for future extension and allow for sufficient room on the proposed site, the area around the depot and stables was made the subject of a purchase order. A length of the foreshore of the river was also acquired, upon which to build a jetty and wharf, to permit the delivery of seaborne coal and the easy removal of ash and other rubbish. The jetty also provided the necessary staging point in the installation of large diameter piping, necessary for drawing off considerable quantities of river water for use in the station for cooling purposes.

The change of plan required Parliamentary approval which was obtained as part of the London County Council (Tramways & Improvements) Act, 1902, authorising the construction of the station at Greenwich and the abandonment of the arrangements made for Camberwell. Later, the Highways Committee of the Council and the Tramways Department decided that the depot space at Camberwell would be more usefully employed as a car shed for housing the new electric cars.

This change of mind meant that it would not be possible for a generating station to be in production for several years. As power would be required to serve the newly-electrified sections as they came into use, considerable temporary generating capacity was required. It had been hoped that the first lines would have been working sometime in 1902, but local generating supply stations were not at that time able to supply greatly increased demand loads at 550 volts d.c. without considerable capital investment. As the LCC had already made it known that it would generate its own power, there was no serious incentive by most power companies and municipalities to seek a load of this kind.

A search was made for suitable premises in which to house sufficient plant to generate the power required for the first electrified lines. After negotiations with the South London Electric Supply Company had been concluded, a temporary station was constructed in a purpose-built engine house on part of the company's premises at Bengeworth Road, Loughborough Junction. The building, ordered at a cost of £4,187 from Messrs. Walter Jones & Sons, Bow, London, was erected by Messrs. Watts, Johnston & Co. and E. Nightingale. After completion of the building, which was ten weeks late, the erection of the first two of three continuous current generating plants began. These machines were supplied by Messrs. Dick, Kerr & Co. Ltd. and each was capable of delivering 2,400 amperes at 625 volts d.c. when running at a speed of 150 rpm. Each generator was directly coupled to a Ferranti 2,500 indicated horsepower (ihp) steam driven engine working at a pressure of 190 lbs at 150 rpm.

The diameter of the high-pressure cylinder was 31 inches and of

Ferranti-Dick, Kerr engines and generators under construction at the temporary generating station, Loughborough Park. (A. D. Packer)

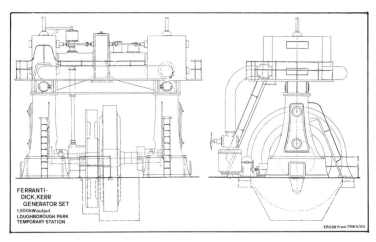

FERRANTI-
DICK, KERR
GENERATOR SET
1,500kW output
LOUGHBOROUGH PARK
TEMPORARY STATION

ERO 88 From TRW 5/03

the low pressure, 62 inches with a stroke of 30 inches. Piston rods measured 6½ inches in diameter; main bearings 18 inches diameter by 36 inches in length; crosshead pins 9 inches in diameter by 13½ inches long. The flywheel weighed 48 tons and was bolted to the generator armature spider. The whole assembly stood 25 feet 4⅛ inches high, 28 feet 1¾ inches deep and when on full condensing load consumed 13½ lbs of steam per ihp/hour and on non-condensing full load used 16½ lbs of steam per ihp/hour.

Three small engines by Bellis & Morcom, of 250 ihp each, drove an equivalent number of exciter dynamos. Cost of this equipment was £25,964, steam piping from Sir Hiram Maxim Electrical & Engineering Co. Ltd. cost £2,268, while a 25-ton capacity electric crane from J. Hitchin & Sons, together with three 10-ton hand cranes, cost £1,477.

Steam for the installation was supplied by the power company at the rate of 1.4d per unit of current generated. It was anticipated that the cost per mile per car would not exceed ½d more than the Council expected to pay for current supplied from a permanent generating station, but this was to prove to be a gross underestimate. It was almost three times that! Even so, the anticipated profit from electric traction in substitution for the horse would amount to a considerable sum, the Council optimistically forecasting £25,000 per annum.

When commissioned in the spring of 1903, the station was operated by LCC Tramways electrical staff. With the eventual addition of a third 1,500 kilowatt machine, it remained in use until after the supply was taken over by the first section of the Greenwich generating station in 1906. On closure of the station, on 19th July 1906, the engines were sold to the power company for a sum a little in excess of £7,000.

In contrast to the d.c. supply generated at Bengeworth Road, the Council entered into an agreement with the London Electric Supply Corporation on 14th October 1902 for the use of part of that company's premises at The Stowage, Deptford in which to erect, for a limited period, two sets of alternating current generating plant which had been intended for installation in the first section of the permanent station. The additional generating capacity was required in order to supply power to the lines to New Cross, Peckham, Old Kent Road, Camberwell and later, Greenwich, prior to the opening of Greenwich generating station. The supply company agreed to provide the steam necessary to run the station, and also to operate and maintain it on behalf of the Council at a cost of 1.65d per unit of power produced.

For this installation, an order was placed in November 1902 with Messrs. Dick, Kerr & Co. Ltd. for the supply of two 1,500 kilowatt three-phase alternators, designed to run at a speed of 150 rpm, to generate current at 6,000/6,600 volts, 25 cps (Hz). Each was to be directly coupled to a Ferranti engine of the type used at Bengeworth Road, also to be supplied by Messrs. Dick, Kerr, together with 13 motor-generators for use in sub-stations and varying in size from 50 kW to 750 kW each, the whole package costing £46,626. On 7th April 1903, British Westinghouse agreed to supply the high tension and exciter switchboards at a cost of £1,257, while the electricity supply company provided the necessary steam piping and switchboard gallery for £2,000 and exhaust tubing for £450. The high tension, low tension and exciter switchboards for the sub-stations at New Cross, Elephant & Castle and Camberwell were supplied by Westinghouse for £5,386.

It was next necessary to consider how power could be supplied to extensions of electrically worked lines in the Southwark and Bermondsey districts in advance of the completion of the permanent station. Arrangements were eventually made with the City of London Electric Lighting Company for a temporary station to be erected at its Bankside, Blackfriars premises. High voltage alternating current was supplied by the company at the rate of 2d per unit generated. Motor-generator sets for supplying current to the tracksides, together with additional machines for the Elephant & Castle sub-station were ordered from Dick, Kerr in April 1904 at a cost of £5,150. Construction of the temporary buildings at a cost of £431 was authorised by the Council on 17th

May and 17th June and the work was carried out by the Tramways Department.

The cable-operated line from Kennington to Streatham was closed to traffic at the end of March 1904 while reconstruction was undertaken to electrify the lines on the conduit system. In this case, temporary arrangements were again necessary for the supply of power, but as the Council already had the steam worked cable machinery in the depot at Telford Avenue, it decided to utilise the boilers to provide steam to drive generators installed in place of the cable winding gear. These machines were part of the original order executed by Dick, Kerr for plant destined to be eventually installed at Greenwich generating station. By 25th May 1904, power was available to the first section of the reconstructed line. The remainder of the line was opened to electric cars on 19th June.

The next project involved the isolated line from the Aldwych Station of the Kingsway Subway to "The Angel" Islington. Due to the delay in commissioning the Holborn and Shoreditch sub-stations, arrangements were made with the County of London Electric Supply Company to provide the necessary power up to 25,000 units a week, at the rate of 1d a unit. The company's station was at Old Street and the Council was afforded facilities to work the switch panels associated with the d.c. supply. Switchgear, cables and ducts were expected to cost £2,000. Current was to go direct to the tramways at Islington, with a switching station (for the time being) located at Queen Street (Holborn) tramway station. Power was supplied prior to the commencement of services on 24th February 1906 and was to remain available until 24th November 1907, if required.

Even though the first section of Greenwich generating station was due to open in May 1906, supplies continued to be taken from outside sources for the northern tramways for some time afterwards. When the line between Aldwych and Islington was extended to Highbury on 16th November 1906, it was arranged with the County of London Electric Supply Company to extend the agreement with the Council to cover this extension at the rate of 1d per unit. A further arrangement was subsequently made with the same company to supply power to work the Stamford Hill to Shoreditch and Bloomsbury to Poplar routes until the completion of certain sub-stations.

In the same way, an agreement was made with the Underground Electric Railway Company of London Ltd. to supply power from their Charing Cross sub-station for a period of six months, to enable the Council to commence working along Victoria Embankment. This was fed to a switchboard installed in the adjacent LCC Victoria Embankment lighting power station. Finally, arrangements were made with the Woolwich Metropolitan Borough Council to supply power to the Woolwich and Plumstead tramway on a temporary basis, at the rate of one penny per unit for the first year and at cost price afterwards.

Apart from arrangements made to meet special requirements it was expected that, as the electric tramways were extended, Greenwich generating station would progressively be able to take the total traction load. Nevertheless, an agreement was made with the London Electric Supply Corporation for it to supply power through Greenwich, to be used for the working of all-night car services "and for certain other special purposes" for which it was considered uneconomical to keep Greenwich station in operation. The "special arrangement" was to be maintained in one of several forms for the whole of the time that the LCC operated the tramway services.

Greenwich Generating Station - Building Work Begins

Parliamentary powers having been obtained to enable the change of location of the generating station to be made, the Council began to acquire additional land upon which to construct the station, wharf and jetty. The properties purchased, for a total of £25,385, comprised:-
1-10 Alfred Place (with adjoining land) and private court.
2-32 and 50-60 (evens) Hoskins Street.
29, 29A, 31 and "The Chapel", Old Woolwich Road.
Elizabeth Cottage.
"The Golden Anchor" public house.
Crowley's Wharf.
Extra sums were also authorised to purchase leases.

One of the results of the compulsory purchase of properties adjacent to the site, was that a number of people living in the houses which had been acquired, had to be found new accommodation before any demolition and reconstruction could begin. A new estate at Hughes Fields, Deptford was developed for this and once this important part of the Council's business was complete, no time was lost in preparing the site for its new use. By December 1902, the foundations and chimney shafts for the first section of the building were under construction; by March 1904, these were complete; erection of the steelwork for the superstructure of the building then being in progress. It took a further two years to complete the building, instal the engines, pump house, outside coal bunkers and jetty. As this section of the station was to be extended almost as soon as it was in operation, a temporary end-screen was erected in order that structural work could continue and not impinge upon the working portion of the station.

Contracts for the preliminary stages of the development of the site were let during the summer of 1902, with the LCC Works Department attending to the formation of the foundations and the construction of the chimneys for £31,300. J. Westwood & Co. of London was entrusted with the structural steelwork for £36,089, while the superstructure was dealt with by H. Lovatt & Co. of London for £52,790. The remainder of the work required necessary to complete the first section was to cost £204,500. The contracts for plant and equipment, which dated from February 1901 were let for a total sum of £344,165. This included £22,782 for boilers supplied by the Stirling Boiler Co. of Edinburgh, £72,590 for d.c. and a.c. plant from Dick, Kerr & Co. of London and £96,713 for reciprocating steam engines from John Musgrave & Sons of Bolton. A number of other manufacturers and suppliers were also involved in providing the many items of equipment, which together completed the work.

The Buildings and Plant

This great complex is the only part of the once-enormous LCC Tramways undertaking to have survived and still to be used for its original purpose, being now used to supply power to the London Underground Railways network. The area of the site is about 3¾ acres, the frontage on the river about 240 feet in length, on Hoskins Street 640 feet and on Old Woolwich Road 300 feet.

A concrete raft 6 feet thick supported the steel girder framework, into which yellow stock bricks and portland stone copings were built, the whole being roofed with grey slates. Ancillary buildings were in the same style, all to the design of Mr. W. E. Riley, F.R.I.B.A., M.Inst. C.E., the Architect to the Council and constructed under his supervision.

The first engine room was 218 feet long and 80 feet wide, with a boiler house of the same size, while the first two chimneys were 250 feet high with inside diameters of 16 feet as measured above the firing doors. The first section cost about 8.6d per cubic foot, or £236,000 in total. Much of the work was done by the LCC Works Department.

Coal supplies were brought to the specially constructed pier by sea-going steamers, each carrying up to 2,000 tons, and unloaded with the assistance of three electric jib cranes, supplied by C. & A. Musker. Special wagons, which were hauled along a standard-gauge light railway by electric locomotives drawing power from a third rail, conveyed the coal from the pier to a large bunker, from where it was distributed to subsidiary bunkers supplying the boilers. The locomotives consisted of box bodies mounted on Brill 21E tramcar trucks using standard tramcar electrical equipment. The wagons, with hinged floors, discharged directly into the main bunker which, with a 2,000 ton capacity, could accept coal at the maximum rate of 1,600 tons a day.

Clean, hard water for the boilers was obtained from specially bored artesian wells, situated within the confines of the generating station. The original boilers installed were described as "the five-drum type" and constructed by the Stirling Boiler Company. Each had a heating surface of 3,650 square feet and an evaporative capacity of about 16,300 lbs of water an hour at 200 pounds per square inch (psi) pressure. Chain-grate mechanical stokers, each giving 60 square feet of grate area were incorporated into the firing mechanism, each group driven by a 25 h.p. electric motor. Six boilers were connected together in two banks on either side of both chimney stacks, allowing for a total of 48 boilers to be in use. After combustion, the residual ash was conveyed by buckets directly to a lower level of the site to be loaded in bulk into barges for disposal.

Engines and Generators

A most unusual type of steam-powered reciprocating engine was employed in the first section of the station. The arrangement, an adaption of a similar type of engine in use in New York and seen by Mr. Rider when on a visit to that city, so impressed him that he decided to utilise the design, but arranged for the construction of the machinery to be undertaken in Britain. The engine itself was known as the "vertical-horizontal" type, consisting of two half-engines, one on either side of the alternator, each half consisting of a vertical high pressure cylinder 33½ inches in diameter and a horizontal low-pressure cylinder 66 inches in diameter.

The stroke of each piston was 48 inches, the two connecting side rods on one side of the engine working on a common overhung crank pin, which was set at an angle of 135° in relation to the crank pin on the other side of the engine, giving eight impulses of thrust per revolution of the alternator, four in the forward direction and four backwards. Engine speed was 94 rpm with steam delivery at 180 psi to the high pressure side.

After the steam was exhausted from the high pressure side of each half-engine, it was passed through a receiver (or re-heat chamber) to be re-heated by live steam direct from the boilers, before passing through the low-pressure cylinder. After re-use the steam was condensed, the resulting water after suitable treatment passing into a hot well for re-use.

Two reasons were given for the use of this type of machine:-
1. It was said to be the nearest thing to turbine operation that could be achieved at that time, with little expected vibration and at economical cost.
2. Water drainage problems were said to be less as the high-pressure cylinders being mounted vertically actually assisted drainage.

So far as the practical results of the first reason were concerned, the vibration generated by the four engines installed proved to be something of a nuisance at full load, resulting in steam turbines being specified for the later extension to the station.

Each engine drove an alternator built by the Electric Construction Company, designed to give an output of 350 amperes per phase with a power factor of 94% at 6,600 volts, 25 cps (Hz), at alternator speed of 94 rpm. A 25% overload factor could be achieved for a maximum of two hours. The alternator armature was stationary, while the cross-fields were mounted on, and revolved around the periphery of the engine fly-wheel. This wheel, with a diameter of 26 feet, weighed approximately 120 tons and, when revolving at the normal engine speed, had a stored-up (kinetic) energy value of about 11,000 foot-tons.

The generated power at 6,600 volts, 25 cps (Hz), was transmitted to sub-stations where it was reduced and converted by means of "rotary transformers" (LCC description) to 550 volts d.c., then distributed to the feeder points placed at half-mile intervals along the lines of route.

By the beginning of 1905, power shortages were being experienced, due to the restricted and unreliable supplies being provided from the various temporary sources and, as the link connection with the London Electric Supply Corporation had already been set up to the main switch-board at Greenwich, considerable calls were made for power from this source. On several occasions, the shortages were so severe that car services had to be reduced for days on end, and the problem was not resolved until the first section of Greenwich Generating Station was brought into use.

It had been calculated that the first part of the station would be capable of providing power for about 750 cars, but with 500 planned for on the south side and 150 on the north side, and a further 268 anticipated at a later date, making a total of 918, the Council concluded that it was essential that the second part of the station would have to be constructed as soon as possible after the first. It had also become obvious that it would be necessary to rely on temporary sources of supply for some time to come.

Meanwhile, contracts for the second portion of the station buildings and equipment were in the course of letting. It was anticipated that, as from August 1905 the work would take approximately 2½ years to complete, but this again was optimistic by about 2 years. Contracts for the steelwork were awarded to E. C. & J. Keay Ltd. of Birmingham for £46,490. 7s.10d; architectural costs were £2,500; general building costs were to be approximately £137,000; while plant and equipment was to cost a further £20,050, which included four turbo-generators of 5,000 kilowatt output each. In all, the completed station was to cost approximately £960,000, exclusive of site costs.

When the station first opened, power was supplied from three of the four sets, the fourth coming into commission early in July 1906, suffering from minor defects which required its withdrawal for a time. To provide service, two machines were running on load with the third as stand-by. This supplied all sub-stations except Streatham, (where the temporary station in the old cable engine house was delivering 400 kW at 550 volts d.c.) and part of the large sub-station at the Elephant & Castle. At certain times of the day, additional power was fed from the Loughborough temporary station until Thursday 19th July 1906, when it closed down. Just prior to this, power requirements were:-

From		
	Greenwich:	5,000 kW
	Deptford:	1,650 kW
	Loughborough:	944 kW
	Total:	7,694 kW

The Official Opening of the Station

After the problems besetting the fourth engine at Greenwich had been analysed, the Council was advised that it would be brought into service by the end of October 1906, when it would then be available to take the first portion of the north side load.

The station was due to be opened with all due ceremony on the afternoon of Saturday 26th May 1906 by the Chairman of the London County Council, Evan Spicer, Esq., after he had ceremonially opened another Council project, the new and spacious Vauxhall Bridge. The intention had been that the Chairman with his retinue would travel across the new bridge by electric tramcar, so performing yet a third ceremony, that of opening the electric tramway from Victoria to Vauxhall. Unfortunately, through an oversight, the Parliamentary powers necessary to allow this section to be used by electric cars had not been obtained. Undaunted, the ceremony went ahead, using horse cars for the journey to the south side of the bridge where, after the obligatory speeches, the party of about 100 people boarded two electric cars to continue the journey to Greenwich.

With the gradual withdrawal of temporary supplies, it was still found necessary to maintain arrangements with the London Electric Supply Corporation. A slightly lower tariff was arranged, the company agreeing to charge 0.75d to 1d per unit instead of 1.65d. Additionally, the company agreed to continue to provide a supplementary supply to Greenwich for working the northern tramways, for working the night services and for any additional power requirements pending the completion of the second section of the generating station. The temporary plant at Deptford was sold to the LESC for £13,000, the plants at Bengeworth Road and Streatham temporary stations were eventually disposed of as surplus material, while the Bankside plant was transferred elsewhere, most of it going to the Elephant & Castle sub-station.

Cost of power generated was approximately 0.676d per unit. Coal to run the station up to 30th June 1907 was purchased at 10/5d per ton. Unusually for that period, the station was opened for public inspection. Many public bodies took a keen interest in the place; some were already complaining about emission of smoke from the chimneys, the Lords Commissioners of the Admiralty being among them as, with their association with the Royal Observatory, they were concerned about what effect smoke would have on observations. A committee was set up to monitor this, consisting of representatives from the LCC and the Admiralty. Sir Benjamin Baker acted on behalf of the Council, the Earl of Rosse represented the Royal Observatory, while the Admiralty had Professor J. A. Ewing to look after its interests.

The special committee reported in December 1906 and made a number of recommendations, including some which suggested certain modifications to plant at the station; as to the way in which and times at which the station should operate so as to avoid any possible interference with the work of the Observatory. These were:-

"a. The question both as regards effects of vibration and obstruction through chimneys, or discharge through chimneys, to be further reviewed after, say, two years, by which time experience should be obtained with the second portion of the station at work.

"b. The generating plant for the second portion to be turbines which, as well as the dynamos, must be of the perfectly balanced type, such as has been proved by trial not to cause vibration.

"c. An undertaking to be obtained that when the plant in the second portion is available for use, the reciprocating engines of the first portion shall not in ordinary circumstances be used after 10 p.m., and their use shall be restricted as far as possible after 8.30 p.m.

"d. Two chimneys of the second portion at present incomplete, not to be higher than 204 feet above the Ordnance Datum.

"e. The discharge of gases from both of these and from the existing chimneys not to be materially hotter than the discharge is now from the existing chimneys, namely, about 250° Fahrenheit.

"f. No further extension to be made beyond the 20,000 kW now contemplated in the equipment of the second portion."

Some of the recommendations of the Committee were incorporated into future policy regarding construction and operation of the station, as will be seen.

During 1907, construction of the superstructure for the second part of the station was put in hand at an estimated cost of £47,940. Total cost of the extension building work was expected to be about £186,000, with a further £150,000 for machinery and plant. As soon as the work was sufficiently advanced to allow the machinery to be installed, two of the four turbo-generators were erected, being commissioned early in 1909, adding 10,000 kW to the output of the station.

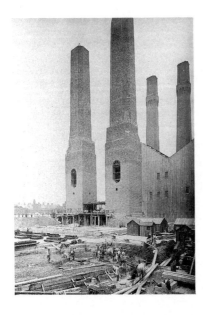

The second section of the Greenwich Generating Station building is seen here under construction in 1906.
(Greater London Photograph Library)

Coal was purchased for 11/- per ton for the year commencing 1st April 1908, which price remained stable for the next two years, with the cost of power generated at the low figure of 0.37d per unit. In March 1910, with the other two turbo-generators in service, power was being generated at 0.35d per unit, with coal at 11/5d per ton. Actual cost of the new equipment was £147,239, of which the turbo-generators accounted for £83,995, with £27,027 for twelve new water-tube boilers and the remainder on many other ancillary items, including pipes, tanks, pumps and switchgear.

The station had taken upwards of eight years to plan, construct and extend to this condition, but, as with so much associated with the LCC Tramways, was to prove to be yet another political football, as it was:-
a. In Greenwich, on the 0° longitude meridian.
b. Too near to the Royal Observatory (according to the Admiralty) for their liking.
c. Disliked by many of the local population because, it was alleged,
   1. Too much smoke was emitted.
   2. Too much gas was emitted.
   3. Too much vibration was generated.
   4. It was too big.
   5. It was there at all.

Further re-Equipment

By 1913, the peak hour loads were such that three of the four reciprocating engines and all four turbines were in use. At the end of March, the cost of power, exclusive of sub-station charges, was 0.315d per unit, while 158,784 tons of coal, at 17/4d per ton, had been consumed.

The Council decided that the time had come for a further extension to be made to the station. On this occasion, the decision was taken to replace the four reciprocating engine sets with four 8,000 kW turbine-driven generators, which would, when completed, give a capacity of 52,000 kW. The estimated cost for this work was £227,000. Reconstruction work would necessitate the removal in the first place of two of the old engines, which would leave the station under-powered. To overcome this difficulty, an agreement was concluded on 6th May 1913 with the London Electric Supply Corporation, for the company to supply up to 2,000 kW of power at a cost of £3 per annum per kW, plus 0.3d per unit for a nine month period. A second agreement, made on 25th November, provided for a further supply of 1,800 kW, at £3 per annum standing charge, but at a unit cost of 0.35d, taken for a period of between four and six months.

Meanwhile, on 6th May 1913, the tender of the British Westinghouse Electric & Manufacturing Co. Ltd. was accepted for the provision of two new turbines and generators at a cost of £50,532. Foundation work for the first of the two commenced at the end of October 1913, Messrs. Kerridge & Shaw Ltd. undertaking this for £7,605, with the stipulation by the Council that work be completed in three months. The first machine was available for service on 27th May 1914 and, at this point, preliminary work for the second stage was put in hand, with Messrs. Kennedy & Donkin being retained as advisors. Tenders were invited at the end of 1914 for the third and fourth of the new generators but, due to problems associated with the outbreak of war, this part of the reconstruction work was to suffer severe delays.

Power shortages still persisted in 1914, resulting in the Council entering into a third agreement with the Corporation on 17th November for additional power to be supplied direct to the Council's Lewisham sub-station up to a maximum of 1,500 kW at £3 per kW per annum and 0.4d per unit, and was considered to be sufficient to enable between 50 and 60 additional cars to be run. The agreement was again revised when the quantity was raised to 3,000 kW as from 1st April 1916, together with an increase in the unit charge so as to reflect the price of coal, which then stood at over 20/- per ton.

Staff Rates of Pay

The rates of pay agreed to for the resident staff at the station, reflected the policy of the Council in paying at or above the usual rates for comparable work in other undertakings. As an employer, the Council was considered to be progressive and fair, but in return, it demanded total loyalty from all sections of the staff. Published rates for various weekly paid grades of employees at Greenwich generating station showed that in 1910-11 the following were in force:-

Boiler House Foreman	£4. 0. 0 to £4.10. 0 per week
Boiler Cleaners	£1.10. 0 to £1.15. 0
Shunters and Tippers	£1.10. 0 to £1.15. 0
Repairs Foreman	£4. 0. 0 to £4.10. 0
Electricians	£3. 0. 0 to £3. 5. 0
Assistant Electricians	£1.15. 0 to £2. 0. 0
Conveyor Drivers	£1.15. 0 to £2. 0. 0
Arc Lamp Trimmers	£1.10. 0 to £1.15. 0
Leading Boiler Scurfer	£1.12. 6 to £1.15. 0
Pump House Attendant	£1.15. 0 to £2. 0. 0
Sub-Station Inspectors	£3. 0. 0 to £4.10. 0

Mishaps

The first reported mishap of any importance occurred on the 27th January 1913 when a high tension cable burned out at 8.25 p.m. putting part of the station out of service for 32 minutes. On the 10th March 1913 a second failure occurred when, at 4.30 p.m., generator No. 7 short-circuited, due to a safety earth wire not being removed after maintenance work had been carried out, and before the machine was run up for service. The result of this action was that a number of cars had to be taken out of service until after 7 p.m. when the machine was run up and put on load. Two days later, machine No. 7 was again in trouble when it failed, possibly as the result of the incident a couple of days before. This time, power supplies were insufficient to maintain a full service, resulting in emergency arrangements being made for allowing standing passengers to travel, up to 15 per car, until full services were resumed on 30th March.

Another serious failure occurred on 14th April 1913 at 8.55 a.m. when No. 2 engine collapsed, resulting in a piston rod being forced through the cylinder cover. Flying metal sliced through a stator winding causing a short-circuit in the cables, closing part of the station. Reduced supply was restored at 11 a.m.; emergency supply obtained from the London Electric Supply Corporation; but even so, a reduced service of cars had to be run, with excess passengers being carried until the repairs were completed on the 10th May and the station was back to normal.

On Friday 11th December 1914 there occurred something of a calamity at the generating station. A transformer which had been in service for several years exploded and ignited. The fire extended to some scaffolding in use by contractors on the replacement work, which in turn ignited some cables, causing a serious conflagration, resulting in loss of power. This damage caused total chaos to services throughout most of London for a considerable time, the only sections maintaining any traffic being on the southern system in the south-east. It was only possible to provide some sort of restricted service as power was once again taken from the London Electric Supply Corporation. It is also quite probable that the feeder cables from the Charing Cross sub-station of the London Underground Railways were still available, even if not generally used, as a restricted service was still able to operate along the Victoria Embankment.

The Council had also stated that "the system has been linked up with another source of supply so as to prevent the complete stoppage of the services in the event of a failure of the Council's own supply. Additional cables have been laid, particularly in the Woolwich area in order to augment the supply of current and thus also increase car services and assist munition workers".

The Great War and Coal Supplies

The outbreak of war on 4th August 1914 had a profound effect on coal supplies to Greenwich, which came mainly from the Tyneside and Scottish coalfields and was seaborne. Soon after the war started, the Firth of Forth was closed to civilian shipping, which effectively prevented any further movement of coal from that area. The Council was then put in the position of having to explore other sources of supply, with the inevitable result that the price went up. In 1914-15, it cost the Council an extra £15,757 above the contractual price of £115,641 to keep a sufficient supply of fuel in hand.

One of the coal contractors was William Cory & Sons Ltd. who, after the war started was charged with the task of obtaining an extra 10,000 tons at contract price plus 1/- per ton, and storing it at the company's wharf at Purfleet, Essex. When it was required for use at Greenwich, it was to be transported in Thames barges at an agreed rate of 4/- per ton. This arrangement was expected to add about £7,500 to station operating costs. To add to the problem of transporting coal from the mining areas, one of the colliers was interned by the War Government (presumably as an "enemy" ship or crew) and difficulty was experienced in obtaining a replacement.

In April 1915, 34,275 tons of coal were obtained on contract for £42,507, while 44,870 tons were purchased on the open market for £46,302. In the next three months, 16,223 tons on contract cost £14,890 and 15,295 tons additionally obtained cost £21,220. From September to December, 28,241 tons were obtained at a total cost of £36,755. The price began to rise sharply in 1916, and it was also becoming difficult to maintain adequate stocks for continuous operation. In an effort to overcome this difficulty, another stockpile was established at Belvedere, Kent, much of which came by rail and was replenished as and when possible. From January to March 1916, 36,180 tons were purchased for £48,038, while from July to September, 33,893 tons cost the Council £51,087.

By 1917 the situation became almost desperate. Due to only two coal carrying ships being allocated to Council service (the S.S. Albert Clement and the S.S. Rhenania) direct supplies to Greenwich were, by the late autumn of that year, deficient by about 1,200 tons a week, necessitating the constant retrieval of reserves from the dumps, which at that time held about 40,000 tons. Further efforts were made to economise on coal by the purchase of coke from other sources (mainly the gas companies) with which to make a coal/coke mixture for firing. For the last three months of 1917, the 19,500 tons of coal used were mixed with 800 tons of coke. This mixture cost the Council £43,000.

Stocks reached their lowest ebb in 1918 with costs going ever higher. In the three months ending 31st March 1918, 25,225 tons of coal and 773 tons of coke cost £46,000 while in the same month the collier S.S. Albert Clement was withdrawn from Council service for military duties, leaving only the Rhenania to carry on. This resulted in even more coke being burned. A supply from the South Metropolitan Gas Company, who offered the Council from 100 to 1,000 tons a week for twelve months, eased the situation somewhat. Even so, the cost had again risen so much that, for the three months ending 30th June, 28,000 tons of coal mixed with 3,400 tons of coke cost £58,000, while the period from July to the end of September saw the use of 24,800 tons of coal and 4,000 tons of coke, costing £58,300. By the time that the end of the war was in sight, things were really bad. Only with great difficulty was sufficient current made available to maintain a very much reduced car service and supply power to war industries as well.

A great strain was then being put on supplies from Greenwich due to the fact that, although some power came to the station from the London Electric Supply Corporation, a large external load was also being imposed upon it. Resulting from an Order issued by the Ministry of Munitions, the LCC was obliged to supply power to Woolwich Arsenal on a regular basis as from 18th January 1918. By the same Order, emergency supplies to West Ham Corporation and St. Pancras Metropolitan Borough Council were also called for as and when required. Looked at in retrospect, Greenwich LCC generating station became one in a chain of power stations supplying current on a sort of "grid" arrangement to all who needed it.

During the years of the war the increased fuel costs progressively caused the unit cost of electricity to go up, as the following table shows.

	1915/16	1916/17	1917/18	1918/19
Coal cost per ton	24/11d	--------	--------	37/7½d to 39/6d
Unit cost	0.588d	0.645d	0.727d	0.804d

The situation regarding coal supplies did not improve much in 1919. Due this time to industrial problems, including a strike of railway workers, 25,000 tons of coke breeze were mixed with coal to maintain output, the total consumption of fuel for the year being approximately 144,000 tons.

Towards the end of 1919, the coaling arrangements were reviewed, and the decision taken to install new handling plant. Duplicate coal chutes from the bunkers into the boiler hoppers were installed, being increased in number to enable twelve more of the boilers to burn coke and other low grade fuels. Cost of this work was £60,000. Despite all this, the difficulty in obtaining supplies of coal extended into 1920 and 1921, while quality was still poor, resulting in coke continuing to be used in large quantities, mixed with the coal. Due to a strike of miners in 1921, the cost of coal to the Council reached an all-time high level of 98/4d a ton, but dropped back dramatically after the strike to settle at about 36/6d. The use of coke was phased out as it, too, rocketed in price and became uneconomic to use. In an effort to further increase flexibility, four of the boilers were fitted with oil burners, which were used at peak periods. After all the problems associated with the war and the post-war strikes, coal prices stabilised towards the end of 1921, the highest being 24/5d a ton, with an average of 18/11d being paid.

Wartime Progress

It will be recalled that the second of the new turbo-generators was being installed when the onset of war seriously slowed down all work for a time. As it was considered essential that machine No. 2 should be completed, the work was pressed ahead as quickly as it was possible to go. In the meantime, it again became necessary to call upon the services of the London Electric Supply Corporation to a considerable degree; this assistance during the spring of 1915 cost the Council £3,525. 9s. 7d. An arrangement was also made between the Council and the London Electric Railway Company of London Ltd. in 1915, when the company agreed to make available an additional supply of current to Woolwich sub-station on a temporary basis. The Western Electric Company contracted to lay the necessary cables to transmit the power.

Machine No. 2 was eventually brought into service in May 1916, which increased demand for steam to a considerable degree, resulting in the Council deciding to alter four of the boilers by the provision of an additional condenser water pipe in each at a total cost of £5,000. The demand for power had increased dramatically to meet the requirements of the Traffic Department, who were charged with operating an almost constant procession of cars to convey large numbers of war workers to and from the many factories, mainly along the riverside areas between Deptford and Plumstead.

A pen-and-ink drawing of the LCC Tramways Generating Station as constructed on the riverside at Greenwich.

Loads were such that it became imperative that the third of the four replacement turbo-generators should be installed. Special arrangements were made with the government departments responsible for authorising the use of scarce resources, in order that this work could go ahead. Progress was slow, but the foundation work for the No. 3 machine was commenced in April 1917 and completed in November. The erection of the generator and ancillary equipment took another year, and the machine was finally commissioned on 12th December 1918 - just over one month after the armistice!

The Post War Years

A serious problem arose in 1920 with corrosion appearing in the blades of the No. 1 turbine set, so advanced that renewal "as quickly as possible" was authorised. A new steam rotor was ordered at a cost of £7,095, which was used to replace the faulty one, the defective rotor then being repaired and placed, in turn, in the other two, to enable their rotors to be attended to.

Authority was finally given in 1921 to go ahead with the provision of the fourth and last 8,000 kW machines. Three new, large boilers were also ordered to replace six smaller ones situated at the northeast end of the station. Contracts for this work were let, with work starting early in 1922. All the new plant was commissioned during 1923. After this was completed, the Council decided to replace the oldest and most troublesome of the 5,000 kW machines with a new one of 15,000 kW capacity, which would allow the other three original turbines to be kept entirely as spare plant, for use only in case of breakdown. In this way, it was hoped that it would once again be possible for the Council to supply almost all the power necessary to keep the tramways operating efficiently.

The installation as at the end of July 1923 consisted of:-

Turbine Set No. 1	Capacity 8,000 kW	Metropolitan Vickers
No. 2	-do-	-do-
No. 3	-do-	-do-
No. 4	-do-	Brown, Boveri
No. 5	5,000 kW	Willans, Dick Kerr
No. 6	-do-	-do-
No. 7	-do-	Westinghouse
No. 8	-do-	-do-

with the No. 4 machine undergoing commissioning tests.

With regard to the new 15,000 kilowatt machine, the tender of Messrs. Richardson, Westgarth & Co. Ltd. was accepted on 4th December 1923 in the sum of £77,467 for the provision of a two-cylinder turbine with Parsons' alternator, together with its own condensing plant containing two condensers. Foundations, pipework and switchgear were all expected to cost a further £8,000. Construction of additional bunkers to hold 10,000 tons of coal was authorised, the tender for this part of the work being accepted on 18th December 1923 at a cost of £34,876. Work started early in 1924, with the machine being finally commissioned and put on load on 24th January 1926, after a construction period of just two years.

The three new large Clayton boilers commissioned in 1923 made it possible, by fitting them with separate ash-handling plant, to operate the station on unwashed fuels, enabling a saving to be made in disposal costs of approximately £5,000 a year. These boilers were also capable of sustaining a high output of between 75,000 to 80,000 lbs of steam per hour, allowing the station to be worked with greater efficiency. Coal costs had also dropped again, the 1924/5 price being averaged at 18/2d a ton as against 22/5d for 1923/4.

More major plant renewals were authorised in 1925, when it was decided to replace the switchgear controlling the works transformer circuits at a cost of £3,386. A further six of the oldest and smallest boilers, with a total evaporative capacity of 90,000 lbs/hour were also to be replaced by three larger ones with a total steam raising capacity of 300,000 lbs/hour. This work, complex and long term, took several years to complete, the boilers finally being commissioned early in 1930, which then made it possible for 27% of the steaming capacity of the station to be obtained from these.

Despite the optimism shown by the Council and its Consultant, Mr. John H. Rider, that the total tramways load could eventually be supplied from Greenwich, it was never possible to achieve this. Due to a problem involving severe voltage drop on the Tooley Street and Rotherhithe end of the route to Greenwich, an agreement was come to with Bermondsey Borough Council in October 1926, whereby the Borough Council would supply the necessary power from its Spa Road generating station, at 0.8d per unit. Provision of switchgear and other plant was to cost approximately £4,350, while cabling was provided and installed by the Enfield Cable Works Ltd. at a cost of £2,775.14 4d. In 1928, however, Bermondsey Council decided to close down its own generating plant and purchase bulk supplies from the London Electric Supply Corporation. The LCC agreed to join the arrangement by taking a supply from the new bulk distribution station and pay £1,160 towards the cost of the new works and to complete the LCC portion at its own expense. The agreement, effective as from 5th February 1929, called for a supply of power based on a maximum demand of 1,000 kW at 600 volts d.c. at a cost of 0.86d per unit delivered to the track switchboard, and was based on the price of coal at 17/6d a ton.

The General Strike of 1926 had a profound effect on the subsequent operation of the station. While only a small load was imposed upon it during the strike, the problems involved in obtaining sufficient and correct supplies of coal were, once again, to force the use of fuels of widely varying characteristics, blended as necessary to obtain the best results that the station staff could achieve. Following the strike, and with the knowledge that considerable re-equipment of the station plant was inevitable, the Council made a fresh agreement with the London Electric Supply Corporation, allowing for a supply of power up to 10,000 kW, instead of the 3,000 previously agreed to in April 1916. The terms of the agreement were that this load could be given by either party to the other in case of emergency or necessity, but no payment would be made. Instead, at the earliest opportunity after the receipt of assistance, the assisted party should return an equal quantity of power to the other.

By 1927 more problems regarding the condition of some of the plant were beginning to show. On 22nd August two interruptions to supply occurred, occasioned by faults on the VHT cables, resulting in the breakdown of the switchgear in the station. This equipment, installed when the station was new in 1906 was carrying loads never envisaged when the plant was designed and engineered. After an enquiry in which Mr. Rider recommended that new equipment be installed, the work was put in hand at an estimated cost of £70,265. A contract for the new armourclad gear in the sum of £46,893 was accepted in May 1928 to be followed in November by the acceptance of a tender for the construction of a new switch-house for £6,440.

The report of the General Manager dated 31st March 1930 showed that operation costs had been reduced in both the generation and distribution services, in spite of further increases in the price of coal. Cost of power for traction purposes including debt charges was 0.687d per unit compared with 0.702d in 1928/9, 0.753d in 1927/8, 0.725d in 1925/6 and 0.864d in 1924/5. The number of units delivered in the year was 216,760,296, with the maximum load on the plant being 55,000 kilowatts. As a matter of interest, 218,254,561 units were delivered in 1931, costing 0.724d per unit.

Again, in 1930, the question of renewal of plant was raised. By then, total capacity of the station was, in theory, 62,000 kilowatts, made up from the total output of one 15,000 kW, four 8,000 kW and three 5,000 kW machines. With the largest out of use, only 47,000 kilowatts was available, with variations in the figures depending which of the machines was out of service for any reason. Maximum load imposed upon the station in 1929 had been 53,000 kW, and it was forecast that, by 1932, it would be likely to be 57,000 kW, which showed that there was not sufficient reserve capacity, even allowing for the arrangements made with the Supply Corporation. There was also an element of obsolescence in some of the equipment; part of it was almost life-expired. The decision was taken to consider the possibility of attaining an ultimate working capacity of 80,000 kW, with a reserve of 20,000 kW, but with an intermediate working capacity of 67,000 kW, with 20,000 kW in reserve. The estimated cost of all this was £450,000. Re-equipment, which was expected to be able to maintain output until 1938, would require:-
1. Ten water-tube boilers and auxiliaries, each of approximately 60,000 lbs/hour evaporative capacity, suitable for supplying steam at 400 psi. at a temperature of 750°F. These were to be supplied by Yarrow & Co. Ltd.
2. Two 20,000 kW (Maximum rating) high pressure turbo-alternators

with condensing plant and auxiliaries, to be supplied by the British Thomson-Houston Company.

Just as arrangements were being made to start the work, the London Power Company, the recent successor to the London Electric Supply Corporation, let it be known on 4th December 1930 that it wished to terminate the previous agreements, whereby the company and the Council helped each other "when necessary". The inference was that as neither party had needed assistance "during the past twelve months", an agreement was no longer necessary. The Council pointed out to the LPC that considerable help was given when company plant was being reconstructed, and it would be equally helpful if the company did the same for the Council during the forthcoming reconstruction work at Greenwich. Eventually, on 5th November 1931, an agreement was reached whereby the Council would pay for power at the rate of 4/- per month per kilowatt, plus 0.35d per unit used, this payment only to be made when power was actually being taken.

In connection with the renewals, expenditure was approved on 8th July 1931; British Thomson-Houston contracted for the turbines for £162,973, while the Council's own Tramways Department was to undertake the preliminary work necessary for generator installation. New pipework and pump equipment was to be supplied by Vickers-Armstrong of Barrow-in-Furness for £27,946 and Drysdale & Co. Ltd., Glasgow, for £4,714.

By the end of 1931, five of the new boilers had been installed, together with auxiliary and ancillary plant, while a 20,000 kW turbo-alternator was put into service in March 1932, replacing one of the 5,000 kW machines. Of the new boilers installed, the first was commissioned on 23rd February, the others being brought into service at intervals during the year. At the end of 1932, seven of the ten were in use, with the second of the 20,000 kW generators coming into service in September. At the end of March 1933, the whole of the work was completed, with all ten boilers in steam. Cost per unit of power for traction purposes in 1932/3 was 0.659d, the number of units delivered was 227.5 millions, while the quantity of coal burned was 183,915 tons.

By June 1933, the total output of the station was generated by the two 20,000 kW British Thomson-Houston alternators; one 15,000 kW Richardson & Westgarth machine; two 8,000 kW Metropolitan-Vickers; one 8,000 kW Metropolitan-Vickers/Parsons and one 8,000 kW Brown-Boveri machines. Steam was supplied from three Clayton & Shuttleworth boilers with an evaporative capacity of 70,000 lbs/hour each; three Clark-Chapman boilers of 75,000 lbs/hour capacity, delivering steam at 200 p.s.i. at a temperature of about 520°f, together with the ten boilers by Messrs. Yarrow, each with a capacity of approximately 60,000 lbs/hour, delivering steam at 400 p.s.i. at 750°F.

Three-phase alternating current at 6,600 volts at 25 cycles per second (Hz) was delivered to the main busbars. All auxiliary power was taken from the main bars as required. Traction supplies were fed to 24 external sub-stations and one within the generating station, each of which converted the high voltage a.c. to 550 volts d.c. for distribution to the lineside sections. Usually, each ½-mile section had its own feeder cables and switches but, in a few instances at the outer ends of the line, two sections were fed from one feeder circuit.

Equipment at the sub-stations, trackside and tracks consisted of 123 converter machines, about 790 miles of cable, 494 miles of conductor tee-rails, 3,140 manholes, 155 miles of duct-line, 440 feeder

Greenwich Generating Station Turbine Hall seen in 1932, just after the completion of modernisation work. (Greater London Photograph Library)

pillars and 3,480 overhead wire traction poles, while many miles of pilot wires to the extremities of the track rails were laid in. On the conduit system, the negative busbars were earthed at the sub-stations, while both positive and negative tee-rails were insulated, which allowed for polarity reversal to be applied from the sub-stations in the event of an earth fault developing on either tee-rail, so placing the fault onto the negative side of the system, and ensuring that services could continue.

On 1st July 1933, ownership of the power station, along with the total tramway undertaking, passed from the London County Council to the London Passenger Transport Board. In the words of the official account of this historic, and to many, unfortunate transfer, "the undertaking was completely self-contained and carried 700 million passengers a year at fares amongst the lowest in the Kingdom. It had a power station with a capacity of 87,000 kilowatts and an annual output approaching 250 million units. The Council transferred an undertaking thoroughly up-to-date and well equipped at all points to continue to play its part in relation to the general passenger transport requirements of London". It seems, with hindsight, to have been a great pity that the successor to the Council did not think likewise!

A Second Generating Station

The Council had intended that there should be a large tramway network in the western suburbs of London which, apart from a few odd lengths, was never built. A site, known as the Pimlico Gasworks, part freehold and part leasehold was purchased under two resolutions of 6th May 1902 and 25th May 1902 for £80,000, plus another £2,000 for legal expenses and £64,000 for an additional parcel of land, with the idea of building a second generating station to serve the proposed new lines. Although much was made of this from time to time, the site was never developed and was ultimately used for other purposes.

The High Tension Cable Network

High tension alternating current at 6,600 volts pressure at a frequency of 25 cps (Hz) was delivered to the main output busbars. From this point it was transmitted to the sub-stations by means of specially designed high tension cables manufactured and supplied by Messrs. Siemens Bros. & Co. Ltd. Initially, about 35 miles, increased in later years to about 45 miles, of three-core, 0.15-inch, paper insulated, lead-covered cable for the main feeders was placed into earthenware ducts laid beneath the streets of the capital. A further 16 ½ miles - later increased to approximately 27 ½ miles - of three-core, 0.075-inch high tension cable was provided to act as inter-station feeders.

At the generating station, a cable tunnel was constructed to enable cables for the south side sub-stations to be carried out of the station and into the main duct lines beneath the streets. For the north side service cables a second tunnel, similar in size to the first, was built to enable the cables to be carried out to a set of ducts which took them to Blackwall Tunnel. A special trough was provided to carry them through the tunnel to the north side of the Thames for distribution to the sub-stations on that side of the river.

Chapter 31
Power Distribution

The Sub-Stations

The special purpose sub-stations which were constructed at key points around the system, were usually not more than about three miles apart in the suburbs, and less in the central areas. The first three to be built were sited at Clapham, within the car shed area; at Brixton Road on part of the site of the cable turning station at No. 20; and at the Elephant & Castle on a site between Dantzic (sic) Street and London Road.

Planning arrangements were also in hand for the purchase of new sites for car sheds at New Cross and Camberwell, both of which were to incorporate sub-stations. So far as the Tooting line was concerned, power was being generated at the temporary station at Loughborough Junction at low voltage d.c., which was fed to Clapham sub-station distribution switches and to part of the switching plant at the Elephant & Castle, where it was distributed to the feeder pillars. The lines to New Cross and Greenwich when completed and put into service received all power supplies from Deptford temporary generating station, with the sub-stations at New Cross, Camberwell and the remainder of the plant at the Elephant & Castle receiving high voltage a.c. to convert to d.c. at the correct voltage for distribution to those lines.

Once a.c. was received at the Elephant & Castle, the d.c. supply from Loughborough Junction was disconnected, leaving that generating plant to supply only the Clapham end of the Tooting line until the Brixton and Streatham line was operational, when d.c. was again fed to the section between Kennington and Brixton.

As the undertaking expanded, so did the need for additional sub-stations. Ultimately there were 26 of them, as now described.

The 14 sub-stations on the south side in 1909 were:-
Battersea, Queen's Road
Brixton, 20 Brixton Road (closed in 1912)
Camberwell, Electric Car Shed
Clapham, Electric Car Shed
Charlton, (inside the Central Repair Depot for sole use there)
Elephant & Castle, Dantzic Street
Forest Hill, Derby Hill
Greenwich (inside the boundary of the generating station)
Lewisham, High Street (near Clock Tower)
New Cross, Electric Car Shed
Stockwell, Stockwell Road (ex-Horse-car Depot)
Streatham, Rear of 31 Streatham Hill
Tooting, Mitcham Road
Wandsworth, "The Gables", East Hill
Three more were added in later years:-
Woolwich, New Road (in 1910)

An interior view of Forest Hill sub-station in 1909, during the erection of one of the motor-generator sets.

Vauxhall, Vauxhall Cross (in 1912, replacing Brixton)
Downham, Bromley Road (in 1924)
One, at Norwood, on ground at the side of the car shed was commissioned as a temporary measure during the 1914-18 war, and dismantled afterwards.

The 10 sub-stations on the north side were:-
Camden Town, 104 Arlington Road
Clapton, Upper Clapton Road
Hackney, Well Street (near Mare Street)
Hammersmith, Electric Car Shed (fed from Wandsworth)
    Ultimately transferred to south side management.
Holborn, Grays Inn Road
Holloway, Warlters Road
Islington, Upper Street
Limehouse, 1 Bloomfield Road, Burdett Road
Mildmay Park, Woodville Road
Shoreditch, 32 Rivington Street, Old Street

All stations had one dedicated feeder cable from Greenwich while additionally, those at the Elephant & Castle, Shoreditch and Holloway each had two. Each station also had a feeder cable to the next nearest station on either side of it. As the south side area was so large, the stations were divided into two distinct groups, viz:-

Group 1.	Camberwell	Group 2.	Battersea
	Downham		Brixton (later Vauxhall)
	Elephant & Castle		Clapham
	Forest Hill		Stockwell
	Greenwich		Streatham
	Lewisham		Tooting

New Cross	Wandsworth
Woolwich	(Hammersmith)
Central Repair Depot	

Those on the north side (excepting Hammersmith) were classified as Group 3.

A temporary sub-station at Queen Street supplied power to the Subway services in 1906/7. The load was later taken over by Holborn sub-station. There were no later additions in LCC days.

Sub-Stations, General

A comprehensive survey of the power generation and distribution system was undertaken by Mr. J. H. Rider, the LCC Tramways Electrical Engineer, in a Paper placed before the Members of the Institution of Electrical Engineers on 25th March 1909. In his report he stated that the Department had a total of 83 motor-generator sets in service, in course of erection, or on order, made up as follows:-

17 motor-generators,	300 kW capacity,	synchronous type
58 motor-generators,	500 kW capacity,	induction type
6 motor-generators,	500 kW capacity,	synchronous type
2 motor-generators,	1,500 kW capacity,	synchronous type
2 rotary converters,	1,500 kW capacity,	synchronous type

The four manufacturers of the sub-station equipment were Messrs. Dick, Kerr & Co. Ltd.; British Westinghouse; The Electrical Construction Co. Ltd.; Siemens Bros. & Co. Ltd., Dynamo Works.

One of the features of LCC sub-station design was the inclusion at each installation of a lead-acid battery of 280 secondary cells. At a nominal two volts per cell, the battery gave 560 volts, which was connected in parallel with the output from the motor-generator sets. This gave a steady bus-bar voltage which would vary very little with the load imposed on it. The battery was used to supply power to the control switchgear as well as providing a standby supply in the sub-station in the event of an emergency. It was not expected, nor was it possible that the battery would be used to supply traction current.

In 1913 the network was almost complete, with only the temporary wartime station at Norwood yet to come and one post-war station to materialise in 1924. With the increase in car mileage due to the continuous rise in the numbers of passengers carried and further extensions to the network, the loads on several of the sub-stations, notably Islington, Holborn, Woolwich, Greenwich, New Cross and Elephant & Castle were so great that further urgent extensions to the plant were necessary, this, in the case of the Elephant & Castle being the second time that such work had been required. A comprehensive scheme was approved on 28th July 1914, whereby existing sub-station machinery was to be re-arranged and additional plant installed at an estimated cost of £48,270. It was planned that the work would be completed by July 1915 but due to the onset of the Great War, it was delayed to some extent.

It has already been mentioned that the Council's system was connected into the supply network of the London Electric Supply Corporation and others, as a safeguard against loss of power for any reason. This became vital in 1914 with the outbreak of the war. The areas which were particularly at risk and in need of such protection were the towns along Thames-side leading to Woolwich and Plumstead, where great activity at the Royal Arsenal and other factories was evident.

It was also realised that the protection of sub-stations and their feeder cables was also necessary in those fateful times, resulting in considerable duplication of the cable network.

The sub-station equipment, like that of the generating station, was greatly overworked during the Great War, with minimum attention due to the shortage of skilled engineering staff, coupled with extreme difficulty in obtaining replacement equipment. As soon as hostilities were over, arrangements were made to clear up the enormous backlog of maintenance of the plant. On 1st March 1921, the post-war programme of renewal and reconstruction commenced. Streatham and Holborn were dealt with first, where existing plant was replaced by a total of seven 1,000 kW rotary converters, the work being completed early in 1923. New machines, of 1,000 kW capacity each, were installed at Hammersmith and Camberwell, the old machines being left in situ for standby purposes. This policy was continued when the Elephant & Castle sub-station was yet again upgraded.

New, additional high tension feeder cables were also provided to serve Shoreditch and Tooting sub-stations, while the re-arrangement of other high tension cables was undertaken. This was done with the object of maintaining the standard of earth return, in order to restrict voltage drop within the limits set by the Board of Trade, as well as improving the reliability of supplies. The Tooting cable was installed in 1922/23, running from Greenwich, via Lewisham sub-station and, together with additional switchgear at Lewisham and Tooting, was commissioned early in 1924.

Further investigations were made by the Council to decide whether any other improvements could be made to the lineside feeder cable network. This resulted in a considerable replacement programme being undertaken, commencing in 1925 and continuing throughout 1926 and into 1927. By the end of March of that year, a total of 700 miles of cables of varying sizes and types were upgraded or replaced. By March 1928 it was 735 miles.

The decision was taken in 1925 to provide a new sub-station at Bromley Road, Downham in order to improve power supply on the line from Catford to Downham, and to provide new facilities on the extension then being planned to Grove Park. The building was available for the installation of cabling, plant and equipment later in the same year. It was ready for service in December 1926 with one 500 kW machine in use, while another was to follow in 1928.

Improvements to and replacements of plant continued to be made during the next few years at New Cross, Greenwich, Forest Hill, Limehouse and Tooting. By the end of 1929, £29,370. 7. 3d was spent on generators, £10,492. 3s. on switchgear and £13,637. 9. 9d on cables and incidental work. A further £65,700 was earmarked over a period of three years for renewals and additions to the high tension and low tension cable network generally.

During the evening of 21st June 1932 a fire broke out in a factory belonging to Messrs. Polikoff Ltd., in Mare Street, Hackney. The conflagration speedily engulfed the roof of the sub-station next door, to be followed by the partial collapse of the factory into the sub-station, extensively damaging the three 750 kW motor-generators and transformers. It was decided to rebuild the structure of the station and to provide new plant at an estimated cost of a little over £10,000 (paid by the Council's insurance fund). Reconstruction work was immediately put in hand and in the meantime the supply of power to the tramways was obtained by switching low tension supplies from neighbouring stations, together with some emergency "teeing-in" to the local feeders. Two 1,000 kW rotary converters replaced the old plant.

As with the remainder of the tramway network, the electricity distribution system passed to the LPTB on 1st July 1933, continuing to play its part in providing the power essential to the efficient working of the system.

Local Line Distribution

Sub-station output was direct current at a pressure of 550 volts, converted from high voltage alternating current by the machinery at each installation. The low voltage d.c. was fed to the trackside within the area of the sub-station by low tension feeder cables, which terminated in Cable Section Feeder Pillars sited on the pavements adjacent to the points where the power was to be fed to the tracks. These cables, together with the high tension cables feeding the sub-stations and the inter-station tie cables, were drawn into nests of earthenware ducts laid beneath the footways.

London, with its conduit system presented many problems in the distribution of power to its complex and very heavily loaded tramway network. Board of Trade Regulations stated that tramway power feeder cable networks must be electrically divided into lengths not exceeding one half mile. On such a system as London this distance in parts of the central area at least, was sometimes less than the statutory half-mile.

The conduit system demanded the use of positive and negative low tension feeder cables between each section feeder pillar and the sub-station. Each pair of distribution cables fed only one section of one half-mile of both "up" and "down" track, even though the feeder pillar connections could be arranged in such a way that either:-
(a) the "city" side or "country" side "up" and "down" tracks could be connected:
(b) both "city" side and "country" side "up" and "down" tracks could be connected:
(c) "city" and "country" "up" could be connected together:
(d) "city" and "country" "down" could be connected together:
(e) the pillar switchgear could be used to link the tracks on either side of it without feeding power into the tracks.

On the conduit system, power was never fed into the conductor tees from more than one feeder box. At complicated junctions such as Gardiners Corner or the Elephant & Castle, it was usual to feed power into the several sets of track from pillars sited up to about 100 yards away from the junction. The tees were "cut" at strategic places so that "double feeding" was not possible.

The reason for "single . feed" arrangements being employed was to guard against a fault condition known as "earthing". This could occur if any one of a number of porcelain insulators carrying the conductor tee-rails in the conduit tube electrically failed for any reason; if metal objects fell or were dropped into the conduit slots; or if a plough on a car collapsed or failed.

Should such a fault occur on the positively charged tee-rail, the circuitry was so arranged that the positive and negative feeders could be reversed at the sub-station. This action would put the fault on the negative side, so allowing the car service to continue in advance of a repair being effected by the electrical engineers. If, however, current was being fed from more than one source, such a switching reversal could cause a short-circuit in the power distribution network with dire results.

When an earth fault occurred on a positively charged tee-rail, the section breaker switch at the sub-station would open and an audible alarm sound. The attendant would, by manipulating double-pole double-throw switches on the control panel, be able to place the fault on to the negative side of the supply. After repair, the circuit could then be restored to normal, although that was not essential.

The negative busbar at each station was maintained at about one ohm above earth potential by means of an infinitely variable adjustable water resistance. In the case of several earth faults occurring at the same time on sections controlled from one station, the attendant would increase the value of the water resistance in order to minimise as far as possible the passage of stray earth return currents. When the faults were cleared, the adjustable resistance was then restored to a nominal one ohm.

Both positive and negative feeder cables were terminated in the pillars with the positive switches normally on the upper panel and the negative on the lower. By means of links at the rear of the panel (only accessible from the rear door, the key of which was held by the electrical staff) any one of four different switching arrangements could be set up. The diagrams show how they were made.

No. 1   shows the feeder box feeding only the left-hand or, say, the "country" tracks.
No. 2   only the right-hand or, say, the "city" tracks.
No. 3   both the left-hand and right-hand tracks.
No. 4   the feeder cable disconnected and the two sets of tracks linked.

The arrangement as shown at either No. 1 or No. 2 was the usual one, so that each pillar only controlled one section of double track of half a mile in length, in one direction only.

The positive and negative cables from the feeder pillar switches were connected to the conductor tee-rail ends at the points where the statutory electrical breaks or gaps were made. The cables, manufactured to Council specification, were of copper core, resin bonded, paper insulated, bitumen filled and lead sheathed types. The main contractor was British Insulated & Helsby Cables Ltd., who also supplied many of the feeder pillars used on the first lines in south London.

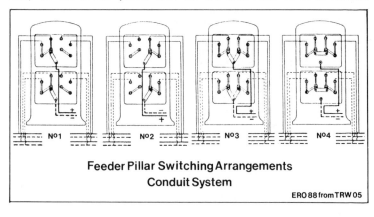

Feeder Pillar Switching Arrangements
Conduit System

ERO 88 from TRW 05

474

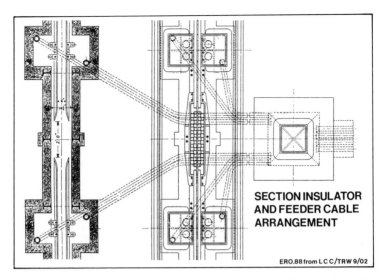

**SECTION INSULATOR
AND FEEDER CABLE
ARRANGEMENT**

ERO.88 from LCC/TRW 9/02

With the overhead wire system, the power was always fed to the wires, while the negative return was always connected to the running rails. However, in a similar way to the arrangements applying to the conduit system, each electrical section was limited to one half-mile. All conections were made from section feeder pillars, which were located alongside heavy duty traction poles, and upon which were fitted special pipes which carried the cables up to the overhead fittings.

A telephone was installed inside each pillar which gave traffic staff, as well as engineers the facility of speaking directly with the sub-station attendant at all times. This system remained in use until, in 1922, a completely new control telephone system was installed on

This LCC section feeder pillar has a cabinet mounted on top of it which contained a private telephone which allowed Traffic Regulators and other staff to speak directly to the Traffic Control Centre. Here, the telephone is being used by the Point Duty Regulator.

475

the northern division of the tramways in order to augment the old arrangement. The new telephones were placed in metal cabinets specially fitted on to the tops of the sections feeder pillars.

A central control office was set up at Hackney, overseeing the whole of the system, for both traffic and engineering staffs. It proved to be of great service to Regulators, enabling them to arrange for diversion and alteration of car services where necessary. The work was completed in 1923 and was so successful that the southern system was similarly dealt with at a cost of £4,200, opening in February 1928 and being controlled from an office at Oval (Kennington).

The Pilot Cables

On the opening of the Greenwich generating station, 26 miles of pilot cable had been installed. The cable, manufactured by British Insulated & Helsby Cables Ltd., consisted of three-core 3/20 copper wire, which was paper insulated and lead covered. Its purpose was to provide continuous testing wires which were laid from the generating station and sub-stations to the furthermost points at the ends of all tracks.

By the time that the network was complete, there was upward of 200 miles of this special type of cable, which played an important part in maintaining the electrical balance of the system.

Chapter 32
The Central Repair Depot

The idea of a Central Repair Depot for the comprehensive overhaul, maintenance and reconstruction work associated with the tramcar fleet was conceived by the Chief Officer of Tramways, Mr. A. L. C. Fell, in 1904. He suggested such a depot and works be founded on "Best American Practice", with riverside and railway access. The proposals of the Chief Officer were brought before the Council in 1904 and formed the basis of debate for almost two years, until an acceptable comprehensive scheme was presented.

The first location to be considered was on a site of about 4½ acres, formerly used by the Battersea Water Works Company and thought to be desirable in all respects. Drawings and specifications were drawn up but, so far as this site was concerned, got no further.

Due to the insistence of the Metropolitan Police that all public service vehicles within the Metropolitan Police District should be thoroughly overhauled and repainted once every twelve months, it fell to the Council to provide facilities on what was to become the grand scale. It was envisaged that the total electric car fleet, both south and north of the Thames, would exceed 1,000 by the end of 1907. By this time the temporary repair works at New Cross were expected to be seriously overloaded and it was becoming a matter of urgency to provide more permanent facilities. At last, on 26th February 1907, the full Council instructed the members of the Highways Committee to report on the matter, which they did on 16th July, recommending the provision of a special building with facilities to deal with all cars and equipment. For this, an estimate of £51,400 was approved for the erection of the first section of suitable buildings, together with another for £16,000 for the provision of machinery, plant and tools.

A freehold site of about seven acres was eventually found, adjacent to the Angerstein Wharf branch line of the South Eastern & Chatham Railway at Charlton in south-east London, and only about 150 yards away from the conduit tramway in Woolwich Road. This site was purchased for £3,850, after which Parliamentary approval was sought in 1908 to construct a branch conduit tramway line from Woolwich Road to the proposed works.

Tenders were called for in 1907 for the erection of the first section of the building on a "schedule of prices" basis, which was expected to cost about £150,000. On 12th November the Council accepted the tender of Chas. Wall Ltd., allowing ten months for completion of the building. Fitting out took about another four months and cost £55,000, after which the Chairman of the Council ceremonially opened the works on 6th March 1909.

By this time it had become apparent that the maximum annual

The main building of the Central Repair Depot is seen here while still under construction. *(Greater London Photograph Library)*

throughput of 600 cars was insufficient, given that it was anticipated that 770 cars would be working on the southern system by March 1910. Authority for an extension to the works was given as a matter of urgency on 13th July 1909, the estimated costs being £47,500 for the building and £11,500 for additional machinery and plant. Chas. Wall Ltd., was again entrusted with the building work, which was considered as a "run-on" from the original construction.

Building work and installation of equipment took another two years, being completed and handed over to the Council in May 1911. It had cost a total of £203,100 to erect the buildings, together with another £66,500 to fit them out and provide all the equipment which would enable up to 1,000 cars a year to be attended to. Finally, on 31st May 1911, the Council contracted with the South Eastern & Chatham Railway for a connection to be made into the railway system, to enable direct deliveries of equipment of all kinds to be made to the depot.

Many functions other than the repair and renovation of tramcars were undertaken by various specialist staffs at Charlton. Plough repair, renovation and some new assembly was undertaken in a specially equipped workshop; traction motors, seats, controller gear and the trucks, both bogie and 4-wheeled rigid types, were attended to on a work-flow basis.

There was a foundry, woodworking shop, blacksmith, welder, wheel turning section, tinsmith, pattern making, armature winding and repair shops and a test room, together with the appropriate sectional stores where everything that could be made, repaired, assembled and fitted was dealt with. The car body overhauling shop with its paint shop and drying room took up almost half the available ground floor space and was approximately 700 feet long and 150 feet wide.

One traverser was initially installed in the main pit running the full length of the building, approximately mid-way between the docking roads, to be followed by a second machine several years later. This

A general view of the body repair shop at the Central Repair Depot.
(Courtesy: R. Elliott)

specially-built shallow traverser was supplied by Appleby's Ltd., and was installed in a pit 16 ft. 6 in. wide and about 6 in. deep. Track gauge was 13 ft. 6 in., with standard LCC conduit work placed centrally between the track, the electrical arrangements being similar to that used for street tracks. A standard car plough supplied power to the traverser motor, while all mechanical and electrical parts were interchangeable with car parts then in use. An unusual feature was the provision of "warping gear" on the traverser (a capstan and winch device for use with steel cables or ropes), by means of which cars, trucks, etc. could be hauled on to or off the tracks or traverser as required.

A second pit was constructed outside the east wall of the depot with access through sliding doorways to each of the tracks in the building. One traverser was placed here. It was also arranged that the conduit slot used to provide power for the external traverser would serve as the power source for a car test track, the rails being laid at 4 ft. 8½ in. gauge along the pit. (This track was still in existence in 1987).

All tools, parts and general items were kept under supervision in a secure stores located between the machine and truck overhauling shops. A narrow gauge railway system, upon which small four-wheeled trolleys were moved around by hand, provided the necessary back-up for the movement of heavy parts and stores. Certain sub-sections of the works were housed on first-floor level, together with offices and a school for apprentices.

During construction of the second section, a third portion was being planned which would, when available, allow 1,800 cars to be attended to in each twelve month period. Expected cost of this new extension was estimated to be about £203,100, with an additional £66,500 for equipment and plant. Given the restrictions of the Kingsway Subway, which could only accommodate single deck cars, the cars which worked entirely on the north side system could not be attended to at Charlton, even though provision appears to have been made for them.

The planned 1913 extension was expected to take about another two years to complete, but had not proceeded very far when the Great War of 1914 put a stop to construction. Eventually, in November 1920, fresh estimates were made of the likely costs for completion of the structural works and equipment. It was decided that a sum of £185,000 (unspent from the pre-war budget) for the building, £1,100 for furnishings and £66,500 for equipment could again be earmarked for the work. A further £116,835 was later added to the estimates, in order to provide funds for the construction of a fourth extension to the building, which was eventually to include a comprehensive central stores section. At that time however, stringent financial restrictions were placed upon the Council with regard to capital spending and, in order to comply with these, the work was carried out in stages over a period of several years.

Piling and foundation work was carried out by J.& W. Stewart, London for £10,800; steelwork by E.C.& J.Keay, Birmingham, £45,598; while Messrs. P. W. Anderson of London obtained the contract to carry out the building work, in the sum of £91,574. Roof glazing was by The British Challenge Glazing Company of Stratford, E., for £4,180; heating and ventilation by Dallow, Roubert & Co. Ltd., Leicester, £4,367; boilers by Davy Bros. Sheffield, £2,565; electric lifts by Holt & Willetts Ltd., Cradley Heath, £1,694, while various specialist firms supplied the large number of other items necessary to equip and furnish the extension.

The enlarged depot building, with the exception of the new stores, came into use in 1926, allowing for all cars to be attended to, both with regard to renovation and repair, complete reconstruction and what was to be known as the "pullmanisation" programme. Several innovative experiments on cars were carried out, together with construction of the famous "Bluebird" (the second 'No. 1') in 1931/2, all of which will be described in the second volume of this history.

Work started in May 1928 on the construction of the new section to house the Central Stores, for which Messrs. Bovis Ltd. gained the contract in the sum of £36,240. The new stores were ceremonially opened for business on 21st November 1928 by the Chairman of the LCC, Lt. Col. C. B. Levita, which finally brought together all branches of this department for the first time. Considerable quantities of stores used by the undertaking were, until then, reposing in many different places, mainly in ex-horse car depots and in small sections of car shed space. These were gradually transferred into the new premises, which allowed the old sites to be used for other purposes or to be disposed of. During autumn 1928, the destination equipment workshops were transferred from Belvedere Road.

An estimate was approved on 22nd May 1928 in the sum of £6,875 for work in connection with the modernisation of the works, which included the installation of slow speed ropeways in the inspection, body and paint shops. It is on record that, on 1st May 1929, although the work was nearing completion, there was an excess expenditure of £3,080 "to make certain alterations and additions which were deemed advisable or necessary during the progress of the works".

The works referred to included the installation of an additional turntable and track at the northern end of the body shop, extra repair and ropeway pits, inspection pits in both the new traverser pits, additional drainage trenches and extra concrete due to the subsidence

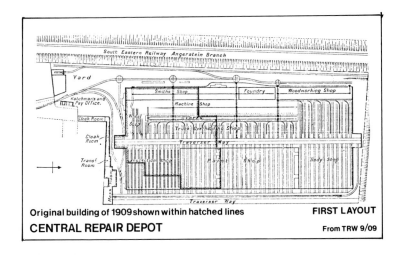

Original building of 1909 shown within hatched lines

CENTRAL REPAIR DEPOT

FIRST LAYOUT

From TRW 9/09

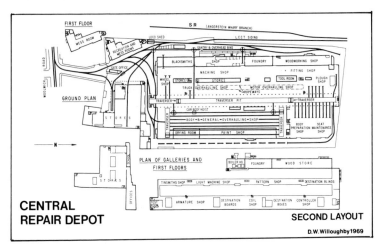

CENTRAL REPAIR DEPOT

SECOND LAYOUT

D.W.Willoughby 1969

of the original levels. Large sections of track were relaid at right angles to the old ones. Other improvements included alteration to the heating and lighting installation in the paint shop.

Two more traversers and two more turntables were also installed in the body and general overhaul shop, together with additional access tracks to the works and stores. A conveyor and two moving tables were also installed in the plough shop, which carried the ploughs and materials along at 20 inches a minute. A maximum of 1,000 ploughs a week could be reconditioned. Staff facilities and accommodation were also completely renewed. The changes may be seen in the two accompanying floor diagrams. With the completion of the works, there was no longer a need for the external traverser, which was eventually removed. All work was completed by June 1929.

In the drive to improve working methods, the Council were mindful of considerable strides that had been made in the development of plant and machinery. A few examples are quoted below from a submission to the Highways Committee from the General Manager, Tramways on 11th July 1929.

1. Vacuum cleaner for car seats, £280. (Previously attended to by beating).
2. Sand handling and moulding box plant for foundry, £1,650, including erection. (Previously attended to by hand).
3. Truck washing plant, £920, inclusive. (Required in connection with the slow speed ropeway).
4. Grit collecting plant for grinding machines, £150 inclusive.
5. Plant for dealing with output of destination boards and advertising matter, £1,000 inclusive. (Consisted of a varnishing machine, drying ovens and sundry apparatus).

The total installed cost of these items was £4,000, against which the Council offset an estimated saving of £870 per annum.

Renovation of Cars

All car movements inside the depot boundaries were made with the assistance of an Andrew Barclay 0-4-0 saddle-tank steam locomotive. When a car entered the works, it would "shoot the plough" at a plough-shift at the entrance to the depot, and then be propelled by the locomotive on to a traverser and conveyed to the inspection shop. On the following morning, the inspection report was compiled, after which the car body was raised by an electric hoist, the trucks run out and replaced by an overhauled set already fitted with reconditioned motors. The car was then connected to the body shop ropeway and moved along the 650-feet long track at the rate of three inches a minute, while the structure of the car body was overhauled. The exception was that any car requiring extensive body repair was dealt with on a stationary road.

The 0-4-0 Andrew Barclay saddletank locomotive which was used at the Central Repair Depot. *(The A. D. Packer collection)*

The workshop crew de-trucking class E/1 car No. 1584.
(Greater London Photograph Library)

The wheel lathe operator is seen here re-profiling the tyres of a pony
wheel set. *(Greater London Photograph Library)*

The plough overhaul shop was kept busy on the continuous repair and reconstruction of worn, damaged and defective ploughs.
(Greater London Photograph Library)

Class E/1 cars on the slow-moving ropeway, being drawn through the paint drying room. Dust free conditions and ducted warm air assisted in the drying process.
(Greater London Photograph Library)

The trucks and motors from the car were conveyed to other shops for overhaul, where a similar ropeway system was used to progress the items through the workshops. After overhaul, the completed trucks were made ready for use beneath other cars.

Seat cushions were removed, together with any other fittings and furniture requiring attention, while the controllers were replaced or otherwise attended to as necessary. Power and lighting cables were tested for their condition, including insulation resistance, while circuit breakers and switches were all removed and calibrated on a specially-designed motor generator set.

On arrival at the end of the overhauling process, the car was next taken to the paintshop, where it was thoroughly washed down and the trucks and lifeguards were spray-painted in black. After connection to the ropeway, one coat of colour was applied, transfers were fixed and the body varnished, the whole process taking about 16 hours.

The scheduled time taken for a complete overhaul and repaint was originally set at 13 days, with each car going through this process once every twelve months. By agreement with the Ministry of Transport and the Metropolitan Police in March 1931, the period between complete overhauls was extended to once every two years. This, together with the expected increased output, resulted in considerable economies, and meant that eight fewer cars would need to be held in the works at any one time. One of the attributed "savings" was, that as the capital value of the eight cars was stated to be £20,240, this sum would be invested in the car services instead of being tied up in the car works.

North side cars, with the exception of the single-deck Subway cars, had always been attended to at workshops at Bow and Holloway car sheds for the annual overhauls and repainting until 1921, when the paint shop was transferred to Hampstead car shed. Parts for replacement purposes were sent from CRD as required, using several electric stores cars which could negotiate Kingsway Subway, together with a number of petrol driven road lorries.

In order to enable cars from the north side system to be driven (or towed) to Charlton, at last making the CRD responsible for the whole fleet, a comprehensive but informal wayleave agreement was concluded with the Metropolitan Electric Tramways Ltd. in September 1926. This allowed the passage of LCC cars over parts of the company system between either Archway Tavern or Manor House and Harlesden, via North Finchley and Cricklewood. The Council expected that out of a gross saving of approximately £4,000 per annum, accrued by central-ising the whole of the overhaul facilities at Charlton, about £2,485 would be spent in transporting the cars between the two systems, resulting in a net saving of £1,515 a year. The company was also to have a reciprocal arrangement with regard to cars belonging to the South Metropolitan Electric Tramways Company being moved to and from the Car Works at Hendon. The agreement remained in force until 1931, when the opening of the deepened Kingsway Subway rendered it redundant so far as the LCC was concerned. However, SMET cars continued to be taken over the western lines of the LCC as and when required.

On completion of an overhaul, each car was taken for a test run out on the Woolwich Road as far as Church Lane, Charlton, a distance of just over half a mile. On its return, it was then driven to Camber-well car shed, where it was checked by the Chief Test Inspector, Traffic and taken for a further test run. If all was satisfactory, it was approved and, if necessary, re-licensed by the police, before being put into service.

Car Licensing

Under special Home Office regulations, the Metropolitan Police Commissioner, as Agent for the Home Sectretary, was empowered to license and delicense all public service vehicles which operated on the streets in the Metropolitan Police District. A department, known as the Public Carriage Office, was staffed by police officers to carry out the work. All tramcars, omnibuses and taxicabs were required to be licensed, following annual overhaul, as being fit for public service.

When new, each tramcar was inspected by a police officer who, when he was satisfied that the vehicle was roadworthy, applied an "approval mark" in a special indelible deep yellow ink to the body-work of the car. This was usually placed on the bulkhead beneath the stairs at the "A" end, at about shoulder height. A large rubber stamp was used to carry out this function, which showed the approval month and year, surmounted by a crown.

Additionally, each car was required to carry a Metropolitan Stage Carriage Plate, a white enamelled oblong metal device, which displayed in black letters and numerals the stage carriage number allocated to the car. These were provided by the police, and were affixed by police officers to the "nearside" rear bulkheads at rocker panel level, adjacent to the entrance steps at one end. A plate gave the necessary license to operate the car in public service. The "Plate Number" was repeated in a similar position at the other end of the car, signwritten in black paint, and also written inside one end of the lower saloon above the offside bulkhead window.

When a car was withdrawn from service for its regular major over-haul, it was delicensed by having the MSC Plate removed by the police before it left its home car shed for the works. On return to its home shed, the inspection, approval and licensing ritual would again be gone through. It cost the LCC 15/- per car per annum for this license.

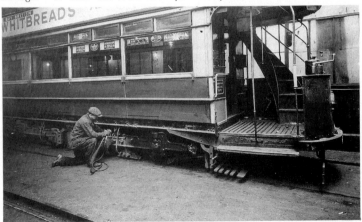

The renovated set of trucks which had been run beneath the car were spray-painted black before the finishing colours were applied to the body of the car. *(Greater London Photograph Library)*

Shortly after the re-opening of the Kingsway Subway in January 1931, arrangements were made between the Council and police that all licensing and delicensing would in future be dealt with at the CRD. This came into effect at the end of March, thereby providing a more centralised control over the duty, with its subsequent economies in staffing, particularly so far as the police were concerned. Henceforward, all inspections were carried out by officers who visited the Works on a regular basis.

The Great War. Production of Armaments

In addition to fulfilling its role as the Central Works for the maintenance of the tramway fleet, the CRD and its staff were called upon to manufacture certain warlike stores during the period of the Great War. The effort was mainly in the production of small parts for shells and guns, in which activity it continued to give service until 16th November 1918.

With regard to military involvement in the affairs of the LCC Tramways, several of the depots and car sheds were requisitioned by the War Department. In the main, it was those buildings which had previously housed horse cars. Plumstead depot was taken over by the Army on 6th August 1914 together with Rye Lane depot at about the same time. Towards the end of hostilities, Hampstead car shed was occupied by the military and used as a motor transport store, being retained by that department until 19th July 1920, when once again, it became a running shed for the tramways.

Postscript

It has been shown that between 1869 and 1899 all the tramway undertakings on the south side of the River Thames were firmly in the hands of private enterprise. When the London County Council took control of these companies, a new era was promised, and attained, for the travelling public. As has been seen in this Volume, the improvements to services offered were not obtained without considerable problems of many kinds being thrown up and overcome.

A similar situation developed on the north side system which, in 1895, 1896 and 1897 had, in the main, been purchased by the Council and leased back to one of the previous owners to operate. Eventually, the lease was revoked by the Council, who then set about electrifying the horse tramway network that had been inherited.

This part of the fascinating history of the Tramways of London will be dealt with in Volume 2, together with the complete story of the horse car companies; a description of the remaining classes of electric cars which made up the passenger rolling stock of the LCC Tramways, together with the road service vehicles used by the Council; routes and services; depots and subsidiary works for the whole of the LCC area; the ticketing arrangements; matters pertaining to staff, together with all relevant Acts of Parliament and several useful tables and appendices.

Events leading up to the transfer of this vast, efficient undertaking to the London Passenger Transport Board on 1st July 1933 will also be described, as will be a short resume of the subsequent fate of the tramway system.

Bibliography

A comprehensive bibliography will be published in Volume 2, and will deal with all aspects of the contents of both volumes of the history. A number of appendices will also be included, with information on finance, operating statistics and other tabular matter.

The Members,
The London Tramways History Group,
December 1988.

The London Tramways History Group

G. E. Baddeley, P. J. Davis, C. E. Holland, D. W. K. Jones, M. B. Leahy,
G. W. Morant, E. R. Oakley, C. S. Smeeton, C. L. Withey.
The Light Rail Transit Association.
The Tramway & Light Railway Society.